Causality and Complex Systems

Causality and Complex Systems

Guest Editors

Jiang Zhang
Peng Cui
Hector Zenil

MDPI

Basel • Beijing • Wuhan • Barcelona • Belgrade • Novi Sad • Cluj • Manchester

Guest Editors
Jiang Zhang
School of Systems Sciences
Beijing Normal University
Beijing
China

Peng Cui
Department of Computer Science
Tsinghua University
Beijing
China

Hector Zenil
School of Biomedical Engineering and Imaging Sciences
King's College London
London
UK

Editorial Office
MDPI AG
Grosspeteranlage 5
4052 Basel, Switzerland

This is a reprint of the Special Issue, published open access by the journal *Entropy* (ISSN 1099-4300), freely accessible at: https://www.mdpi.com/journal/entropy/special_issues/causality_complex_systems.

For citation purposes, cite each article independently as indicated on the article page online and as indicated below:

Lastname, A.A.; Lastname, B.B. Article Title. *Journal Name* **Year**, *Volume Number*, Page Range.

ISBN 978-3-7258-6790-5 (Hbk)
ISBN 978-3-7258-6791-2 (PDF)
https://doi.org/10.3390/books978-3-7258-6791-2

Contents

About the Editors

Jiang Zhang

Jiang Zhang is a professor in the School of Systems Science, Beijing Normal University, and the founder of Swarma Club and Swarma Research. His major research interests include causal emergence, scaling laws in complex systems, and machine learning on complex networks.

Peng Cui

Peng Cui is an Associate Professor with tenure at Tsinghua University. He received his PhD degree from Tsinghua University in 2010. His research interests include causal inference and stable learning, network representation learning, and social dynamics modeling. He has published more than 100 papers in prestigious conferences and journals in machine learning, data mining and multimedia. His recent research won five best paper awards and was selected for the Best of KDD Special Issues in 2014 and 2016, respectively. He is (was) the Associate Editor of *IEEE TKDE, IEEE TBD, ACM TIST, ACM TOMM, DMKD* and *KAIS*, etc., and the program co-chair of ACM CIKM19 and MMM2020. He is a Distinguished Member of ACM and CCF, as well as a Senior Member of IEEE.

Hector Zenil

Hector Zenil holds PhDs in Logic and Epistemology from Université Paris 1 Panthéon-Sorbonne and in Computer Science from the University of Lille. He was a faculty member and Senior Researcher at the Structural Biology Group, Department of Computer Science, Oxford University, at The Alan Turing Institute in London and at the Department of Chemical Engineering and Biotechnology at the University of Cambridge. He introduced the field of Algorithmic Information Dynamics. He received the Charles François Prize in 2024 from the International Academy for Systems and Cybernetic Sciences at the World's Conference on Complex Systems. He is the managing editor of the first journal in complexity science, *Complex Systems*, founded in 1984 by Stephen Wolfram, and of the journals *Complexity* (Wiley), *PLoS Complex Systems*, and the *Complex Systems* book series by Springer Nature.

Preface

We are pleased to introduce this Special Issue of *Entropy*, titled "Causality and Complex Systems", which explores the intricate relationships between causality and complexity. This collection of research papers aims to illuminate how causal mechanisms operate in complex systems, with a particular focus on emergent causality and its implications across diverse fields.

This issue delves into the interplay between causality and complexity, addressing themes such as causal discovery, causal emergence, downward causality, and the applications of machine learning and information theory in elucidating causal dynamics. It covers a wide range of topics, from theoretical frameworks to practical applications, with the goal of advancing our understanding of causality in dynamic, interconnected systems.

The primary objective of this Special Issue is to present innovative methodologies for causal discovery and inference, bridging the gap between theoretical concepts and practical applications. By exploring how emerging causal relationships at the macro-level inform system behavior, this issue aims to provide insights that can lead to better models and interventions.

The study of causality in complex systems is essential due to the prevalence and intricacy of such systems in various domains. As our ability to model and analyze these systems evolves, the need for sophisticated tools to uncover causal structures grows. This Special Issue addresses this need by presenting advanced methodologies to comprehend causality and complexity effectively.

This Special Issue is intended for researchers, academics, and professionals working in the fields of complex systems, causality, machine learning, and information theory. It also serves as a valuable resource for graduate students exploring the latest developments in causal dynamics within complex systems.

We extend our gratitude to the contributors of this Special Issue for their insightful research and dedication to advancing the field. Their work has significantly enhanced our understanding of causality in complex systems.

We acknowledge the efforts of the editorial team, anonymous reviewers, and MDPI for their support and commitment to academic rigor, ensuring the high quality of this issue. Their contributions have been instrumental in facilitating the dissemination of cutting-edge research to a global audience.

This Special Issue represents a collaborative effort to deepen our understanding of causality in complex systems, fostering further exploration and innovation.

Jiang Zhang, Peng Cui, and Hector Zenil
Guest Editors

entropy

MDPI

Review

Emergence and Causality in Complex Systems: A Survey of Causal Emergence and Related Quantitative Studies

Bing Yuan [1,†], Jiang Zhang [1,2,*,†], Aobo Lyu [3], Jiayun Wu [4], Zhipeng Wang [2], Mingzhe Yang [2], Kaiwei Liu [2], Muyun Mou [2] and Peng Cui [4]

1 Swarma Research, Beijing 100085, China; yuanbing_cn@hotmail.com
2 School of Systems Sciences, Beijing Normal University, Beijing 100875, China; wangzhipeng@mail.bnu.edu.cn (Z.W.); ymp66393866@163.com (M.Y.); 202221250005@mail.bnu.edu.cn (K.L.); moumuyun@mail.bnu.edu.cn (M.M.)
3 Department of Electrical and Systems Engineering, Washington University, St. Louis, MO 63130, USA; aobo.lyu@wustl.edu
4 Department of Computer Science and Technology, Tsinghua University, Beijing 100084, China; jiayun.wu.work@gmail.com (J.W.); cuip@tsinghua.edu.cn (P.C.)
* Correspondence: zhangjiang@bnu.edu.cn
† These authors contributed equally to this work.

Abstract: Emergence and causality are two fundamental concepts for understanding complex systems. They are interconnected. On one hand, emergence refers to the phenomenon where macroscopic properties cannot be solely attributed to the cause of individual properties. On the other hand, causality can exhibit emergence, meaning that new causal laws may arise as we increase the level of abstraction. Causal emergence (CE) theory aims to bridge these two concepts and even employs measures of causality to quantify emergence. This paper provides a comprehensive review of recent advancements in quantitative theories and applications of CE. It focuses on two primary challenges: quantifying CE and identifying it from data. The latter task requires the integration of machine learning and neural network techniques, establishing a significant link between causal emergence and machine learning. We highlight two problem categories: CE with machine learning and CE for machine learning, both of which emphasize the crucial role of effective information (EI) as a measure of causal emergence. The final section of this review explores potential applications and provides insights into future perspectives.

Keywords: causality; emergence; causal emergence; causal emergence identification; effective information; machine learning

1. Introduction

Economic growth, environmental protection, sustainable development, the global climate crisis, social inequality, and many other issues are all intertwined with complex systems [1,2]. Therefore, gaining a deep understanding of how complex systems operate, evolve, grow, stabilize, and collapse is of paramount importance. However, this task is exceptionally challenging due to the fact that complex systems consist of diverse and heterogeneous agents that interact through complex nonlinear relationships [3]. Moreover, they all exhibit emergent phenomena, which are highly common in complex systems but carry a sense of mystery [4].

How did the first living cell emerge from the collisions between various molecules in the Earth's early environment [5]? How does the cognitive concept of "I" emerge from the intricate interactions among countless neurons in our brain [6]? How do large neural language models suddenly exhibit emergent abilities [7]? These fundamental questions revolve around the concept of emergence in complex living, cognitive, and artificial systems. Emergence refers to the phenomenon where macroscopic properties and phenomena cannot be solely attributed to or explained by the properties of individual components [4,8–10]. This presents a formidable challenge to the traditional reductionist perspective while also shedding light on the underlying reasons for the enigmatic nature of emergent phenomena.

However, as elucidated by Bedau's theory of weak emergence [10], many emergent phenomena can be comprehended through the interactions among the individuals within the system [4]. Complex systems, in fact, consist of extensive networks of interacting components [11]. Within these networks, even a minor cause, such as a perturbation of a single unit, can propagate through the interconnected network, resulting in a collective effect. The phenomenon described is commonly known as the butterfly effect [12], which provides an explanation for the occurrence of emergence. On the other hand, emergent properties, such as homeostasis [13], can stabilize the system itself, thereby preserving the locality of causal effects and preventing the observation of macro-level effects. These phenomena demonstrate that complex systems achieve interactions through causal laws, where numerous local causal laws form interconnected causal networks as a whole. And this whole possesses unique causal characteristics.

Causality, or causation, refers to the connection between a cause and its resulting effect [14–16]. It describes the phenomenon in which an event, known as the cause, leads to another event, known as the effect. Traditional studies of causality have typically focused on the causal relationship between two or a few variables. However, the unique characteristics of causality in complex systems present new challenges to classical causal science due to the vast number of variables involved and the presence of emergent phenomena. In complex systems, it is possible for one cause to have multiple effects, and conversely, one effect may be influenced by a multitude of causes. Furthermore, in complex systems, causality often exhibits cross-level properties, which are closely associated with emergence.

Emergence and causation interconnect with each other. On one hand, emergence is the causal effect of complex and nonlinear interactions between components in complex systems [8,9]. On the other hand, emergent properties may have causal effects on individuals in complex systems [4,17]. For example, the price of fossil fuel is the emerging result of the interactions between buyers and sellers in the market. At the same time, the price may also provide feedback to the market: it can affect the decision making of each individual.

Furthermore, we can understand emergence through the perspective of causation. What emergence means is that some phenomena and properties on the macroscopic level can not be attributed to the microscopic properties [18]. Thus, emergent properties or phenomena lose their direct explanations as usual but may be attributed to the causes on the macro-level, as pointed out by [19]. Therefore, new causalities can be observed on larger scales.

In conclusion, gaining a deep understanding of emergence is crucial in the field of complex system studies. Specifically, the development of a quantitative theory of emergence is on the verge of emerging. Such a theory holds the potential to address significant challenges, including the origins of life [20], the emergence of novel capabilities in large neural network models [7], and the potential for intelligence, consciousness, and free will to arise in artificial systems [21]. Causality not only exhibits a profound connection with emergence but is also considered by many researchers as one of the most crucial perspectives for quantitatively comprehending emergence [18,19,22,23].

Two primary challenges take precedence in understanding emergence from a causal perspective. The first is establishing a quantitative definition of emergence, whereas the second involves identifying emergent behaviors or phenomena through data analysis.

To address the first challenge, two prominent quantitative theories of emergence have emerged in the past decade. The first is Erik Hoel et al.'s theory of causal emergence [19], whereas the second is Fernando E. Rosas et al.'s theory of emergence based on partial information decomposition [24].

Hoel et al.'s theory of causal emergence specifically addresses complex systems that are modeled using Markov chains. It employs the concept of effective information (EI) to quantify the extent of causal influence within Markov chains and enables comparisons of EI values across different scales [19,25]. Causal emergence is defined by the difference in the EI values between the macro-level and micro-level. Several examples of discrete Markov chains have been shown to exhibit causal emergence if their EI values of macro-level dynamics are larger than those of micro-level dynamics. Hoel and other researchers further extended the measures of effective information and causal emergence for dynamical systems with continuous variables [26] and complex networks [27]. Other measures are also possible for quantifying causal effects and, consequently, causal emergence. In [28], Comolatti and Hoel systematically compared several causal effect measures and concluded that causal emergence is independent of the selection of the measure.

However, in Hoel's theory of causal emergence, it is essential to establish a coarse-graining strategy beforehand. Alternatively, the strategy can be derived by maximizing the effective information (EI) [19]. However, this task becomes challenging for large-scale systems due to the computational complexity involved. To address these problems, Rosas et al. introduced a new quantitative definition of causal emergence [24] that does not depend on coarse-graining methods, drawing from partial information decomposition (PID)-related theory. PID is an approach developed by Williams et al., which seeks to decompose the mutual information between a target and source variables into non-overlapping information atoms: unique, redundant, and synergistic information [29]. Based on this groundwork, Rosas further developed the concept and introduced a theory called ϕID to decompose the mutual information between multiple target and source variables [30]. This framework provides a quantitative definition of causal emergence by measuring the positive synergy information between the source and target variables based on the inherent characteristics of the system.

The second challenge pertains to the identification of emergence from data. In an effort to address this issue, Rosas et al. derived a numerical method [24]. However, it is important to acknowledge that this method offers only a sufficient condition for emergence and is an approximate approach. Another limitation is that a coarse-grained macro-state variable should be given beforehand to apply this method. Hence, there is a need for the development of new methods.

Recently, artificial intelligence, propelled by the rapid advancements in machine learning and deep neural network technology, has witnessed significant progress. In the context of causal emergence, there are two key aspects to consider. Firstly, machine learning and neural network technology can be employed to address the challenge of identifying causal emergence. By leveraging these tools, we can develop approaches to effectively detect and analyze causal emergence phenomena. Secondly, the concepts and techniques from causal emergence can be introduced into machine learning to enhance the generalization capabilities of models. This integration can potentially improve the ability of machine learning algorithms to generalize well beyond the training data, leading to more robust and adaptable systems.

In a recent study by Zhang et al. [31], a machine learning framework named the Neural Information Squeezer (NIS) was introduced to address the challenge of identifying causal emergence using Hoel et al.'s framework. Remarkably, the NIS neural network, functioning as a "machine observer" equipped with an internal model, exhibits a remarkable ability to identify causal emergence across various types of data. In the latest updated version of this work, the Neural Information Squeezer Plus (NIS+) has been developed to directly maximize the critical measure of causal emergence theory, namely effective information (EI) [32]. Through extensive experiments conducted on both simulated data and real brain data, the NIS+ has demonstrated its ability to automatically find emergent macro-variables and macro-dynamics. Consequently, the NIS+ enables quantifying causal emergence in data with the learned macro-dynamics. The results of these experiments highlight the effectiveness and potential of the NIS+ in capturing and analyzing causal emergence phenomena.

Furthermore, the NIS+ showcases superior performance in terms of generalization ability by directly maximizing effective information (EI). This brings forth a second question:

can we leverage the measure of causation, EI, in the context of causal emergence, to enhance the generalization capability of neural networks for out-of-distribution scenarios? This concept is referred to as causal emergence for machine learning. By exploring this idea, we aim to bridge the gap between causal emergence and machine learning, potentially unlocking new avenues for improving the generalization abilities of machine learning.

Finally, in Section 5, we address several important and related issues. Firstly, we explore the similarities and differences between two emerging fields: causal emergence and causal representation learning [33]. This comparison sheds light on the interplay between these two domains. Secondly, we delve into a philosophical problem concerning ontological or epistemological causality and emergence, providing insights into the underlying philosophical implications. Lastly, we discuss the potential applications of causal emergence in complex systems and how it contributes to our understanding of complex systems from a causal emergence perspective. These discussions broaden the scope of this paper and offer intriguing avenues for future research.

This paper aims to provide a comprehensive review of the latest research on the quantitative theory and applications of causal emergence and related works. It also explores the connections between causal emergence, machine learning, and complex systems. The subsequent section delves into the background of causal emergence, with a particular focus on the interplay between causation and emergence in complex systems. In Section 3, various quantitative theoretical frameworks are introduced, including Crutchfield et al.'s computational mechanics [22], Seth et al.'s Granger causal emergence [23], Hoel et al.'s causal emergence theory, and Rosas et al.'s theory of emergence based on information decomposition. Additionally, related concepts such as the coarse-graining strategy, measures of effective information, and partial information decomposition are discussed, and a comparative analysis of these theories is presented. Section 4 addresses the connection between causal emergence theory and machine learning. It explores the use of machine learning and neural network techniques for identifying causal emergence and extends the measure of effective information (EI) to machine learning problems. Finally, this paper delves into other important topics and potential applications in the fields of machine learning and complex systems.

2. Background: From Causality to Emergence

2.1. Causality

Causality, which is a fundamental concept in many fields, including philosophy, natural science, and social science, refers to the relationship between a pair of events, where the first event (cause) can influence the second one (effect) [14–16]. The relationship between cause and effect can exhibit either deterministic or probabilistic characteristics. In deterministic causality, the cause will always produce the same effect, whereas in probabilistic causality, the cause will only produce the effect with a certain probability.

In most physical systems governed by differential equations or Markovian dynamics, whether deterministic or probabilistic, causality is inherent. This arises from the fact that manipulating a variable within the system can result in observable changes in other variables, albeit with probabilistic outcomes. As pointed out by Y. Iwasaki and H. A. Simon [34], one physical mechanism may correspond to several possible causal structures because causal graphs describe local causal interactions, whereas mechanisms are the global constraints for all variables. We further discuss the relationship between Markovian dynamics and causal models in detail below.

If we do not know the physical mechanism of a system, how can we model the causality behind the system? There are several parallel theoretical frameworks that can be used to do this. For example, Judea Pearl utilized probabilistic graphic models (e.g., Bayesian network, causal graph, and structural causal model) to characterize causal interactions [15,16]. In these models, nodes represent random variables and acyclic links represent causal interactions. Pearl distinguished and quantified three levels of causality in different models. The first level is association, i.e., the correlation between variables, which can be modeled using

Bayesian networks [35]. The second level is intervention, which can be characterized using causal graph models [16]. The difference between a causal graph and a Bayesian network is that the former enables defining a special operator, called a "do" operator, to simulate the interventions performed by the experimenter. The last level is counterfactual, which can be quantified using structural causal models [15]. The distinguishing characteristic of a structural causal model is that all interactions within a causal graph can be described by a set of deterministic functions that involve the input variables and unknown components, thereby introducing uncertainty. Counterfactual causal inferences, that is, inferences under an imaginary scenario, can be conducted only on structural causal models. The different types of causal models and the corresponding causal hierarchy in Pearl's theory are shown in Figure 1.

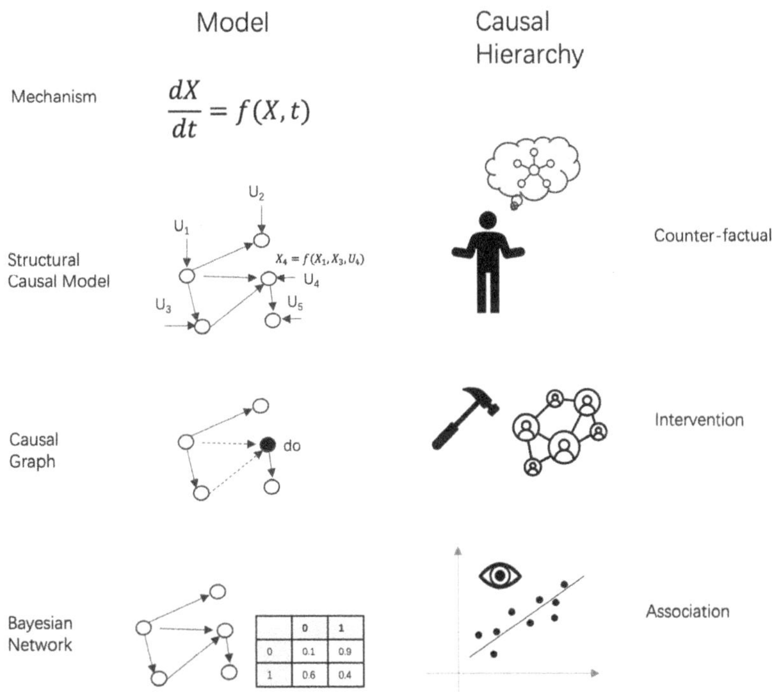

Figure 1. The causal models (**left**) column and the corresponding causal hierarchy (**right**) column.

Another quantitative framework for causal inference is Donald B Rubin's "potential outcome" theory, which operates at the counterfactual level [36]. According to this theory, each individual has two potential outcomes: the outcome that would be observed if the individual receives the treatment, and the outcome that would be observed if the individual does not receive the treatment. Rubin's theory suggests that the causal effect of a treatment can be estimated by comparing the difference between the observed outcome and the unobserved potential outcome for each individual.

Researchers have also developed a bundle of methods, named causal discovery algorithms [37], to automatically discover the causal relations between variables merely from data. For example, constraint-based algorithms [38] and score-based algorithms [39] for causal discovery are two typical representations. Causal discovery has emerged as an interdisciplinary area at the intersection of machine learning, causal inference, and statistics.

Due to the uncertainty and ambiguity behind the discovered causal relations, measuring the degree of causal effect between two variables is another important problem. Numerous independent historical studies have addressed the issue of causation measurement. These include Hume's concept of constant conjunction [40], Eells' and Suppes' measures of causation as probability raising [41,42], and Judea Pearl's measures of causation [16]. Effective information (EI) in the framework for causal emergence is also an indicator for measuring causal effect, and we explain this point in Section 3.5.3. All these measures can be roughly decomposed into two causal primitives, which characterize the necessary causation and sufficient causation, respectively [43].

It is crucial to differentiate between Markovian dynamics or dynamical mechanism models and the causal models introduced above. In current causal emergence theories [19,24], Markovian dynamics, rather than causal models, including causal graphs and structural causal models, play a central role. There are several distinctions between Markovian dynamics and these causal models.

Firstly, in Markovian dynamics, the temporal evolution of one or multiple variables is typically described, with causal relationships between these variables extending across different points in time. Consequently, all variables are dependent on time, and a variable at one time step can causally impact another variable at the subsequent time step. Conversely, the aforementioned causal models do not explicitly incorporate the element of time. In these models, neither the variables nor the causal relationships are explicitly defined as functions of time.

Secondly, it is worth noting that circular interaction structures, including self-looped interactions, may exist in Markovian dynamics. However, such circular structures are typically not permitted in the causal models we introduced. This distinction arises from the fact that both causal graph models and structural causal models are constructed based on directed acyclic graphs (DAGs) [16]. However, this issue can be resolved by converting Markovian dynamics into DAGs. The initial step involves introducing static causal variables at each time step. Consequently, the same variable in Markovian dynamics can be transformed into a set of different variables at different time steps. This expansion allows for causal relationships across time steps while eliminating circular structures in causal graphs [44].

Given the limitations of conventional causal models based on directed acyclic graphs (DAGs) [45], there is a need for new representation methods. For instance, Richardson [46] expanded the causal modeling approach to include DAGs. Spirtes [47] discussed DAG representations of feedback models and applied them to economic processes. Lacerda et al. also developed a method utilizing independent components analysis to discover cyclic causal models [48]. Furthermore, Forré and Mooij introduced a novel causal discovery method for nonlinear structural causal models with cycles and latent confounders [49]. George T.H. Ellison proposed a methodology that leverages domain knowledge to extract DAGs from temporal relationships among multiple variables [50]. Causal discovery methods can also be extended to temporal data by segregating various temporal data analysis tasks, such as classification, clustering, and prediction. Recently, Gong et al. provided a comprehensive review of these techniques in [51]. These advancements have the potential to broaden the range of available causal models.

In summary, causality is a fascinating interdisciplinary topic spanning several subjects. Numerous quantitative frameworks and measures have been developed in recent decades.

2.2. Emergence

Emergence, known as "the whole is greater than the sum of parts" [52], is a central concept in many philosophical and theoretical discussions about the nature of complexity and the relationship between micro- and macro-levels of organization. Therefore, the scale of a system (micro or macro) and the cross-level interactions must be considered when we discuss emergence. This may increase the complexity of the study of emergence [53–59].

Although many examples of emergence have been pointed out in various fields [4,59], including the herding behaviors of birds [60], collective behaviors of simple computer programs [61], and emerging ability of large language models [7], a unifying understanding of this phenomenon does not exist right now. People try to understand emergence from different aspects, including self-organization [62], order out of disorder [63], and causality. In this review, we mainly focus on the last point of view.

Emergence has deep connections with causation [10,18,64,65]. First, emergence emphasizes the new properties arising from the interactions between the components in the system, rather than the components themselves. Consequently, all emergent properties and processes at the macro-level can, in principle, be comprehended as the causal effects resulting from interactions between individuals at the micro-level. This is what the philosophical notion of "supervenience" tries to describe.

However, this does not mean that all emergent phenomena at the macro-level can be easily attributed to micro-level individuals and their interactions. Two major reasons can account for this. The first reason is due to the principle of computational irreducibility proposed by Wolfram [66], which claims that although we know emergent properties arise from a set of simple rules, there is no shortcut, in principle, to predict the results other than implementing the rules. For example, the complex behaviors (e.g., herding and aligning) of the Boid model are the results of simple rules, but these behaviors cannot be reduced to individual behaviors simply without simulating them [60].

The second reason is that emergent behaviors may be determined by other emergent properties at the macro-level [19,24]. For example, although the price of rice in the market is determined by all the interactions (bargaining) between buyers and sellers, it is also the causal effect of the price of fossil oil because severe shortages of fossil oil can cause inflation. Therefore, the cause of one emergent property (rice price) is another emergent macro-level coarse-grained variable. This means new causation can be observed between macro-level coarse-grained variables, as pointed out by the theory of causal emergence. Interestingly, the causation at different levels must be consistent to explain the micro-level event of fluctuating rice prices. Otherwise, a double causation [67] fallacy may appear. This consistency between causality at different scales is called the causal equivalence principle in Yurchenko's latest article [68].

In order to better understand emergence, Bedau et al. [10,65] classified emergence into three categories according to the causal interactions between the micro- and macro-levels: nominal emergence [69,70], weak emergence [10,71], and strong emergence [17,72].

Of these categories, the notion of nominal emergence is the least controversial. It can be described as a kind of property that can be possessed by macro-level patterns or processes but not by their micro-level components [69,70]. For example, pixel patterns on a screen are nominal emergent properties. We can consider such nominal emergent patterns as "supervenient" because all macro-level properties derive from individuals.

Weak emergence refers to macro-level properties or processes that derive through interactions between individual components in a complicated way such that they cannot be easily reduced to micro-level properties due to the principle of computational irreducibility [10,71]. For weak emergent patterns or processes, the causes may come from both the micro- and macro-levels; therefore, emergent causation may coexist with micro-level causation.

In the discourse surrounding emergence, weak emergence is generally more widely accepted than strong emergence. However, there are some concepts and descriptions that remain somewhat ambiguous [73]. For instance, in Bedeau's original definition, a property is considered weakly emergent if and only if it can be derived from micro-dynamics through simulation. Nevertheless, the term "simulation" itself can be interpreted in different ways—whether it refers to digital simulations or analog simulations is not explicitly implied. Bedeau further elaborated on this concept by stating that if a macro-level property can, in principle, be simulated without requiring an actual simulation, then it can be considered weakly emergent [10]. However, even this explanation is not entirely clear-cut.

There are more debates on strong emergence, which refers to properties or processes at the macro-level that cannot, in principle, be reduced to micro-level properties, including the interactions of individuals [17,72]. Thus, Boid's collective behaviors are not strongly emergent because they are the result of interactions within the Boid model. This notion is controversial because it rejects any mechanistic explanations for strong emergent properties, which cannot be explained by micro-level variables. Furthermore, it raises some long-standing philosophical debates about "causal fundamentalism" [74] and "supervenience" [75], and the existence of strong emergence remains an open problem due to the scarcity of concrete examples.

Jochen Fromm further explained strong emergence as the causal effect of downward causation [18]. Consider a system that contains three different scales: micro, meso, and macro. Downward causation refers to the causal power from the macro-level to the meso-level or from the meso-level to the micro-level. Consequently, although the strong emergent properties or processes at the meso-level are supervenient to micro-level properties and interactions, their causes derive from the macro-level and, therefore, second-order patterns or processes. However, there are many debates on the notion of downward causation itself, e.g., [64,68].

In summary, there are three types of causation based on their cross-level properties, which are associated with emergence, as depicted in Figure 2:

1. Upward causation: This involves the supervenience relation, where macro-level effects can be attributed to micro-level variables.
2. Intra-level causation: This refers to causal effects occurring within the same scale or level.
3. Downward causation: Here, macro-level properties influence micro-level properties.

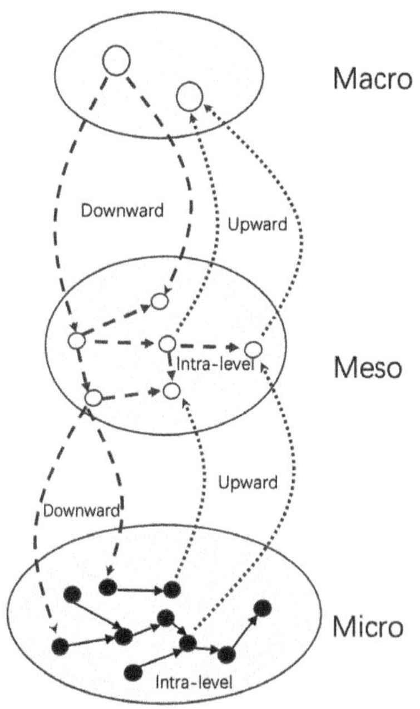

Figure 2. The various types of causation that exist within multi-scale complex systems. In this figure, solid arrows represent common causation, which is generally accepted without much controversy. Dotted arrowed lines indicate a form of "causation" driven by supervenience, whereas dashed arrowed lines represent emergent causation, occurring either at an intra-level or downward.

In Figure 2, the black solid lines represent causation without controversy. However, according to a recent paper by Yurchenko [68], the causation represented by the dashed and dotted lines (except the intra-level ones in the meso-level) may not actually be causality but rather reasons or explanations. Yurchenko introduced the term "reason" to distinguish it from the conventional understanding of causality, as cross-level causal effects may not possess causal powers. Instead, they serve as reasons or explanations from the perspective of an observer. Yurchenko accepted intra-level causation at the meso- or macro-level as "real", similar to causation at the micro-level. He even coined the term "causal equivalent principle" to represent the idea that all intra-level causations, except those that are cross-level, should be accepted and are equivalent to each other.

However, other scholars think that compared to the causal relationship at the micro-level, the intra-level causation at the meso- or macro-level is problematic because the coarse-graining strategy is relevant [76–78]. As demonstrated in the numeric example in Section 3.5.4, the causation measured by EI is dependent on the coarse-graining method. Hoel et al. tried to avoid this problem by introducing EI maximization. Indeed, EI maximization serves as an objective standard for selecting coarse-graining and macro-dynamics; however, a unique solution is required. We discuss this problem further in Section 5.2.

3. Quantifying Emergence by Causality

Since causality and emergence have a strong connection and causality has multiple quantitative frameworks and measures, it becomes natural to use causality to quantify emergence. In this section, we review several frameworks used to quantify multi-scale causality and emergence.

3.1. Early Related Works

Before the theory of causal emergence was proposed by Hoel et al., some works introduced very similar ideas to causal emergence theory. For example, Crutchfield et al.'s computational mechanics theory considered causal states, which are the partitions of the state space and may have good predictions. Furthermore, Seth et al. proposed G-causality to quantify emergence using Granger's causality. We discuss them in detail below.

3.2. Computational Mechanics

The theory of computational mechanics proposed by Crutchfield, Shalizi, and Feldman et al. tried to formulate this kind of emergent causation in a quantitative framework [22]. In some sense, computational mechanics can be understood as the inverse of statistical mechanics. This is because statistical mechanics derives macro-level consequences from micro-dynamics, whereas the inverse process is performed by computational mechanics, which constructs a minimal causal model from the observations of a stochastic process that can generate the observed time series.

Let us assume that the stochastic process under consideration can be represented as $\overleftrightarrow{s}$. We can divide it into two segments beginning from time step t: the history before t, denoted as $\overleftarrow{s_t}$, and the future after t, denoted as $\overrightarrow{s_t}$. If the process is stationary, we can remove the denotation of t. Thus, all possible histories $\overleftarrow{s}$ form a set, denoted as $\overleftarrow{S}$, and all futures $\overrightarrow{s}$ form a set, denoted as $\overrightarrow{S}$.

We aim to establish a model that can reconstruct and predict observed random sequences, with a higher accuracy being desirable. However, the randomness of the sequences prevents us from achieving a perfect reconstruction unless we record every randomly occurring character. This would make the model excessively long. To preserve useful information as concisely as possible, we need a coarse-grained mapping that captures the ordered structure in the random sequences, known as patterns [63]. We can partition $\overleftarrow{S}$ into mutually exclusive and jointly comprehensive subsets that form a set $\mathcal{R}$. Any subset $R \in \mathcal{R}$ is called a "state". We define a function from histories to states as $\eta : \overleftarrow{S} \rightarrow \mathcal{R}$. Thus, η is a method that can partition the history into mutually exclusive and jointly comprehensive subsets.

For a set of states $\mathcal{R}$, we can measure its simplicity using a complexity metric. Intuitively, the larger the cardinality of $\mathcal{R}$, the more complex it is. Additionally, we need to consider its distribution. For example, if one state occurs frequently while others occur rarely, it is less complex compared to a situation with a uniform distribution. Therefore, we can define the **statistical complexity** C_μ of a set of states using Shannon entropy [79]:

$$C_\mu(\mathcal{R}) \triangleq -\sum_{\rho\in\mathcal{R}} P(\mathcal{R}=\rho)\log_2 P(\mathcal{R}=\rho). \quad (1)$$

When constructing predictive models using a set of states, the statistical complexity refers to the size of the model.

What kind of state set can achieve the best balance between predictiveness and parsimony? We can introduce an equivalent relationship called **causal equivalence** [63]. Concretely, we say $\overleftarrow{s}$ and $\overleftarrow{s}'$ are causally equivalent if and only if:

$$P(\overrightarrow{s}|\overleftarrow{s}) = P(\overrightarrow{s}|\overleftarrow{s}')$$

This equivalent relationship can partition all the histories into equivalent classes, and they are defined as **causal states**. We denote all the causal states of a history $\overleftarrow{s}$ as $\epsilon(\overleftarrow{s})$, where $\epsilon : \overleftarrow{S} \to 2^{\overleftarrow{S}}$ is a function that can map a history $\overleftarrow{s}$ to the causal state $\epsilon(\overleftarrow{s}) \in 2^{\overleftarrow{S}}$, which is a subset of the histories.

For any two causal states $\mathcal{S}_i$ and $\mathcal{S}_j$, we can define **causal transitions** as a set of labeled probabilities $T_{ij}^{(s)}$ that represent the transition from the causal state S_i to the causal state S_j while emitting the symbol $s \in \mathcal{A}$ [63]:

$$T_{ij}^{(s)} \equiv \mathrm{P}(\mathcal{S}' = \mathcal{S}_j, \overrightarrow{\mathcal{S}}'^{L=1} = s|\mathcal{S} = \mathcal{S}_i),$$

where $\mathcal{S}$ is the current causal state, $\mathcal{S}'$ is its successor, and $\overrightarrow{\mathcal{S}}'^{L=1} = s$ denotes all the sequences of length $L = 1$, in which the first symbol emitted is s (we use slightly different symbols from those in [79]). Hence, by combining: $\mathcal{S}' = \mathcal{S}_j$ and $\overrightarrow{\mathcal{S}}'^{L=1} = s$, we ensure that all subsequent causal states will have the identical initial emitted symbol s. We denote the set $\{T_{ij}^{(s)} : s \in \mathcal{A}\}$ by T. The definition of causal transitions leads to a direct conclusion: $T_{ij}^{(s)} = \mathrm{P}(\overleftarrow{s}s \in \mathcal{S}_j|\overleftarrow{s} \in \mathcal{S}_i) = \frac{\mathrm{P}(\overleftarrow{s}\in\mathcal{S}_i,\overleftarrow{s}s\in\mathcal{S}_j)}{\mathrm{P}(\overleftarrow{s}\in\mathcal{S}_i)}$, where $\overleftarrow{s}s$ is read as the semi-infinite sequence obtained by concatenating the history $\overleftarrow{s}$ and the symbol s [79].

The **ϵ-machine** of a process is defined as the ordered pair $\{\epsilon, T\}$, where ϵ is the causal state function (which can map a state s to the partition $\epsilon(s)$), and T is the set of the transition matrices (the dynamics) for the states defined by ϵ.

Up until now, we have defined ϵ-machine, which is a pattern discovery machine where the patterns are unraveled from the set of histories. The remaining task is to show that it is, in some sense, optimal. It has the important properties of being minimally predictive, maximally statistically complex, and minimally stochastic [79].

We compare the causal state $\mathcal{S}$ to any state $R \in 2^{\overleftarrow{S}}$ to show that for the purpose of predicting the future, the causal states do a better job, i.e., they provide more information. This property can be formulated as a mathematical theorem, called **the maximal predictability theorem**. It is stated as follows: if $\mathcal{S}$ is the causal state given by ϵ, then for any other state $R \in 2^{\overleftarrow{S}}$ and all $L \in \mathbb{Z}^+$, we have:

$$H[\overrightarrow{\mathcal{S}}^L|R] \geq H[\overrightarrow{\mathcal{S}}^L|\mathcal{S}].$$

where $H(\cdot|\cdot)$ is the conditional entropy, and $\overrightarrow{\mathcal{S}}^L$ is the L-length sequences for future. Thus, the inequality shows that the uncertainty of $\overrightarrow{\mathcal{S}}^L$ given the causal state $\mathcal{S}$ is less than all other states.

After achieving optimal predictiveness, the causal state set remains the one with minimal statistical complexity. We first introduce the notion of **prescient rivals** denoted as $\hat{\mathcal{R}}$, which are the states that are as predictive as the causal states; viz., for all $L \in \mathbb{Z}^+$, $H[\overrightarrow{S}^L|\hat{\mathcal{R}}] = H[\overrightarrow{S}^L|\mathcal{S}]$.

Next, we present the **minimum statistical complexity theorem**: for all prescient rivals $\hat{\mathcal{R}}$,

$$C_\mu(\hat{\mathcal{R}}) \geq C_\mu(\mathcal{S}) \tag{2}$$

Next, we show that the causal states are **minimally stochastic**. That is to say, compared with other competitors with the same ability to predict the future, the causal states and their transition dynamics have the least uncertainty. Then, we have the **minimal stochasticity theorem**, which is expressed as follows: for all prescient rivals $\hat{\mathcal{R}}$,

$$H[\hat{\mathcal{R}}'|\hat{\mathcal{R}}] \geq H[\mathcal{S}'|\mathcal{S}].$$

where $\mathcal{S}'$ and $\hat{\mathcal{R}}'$ are the next causal state of the process and the next state, respectively. This means that the causal state and ϵ-machine provide the best intrinsic determinism.

Since the causal state set is considered the best, how can we compute the causal states and ϵ-machine from the observed data? The authors of [63] introduced a **hierarchical machine reconstruction algorithm**; however, the details are not reiterated here.

Although this algorithm may not be applicable to all operational scenarios, the authors presented numerical computational results and corresponding machine reconstruction pathways for chaotic dynamics, hidden Markov models, and cellular automata as examples [63,79].

It is interesting to compare the theory of computational mechanics with causal emergence. Indeed, we can understand that all the histories $\overleftarrow{s}$ are micro-level states, and all the states $R \in \mathcal{R}$ are macro-states. Thus the function η that can map a history $\overleftarrow{s}$ to a state R is a possible coarse-graining strategy.

It is worth pointing out that the causal state $\epsilon(\overleftarrow{s})$ is the special state that can have at least the same predictive power as the micro-state $\overleftarrow{s}$, i.e., the full history. Therefore, ϵ is similar to the notion in the effective coarse-graining strategy in [31] (see Section 3.6.5), and the causal transitions T represent the corresponding effective macro-level dynamics. The feature of minimal stochasticity characterizes the deterministic property of the macro-dynamic. This property is characterized by effective information (EI) in causal emergence theory.

Although a clear definition and quantitative theory of emergence were not provided, the authors discussed the relationship between computational mechanics and emergence [63,80]. In [63], the authors explained that emergence can be conceptualized as a dynamic process in which a pattern acquires the ability to predictably adapt to different environments, as observed by an external observer. Additionally, they differentiated intrinsic emergence from emergence itself, as intrinsic emergence goes beyond the mere production of patterns and encompasses the formation of an embedded observer within the system through these patterns.

3.3. G-Emergence Theory

G-emergence theory, proposed by Seth in 2008 [23], is one of the earliest works on a quantitative measure of emergence. His basic idea is to use nonlinear Granger causality to measure weak emergence in complex systems.

Granger causality (G-causality) is formally defined as follows: Given two time series A and B, if the past values of B can help predict the future values of A, beyond what can be forecasted using the past values of A, then B is said to be "Granger-cause" of A. This implies the existence of Granger causality between A and B.

When applying a bivariate autoregressive model for predictions, residual terms are included in the equations of the two variables. Then, the residuals can be utilized to quantify the extent of the causal effect in G-causality. The degree of B being the G-cause of A is quantified by the logarithmic of the ratio of the two variances of residuals. One is the residual of the autoregression model of A if all the terms of B are omitted, and the other is the residual of the full prediction model, as shown in Figure 3. In addition, in [23], the author also defined G-autonomous as the ability of past values in a time series to predict its own future values. And the degree of G-autonomous can be measured in a similar way as G-causality.

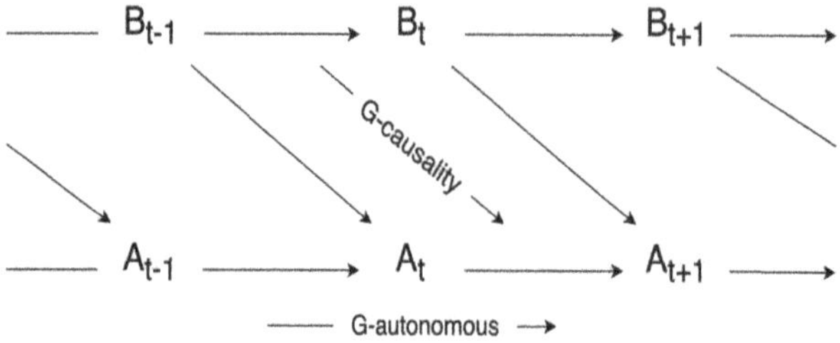

Figure 3. G-causality and G-autonomous.

With these two basic notions in G-causality, as shown in Figure 4, the author defined G-emergence on macro-variables as follows: a macro-variable M is G-emergent from a set of micro-variables $\{m\}$ if and only if (i) M is G-autonomous with respect to $\{m\}$, and (ii) $\{m\}$ is G-cause of M. The degree of G-emergence can also be quantitatively measured by multiplying the degree of G-autonomous of M and the average of G-causes of $\{m\}$ on M.

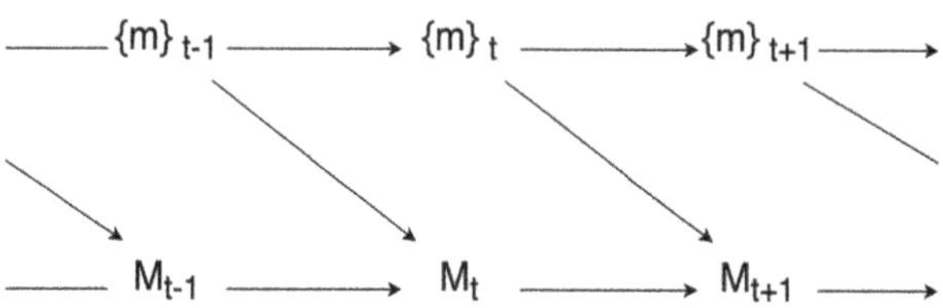

Figure 4. G-autonomous.

The author tested the G-emergence theory on the Boid model. This model is a famous artificial life model that simulates the flocking behavior of birds using three simple rules: cohesion, alignment, and separation [60]. These basic rules are realized by the virtual forces exerted on each bird, and the strength of each force can be controlled. The author found that by increasing the strength of cohesion, the G-emergence of the entire flock also increased. Here, the macro-variable is selected as the center of the flock (center of mass), and each bird is a micro-variable. The author also discovered a downward causality phenomenon in this simple model: the center of mass can be used to predict each individual bird. However, the author did not distinguish downward causation from other common causality in their work because Granger's causality is not a real causal relationship.

Seth's G-emergence theory was the first attempt to quantify the emergence phenomenon via a causality measure. However, the causality measure that the author used was Granger causality, which is not a strict causal measure, and it also depends on the regression method to be used. Furthermore, the measure is defined on variables but not dynamics, which means the result depends on the selection of variables.

3.4. Other Quantitative Theories of Emergence

There are alternative means of measuring emergence that do not require relying on causality. Two different methods have been discussed by the scholars. One is to understand emergence as a process from disorder to order, and the other is to understand emergence from the perspective that "the whole is greater than the sum of parts".

For example, Moez Mnif and Christian Müller-Schloer used Shannon entropy [81] to measure order and disorder. In a self-organized process, emergence occurs when there is an increase in order. This increase can be quantified by measuring the Shannon entropy difference between the initial state and the final state, denoted as $H_{start} - H_{end}$. However, this definition has two limitations. Firstly, the measurement of entropy, denoted as H, is dependent on the abstract level of observation. Therefore, it is necessary to account for the entropy increase resulting from a change in the observer's abstract level. Secondly, the choice of the initial condition of the system is arbitrary. To address this limitation, one approach is to measure the relative level of Shannon entropy compared to the maximum entropy distribution. Finally, emergence can be quantified by:

$$Emergence = H_{max} - H - \Delta H_{view}, \tag{3}$$

where H_{max} is the maximized entropy of the system. If no prior information is available, the maximum entropy, denoted as H_{max}, corresponds to the Shannon entropy of an equal probability distribution. On the other hand, H represents the Shannon entropy of the system at the final moment of a self-organization process. Additionally, ΔH_{view} represents the entropy increase during this process resulting from a change in the observer's abstraction level. It should be noted that if the observer does not alter their abstraction level, this term would be zero. We can also normalize this quantity by dividing H_{max} such that different features can be compared by the normalized quality. For a multivariate system, the authors suggested employing a radar plot to visualize the emergence fingerprint of the dynamical process, which showcases the normalized emergence measure across various variables. Then, the authors applied this method to a simulated system of chickens. M. Tang and X. Mao applied this indicator to artificial society models [82].

Inspired by Moez Mnif and Christian Müller-Schloer's work, ref. [83] suggested using the divergence measure between two probability distributions to better quantify emergence. They understood emergence as being *an unexpected or unpredictable change of the distribution underlying the observed samples*. However, this method suffers from computational complexity and estimation accuracy. To address these problems, ref. [84] further proposed an approximating method using the Gaussian mixture model to estimate the density and introduced Mahalanobis distance to characterize the divergence between data and Gaussian components, leading to better results. In [85], the authors systematically compared the three aforementioned methods and applied them to a simple test example. Another Shannon entropy-based emergence measure was proposed by Holzer and de Meer et al. [86,87]. They considered a complex system as a self-organization process in which different individuals interact with communications. Emergence can then be measured based on a ratio between the Shannon entropy measure on all communications between agents and the total summation of the Shannon entropy for each communication as a separate source.

Unlike the aforementioned methods, refs. [88,89] proposed a method to quantify emergence based on the idea that "the whole is greater than the sum of its parts", defining emergence from the interaction rules and states of agents instead of the overall statistical measure of the whole system. Specifically, this measure consists of two terms that are subtracted from each other. The first term characterizes the collective states of the entire system, whereas the second term represents the summation of the individual states of all its constituent parts. This measure emphasizes the emergence that arises from the interactions and collective behavior of the system. This method was then tested on the example of bird flock simulation.

3.5. *Erik Hoel's Causal Emergence Theory*

3.5.1. Basic Idea

The first quantitative emergence theory based on Markov dynamics and causality measures through intervention was Erik Hoel's causal emergence theory.

In this framework, system properties can be characterized at various levels, ranging from micro to macro. If a system exhibits stronger causality at the macro-level than at the micro-level, it demonstrates causal emergence. Causality is reflected between successive states during the system's evolution. The strength of a system's causality reveals the extent to which its future state is influenced by its current state. The basic idea of causal emergence is illustrated in Figure 5.

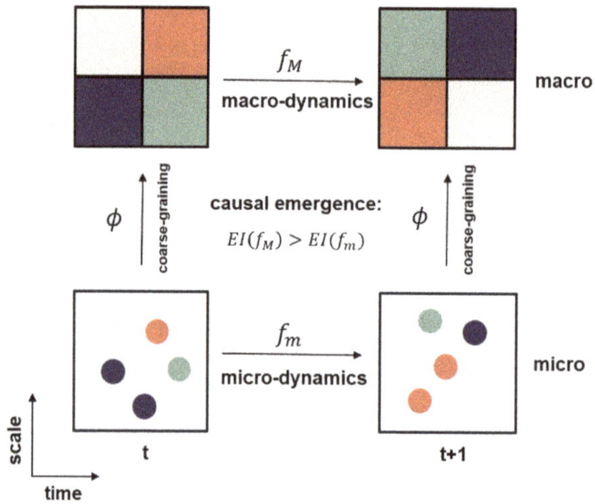

Figure 5. The basic idea of Erik Hoel's causal emergence theory. The colored circles represent micro-states, whereas the colored squares represent macro-states.

For example, statistical mechanics is a typical theory of causal emergence. At the micro-level, a huge number of molecules collide and exhibit random behaviors such that probabilistic language must be used to describe them. However, if we coarse-grain the whole system into several thermodynamic physical variables like pressure, temperature, etc., we can use very concise and exact thermodynamic equations to describe their behaviors. Therefore, thermodynamic laws have a stronger causal effect than micro-level molecular dynamics.

Formal tools are used to describe the elements in Hoel's causal emergence theory. Typically, it employs discrete Markov models to describe the micro-dynamics of systems, and the corresponding macro-level systems with different Markov dynamics can be derived by coarse-graining the micro-systems. Additionally, the inherent strength of the causal effect of the Markov model can be measured with effective information (EI), indicating how effectively a particular state influences the future state of a system.

EI is an intrinsic property of a system's dynamics and can be quantified by the transitional probability matrix (TPM). A coarse-graining strategy is a function that maps a set of micro-states into a particular macro-state, allowing for the derivation of a new dynamical model described by TPM from the micro-level TPM. The effective information of the coarse-grained model can also be computed. The phenomenon of causal emergence implies that as we coarse-grain microscopic states, the amount of effective information transmitted from the current state to the next state can possibly increase. At a certain macroscopic scale of coarse-graining, the effective information reaches a maximum; this scale represents the point at which the system state has the maximum causal power to predict future states in the most reliable and effective way.

To illustrate causal emergence, let us look at a particular Markov chain model with four possible states, whose transition probability matrix (TPM) is:

$$S_m = \begin{bmatrix} 1/3 & 1/3 & 1/3 & 0 \\ 1/3 & 1/3 & 1/3 & 0 \\ 1/3 & 1/3 & 1/3 & 0 \\ 0 & 0 & 0 & 1 \end{bmatrix} \tag{4}$$

In this model, if we take the first three states as group 1 and the last state as group 2, anyone in group 1 can transition to any of the three states in the same group with equal probability at the next moment. However, because there is only one state in group 2, so the fourth state will always stay in its position. Intuitively, we can conclude that the future states are not fully determined by the current states, and uncertainty mainly arises from group 1.

However, if we merge the first three states in group 1 into one new state and keep the fourth state in group 2 as it is, we obtain a coarse-grained Markov model with two states, represented by the following TPM:

$$S_M = \begin{bmatrix} 1 & 0 \\ 0 & 1 \end{bmatrix} \quad (5)$$

Now, the future states of the new system can be fully determined by the current states. This shows that we can eliminate the uncertainty of a nondeterministic system by performing coarse-graining over the system states.

3.5.2. About Coarse-Graining

The example above illustrates how a system's determinism can increase as it is coarse-grained. Coarse-graining is a process that simplifies the description of a system by grouping its components into larger, more slowly varying units. It is often used to identify the essential features of a system that determine its macroscopic behavior, without being burdened by the details of micro-scale interactions. Unlike dimension reduction techniques, such as PCA and SVD, coarse-graining takes into account the system's features at different spatial and temporal scales. Coarse-graining also differs from renormalization. In physics, the renormalization group method was invented to eliminate infinities in integrals. It is also used to coarse-grain a system such that the Hamiltonian or partition functions are similar between micro- and macro-levels [90,91]. However, the coarse-graining method does not have this requirement in general. Although both techniques are designed to describe a system from a coarse-grained level, coarse-graining focuses more on the states of the system, whereas renormalization cares about dynamics, system rules, partition functions, etc. Renormalization is frequently used in physics and the study of phase transitions to explore critical phenomena and symmetry breaking. These are aspects that coarse-graining typically does not consider.

Given a transitional probability matrix (TPM), there are many ways to partition the state space for coarse-graining the system. What kind of coarse-graining strategies are more reasonable? In [19,25], the authors suggested selecting an appropriate coarse-graining method by maximizing the effective information of the coarse TPM. In the literature, there is another criterion for selecting a coarse-graining strategy called lumpability, where the lumpability of a TPM refers to the coarse-grained TPM exhibiting similar dynamics and observation statistics [92]. Commutativity is another requirement that requires the operations of coarse-graining and state transitions to be commutative [93]. There are also other discussions or reasonable model reductions of Markov or hidden Markov models [94–96].

3.5.3. About Effective Information

In order to quantify emergence, a widely used method is to calculate the mutual information between the past states and future states of a system. This mutual information defines the upper limit of the information being transferred from the past to the future. If the mutual information is high, it suggests that a significant amount of information about the past is retained in the future.

$$I(X_t; X_{t+1}) = \sum P(X_t, X_{t+1}) \log \frac{P(X_t, X_{t+1})}{P(X_t)P(X_{t+1})} \quad (6)$$

One limitation of utilizing mutual information is that the resulting value may fluctuate in response to changes in the joint probability of data. This can make it difficult to obtain a consistent outcome if the system is exposed to different inputs.

Effective Information (EI)

To address this limitation, Hoel introduced the concept of effective information to measure the causal effect of the current state on the future state of a system. Effective information is a scoring metric based on mutual information and can be calculated from the system's transition probability matrix (TPM), which is invariant to the input data.

By "intervening" in the current state distribution to follow the uniform distribution (the distribution of maximum entropy), denoted as I_D, the TPM enables the prediction of the future state distribution E_D at the next moment. The effective information (EI) of the system is defined as the mutual information between I_D and E_D, which can be expressed as

$$EI \equiv I(I_D; E_D) = I(X_t; X_{t+1})|_{do(X_t)\sim U} \tag{7}$$

The probability distribution of the random variable X_t, representing the initial state, is denoted as $do(X_t) \sim U$, indicating that it follows a uniform distribution. Hoel adopted the notion of the "do" operator from Judea Pearl's causal analysis framework [25]. It is worth noting that in Pearl's context, the do operator is typically used to assign a specific value to the intervened variable rather than applying a distribution [16].

Another point that needs clarification is that the "do" operator used here is purely a mathematical construct that specifies the distribution of X_t. It does not imply the need for actual intervention in the system. However, the imaginary "do" operation is equivalent to a real intervention in the context of this scenario, given that the dynamical mechanism (TPM) is provided. Consequently, we can perform any desired intervention on the system, just as in computer simulations.

The second issue pertains to why we apply the "do" operator to a uniform distribution. In [19], Hoel et al. claimed that the distribution should be the maximum entropy distribution, which is the most reasonable selection for the input variable X_t if we have no prior information about the input variable [97]. As we know, uniform distribution can be derived by maximizing entropy if there is no constraint.

The authors of this review believe that applying the "do" operator to a uniform distribution ensures that the objective measured by EI solely reflects the dynamical mechanism itself, i.e., the TPM, and is independent of any input data.

This point can be clearer if we re-express EI as a function of the TPM of the system (see Appendix A for the detailed derivation):

$$EI = \frac{1}{N}\sum_{i,j} TPM(i,j)\log_2\left(\frac{N \times TPM(i,j)}{\sum_k TPM(k,j)}\right), \tag{8}$$

where $TPM(i,j)$ represents the transitional probability of the system from the state i to the state j.

Therefore, effective information offers a solution to the aforementioned limitation of mutual information. Given that the TPM can capture the inherent nature of a system, EI is likewise an intrinsic property of the system.

However, if we apply the "do" operator to the system using different distributions, EI will depend on the chosen distribution, and certain transition probabilities of specific rows may carry greater weight in the average calculation. Consequently, deriving a simple expression solely based on the transitional probability matrix (TPM) may not be possible. Furthermore, if there is no "do" operator, the effects of the dynamical mechanism and the input distribution in EI would not be distinguishable or separated, as the mutual information is a function of the input distribution $p(X_t)$.

The Derived Measures of EI

Furthermore, we can calculate the EIs for the TPMs of both macro- and micro-dynamics, and their difference is defined as the measure of causal emergence, that is,

$$CE = EI(TPM_M) - EI(TPM_m), \tag{9}$$

where TPM_M represents the TPM of macro-level dynamics, and TPM_m represents the TPM of micro-level dynamics. CE measures the degree of causal emergence. If $CE > 0$, then causal emergence occurs; otherwise, it does not occur.

However, there is a limitation for EI and CE when comparing two dynamics that differ significantly in size. This is because the value of effective information relies on the number of possible states within the system, denoted as N, with an upper bound of $\log_2(N)$. To facilitate comparisons between different coarse-graining strategies and scales, effective information is often normalized, resulting in a metric known as the effect coefficient Eff.

$$Eff = \frac{EI}{\log_2(N)} \tag{10}$$

The value of the effect coefficient is always between 0 and 1, representing the proportion of effective information being transferred from current states to future states. If the information is fully transferred, the effect coefficient is 1.

In addition to characterizing causal emergence, the effect coefficient can be further broken down into two meaningful components: "*Determinism*", which represents the certainty of a current state evolving into a certain state or diverging into multiple states in the next moment, and "*Degeneracy*", which represents the possibility of multiple current states converging into one state in the next moment.

$$Eff = Determinism - Degeneracy \tag{11}$$

where both "*Determinism*" and "*Degeneracy*" can be defined in terms of the TPM (refer to Equations (8) and (10)):

$$\begin{aligned} Determinism &= \frac{1}{N\log_2(N)}\sum_{i,j} TPM(i,j)\log_2(N \times TPM(i,j)) \\ Degeneracy &= \frac{1}{N\log_2(N)}\sum_{i,j} TPM(i,j)\log_2(\sum_{k} TPM(k,j)) \end{aligned} \tag{12}$$

It should be noted that the determinism of a system is always greater than its degeneracy, as the lower bound of the effect coefficient is 0. The following examples illustrate what determinism and degeneracy look like in systems with varying TPMs.

In Figure 6, the square cells represent the elements of the TPM, and the grayscale areas represent the values of the TPM elements. Example (a) is a bijective system, meaning that all information from current states can be transferred to future states without loss. It is fully deterministic with zero degeneracy. Example (b) is an extreme case where all current states lead to only one future state, illustrating that high determinism does not necessarily imply a high effect coefficient. Systems (c) and (d) differ but have the same effect coefficients. Finally, system (e) is a coarse-grained version of either system (c) or (d), demonstrating two important points: first, different microscopic systems can be coarse-grained to the same macroscopic system, and second, causal emergence can be quantitatively captured from coarse-graining by the increased effect coefficient.

One limitation of EI is its global nature, as highlighted by the fact that the summation of additional terms encompasses the entire state space, as defined in Equation (8). Therefore, ref. [98] proposed the concept of flickering emergence, which decomposes EI into each term added in Equation (8). This new feature can characterize the local properties of Markov dynamics.

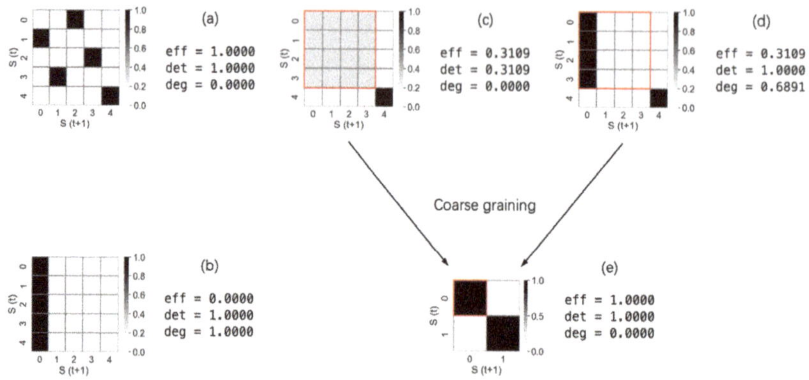

Figure 6. Examples of effect coefficient, determinism, degeneration, and how coarse-graining can change them. (**a**) Deterministic system with zero degeneracy; (**b**) Deterministic system with zero effect coefficient due to high degeneracy; (**c**) Partially deterministic system; (**d**) Deterministic system with low effect coefficient; (**e**) Coarse-grained system from (**c**) or (**d**), resulting in a fully deterministic system with a high effect coefficient.

Comparison with Other Measures of Causation

Hoel's theory of causal emergence is based on effective information, however, is the selection of EI necessary for measuring causation? Is causal emergence a phenomenon that depends on the selection of the measure of causation? To address this problem, in Comolatti and Hoel's work [28], a systematic comparison was conducted between effective information (EI) and other measures of causation that are widely applied in various fields, ranging from philosophy to genetics.

The findings of this comparison revealed that causal emergence is not merely a peculiar phenomenon limited to a specific measure. Instead, it exhibits commonalities and shared characteristics across different measures and fields of study. EI is not the sole measure for capturing causal emergence; there are other measures of causation that can also reveal the phenomenon of causal emergence. This suggests that the concept of causal emergence has broader applicability and relevance. We introduce this work in detail below.

Firstly, Hoel highlighted that causation is not merely a singular relationship between a cause and an effect. Instead, it encompasses two fundamental dimensions known as *causal primitives*: sufficiency and necessity.

The sufficiency aspect of causation refers to the scenario where the occurrence of the cause guarantees the occurrence of the effect. In other words, whenever the cause happens, the effect is also observed. This sufficiency dimension, denoted as $suff$, can be formally defined as the probability of the effect e occurring given the condition that the cause c has occurred:

$$suff(e,c) = P(e|c). \tag{13}$$

In addition, a necessary (*nec*) relation in causation refers to the absence of the effect implying the absence of the cause. In other words, when the effect does not occur, it indicates that the cause also does not occur. This can be understood as a kind of causal effect measure for the counterfactual. This necessary dimension, denoted as *nec*, can be quantitatively defined as the probability that the effect e does not occur when the condition that the cause c has not occurred is given by:

$$nec(e,c) = 1 - P(e|C/c), \tag{14}$$

where C/c represents the set of all possible causes in C but with the particular cause c being excluded. Therefore, $P(e|C/c)$ represents the probability that e occurs if other causes except c occur.

With these causal primitives defined, Hoel compared different measures of causation, including Hume's constant conjunction [40], Cheng's causal attribution [99], Eells's measure of causation as probability raising [41], Suppes's measure of causation as probability raising [42], and Judea Pearl's measures of causation [16]. The finding was that all of these measures can be expressed as the two causal primitives.

For example, Cheng's causal attribution can be expressed as:

$$CS_{cheng} = \frac{suff(e,c) + nec(e,c) - 1}{nec(e,c)} \tag{15}$$

With this understanding, a natural question arises: Can effective information (EI) be expressed using causal primitives? The answer is affirmative. However, to clarify this point, two important distinctions need to be made. Firstly, in most measures of causation, the causal variables are binary, whereas EI is defined for variables with multiple values. Secondly, EI is an information-theoretic measure, whereas others are probabilistic measures. Despite these distinctions, EI can still be expressed using causal primitives.

To understand this, let us examine the equivalent measure of EI: normalized effective information (Eff) in Equation (11). This measure contains two terms. The first term is *determinism*, and the second one is *degeneracy*. These two terms can be expressed as $suff$ and nec:

$$determinism = 1 - \frac{\sum_{c\in C} P(c)H(e|c)}{\log_2 N}, \tag{16}$$

where $H(e|c) \equiv -\sum_{e\in E} P(e|c)\log_2 P(e|c)$ is the Shannon entropy of the conditional probability $P(e|c)$, which is $suff(e,c)$, and $P(c), \forall c \in C$ is the distribution of all causes. In the definition of EI (Equation (7)), this distribution is intervened as a uniform distribution such that equal weights are assigned to causes $c \in C$. It is not hard to see that *determinism* is an information metric for $suff(e,c)$ and is averaged for all causes. Furthermore, as $suff(e,c) = P(e|c)$ increases and approaches one, indicating the emergence of causal effect, the value of H decreases, whereas determinism concurrently increases. Thus, the determinism term in EI plays a similar role to that of $suff$ in causal primitives.

Another term is *degeneracy*, which can be re-written as:

$$degeneracy = 1 - \frac{H(e|C)}{\log_2 N}, \tag{17}$$

where $H(e|C) \equiv -\sum_{e\in E} P(e|C)\log_2 P(e|C)$ is also the Shannon entropy of the conditional probability $P(e|C)$, which is calculated by averaging the causal effect for all elements in C as $P(e|C) = \sum_{c\in C} P(c)P(e|c)$. The entropy $H(e|C)$ serves as a measure of the average causal effect for counterfactuals, as $P(e|C)$ can be interpreted as $P(e|C/c)$. This is due to the approximation $P(e|C) \approx P(e|C/c)$ when the number of elements in C is significantly large, and C certainly encompasses C/c. Consequently, *degeneracy* in EI acts as the counterpart to nec in causal primitives.

Therefore, EI or eff is a valuable measure of causation, particularly in cases where the cause and effect variables are not limited to binary values.

Comolatti and Hoel [28] conducted additional experiments to investigate the phenomenon of causal emergence using various Markovian dynamics, employing different measures of causation, as discussed above. Their findings revealed the widespread occurrence of causal emergence, regardless of the specific measure of causation employed.

3.5.4. Examples of Causal Emergence

The example above demonstrates a coarse-graining strategy that is intuitive, as it involves aggregation at the state level. However, in reality, coarse-graining often occurs among variables, and the combination of these variables produces different states. Let us look at a more complicated example of a boolean network, given in [19], and inspect the causal emergence when coarse-graining its state transition mechanism. A, B, C, and D are four binary variables whose state transition relations are shown in Figure 7a.

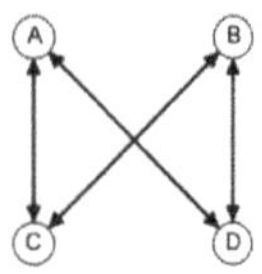

(a)

C or D / AB	0	1
00	0.7	0.3
01	0.7	0.3
10	0.7	0.3
11	0.0	1.0

(b)

CD / AB	00	01	10	11
00	0.49	0.21	0.21	0.09
01	0.49	0.21	0.21	0.09
10	0.49	0.21	0.21	0.09
11	0.00	0.00	0.00	1.00

(c)

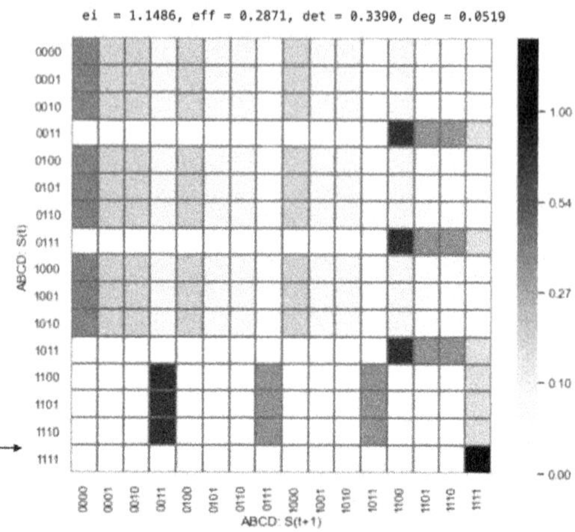

(d)

Figure 7. The mechanism and transition probability matrix of a boolean network. Each variable's next state is determined by the combination of the current states of two other variables, as shown in the boolean network (**a**). If we examine an atomic subsystem with two inputs and one output, such as AB →C, the next state of C depends on the present states of A and B. If A = 0 and B = 0, the probability of C being 1 is 70%, whereas the probability of it being 0 is 30%, as indicated in the table (**b**). This same microscopic dynamics applies to other atomic subsystems such as AB→D, CD→A, and CD→B. When we expand to a subsystem of two inputs and two outputs, AB→ CD and CD→AB, we obtain the transition probability matrix (TPM), as demonstrated in the table (**c**). Finally, we extend to the dynamics of the entire system ABCD→ABCD, whose TPM is represented as a heatmap (**d**). The effective information and relative metrics of the entire system are as follows: $EI_{mi} = 1.1486$, $Eff = 0.2871$, $Determinism = 0.3390$, $Degeneracy = 0.0519$

In order to demonstrate how different coarse-graining strategies can impact effective information, we can combine two micro-states into a single macro-state. For example, we can define $\alpha = (A, B)$ and $\beta = (C, D)$ as coarse-grained variables at the macro-level, where their values can be either 'off' or 'on'. Using various aggregation strategies, as illustrated in (a)/(b) and (d)/(e) in Figure 8, we can construct the TPMs for the resulting coarse-grained systems. The TPM and the corresponding metrics are presented in Figure 8c,f, respectively.

The effective information values for the two macroscopic systems are $EI_{ma1} = 1.55$ and $EI_{ma2} = 0.18$, respectively. It is evident that the effective information has increased in the first coarse-graining scenario ($EI_{ma1}(1.55) > EI_{mi}(1.15)$), whereas it has decreased in the second case ($EI_{ma2}(0.18) < EI_{mi}(1.15)$). Thus, causal emergence is observed in the first coarse-graining scenario. This implies that (1) proper coarse-graining can lead to causal emergence in a macroscopic system, and (2) not all coarse-graining approaches result in higher effective information. This example illustrates that coarse-graining can play an important role in emergence, and effective information is a well-defined quantification method. This gives us the opportunity to identify causal emergence in a given system. This raises the following question: What coarse-graining strategy can generate the maximum effective information? We address this question in Section 4.

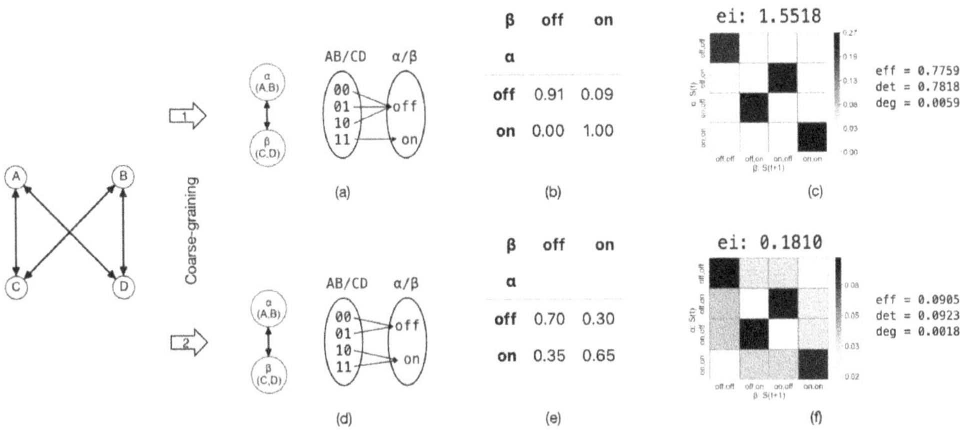

Figure 8. An example showing how different coarse-graining strategies applied to the same boolean network, shown in Figure 7, can lead to different boolean dynamics. (**a**) Coarse-graining strategy 1. (**b**) Macro-dynamics resulting from strategy 1. (**c**) The corresponding heatmap of the TPM and the effective information metrics of the macroscopic system using method 1. (**d**) Coarse-graining strategy 2. (**e**,**f**) The macro-dynamics and TPM corresponding to coarse-graining strategy 2 in (**d**), respectively.

3.5.5. Extensions to Continuous Systems

Effective information and its associated metrics have been shown to be useful in quantifying causal emergence. However, there are some limitations to be aware of. First, the method is only applicable to discrete-state systems. Second, knowledge of the system's transition probability matrix (TPM) is required to calculate the effective information metrics. Efforts have been made to apply or extend the concepts of effective information to continuous systems [26,31,100].

Ordinal Partition Network

One approach to incorporating effective information in continuous systems is to transform the continuous variables into discrete ones using the ordinal partition network (OPN) method [100]. The basic idea is to transform the time-series data generated by a continuous dynamical system into a sub-time series of dimensionality d with discrete values and then establish a transition probability matrix (TPM) between these discrete series. This approach involves three steps: firstly, sampling the original time series with a specified time interval τ to create sub-time series of dimensionality d; secondly, ranking these sub-series based on their values; and finally, utilizing the d-dimensional vectors of rank orders to represent the original sub-series. By employing rank orders, this method ensures that the values are restricted to integers within a certain range.

In [100], the author applied the OPN method to the Rossler chaotic attractor system. By quantifying effective information, he noticed that effective information (such as determinism and degeneracy) was sensitive to the critical phase transition between period and chaos [100].

Causal Geometry

Alternatively, Pavel Chvykov and Erik Hoel extended the causal emergence framework to continuous systems and proposed the concept of causal geometry [26].

To understand the basic idea of this work, we suppose the continuous system considered is a continuous functional map and assume that the uncertainties are small disturbances added to this deterministic function, that is,

$$y = f(x) + \varepsilon, \tag{18}$$

where x is the input variable defined on the interval $[-L/2, L/2]$, L is a very large constant, y is the output variable, and ε is a Gaussian noise with a zero mean and standard deviation $\epsilon \ll L$. Then, an approximate form of the effective information for such a continuous system can be obtained using the Gaussian integral.

$$EI \approx \ln(\frac{L}{\sqrt{2\pi e}}) + \frac{1}{2L}\int_{-L/2}^{L/2} \ln\left(\frac{f'(x)}{\epsilon}\right)^2 dx. \tag{19}$$

The reason we set the domain of x to $[-L/2, L/2]$ is to guarantee that the Gaussian integral can be implemented and to simplify the definition of a uniform distribution on it.

This form can be easily generalized to a dynamical system with discrete time steps once we replace x and y with $x(t)$ and $x(t+1)$, respectively. The formula can also be extended to higher dimensions, with $\mathbf{x}$ and $\mathbf{y}$ represented in bold. Suppose $\mathbf{x} \in [-L/2, L/2]^n \subset \mathcal{R}^n$ and $\mathbf{y} \in \mathcal{R}^m$, where n and m are positive integers. Equation (19) can be generalized to the following form:

$$EI \approx \ln(\frac{L^n}{(2\pi e)^{m/2}}) + \frac{1}{2}\mathbb{E}_{\mathbf{x}\sim U([-\frac{L}{2},\frac{L}{2}]^n)} \ln\left|\det\left(\frac{\partial_{\mathbf{x}} f(\mathbf{x})}{\Sigma^{1/2}}\right)\right|^2, \tag{20}$$

where Σ is the covariance matrix of the Gaussian noise ε, $U([-L, L]^n)$ represents the uniform distribution on the hypercube $[-L, L]^n$, $|\cdot|$ is the absolute value operation, and det is the determinant.

Note that the conditional distribution of $\mathbf{y}$ given $\mathbf{x}$ is a Gaussian distribution, that is, $p(\mathbf{y}|\mathbf{x}) = \mathcal{N}(f(\mathbf{x}), \Sigma)$. Thus, the term in the expectation in Equation (20) can be written as:

$$\left|\det\left(\frac{\partial_{\mathbf{x}} f(\mathbf{x})}{\Sigma^{1/2}}\right)\right|^2 = \left|\det\left(\mathbb{E}_{\mathbf{y}|\mathbf{x}}[\partial_\mu \partial_\nu \ln p(\mathbf{y}|\mathbf{x})]\right)\right|, \tag{21}$$

and this corresponds to the determinant of the negative Fisher information metric for the distribution $p(\mathbf{y}|\mathbf{x})$:

$$g_{\mu\nu} \equiv -\mathbb{E}_{\mathbf{y}|\mathbf{x}}[\partial_\mu \partial_\nu \ln p(\mathbf{y}|\mathbf{x})], \tag{22}$$

which measures the sensitivity of the logarithmic $p(\mathbf{y}|\mathbf{x})$ to changes in $\mathbf{x}$, where $\partial_\mu \equiv \frac{\partial}{\partial \mathbf{x}_\mu}$ represents the partial derivative with respect to the μth component of $\mathbf{x}$. Therefore, we have defined a distance metric for the Riemann manifold $\mathcal{M} = \{p(\mathbf{y}|\mathbf{x})\}$ on the parameter space $\mathbf{x} \in [-L/2, L/2]^n$, encompassing all possible distributions of $p(\mathbf{y}|\mathbf{x})$. This is the origin of the term "geometry" in this framework.

Finally, we can obtain an expression for EI with the Fisher information metric:

$$EI \approx \ln\frac{L^n}{(2\pi e)^{m/2}} - \frac{1}{2}\mathbb{E}_{\mathbf{x}\sim U([-\frac{L}{2},\frac{L}{2}]^n)} \ln|\det(g_{\mu\nu})|. \tag{23}$$

This formula can be generalized to cases where $p(\mathbf{y}|\mathbf{x})$ is a non-Gaussian distribution. Once the distribution function is known, we can obtain its Fisher information metric, and then EI can be calculated using Equation (23). The reason behind this is that the whole manifold $p(\mathbf{y}|\mathbf{x})$ for any $\mathbf{x}$ can be understood as a concatenation of local Gaussian distributions.

In [26], the authors considered a more general case in which intervention noise is added to the input (intervention) variable x in Equation (19). The intervention noise is denoted as $\xi \sim \mathcal{N}(0, \delta^2)$, where δ is the standard deviation of ξ. In contrast, ε is called observational noise distinguishing it from ξ, and is added to the output (observational) variable y according to Equation (19). Finally, if two kinds of noise are both considered and if $L = 1$ and $\epsilon \ll 1$, Equation (19) becomes:

$$EI \approx -\frac{1}{2}\int_{-1/2}^{1/2} \ln\left[\left(\frac{\epsilon}{f'(x)}\right)^2 + \delta^2\right] dx. \tag{24}$$

This is the formula for EI for the continuous mapping function (Equation (18)) given by [26]. Using this equation and a logistic function for $f(x)$, the authors compared the EIs of a more continuous map (Equation (18)) and a more discrete map with an adjustable parameter in the logistic function. They discovered that when the noise level is low, the continuous map can exhibit higher EI compared to the discrete map. However, as the noise level increases, discretizing the mapping function can lead to a model with higher EI. This phenomenon helps explain why digital circuits eventually outperform analog circuits in mitigating noise interference; the binarization and coarse-graining strategy of digital circuits suppresses the propagation and diffusion of noise.

To generalize the information geometry to the case with intervention noise and observational noise, let us introduce a new intermediate variable $\theta \in \Theta \subset \mathcal{R}^l$ with dimensionality l such that we cannot control $\mathbf{y}$ by directly intervening $\mathbf{x}$. Instead, we can intervene $\mathbf{x}$ to influence θ and indirectly affect $\mathbf{y}$. Therefore, the three variables form a Markov chain: $\mathbf{x} \to \theta \to \mathbf{y}$.

In this case, two manifolds can be obtained: the effect manifold $\mathcal{M}_E = \{p(\mathbf{y}|\theta)\}_{\theta\in\Theta}$ with metric $g_{\mu\nu} = -\mathbb{E}_{p(\mathbf{y}|\theta)}\partial_\mu\partial_\nu \ln p(\mathbf{y}|\theta)$ and the intervention manifold $\mathcal{M}_I = \{\tilde{q}(\mathbf{x}|\theta)\}_{\theta\in\Theta}$ with metric $h_{\mu\nu} = -\mathbb{E}_{\tilde{q}(\mathbf{x}|\theta)}\partial_\mu\partial_\nu \ln \tilde{q}(\mathbf{x}|\theta)$, where $\tilde{q} \equiv \frac{q(\theta|\mathbf{x})}{\int q(\theta|\mathbf{x})dx}$ and $\partial_\mu = \partial/\partial\theta_\mu$. These two manifolds together are called causal geometry.

Finally, the EI calculation formula for causal geometry is:

$$EI_g = \ln\frac{V_I}{(2\pi e)^{n/2}} - \frac{1}{2V_I}\int_\Theta \sqrt{|\det(h_{\mu\nu})|}\ln\left|\det\left(I_n + \frac{h_{\mu\nu}}{g_{\mu\nu}}\right)\right| d^l\theta, \tag{25}$$

where we have set $L = 1$ and $m = l = n$ to reduce the number of free parameters, and I_n is the identity matrix with size n, $V_I = \int_\Theta \sqrt{|\det(h_{\mu\nu})|} d^l\theta$.

EI Calculation for Neural Networks

One of the application areas for continuous EI is neural networks. In [101], the authors applied EI to analyze the causal effects for different layers of neural networks and compared the results with the information bottleneck theory. The method they used to calculate EI was to convert continuous variables into discrete ones by dividing the domains of the input and output variables into small regions. However, this method has high computational complexity and is challenging to extend to high dimensions.

In [31], the authors proposed a new numeric method for calculating EI on neural networks. The basic idea behind this method is to understand a well-trained feed-forward neural network as a stochastic mapping, following:

$$\mathbf{y} = f(\mathbf{x}) + \varepsilon, \tag{26}$$

where $\mathbf{x} \in \mathcal{R}^n$ is the input variable, $\mathbf{y} \in \mathcal{R}^m$ is the output variable, and $f : \mathcal{R}^n \to \mathcal{R}^m$ is the deterministic map of the neural network. Additionally, ε is a Gaussian noise with a mean of zero and a covariance matrix $\Sigma = diag(\sigma_1^2, \sigma_2^2, \cdots, \sigma_m^2)$, where σ_i is the mean square error on dimension i across the entire training dataset. In this way, the neural network can be regarded as a Gaussian distribution $p(\mathbf{y}|\mathbf{x}) = \mathcal{N}(f(\mathbf{x}), \Sigma)$.

Therefore, Equation (20) can be used on this neural network to calculate EI. In [31], the authors used the Monte Carlo integration method to estimate the expectation in Equation (20). This technique significantly reduces the computational complexity.

However, when the authors compared the results calculated using Equation (20) for various neural networks with different dimensions, they obtained unreasonable results: EI increased with the number of dimensions. Thus, causal emergence was not always observed because micro-dynamics exhibited unreasonably larger EI. Another drawback of Equation (20) is that the parameter L always dominates the value of the expression and should be removed from the equation. One way to solve this issue is to use Eff instead of EI (see Equation (10)). However, not all Ls in Equation (20) can be eliminated. Therefore, the authors introduced the notion of dimension-averaged EI, defined as

$$dEI \equiv \frac{EI}{m} \tag{27}$$

which simply divides EI by the dimension of the output variable $\mathbf{y}$. By using dimension-averaged EI, L can be removed when calculating dimension-averaged causal emergence for the neural networks f_M and f_m representing macro- and micro-dynamics, respectively, given by

$$dCE(f_M, f_m) \equiv \frac{EI(f_M)}{n_M} - \frac{EI(f_m)}{n_m}, \tag{28}$$

where dCE is the dimension-averaged causal emergence measure. If we incorporate Equation (20) into Equation (28), we obtain:

$$dCE \approx \frac{\mathbb{E}_{\mathbf{x}_M} \log|\det(\partial_{\mathbf{x}_M} f_M)| + \sum_{i=1}^{x_M} \log \sigma_{i,M}^2}{n_M} - \frac{\mathbb{E}_{\mathbf{x}_m} \log|\det(\partial_{\mathbf{x}_m} f_m)| + \sum_{i=1}^{x_m} \log \sigma_{i,m}^2}{n_m}, \tag{29}$$

in which L is eliminated.

3.5.6. Causal Emergence in Complex Networks

Many complex systems can be represented by networks; therefore, applying the framework for causal emergence to networks is necessary. However, two problems should be solved in advance to apply Hoel's framework: one is to assign dynamics to the studied network because networks are static structures without any dynamical properties and the other is to coarse-grain the network.

Klein and Hoel [27] addressed the first problem by considering random walks on complex networks. Subsequently, the TPM of the system was defined based on the transfer probabilities between nodes of a large number of random walkers. Due to the good mathematical properties of the random walk dynamics on graphs, the authors established an explicit expression for EI on networks, and the final form only relied on the weighted normalized adjacency matrix $w_{ij}(\sum_j w_{ij} = 1)$ of the network. The expression is as follows:

$$EI = H(\langle W_i^{out} \rangle) - \langle H(W_i^{out}) \rangle. \tag{30}$$

where $H(\langle W_i^{out} \rangle)$ represents the Shannon entropy calculated from the distribution of the averaged out-weights across all nodes ($W_i^{out} \equiv \{w_{ij} | j = 1, 2, \ldots, N\}$), which characterizes the determinism of the random walk dynamics; $\langle H(W_i^{out}) \rangle$ is the average Shannon entropy for all nodes, which characterizes the degeneracy of the dynamics; and $H(W_i^{out})$ is the uncertainty of node i.

To address the second problem, in [27], the greedy algorithm was used to group nodes to form a macro-network. It is worth noting that when merging micro-nodes into macro-nodes, the TPM of the resulting macro-network can be derived by merging the probabilities from the TPM of the micro-level. To ensure that the grouped macro-network maintains the same random walk dynamics as the original one, a dynamic consistency test is implemented.

In the experimental section, the aforementioned paper explored the application of a greedy search for identifying causal emergence in complex networks. Experiments were conducted on artificial networks as well as four types of real networks. In the case of ER random networks, the size of effective information was solely dependent on the connection probability p and converged to $-\log_2 p$ with the increase in network size. Additionally, a significant finding was the presence of a phase transition point, where the average degree of the network reached approximately $\log_2 N$. Beyond this point, the random network structure did not contain additional information with increasing size. In the case of preferential attachment (PA) networks, when $\alpha < 1.0$ (α represents the degree of preferential attachment), the effective information of the network increased as the network size expanded. Conversely, when $\alpha > 1.0$, the opposite was observed. The scale-free network corresponding to $\alpha = 1.0$ represented the critical boundary of growth. Regarding real networks, the authors found that biological networks exhibited the lowest EI due to the presence of significant noise, which can be removed through effective coarse-graining, and causal emergence was the most significant compared to other types of networks. However, technical networks exhibited sparsity and non-degeneracy, resulting in higher average efficiency and more specific node relationships. Consequently, they exhibited the highest EIs among the studied networks.

The network coarse-graining method mentioned above is the greedy algorithm. However, when the network is very large, the efficiency of this method remains considerably low. Following that, Griebenow et al. [102] introduced a spectral clustering-based approach for identifying causal emergence within networks. More specifically, the method involved performing eigenvalue decomposition of the TPM, followed by constructing a similarity matrix using the eigenvectors of the nodes. The OPTICS algorithm was employed to cluster the nodes, and nodes belonging to the same cluster were aggregated into a macro-node. Subsequently, the maximum value of EI was selected by utilizing the linear search distance hyperparameter ϵ. In their paper, the authors additionally proposed a gradient descent algorithm based on deep learning. This approach encompassed several steps, beginning with the random initialization of a grouping matrix. Then, this matrix was used to construct a macro-network by combining the micro-networks. Finally, the grouping strategies were automatically learned through the process of maximizing effective information within the macro-network. However, this method often falls into the local optimal solution.

3.5.7. Other Applications

Once the method for quantifying causal emergence in complex systems is developed, it can be applied across various fields that possess abundant network data. The first type of network studied was biological networks.

As previously discussed, biological networks are full of noise, which poses challenges in comprehending their internal operating principles. On one hand, such noise arises from inherent fluctuations within the system itself, whereas on the other hand, it can be introduced through measurement or observation processes. Consequently, Klein et al. [103] further explored the relationship between noise, degeneracy, and certainty in biological networks and their specific meanings. For instance, in gene expression networks, highly deterministic relationships indicate that the expression of one gene almost invariably leads to the expression of another gene. Simultaneously, degeneracy is a prevalent phenomenon in the evolutionary processes of biological systems. Due to these two factors, it remains unclear at which scale biological systems should be analyzed to gain a deeper understanding of their functions.

To address this, Klein et al. [104] conducted an analysis of protein interaction networks across more than 1800 species. They employed EI as a measure for assessing the levels of noise and uncertainty in protein interactions. The findings revealed that the macro-scale network exhibited lower levels of noise and degeneracy. Additionally, the nodes within the macro-scale interaction group demonstrated greater resilience compared to the nodes that were not part of the macro-scale interaction group. Through robust analysis, the authors demonstrated that eukaryotes exhibited a stronger degree of causal emergence compared to archaea. Additionally, to address the 'deterministic paradox,' the authors introduced the concepts of the neutral process and the selection process in biological evolution. The neutral process operates at the micro-scale, leveraging mutations to promote interactions and enhance species diversity. On the other hand, the selection process operates at the macro-scale, effectively eliminating noise that hampers system operation and efficiency. Therefore, in order to adapt to the demands of evolution, it becomes essential for evolved biological systems to function across multiple scales.

Hoel et al. [43] conducted further research on the causal emergence within biological systems. The authors elaborated that macro- and micro-systems exist widely in biological systems. For example, the micro-scale of a group of cells can involve potential ion channel changes, whereas the macro-scale corresponds to the membrane potential changes of cells. Furthermore, the authors utilized EI to analyze gene regulatory networks, aiming to identify the most informative models for controlling mammalian heart development. By quantifying the causal emergence within the largest component of the gene network of Saccharomyces cerevisia, it was revealed that informative macro-scale structures were prevalent across biological systems. Additionally, the authors emphasized the importance of evolutionary systems operating at multiple scales due to the significant advantages they offer. Natural selection requires variation between populations, and degradation observed in biological systems serves as a crucial factor for evolution. Degradation provides the conditions for the evolutionary process. However, organisms also need to maintain predicted consistency in phenotype, behavior, and structure to ensure survival and reproduction. Consequently, evolved systems need to operate at multiple scales, and the function of multi-scale systems is malleable in changing environments.

Swain et al. [105] conducted an investigation into the impact of ant colony interaction history on task assignment and task switching. They employed effective information to examine how noise information propagates among ants and explored the relationship between EI and the proportion of ants assigned to different tasks within ant colonies. The study revealed that the extent of historical interaction between ant colonies influenced task assignment. Additionally, the specific type of ant colony involved in an interaction determined the level of noise present within that interaction. For example, the interactions between foragers displayed significantly higher levels of noise when contrasted with interactions between nurses or cleaners. Furthermore, even when ants switched functional groups, the cohesion within ant colonies ensured the stability of the overall colony, and different functional ant colonies also played different roles in maintaining group cohesion.

The EI indicator and causal emergence theoretic framework can also be applied to artificial systems. For example, Marrow et al. [101] quantified and monitored the changes in the causal structure of neural networks during training, in which EI was employed to evaluate the degree of causal influence of nodes and edges on downstream tasks at each layer. By observing the changes in EI, including determinism (sensitivity) and degeneracy, throughout model training, the generalization ability of the model could be determined, thus helping better understand and explain the working principle of neural networks.

Varley et al. [100] attempted to apply the causal emergence framework to both discrete cellular automata and continuous Rossler systems. In the case of cellular automata systems, the authors select 88 unique rules corresponding to four types: static, periodic, chaotic, and complex. By considering each state as a node, where each state determines the subsequent state, a directed state transition graph is constructed. The analysis revealed that rules 1, 2, and 4 correspond to the strongest causal emergence of dynamics. Notably, the network constructed by these three rules exhibited a significant presence of star and spoke motifs. In addition, the authors also draw some quantitative conclusions, for example, among the 17 rules belonging to the third and fourth categories, 30% exist causal emergence, 70% show causal degradation, and the CE of cellular automata with the same rules remained relatively consistent across different sizes.

Furthermore, the authors employed the OPN algorithm to transform the continuous system into a discrete-state transition graph for comparative analysis (see Section 3.5.5). They found that chaos dynamics demonstrated a correlation with low determinism, and the variations in the degeneracy and efficiency coefficients aligned with the changes observed in the determinism curve.

3.5.8. Critiques

In the extensive literature on causality and emergence, Hoel's theory has attracted attention for linking emergence and causality through interventionism, introducing the concept of causal emergence in a quantitative manner. However, Dewhurst [77] provided a philosophical clarification of Hoel's theory, arguing that it was epistemological rather than metaphysical. This suggests that Hoel's macroscopic causality is merely a causal explanation based on information theory, rather than involving "genuinely novel causal powers". This also raises concerns about the assumption of a uniform distribution, as there is no empirical basis to favor it over other distributions.

The computation of Hoel's effective information relies on two premises: (1) knowledge of the system's microscopic dynamics, and (2) knowledge of the coarse-graining scheme. However, in practice, it is rare for both conditions to be simultaneously satisfied, especially in observational studies where both are unknown. This limitation hinders the practical applicability of Hoel's theory.

It has been pointed out that Hoel's theory neglects the constraints on coarse-graining methods, and certain coarse-graining methods can lead to ambiguity [78]. Additionally, the combination of some coarse-graining operations over states and coarse-graining operations over time does not exhibit commutativity. For instance, by assuming $A_{m\times n}$ is a coarse-graining operation over states (merging n states into m states), and $(\cdot)\times(\cdot)$ is a coarse-graining operation over time (combining two time steps into one), the equation $A_{m\times n}(TPM_{n\times n}) \times A_{m\times n}(TPM_{n\times n}) = A_{m\times n}(TPM_{n\times n} \times TPM_{n\times n})$ does not always hold. This indicates that certain coarse-graining operations can result in a discrepancy between the evolution of macroscopic states and the coarse-grained states of the evolved microscopic systems. It implies the need for consistent constraints on coarse-graining strategies.

This means that solely maximizing EI may raise some problems, and further constraints must be added to the framework. We discuss this problem in Section 4.1.1.

3.6. *Fernando E. Rosas's Quantification of Causal Emergence*

3.6.1. Basic Idea

In Hoel's framework, it is essential to find a coarse-graining strategy in order to determine the occurrence of causal emergence, and the outcome is influenced by the choice of the coarse-graining method. Although it has been suggested by Hoel [19,25] that an optimal strategy can be identified by maximizing EI, certain issues have been raised by Dewhurst [77]. EI is a global measure because it requires the input variable X to be a uniform distribution over the whole domain [24]. However, many regions are not observable from the data. Consequently, there is a pressing need for an alternative theoretical framework for causal emergence that does not rely on a coarse-graining method.

In response, Fernando E. Rosas took an approach that did not require a coarse-graining strategy as a prerequisite, attempting to break down excess entropy—the mutual information between a system's past and future states—into non-overlapping parts to identify the information components most relevant to causal emergence. To accomplish this, he relied on the partial information decomposition (PID) framework proposed by Williams and Beer, which provides a method for the non-overlapping decomposition of joint mutual information [29]. Below, we introduce Williams and Beer's theoretical framework.

3.6.2. Partial Information Decomposition

The partial information decomposition (PID) framework investigates the general informational relationship between source variables and a target variable. To simplify the problem description without sacrificing generality, let us consider a system with two input variables (X_1, X_2) and one output variable (Y) as an example, as depicted in the Venn diagram below.

The mutual information between the target variable and individual source variables, $I(X_1;Y)$ and $I(X_2;Y)$, as well as the mutual information between the target variable and the joint source variable, $I(X_1,X_2;Y)$, exhibits a complex relationship. Intuitively, one cannot be converted to another. Nonetheless, it is an intuitive notion that the overlapped circular plates of $I(X_1;Y)$ and $I(X_2;Y)$ divide the oval region of $I(X_1,X_2;Y)$ into four adjacent non-overlapping regions, representing the three types of information components of $I(X_1,X_2;Y)$:

$$I(X_1,X_2;Y) = Red(X_1,X_2;Y) + Un(X_1;Y|X_2) + Un(X_2;Y|X_1) + Syn(X_1,X_2;Y) \quad (31)$$

Specifically:

- *Red*: Redundant information refers to the information held by both sources;
- *Un*: Unique information refers to the information held by one source but not the other;
- *Syn*: Synergistic information is the information held by all sources together, but not any individual one.

If we can identify variable representations corresponding to these information components, the non-overlapping feature in the Venn diagram indicates their independence from one another.

For a more intuitive understanding, let us consider a few simple toy examples.

Case 1, $Y = X_1 = X_2$: This is a scenario in which a single source variable can predict the target variable, and the addition of another source variable does not enhance the prediction of the target variable. In this case, we have $I(X_1,X_2;Y) = Red(X_1,X_2;Y)$, as depicted in Figure 9b.

Case 2, $Y = X_1 \oplus X_2, X_1 \perp X_2$: In another scenario, neither of the source variables can predict the target variable individually, but together, they can predict the target variable synergistically. In this case, $I(X_1,X_2;Y) = Syn(X_1,X_2;Y)$, as depicted in Figure 9c.

Case 3, $Y = X_1, X_1 \perp X_2$: In this scenario, the target variable can be predicted by one of the source variables but not the other, which implies $I(X_1,X_2;Y) = Un(X_1;Y|X_2)$, as depicted in Figure 9d.

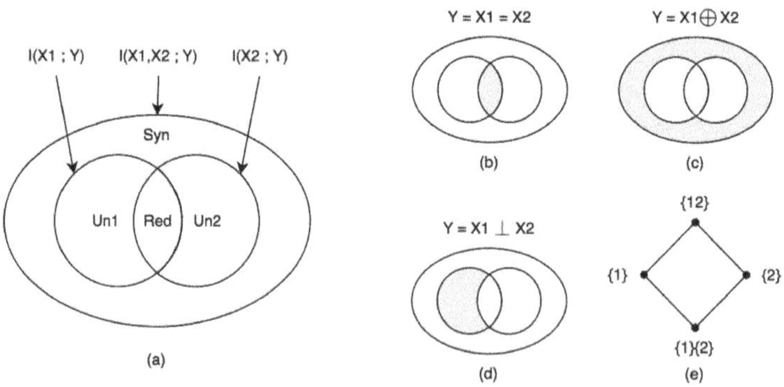

Figure 9. Venn diagram of PID. (**a**) Relationship of mutual information between Y and X1, X2. (**b–d**) Examples showing that joint mutual information is solely contributed by redundant, synergistic, and unique information. (**e**) Redundancy lattice representation of (**a**).

For general cases, Williams and Beer presented a method for calculating redundant information, defined as Red_{min}. This method reflects the concept of redundancy, identifying it as the shared information across all sources, which is equivalent to the minimum amount of information contributed by any single source:

$$Red_{min}(X_1,X_2;Y) \sum_{y \in \mathcal{Y}} P(Y=y) \min_{Xi} I(Y=y;X_i) \quad (32)$$

Figure 9e presents an alternative way of visualizing the PID framework, known as the redundancy lattice [29]. In this representation, $\{12\}$ denotes synergistic information, $\{1\}$ and $\{2\}$ denote unique information, and $\{1\}\{2\}$ denotes redundant information. In the subsequent sections, we demonstrate that the ϕID framework employs the notation of the redundancy lattice.

Although the PID framework remains compatible with scenarios involving more than two source variables, it should be noted that the corresponding Venn diagrams and redundancy lattices for these scenarios can become substantially more complicated and difficult to decipher, as discussed in [29].

3.6.3. Integrated Information Decomposition

The PID framework provides a useful framework for analyzing the non-overlapping information composition in a multivariate system. However, its application to causal analysis of dynamic systems is limited by the fact that it only allows for a single target variable. This limitation prevents the framework from fully capturing the transitions of multiple states across time steps. To address this challenge, Fernando E. Rosas developed Integrated Information Decomposition (ϕID) [30], which takes its name from Integrated Information Theory (IIT) [21]. This extension of PID provides a more comprehensive method for analyzing dynamic systems.

To introduce Rosas's framework clearly, we consider a system with only two variables. All the definitions and calculations can be generalized to systems with more variables.

The objective of the ϕID framework is to decompose excess entropy into non-overlapping information components. In a two-variable Markovian system, excess entropy is given by $E = I(X_t^1, X_t^2; X_{t+1}^1, X_{t+1}^2)$, where X_t^1 and X_t^2 represent the current states, and X_{t+1}^1, X_{t+1}^2 represent the future states. From a causation perspective, X_t^1 and X_t^2 represent causes, whereas X_{t+1}^1 and X_{t+1}^2 represent effects.

Rosas first noted that mathematically, the PID framework is symmetric with respect to the source and target variables. There are two viewpoints for analyzing the above Markovian system with PID. One viewpoint takes X_{t+1}^1 and X_{t+1}^2 together as the target variable (aiming to decompose the "cause" to elements), whereas the other viewpoint takes X_t^1 and X_t^2 together as the target variable (aiming to decompose the "effect" to elements). The redundancy lattices of these perspectives are illustrated in Figure 10a,b, and respectively, are referred to as "forward PID" and " PID".

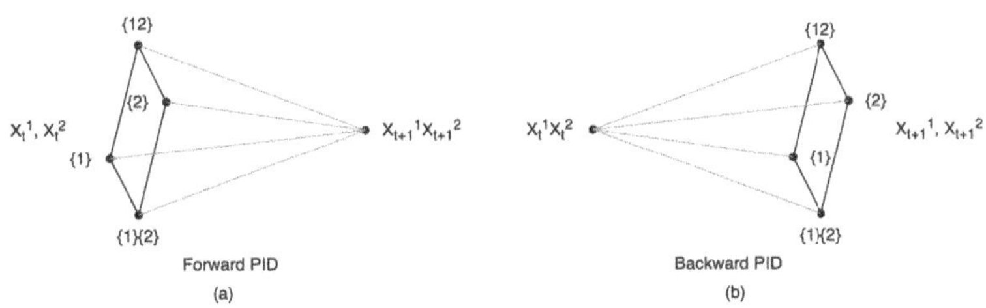

Figure 10. (**a**) Redundancy lattice of "forward PID" and its target variable $X_{t+1}^1X_{t+1}^2$. (**b**) Redundancy lattice of "backward PID" and its target variable $X_t^1X_t^2$.

Next, Rosas introduced the ϕID framework, consolidating forward PID and backward PID into a single framework. In this framework, the one-to-many relationship in PID was expanded to include many-to-many relationships. He built full connections between the elements of the redundancy lattices of forward PID and backward PID. This approach generates 16 relations between the source and target, as depicted by the colored lines in Figure 11a (each color corresponds to a specific source element of X_t). These relations are referred to as "ϕID atoms" and can be represented as vertices in a lattice, as shown in Figure 11b. This more complex lattice is referred to as the double-redundancy lattice because it is a "product" of two redundancy lattices (of forward PID and backward PID).

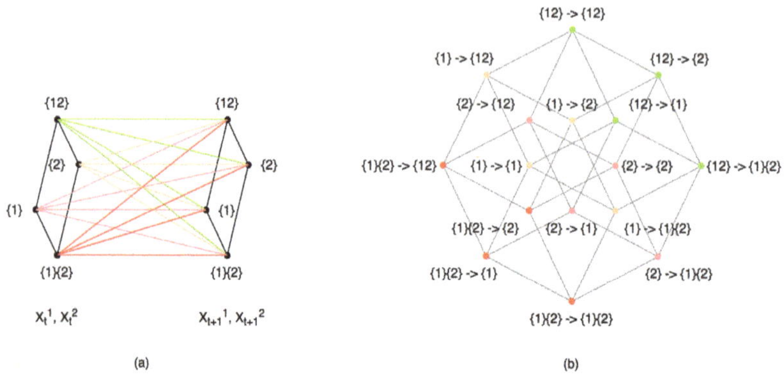

Figure 11. (**a**) Relationships between redundancy lattices of forward PID and backward PID. (**b**) Double-redundancy lattice, whose vertices correspond to the edges in (**a**). Distinct colors of dots and lines are employed to distinguish the source elements of X_t.

In the double-redundancy lattice, each vertex is defined as a "ϕID atom", denoted as $I_\partial^{\alpha\to\beta}, \alpha, \beta \in \mathcal{A}$, where $\mathcal{A} = \{\{\{1\}\{2\}\}, \{1\}, \{2\}, \{12\}\}$. For instance, the ϕID atom of the vertice $\{12\} \to \{12\}$ is denoted as $I_\partial^{\{12\}\to\{12\}}$. The ϕID atom represents the broken-down information transmitted from the cause elements to the effect elements, and their cumulative sum amounts to the excess entropy of the entire system. Consequently, the formal definition of Integrated Information Decomposition (ϕID) is:

$$\mathbf{E} = I(\mathbf{X_t}; \mathbf{X_{t+1}}) = \sum_{\alpha,\beta\in\mathcal{A}} I_\partial^{\alpha\to\beta} \tag{33}$$

The main advantage of ϕID is that it can provide a more fine-grained analysis of complex systems compared to PID by introducing the temporal dynamic. By decomposing the mutual information of the system at different times, ϕID provides another approach for the quantitative study of causal emergence.

3.6.4. Reconciling Emergences

Building upon the concept of synergistic information in the PID framework, Rosas introduced a quantitative definition of causal emergence using the ϕID framework to tackle the challenge of identifying an appropriate coarse-graining strategy. The definition includes two aspects: firstly, determining whether the system has the capacity to generate causal emergence, and secondly, assessing the occurrence of causal emergence given a specific macroscopic feature.

Regarding a system's capacity to exhibit causal emergence, this definition establishes a connection between causal emergence and synergistic relationships among variables across different time points. Consequently, a system denoted as X_t is said to possess the capacity for causally emergent features if and only if:

$$Syn(X_t; X_{t+1}) > 0 \tag{34}$$

In this context, causal emergence is understood as the synergistic effect between variables at preceding and subsequent moments within a Markovian dynamics system.

Then, Rosas further divided causal emergence into two parts in the ϕID framework, downward causality and causal decoupling, based on the distinct characteristics of the information atoms. Among the sixteen ϕID atoms obtained by decomposing the mutual information $I(X_t; X_{t+1})$ using ϕID, there are four information atoms corresponding to the synergistic effect, which is regarded as the composition of causal emergence. These atoms are denoted as $I_\partial^{\{12\}\to\alpha}(X_t, X_{t+1}), \alpha \in \mathcal{A} = \{\{\{1\}\{2\}\}, \{1\}, \{2\}, \{12\}\}$.

Downward causality is denoted as $\mathcal{D}(X_t, X_{t+1})$, encapsulating the information atoms that exclusively manifest a synergistic effect in forward PID, as shown in Figures 12 and 13:

$$\mathcal{D}(X_t, X_{t+1}) := \sum_{\alpha \in A/\{12\}} I_\partial^{\{12\}\to\alpha}(X_t, X_{t+1}) \tag{35}$$

While causal decoupling is denoted as $\mathcal{G}(X_t, X_{t+1})$, pinpointing the specific information atom where both forward and backward PID exhibit synergy:

$$\mathcal{G}(X_t, X_{t+1}) := I_\partial^{\{12\}\to\{12\}}(X_t, X_{t+1}) \tag{36}$$

Since ϕID is a non-overlapping decomposition of all information, this classification takes into account all cases of causal emergence, that is,

$$Syn(X_t; X_{t+1}) = \mathcal{G}(X_t, X_{t+1}) + \mathcal{D}(X_t, X_{t+1}). \tag{37}$$

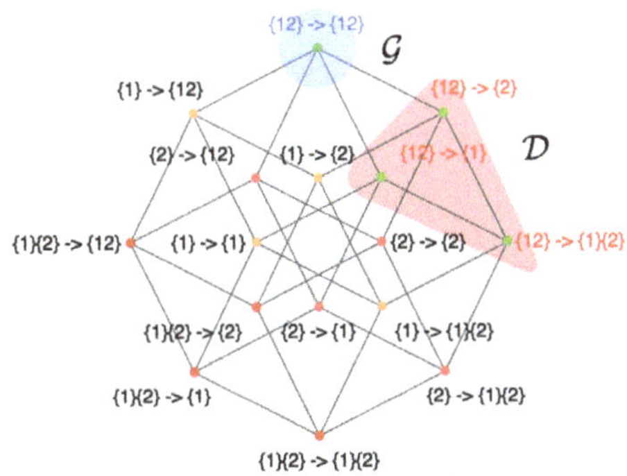

Figure 12. Causal decoupling ($\mathcal{G}$) and downward causation ($\mathcal{D}$) are represented by a double-redundancy lattice. Distinct colors of dots are employed to distinguish the source elements of X_t, (colors are corresponding to Figure 11).

In addition to that, Rosas also provided an approach to quantify the causal emergence of a specific macro-variable, i.e., a coarse-graining strategy. If a system has the capacity to generate causal emergence, there can be some macroscopic features that exhibit causal emergence. A feature variable V is said to be supervenient on the underlying system if it does not provide any predictive power for future states at times $t+1$ when the complete state X of the system at time t is known with perfect precision. This is equivalent to V_t being statistically independent of X_{t+1} given X_t. Then, for a system described by X_t, a supervenient feature V_t is said to exhibit causal causation if:

$$Un(V_t; X_{t+1}|X_t) > 0. \tag{38}$$

For this definition, the system's capacity of causal emergence is required, where $Syn(X_t; X_{t+1}) > 0$, since $Un(V_t; X_{t+1}|X_t) \leq Syn(X_t; X_{t+1})$ holds for any supervenient feature V_t. Corresponding to the classification of the system's capacity, the downward causation (as indicated by the red dotted line in Figure 13) of a feature variable V exists when

$$\begin{gathered} Un(V_t; X^1_{t+1}|X_t) > 0 \\ or \\ Un(V_t; X^2_{t+1}|X_t) > 0 \end{gathered} \tag{39}$$

and causal decoupling (as indicated by the blue dotted line in Figure 13) exists when

$$Un(V_t; V_{t+1}|X_t, X_{t+1}) > 0, \tag{40}$$

which also depends on the capacity of the system. Furthermore, V_t is said to have pure causal decoupling if $Un(V_t; X^{\alpha}_{t+1}|X_t) = 0$ and $Un(V_t; X_{t+1}|X_t) > 0$. If all the emergent features exhibit pure causal decoupling, the system is said to be perfectly decoupled.

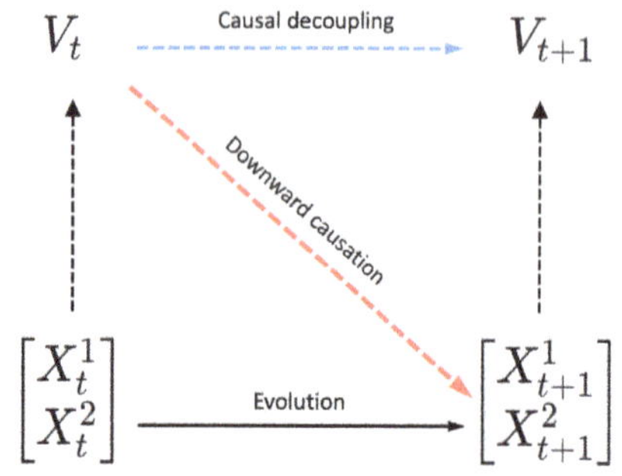

Figure 13. Synergistic causes can be further divided into causal decoupling and downward causation.

Although a rigorous quantitative definition for causal emergence was proposed, the mathematical formulations used in ϕID can be complex and computationally demanding, making it difficult to apply the method to real-world systems. Also, In addition, the inconsistency in PID calculation causes the definition of causal emergence to depend on a specific PID calculation. To address these problems, Rosas relaxed the calculation of causal emergence and established a identification criteria based one the sufficient conditions of causal decoupling and downward causation.

Specifically, to avoid exploring the specific quantitative methods of synergistic and redundant information, this criteria repeatedly subtracts redundant information, making the result a sufficient condition for causal emergence, which lose some of its generality but improves the reliability. The three indicators to be used are:

$$\Psi_{t,t+1}(V) := I(V_t; V_{t+1}) - \sum_j I(X_t^j; V_{t+1}), \tag{41}$$

which measures the mutual information between macro-variables across two time steps minus the mutual information between each micro-state and macro-state.

$$\Delta_{t,t+1}(V) := \max_j \left(I(V_t; X_{t+1}^j) - \sum_i I(X_t^i; X_{t+1}^j)) \right), \tag{42}$$

which is the maximum of the difference between mutual information of V_t and X_{t+1}^j and the summation of the mutual information of X_t^i and X_{t+1}^j.

$$\Gamma_{t,t+1}(V) := \max_j I(V_t; X_{t+1}^j), \tag{43}$$

which is the maximum mutual information between V_t and X_{t+1}^j. For the above indicators, V is a predefined macro-variable, but the specific method for finding such a macro-variable is not discussed in [24].

The specific usage of the indicators are as follows: Firstly, $\Psi_{t,t+1}(V) > 0$ is a sufficient condition for the causal emergence of V_t. Secondly, $\Delta_{t,t+1}(V) > 0$ is a sufficient condition for V_t to show downward causation. Thirdly, $\Psi_{t,t+1}(V) > 0$ and $\Gamma_{t,t+1}(V) = 0$ together constitute a sufficient condition for causal decoupling.

In summary, Rosas proposed an approach to quantitatively characterize and classified causal emergence based on ϕID by establishing the relationship between causal emergence and the synergistic effect of variables at different time points and further categorized causal emergence. The definition not only provides an objective assessment of a system's capacity for causal emergence but also enables the measurement the causal emergence associated with a specific macro-feature. His significant contributions include bridging the gap between the study of causal emergence and quantitative empirical research, classifying the different types of causal emergence, and complementing philosophical discussions on the topic.

The PID and ϕID frameworks hold the potential for explaining data in various applications. For instance, Luppi et al. recently employed the ϕID method to analyze brain BOLD signals [106], aiming to identify the synergistic core of the brain. Their findings revealed that synergistic information facilitates the integration of different brain regions, whereas redundancy contributes to robustness. This study offers valuable insights into understanding the underlying mechanisms of the brain.

The advancement of partial information decomposition techniques allows for further analysis of the mutual information between variables, enabling a deeper understanding of system properties from multiple perspectives. In a study by Varley et al. [107], the authors applied partial information decomposition to decompose the mutual information of a system. They calculated an indicator of synergy bias to assess how synergistic information is distributed across different levels of the system using the method proposed by Williams and Beer [29]. A higher synergy bias indicated a greater amount of partial information involved in synergistic relationships. Subsequently, the authors observed that in certain systems exhibiting causal emergence, when the system is simplified or reduced, the synergy bias increases. This suggests that as we coarse-grain the system, partial information undergoes a transformation from redundancy to synergy. The overall conclusion drawn was that emergence can be understood as a form of information conversion.

3.6.5. Causal Emergence Identification from Data

In the previous sections, we introduced several works on quantifying emergence through causality and other information-theoretic concepts. All of these works tried to propose quantitative measures, conceptual frameworks, and numeric examples based on Markovian dynamics for causal emergence. However, in practical applications, for a theoretical framework to be implemented, we need to automatically identify causal emergence from real data, especially time-series data of dynamic systems, and provide explanations for the results.

The first method for causal emergence identification was introduced in Rosas's paper on causal emergence [24] and involves the three indicators defined by Equations (41)–(43), as mentioned in Section 3.6.4. The identification criteria were exemplified in three case studies, leading to the following conclusions: particle collisions emerge as a distinctive feature within Conway's Game of Life, flock dynamics emerge as a characteristic feature in simulated bird behavior, and the representation of motor behavior in the cortex emerges from neural activity.

Although these three indicators avoid the problem of redundant information calculation, it is important to note that they serve as sufficient conditions, rather than as definitive proof of emergence. In other words, indicators greater than 0 can suggest the presence of emergence, but indicators less than 0 do not necessarily imply the absence of emergence. The construction of this indicator faces challenges in identifying emergence in systems with significant redundant information or a large number of variables, which is often the case in many real-world systems. Additionally, a limitation of this method is the requirement of a predetermined coarse-grained variable V, and different choices of this variable can significantly impact the results. As a result, the development of an automatic coarse-graining strategy based on data remains an unresolved issue.

As a result, the current theoretical frameworks for causal emergence lack a practical and effective identification algorithm. Although previous studies have proposed methods based on static network structures and approximations for information decomposition, there is still a need for a comprehensive approach that can be applied to general Markovian dynamic systems. One of the main challenges is the necessity to search for all possible functions of coarse-graining or decomposing subsets within the data to identify causal emergence in complex systems. However, conventional numerical methods are unable to handle the computational costs associated with such an extensive search in a vast functional space. Therefore, the development of new methods is imperative to address these issues.

In Section 4, we explore the application of machine learning techniques to address the challenge of identifying causal emergence within time-series data.

3.6.6. Comparison with Hoel's Framework

When comparing Hoel's framework to Rosas's quantification framework for causal emergence, several clear advantages can be observed in the latter. Firstly, Rosas's theory does not require a predetermined coarse-graining method, making it more mathematically rigorous and formal. Secondly, it offers a detailed decomposition of causal emergence, specifically downward causation and causal decoupling. Lastly, it effectively avoids cases of fake causal emergence, where the macro-variable depends solely on unique or redundant information from the micro-variables.

However, there are also some disadvantages to consider. Firstly, in order to obtain the full information lattice, a systematic iteration of all variable compositions is required. Additionally, despite the use of Formula (38), it is necessary to define a macro-variable. Unfortunately, the authors do not provide any method to identify such a variable. Secondly, all the mutual information and its decomposition are based on correlations rather than causality. It is crucial to discuss how to incorporate causal elements, such as intervention and counterfactuals, into the framework.

Finally, the issue of identifying whether causal emergence occurs in a system based on the given time-series data of its behaviors has not been addressed in the preceding discussion. To address this problem, the application of emerging technologies in machine learning and artificial intelligence is required. These technologies can provide valuable tools and techniques for detecting and analyzing causal emergence.

4. Causal Emergence and Machine Learning

Recently, newly emerging machine learning technologies have made significant breakthroughs in addressing a range of important and challenging problems [108–116]. Examples include defeating human champions in complex games like Go [108,109], predicting the intricate structures of protein folding [110], and generating human language using large language models [117]. These achievements have been made possible through the application of machine learning methods, which leverage well-designed neural network architectures and automatic differentiation techniques.

However, there is a crucial limitation of conventional machine learning: it can only capture the information or associations within the data, without being able to uncover the underlying causal relationships. According to the theory of causal hierarchy by Judea Pearl [15,16,118], causality is very different from association because the former always represents a more stable relationship that is invariant in different environments, whereas the latter may be more dependent on contexts and reflects the limitation of the data. Therefore, it is necessary to develop new machine learning frameworks to incorporate the consideration of causality [33,118,119]. Numerous studies have provided evidence to show that incorporating aspects of causality can lead to improved performance in machine learning tasks, including out-of-distribution generalization, adaptation to diverse environments, and handling interventions [118,120,121].

Machine learning and causal inference are also connected to causal emergence in two aspects, which we call "causal emergence with machine learning" and "causal emergence for machine learning". On one hand, machine learning can be employed to address the challenge of identifying causal emergence from data, referred to as "causal emergence with machine learning". On the other hand, causal emergence theory and effective information (EI) measures have potential applications in the field of machine learning, known as "causal emergence for machine learning". However, the extension depends on a deeper understanding of how causal emergence theory is related to causality.

4.1. Causal Emergence with Machine Learning

In Section 3.6.5, we discussed the challenge of identifying causal emergence. Although Rosas et al. presented a method to address this issue by calculating an approximate measure of causal emergence based on their theoretical framework (Equation (41)), the method requires the availability of a macro-variable, denoted as V_t, which needs to be defined in advance. However, defining this variable in a general sense when confronted with data remains challenging. Hence, the question arises of whether we can leverage machine learning to automatically learn the macro-variable. In this section, we explore two recent approaches that utilize machine learning and neural network techniques to address the problem of causal emergence identification from the perspective of Heol et al.'s theoretical framework for EI maximization. These methods aim to learn the coarse-graining strategy, macro-variable, and macro-dynamics directly from the data, eliminating the need for explicit definitions. By leveraging the power of machine learning, we can potentially overcome the limitations of manual variable definition and enable a more automated and data-driven approach to identifying causal emergence.

4.1.1. Neural Information Squeezer (NIS)

The first work we introduce has just been published in this special issue. In this paper, the authors formulated the problem of causal emergence identification in continuous Markov dynamics. Suppose the time-series data $x_1, x_2, \ldots, x_T$ are generated by a stochastic dynamical system continuously, which can be described by a differential equation,

$$\frac{dx}{dt} = g(x(t), \xi), \tag{44}$$

where ξ is a Gaussian noise. The time series $\{x_t\}$ represents the observations of the micro-states of the system. The problem we confront is identifying whether causal emergence occurs for the original system. We also want to know the appropriate coarse-graining strategies, the macro-dynamics corresponding to the chosen coarse-graining method, and the dimension of the phase space at the macro-level when the causal emergence occurs.

To address this problem, the authors proposed a mathematical framework by converting the original issue into an optimization problem for functions. Specifically, the goal is to find the appropriate coarse-graining strategy ϕ_q, defined on $\mathcal{R}^p \to \mathcal{R}^q$, where $q < p$ is the dimension of the macro-states. Additionally, the aim is to determine the macro-level Markov dynamics f, defined on $\mathcal{R}^q \to \mathcal{R}^q$ with the random noise ζ, by maximizing $\mathcal{J}$—the dimension-averaged EI of the macro-dynamics (see Equation (27)). This is expressed as,

$$\max \mathcal{J}(\hat{f}_{\phi_q}), \tag{45}$$

However, this problem has a trivial solution, e.g., ϕ is a constant map for all micro-states, and the macro-dynamic is an identity. Surprisingly, this solution has a large EI because the identity map has the largest determinism and lowest degeneracy among all q-dimensional functions. This is trivial because too much information has been abandoned by the coarse-graining strategy such that the macro-dynamic is useless.

To address the problem, the authors added a reasonable constraint to the original optimization framework, called the effectiveness requirement. A coarse-graining strategy and its corresponding macro-dynamics are considered effective if there exists another decoarse-graining function $\phi^\dagger$ such that the functions ϕ, f, and $\phi^\dagger$ can predict the micro-state, instead of the macro-state, in the next time step based on the state in the previous step. The constraint can be written as,

$$||\phi^\dagger(f(\phi(x_t))) - x_{t+1}|| < \epsilon, \tag{46}$$

for all time steps t, where ϵ is a given constant. This way, an effective coarse-graining strategy and macro-dynamics not only maximize the EI but also reproduce the original micro-dynamics as much as possible.

This constraint is an important complement to the framework for EI maximization because the decoarse-graining function $\phi^{\dagger}$ can map macro-states back to micro-states, addressing the problem of the ambiguity of macro-states. This constraint also ensures commutativity. To demonstrate this, we can apply $(\phi^{\dagger})^{-1} \approx \phi$ to both sides of Equation (46), resulting in $||f(\phi(x_t)) - \phi(x_{t+1})|| < \phi(\epsilon)$.

However, the problem is still hard to solve. In [31], the authors proposed a two-stage method, which can minimize the prediction error under a given dimension q of macro-states in the first step and maximize EI for different values of q in the second step. The first step can be solved by training a neural network, and the second step converts the complex functional optimization problem into a line search in one-dimensional space.

To realize the abstract mathematical framework, the authors proposed an encoder-dynamics learner-decoder framework for neural networks, named the Neural Information Squeezer (NIS), vividly describing the basic working principle of the framework as depicted in Figure 14.

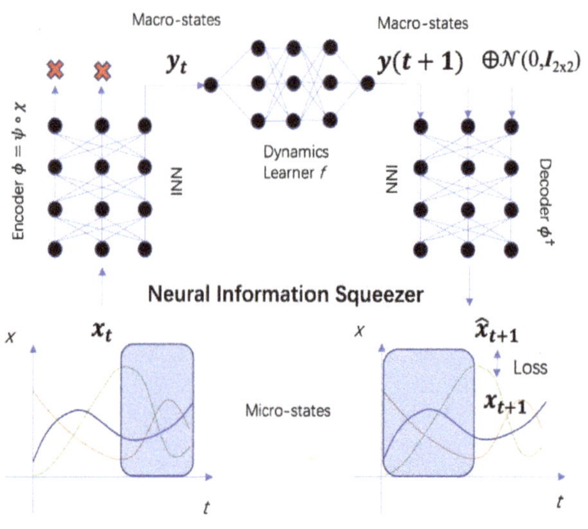

Figure 14. The architecture and workflow of the Neural Information Squeezer (NIS). The NIS consists of three main components: an encoder ϕ, a dynamics learner f, and a decoder $\phi^{\dagger}$. The encoder ϕ comprises an invertible neural network ψ and a projection operator χ, which simply discards fixed dimensions output by ϕ. On the other hand, the decoder $\phi^{\dagger}$ incorporates the same invertible neural network as the encoder but implements its inverse ψ^{-1}. In cases where the input is incomplete, it can be complemented using Gaussian random noise.

In order to reduce the complexity of the encoder and decoder, corresponding to ϕ and $\phi^{\dagger}$, respectively, the authors used an invertible neural network to implement the encoder and inverted the input-output workflow of the same neural network to implement the decoder. Concretely, the encoding process was decomposed into two computation steps: information conversion with the invertible neural network $\psi : \mathcal{R}^p \to \mathcal{R}^q$ on a p-dimensional input space, and information discarding with a simple projection operation. This is expressed as:

$$\phi(x) = \chi_q(\psi(x)), \tag{47}$$

where χ_q is the projection operator that projects a $p > q$-dimensional vector into a q-dimensional vector, retaining dimensions from 1 to q. The decoding process also consists of two stages: randomly sampling Gaussian noise to complete the details of macro-states, and information conversion but in an inverted way, that is,

$$\phi^{\dagger}(x) = \psi^{-1}(x \bigoplus \zeta), \tag{48}$$

where $\zeta \sim \mathcal{N}(0, I_{p-q})$ is a $p-q$-dimensional standard Gaussian random vector, and $\bigoplus$ is the operation of vector concatenation.

The adoption of an invertible neural network in the framework serves two main purposes. Firstly, by inverting the workflow of the neural network ψ to obtain the decoder $\phi^{\dagger}$, a significant reduction in the number of parameters is achieved. This reduction can lead to improved efficiency and computational benefits. Secondly, the use of invertible functions in the neural network provides favorable mathematical properties that facilitate the analysis of the entire framework in a tractable manner. These properties enable researchers to gain insights and understand the characteristics of the framework more easily.

This architectural design with an invertible neural network not only reduces the complexity of computation but also separates the input information from the micro-states into noise and EI for prediction. The authors proved a mathematical theorem stating that, as the neural network converges through training, the mutual information between adjacent macro-states tends to approach the mutual information of two adjacent-step micro-states in the data. This means that all the information discarded by the encoder is almost irrelevant to the prediction. All the useful information converges into the information bottleneck within the macro-level dynamics learner. Another theorem demonstrates that the degree of information compression for micro-states increases as we reduce the dimension of the macro-states. Thus, the macro-state dynamics learner, acting as a narrower information bottleneck, progressively discards more and more extraneous information from the original micro-state data.

To address the problem of causal emergence identification, we first optimize the neural networks, and the dimension-averaged EI, $\mathcal{J}_q$, can be obtained for different q. When $q = p$, the derived $\mathcal{J}_p$ is the dimension-averaged EI for the micro-dynamics. Finally, the calculation of

$$\Delta\mathcal{J} = \mathcal{J}_q - \mathcal{J}_p \tag{49}$$

is the measure of dimension-averaged causal emergence (see Equation (28)). If $\Delta\mathcal{J} > 0$, we can state that causal emergence occurs.

Numeric examples are provided to show the effectiveness of the whole framework. Interestingly, the Neural Information Squeezer can handle time-series data with discrete micro-states, even though the whole framework was initially designed for continuous dynamical systems. Particularly, the model determines the same coarse-graining strategy and macro-level dynamic as illustrated in the example of a boolean network with four nodes in Hoel's original paper, although no information about node grouping and state mapping was provided in the framework.

It is also interesting to compare the NIS with the frameworks and models mentioned in previous sections. Compared to the theory of computational mechanics, the NIS can be treated as a kind of ϵ-machine because any encoded macro-states can be understood as states. When the whole framework is well trained, such that it can precisely predict future micro-states, the encoded macro-states converge to effective states, which can be treated as causal states in computational mechanics. However, the objective that maximizes the effective information (EI) in the NIS has no correspondence.

The NIS also shares a similarity with G-emergence because it adopts the ideas of Granger causality: the effective macro-state is optimized by predicting the micro-state in the next time step. However, there are several obvious differences between the two frameworks. In the theory of G-emergence, the macro-state must initially be selected manually, although it is optimized automatically. In addition, the NIS uses neural networks to predict future states, whereas G-emergence uses auto-regressive techniques to fit the data. Due to the universal approximate theorem (see [122,123]), neural networks are more advantageous.

The NIS provides a solution for causal emergence identification from data, and it is the first solution for addressing the problem of the automatic construction of the coarse-graining strategy and macro-dynamics from data for causal emergence identification.

Another important benefit of the NIS is that it essentially addresses a generalized causal emergence identification problem, extending beyond mere justification. This is because following training, the NIS not only identifies whether causal emergence occurs but also obtains a neural network for coarse-graining the data and another for simulating the macro-dynamics. This can provide us with richer information compared to a mere justification.

4.1.2. Neural Information Squeezer Plus (NIS+)

One of the biggest problems of the NIS is that it does not directly address the EI maximization problem by optimizing the neural networks (encoder, decoder, and dynamics learner). Instead, it searches for the optimal dimension of the macro-state space q such that EI can be maximized. Therefore, for a given q, the neural networks are optimal for reconstructing the micro-dynamics (minimizing Equation (46)) but not for EI. In addition, the NIS cannot support complex computations such as coarse-graining functions involving multiple steps of information conversion and discarding.

To address these problems, the NIS+ was proposed, as discussed in [32]. Mathematically, the problem of EI maximization can be transformed into a machine learning problem based on the definition of EI and the variational inequality and probability reweighting technique. After this conversion, the minimization problem can be solved by training three neural networks ψ_ω, f_θ, and $g_{\theta'}$ with parameters ω, θ, and θ', respectively. Formally, the minimization problem without constraints can be written as:

$$\min_{\omega,\theta,\theta'} \sum_{t=1}^{T-1} w(\mathbf{x}_t)||\mathbf{y}_t - g_{\theta'}(\mathbf{y}_{t+1})|| + \lambda||\hat{\mathbf{x}}_{t+1} - \mathbf{x}_{t+1}||, \tag{50}$$

where $\mathbf{y}_t = \phi(\mathbf{x}_t) = Proj_q(\psi_\omega(\mathbf{x}_t))$ and $\mathbf{y}_{t+1} = \phi(\mathbf{x}_{t+1}) = Proj_q(\psi_\omega(\mathbf{x}_{t+1}))$ are the macro-states. λ is a Lagrangian multiplier, which is regarded as a hyperparameter in experiments. $w(\mathbf{x}_t)$ is the inverse probability weight, which is defined as:

$$w(\mathbf{x}_t) = \frac{\tilde{p}(\mathbf{y}_t)}{p(\mathbf{y}_t)} = \frac{\tilde{p}(\phi(\mathbf{x}_t))}{p(\phi(\mathbf{x}_t))}, \tag{51}$$

where $\tilde{p}$ is the new distribution of macro-states $\mathbf{y}_t$ after intervention for $do(\mathbf{y}_t \sim \mathcal{U}_q)$, and p is the natural distribution of the data. In practice, $p(\mathbf{y}_t)$ is estimated through kernel density estimation (KDE) [124]. The approximated distribution, $\tilde{p}(\mathbf{y}_t)$, is assumed to be a uniform distribution, which is characterized by a constant value. Consequently, the weight w is computed as the ratio of these two distributions. Theorems have been proven to ensure the correctness of this conversion. The overall framework for the NIS+ is depicted in Figure 15.

Additionally, to apply the NIS+ to data generated by complex systems like multi-agent systems and cellular automata, the structures of the encoder can be extended by defining two kinds of combinations: stacking the basic encoder and concatenating the basic encoder. Here, a basic encoder is the composition of an invertible neural network and a projection operation. By inverting the directions of all the basic encoders and supplementing empty inputs with Gaussian noise vectors, we can obtain the corresponding decoder.

Serious numerical experiments have demonstrated that the NIS+ can automatically learn emergent dynamics and the coarse-graining strategy from data and can integrate these results to identify causal emergence.

For instance, in experiments utilizing training data generated by introducing Gaussian noise to SIR dynamics, the NIS+ demonstrated superior performance compared to the NIS in recovering the vector field of derivatives that aligned with the actual macro-level

SIR dynamics. To assess the ability of the NIS+ to learn emergent dynamics, the authors generated data based on macro-states using the SIR dynamics as the ground truth. However, the NIS+ cannot directly utilize this data; only micro-level noisy data can be employed. These micro-level data were generated by introducing Gaussian noise to the macro-states.

In the experiments conducted with the Boid model, training data were generated using the renowned Boid model, which simulates the herding behavior of birds. Both the NIS+ and NIS demonstrated the ability to automatically learn macro-level states and dynamics. In this simulation, the authors divided all artificial birds (boids) into two distinct groups. Interestingly, the learned macro-states could also be categorized into two groups. Within each group, the predicted trajectories generated by the learned macro-dynamics of this group accurately followed the center of the boid groups.

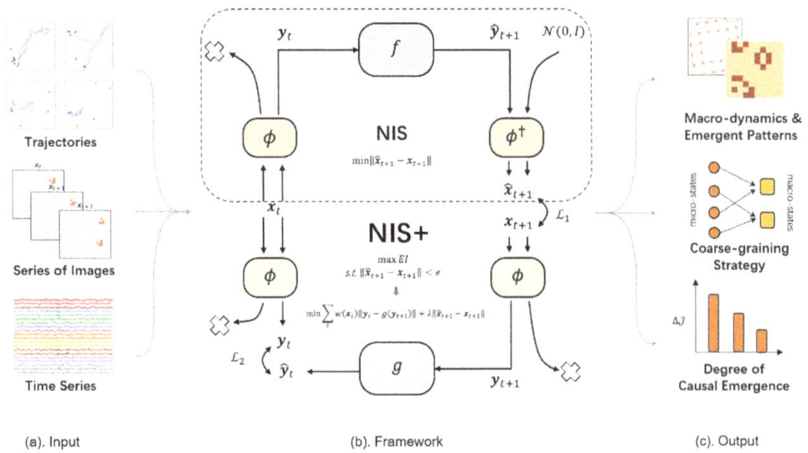

Figure 15. The workflow and architecture of our proposed framework, the Neural Information Squeezer Plus (NIS+), for discovering causal emergence within data. (**a**) Various forms of input data. (**b**) The framework for our proposed model, the NIS+, incorporates our previous model, the NIS. The boxes represent functions or neural networks, and an arrow pointing to a cross represents the operation of information discarding. x_t and x_{t+1} represent the observational data of micro-states, whereas $\hat{x}_{t+1}$ represents the predicted micro-state. $y_t = \phi(x_t)$ and $y_{t+1} = \phi(x_{t+1})$ represent the macro-states obtained by encoding the micro-states using the encoder. $\hat{y}_t = \phi(\hat{x}_t)$ and $\hat{y}_{t+1} = \phi(\hat{x}_{t+1})$ represent the predicted macro-states obtained by encoding the predictions of micro-states. The mathematical problems that each framework aims to solve are also illustrated in the figure. (**c**) The various output forms of the NIS+, which include the learned macro-dynamics, captured emergent patterns, functions of coarse-graining, and the degree of causal emergence.

The ability to capture emergent patterns was verified through experiments conducted in the "Game of Life". The NIS+ demonstrated the capability to automatically discover both static and dynamic patterns, such as the "glider", within the learned latent space. Additionally, when clear emergent patterns appeared in the data, larger effective information (EI) was observed for the learned emergent macro-dynamics.

Across all the training data generated through simulations, the NIS+ outperformed comparative models, including the NIS, variational autoencoders, and feed-forward neural networks, in experiments testing the model on data distributions that differed from the training data.

The paper also presented results on real data. Two sets of real fMRI time-series data from human subjects were used. The first dataset, AOMIC ID1000 [125], contained fMRI scanning data collected while subjects watched the same movie clip. As a comparison, another fMRI dataset, AOMIC PIOP2 [125], containing resting-state data from 50 subjects, was also utilized. The primary training objective was to predict the fMRI signal at the next time step using the learned macro-dynamics and decoder while simultaneously maximizing the effective information (EI) of the macro-level dynamics. Ultimately, a one-dimensional macro-state was found to represent all 100-dimensional micro-state data. Through attribution analysis, the authors found that micro-level signals with larger weights contributing to the one-dimensional macro-state were located in areas associated with visual tasks. However, in the comparison dataset with resting-state data, seven-dimensional macro-states were found to represent the micro-states, and attribution experiments revealed that micro-states with larger weights were distributed across different brain areas.

After the macro-dynamics and coarse-graining strategy were learned, the EIs at both the macro-level and micro-level could be calculated so that causal emergence could be quantified. The experiments showed that the measure of causal emergence depends on different types of noise. If noise was added to the observational data (micro-state), the degree of causal emergence increased with the level of noise. In contrast, if the noise was from the dynamical mechanism, i.e., added to macro-states, the degree of causal emergence decreased with the level of noise. This implies that coarse-graining can learn to eliminate noise in raw data so that better macro-dynamics with larger EI can emerge. However, if the noise is from the internal dynamics, it cannot be removed through coarse-graining.

4.2. Why Is Causal Emergence "Causal"?

In the previous sections, we discussed two frameworks that utilize machine learning and neural network techniques to address the challenge of causal emergence identification. Both frameworks place significant emphasis on maximizing EI to learn the coarse-graining strategy and macro-dynamics. Notably, the NIS+ framework extends the NIS approach to achieve real EI maximization, whereas the NIS relies on adjusting the hyperparameter q to optimize EI.

Moreover, the NIS+ has demonstrated an additional capability to generalize data distributions that differ from the training data. This suggests that the NIS+ can learn an invariant causal mechanism that is independent of the input distribution shifts through EI maximization. However, before extending this method to other machine learning scenarios, an essential question needs to be addressed: Is there a genuine relationship between causal emergence, EI maximization, and causality itself?

In the previous sections, we introduced two theoretical frameworks of causal emergence: Hoel's framework and Rosas's framework. In both frameworks, the measurement of causal emergence heavily relies on mutual information. However, it is crucial to acknowledge that mutual information primarily quantifies correlation rather than causality. So why do the authors assert that their theories pertain to "causal" emergence?

The key point lies in the research objectives of these frameworks, which focus on a Markov dynamical system. In this context, the dynamical mechanism is assumed to be known, and confounding variables are not considered. Under this assumption, measures related to correlation can effectively indicate causality. While mutual information itself is not a direct measure of causality, it can serve as a proxy for causality when the underlying dynamics are well understood and confounding factors are absent. Therefore, in the context of these frameworks, the use of mutual information as a measure for causal emergence is justified because it captures the relationships between variables in a way that aligns with the assumed known dynamics of the system.

When comparing the two frameworks, Hoel's framework can be considered more "causal" than Rosas's framework. This is because Hoel's framework introduces the do operator in the definition of effective information (EI), as expressed in Equation (7). The do operator allows for interventions and represents a causal manipulation of variables, which strengthens the causal interpretation of the framework. Furthermore, the significance of EI lies in its deep connections with other measures of causation proposed in various fields [28]. According to the information in Section 3.5.3, these measures aim to quantify the causal impact of an intervention or treatment on an outcome. By incorporating the do operator, EI aligns with these causal effect measures and provides a valuable tool for assessing causal relationships.

Furthermore, let us delve into the application background of the NIS and NIS+ to understand why these frameworks, based on EI maximization, are considered causal. Firstly, the input data in both frameworks, denoted as x_t, are generated by a Markovian dynamical system, with no other confounding factors considered, apart from the system itself. As a result, the state of two consecutive time steps, represented as x_t and x_{t+1}, without loss of generality, can be modeled by a simple causal diagram $x_t \to x_{t+1}$ due to the Markovian property. This causal diagram naturally adheres to the exogeneity assumption in causal inference [16], indicating the absence of any confounders between the two states. Consequently, the "do" operator in EI can be replaced with conditional probability, which can be estimated from observations.

Taking all these aspects into consideration, we conclude that the theoretical frameworks of causal emergence and the machine frameworks for causal emergence identification, namely the NIS and NIS+, are indeed related to causality. Moreover, they can be extended to other scenarios within the realm of machine learning. We further explore and discuss this point in the subsequent sections.

4.3. *Causal Emergence for Machine Learning*

In this sub-section, we introduce how causal emergence can enhance machine learning in out-of-distribution scenarios. It turns out that the *do* intervention introduced in EI captures the causal dependency from the data generation process and thus complements correlation-based machine learning algorithms.

4.3.1. Out-of-Distribution Generalization

As demonstrated in the previous subsection, the measurement of causal emergence by vanilla effective information [19] is defined for stationary dynamics systems in a self-supervised fashion since the input (cause) space and the output (effect) space share the support. However, Hoel generalized effective information to general input-output systems [26] (see Section 3.5.5), where the cause and the effect space take arbitrary support, which could either be discrete or continuous. Empowered by the general notation of EI, causal emergence could be applied in supervised machine learning to evaluate the strength of causation between the feature space $\mathcal{X}$ (or its learned representation) and the target space $\mathcal{Y}$, thus enhancing the prediction from the cause (feature) to the effect (target). It is worth noting that a direct fitting from $\mathcal{X}$ to $\mathcal{Y}$ on the observations suffices for common prediction tasks with an i.i.d. assumption, implying that the training and test data are independently and identically distributed.

However, if samples are drawn from outside the training distribution, it is essential to learn a representation space that generalizes from the training to the test environment, known as out-of-distribution (OOD) generalization. Due to the common belief that causal relations generalize better than statistical correlations [126], causal emergence theory could serve as a criterion for the causation embedded in the representation space. The occurrence of causal emergence indicates the revelation of potential causal factors of the target, thus producing a robust representation space with regard to out-of-distribution generalization.

Introduction to OOD

Before the detailed discussion of the connection between causal emergence and OOD generalization, we begin with a brief introduction to the latter topic. Out-of-distribution generalization toward arbitrary distributional shifts is generally considered impossible [127]. Therefore, it is commonly assumed that there exists an underlying causal mechanism governing the data generation process, which remains invariant to distributional shifts. Formally, according to Pearl's Structural Equation Model [16], which causally formulates data generation, the target Y is supposed to be generated from a part of the feature X, i.e., $Y = f(X_c, \epsilon)$, where X_c represents the selected features or a representation of X, and

ϵ is a random noise independent of (X, Y). Obviously, X_c is the true cause of the target, and the causal mechanism f is presumed to be invariant across training and test environments. On the other hand, the raw feature X might comprise a mixture of causal variables and non-causal variables. The latter could arise from confounding, selection bias, or anti-causal mechanisms, all of which introduce spurious correlations between the target and non-causal variables. The strength and direction of these spurious correlations vary across environments, resulting in distributional shifts that hamper the out-of-distribution performance of machine learning techniques. As a remedy, a prominent branch of OOD algorithms [126,128–130] learns an invariant representation space distilling the causal variables from the raw feature space. Typically, a metric of the representation is devised to verify the stability of the correlation between the learned representation space and the target and is adopted as a regularization for the optimization objective to encourage the representation learner to extract causal variables from features. The paradigm for invariant representation learning can be expressed as [131]:

$$\min_{f,\phi} \mathcal{R}(f(\phi(X)), Y) + \lambda \ell_{reg}(\phi), \tag{52}$$

where $\phi(X)$ is the learned representation, f is the learned predictor, $\mathcal{R}$ is the task-specific risk function, and ℓ_{reg} is the regularization.

Representation learning-based OOD algorithms are diversified in their constraints on the representation space characterized by the regularizers. Each metric of the representation fits a specific data generation pattern and does not guarantee to filter out the causal variables when the setting is violated. However, causal emergence potentially offers a united metric of representation for OOD generalization rooted in causality theory.

Before diving into the application of causal emergence, we first discuss the representative regularizers of representation learning and their limitations. Domain-invariant representation learning proposes an aligned feature space with the constraint $g(X) \perp \mathcal{E}$, where $\mathcal{E}$ denotes the environment index for training and test environments. The regularization is implemented by the metric of Maximum Mean Discrepancy (MMD) distance of representation across environments [132] or an adversarial classifier for the environment index [130]. However, the alignment constraint provides a generalization guarantee only for a covariate shift [129], where the distribution shift is restricted to the features X without perturbing $P(Y|X)$. On the other hand, invariant risk minimization [126,133] pursues an invariant conditional distribution $P(Y|g(X))$ of the representation across environments, which translates to $Y \perp \mathcal{E} \mid g(X)$. Invariant risk minimization has been proven to recover the causal variable in a data generation process where the non-causal variable is anti-causally generated by the target but is reported to fail under a covariate shift [134]. Further, conditional invariant representation [128,132] is designed specifically for image classification where the target is modeled as the cause of the feature instead of the effect. The conditional independence $g(X) \perp \mathcal{E} \mid Y$ is enforced on the representation space.

It has been theoretically proven that any statistical independence regularization is valid for a subgroup of Structural Equation Models, and it does not generalize across all data generation processes [135]. As a result, the metric of representation manages to capture the causation between the representation space and the target variable only if a specific causal graph of data generation is given, hindering the general applicability of invariant representation learning. Worse still, the existence of the environment index $\mathcal{E}$ in the independence regularizers introduces the necessity of multiple environments for training procedures, increasing the data collection and labeling expenses. To this end, there is active demand for a unified and general metric of representation for OOD generalization, for which causal emergence might be a good candidate.

Causal Emergence and OOD

The link between OOD generalization and causal emergence can be attributed to the do intervention of effective information. By definition [16], intervening in the feature distribution with $do(X)$ modifies the structural equations of all the variables in the feature space to a constant value, whereas the equation for the target remains intact as $Y = f(X_c)$. On one hand, the assumption of the causal mechanism's invariance to distributional shift is respected since the causal correlation between causal variables and the target is reserved. On the other hand, the spurious correlation between non-causal variables and the target is removed by the intervention. For example, a non-causal variable anti-causally correlated with the target leads to a structural equation as $X_n = h(Y, \epsilon)$, and $do(X_n)$ replaces the equation with $X_n = U$, where $U \sim U_{max}$, and U_{max} represents the maximum entropy distribution on the domain of X_n. As a result, X_n is no longer caused by Y, and the spurious correlation vanishes. In another example, if a non-causal variable is correlated with the target by a confounder E (probably in the feature space), the structural equation takes the form of $X_n = \phi(E, \epsilon)$ and $Y = f(X_c, E, \epsilon)$. Then, the do intervention would modify the equation to $X_n = U$ and confounding ceases to exist. In summary, the intervention introduced by EI captures the causal correlation between features and the target while suppressing the spurious correlation. It renders EI an ideal metric to assess the causality contained in the representation space and, thus, the generalization of the induced algorithm.

Recall that an increment in effective information implies the occurrence of causal emergence. Therefore, we propose a conjecture that out-of-distribution generalization could be achieved simultaneously with maximizing EI (or normalized EI) for representation learning. Notably, Shannon's mutual information holds the property that any representation has no gain of mutual information with the target over the raw feature space, i.e., $I(g(X); Y) \leq I(X; Y)$, as per the data processing theorem. Thus, direct fitting inclines to absorb as much information with the target as possible into the representation space. In contrast, EI (or normalized EI) would possibly peak at a medium stage of abstraction of raw features, coinciding with the philosophy of OOD generalization that less could be more. Ideally, at the peak of EI (or normalized EI) where causal emergence occurs, all non-causal features are excluded, and the causal features are revealed, resulting in the most informative representation while remaining invariant to distributional shifts.

The removal of spurious correlations and recovery of causal mechanisms by manipulating feature distributions are principles shared by the reweighting technique widely adopted in the OOD literature. For instance, stable learning [136–138] is designed for scenarios where collinearity exists in input variables, causing spurious correlations between non-causal variables and the target. It achieves this by reweighting training samples to decorrelate the features, thus reducing collinearity and eliminating spurious correlations. Similar to EI, stable learning is free of environment index labeling. Further, both sample reweighting and feature decorrelation share the philosophy of distribution intervention. In this sense, EI could be viewed as an information-theoretic abstraction of reweighting-based debiasing techniques for OOD generalization.

5. Discussion and Perspectives

We have presented several quantitative theoretical frameworks on causal emergence. However, there are numerous unexplored problems and implications that warrant further discussion. In this section, we address four key topics for future research: causal emergence and causal representation learning, ontological and epidemiological causality and emergence, potential applications in complex systems, and understanding complex systems from the perspective of causal emergence.

5.1. Causal Emergence and Causal Representation Learning

Causal representation learning (CRL) is an emerging field in artificial intelligence (AI) [33] that combines two important fields in AI: representation learning and causal inference. Representation learning aims to extract important features (or representations) hidden in data to make predictions automatically [139]. It can be regarded as a typical application of deep learning and has achieved remarkable success in various domains such as image classification [111], face recognition [112], language understanding [113–115], and game playing [109,116]. However, conventional representation learning suffers from a critical limitation: it can only capture the information of associations within the data but not the underlying causal relationships. Therefore, it is important to consider causality in representation learning.

To address the problem, CRL tries to combine the advantages of the two sub-fields: representation learning and causal inference to extract the important features and the relationships with causation behind data automatically [33].

A typical CRL scenario is depicted in Figure 16. Suppose there is a set of variables and causal mechanisms (including causal graphs and structural equations) that describes how the world of robotic arms and colorful blocks works. However, these mechanisms are not directly observable for the agent undergoing causal representation learning. Instead, what the agent can observe is a set of images generated by robotic arms and blocks. The objective of a causal learning framework is to extract the causal variables and mechanisms from the observed images, and the variables and mechanisms can be used to implement other downstream tasks, for example, causal relationship discovery [140] and predictions in different environments [120] or domains [118,121].

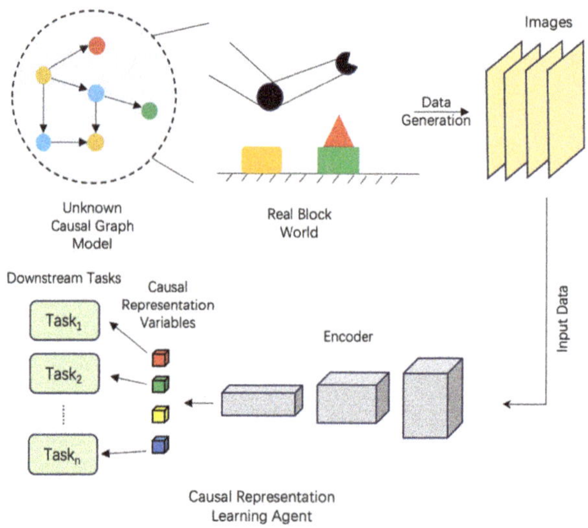

Figure 16. Illustration of the workflow of a typical causal representation learning (CRL) agent. The top panel depicts a real block world with a robotic arm and the corresponding causal graph, representing relationships between variables in the real world, which is totally unknown to the agent. Additionally, the data are presented as images generated by the block world. The bottom panel depicts the structure of the causal representation learning agent. It utilizes a convolutional neural network (CNN) to extract meaningful representations from the data and perform downward tasks based on these representations. The encoder plays a crucial role in capturing relevant features and patterns from the input data, enabling the agent to learn and understand causal relationships.

When comparing Figures 14 and 15 with Figure 16, we found that as a framework for machine learning, Neural Information Squeezer Plus can be regarded as a kind of CRL framework. Thus, with the NIS and NIS+, we effectively employ CRL to address the problem of identifying causal emergence (CE). Both CE and CRL frameworks feature an encoder and decoder designed to represent raw data as causal variables. Latent causal mechanisms can be learned in both frameworks. In this section, we compare the similarities and differences between these two emerging fields.

5.1.1. Similarities

It is interesting to compare the tasks of causal emergence identification within the theoretical framework of Erik Hoel and causal representation learning. Actually, the task of causal emergence identification can be understood as a task of causal representation learning, where the macro-variables are the causal variables, the macro-dynamics are the causal mechanisms, and the coarse-graining strategy is an encoding process that transforms the original data into representations. Within this framework, EI can be understood as a measure of the strength of the causal effect on the mechanism. To identify causal emergence, we need to learn the appropriate causal variables to represent data and discover causal mechanisms at the macro-level (in the representational latent space) to ensure that the EI of the learned causal mechanism in the latent space is larger than that of the original data. Table 1 shows a detailed comparison of causal emergence identification and causal representation learning.

Table 1. Comparison of causal emergence identification and causal representation learning.

	Causal Emergence Identification	**Causal Representation Learning**
Data	Observations (time series) of micro-states	Raw data generated by some causal mechanism in real life
Latent variables	Macro-states	Causal representations
Causal mechanism	Macro-dynamics	Causal mechanisms
Mapping between data and latent variables	Coarse-graining	Representation
Optimization for causality	EI maximization	Prediction loss, disentanglement
Objective	Finding an optimal coarse-graining strategy and a macro-dynamic that has a stronger causal effect	Finding an optimal representation of the raw data to ensure that the independent causal mechanism can be realized by the representations

With these similarities, the technologies and concepts from both fields can learn from each other. For example, the techniques of causal representation learning can be applied to discover causal emergence.

On the other hand, the learned abstract causal representations can be viewed as macro-states, which enhances the explainability of causal representation learning. This perspective suggests that CRL essentially uncovers hidden causal emergent features within the data.

Moreover, these similarities between emergent phenomena and CRL contribute to a deeper understanding of emergence itself. By applying CRL frameworks to data generated by dynamical systems exhibiting emergent phenomena, we can extract more profound causal structures. These profound causal structures may serve as the origins of the mysteries surrounding emergence. By delving into the depths of CRL and uncovering the hidden causal relationships within complex systems, we can gain insights into the mechanisms behind emergent phenomena. These causal structures may provide a foundation for understanding the emergence of novel properties and behaviors that arise from the interactions of simpler components.

5.1.2. Differences

However, there are several theoretical differences between CRL and causal emergence. The biggest difference is that CRL assumes that there is a real causal mechanism behind the data, and the data are generated by this causal mechanism [33]. In contrast, for causal emergence identification, the emergent variables and mechanisms at the macro-level are just handy ways to observe and understand data, and "real causality" may not exist. The differences are illustrated in Figure 17.

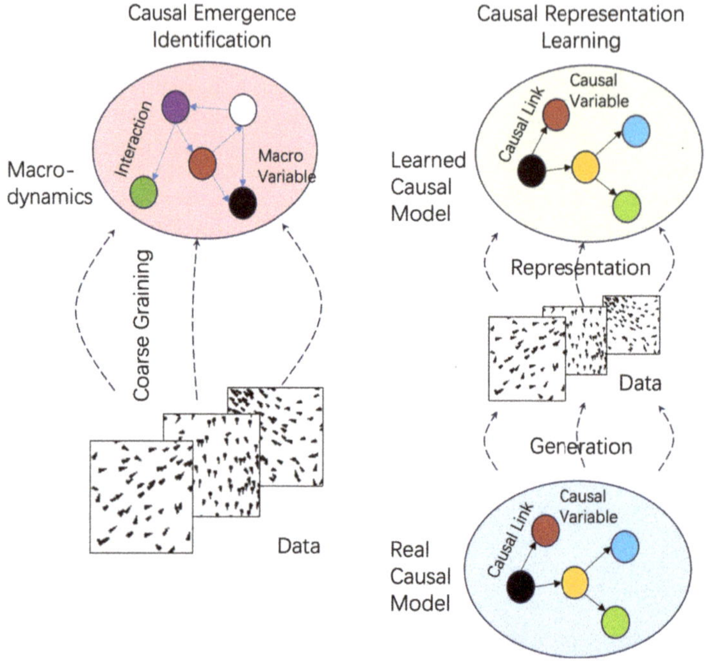

Figure 17. Comparison of causal emergence identification and causal representation learning. All the potential co-founders are ignored. The black arrows represent causal relations, whereas the blue arrows represent interactions between macro-variables. The dashed lines with arrows represent the information flows for coarse-graining, representation, or data generation.

However, if an epistemological perspective is adopted, this difference disappears because both approaches extract meaningful information from observational data to obtain representations with stronger causal effects.

Another major difference is that the causal mechanism for macro-states in causal emergence is a dynamical system. Therefore, if the dynamics in the macro-state space are on a network, circular structures may exist because the state variables will be iterated in the dynamical system. As a result, feedback and circular indirect interactions are allowed in such a model. However, the causal mechanism is always represented by a structural causal model in CRL. Although these models are always directed acyclic graphs, loops or circular structures are not allowed. However, these differences are not important because Markovian dynamics can always be converted to causal models, as mentioned in Section 2.1.

Finally, unknown co-founders are always ignored in causal emergence, whereas they play very important roles in causal structural models.

In summary, there are deep connections between causal emergence and CRL. On one hand, the machine learning framework for causal emergence identification exhibits similar structures to the frameworks for CRL. And even the concepts can establish one-to-one correspondence, as shown in Table 1. Therefore, the ideas and techniques of both sides can learn from each other.

On the other hand, studies of causal emergence can provide new perspectives and insights for causal representation learning algorithms. For example, we can interpret the learned representations and causal mechanisms as emergent causal laws. The maximization of EI may improve the efficiency of learning the causalities for both CRL and reinforcement learning agents.

5.2. Ontological and Epistemological Causality and Emergence

Although machine learning techniques have facilitated the learning of causal structures and models, as well as the exploration of emergent properties and causation, it is important to consider whether the results obtained through machine learning reflect ontological causality and emergence or if they are merely epistemological phenomena.

Here, ontological causality refers to the causal relationships that exist in objective reality, independent of our knowledge or understanding. Ontological causality explores the fundamental mechanisms and interactions that give rise to causal effects in the world. Similarly, ontological emergence is concerned with the objective existence of emergent properties and their underlying mechanisms.

Epistemological causality, on the other hand, focuses on our knowledge and understanding of causality. It deals with how we perceive, model, and explain causal relationships based on our observations and experiences, but the causality may not exist in the real world. Epistemological emergence, akin to epistemological causality, focuses on our comprehension and elucidation of emergent phenomena. In other words, epistemological causality and emergence depend on an observer, and different observers may have distinct perspectives about causality and emergence for a particular objective phenomenon.

There has been a longstanding debate regarding the ontological and epistemological aspects of causality and emergence throughout history [17,22,68,76]. The authors of [68] highlighted that the concept of "causation" in the literature is often vague and should be differentiated into "cause" and "reason", aligning with ontological and epistemological causality. "Cause" means genuine cause that sufficiently causes the effects (causal closure principle [141] and exclusion principle [142]), whereas "reason" serves as a mere explanation for individuals to comprehend the effects. Reason may not possess the same level of rigor as genuine cause, but it does offer a certain degree of predictability that individuals find valuable in certain circumstances.

However, distinguishing between them, particularly when addressing specific phenomena, remains a challenging task. One such controversial concept is downward causation, which has sparked extensive discussions. The question of whether downward causation exists objectively or not remains open. In [24], Rosas argued that downward causation not only exists independently of particular observers but also provides a characterization of the phenomenon through quantified measures using information decomposition. However, Yurchenko proposed that it is important to differentiate between two separate concepts: causality and reasoning. According to this perspective, downward causation falls under the category of "reason" rather than causation. In this context, causality and reasoning can be seen as representing ontological and epistemological causality, respectively.

Similarly, debates persist regarding the nature of causal emergence. The question arises as to whether causal emergence is a genuine phenomenon that exists independently of particular observers [77]. In Section 3.5.4, we highlighted that different coarse-graining strategies can lead to distinct macro-dynamic mechanisms with varying measures of EI. In essence, different coarse-graining strategies can be seen as representing different observers. However, Hoel's theory proposes a criterion to differentiate between coarse-graining methods, namely EI maximization. Consequently, for a given set of Markovian dynamics, only the coarse-graining strategy and corresponding macro-dynamics that maximize the EI measure can be considered as an objective outcome. Nevertheless, a challenge arises when multiple solutions exist that maximize EI, introducing a degree of subjectivity [77]. The authors of [31,32] addressed this issue by introducing constraints on prediction errors in micro-states, which partially alleviates the problem. However, the question of whether optimal results have unique solutions remains an open problem that requires further investigation.

Similarly, although the incorporation of machine learning cannot resolve debates surrounding ontological and epistemological causality and emergence, it can provide objective standards that help mitigate subjectivity. This is because machine learning algorithms strive to optimize objective functions. Thus, machine learning agents can be viewed as "objective" observers that make judgments on causality and emergence. This represents an additional advantage of incorporating machine learning. However, the issue of unique solutions is crucial in this approach and warrants further attention.

Are the machine learning results ontological or epistemological? The answer is that the results are epistemological and depend on machine learning algorithms. However, this does not mean that all the results of machine learning are meaningless since if the learning agents are well trained and the defined mathematical objectives are effectively optimized, the results can also be considered objective and independent of the algorithms.

It is intriguing to pose the same question regarding human cognition. Do all cognitive results in the human brain, encompassing causality, coarse-graining strategies, and macro-dynamics, reflect objective reality, or are they purely epistemological? Firstly, answering this question is exceedingly challenging. Secondly, the cognitive results specific to a particular human brain must objectively manifest within the neural network structures. Thus, for that brain, these results are ontological. Similar reasons hold for machine learning. The cognitive results of machine learning algorithms are recorded by the structures and parameters in neural networks. Therefore, studying these structures may reveal the properties of the original systems, and the nature of the interactions between the observer and the observed objects can be objectively reflected by machines.

Furthermore, the integration of machine learning can assist in establishing a theoretical framework for modeling observers and studying the interactions between the observer and the corresponding observed complex systems. This framework allows us not only to explore the hard problems regarding causality and emergence but also to understand the limitations and boundaries of the observer. One example of this research is the emergent classicality of quantum systems from the information bottleneck formed by machine learning algorithms [143].

5.3. Potential Applications in Complex Systems

In Section 4, we discussed the techniques related to causal emergence identification, machine learning, and causal inference. In this sub-section, we discuss the potential applications of these techniques in complex systems. Complex systems can be understood as a large network, with events connected by causal links. Automatically discovering the complex causal relationships from data is a challenging problem.

The research area of causal discovery has tried to address this problem in various ways [144–149]. However, additional challenges may arise when applying these causal discovery methods in complex systems because circular causal structures and cross-level causation may exist.

Circular causal structures widely exist in complex dynamical systems due to the feedback effect. That is, one variable may affect itself via a direct self-loop feedback or a long chain forming a circle. This circular causal structure may pose a challenge to existing methods of causality because most of these methods study directed acyclic causal graphs. However, recent progress has seen the development of some methods for discovering these circular structures in a data-driven manner, e.g., [46–49,150–153].

Another aspect is that higher-level or cross-level causation may exist if the ingredients of scale and coarse-graining are considered. For example, downward causation describes the causal effect between macro-level and micro-level variables. Thus, the causal connections may be cross-level. If causal emergence occurs in a complex system, some strong causality may be found between macro-variables. All of these factors in complex systems present new challenges. The machine learning methods discussed in Section 4.1.1 can address the question of whether higher-level causality exists at the macro-level. However, it is important to note that this is a global property. It must be further developed and extended to find a local causal relationship between macro-variables or macro-variables and micro-variables [98]. Moreover, existing methods of causal discovery must be extended to consider the method of grouping a set of variables or coarse-graining a system. For example, ref. [154] proposed a coarse-to-fine causal discovery algorithm based on Granger causality and a graph neural network. The grouping process of variables is from coarse to fine, which can improve the efficiency of the algorithm. Other multi-level causal discovery methods were proposed and discussed in [155–157].

Another interesting problem is emergence detection. In complex dynamical systems, various higher-level patterns, such as waves, periodic oscillations, and solitons, are ubiquitous. For instance, in the climate system, typhoons and tornadoes are emergent vortex structures. In urban areas, traffic jams also emerge as a result of interactions among a large number of cars. Social riots are another example of emergent events in higher levels of human society. Identifying these emergent patterns at an early stage is crucial and significant [81,81,158–162]. Therefore, there is an urgent need for a method that can automatically detect these emergent patterns and even provide early warning signals.

In this review, we mainly focus on the emergence of causality; however, we are not limited to this specific type of emergence. More macroscopic or global-level properties could also be emergent, although causal emergence may be the most important one. For example, in [163], the authors discussed the concept of emergent information closure, which refers to the idea that the encoded information within an agent can form a closed system that is not influenced by the external world. The authors then argued that this agent with information closure can be regarded as a kind of consciousness. Symmetry may be another interesting property within some complex systems, and it may be emergent. For example, any single trajectory of a large number of random walkers in a two-dimensional Euclidean space is random. Nevertheless, the Gaussian distribution surface describing how the number of walkers falling in each small region changes with different locations is isotropic. This kind of symmetry can only be found at the macro-level and, thus, it is emergent. It would be interesting and useful to deploy a method for automatically discovering this kind of emergent symmetry. The framework for the NIS can be extended to address the problem of emergent symmetry identification if the optimized objective, EI, is replaced with a measure of isotope or more general symmetry [164]. Similarly, we can also find other emergent symmetries using this framework once their measurement and optimization are possible.

However, it is crucial to acknowledge the inherent limitations of applying machine learning techniques to causal discovery and emergence identification problems. For instance, in [45], the authors highlighted the existence of 'statistically equivalent' but causally distinct DAGs, implying that different causal structures can be constructed to account for the same dataset. Consequently, when utilizing machine learning techniques to uncover causality and emergent properties, similar challenges need to be addressed. Further research in this direction warrants significant attention to overcome these obstacles.

5.4. Understanding Complex Systems from Causal Emergence

A profound understanding of causal emergence and emergent causality can provide insights into understanding various mysterious phenomena in complex systems, including living systems, social systems, climate systems, ecosystems, and more. Significantly, fundamental questions, such as free will [68], consciousness [165], and life, are all intricately connected to emergent causation [166]. For instance, free will can be viewed as an emergent form of downward causation [68]. Social phenomena can be comprehended through the lens of causal emergence [167]. Interestingly, both the EI and ϕID frameworks for causal emergence have connections with one of the theories of consciousness, namely the integrated information theory [168]. However, understanding these abstract concepts and phenomena in the context of causal emergence is merely an initial step.

For a specific system, there are three problems that should be addressed in future studies: (1) When does causal emergence occur? (2) How does emergent causality have functional effects on the system? (3) How does emergent causality change when the system is changed to adapt to the environment? We discuss these problems one by one.

We still do not know when causal emergence will occur and how the measure of causal emergence changes with some key parameters of a system. In [32], the authors showed how the measure of causal emergence changes with different noises in the Boid model (see the relevant discussion in Section 4.1.2). It is reasonable to expect that there is a phase transition of emergent causality within a complex system when some key parameter changes because the causality or strength of the causal effect is also a global property, and it may be dependent on some order parameters.

If causal emergence occurs in the system, how does the emergent causation affect the parts and the whole of the system? For example, the emergent "I" can be understood as an emergent macro-variable [68]. How does "I" influence the part, say the foot, to move? This problem is non-trivial because it relates to the problem of mind–body interaction. It is important to study the information flows at both the macro-level and micro-level together to understand this phenomenon.

Finally, what is the relationship between adaptation and emergence [4,169,170]? Sometimes, when we refer to a property as emergent, we essentially mean that this property can be developed through adaptation. Therefore, adaptation or evolution serves as a causal force for certain emergent properties. This concept also applies to emergent causality. For instance, downward causation, which is commonly found in complex systems, emerges as a result of adaptation and evolution. The next crucial question is, how can we evolve an emergent property or causation? This problem resembles the issue of designing emergence [171–173]. However, our aim here is to seek an explanation rather than a design. We want to understand the specific environment and manner in which the observed emergent causation can be evolved through adaptation.

All these problems require further studies in the future. However, these problems are just a few of the more interesting problems that need to be addressed.

Author Contributions: Conceptualization, J.Z.; methodology, J.Z., B.Y. and P.C.; writing, B.Y., J.Z., A.L., J.W., Z.W., M.Y., K.L. and M.M. All authors have read and agreed to the published version of the manuscript.

Funding: This work was supported in part by National Natural Science Foundation of China (No. 62141607, U1936219).

Institutional Review Board Statement: Not applicable.

Data Availability Statement: No data available.

Acknowledgments: This work is inspired by the insightful discussions held in the "Causal Emergence" series reading groups organized by Swarma Club and the "Swarma-Kaifeng" Workshop. We would like to extend our sincere gratitude to Professors Yizhuang You, Jing He, Dr. Chaochao Lu, and Dr. Yanbo Zhang for their invaluable contributions and insightful discussions. We express our appreciation for the support from the Save 2050 Programme, a joint initiative of Swarma Club and X-Order. Additionally, we are grateful for the support received from Swarma Research.

Conflicts of Interest: The authors declare no conflicts of interest.

Appendix A. Calculation of EI with Transition Probability Matrix

Calculating effective information (EI) requires knowledge of the joint probability distribution of the system. The state transition probability matrix (TPM) defines the probability of transitioning from one state of the system to another. Specifically, the j_{th} element of the i_{th} row in the TPM, denoted by $TPM(i,j)$, represents the probability of the system being in state s_j at time $t+1$, given that it is in state s_i at time t (i.e., $P(X_{t+1} = s_j | X_t = s_i)$).

$$TPM(i,j) = P(X_{t+1} = s_j | X_t = s_i) = \frac{P(X_{t+1} = s_j, X_t = s_i)}{P(X_t = s_i)} \tag{A1}$$

Assuming we can "force" the system to conform to a maximum entropy distribution (i.e., uniform distribution) with N states, the probability of being in any given state i at time t, denoted by $P_u(X_t = s_i)$, is $\frac{1}{N}$.

As a result, the TPM can be expressed as the product of the joint probability of the system's maximum entropy distribution, denoted by $P_u(X_{t+1} = s_j, X_t = s_i)$, and the total number of states, which is N, as demonstrated below.

$$TPM(i,j) = \frac{P_u(X_{t+1} = s_j, X_t = s_i)}{P_u(X_t = s_i)} = \frac{P_u(X_{t+1} = s_j, X_t = s_i)}{1/N} = N \times P_u(X_{t+1} = s_j, X_t = s_i) \quad \text{(A2)}$$

Hence, the TPM of the system can be used to express both the joint probability and marginal probability at time $t+1$ of the system's maximum entropy distribution.

$$\therefore P_u(X_{t+1} = s_j, X_t = s_i) = \frac{1}{N} TPM(i,j) \quad \text{(A3)}$$

$$\therefore P_u(X_{t+1} = s_j) = \sum_i P_u(X_{t+1} = s_j, X_t = s_i) = \frac{1}{N} \sum_i TPM(i,j) \quad \text{(A4)}$$

Using this relationship, EI can be calculated directly with the TPM.

$$\begin{aligned} EI = I(I_D; E_D) &= I(X_t; X_{t+1})|_{do(X_t)\sim U} \\ &= \sum_{i,j} P_u(X_{t+1} = s_j, X_t = s_i) \log_2 \left(\frac{P_u(X_{t+1} = s_j, X_t = s_i)}{P_u(X_{t+1} = s_j) P_u(X_t = s_i)} \right) \\ &= \sum_{i,j} \frac{1}{N} TPM(i,j) \log_2 \left(\frac{\frac{1}{N} TPM(i,j)}{\frac{1}{N} \sum_k TPM(k,j) \times \frac{1}{N}} \right) \\ &= \frac{1}{N} \sum_{i,j} TPM(i,j) \log_2 \left(\frac{N \times TPM(i,j)}{\sum_k TPM(k,j)} \right) \end{aligned} \quad \text{(A5)}$$

References

1. Ledford, H. How to solve the world's biggest problems. *Nature* **2015**, *525*, 308–311. [CrossRef] [PubMed]
2. Mensah, P.; Katerere, D.; Hachigonta, S.; Roodt, A. *Systems Analysis Approach for Complex Global Challenges*; Springer: Berlin/Heidelberg, Germany, 2018.
3. Bar-Yam, Y. General features of complex systems. In *Encyclopedia of Life Support Systems (EOLSS)*; UNESCO, EOLSS Publishers: Oxford, UK, 2002; Volume 1.
4. Holland, J.H. *Emergence: From Chaos to Order*; OUP: Oxford, UK, 2000.
5. Artime, O.; De Domenico, M. From the origin of life to pandemics: Emergent phenomena in complex systems. *Philos. Trans. R. Soc. A* **2022**, *380*, 20200410. [CrossRef] [PubMed]
6. Lagercrantz, H.; Changeux, J.P. The emergence of human consciousness: From fetal to neonatal life. *Pediatr. Res.* **2009**, *65*, 255–260. [CrossRef] [PubMed]
7. Wei, J.; Tay, Y.; Bommasani, R.; Raffel, C.; Zoph, B.; Borgeaud, S.; Yogatama, D.; Bosma, M.; Zhou, D.; Metzler, D.; et al. Emergent abilities of large language models. *arXiv* **2022**, arXiv:2206.07682.
8. Anderson, P.W. More is different: Broken symmetry and the nature of the hierarchical structure of science. *Science* **1972**, *177*, 393–396. [CrossRef] [PubMed]
9. Meehl, P.E.; Sellars, W. The concept of emergence. *Minn. Stud. Philos. Sci.* **1956**, *1*, 239–252.
10. Bedau, M.A. Weak emergence. *Philos. Perspect.* **1997**, *11*, 375–399. [CrossRef]
11. Albert, R.; Barabási, A.L. Statistical mechanics of complex networks. *Rev. Mod. Phys.* **2002**, *74*, 47. [CrossRef]
12. Wikipedia. Butterfly Effect—Wikipedia, The Free Encyclopedia. 2023. Available online: https://en.wikipedia.org/wiki/Butterfly_effect (accessed on 27 September 2023).
13. Wikipedia. Homeostasis—Wikipedia, The Free Encyclopedia. 2023. Available online: https://en.wikipedia.org/wiki/Homeostasis (accessed on 4 October 2023).
14. Granger, C.W. Investigating causal relations by econometric models and cross-spectral methods. *Econom. J. Econom. Soc.* **1969**, *37*, 424–438. [CrossRef]
15. Pearl, J. *Models, Reasoning and Inference*; Cambridge University Press: Cambridge, UK, 2000; Volume 19.
16. Pearl, J. *Causality*; Cambridge University Press: Cambridge, UK, 2009.
17. Kim, J. 'Downward causation' in emergentism and nonreductive physicalism. In *Emergence or Reduction*; Walter de Gruyter: Berlin, Germany, 1992; pp. 119–138.
18. Fromm, J. Types and forms of emergence. *arXiv* **2005**, arXiv:nlin/0506028.
19. Hoel, E.P.; Albantakis, L.; Tononi, G. Quantifying causal emergence shows that macro can beat micro. *Proc. Natl. Acad. Sci. USA* **2013**, *110*, 19790–19795. [CrossRef] [PubMed]

20. Ellis, G.F. Efficient, formal, material, and final causes in biology and technology. *Entropy* **2023**, *25*, 1301. [CrossRef] [PubMed]
21. Oizumi, M.; Albantakis, L.; Tononi, G. From the phenomenology to the mechanisms of consciousness: Integrated information theory 3.0. *PLoS Comput. Biol.* **2014**, *10*, e1003588. [CrossRef] [PubMed]
22. Crutchfield, J.P.; Young, K. Inferring statistical complexity. *Phys. Rev. Lett.* **1989**, *63*, 105. [CrossRef] [PubMed]
23. Seth, A.K. Measuring emergence via nonlinear Granger causality. *alife* **2008**, *2008*, 545–552.
24. Rosas, F.E.; Mediano, P.A.; Jensen, H.J.; Seth, A.K.; Barrett, A.B.; Carhart-Harris, R.L.; Bor, D. Reconciling emergences: An information-theoretic approach to identify causal emergence in multivariate data. *PLoS Comput. Biol.* **2020**, *16*, e1008289. [CrossRef]
25. Hoel, E.P. When the Map Is Better Than the Territory. *Entropy* **2017**, *19*, 188. [CrossRef]
26. Chvykov, P.; Hoel, E. Causal geometry. *Entropy* **2020**, *23*, 24. [CrossRef]
27. Klein, B.; Hoel, E. The emergence of informative higher scales in complex networks. *Complexity* **2020**, *2020*, 8932526. [CrossRef]
28. Comolatti, R.; Hoel, E. Causal emergence is widespread across measures of causation. *arXiv* **2022**, arXiv:2202.01854.
29. Williams, P.L.; Beer, R.D. Nonnegative decomposition of multivariate information. *arXiv* **2010**, arXiv:1004.2515.
30. Mediano, P.A.; Rosas, F.; Carhart-Harris, R.L.; Seth, A.K.; Barrett, A.B Beyond integrated information: A taxonomy of information dynamics phenomena. *arXiv* **2019**, arXiv:1909.02297.
31. Zhang, J.; Liu, K. Neural information squeezer for causal emergence. *Entropy* **2022**, *25*, 26. [CrossRef]
32. Yang, M.; Wang, Z.; Liu, K.; Rong, Y.; Yuan, B.; Zhang, J. Finding emergence in data: Causal emergence inspired dynamics learning. *arXiv* **2023**, arXiv:2308.09952 .
33. Schölkopf, B.; Locatello, F.; Bauer, S.; Ke, N.R.; Kalchbrenner, N.; Goyal, A.; Bengio, Y. Toward causal representation learning. *Proc. IEEE* **2021**, *109*, 612–634. [CrossRef]
34. Iwasaki, Y.; Simon, H.A. Causality and model abstraction. *Artif. Intell.* **1994**, *67*, 143–194. [CrossRef]
35. Sucar, L.E. *Probabilistic Graphical Models*; Advances in Computer Vision and Pattern Recognition; Springer: London, UK, 2015; Volume 10, p. 1 .
36. Rubin, D.B. Causal inference using potential outcomes: Design, modeling, decisions. *J. Am. Stat. Assoc.* **2005**, *100*, 322–331. [CrossRef]
37. Malinsky, D.; Danks, D. Causal discovery algorithms: A practical guide. *Philos. Compass* **2018**, *13*, e12470. [CrossRef]
38. Spirtes, P.; Glymour, C.; Scheines, R. *Causation Prediction and Search*, 2nd ed.; MIT Press: Cambridge, MA, USA, 2000.
39. Chickering, D.M. Learning equivalence classes of Bayesian-network structures. *J. Mach. Learn. Res.* **2002**, *2*, 445–498.
40. Hume, D. An enquiry concerning human understanding. In *Seven Masterpieces of Philosophy*; Routledge: Abingdon, UK, 2016; pp. 183–276.
41. Eells, E. *Probabilistic Causality*; Cambridge University Press: Cambridge, UK, 1991; Volume 1.
42. Suppes, P. A probabilistic theory of causality. *Br. J. Philos. Sci.* **1973**, *24*, 409–410.
43. Hoel, E.; Levin, M. Emergence of informative higher scales in biological systems: A computational toolkit for optimal prediction and control. *Commun. Integr. Biol.* **2020**, *13*, 108–118. [CrossRef]
44. Koller, D.; Friedman, N. *Probabilistic Graphical Models: Principles and Techniques*; MIT Press: Cambridge, MA, USA, 2009.
45. Textor, J.; Van der Zander, B.; Gilthorpe, M.S.; Liśkiewicz, M.; Ellison, G.T. Robust causal inference using directed acyclic graphs: The R package 'dagitty'. *Int. J. Epidemiol.* **2016**, *45*, 1887–1894. [CrossRef] [PubMed]
46. Richardson, T.S. A discovery algorithm for directed cyclic graphs. *arXiv* **2013**, arXiv:1302.3599.
47. Spirtes, P.L. Directed cyclic graphical representations of feedback models. *arXiv* **2013**, arXiv:1302.4982.
48. Lacerda, G.; Spirtes, P.L.; Ramsey, J.; Hoyer, P.O. Discovering cyclic causal models by independent components analysis. *arXiv* **2012**, arXiv:1206.3273.
49. Forré, P.; Mooij, J.M. Constraint-based causal discovery for non-linear structural causal models with cycles and latent confounders. *arXiv* **2018**, arXiv:1807.03024.
50. Ellison, G.T. Using Directed Acyclic Graphs (Dags) to Represent the Data Generating Mechanisms of Disease and Healthcare Pathways: A Guide for Educators, Students, Practitioners and Researchers. In *Teaching Biostatistics in Medicine and Allied Health Sciences*; Springer: Berlin/Heidelberg, Germany, 2023; pp. 61–101.
51. Gong, C.; Yao, D.; Zhang, C.; Li, W.; Bi, J. Causal Discovery from Temporal Data: An Overview and New Perspectives. *arXiv* **2023**, arXiv:2303.10112.
52. Pepper, S.C. Emergence. *J. Philos.* **1926**, *23*, 241–245. [CrossRef]
53. Winning, J.; Bechtel, W. Complexity, control and goal-directedness in biological systems. In *The Routledge Handbook of Emergence*; Routledge: Abingdon, UK, 2019; p. 134.
54. Hendry, R.F. Substance and structure. In *The Routledge Handbook of Emergence*; Routledge: Abingdon, UK, 2019; p. 339.
55. Huxley, T.H. *Evolution and Ethics 1893–1943*; Pilot Press: King's Lynn, UK, 1947.
56. Mill, J.S. Of the Composition of Causes. In *A System of Logic, Ratiocinative and Inductive: Being a Connected View of the Principles of Evidence, and the Methods of Scientific Investigation*; Cambridge Library Collection—Philosophy; Cambridge University Press: Cambridge, UK, 2011; Volume 1, pp. 425–436. [CrossRef]
57. Gibb, S.; Hendry, R.F.; Lancaster, T. *The Routledge Handbook of Emergence*; Routledge: Abingdon, UK, 2019.
58. Ross, W.D.; Smith, J.A. *The Works of Aristotle: Metaphysica, by WD Ross*; Clarendon Press: Cambridge, UK, 1908; Volume 8.
59. Holland, J.H. *Hidden Order: How Adaptation Builds Complexity*; Addison Wesley Longman Publishing Co., Inc.: Boston, MA, USA, 1996.

60. Reynolds, C.W. Flocks, herds and schools: A distributed behavioral model. In Proceedings of the 14th Annual Conference on Computer Graphics and Interactive Techniques, Anaheim, CA, USA, 27–31 July 1987; pp. 25–34.
61. Gardner, M. The Fantastic Combinations of Jhon Conway's New Solitaire Game'Life. *Sc. Am.* **1970**, *223*, 20–123.
62. Luhmann, N. *Social Systems*; Stanford University Press: Redwood City, CA, USA, 1995.
63. Crutchfield, J.P. The calculi of emergence: Computation, dynamics and induction. *Phys. D Nonlinear Phenom.* **1994**, *75*, 11–54. [CrossRef]
64. Bedau, M.A.; Humphreys, P. *Emergence: Contemporary Readings in Philosophy and Science*; MIT Press: Cambridge, MA, USA, 2008.
65. Bedau, M. Downward causation and the autonomy of weak emergence. *Principia Int. J. Epistemol.* **2002**, *6*, 5–50.
66. Wolfram, S. *A New Kind of Science*; Wolfram Media Champaign: Champaign, IL, USA, 2002; Volume 5.
67. Merton, R.K. *The Sociology of Science: Theoretical and Empirical Investigations*; University of Chicago Press: Chicago, IL, USA, 1973.
68. Yurchenko, S.B. Can there be a synergistic core emerging in the brain hierarchy to control neural activity by downward causation? *TechRxiv* **2023** . [CrossRef]
69. Harré, R. *The Philosophies of Science*; Oxford University Press: New York, NY, USA , 1985.
70. Baas, N.A. Emergence, hierarchies, and hyperstructures. In *Artificial Life III, SFI Studies in the Science of Complexity, XVII*; Routledge: Abingdon, UK, 1994; pp. 515–537.
71. Newman, D.V. Emergence and strange attractors. *Philos. Sci.* **1996**, *63*, 245–261. [CrossRef]
72. O'Connor, T. Emergent properties. *Am. Philos. Q.* **1994**, *31*, 91–104.
73. Héder, M.; Paksi, D. A Criticism of Weak Emergence. *Polanyiana* **2019**, *28*, 1–2
74. Jackson, F.; Pettit, P. In defense of explanatory ecumenism. *Econ. Philos.* **1992**, *8*, 1–21. [CrossRef]
75. Kim, J. Making sense of emergence. *Philos. Stud. Int. J. Philos. Anal. Tradit.* **1999**, *95*, 3–36.
76. Bonabeau, E.; Dessalles, J.L. Detection and emergence. *arXiv* **2011**, arXiv:1108.4279.
77. Dewhurst, J. Causal emergence from effective information: Neither causal nor emergent? *Thought J. Philos.* **2021**, *10*, 158–168. [CrossRef]
78. Eberhardt, F.; Lee, L.L. Causal emergence: When distortions in a map obscure the territory. *Philosophies* **2022**, *7*, 30. [CrossRef]
79. Shalizi, C.R. *Causal Architecture, Complexity and Self-Organization in Time Series and Cellular Automata*; The University of Wisconsin-Madison: Madison, WI, USA, 2001.
80. Shalizi, C.R.; Moore, C. What is a macrostate? Subjective observations and objective dynamics. *arXiv* **2003**, arXiv:cond-mat/0303625.
81. Mnif, M.; Müller-Schloer, C. Quantitative emergence. In *Organic Computing—A Paradigm Shift for Complex Systems*; Springer: Basel, Switzerland, 2011; pp. 39–52.
82. Tang, M.; Mao, X. Information entropy-based metrics for measuring emergences in artificial societies. *Entropy* **2014**, *16*, 4583–4602. [CrossRef]
83. Fisch, D.; Jänicke, M.; Sick, B.; Müller-Schloer, C. Quantitative emergence–A refined approach based on divergence measures. In Proceedings of the 2010 Fourth IEEE International Conference on Self-Adaptive and Self-Organizing Systems, Budapest, Hungary, 27 September–1 October 2010; IEEE Computer Society: Washington, DC, USA, 2010; pp. 94–103.
84. Fisch, D.; Fisch, D.; Jänicke, M.; Kalkowski, E.; Sick, B. Techniques for knowledge acquisition in dynamically changing environments. *ACM Trans. Auton. Adapt. Syst. (TAAS)* **2012**, *7*, 1–25. [CrossRef]
85. Fisch, D.; Jänicke, M.; Müller-Schloer, C.; Sick, B. Divergence measures as a generalised approach to quantitative emergence. In *Organic Computing—A Paradigm Shift for Complex Systems*; Springer: Basel, Switzerland, 2011; pp. 53–66.
86. Holzer, R.; De Meer, H.; Bettstetter, C. On autonomy and emergence in self-organizing systems. In *International Workshop on Self-Organizing Systems, Proceedings of the Third International Workshop, IWSOS 2008, Vienna, Austria, 10–12 December 2008* ; Springer: Berlin/Heidelberg, Germany, 2008; pp. 157–169.
87. Holzer, R.; de Meer, H. Methods for approximations of quantitative measures in self-organizing systems. In Proceedings of the Self-Organizing Systems: 5th International Workshop, IWSOS 2011, Karlsruhe, Germany, 23–24 February 2011; Proceedings 5; Springer: Berlin/Heidelberg, Germany, 2011; pp. 1–15.
88. Teo, Y.M.; Luong, B.L.; Szabo, C. Formalization of emergence in multi-agent systems. In Proceedings of the 1st ACM SIGSIM Conference on Principles of Advanced Discrete Simulation, Montreal, QC, Canada, 19–22 May 2013; pp. 231–240.
89. Szabo, C.; Teo, Y.M. Formalization of weak emergence in multiagent systems. *ACM Trans. Model. Comput. Simul. (TOMACS)* **2015**, *26*, 1–25. [CrossRef]
90. Christensen, K.; Moloney, N.R. *Complexity and Criticality*; World Scientific Publishing Company: Singapore, 2005; Volume 1.
91. McComb, W.D. *Renormalization Methods: A Guide for Beginners*; OUP Oxford: Cambridge, UK, 2003.
92. Kemeny, J.; Snell, J. *Finite Markov Chains: With a New Appendix "Generalization of a Fundamental Matrix"*; Undergraduate Texts in Mathematics; Springer: New York, NY, USA, 1983.
93. Pfante, O.; Bertschinger, N.; Olbrich, E.; Ay, N.; Jost, J. Comparison between different methods of level identification. *Adv. Complex Syst.* **2014**, *17*, 1450007. [CrossRef]
94. Kotsalis, G.; Megretski, A.; Dahleh, M.A. Balanced truncation for a class of stochastic jump linear systems and model reduction for hidden Markov models. *IEEE Trans. Autom. Control* **2008**, *53*, 2543–2557. [CrossRef]
95. White, L.B.; Mahony, R.; Brushe, G.D. Lumpable hidden Markov models-model reduction and reduced complexity filtering. *IEEE Trans. Autom. Control* **2000**, *45*, 2297–2306. [CrossRef]

96. Wolpert, D.H.; Grochow, J.A.; Libby, E.; DeDeo, S. Optimal high-level descriptions of dynamical systems. *arXiv* **2014**, arXiv:1409.7403.
97. Jaynes, E.T. Information theory and statistical mechanics. *Phys. Rev.* **1957**, *106*, 620. [CrossRef]
98. Varley, T.F. Flickering emergences: The question of locality in information-theoretic approaches to emergence. *Entropy* **2022**, *25*, 54. [CrossRef]
99. Cheng, P.W.; Novick, L.R. Causes versus enabling conditions. *Cognition* **1991**, *40*, 83–120. [CrossRef] [PubMed]
100. Varley, T.F. Causal emergence in discrete and continuous dynamical systems. *arXiv* **2020**, arXiv:2003.13075.
101. Marrow, S.; Michaud, E.J.; Hoel, E. Examining the Causal Structures of Deep Neural Networks Using Information Theory. *Entropy* **2020**, *22*, 1429. [CrossRef] [PubMed]
102. Griebenow, R.; Klein, B.; Hoel, E. Finding the right scale of a network: Efficient identification of causal emergence through spectral clustering. *arXiv* **2019**, arXiv:1908.07565.
103. Klein, B.; Swain, A.; Byrum, T.; Scarpino, S.V.; Fagan, W.F. Exploring noise, degeneracy and determinism in biological networks with the einet package. *Methods Ecol. Evol.* **2022**, *13*, 799–804. [CrossRef]
104. Klein, B.; Hoel, E.; Swain, A.; Griebenow, R.; Levin, M. Evolution and emergence: Higher order information structure in protein interactomes across the tree of life. *Integr. Biol.* **2021**, *13*, 283–294. [CrossRef] [PubMed]
105. Swain, A.; Williams, S.D.; Di Felice, L.J.; Hobson, E.A. Interactions and information: Exploring task allocation in ant colonies using network analysis. *Anim. Behav.* **2022**, *189*, 69–81. [CrossRef]
106. Luppi, A.I.; Mediano, P.A.; Rosas, F.E.; Holland, N.; Fryer, T.D.; O'Brien, J.T.; Rowe, J.B.; Menon, D.K.; Bor, D.; Stamatakis, E.A. A synergistic core for human brain evolution and cognition. *Nat. Neurosci.* **2022**, *25*, 771–782. [CrossRef]
107. Varley, T.F.; Hoel, E. Emergence as the conversion of information: A unifying theory. *Philos. Trans. R. Soc. A* **2022**, *380*, 20210150. [CrossRef]
108. Silver, D.; Huang, A.; Maddison, C.J.; Guez, A.; Sifre, L.; Van Den Driessche, G.; Schrittwieser, J.; Antonoglou, I.; Panneershelvam, V.; Lanctot, M.; et al. Mastering the game of Go with deep neural networks and tree search. *Nature* **2016**, *529*, 484–489. [CrossRef]
109. Dabney, W.; Kurth-Nelson, Z.; Uchida, N.; Starkweather, C.K.; Hassabis, D.; Munos, R.; Botvinick, M. A distributional code for value in dopamine-based reinforcement learning. *Nature* **2020**, *577*, 671–675. [CrossRef] [PubMed]
110. Senior, A.W.; Evans, R.; Jumper, J.; Kirkpatrick, J.; Sifre, L.; Green, T.; Qin, C.; Žídek, A.; Nelson, A.W.; Bridgland, A.; et al. Improved protein structure prediction using potentials from deep learning. *Nature* **2020**, *577*, 706–710. [CrossRef] [PubMed]
111. LeCun, Y.; Bengio, Y.; Hinton, G. Deep learning. *Nature* **2015**, *521*, 436–444. [CrossRef] [PubMed]
112. Wang, H.; Wang, Y.; Zhou, Z.; Ji, X.; Gong, D.; Zhou, J.; Li, Z.; Liu, W. Cosface: Large margin cosine loss for deep face recognition. In Proceedings of the IEEE Conference on Computer Vision and Pattern Recognition, Salt Lake City, UT, USA, 18–23 June 2018; pp. 5265–5274.
113. Mikolov, T.; Chen, K.; Corrado, G.; Dean, J. Efficient estimation of word representations in vector space. *arXiv* **2013**, arXiv:1301.3781.
114. Devlin, J.; Chang, M.W.; Lee, K.; Toutanova, K. Bert: Pre-training of deep bidirectional transformers for language understanding. *arXiv* **2018**, arXiv:1810.04805.
115. Vaswani, A.; Shazeer, N.; Parmar, N.; Uszkoreit, J.; Jones, L.; Gomez, A.N.; Kaiser, Ł.; Polosukhin, I. Attention is all you need. In Proceedings of the Advances in Neural Information Processing Systems 30 (NIPS 2017), Long Beach, CA, USA, 4–9 December 2017; Curran Associates Inc.: Red Hook, NY, USA, 2017.
116. Mnih, V.; Kavukcuoglu, K.; Silver, D.; Rusu, A.A.; Veness, J.; Bellemare, M.G.; Graves, A.; Riedmiller, M.; Fidjeland, A.K.; Ostrovski, G.; et al. Human-level control through deep reinforcement learning. *Nature* **2015**, *518*, 529–533. [CrossRef]
117. Fan, L.; Li, L.; Ma, Z.; Lee, S.; Yu, H.; Hemphill, L. A bibliometric review of large language models research from 2017 to 2023. *arXiv* **2023**, arXiv:2304.02020.
118. Cui, P.; Athey, S. Stable learning establishes some common ground between causal inference and machine learning. *Nat. Mach. Intell.* **2022**, *4*, 110–115. [CrossRef]
119. Kaddour, J.; Lynch, A.; Liu, Q.; Kusner, M.J.; Silva, R. Causal machine learning: A survey and open problems. *arXiv* **2022**, arXiv:2206.15475.
120. Peters, J.; Bühlmann, P.; Meinshausen, N. Causal inference by using invariant prediction: Identification and confidence intervals. *J. R. Stat. Soc. Ser. B Stat. Methodol.* **2016**, *78*, 947–1012. [CrossRef]
121. Kuang, K.; Cui, P.; Athey, S.; Xiong, R.; Li, B. Stable prediction across unknown environments. In Proceedings of the 24th ACM SIGKDD International Conference on Knowledge Discovery & Data Mining, London, UK, 19–23 August 2018; pp. 1617–1626.
122. Hornik, K. Approximation capabilities of multilayer feedforward networks. *Neural Netw.* **1991**, *4*, 251–257. [CrossRef]
123. Teshima, T.; Ishikawa, I.; Tojo, K.; Oono, K.; Ikeda, M.; Sugiyama, M. Coupling-based invertible neural networks are universal diffeomorphism approximators. *Adv. Neural Inf. Process. Syst.* **2020**, *33*, 3362–3373.
124. Rosenblatt, M. Remarks on some nonparametric estimates of a density function. *Ann. Math. Stat.* **1956**, *27*, 832–837. [CrossRef]
125. Snoek, L.; van der Miesen, M.M.; Beemsterboer, T.; Van Der Leij, A.; Eigenhuis, A.; Steven Scholte, H. The Amsterdam Open MRI Collection, a set of multimodal MRI datasets for individual difference analyses. *Sci. Data* **2021**, *8*, 85. [CrossRef] [PubMed]
126. Arjovsky, M.; Bottou, L.; Gulrajani, I.; Lopez-Paz, D. Invariant risk minimization. *arXiv* **2019**, arXiv:1907.02893.
127. Ye, H.; Xie, C.; Cai, T.; Li, R.; Li, Z.; Wang, L. Towards a theoretical framework of out-of-distribution generalization. *Adv. Neural Inf. Process. Syst.* **2021**, *34*, 23519–23531.

128. Huh, D.; Baidya, A. The Missing Invariance Principle found–the Reciprocal Twin of Invariant Risk Minimization. *Adv. Neural Inf. Process. Syst.* **2022**, *35*, 23023–23035.
129. Zhao, H.; Des Combes, R.T.; Zhang, K.; Gordon, G. On learning invariant representations for domain adaptation. In Proceedings of the International Conference on Machine Learning, PMLR, Long Beach, CA, USA, 9–15 June 2019; pp. 7523–7532.
130. Ganin, Y.; Ustinova, E.; Ajakan, H.; Germain, P.; Larochelle, H.; Laviolette, F.; Marchand, M.; Lempitsky, V. Domain-adversarial training of neural networks. *J. Mach. Learn. Res.* **2016**, *17*, 1–35.
131. Wang, J.; Lan, C.; Liu, C.; Ouyang, Y.; Qin, T.; Lu, W.; Chen, Y.; Zeng, W.; Yu, P. Generalizing to unseen domains: A survey on domain generalization. *IEEE Trans. Knowl. Data Eng.* **2022**, *35*, 8052–8072. [CrossRef]
132. Li, Y.; Gong, M.; Tian, X.; Liu, T.; Tao, D. Domain generalization via conditional invariant representations. In Proceedings of the AAAI Conference on Artificial Intelligence, New Orleans, LA, USA, 2–7 February 2018; Volume 32.
133. Koyama, M.; Yamaguchi, S. Out-of-distribution generalization with maximal invariant predictor. *arXiv* **2020**, arXiv:2008.01883.
134. Ahuja, K.; Caballero, E.; Zhang, D.; Gagnon-Audet, J.C.; Bengio, Y.; Mitliagkas, I.; Rish, I. Invariance principle meets information bottleneck for out-of-distribution generalization. *Adv. Neural Inf. Process. Syst.* **2021**, *34*, 3438–3450.
135. Kaur, J.N.; Kiciman, E.; Sharma, A. Modeling the data-generating process is necessary for out-of-distribution generalization. *arXiv* **2022**, arXiv:2206.07837.
136. Shen, Z.; Cui, P.; Zhang, T.; Kunag, K. Stable learning via sample reweighting. In Proceedings of the Proceedings of the AAAI Conference on Artificial Intelligence, New York, NY, USA, 7–12 February 2020; Volume 34, pp. 5692–5699.
137. Shen, Z.; Cui, P.; Liu, J.; Zhang, T.; Li, B.; Chen, Z. Stable learning via differentiated variable decorrelation. In Proceedings of the 26th ACM Sigkdd International Conference on Knowledge Discovery & Data Mining, Virtual, 6–10 July 2020; pp. 2185–2193.
138. Zhang, X.; Cui, P.; Xu, R.; Zhou, L.; He, Y.; Shen, Z. Deep stable learning for out-of-distribution generalization. In Proceedings of the IEEE/CVF Conference on Computer Vision and Pattern Recognition, Nashville, TN, USA, 20–25 June 2021; pp. 5372–5382.
139. Bengio, Y.; Courville, A.; Vincent, P. Representation learning: A review and new perspectives. *IEEE Trans. Pattern Anal. Mach. Intell.* **2013**, *35*, 1798–1828. [CrossRef] [PubMed]
140. Monti, R.P.; Zhang, K.; Hyvärinen, A. Causal discovery with general non-linear relationships using non-linear ica. In Proceedings of the Uncertainty in Artificial Intelligence, PMLR, Tel Aviv, Israel, 22–25 July 2019; pp. 186–195.
141. Clayton, P.; Davies, P. *The Re-Emergence of Emergence: The Emergentist Hypothes*; Oxford University Press: Oxford, UK, 2006.
142. Kim, J. *Physicalism, or Something Near Enough*; Princeton University Press: Princeton, NJ, USA, 2007.
143. Zhang, Z.; You, Y.Z. Observing Schrödinger's Cat with Artificial Intelligence: Emergent Classicality from Information Bottleneck *arXiv* **2023**, arXiv:2306.14838.
144. Glymour, C.; Zhang, K.; Spirtes, P. Review of causal discovery methods based on graphical models. *Front. Genet.* **2019**, *10*, 524. [CrossRef] [PubMed]
145. Zanga, A.; Ozkirimli, E.; Stella, F. A survey on causal discovery: Theory and practice. *Int. J. Approx. Reason.* **2022**, *151*, 101–129. [CrossRef]
146. Donges, J.F.; Zou, Y.; Marwan, N.; Kurths, J. The backbone of the climate network. *Europhys. Lett.* **2009**, *87*, 48007. [CrossRef]
147. Kalisch, M.; Bühlman, P. Estimating high-dimensional directed acyclic graphs with the PC-algorithm. *J. Mach. Learn. Res.* **2007**, *8*, 613–636.
148. Zheng, X.; Aragam, B.; Ravikumar, P.K.; Xing, E.P. Dags with no tears: Continuous optimization for structure learning. *Adv. Neural Inf. Process. Syst.* **2018**, *31* 9472–9483. .
149. Zhu, S.; Ng, I.; Chen, Z. Causal discovery with reinforcement learning. *arXiv* **2019**, arXiv:1906.04477.
150. Rantanen, K.; Hyttinen, A.; Järvisalo, M. Learning optimal cyclic causal graphs from interventional data. In Proceedings of the International Conference on Probabilistic Graphical Models, PMLR, Skørping, Denmark, 23–25 September 2020; pp. 365–376.
151. Zhang, Z.; Zhao, Y.; Liu, J.; Wang, S.; Tao, R.; Xin, R.; Zhang, J. A general deep learning framework for network reconstruction and dynamics learning. *Appl. Netw. Sci.* **2019**, *4*, 110. [CrossRef]
152. Pamfil, R.; Sriwattanaworachai, N.; Desai, S.; Pilgerstorfer, P.; Georgatzis, K.; Beaumont, P.; Aragam, B. Dynotears: Structure learning from time-series data. In Proceedings of the International Conference on Artificial Intelligence and Statistics, PMLR, Palermo, Italy, 26–28 August 2020; pp. 1595–1605.
153. Vowels, M.J.; Camgoz, N.C.; Bowden, R. D'ya like dags? a survey on structure learning and causal discovery. *ACM Comput. Surv.* **2022**, *55*, 1–36. [CrossRef]
154. Cheng, Y.; Li, L.; Xiao, T.; Li, Z.; Suo, J.; He, K.; Dai, Q. CUTS+: High-dimensional Causal Discovery from Irregular Time-series. *arXiv* **2023**, arXiv:2305.05890.
155. Wang, D.; Chen, Z.; Ni, J.; Tong, L.; Wang, Z.; Fu, Y.; Chen, H. Hierarchical graph neural networks for causal discovery and root cause localization. *arXiv* **2023**, arXiv:2302.01987.
156. Zhang, Q.; Zhang, C.; Cheng, S. Wavelet Multiscale Granger Causality Analysis Based on State Space Models. *Symmetry* **2023**, *15*, 1286. [CrossRef]
157. Fan, C.; Wang, Y.; Zhang, Y.; Ouyang, W. Interpretable Multi-Scale Neural Network for Granger Causality Discovery. In Proceedings of the ICASSP 2023-2023 IEEE International Conference on Acoustics, Speech and Signal Processing (ICASSP), Rhodes Island, Greece, 4–10 June 2023; IEEE: Piscataway, NJ, USA, 2023; pp. 1–5.
158. Haugen, R.A.; Skeie, N.O.; Muller, G.; Syverud, E. Detecting emergence in engineered systems: A literature review and synthesis approach. *Syst. Eng.* **2023**, *26*, 463–481. [CrossRef]

159. O'toole, E.; Nallur, V.; Clarke, S. Decentralised detection of emergence in complex adaptive systems. *ACM Trans. Auton. Adapt. Syst. (TAAS)* **2017**, *12*, 1–31. [CrossRef]
160. O'Toole, E.; Nallur, V.; Clarke, S. Towards decentralised detection of emergence in complex adaptive systems. In Proceedings of the 2014 IEEE Eighth International Conference on Self-Adaptive and Self-Organizing Systems, London, UK, 8–12 September 2014; IEEE: Piscataway, NJ, USA, 2014, pp. 60–69.
161. Pazho, A.D.; Noghre, G.A.; Purkayastha, A.A.; Vempati, J.; Martin, O.; Tabkhi, H. A Survey of Graph-based Deep Learning for Anomaly Detection in Distributed Systems. *arXiv* **2022**, arXiv:2206.04149.
162. Liu, R.; Wu, Z.; Yu, S.; Lin, S. The emergence of objectness: Learning zero-shot segmentation from videos. *Adv. Neural Inf. Process. Syst.* **2021**, *34*, 13137–13152.
163. Chang, A.Y.; Biehl, M.; Yu, Y.; Kanai, R. Information closure theory of consciousness. *Front. Psychol.* **2020**, *11*, 1504. [CrossRef]
164. Liu, Z.; Tegmark, M. Machine learning hidden symmetries. *Phys. Rev. Lett.* **2022**, *128*, 180201. [CrossRef] [PubMed]
165. Tononi, G.; Koch, C. Consciousness: Here, there and everywhere? *Philos. Trans. R. Soc. B Biol. Sci.* **2015**, *370*, 20140167. [CrossRef] [PubMed]
166. Walker, S.I. Top-down causation and the rise of information in the emergence of life. *Information* **2014**, *5*, 424–439. [CrossRef]
167. Elder-Vass, D. *The Causal Power of Social Structures: Emergence, Structure and Agency*; Cambridge University Press: Cambridge, UK, 2010.
168. Tononi, G.; Boly, M.; Massimini, M.; Koch, C. Integrated information theory: From consciousness to its physical substrate. *Nat. Rev. Neurosci.* **2016**, *17*, 450–461. [CrossRef]
169. Holland, J.H. Hidden order. In *Business Week-Domestic Edition*; Addison-Wesley: Boston, MA, USA, 1995; p. 21.
170. Holland, J.H. *Adaptation in Natural and Artificial Systems: An Introductory Analysis with Applications to Biology, Control, and Artificial Intelligence*; MIT Press: Cambridge, MA, USA, 1992.
171. Adamatzky, A.; Chen, G.; Bazzan, A.L.C.; Brasil, R.; Burguillo, J.C.; Corchado, E.; Davendra, D.; Lampinen, J.; Middendorf, M.; Ott, E.; et al. *Emergence, Complexity and Computation*; Springer: Berlin/Heidelberg, Germany, 2022; p. 10624.
172. Kreyssig, P.; Dittrich, P. Emergent control. In *Organic Computing—A Paradigm Shift for Complex Systems*; Springer: Basel, Switzerland, 2011; pp. 67–78.
173. Mitchell, M.; Hraber, P.; Crutchfield, J.P. Revisiting the edge of chaos: Evolving cellular automata to perform computations. *arXiv* **1993**, arXiv:adap-org/9303003.

entropy

MDPI

Perspective

Efficient, Formal, Material, and Final Causes in Biology and Technology

George F. R. Ellis

Mathematics Department, The New Institute, University of Cape Town, 20354 Hamburg, Germany; george.ellis@uct.ac.za

Abstract: This paper considers how a classification of causal effects as comprising efficient, formal, material, and final causation can provide a useful understanding of how emergence takes place in biology and technology, with formal, material, and final causation all including cases of downward causation; they each occur in both synchronic and diachronic forms. Taken together, they underlie why all emergent levels in the hierarchy of emergence have causal powers (which is Noble's principle of biological relativity) and so why causal closure only occurs when the upwards and downwards interactions between all emergent levels are taken into account, contra to claims that some underlying physics level is by itself causality complete. A key feature is that stochasticity at the molecular level plays an important role in enabling agency to emerge, underlying the possibility of final causation occurring in these contexts.

Keywords: Aristotle; causation; emergence; causal closure; downwards causation

1. Introduction

Fully understanding causation and fully explaining why complex systems are the way they are and behave the way they do requires holistic, historical, contextual, and extended views of causation across levels. As Aristotle was the first person we know of to articulate this holistic view, it is worth exploring whether, taking into account scientific discoveries made since his time, revisiting his understandings might be useful to us today. I suggest here that useful light is thrown on the way that life emerges from the underlying physics and molecular biology by considering updated versions of his four types of causation—efficient, formal, material, and final (Shields 2022 [1])—and that the same is true for understanding the emergence of technology (Arthur 2009 [2]), specifically digital computers. This argument gives strong support to an emergentist position in biology and technology.

This paper is not a disquisition on Aristotle's views as such. Rather, it uses the basic notions of his four kinds of causation as a foundation for providing a useful, fine-grained view of the nature of causation in these contexts. The paper is also not a discussion of the contentious issue of whether any variety of strong or weak emergence occurs. The concern is how emergence that occurs in these contexts is characterized by genuinely effective laws relating emergent concepts and variables without considering the logically separate issue of whether this emergent higher-level behavior can be uniquely predicted from lower-level elements and laws alone.

The paper also does not include a discussion of causation in the cosmological context, where the nature of final causation becomes a controversial issue.

What this paper does do, is firstly, claim that in the specific cases of concern, there are verifiable same-level laws of behavior characterizing causation at every emergent level, specified in terms of variables applicable at that level. This is shown to be true by providing specific examples from various contexts where it indeed occurs, as can be demonstrated by suitable experiments. Existence of these effective laws is how the different emergent levels (and associated academic disciplines) are identified. Why are they considered effective laws? Because whatever their origin, they reliably determine outcomes given suitable initial data and boundary conditions. This may be claimed to be a useful updated concept of efficient causation. How does efficient causation arise? By coarse-graining lower-level variables and dynamics (i.e., viewing them at a larger scale) or black-boxing lower-level logical relations. This results in both formal and material causation occurring at the relevant emergent level, and possibly final causation as well; thus, these are aspects enabling efficient causation, occurring concurrently. Formal and material causation are associated with symmetry breaking. Specific outcomes are determined by setting boundary and initial conditions, including those provided by higher levels (Noble 2012 [3]). Secondly, a key point is that any of these forms of causation can take place in either synchronic or diachronic forms: they can be time independent or time dependent. Thirdly, downwards causation can take place via any of suitably generalized formal, material, and final causation, contrary to claims that downward causation cannot occur. Thus, causal closure can only occur when all levels related by upwards emergence and downwards causation are included in the set considered. No physics level (of which there are a number) is causally complete by itself.

Why is this worth doing? Not only because Aristotle gave the germ of the idea in each case, which is indeed true, and so provides a link back to long before Galileo Galilei, Isaac Newton, and other such pioneers, but because it gives a viewpoint on emergence that is more comprehensive in its ambit than most other approaches.

This section looks at Aristotle's four causes (Section 1.1), scientific discoveries since then (Section 1.2), the theme of updated versions of Aristotle's causes (Section 1.3), and then gives a brief outline of this paper (Section 1.4).

1.1. Aristotle's Four Causes (This account is due to Christoph Horn (Bonn). I thank him for it)

Aristotle's account of the four causes is given in *Physics* II 3 and in *Metaphysics* V 2. Whereas our modern concept of a cause refers to an event under the influence of which a certain state of the world is brought about, Aristotle presents his general idea of causes (*aitiai*) as the answer to the why-question (*to dia ti*) in general. Aristotle's account of causality comprises four ways to explain a given state of the world. He identifies four kinds of entities which can be used in an explanation:

- **The material cause**: "that out of which", e.g., the bronze of a statue or the silver that makes a bowl.
- **The formal cause**: "the form", "the account of what-it-is-to-be", e.g., the shape of a statue.
- **The efficient cause**: "the primary source of the change or rest", e.g., the artisan, the art of bronze-casting the statue, the man who gives advice, the father of the child.
- **The final cause**: "the end or the good, that for the sake of which a thing is done", e.g., health is the end of walking, losing weight, purging, drugs, and surgical tools.

Causation appears in different meanings, as Aristotle claims, and it may be that all four causes appear in the explanation of an entity or a fact (*Phys.* 195 a 3–5). In the case of an artifact such as a bronze statue or a silver bowl, the bronze and the silver explain the things as their *material cause*. The material cause is directly interrelated with the *formal cause*, i.e., the shape of the statue or the bowl. Additionally, Aristotle introduces *the efficient cause* as that which is what produces the statue. He thinks that this is both the artisan and the technique of processing the material. The *final cause* is the end or the good for which the craftsman produced the artifact. Aristotle explicitly says that this "good" need not be a real good; it suffices that the agent considers something as a good.

1.2. Scientific Discoveries since Then

Our understanding of the functioning of the natural and biological world is now based on two ideas: firstly, that there are some fundamental immutable laws of nature that underlie how all matter behaves, and secondly, that complex systems such as plants and animals and ecosystems and digital computers arise through very complex combinations of various kinds of particles or fields subject to those basic physical laws.

Basic Constituents and Laws: Everything we see around us is composed of particles that are subject to forces that determine how they move. This is explained clearly in the famous *Feynman Lectures in Physics*, Volumes I and II (Feynman 2013 [4]).

Constitution of matter: One of the most fundamental discoveries ever made is that everything is made of extremely small atoms—a fact that is far from obvious. They, in turn, are made of smaller particles (protons, neutrons, and electrons, characterized by their mass **m** and electric charge **e**), with the first two made up of even smaller particles called quarks. Atoms consist of a small nucleus comprising a number **N** of positively charged protons and an approximately equal number of uncharged neutrons, surrounded (in the neutral state) by a cloud of **N** negatively charged electrons that occur in shells at increasing distance from the nucleus (**N** is the atomic number). Combinations of atoms can form gases, liquids, glasses, crystals, or molecules.

Quantum theory (Feynman 2013 [4]: Volume III) shows that all matter has both a particulate and wave like nature; even light is made of particles ("photons"). Special relativity shows that mass **m** and energy **E** can be transformed into each other according to the famous Einstein formula $\mathbf{E} = \mathbf{m}\,\mathbf{c}^2$, where **c** is the speed of light.

The four forces acting on particles are gravity, electromagnetism, the weak force, and the strong force, which can be represented as fields filling space ("the gravitational field", "the electromagnetic field"), thereby solving the puzzle as to how they can act at a distance. Electric and magnetic fields interact with each other in such a way that they can create electromagnetic waves that travel at the speed of light **c**, with a wavelength $\boldsymbol{\lambda}$ that can range from the very long (radio waves) to the very short (X-rays and γ-rays), including light itself: the part of the electromagnetic spectrum that is visible to us, with different colors corresponding to different wavelengths.

Chemical elements: Combining these basic components gives rise to substances of various kinds that are the link to higher-order complexity. In Aristotle's case, these were earth, air, fire, and water, not considered as elementary in their own right but as a heap or foundation for complex possibilities (Sokolowski 1970 [5]).

Nowadays, elementary particles are understood to give rise to atoms of various kinds that are characterized as chemical elements such as hydrogen, carbon, nitrogen, oxygen, iron, and so on. They are nature's building blocks (Emsley 2011 [6]), with chemical properties that depend on their atomic number **N** via the column they belong to in the ***Periodic Table of the Elements*** (Scerri 2019 [7]).

Biomolecules: Atoms can be combined into the carbon-based organic molecules that are the foundation of life. Particularly important are macromolecules (Lehn 2004 [8]): on the one hand, nucleic acids DNA and RNA are the basis of storing and reading genetic information (Watson et al., 2014 [9]), and on the other hand, the proteins are the workhorses of molecular biology (Petsko and Ringe 2004 [10], Wagner 2014 [11]).

Complex systems: Basic principles: Modular hierarchical structures underlie the emergence of complexity in general, and of life in particular, for very good reasons (Booch et al., 2007 [12]), as discussed in Section 2. Through downward causation (Pezzulo and Levin 2016 [13], Vooshholz and Gabriel 2021 [14]), all emergent levels have causal powers (Noble 2012 [3]). They are adapted to their environments to greater or lesser degree by evolutionary, developmental, and functional mechanisms; a different environment will result in different structure and function at each level.

Complex systems: Biology: Emergent laws arise out of these foundations, through coarse-graining, symmetry breaking (Anderson 1972 [15]), or black boxing (Marshall et al., 2018 [16]). As regards to biology (Campbell and Reece 2005 [17]), there are well-established effective laws for:

1. Physical chemistry (Atkins and de Paula 2011 [18]);
2. Macromolecular chemistry (Lehn 2004 [8]);
3. Molecular biology (Watson et al., 2014 [9]);

4. Cell biology (Allen and Cowling 2011, Alberts et al., 2015 [19,20]), including cell signaling networks (Berridge 2014 [21]), metabolic networks (Jeong et al., 2000 [22]), and gene regulatory networks (Karlebach and Shamir 2008 [23]);
5. Physiology (Hall and Hall 2020 [24], Davies 2021 [25]);
6. Neuroscience (Kandel 1991 [26], Churchland and Sejnowski 1994 [27], Kandel et al., 2000 [28], Kandel 2012 [29]);
7. The psychological level in some instances (Franklin et al., 2013, 2016 [30,31], Jacob et al., 2023 [32]).

These are often called "special sciences". Putting them together, one arrives at the hierarchy of emergence depicted in Figure 1 below. There are also emergent laws for origins of these entities, firstly as regards evolution, occurring on long timescales, with some species dying out and new species coming into being through the processes of natural selection (Darwin 2019 [33], Campbell 1974 [34], Dobzhansky 2013 [35], Wagner 2014 [11]). Development occurs on shorter timescales (Gilbert 2001 [36], Wolpert et al., 2002 [37], Gilbert 2019 [38]). These interact in an EVO–DEVO way (Gilbert et al., 1996 [39], Oyama et al., 2001 [40], Carroll 2005, 2008 [41,42]). These processes operate simultaneously as regards all the aspects 1.–6. enumerated above (Ellis 2023 [43]: §3.2). A key feature is that information flows play an important role in biological function (Nurse 2008 [44], Farnsworth et al., 2013 [45], Farnsworth 2022 [46]).

Complex systems: Engineering, computers, the internet: Complex systems created by human beings arise on the same foundation of particles and atoms, designed on the basis of the same principles of modular hierarchical structuring (Booch et al., 2007 [12]). This provides the foundations of technology (Arthur 2009 [2]) and engineering (Blockley 2012 [47]) based in the principles of engineering design (Dieter and Schmidt 2021 [48]).

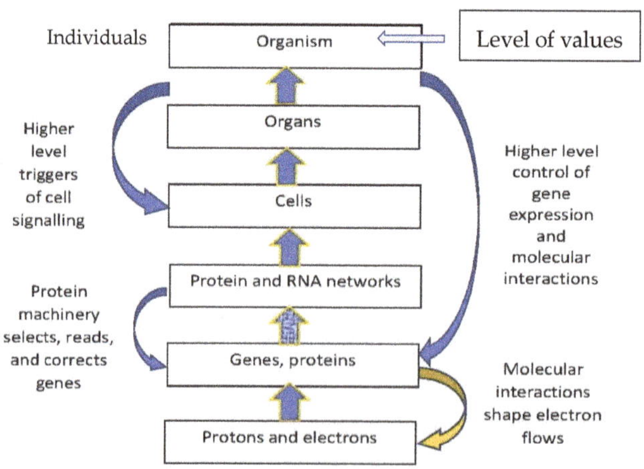

Figure 1. The interplay between bottom-up and top-down interactions in an individual (Ellis and Noble 2023 [49]). Causal closure occurs because the upwards arrows range from the bottom physics level to the level of the whole individual, and the downward arrows reach all the way down again, linking all levels (Ellis 2020a [50]). Values, related to final causation, occur at the level of the individual person. There is a higher level ("Society") not shown here.

1.3. Updated Versions of Aristotle's Causes

The central theme of this paper is that updating Aristotle's four causes to take into account these more recent discoveries will form an important resource for understanding complex emergence these cases and that doing so validates the emergentist viewpoint: each of the emergent levels in the hierarchy of existence has real causal powers (Clayton and Davies 2006 [51], Murphy et al., 2009 [52], Noble 2012, 2016 [3,53], Ellis 2020a [50], O'Connor 2021 [54]).

Previous references that have looked at this issue include Ackoff (1973) [55], Juarrero (2002) [56], Noble 2016 [53], Ellis 2012 [57], Tabaczek 2013 [58], Ellis 2016 [59], Hofmeyr 2017, 2018 [60,61], and Noble and Noble 2021 [62]. This paper develops, in depth, the way generalized versions of Aristotle's four causes enable emergence in biology and technology, by showing in detail how formal and material causes enable downwards causation, which together with upwards emergence underlies the way efficient causation occurs at every emergent level in the hierarchy (Noble 2012 [3], Ellis 2020a [50]) and hence allows final causation as well.

Causation: What notion of causation do we use in the following discussion? It will be defined in terms of ***difference making***, whether experimental or counterfactual (Menzies and List 2010 [63], Kment 2010 [64], Pietsch 2016 [65]), but noting that determining what is in fact making a difference may require in depth investigation (Pearl and Mackenzie 2018 [66]). One way to achieve better assessments of causation is to construct multi-factorial models, from which the causal role of each factor can then be unraveled through defining all the conditionals under which the causal role of any particular factor can be deduced (I thank Denis Noble for this comment). This also assumes that time passes with a unique direction of time, which is indeed the case on our current cosmological view (Ellis 2022 [67]), despite some counter claims based in the idea of a block universe. Thus, there is no ambiguity as regards to causes preceding effects.

1.4. This Paper

The sections that follow are: Section 2—The hierarchy of existence; Section 3—Efficient causation; Section 4—Formal causation; Section 5—Material causation; Section 6—Final causation; Section 7—The outcome: the significance of Aristotelian causation, updated.

2. The Hierarchy of Existence

Putting together the scientific understandings just discussed (Section 1.3), we understand emergent systems as being adaptive modular hierarchical structures. These form the context for the functioning of the four causes. I discuss now modular hierarchical structures (Section 2.1), the issue of reductionism and emergence in this context (Section 2.2), and the relation to the four causes (Section 2.3).

2.1. A Current View: Modular Hierarchical Structures

Biology—Structure enables function (Brewer and Burrow 1980 [68]), which is central to biology (Hartwell et al., 1999 [69]) (See *Human Biology*, Chapter 10: Structure Determines Function (Salt Lake City College) for many examples.). If we conjoin the effective laws **1–7** discussed in Section 1.3, we get the hierarchical structure represented in Figure 1. It is modular, with each level being made up of semi-autonomous components interacting with each other.

Why modular?—The basic principle underlying complex emergence is to break up a complex task at level **L** into simpler tasks, create modules at level **L-1** to handle the simpler tasks, then combine the outcomes of the modules to handle the higher-level task. The modules at level **L-1** in turn can be broken up into sub-modules to handle even simpler tasks, till a level **L0** is reached, where the needed action is so simple it can be fully handled at that level, in general, the interaction at that level will be linear (Ellis 2023 [43]).

Why hierarchical?—Hierarchy naturally emerges on carrying out an integration of the modules. Vast numbers of modular components are involved at lower levels. The number of cells in a human body is 10^{13}, number of proteins in a cell is 10^{7}, number of atoms in a cell is 10^{14}, number of atoms in a human is 10^{27}. The lower levels have a highly dynamic nature: molecules in air at normal room temperature are moving at between 300 to 400 m per second. A biomolecule collides 10^{13} times a second with water molecules at room temperatures (see *"Cells are very fast and crowded places"* by Ken Shirriff), as is evidenced by Brownian Motion (Hoffmann 2012 [70]). Macromolecules change shape as they carry out biological functions.

Nature of the modules: Key features of modules are characterized by (Booch et al., 2007 [12]) as follows:

- **Boundaries and binding:** they have some kind of boundary limiting their extent and are more tightly bound with faster internal interactions than the weaker strength and slower speed of interaction between modules.
- **Information hiding**: a user of a module does not need to know the internal variables and mechanisms of the module; all they are concerned with is that it carries out its required tasks.
- **Abstraction (black boxing)**: the functioning of the module can be characterized by an abstract description relating the input variables to output variables (Ashby 2013 [71]), summarized by a suitable label/name.
- **Interfaces:** control transfer of energy and information in and out of a module according to a protocol.
- **Multiple realizability:** A key feature is the multiple realizability of a module's internal structure consistent with its abstract description and interface protocols (Gillett 2002 [72], Piccinini and Maley 2014 [73], Batterman 2018 [74], Bickle 2020 [75]). This is an inevitable result of evolutionary origins (Edelman and Gally 2001 [76]).
- **Origin**: Modularity makes possible the coming into being of very complex structures through the inheritance of modules with variation and selection; otherwise, it is simply not practicable (Simon 2019 [77]).

Function: The definition of function in biology has been subject to some debate. We use an ***organizational account*** of biological functions (Mossio et al., 2009 [78], Farnsworth et al., 2017 [79], Ellis and Kopel 2019 [80]); in essence, functions are there in order to enable the organism as a whole to function on a day-to-day basis and the whole is organized to make this possible. Thus, this definition does not depend on evolutionary origins (see the discussion in Gardner 2009 [81].

Technology: The same principles apply to technology (Arthur 2009 [2], pp. 32–43), including digital computers (Tanenbaum and Austin 2013 [82], Ellis 2016: §2 [59]) and materials (Fratzl and Weinkamer 2007 [83], Chen et al., 2021 [84]). In these cases, we might refer to *structure and dynamics* (Dove 2013 [85]) rather than *structure and function* (Brewer and Burrow 1980 [68]), although in all cases it might be appropriate to still use the term "function", e.g., in the case of manufactured materials (Miodownik 2014 [86]) and in the case of digital computers (Ellis and Drossel 2019 [87]), as they all serve a purpose. In each case, there is a hierarchy of emergence similar to that shown in Figure 1 (Batterman 2013 [88], Ellis 2016 [59], Ellis and Drossel 2019 [87]).

2.2. Reductionism and Holism

The emergent whole arises out of the parts: it could not exist without them. Given the context of the emergent hierarchy (Figure 1), the issue arises of how the emergence of the higher levels from the lower levels occurs, both diachronically (over time) and synchronically (at each time). This occurs diachronically by assembly in *chemical processes* (Atkins and de Paula 2011 [18]), *developmental processes* (Gilbert 2019 [38]), or *manufacturing* (Kaeslin 2008 [89]), each case involving symmetry breaking (Anderson 1972 [15]). It occurs synchronically by *coarse-graining* (Flack 2017 [90]) or *Black boxing* (Ashby 2013 [71], Marshall et al., 2018 [16]) via logical combinations of variables, as in digital computers (Booch et al., 2007 [12], Dasgupta 2016 [91]).

There are two essentially opposing views about the resultant emergent levels that have been strongly debated for many decades:

A reductionist view: The whole is *nothing but the sum of the parts*, even if we cannot actually predict outcomes at macrolevels from details at microlevels. It is claimed by some physicists that, in reality, nothing takes place except interactions between particles (Greene 2020 [92], Carroll 2021 [93], Hossenfelder 2022 [94]). No essential dynamics takes place at any higher levels.

An emergentist or holistic view: Irreducible emergent entities arise that are *more than the sum of the parts*: summation of lower-level effects does not suffice to explain emergence (Clayton and Davies 2006 [51], O'Connor 2021 [54]), with various kinds of emergence proposed (Cunningham 2001 [95], Chalmers 2006 [96], Brigandt and Love 2023 [97]). Paoletti (2020) [98] characterizes emergence as partial and qualified dependence of the emergent entities on the entities in their emergence bases. Santos (2021) [99] characterizes it in terms of a relation of both partial dependence and partial independence (the latter being conceived in terms of a relative irreducibility or autonomy) between a given entity (the putative "emergent") and the entities with respect to which it may be said to be emergent (the "emergence base"). This emergence is enabled by downward causation occurring in addition to bottom-up causation (Noble 2012 [3], Ellis 2012 [57]). The summary slogan that captures the emergentist theme is:

"The whole is greater than the sum of its parts."

This is a common claim nowadays amongst those studying complex systems, see for example Ackoff (1973) [55], Tanaka et al. (1998) [100], Glaser and Glaser (2000) [101], Galatzer-Levy (2002) [102], Davison et al. (2006) [103], Pérez-Dorado et al. (2012) [104], Matthews and Guarné (2013) [105], Kornblith et al. (2014) [106], Taylor and Wood (2019) [107], and Fang and Hu (2022) [108]. However, it is denied not just by some reductionist physicists, as mentioned above, but also by reductionist philosophers (Kim 2005 [109]), biologists (Dawkins 2016 [110]), and neuroscientists (Crick 1994 [111]), denying the possibility of free will (Harris 2012 [112], Caruso 2012 [113]).

We note here that there is a major problem with these claims: ***they cannot all be right***! If physics unequivocally causes all, then neither genes nor neurons have any real causal powers; whereas if either of these emergent entities have real causal powers, then it is not true that physics by itself determines all. These claims contradict each other.

Which of them, if any, is correct? The solution is that *all emergent levels have real causal powers* (Noble 2012, 2016 [3,53], Ellis 2020a [50], Noble and Ellis 2022 [114]), as discussed in §3. Consequently, these levels exist ontologically, not just epistemologically: we reliably determine this ontological nature by suitable experiments. This is supported by Simpson and Horsely (2022) [115], who state:

> *"We argue that the causal powers of many systems are determined by) higher-level, macroscopic properties that are neither reducible nor weakly emergent, and that contemporary physics is compatible with some kind of pluralism that affirms that these entities are robustly real."*

Again, I note that I am not concerned here with the debate about the difference between weak and strong concepts of emergence, that is, the question of whether one can uniquely determine higher-level outcomes on the basis of lower-level dynamics and variables alone. Rather, the claim is that verifiable emergent-level dynamics does indeed occur at higher levels, causally affecting outcomes, and indeed this is why such emergent levels are recognized as existing and being characterized by "special sciences"—which indisputably exist as academic disciplines. Their basis in lower-level dynamics is indeed true, but that lower-level dynamics is influenced in a downward way through mechanisms I discuss is how interlevel relations are coordinated and leads to causal closure.

2.3. Relation to the Four Kinds of Causes

Given the context of the hierarchy of emergence (Figure 1) that I have just sketched, with the associated effective laws (Section 1.3), we can now state the main theses that will be developed in what follows. They relate to the hierarchy of emergence as follows: ***efficient causation*** occurs at every emergent level in biology and technology (Noble 2012 [3], Ellis 2020a [50], Ellis and Noble 2023 [49]). Although it is enabled by both formal and material causation, they can each be distinguished from the other. This same level causation is enabled by the ***interplay of upwards and downwards causation*** between emergent levels. Upwards causation takes place by ***coarse-graining***, including ***structural emergence*** and ***black boxing***. The two key forms of downward causation enabling this are ***formal causation*** and ***material causation***, which occur in both synchronic and diachronic forms. ***Final causation*** is a further form of downward causation in the cases of intelligent beings (Noble and Ellis 2022 [114]) and so for the social structures and artefacts they create (Ellis and Drossel 2019 [87], Ellis and Noble 2023 [49]). ***Causal closure*** only occurs when all inter-level linkages generated by all these forms of causation are taken into account (Montevil and Mossio 2015 [116], Ellis 2020 [117]). No physical level is, by itself, causally complete, as claimed by some (Kim 2005 [109], Hossenfelder 2022 [94]). Such a claim ignores all the factors that lead to specific physical outcomes at a particular time and place. Physical laws per se, expressed for example by Newton's laws of motion and by Maxwell's equations, do not lead to any specific outcomes at all.

2.4. Is This Persuasive?

I have received the following comment from a referee:

> *"But there is little work done to actually prove, to a skeptical reader, that this is indeed the right way to think about things. The rejoinder could always be that such causal descriptions are merely convenient and that all the real work is still being done at the level of physical forces—it's just too complicated for us to grasp".*

My response is that whereas real work is certainly being conducted at the level of physical forces, "real work" is also being conducted at each emergent level, as is shown by all the examples given. It is, for example, an undoubted fact that genes can be read by cell machinery in such a way as to produce proteins, following well-established causal relations, and that the pumping of blood by the heart keeps cells alive, as proven by physiological studies. These are factual statements proven over and over again by experiments and indeed by biological functioning in daily life. They are independent of any views on reduction and emergence. The idea that any given level has some causal independence from the goings-on at lower levels relies on ideas of hierarchy, modularity, coarse-graining, multiple realizability, and causal protectorates, which I argue in this paper. Yates (2017) [118] contends that examples such as those I give demonstrate the reality of strong emergence. O'Connor (2021) [54] comments:

> *"A skeptic might press that the effects Yates cites as pointing to a distinctive kind of higher-level causal power are themselves all higher-level. Assuming that all macroscopic properties are microphysically realized, if one were able to take a wide-angle view of the evolving process in purely micro-physical terms throughout (including in characterizing the targeted token effects), it's not clear that reference to anything other than the features of and basic relations among microphysical entities is required for explanation. It might well be the case that to explain the token effects under their macroscopic description requires equally macroscopic appeal to molecular geometry (where a given geometric shape is multiple realizable by distinct spatial arrays of atoms). But such explanatory irreducibility is, as we've seen, the hallmark of forms of weak emergence."*

However, as stated above, I am not here concerned with the distinction between strong and weak emergence but rather that the higher levels are indeed examples of emergence whether strong or weak, and that is confirmed by giving examples where it is indeed true. In any case, an Aristotelian approach to emergence is helpful at this point, since the Aristotelian can insist that we cannot fully describe the microscopic level except in terms of the specific ways in which that level is informed and structured by higher levels.

3. Efficient Causation

This section looks at how an updated version of efficient causation works out in the context of our present-day understandings of science. It considers the nature of an updated version of efficient causation (Section 3.1) and how this works out in biology (Section 3.2) and technology and digital computers (Section 3.3). It finally considers abstract causation (Section 3.4).

3.1. Updated Version of Efficient Causation

Aristotle's concept of efficient causation was presented in Section 1.2. He was not in a position to differentiate the different levels of emergence indicated in Figure 1, as the relevant scientific results leading to that hierarchy were not then known. Given this hierarchy, we follow (Noble 2012 [3]), Ellis (2020a) [50], and (Ellis and Noble 2023 [49]) by proposing the following updated version.

Each emergent level **L** for a system **S** is characterized by suitable variables $\mathbf{X^i}_\mathbf{L}(\mathbf{t})$ at time **t** (Anderson 1972 [15]). In this context, our updated definition of material causation is:

> ***Efficient causation*** *takes place at an emergent level* **L** *in the hierarchy of emergence of a system* **S** *when effective laws* $\mathbf{E_L}(\mathbf{X^i}_\mathbf{L}(\mathbf{t}))$ *at level* **L** *determine the values at times* $\mathbf{t} > \mathbf{t_0}$ *of the relevant variables* $\mathbf{X^i}_\mathbf{L}(\mathbf{t})$ *at that level from initial data* $\mathbf{X^i}_\mathbf{L}(\mathbf{t_0})$ *at time* $\mathbf{t_0}$*. This is a characterization of causation at that level.*

The effective laws may be deterministic, as in Newton's laws of motion and Maxwell's equations, or probabilistic, as in the case of statistical mechanics and quantum physics; they may even involve chaotic dynamics (Shen et al., 2021 [119], Neyrinck et al., 2022 [120]). Some key points:

- Emergent levels are *defined* by the existence of efficient causation (i.e., well-established effective theories) and associated variables at that level. It will generally take place via a combination of formal and material causation at that level.
- Efficient causation at an emergent level **L** is enabled by a combination of upward and downwards causation between levels, the latter occurring via formal and material causation, as we discuss below.
- All these effective levels and associated laws are needed in order that the system functions: if any of them are missing, it will not work. This is Noble's *principle of biological relativity* (Noble 2012, 2022 [3,121]), which can be extended to emergent contexts of technology (Ellis 2020a [50]).
- There can be no efficient physical causes without some non-random organization of stuff—a directionality of physical forces arises from physical inhomogeneities. Thus, the notion is intimately linked with the idea of symmetry breaking (Anderson 1972 [15]).

Some physicists and philosophers only recognize efficient causation at an underlying physics level without prescribing what that level is (they face the embarrassment that we do not know what the bottom-most physics level is). For practical purposes in biology and engineering and indeed everyday life, the relevant underlying effective physics theory is the level of the time-dependent Schrodinger equation for electrons and nuclei, set out in Laughlin and Pines (2000) [122]. However, that is emergent from lower physical levels: it is based in a lower level, the level of the standard model of particle physics (Oerter 2006 [123]) (described in Wikipedia here: https://en.wikipedia.org/wiki/Standard_Model (accessed on 11 June 2023)), itself believed to be based in some (as yet unknown) lower level, that of a "Theory of Everything" (perhaps string theory/M theory, perhaps not). In contrast, we claim that efficient causation takes place and is causally effective at every emergent level L.

3.2. Biology

Broad categories of such emergent laws were given in Examples **2–6** listed in Section 1.3. Some specific cases with well-defined effective theories are cell signaling processes (Berridge 2014 [21]), gene regulatory networks (Davidson and Erwin 2006 [33], Karlebach and Shamir 2008 [23]), metabolic networks (Jeong et al., 2000 [22]), the heart (Noble 2002 [124], Fink and Noble 2008 [125]), nerve cells and behavior (Kandel 1991, 2001 [26,126]), and neural networks (Churchland and Sejnowski 1994 [27], Carpenter and Grossberg 1987, 1988 [127,128]).

3.3. Digital Computers and Technology

Digital computers are designed according to the precepts of modular hierarchical structures (Simon 2019 [77], Booch et al., 2007 [12]). The emergent levels are characterized in Tanenbaum and Austin (2013) [82]: there is a tower of virtual machines, linked by compilers or interpreters (Ellis 2016: §2, [59]). Algorithms drive what happens (Dasgupta 2016 [91], Ellis and Drossel 2019 [87]), and they too are hierarchically structured in a modular way.

All engineering (Blockley 2012 [47]) is similarly based in modular hierarchical structures, for very good reasons (Simon 2019 [77]). For example, an aircraft is a hugely complex structure (see for an indication of this hierarchy https://mae.ufl.edu/haftka/structures/FAA.pdf (accessed on 11 June 2023)), including many computers. Each form of engineering is based in some technology (Bronowski 2011 [129], Arthur 2009 [2]), which is the effective causation enabling that engineering practice. Thus, there is *civil engineering*, enabling stable structures (bridges, roads, tunnels, buildings, dams) to exist, based in the design and construction of structures so as to ensure their stability; *mechanical engineering*, based in the control of energy and particularly thermodynamics; *electrical engineering*, based in the control of the flow of electrons and associated magnetic fields; *electronic engineering*, based in logical operations enabled by transistors and integrated circuits; *chemical engineering*, based in the control of chemical interactions and purification processes; *biotechnology*, based in molecular biology interactions and particularly now the use of CRISP-R; *nuclear engineering*, based in nuclear interactions; *information technology*, based in digital computers and nowadays engaging in AI projects. The latter is more than computer science: it refers to how to gather, analyze, sort, and use information productively.

In each case, efficient causation takes place at multiple levels in an integrated way involving both material and formal causation at each level, the higher levels being designed to shape the lower-level dynamics so as to produce the desired higher-level outcome (Dieter and Schmidt 2021 [48]). The emergent results (e.g., an aircraft flies with specific performance capabilities) are determined and verified as effective laws at the integral emergent level, which can be determined without any knowledge of the lower-level structures and dynamics (a pilot does not have to be a quantum physicist). All these examples are clear cases of the whole being greater than the sum of the parts: it is the specific organization of the parts that leads to the desired outcomes. Each of these technologies has emerged through an evolutionary process (Arthur 2009 [2]), exploring the possibilities within the boundaries allowed by physical constraints (Vogel 2000 [130]).

3.4. Abstract Causation

Because of our symbolic abilities (Deacon 1998 [131]), in the case of human beings, abstract causation takes place: that is, ***abstract entities have causal powers***. This occurs through the interactions between individuals and the society in which they live, for it is through that interaction that causal powers of abstract entities arise. They do not arise because of any individual's brain state, because it is *socially shared concepts* that have the causal power (Murphy and Brown 2007 [132]).

An example is the ***rules of chess***, which are abstract concepts stated as formal rules. These do not derive their causal power though being instantiated in any one specific person's brain: these powers arise from them being instantiated in the brains of every person who plays chess. Furthermore, they are not only instantiated in neural states in brains: they are instantiated in chess books, in algorithms in computer programs, talks given on the internet, in the moves on a chess board, and so on. Conceptually, the rules of chess are the abstract *equivalence class of all such instantiations* (Noble and Ellis 2022 [114], Ellis and Noble 2023 [49]).

Other examples are, *plans* enabling the creation of artifacts such as buildings, bridges, aircraft, computers (Ellis 2016 [59]); *money*, used as a medium of exchange or a store of value (Davidson 1972 [133]); *signs*, such as those indicating restrooms for males and females; *laws*, such as those for motor vehicle behavior at traffic intersections, instantiated by stop signs and by traffic lights that cause drivers to stop when red and allow them to move when green; and *legal agreements*, underlying the existence of organizations such as closed corporations (Harari 2014 [134]). In each case, the entity is abstract because it is multiply realizable, for example plans for an aircraft can be talked about, drawn on paper, instantiated in computer programs, and listed in a formal specification; the abstract concept is not the same as any specific one of these instantiations. Each of them in turn have causal powers through the brain functioning underlying mental causation (Menzies 2003 [135], Robb and Heil 2021 [136]) and taking place in a social context (Aberle et al., 1950 [137]) that determines the appropriate functioning of these abstract entities.

The key point them is that ***these can all be regarded as forms of efficient causation taking place at the level of the individual person in Figure 1***, occurring in the current social context that both enables it to occur and provides constraints on what kinds of abstract causation are allowed.

4. Formal Causation

Aristotle's concept of formal causation was presented in Section 1.2. This section looks at how an updated version of formal causation works in the context of our present-day understandings of science. It considers an updated version of formal causation (Section 4.1), formal causation and life (Section 4.2), in artefacts and engineering (Section 4.3), oscillators (Section 4.4), feedback control/homeostasis (Section 4.5), and adaptive brain networks and ion channels (Section 4.6).

4.1. Updated Version of Formal Causation

Structure, which can be labelled "form", underlies function at every emergent level in biology (Brewer and Burrow 1980 [68], Wainwright 1998 [138]) and engineering (Blockley 2012 [47]). In agreement with Aristotle's understanding, this can be suitably labelled "formal causation". It takes place either synchronically (the form is unchanging and shapes interactions in a fixed way) or diachronically (with form responding dynamically to changing conditions). Form has causal powers by imposing constraints at higher levels which then entrain lower-level variables. Crucially, it can occur at any single level **L**, then being a mechanism whereby efficient causation takes place at that level by setting constraints at that level, but also acts down to shape what happens at lower levels **L** − **N** by setting symmetry breaking constraints at those levels. Because of this possibility, efficient causation at level **L** can be shaped by formal causation at higher levels **L** + **M**. Our updated definition of formal causation in the context of the relevant hierarchy of emergence is:

> ***Formal causation*** *takes place at an emergent level* **L** *in the hierarchy of emergence of a system* **S** *when the variables* $\mathbf{X^i_L(t)}$ *in the effective laws* $\mathbf{E_L(X^i_L(t))}$ *at level* **L** *of* **S** *obey constraints* $\mathbf{C(X^i_L(t),t) = 0}$*. The constraints may depend on time via higher level variables* $\mathbf{X^i_M(t)}$*,* $\mathbf{M > L}$*: then* $\mathbf{C(X^i_L(t),t) = F(X^i_L(t), X^i_M(t)) = 0}$*. Such constraints determine the shapes of entities and perhaps how that shape changes with time.*

Indeed, *constraints are causes* (Juarrero 2002 [56]), given our definition of causality. There is a paradox here: without constraints, one just has particles randomly bumping into each other. Adding constraints can generate functionality (Deacon 2006 [139]); for example, an electric wire channels electrons from point A to point B along the wire, the point being that the electrical resistance orthogonal to the direction of the wire is essentially infinite because of its insulating sheathing. Thus, its function is to channel the flow of electrons at the electron level in order to fulfil some function at a higher level. Because of this constraint, the electrons do not diffuse randomly in all directions, as occurs in Brownian motion.

Because it's effect chains down from the level **L**, *constraints at level* **L** *affect all lower levels* **N** < **L**. Thus, formal causation at level L exerts a form of ***downward causation*** (Noble 2008, 2012 [3,140]). There are a great many detailed ways constraints at a higher level can be realized at lower levels. Thus, as is usual in downward causation, one has ***multiple realizability*** of higher-level constraints at lower levels.

Static (synchronic) or dynamic (diachronic) formal causation: if $\partial C(X^i_L(t),t)/\partial t = 0$ in the interval I: $t_1 < t < t_2$, then *formal causation is static* during I, remaining unchanged during I; if $\partial C(X^i_L(t),t)/\partial t \neq 0$ *in I*, then *it is dynamic* during I.

When the constraints depend on time via higher level variables, dynamic formal causation enables ***contextual branching of dynamics to meet higher level needs***. As an example, consider electric wiring joining one terminal of a battery to a switch, then a light, and then the other terminal of the battery. The following branching dynamics arise at the macrolevel from the constraints created by the circuit:

$$\text{IF \{switch is on\} THEN \{light shines\} ELSE \{not\}.} \tag{1}$$

The resulting macro- to microlevel relation is:

$$\text{IF \{switch is on\} THEN \{electrons flow in wire and lamp\} ELSE \{not\},} \tag{2}$$

whereas the companion micro- to macrolevel relation is:

$$\text{IF \{electrons flow in lamp\} THEN \{lamp shines\} ELSE \{not\}.} \tag{3}$$

Thus, macrolevel constraints control microlevel dynamics, which then cause macrolevel events through the closed form of the circuit at the macrolevel when the switch is closed but its open form if the switch is open (a macrolevel difference in circuit topology that cannot be described at the microlevel). The higher-level need being met is to attain the right level of light in the room. This also demonstrates how the human mind/brain can downwardly control the flow of electrons in a wire by changing the switch setting, which happens every time someone turns a light on or off.

Is formal causation always associated with function? Not necessarily; there are a multitude of natural forms out there—planets, rocks, mountains, rivers, lakes, oceans—that can have complex forms and associated formal causation without associated functions. However, all living systems are associated with functions (Hartwell et al., 1999) [69], as are all artefacts (Simon 2019 [77]), engineering systems (Blockley 2012 [47]), organizations (Etzioni 1964 [141]), and social structures (Elder-Vass 2010 [142]), so formal causation in all these contexts will be associated with function. In all the latter cases, this occurs via agency exerted by the human mind in a social context (Murphy and Brown 2007 [132], Noble and Noble 2021 [62]).

4.2. Formal Causation and Life

Our bodies have an immensely complex emergent form, characterized by our physiology (Hall and Hall 2020 [24], Davies 2021 [25]), that enables our functioning. This occurs via time-dependent formal causation enabled by that very complex modular hierarchical structuring. Crucially, the link between physics and biology is macromolecular chemistry (Lehn 2004 [8]), where it is the conformational change of macromolecules—a change of shape—together with the lock and key mechanism of molecular recognition (Behr 2008 [143]) that is the key principle of molecular biology in general and catalysis by enzymes in particular.

4.3. Formal Causation: Artefacts and Engineering

A vase or jug contains water because of its "container" shape; it would not do so if that shape were different because of a crack or hole in it. The shape of the vase causes the water to be contained. A pipe leads water from one place to another; its form prevents the water from spreading out sideways and takes it to its appointed destination. Similar examples on a larger scale are a tunnel, a bridge, an aircraft landing strip, and a dam, each designed with function in mind. The shape of a piano or cello is carefully designed to produce specific kinds of musical sounds through its shape (and its constituent material: material causation also takes place).

A building is another example, providing shelter and functional spaces of various kinds (cooking, sleeping, relaxing, bathing, and so on). In this case, *dynamic* formal causation can take place, as doors may open and close, allowing ingress and egress or not, curtains may be open or drawn, allowing light in from outside or not, and so on. Thus, the nature of the constraints resulting in formal causation can be adjusted to meet needs that vary with time.

Each form of engineering (Blockley 2012 [47]) is based in formal causation associated with its underlying technology (Arthur 2009 [2]) and has been designed to be that way through the general principles of engineering design enabling the desired outcomes (Dieter and Schmidt 2021 [48]) (for a great discussion of a specific case, see the aircraft design process on Wikipedia). Thus, electrical engineering is based in wires, resistors, capacitors, electromagnetic coils, magnets switches, relays, light bulbs and LEDs, sensors, batteries, electric motors, and dynamos. The specific configurations of these components is the formal cause of outcomes such as for automobile ignition systems, lighting systems, functioning of domestic appliances, and so on. Electronic engineering, based additionally in transistors and integrated circuits and further components such as microphones, loudspeakers, and digital cameras based in charge-coupled devices (CCDs), allows the construction of music systems, digital computers, electronic alarm systems, automatic pilots, etc.

In both cases, one has *dynamical formal causation* allowing very complex conditional branching of dynamics of modular hierarchical structures to produce the desired functionality. A key issue here is how to design a suitable user interface for such systems, which is a complex topic in its own right (Norman 1986, 2013 [144,145]) relating formal to final causation.

4.4. Formal Causation: Oscillators

Oscillators are a key emergent feature of engineering, biology, brain function, and social life, where they underlie clocks. They are all outcomes of formal causation of varied kinds, occurring because of the shapes of emergent structures.

In engineering, examples are that steam engines, petrol engines, and diesel engines are all powered by recurrent mechanical cycles generated by the shapes of the mechanical components and their interlocking structure. Electronic oscillators are widely used, for example in radios, inverters, digital games, and computers. The functioning of digital computers is centrally based on an IPO cycle: input $\rightarrow$ process $\rightarrow$ output, generated by an electronic oscillator. It has a system clock with various functions.

The principles of biological oscillators are set out in Novak and Tyson (2008) [146] and Li and Yang (2018) [147]. They occur in cells, where cell-cycle clocks and switches underlie cell development processes (Tyson and Novak 2022 [148]); the heart (Noble 2002 [124], Fink and Noble 2008 [125]) and lungs, where each have regular cycles that jointly keep us alive by providing our cells with the oxygen and nutrients they need; and nervous system. The stomatogastric ganglion of the spiny lobster (Churchland and Sejnowski 1994 [27]) controls gastric mill muscles that open and close a set of three teeth in a kind of chewing behavior. This repetitive behavior is generated by small neural circuits that essentially forms an oscillator (Daur et al., 2016 [149]). Metastable oscillatory modes emerge from synchronization in the brain spacetime connectome (Cabral et al. (2022) [150], and adaptive resonant networks occur in the brain (Carpenter and Grossberg 1987, 1988 [127,128]).

4.5. Formal Causation: Feedback Control/Homeostasis

A crucial feature of engineering and biology is feedback control, labelled *cybernetics* in an engineering context (Wiener 1961 [151], Ashby 1964 [152]) and *homeostasis* in a biological context (Modell et al., 2015 [153], Hall and Hall 2020 [24], Ellis and Nobel 2023 [49]). The problem is to maintain stability or attain a desired goal in the face of ongoing perturbing influences. The solution is to make continual adjustments to counteract the effect of such disturbances using information flows to attain the desired outcomes.

The Basic Principle: Suppose a system **S** is in a state **SS**, the desired state is **DS**, and **SS** is measured by a sensor **M** to be different from **DS**, so there is an error **ES:= DS − SS** between the desired and actual state. This error is sent by a controller **C** via a physical connection to an activator **A** that can alter the system state **S** in such a way as to reduce the magnitude $|\mathbf{ES}|$ of the error **ES**. This is performed until the error **ES** is less than some threshold $\mathbf{\Delta S}$ below which the difference does not matter. Then, the activator is turned off.

Example: A thermostat for a room has a controller **C** where you set the desired temperature **DT** and a sensor **M** that determines **T**. The controller can turn on a heater **A**, which will increase the temperature **T** until $|\mathbf{DT} - \mathbf{T}| < \mathbf{\Delta T}$. The **branching logic** that emerges is:

$$\text{IF } \{|\mathbf{DT} - \mathbf{T}| > \mathbf{\Delta T}\} \text{ THEN } \{\mathbf{C} \text{ activates } \mathbf{A}\} \textbf{ ELSE } \{\mathbf{A} \text{ is turned off}\}. \quad (4)$$

This is formal causation because the logic (4) emerges from the specific form of the system: the emergent macrolevel loop that connects the components **M**, **C**, and **A**. If the form is changed by disconnecting the activator, then the outcome is different: all the parts are still there but the topology of the circuit is open, not closed; the circuit form is changed, and no homeostatic action takes place. It is downward causation because the system acts to attain the desired temperature **DT** at the macrolevel, thereby controlling the average molecular speed $\mathbf{<v^2>}$ at the microlevel downwardly, because $\mathbf{<v^2> = \alpha\, T}$ where α **= 3R/M**.

Homeostasis is a central principle in control engineering, organizations (Penrose 1952 [154], Scott and Davis 2007: pp. 90–93 [155], Damasio and Damasio 2016 [156]), and biology at every level. We have homeostatic systems for pH levels, blood glucose, iron levels, levels of blood gases, calcium and sodium concentrations, and cell membrane potentials at the microlevel and body temperature, blood pressure, normal heart rate, and fluid balance at the macrolevel; you are ill if any of these quantities are out of bounds, which is why these levels are used for medical diagnoses of health.

4.6. Formal Causation: Adaptive Brain Networks and Ion Channels

The central nervous system (CNS) has several layers of structure (Churchland and Sejnowski 1994: Figure 1.4 [27]), namely, molecules, synapses, neurons, networks, maps, systems, and the CNS as a whole. Systems have topographic maps, layers, and columns and contain local networks. Neurons have a complex structure of axons, a nucleus, and dendrites, joined to other neurons by synapses, so forming networks (Churchland and Sejnowski 1994: pp. 27–60 [27]). These networks are shaped by our life experiences through various mechanisms of brain plasticity, resulting in the unique total set of synaptic connections that make each of us the individual that we are: this is the dynamic form of our individual brain. The connections synaptic strengths are continually changing as we interact with the physical and social world around us. This is the time-dependent formal cause of all the brain dynamics underlying our thought and actions (Leopold 2023 [157]).

At the neuronal level, action potential spike chains convey signals from one neuron to another, enabled at the molecular level by flow of sodium and potassium ions through the cell membrane, controlled by voltage-gated ion channels. These are proteins imbedded in the cell membrane that change conformation in response to the voltage across the cell membrane in according to the way supramolecular chemistry works by conformational changes (Lehn 2004 [8]). These changes reach down to affect the level of electrons by changing constraints in the underlying Hamiltonian (Ellis and Kopel 2019 [80]), thus enabling contextual branching logic to emerge from the underlying physics at the neural level and hence at the emergent network levels (Kandel et al., 2000 [28]).

5. Material Causation

Aristotle's concept of material causation was presented in Section 1.2. This section considers an updated version of material causation (Section 5.1) and then its application at the basis of engineering, technology, and daily life (Section 5.2) and how it occurs in metabolism and the cardiovascular system (Section 5.3), in gene regulatory networks and developmental processes (Section 5.4), and in adaptive selection and evolutionary processes (Section 5.5).

5.1. Updated Version of Material Causation

Material causation either takes place synchronically (statically): materials are there at the present time due to previous processes, or diachronically (dynamically): material stuff is continually being altered to fit same-level or higher-level needs, their existence and nature is due to ongoing dynamic processes. This dynamic aspect is key to biology. Either can occur at level **L**: efficient causation takes place at that level through the nature of the material stuff present at that level. In the dynamic case, it can also act down to shape the nature of material stuff at lower levels **L − N**. Because of this possibility, conversely, efficient causation at level **L** can be shaped by material causation at higher levels **L + M**.

The proposed updated definition of material causation in the context of the relevant hierarchy of emergence is:

> ***Material causation*** *takes place at an emergent level* **L** *in the hierarchy of emergence of a system* **S** *when a set of variables* $\{\mathbf{X}^i{}_L(t)\}$ *characterizes the nature of material stuff at level* **L** *of* **S**. *This underlies the possible emergent set of such variables* $\{\mathbf{X}^i{}_N(t)\}$ *at levels* $N > L$ *of* **S**. *Material causation is* ***static*** *in an interval* $\mathbf{I} = [\mathbf{t1}, \mathbf{t2}]$ *if the set of variables* $\{\mathbf{X}^i{}_L(t)\}$ *is constant in that interval and is* ***dynamic*** *if* $\{\mathbf{X}^i{}_L(t)\}$ *changes during this time.*
>
> *It affects higher levels* **L > M** *upwardly and can affect* ***lower levels N < L*** *downwardly.*

Static material causation occurs at a level L simply through the existence of the materials out of which structures are made. Those materials came into being either naturally through geological processes, as in the case of igneous, sedimentary, and metamorphic rocks, through developmental processes in biology, or artificially through manufacturing processes as in the case of steel, glass, plastics, paper, cloth, and so on (Miodownik 2014 [86]). These materials at level **L** determine what material can exist at levels **M > L**.

Dynamic material causation occurs at a level L ***either*** if the set of variables $\{\mathbf{X}^i{}_L(\mathbf{t})\}$ at level **L** at time **t** are altered by same-level interactions at level **L or** if higher-level variables $\mathbf{X}^i{}_M(\mathbf{t})$ (**M > L**) shape a new set of variables $\{\mathbf{X}^i{}_L{}^\#(\mathbf{t}')\} = \{\{\mathbf{X}^i{}_L{}^\#(\mathbf{t}'), \mathbf{X}^i{}_M(\mathbf{t}')\}$ at level L; this is ***dynamic downward material causation*** (**DDM**). It takes place by:

DDM1: ***creating*** or ***importing*** new elements;
DDM2: ***sustaining*** or ***altering*** elements already in place;
DDM3: ***deleting*** or ***exporting*** elements.

This downward action to shape the parts to fit higher-level needs is labeled "Machresis" by Gillett (2002) [72]. It leads to the key idea of "*understanding the parts in terms of the whole*" (Cornish Bowden et al., 2004 [158]). There is a key contrast between biology and statistical physics here; nothing like this occurs in the billiard ball model of kinetic theory, which is the paradigm often shaping physicalist thought. However, it occurs in the creation of quasi-particles such as phonons in solid-state physics and Cooper pairs in superconductivity (S Simon 2013 [159], Ellis 2020a [50]).

Dynamic material causation enables a ***contextual branching of dynamics*** through the three DDMn operations listed. The generic form that this takes is: set a selection criterion **C** for desired properties of the variable set $\{\mathbf{X}^i{}_L(\mathbf{t})\}$ at level **L**, where **C** can be a criterion either in terms of the variables at level **L** or in terms of resultant emergent variables at a level **M > L**. Then:

$$\text{IF \{the set } \{\mathbf{X}^i{}_L(\mathbf{t})\} \text{ does not satisfy } \mathbf{C}\} \text{ THEN \{vary } \{\mathbf{X}^i{}_L(\mathbf{t})\} \text{ to give a new set } \{\mathbf{X}^i{}_L{}^\#(\mathbf{t}')\}\} \quad (5)$$

where the variation is produced by one of {DDM1, DDM2, DDM3}, either in a directed manner or by a randomization process, to provide the new set of variables $\{\mathbf{X}^i{}_L{}^\#(\mathbf{t}')\}$ to select from. Then:

$$\text{IF \{the set } \{\mathbf{X}^i{}_L{}^\#(\mathbf{t}')\} \text{ does not satisfy C\} THEN \{repeat\} ELSE \{stop\}}. \quad (6)$$

This is an iterated search procedure in the space of possible variables to find a set of underlying variables that satisfy the selection criteria. It is central in Darwinian evolution

(Section 5.5) and in engineering design (Dieter and Schmidt 2021 [48]). Note the role of randomness here: it is a key element in many optimal search procedures (Palmer 2022 [160], Ellis and Noble 2023 [49]). The nature of the variables $\{\mathbf{X}^i{}_L(t)\}$ at every lower level is potentially changed by this mechanism.

Is material causation always associated with function? Not necessarily; there are a multitude of natural forms out there—planets, rocks, mountains, rivers, lakes, oceans—comprised of many kinds of matter that affect outcomes materially but without associated functions. However, all living systems are associated with functions (Hartwell et al., 1999 [69]), as are all artefacts (Simon 2019 [77]), engineering outcomes (Blockley 2012 [47]), organizations (Etzioni 1964 [141]), and social structures (Elder-Vass 2010 [142]), so material causation in all these contexts will be associated with function.

5.2. Material Causation: Materials at the Basis of Engineering, Technology, and Daily Life

Every branch of engineering or technology relies on materials that are shaped by a manufacturing process to in order to play a role in performing some function. These are selected for engineering design (Dieter and Schmidt 2021 [48]) and underlie daily existence (see *"Stuff matters"* Miodownik (2014) [86] for a brilliant description). A key form of material causation is constituted by *purification processes*: centrifuges, filtration, titration, fractionation columns, and so on, carried out in production plants creating pure substrates of a highly specific kind that can then be shaped by manufacturing processes to result in the desired formal causation. This is a central function of chemical engineering and the pharmaceutical industry. Manufacturing processes provide from this basis the components that are then assembled into systems (Dieter and Schmidt 2021 [48]). This involves molding plastics according to specification, weaving, knitting, or crocheting to turn one-dimensional threads into two-dimensional cloth that can then be made into clothes, and so on, providing the components needed for the next level up (Miodownik 2014 [86]). These are all cases of **static material causation** because once the relevant system (a weaving loom, distillery, chemical plant, injection mold) has produced the relevant component, it does not then change it continually in an active way.

5.3. Dynamic Material Causation: Metabolism and the Cardiovascular System

Metabolism is the set of reactions whereby organisms are provided with the nutrients they need to survive, converting food to provide energy in the form of ATP and to provide the amino acids, monosaccharides, and nucleotides needed for constructing proteins, carbohydrates, and nucleic acids. Metabolic networks (Jeong et al., 2000 [161]) at the cellular level carry out these processes and so keep cells functioning. They include the citric acid cycle, which oxidizes nutrients to produce usable chemical energy in the form of ATP. They interact with genetic regulatory networks (Goelzer et al., 2008 [162]) in a complex way to respond to changes in environmental conditions (Buescher et al., 2012 [163]). Overall, this is **DDM1:** ongoing dynamic creation of needed lower-level elements (sets of biomolecules) by a next level system (the metabolic network) to meet cellular needs in a contextual way.

The cardiovascular system, including the heart and **the lungs** at the physiological systems level, keeps us alive by enabling cells (the basic units of life) to survive. If the system fails, it can cause a heart attack; cells die at the cellular level and damage at the physiological level can be a stroke where parts of the brain become damaged or die. Overall, this is **DDM2:** dynamically sustaining viability of lower-level elements through functioning of higher-level structures.

5.4. Dynamic Material Causation: Developmental Processes and Gene Regulatory Networks

Developmental processes produce the hierarchy of cells, tissues, and physiological systems (Figure 1). They have to create the right kinds of cells in the right place at the right time to give the right tissue, and cell types are determined by specific proteins. How are these determined so as to give structure that results in the desired function? This is facilitated by **gene regulatory networks** (Jacob and Monod 1961 [164], Monod et al., 1963 [165],

Davidson and Erwin 2006 [166], Karlebach and Shamir 2008 [23]). These networks control the way genes are read at the molecular level to produce specific proteins as needed. This is a form of **DDM1**: creation of proteins that were not there before through the molecular biology of the gene (Watson et al., 2014 [9]) in the context of the cell (Alberts et al., 2015 [19]). **Developmental systems** (Oyama et al., 2001 [40]) are the next level up, using positional information to control the reading of genes via gene regulatory networks and so determining what type of cell should come into being and where: should they be stem cells? bone cells? blood cells? muscle cells? fat cells? nerve cells? and so on. They become these various types of cells by modification of pluripotent cells according to the position in the embryo (Gilbert 2001 [36], Wolpert et al., 2002 [37], Gilbert 2019 [38]). Again, cell shapes and sizes are determined developmentally. This is a form of **DDM2**: modification of the nature of entities that already exist. Then, **apoptosis** is a form of **DDM3**: programmed cell death in multicellular organisms.

5.5. Dynamic Material Causation: Adaptive Selection and Evolutionary Processes

Natural selection (Darwin 2019 [33], Dobzhansky 2013 [35]) occurs via replication of living beings with variation of properties at the macrolevel (phenotype) due to variation at the molecular (genotype) level, resulting in different survival and replication probabilities of different phenotypes. Over the course of time, those with a comparative survival advantage tend to replace the others and their genotypes then dominate the gene pool. Thus, natural selection can provide a naturalistic explanation for apparent design (Gardner 2009 [81]). This is a case of downward causation (Campbell 1974 [34]) from the environment to organisms to gene regulatory networks to genes to proteins. This can be considered as either **DDM1**: a process creating genomes that were not there before, or **DDM2**: a process altering genes that are already present in the gene pool. Which is appropriate depends on when one gene is different from another (Kaplow et al., 2022 [167]).

The system **S** is a population, so the statistics of survival and reproduction are key. It is individuals that survive and pass on their genes in a mutated way but it is populations that get selected for at the macrolevel, with this outcome chaining down to the individual level and then the gene level. It is an example of the generic principles of adaptive selection: creating order from disorder according to some selection criterion (see (5) and (6)), with stochasticity/randomness of variation providing the variety to choose from. Mutation and genetic recombination supply the needed genetic diversity. Genotype to phenotype maps for proteins, metabolic networks, and gene regulatory networks result from this process, each selected in an evolutionary way. The huge degeneracy of these maps (Wagner 2014 [11]) is key in explaining how exploration of these spaces can take place in the evolutionary time available. Developmental systems are created by evolution and then in turn shape evolutionary outcomes; overall, it is a circular interactive process because each influences the other, leading to the EVO–DEVO view of how evolution takes place (Gilbert et al., 1996 [39], Carroll 2005, 2008 [41,42], Davidson and Erwin 2006 [166], Collins et al., 2007 [168]). Friston et al. (2023) [169] express it this way:

> *"We treat the slow phylogenetic process (natural selection) as furnishing top down constraints (i.e., top-down causation) on fast phenotypic processes (action selection). In turn, the active exchange of the phenotype with its environment provides evidence that is assimilated by natural selection (i.e., bottom-up causation). This multi-scale ontological account is licensed by describing both phylogenetic and phenotypic processes as selecting (extended) genotypes and (extended) phenotypes with the greatest fitness; where fitness is quantified with (free energy) functionals of probability density functions (a functional is a function of a function)."*

A key point resulting from these two comments is the following:

> ***Selection shapes all emergent levels L in Figure 1 simultaneously***. *It has to do so, because they all work together to enable the organism to function (Noble 2012 [3], Ellis 2020 [117]). Selection is therefore not confined to either the gene level or the*

> *organism level: it is a process of selection of effective causation at all emergent levels from the macromolecular level up.* (It does not of course affect the physics or physical chemistry levels. These are determined by the laws of physics.)

This is an extension of Noble's *principle of biological relativity* (Noble 2012 [3]) from organism structure and function to organism evolution. Thus, physiological systems, tissues, cells, and proteins are all the subject of selection (Wagner 2014 [11]).

Major transitions in evolution (Szathmáry and Maynard Smith 1995 [170]) correspond to changes in the emergent hierarchy, perhaps reflecting new uses of information and higher levels of cooperation through addition of a new emergent level. Thus, ***the hierarchy itself evolves***.

Overall, the process generically results in better adaptation at the macrolevel, even if that adaptation is hard to see at the molecular level because of the multiple realizability of macrolevel structures at the microlevel. Adaptation can be regarded as organism design (Gardner 2009 [81])—which was Darwin's great discovery (Darwin 2019 [33], Dobzhansky 2013 [35]). However, genetic drift also takes place: some mutations that do not significantly affect survival rates also occur, so not all emergent features are optimally adapted (e.g., the relation of the optic nerve to the eye). Thus, evolutionary history is embodied in outcomes.

The same evolutionary principles apply to technologies (Arthur 2009 [2]) and resulting engineering applications (Vogel 2000 [130], Blockley 2012 [47]). Indeed, they apply to design processes in engineering (Dieter and Schmidt 2021 [48]).

6. Final Causation

The ultimate driver of all these dynamics is purposeful goals, which is where final causation comes in. Aristotle's concept of final causation was presented in Section 1.2. This section looks at how an updated version of final causation works out in the context of our present-day understandings of science. It considers an updated version of final causation (Section 6.1), the case of individuals (Section 6.2), the case of organizations and resultant technology (Section 6.3), and the foundations of agency (Section 6.4).

6.1. Updated Version of Final Causation

Essentially, final causation refers to the *reason* that things happen: *Why did it occur?* This is the issue of function or purpose in living beings, individual life, in society and organizations, and hence in technology. The proposed updated version of final causation is:

> **Final causation** *occurs when values, purpose, or meaning ("Telos") shape decisions made by organisms, individuals, groups, or organizations and hence shape their actions, with consequent material outcomes at the macrolevel (personal or organizational) that chain down to affect outcomes at all underlying physical levels.*

In fact, as a referee comments, all living beings have at least an implicit purpose and normativity due to the tautological consequences of natural selection, which gives a value to things that favor persistence.

It is a key form of downward causation, shaping physical outcomes to achieve high-level purposes. The way this happens in the case of individuals is discussed in depth in Noble and Ellis (2022) [114] and in the case of organizations in Carney (2021) [171] and Ellis and Noble (2023) [49]. It may occur through a rational process of meta-analysis (Murphy and Brown 2007 [132]), leading to the view of *The Good Society* (Bellah et al., 1985 [172]) or to be based in narratives embodying values (Kay and King 2020 [161], Johnson et al., 2020 [173]). Again, multiple realizability occurs: there are many ways desired higher-level values can be achieved at lower levels.

As regard to final causation, a referee comments as follows:

> *"What is ontologically prior? The metaphysical question is this: are values and meaning just a special cause of final cause (as Aristotle thought), or do they figure in the very definition of final cause (as Ellis proposes)? Which is ontologically prior to which? If*

Ellis were to embrace Aristotle's more expansive definition of teleology, this wouldn't negate any of what he describes about the irreducible role of final causation in the human and social sciences. For Aristotle, the question becomes this: are there real (and even irreducible) powers at the peculiarly human and rational level? If powers exist at that level, like the power of reasoning well or a sensitivity to the real value of actions or states, then final causation also obtains".

One could indeed propose this as an alternative to what I suggest here. However, my position is that values are indeed the final cause in human life and hence in technology (Noble and Ellis 2022 [114]). On this view, irreducible powers at the peculiarly human and rational level are the foundation of final causation, enabling it to occur, rather than being final causation itself.

6.2. The Case of Individuals

Final causation in the case of an individual essentially corresponds to self-actualization in Maslow's hierarchy of needs (Maslow 1943 [174]), updated in Heylighen (1992) [175], and is based in processes of metacognition (Murphy and Brown 2007 [132]), where people have responsibility for creating and sustaining normativity (MacIntyre 1984 [176], Heyes 2022 [177]). There may be major life choices such as to be a doctor or teacher or engineer or artist. Once made, this is the final cause that then shapes all further decisions in a hierarchical fashion: what education is needed to make this possible? Where to obtain that education? How to pay for it?, and so on, reaching down to influencing material outcomes such as molecular changes in a patient's body or paint being applied to a surface. Final causation may also take the form of issues such as a concern for keeping healthy, chaining down to taking exercise, not smoking, joining a gym, and so on, or wishing to travel to distant places to experience them, resulting in learning a foreign language and booking a ticket. Above all, final causation relates to ethical stances and value choices, where values can be envisaged as lying on a scale from extreme selfishness and self-centeredness on the one hand to extreme generosity and a willingness to be self-sacrificial on the other (Ellis and Noble 2023 [49]). These shape all that one does, including one's interaction with a community.

6.3. The Case of Organizations and Resultant Technology

All organizations have a purpose, otherwise they would not exist. Problem definition is a complex process (Dieter and Schmidt 2021: p. 10 [48]). Deciding what organizational purpose is, is a key part of management (Drucker 2012 [178]) and leadership (Burns 2004, 2010 [179,180]). The result is a hierarchy of goals (Etzioni 1964: pp. 6–8 [141], Mohr 1973 [181]) that supply the value premises that underlie decisions (Simon 2013 [182] and Scott and Davis 2007: pp. 53–56 [155]). In this hierarchical structure of ends,

"Each member of a set of behavior alternatives Is weighted in terms of a comprehensive scale of values—the "ultimate" ends" (Scott and Davis 2007: p. 54 [155]),

which is nothing other than the organizational final cause. One should note here the multidimensional nature of goals: they have a cognitive function, a motivational function, a symbolic function, a justification function for actions taken, and an evaluator function (Scott and Davis 2007: p. 184 [155]). Additionally, they have a normative nature: they relate to what is desirable in a moral sense, which is where transformational leadership arises (Burns 2004, 2010 [179,180]). Note that the fact there is such a moral dimension does not imply that actions of any particular individual, group, or organization will necessarily be morally good, rather that they will lie somewhere on the moral spectrum presented in Ellis and Noble (2023) [49] whether they make this explicit or not, and this will be a key aspect of the final causation taking place.

Those values, whatever they are, will be changing physical outcomes. They change judicial, political, economic, social, and health outcomes (Etzioni 2010 [183]). Overall, Carney (2021) [171] is a profound examination of final causation in social and organizational contexts. The point then is that this all relates to final causation in technology, for all technology has been developed for some purpose, and will result in real-world occurrences that reflect those purposes to a greater or level degree; the case of digital computers, the internet, and outcomes such as the existence of Amazon to simplify purchasing and social media to enable social contact is a case in point.

6.4. Foundations of Agency and Free Will

Clearly, final causation does not make sense unless we have sufficient agency to make meaningful choices between different the options available to us (Dennett 2015 [184]).

Strong arguments that this is so include those by Murphy and Brown (2007) [132], Ismael (2016) [185], List (2019) [186], and Potter and Mitchell (2022) [187] (they present a framework of eight criteria that, collectively, describe a system that overcomes the challenges concerning agent causality in an entirely naturalistic and non-mysterious way. The criteria are: (1) thermodynamic autonomy, (2) persistence, (3) endogenous activity, (4) holistic integration, (5) low-level indeterminacy, (6) multiple realizability, (7) historicity, (8) agent-level normativity). Multiple realizability of higher-level states at lower levels plays a key role (List 2019 [186]), as does the fact that we are open systems so it is impossible that detailed knowledge of the state $\mathbf{\Sigma}$: = $(\mathbf{p}_i,\mathbf{q}_j)$ of every single particle in our bodies at time $\mathbf{t}_0$ can determine our future human actions, because those actions are responses to external information $\mathbf{\Phi}$ from the outside world at time $\mathbf{t} > \mathbf{t}_0$ that is not contained in $\mathbf{\Sigma}$. However, these arguments need to be buttressed by including the way that huge randomness at the molecular level allows downwards selection of outcomes at those levels that fulfil higher-level purposes (Noble and Noble 2018, 2021 [62,188]) in line with the way that molecular machines work (Hoffmann 2012 [70], Brown and Sivak 2019 [189]). It also needs to include the fact of biological emergence of purpose, as Ball (2023: pp. 7, 12) [190] comments:

> *"The distinction between physics and biology is sometimes illustrated* via *the thought experiment of repeating Galileo's (almost certainly apocryphal) Tower of Pisa experiment by dropping a cannonball and a pigeon. To the extent that we can predict what the pigeon will do at all, we implicitly invoke its agency. To explain why it does not simply plummet, it is not enough to invoke aerodynamics; we must also in effect allow that the pigeon does not want to plummet. It manifests its agency by virtue of having goals. . . . Agency evolves precisely because living organisms are liable to encounter challenges that evolution itself is too slow to adapt to."*

Our claim now will be:

> ***Free Will:*** *In the context of the modular hierarchical structure of human life, with multiple realizability of higher-level functions occurring in the context of huge numbers of molecules at the cellular level in a highly dynamic environment (§2.2) and with humans being open systems, dynamic formal and material downward causation underlie the existence of free will.*

This is the essential content of Noble and Noble 2018, 2021 [62,188], Ellis (2021) [191], and Ellis and Noble 2023 [49]. It allows the metacognition and reflection on purpose that is the key element of final causation (Murphy and Brown 2007 [132]). It does not in any way undermine standard physics as set out in Carroll 2022 [192].

Physical indeterminacy at the lowest levels is essential to provide some causal slack in the system, whereby macroscopic organization can have any kind of real causal influence over the go of things. There is even literature from Aristotle himself on chance as a "fifth cause", though it is admittedly confusing and contentious. This counters claims that, for example, the standard model of particle physics is "causally comprehensive" and any talk of causes at higher levels is just a convenient fiction. Since supervenience is merely a matter of a kind of robust correlation, the fact that the emergent properties supervene on the physical base does not mean that the emergent properties are wholly dependent on or wholly grounded by the microphysical. If the emergent properties are truly equally fundamental in our ontology, some special reason must be given for thinking that the emerging properties can vary only if the base properties do. However, the horizontal causal connections between emergent properties can be stochastic or probabilistic, so two worlds can come over time to vary at the emergent level without undergoing any difference at the base level (I thank a referee for the comments in this paragraph). Biology fulfils these conditions because there is major stochasticity at the molecular level (Section 1.4).

7. The Outcome

In this section I conclude the discussion of an updated version of Aristotelian causation by considering the four causes and emergence (Section 7.1), a specific example (Section 7.2), causal closure (Section 7.3), and how physics by itself does not give all the answers (Section 7.4).

7.1. The Four Causes and Emergence

One can propose that the four causes relate to emergence in the following ways:

- Stating that efficient causation occurs at each higher level is essentially the claim that emergence does indeed occur. Novelty arises at each higher level because the nature of efficient causation is different at each emergent level.
- Stating that material causation occurs is essentially stating that supervenience occurs over a material basis.
- Stating that formal causation occurs is essentially the statement that constraints break symmetries and thereby shape outcomes.
- Stating that final causation occurs is a statement that in the case of humans and the abstract and material artefacts they create, purpose and values play a key role in determining outcomes.
- The same level relations between the four causes are that both material and formal causation often play a role in efficient causation at each level. The exception is abstract causation in the case of intelligent beings and organizations.
- The interlevel relations that relate efficient causation at different levels in biology and technology are mediated by static and dynamic material and formal causation.
- Final causation plays a key role in determining what happens at all levels in the cases of human beings, organizations, and technology: it, in effect, provides a topmost level of causation via its associated values, as indicated in Figure 1.
- In each case, outcomes are determined contextually via initial and boundary conditions for the effective laws characterizing efficient causation at each level. The effective laws do not by themselves determine any outcomes at all and that applies inter alia to the efficient causation characterized by physical laws such as Newton's laws of motion, Maxwell's equations, and so on. They determine possibilities but not specific outcomes in particular contexts.

7.2. A Specific Example

An example of the interactions between the various kinds of causation is given by an example developed from a talk given by Russell Ackoff, namely:

Why is an aircraft flying from Hamburg to London?

If carefully considered, it turns out that all forms of Aristotelian causation are involved, as indicated in Table 1.

Final causation arises at **Level L8**, that of the founder and shareholders. They decide the purpose of the company, which is its final cause (cf. Mayer 2018 [193]) from which all else follows. ***Efficient and material causation*** take place at **Level L7**, the level of managers, who timetable flights (efficient causation) and arrange for aircraft and fuel to be available (material causation). Efficient and material causation occur at **Level L6**: the level where engineers design the plane and then manufacture it. A fundamental reason that the plane flies is because it was designed to fly, whereas a house does not fly because it was not so designed. ***Final causation*** occurs again at **Level L5**: the passengers desire the trip because of some final cause or other (family loyalty, a wish to travel, the purpose of a business they run, and so on). ***Efficient causation*** occurs at **Level L4**: the plane flies because the pilot controls the aircraft, opening the throttle, adjusting the height and heading, etc. ***Formal causation*** occurs at **Level L3**, because it is the shape of the wing that makes the plane fly rather than drop out of the sky; much money is spent on researching optimal wing shape. ***Material causation*** also occurs at **Level L3**, because the strength of the wing depends on the materials out of which it is made. ***Efficient causation*** takes place at **Level L2**: Bernoulli's principle determines the lift that the wing (with its specific shape, so formal causation) will generate when flying at a specific speed, because air molecules are moving faster above the wing than below, and that is based in the kinetic theory of molecular behavior. ***Efficient causation*** at **Level L1** is how the underlying physics enables it all to happen.

Table 1. Causal factors when a plane flies from London to Hamburg.

Level	Agent	Causation	Nature
L8	Founder Shareholders	Final	Provide a service; Make a profit
L7	Management	Efficient Material	Timetable flights; Buy aircraft; Arrange fuel supply
L6	Engineers	Efficient, Material	Design the plane; Manufacture it
L5	Passengers	Final	Need for trip
L4	Pilot	Efficient	Control aircraft
L3	Wing	Formal Material	Provides lift; Provides strength
L2	Fluid Flow	Efficient	Bernoulli's principle
L1	Molecules	Efficient	Kinetic theory

All the four forms of causation are at work. The plane will not be flying unless they all are determining outcomes in a coherent way simultaneously. Physical causation is simply one of the many causes entering the picture.

7.3. Causal Closure

From this, it follows that causal closure only occurs when all levels linked by upward and downward causation, and the interactions between them occurring via formal and material causation, are taken into account (Ellis 2020 [117]). The plane will not be flying if any of these levels or types of causation are missing because of the interlevel links between them. Thus, it is not true that the physical level by itself is causally closed, as some claim.

Further examples of causal closure in emergent contexts are, biological organization as closure of constraint (Mossio and Moreno 2010 [194], Montévil and Mossio 2015 [158]); smoking causes lung cancer, driven by advertising and social pressure but arising through molecular biology processes (Ellis and Noble 2023 [49]); determination of values occurs by circular interaction between individuals and society (Ellis and Noble 2023 [49]); the emergence of functionality over time due to natural selection, which is instantiated in some particular molecular configurations of a system meeting specific emergent biological needs, that is, via efficient and material and formal causes. As Aristotle argued, these explanations at different levels and over different timescales are not in contrast with each other—they are all required to fully explain the behavior of the system. A referee argues,

> *"Aristotelians contend, there is no microscopic world that can be exhaustively described in exclusively microscopic terms, because of the irreducible role of macroscopic constraints. This fact renders the usual definition of supervenience (whether global or local) inapplicable, since that definition presupposes that we can disentangle emergent and base*

properties and facts from each other. Aristotelians should reject the talk of disjoint "levels" of reality in favor of pluralistically-described indivisible whole."

My viewpoint, defended above, is that the first two claims here are indeed true and are what is defended in this paper. Where I disagree is the third claim. I agree that the whole acts as an indivisible entity, in the sense that causal closure takes place: outcomes are only determined when all interacting levels are taken into account and in that sense form an integral whole. Nevertheless, that whole does indeed have determinable separate levels, each with real causal powers. This fact is demonstrated by all the examples given here (and is the reason those examples are given). They are solid evidence this claim is true.

7.4. Physics by Itself Does Not Give All the Answers

Greene (2020) [92], Carroll (2021) [93], and Hossenfelder (2022) [94] use titles in articles and books claiming that physics can provide answers to all the biggest questions in the universe. They believe that only efficient causation occurs and that only at some underlying not specified physics level (the problematic issue is that we do not know what the bottom-most physical level is, assuming there is one). Thus, they operate in a framework that does not take into account three of the four Aristotelian causes and takes into account only one level of efficient causation. This viewpoint is unable to explain even so simple an issue as why a teapot exists (Ellis 2005 [195]), nor can it explain neuroscience outcomes (Grasso et al., 2021 [196]). It is the existence of such reductionist viewpoints (Horgan 2023 [197]) that make it important to explicate the various other kinds of causes that demonstrably occur in the real world. This can be systematized by an approach generalizing Aristotle's causes to be both synchronic and diachronic.

The ***possibilities*** of biological and technological emergent outcomes are built into the laws of physics. ***Specific outcomes*** depend both on those laws and on contextual and historical factors that are not implied by them. Aristotle's four causes are all implicated in specific real-world outcomes. Why the laws of physics exist, and why they have the nature they do, is the deep underlying metaphysical question that cannot be answered by science.

Funding: This research is supported by the University of Cape Town Research Committee.

Institutional Review Board Statement: Not applicable.

Data Availability Statement: Not applicable.

Acknowledgments: I thank two anonymous referees whose comments have led to substantial improvements in this paper.

Conflicts of Interest: The authors declare no conflict of interest.

References

1. Shields, C. Aristotle. In *The Stanford Encyclopedia of Philosophy*; Zalta, E.N., Ed.; Stanford University: Stanford, CA, USA, 2022. Available online: https://plato.stanford.edu/archives/spr2022/entries/aristotle/ (accessed on 11 June 2023).
2. Arthur, W.B. *The Nature of Technology: What It Is and How It Evolves*; Simon and Schuster: New York, NY, USA, 2009.
3. Noble, D. A theory of biological relativity: No privileged level of causation. *Interface Focus* **2012**, *2*, 55–64. [CrossRef] [PubMed]
4. Feynman, R. *The Feynman Lectures in Physics: Volume I: Mainly Mechanics, Radiation, and Heat, Volume II: Mainly Electromagnetism and Matter, Volume III: Quantum Mechanics*; Addison Wesley: Boston, MA, USA, 2013.
5. Sokolowski, R. Matter, elements and substance in Aristotle. *J. Hist. Philos.* **1970**, *8*, 263–288. [CrossRef]
6. Emsley, J. *Nature's Building Blocks: An AZ Guide to the Elements*; Oxford University Press: Oxford, UK, 2011.
7. Scerri, E. *The Periodic Table: Its Story and Its Significance*; Oxford University Press: Oxford, UK, 2019.
8. Lehn, J.M. Supramolecular chemistry: From molecular information towards self-organization and complex matter. *Rep. Prog. Phys.* **2004**, *67*, 249. [CrossRef]
9. Watson, J.D.; Baker, T.A.; Gann, A.; Bell, S.P.; Levine, M.; Losick, R.M. *Molecular Biology of the Gene*; Pearson: Boston, MA, USA, 2014.
10. Petsko, G.A.; Ringe, D. *Protein Structure and Function*; Oxford University Press: Oxford, UK, 2004.
11. Wagner, A. *Arrival of the Fittest: Solving Evolution's Greatest Puzzle*; Penguin: London, UK, 2014.
12. Booch, G.; Maksimchuk, R.A.; Engle, M.W.; Young, B.J.; Connallen, J.; Houston, K.A. *Object-Oriented Analysis and Design with Applications*; Addison Wesley: Boston, MA, USA, 2007.

13. Pezzulo, G.; Levin, M. Top-down models in biology: Explanation and control of complex living systems above the molecular level. *J. R. Soc. Interface* **2016**, *13*, 20160555. [CrossRef] [PubMed]
14. Vooshholz, J.; Gabriel, M. *Top-Down Causation and Emergence*; Springer: Cham, Germany, 2021.
15. Anderson, P.W. More is different: Broken symmetry and the nature of the hierarchical structure of science. *Science* **1972**, *177*, 393–396. [CrossRef] [PubMed]
16. Marshall, W.; Albantakis, L.; Tononi, G. Black-boxing and cause-effect power. *PLoS Comput. Biol.* **2018**, *14*, e1006114. [CrossRef] [PubMed]
17. Campbell, N.A.; Reece, J.B. *Biology*; Benjamin Cummings: San Francisco, CA, USA, 2005.
18. Atkins, P.; De Paula, J. *Physical Chemistry for the Life Sciences*; Oxford University Press: New York, NY, USA, 2011.
19. Alberts, B. *The Molecular Biology of the Cell*; Garland Science: New York, NY, USA, 2015.
20. Allen, T.; Cowling, G. *The Cell: A Very Short Introduction*; Oxford University Press: Oxford, UK, 2011.
21. Berridge, M.J. *Cell Signalling Biology*; Portland Press: London, UK, 2014.
22. Jeong, H.; Tombor, B.; Albert, R.; Oltvai, Z.N.; Barabási, A.L. The large-scale organization of metabolic networks. *Nature* **2000**, *407*, 651–654. [CrossRef]
23. Karlebach, G.; Shamir, R. Modelling and analysis of gene regulatory networks. *Nat. Rev. Mol. Cell Biol.* **2008**, *9*, 770–780. [CrossRef]
24. Hall, J.E.; Hall, M.E. *Guyton and Hall Textbook of Medical Physiology*; Elsevier Health Sciences: London, UK, 2020.
25. Davies, J.A. *Human Physiology: A Very Short Introduction*; Oxford University Press: Oxford, UK, 2021.
26. Kandel, E.R. Nerve cells and behavior. *Princ. Neural Sci.* **1991**, *3*, 18–32. [CrossRef]
27. Churchland, P.S.; Sejnowski, T.J. *The Computational Brain*; MIT Press: Cambridge, MA, USA, 1994.
28. Kandel, E.R.; Schwartz, J.H.; Jessell, T.M.; Siegelbaum, S.; Hudspeth, A.J.; Mack, S. (Eds.) *Principles of Neural Science*; McGraw-Hill: New York, NY, USA, 2000.
29. Kandel, E.R. *The Age of Insight: The Quest to Understand the Unconscious in Art, Mind, and Brain, from Vienna 1900 to the Present*; Random House: New York, NY, USA, 2012.
30. Franklin, S.; Madl, T.; D'mello, S.; Snaider, J. LIDA: A systems-level architecture for cognition, emotion, and learning. *IEEE Trans. Auton. Ment. Dev.* **2013**, *6*, 19–41. [CrossRef]
31. Franklin, S.; Madl, T.; Strain, S.; Faghihi, U.; Dong, D.; Kugele, S.; Snaider, J.; Agrawal, P.; Chen, S. A LIDA cognitive model tutorial. *Biol. Inspired Cogn. Archit.* **2016**, *16*, 105–130. [CrossRef]
32. Jacob, A.; Kugele, S.; Newen, A.; Franklin, S. Modeling interactions between the embodied and the narrative self: Dynamics of the self-pattern within LIDA. *Cogn. Syst. Res.* **2023**, *81*, 25–36.
33. Darwin, C. *On the Origin of Species by Means of Natural Selection, or, the Preservation of Favoured Races in the Struggle for Life*; Natural History Museum: New York, NY, USA, 2019.
34. Campbell, D. Downward causation in hierarchically organised biological systems. In *Studies in the Philosophy of Biology: Reduction and Related Problems*; Ayala, F.J., Dobhzansky, T., Eds.; University of California Press: Berkeley, CA, USA, 1974; pp. 179–186.
35. Dobzhansky, T. Nothing in biology makes sense except in the light of evolution. *Am. Biol. Teach.* **2013**, *75*, 87–91. [CrossRef]
36. Gilbert, S.F. Ecological developmental biology: Developmental biology meets the real world. *Dev. Biol.* **2001**, *233*, 1–12. [CrossRef] [PubMed]
37. Wolpert, L.; Tickle, C.; Arias, A.M. *Principles of Development, Version 2023/06/08*; Oxford University Press: New York, NY, USA, 2002.
38. Gilbert, S. *Developmental Biology*; Sinauer Associates: Sunderland, MA, USA, 2019.
39. Gilbert, S.F.; Opitz, J.M.; Raff, R.A. Resynthesizing evolutionary and developmental biology. *Dev. Biol.* **1996**, *173*, 357–372. [CrossRef] [PubMed]
40. Oyama, S.; Griffiths, P.E.; Gray, R.D. *Cycles of Contingency: Developmental Systems and Evolution*; MIT Press: Cambridge, MA, USA, 2001.
41. Carroll, S.B. *Endless Forms Most Beautiful: The New Science of Evo Devo and the Making of the Animal Kingdom*; WW Norton & Company: New York, NY, USA, 2005.
42. Carroll, S.B. Evo-Devo and an Expanding Evolutionary Synthesis: A Genetic Theory of Morphological Evolution. *Cell* **2008**, *134*, 25–36. [CrossRef]
43. Ellis, G. Quantum physics and biology: The local wavefunction approach. *J. Phys. Conf. Ser. (IOP Publ.)* **2023**, *2533*, 012019. [CrossRef]
44. Nurse, P. Life, logic and information. *Nature* **2008**, *454*, 424–426. [CrossRef]
45. Farnsworth, K.D.; Nelson, J.; Gershenson, C. Living is information processing: From molecules to global systems. *Acta Biotheor.* **2013**, *61*, 203–222. [CrossRef]
46. Farnsworth, K.D. How an information perspective helps overcome the challenge of biology to physics. *Biosystems* **2022**, *217*, 104683. [CrossRef]
47. Blockley, D. *Engineering: A Very Short Introduction*; Oxford University Press: Oxford, UK, 2012.
48. Dieter, G.E.; Schmidt, L.C. *Engineering Design*; McGraw Hill: New York, NY, USA, 2021.
49. Ellis, G.; Noble, D. Economics, Society, and the Pre-eminent Role of Values. *Theor. Biol. Forum* **2023**, *115*, 45–70.
50. Ellis, G. Emergence in solid state physics and biology. *Found. Phys.* **2020**, *50*, 1098–1139. [CrossRef]

51. Clayton, P.; Davies, P. (Eds.) *The Re-Emergence of Emergence*; Oxford University Press: Oxford, UK, 2006.
52. Murphy, N.; Ellis, G.; O'Connor, T. (Eds.) *Downward Causation and the Neurobiology of Free Will*; Springer Science & Business Media: Berlin/Heidelberg, Germany, 2009.
53. Noble, D. *Dance to the Tune of Life: Biological Relativity*; Cambridge University Press: Cambridge, MA, USA, 2016.
54. O'Connor, T. Emergent Properties. In *The Stanford Encyclopedia of Philosophy*; Zalta, E.N., Ed.; Stanford University: Stanford, CA, USA, 2021. Available online: https://plato.stanford.edu/archives/win2021/entries/properties-emergent/ (accessed on 11 June 2023).
55. Ackoff, R. Science in the Systems Age: Beyond IE, OR, and MS. *Oper. Res.* **1973**, *21*, 661–671. [CrossRef]
56. Juarrero, A. *Dynamics in Action: Intentional Behavior as a Complex System*; MIT Press: Cambridge, MA, USA, 2002.
57. Ellis, G. Top-down causation and emergence: Some comments on mechanisms. *Interface Focus* **2012**, *2*, 126–140. [CrossRef] [PubMed]
58. Tabaczek, M. The metaphysics of downward causation: Rediscovering the formal cause. *Zygon* **2013**, *48*, 380–404. [CrossRef]
59. Ellis, G. *How Can Physics Underlie the Mind. Top-Down Causation in the Human Context*; Springer: Berlin/Heidelberg, Germany, 2016.
60. Hofmeyr, J.-H. Basic biological anticipation. In *Handbook of Anticipation*; Poli, R., Ed.; Springer: Cham, Germany, 2017.
61. Hofmeyr, J.-H. Causation, constructors and codes. *Biosystems* **2018**, *164*, 121–127. [CrossRef] [PubMed]
62. Noble, R.; Noble, D. Can reasons and values influence action: How might intentional agency work physiologically? *J. Gen. Philos. Sci.* **2021**, *52*, 277–295. [CrossRef]
63. Menzies, P.; List, C. The Causal Autonomy of the Special Sciences. In *Emergence in Mind*; Oxford University Press: Oxford, UK, 2010. Available online: https://philpapers.org/rec/MENTCA (accessed on 11 June 2023).
64. Kment, B. Causation: Determination and Difference-Making. *Noûs* **2010**, *44*, 80–111. [CrossRef]
65. Pietsch, W. A difference-making account of causation. In Proceedings of the 5th Biennial Conference of the European Philosophy of Science Association, Duesseldorf, Germany, 23–26 September 2015.
66. Pearl, J.; Mackenzie, D. *The Book of Why: The New Science of Cause and Effect*; Basic Books: New York, NY, USA, 2018.
67. Ellis, G. Physical time and human time. *arXiv* **2022**, arXiv:2210.10107.
68. Brewer, C.V.; Burrow, C.D. *Life: Form and Function*; MacMillan: New York, NY, USA, 1980.
69. Hartwell l Hopfield, J.; Leibler, S.; Murray, A. From molecular to modular cell biology. *Nature* **1999**, *402*, C47–C52. [CrossRef]
70. Hoffmann, P. *Life's Ratchet: How Molecular Machines Extract Order from Chaos*; Basic Books: New York, NY, USA, 2012.
71. Ashby, W.R. *Design for a Brain: The Origin of Adaptive Behaviour*; Springer Science & Business Media: Berlin/Heidelberg, Germany, 2013.
72. Gillett, C. The metaphysics of realization, multiple realizability, and the special sciences. *J. Philos.* **2002**, *100*, 591–603.
73. Piccinini, G.; Maley, C.J. The metaphysics of mind and the multiple sources of multiple realizability. In *New Waves in Philosophy of Mind*; Palgrave Macmillan: London, UK, 2014; pp. 125–152.
74. Batterman, R.W. Autonomy of theories: An explanatory problem. *Noûs* **2018**, *52*, 858–873. [CrossRef]
75. Bickle, J. Multiple Realizability. In *The Stanford Encyclopedia of Philosophy*; Edward, N.Z., Ed.; Stanford University: Stanford, CA USA, 2020. Available online: https://plato.stanford.edu/archives/sum2020/entries/multiple-realizability/ (accessed on 11 June 2023).
76. Edelman, G.M.; Gally, J.A. Degeneracy and complexity in biological systems. *Proc. Natl. Acad. Sci. USA* **2001**, *98*, 13763–13768. [CrossRef] [PubMed]
77. Simon, H.A. *The Sciences of the Artificial*; MIT Press: Cambridge, MA, USA, 2019.
78. Mossio, M.; Saborido, C.; Moreno, A. An organizational account of biological functions. *Br. J. Philos. Sci.* **2009**, *60*, 813–841. [CrossRef]
79. Farnsworth, K.D.; Albantakis, L.; Caruso, T. Unifying concepts of biological function from molecules to ecosystems. *Oikos* **2017**, *126*, 1367–1376. [CrossRef]
80. Ellis, G.; Kopel, J. The dynamical emergence of biology from physics: Branching causation via biomolecules. *Front. Physiol.* **2019**, *9*, 1966. [CrossRef] [PubMed]
81. Gardner, A. Adaptation as organism design. *Biol. Lett.* **2009**, *5*, 861–864. [CrossRef]
82. Tanenbaum, A.S.; Austin, T. *Structured Computer Organisation*; Pearson: Boston, MA, USA, 2013.
83. Fratzl, P.; Weinkamer, R. Nature's hierarchical materials. *Prog. Mater. Sci.* **2007**, *52*, 1263–1334. [CrossRef]
84. Chen, Y.; Ma, Y.; Yin, Q.; Pan, F.; Cui, C.; Zhang, Z.; Liu, B. Advances in mechanics of hierarchical composite materials. *Compos. Sci. Technol.* **2021**, *214*, 108970. [CrossRef]
85. Dove, M.T. *Structure and Dynamics: An Atomic View of Materials*; Oxford University Press: Oxford, UK, 2003.
86. Miodownik, M. *Stuff Matters: The Strange Stories of the Marvellous Materials that Shape Our Man-Made World*; Houghton MIflin: Boston, MA, USA, 2014.
87. Ellis, G.; Drossel, B. How Downwards Causation Occurs in Digital Computers. *Found. Phys.* **2019**, *49*, 1253–1277. [CrossRef]
88. Batterman, R. The tyranny of scales. In *Oxford Handbook of Philosophy of Physics*; Oxford University Press: Oxford, UK, 2013; pp. 255–286.
89. Kaeslin, H. *Digital Integrated Circuit Design, from VLSI Architectures to CMOS Fabrication*; Cambridge University Press: Cambridge, MA, USA, 2008.

90. Flack, J.C. Coarse-graining as a downward causation mechanism. *Philos. Trans. R. Soc. A Math. Phys. Eng. Sci.* **2017**, *375*, 20160338. [CrossRef] [PubMed]
91. Dasgupta, S. *Computer Science: A Very Short Introduction*; Oxford University Press: Oxford, UK, 2016.
92. Greene, B. *Until the End of Time: Mind, Matter, and Our Search for Meaning in an Evolving Universe*; Knopf: New York, NY, USA, 2020.
93. Carroll, S.M. Consciousness and the Laws of Physics. *J. Conscious. Stud.* **2021**, *28*, 16–31. [CrossRef]
94. Hossenfelder, S. *Existential Physics: A Scientists Guide to Life's Biggest Questions*; Viking: New York, NY, USA, 2022.
95. Cunningham, B. The re-emergence of 'emergence'. *Philos. Sci.* **2001**, *68*, S62–S75. [CrossRef]
96. Chalmers, D.J. Strong and weak emergence. In *The Re-Emergence of Emergence*; Oxford University Press: Oxford, UK, 2006; pp. 244–256.
97. Brigandt, I.; Love, A. Reductionism in Biology. In *Stanford Encyclopedia of Philosophy*; Zalta, E.N., Nodelman, U., Eds.; Stanford University: Stanford, CA, USA, 2023. Available online: https://plato.stanford.edu/archives/sum2023/entries/reduction-biology/ (accessed on 11 June 2023).
98. Paoletti, M.P. Emergent powers. *Topoi* **2020**, *39*, 1031–1044. [CrossRef]
99. Santos, G. Integrated-structure emergence and its mechanistic explanation. *Synthese* **2021**, *198*, 8687–8711. [CrossRef]
100. Tanaka, J.W.; Kay, J.B.; Grinnell, E.; Stansfield, B.; Szechter, L. Face recognition in young children: When the whole is greater than the sum of its parts. *Vis. Cogn.* **1998**, *5*, 479–496. [CrossRef]
101. Glaser, J.R.; Glaser, E.M. Stereology, morphometry, and mapping: The whole is greater than the sum of its parts. *J. Chem. Neuroanat.* **2000**, *20*, 115–126. [CrossRef] [PubMed]
102. Galatzer-Levy, R.M. Emergence. *Psychoanal. Inq.* **2002**, *22*, 708–727. [CrossRef]
103. Davison, K.S.; Siminoski, K.; Adachi, J.D.; Hanley, D.A.; Goltzman, D.; Hodsman, A.B.; Josse, R.; Kaiser, S.; Olszynski, W.P.; Papaioannou, A.; et al. Bone strength: The whole is greater than the sum of its parts. *Semin. Arthritis Rheum.* **2006**, *36*, 22–31. [CrossRef] [PubMed]
104. Pérez-Dorado, I.; Galan-Bartual, S.; Hermoso, J.A. Pneumococcal surface proteins: When the whole is greater than the sum of its parts. *Mol. Oral Microbiol.* **2012**, *27*, 221–245. [CrossRef]
105. Matthews, L.; Guarné, A. Dbf4: The whole is greater than the sum of its parts. *Cell Cycle* **2013**, *12*, 1180–1188. [CrossRef] [PubMed]
106. Kornblith, L.Z.; Howard, B.M.; Cheung, C.K.; Dayter, Y.; Pandey, S.; Busch, M.P.; Pati, S.; Callcut, R.A.; Vilardi, R.F.; Redick, B.J.; et al. The whole is greater than the sum of its parts: Hemostatic profiles of whole blood variants. *J. Trauma Acute Care Surg.* **2014**, *77*, 818–827. [CrossRef] [PubMed]
107. Taylor, R.; Wood, P.A. A million crystal structures: The whole is greater than the sum of its parts. *Chem. Rev.* **2019**, *119*, 9427–9477. [CrossRef] [PubMed]
108. Fang, S.; Hu, Y.H. Thermo-photo catalysis: A whole greater than the sum of its parts. *Chem. Soc. Rev.* **2022**, *51*, 3609–3647. [CrossRef] [PubMed]
109. Kim, J. *Physicalism, or Something Near Enough*; Princeton University Press: Princeton, NJ, USA, 2005.
110. Dawkins, R. *The Selfish Gene*; Oxford University Press: Oxford, UK, 2016.
111. Crick, F. *The Astonishing Hypothesis*; Scribner: New York, NY, USA, 1994.
112. Harris, S. *Free Will*; Simon and Schuster: New York, NY, USA, 2012.
113. Caruso, G.D. *Free Will and Consciousness: A Determinist Account of the Illusion of Free Will*; Lexington Books: Washington, DC, USA, 2012.
114. Noble, D.; Ellis, G. Biological Relativity Revisited: The pre-eminent role of values. *Theor. Biol. Forum.* **2022**. [CrossRef]
115. Simpson, W.M.; Horsley, S.A. Toppling the Pyramids: Physics without physical state monism. In *Powers, Time and Free Will*; Springer International Publishing: Cham, Germany, 2022; pp. 17–50.
116. Montévil, M.; Mossio, M. Biological organisation as closure of constraints. *J. Theor. Biol.* **2015**, *372*, 179–191. [CrossRef] [PubMed]
117. Ellis, G. The causal closure of physics in real world contexts. *Found. Phys.* **2020**, *50*, 1057–1097. [CrossRef] [PubMed]
118. Yates, D. Demystifying Emergence. *Ergo Open Access J. Philos.* **2017**, *3*, 809–841. [CrossRef]
119. Shen, B.-W.; Pielke Sr, R.A.; Zeng, X.; Baik, J.-J.; Faghih-Naini, S.; Cui, J.; Atlas, R.; Reyes, T. Is weather chaotic? Coexisting chaotic and non-chaotic attractors within Lorenz models. In *13th Chaotic Modeling and Simulation International Conference*; Springer International Publishing: Berlin/Heidelberg, Germany, 2021; Volume 13, pp. 805–825.
120. Neyrinck, M.; Genel, S.; Stücker, J. Boundaries of chaos and determinism in the cosmos. *arXiv* **2022**, arXiv:2206.10666.
121. Noble, D. How the Hodgkin Cycle became the Principle of Relativity. *J. Physiol.* **2022**, *600*, 5171–5177. [CrossRef]
122. Laughlin, R.B.; Pines, D. The theory of everything. *Proc. Natl. Acad. Sci. USA* **2000**, *97*, 28–31. [CrossRef] [PubMed]
123. Oerter, R. *The Theory of Almost Everything: The Standard Model, the Unsung Triumph of Modern Physics*; Penguin: London, UK, 2006.
124. Noble, D. Modelling the heart—From genes to cells to the whole organ. *Science* **2002**, *295*, 1678–1682. [CrossRef] [PubMed]
125. Fink, M.; Noble, D. Noble model. *Scholarpedia* **2008**, *3*, 1803. [CrossRef]
126. Kandel, E.R. The molecular biology of memory storage: A dialogue between genes and synapses. *Science* **2001**, *294*, 1030–1038. [CrossRef] [PubMed]
127. Carpenter, G.A.; Grossberg, S. A massively parallel architecture for a self-organizing neural pattern recognition machine. *Comput. Vis. Graph. Image Process.* **1987**, *37*, 54–115. [CrossRef]
128. Carpenter, G.A.; Grossberg, S. The ART of adaptive pattern recognition by a self-organizing neural network. *Computer* **1988**, *21*, 77–88. [CrossRef]

129. Bronowski, J. *The Ascent of Man*; Random House: New York, NY, USA, 2011.
130. Vogel, S. *Cats' Paws and Catapults: Mechanical Worlds of Nature and People*; WW Norton & Company: New York, NY, USA, 2000.
131. Deacon, T. *The Symbolic Species: The Co-Evolution of Language and the Brain*; WW Norton: New York, NY, USA, 1998.
132. Murphy, N.; Brown, W. *Did My Neurons Make Me Do It?* Oxford University Press: Oxford, UK, 2007.
133. Davidson, P. Money and the real world. *Econ. J.* **1972**, *82*, 101–115. [CrossRef]
134. Harari, Y.N. *Sapiens: A Brief History of Humankind*; Random House: New York, NY, USA, 2014.
135. Menzies, P. The Causal Efficacy of Mental States. In *Physicalism and Mental Causation*; Imprint Academic: Charlottesville, VA, USA, 2003; pp. 195–224.
136. Robb, D.; Heil, J. Mental Causation. In *The Stanford Encyclopedia of Philosophy*; Zalta, E.N., Ed.; Stanford University: Stanford, CA, USA, 2021.
137. Aberle, D.F.; Cohen, A.K.; Davis, A.K.; Levy, M.J., Jr.; Sutton, F.X. The functional prerequisites of a society. *Ethics* **1950**, *60*, 100–111. [CrossRef]
138. Wainwright, S.A. Form and function in organisms. *Am. Zool.* **1988**, *28*, 671–680. [CrossRef]
139. Deacon, T.W. Emergence: The hole at the wheel's hub. In *The Re-Emergence of Emergence: The Emergentist Hypothesis from Science to Religion*; Clayton, P., Davies, P.C.W., Eds.; Oxford University Press: Oxford, UK, 2006; pp. 111–150.
140. Noble, D. *The Music of Life: Biology Beyond Genes*; Oxford University Press: Oxford, UK, 2008.
141. Etzioni, A. *Modern Organizations*; Prentice Hall: Upper Saddle River, NJ, USA, 1964.
142. Elder-Vass, D. *The Causal Power of Social Structures: Emergence, Structure and Agency*; Cambridge University Press: Cambridge, MA, USA, 2010.
143. Behr, J.P. (Ed.) *The Lock-and-Key Principle: The State of the Art—100 Years on*; Wiley: New York, NY, USA, 2008.
144. Norman, D. User Centered System Design. In *New Perspectives on Human-Computer Interaction*; Lawrence Erlbaum: Mahwah, NJ, USA, 1986.
145. Norman, D. *The Design of Everyday Things: Revised and Expanded Edition*; Basic Books: New York, NY, USA, 2013.
146. Novak, B.; Tyson, J.T. Design Principles of Biochemical Oscillators. *Nat. Rev. Mol. Cell Biol.* **2008**, *9*, 981–991. [CrossRef]
147. Li, Z.; Yang, Q. Systems and synthetic biology approaches in understanding biological oscillators. *Quant. Biol.* **2018**, *6*, 1–14. [CrossRef] [PubMed]
148. Tyson, J.J.; Novák, B. Time-keeping and decision-making in the cell cycle. *Interface Focus* **2022**, *12*, 20210075. [CrossRef] [PubMed]
149. Daur, N.; Nadim, F.; Bucher, D. The complexity of small circuits: The stomatogastric nervous system. *Curr. Opin. Neurobiol.* **2016**, *41*, 1–7. [CrossRef]
150. Cabral, J.; Castaldo, F.; Vohryzek, J.; Litvak, V.; Bick, C.; Lambiotte, R.; Friston, K.; Kringelbach, M.L.; Deco, G. Metastable oscillatory modes emerge from synchronization in the brain spacetime connectome. *Commun. Phys.* **2022**, *5*, 184. [CrossRef]
151. Wiener, N. *Cybernetics: Or Control and Communication in the Animal and the Machine*, 2nd revised ed.; MIT Press: Camb, MA, USA, 1961.
152. Ashby, W.R. *An Introduction to Cybernetics*; Chapman and Hall: Boca Raton, FL, USA, 1964.
153. Modell, H.; Cliff, W.; Michael, J.; McFarland, J.; Wenderoth, M.P.; Wright, A. A physiologists view of homeostasis. *Adv. Physiol. Educ.* **2015**, *39*, 259–266. [CrossRef]
154. Penrose, E.T. Biological Analogies in the Theory of the Firm. *Am. Econ. Rev.* **1952**, *42*, 804–819.
155. Scott, W.R.; Davies, G.F. *Organizations and Organizing: Rational, Natural, and Open Systems Perspectives*; Pearson Education: Upper Saddle River, NJ, USA, 2007.
156. Damasio, A.; Damasio, H. Exploring the concept of homeostasis and considering its implications for economics. *J. Econ. Behav. Organ.* **2016**, *126*, 125–129. [CrossRef]
157. Leopold, D.A. A redrawn map for the human motor cortex. *Nat. News Views* **2023**, *617*, 253–254. [CrossRef]
158. Cornish-Bowden, A.; Cárdenas, M.L.; Letelier, J.C.; Soto-Andrade, J.; Abarzúa, F.G. Understanding the parts in terms of the whole. *Biol. Cell* **2004**, *96*, 713–717. [CrossRef]
159. Simon, S.H. *The Oxford Solid State Basics*; Oxford University Press: Oxford, UK, 2013.
160. Palmer, T.N. *The Primacy of Doubt*; Basic Books: New York, NY, USA, 2022.
161. Kay, J.; King, M. *Radical Uncertainty: Decision Making for an Unknowable Future*; The Bridge Street Press: London, UK, 2020.
162. Goelzer, A.; Bekkal Brikci, F.; Martin-Verstraete, I.; Noirot, P.; Bessières, P.; Aymerich, S.; Fromion, V. Reconstruction and analysis of the genetic and metabolic regulatory networks of the central metabolism of Bacillus subtilis. *BMC Syst. Biol.* **2008**, *2*, 20. [CrossRef]
163. Buescher, J.M.; Liebermeister, W.; Jules, M.; Uhr, M.; Muntel, J.; Botella, E.; Hessling, B.; Kleijn, R.J.; Le Chat, L.; Lecointe, F.; et al. Global network reorganization during dynamic adaptations of Bacillus subtilis metabolism. *Science* **2012**, *335*, 1099–1103. [CrossRef] [PubMed]
164. Jacob, F.; Monod, J. Genetic regulatory mechanisms in the synthesis of proteins. *J. Mol. Biol.* **1961**, *3*, 318–356. [CrossRef] [PubMed]
165. Monod, J.; Changeux, J.P.; Jacob, F. Allosteric proteins and cellular control systems. *J. Mol. Biol.* **1963**, *6*, 306–329. [CrossRef] [PubMed]
166. Davidson, E.H.; Erwin, D.H. Gene regulatory networks and the evolution of animal body plans. *Science* **2006**, *311*, 796–800. [CrossRef] [PubMed]

167. Kaplow, I.M.; Lawler, A.J.; Schäffer, D.E.; Srinivasan, C.; Sestili, H.H.; Wirthlin, M.E.; Phan, B.N.; Prasad, K.; Brown, A.R.; Zhang, X.; et al. Relating enhancer genetic variation across mammals to complex phenotypes using machine learning. *Science* **2022**, *380*, 644. [CrossRef]
168. Collins, J.P.; Gilbert, S.; Laubichler, M.D.; Müller, G.B. Modeling in EvoDevo: How to integrate development, evolution, and ecology. In *Modelling Biology*; MIT Press: Cambridge, MA, USA, 2007; pp. 355–378.
169. Friston, K.; Friedman, D.A.; Constant, A.; Knight, V.; Parr, T.; Campbell, J.O. A variational synthesis of evolutionary and developmental dynamics. *arXiv* **2023**, arXiv:2303.04898. [CrossRef] [PubMed]
170. Szathmáry, E.; Maynard Smith, J. The major evolutionary transitions. *Nature* **1995**, *374*, 227–232. [CrossRef]
171. Carney, M. *Values: An Economist's Guide to Everything that Matters*; William Collins: London, UK, 2021.
172. Bellah, R.N.; Madsen, R.; Tipton, S.M.; Sullivan, W.M.; Swidler, A. *The Good Society*; Alfred Knopf: New York, NY, USA, 1985.
173. Johnson, S.; Bilovich, A.; Tuckett, D. Conviction narrative theory: A theory of choice under radical uncertainty. *Behav. Brain Sci.* **2020**, *46*, e82. [CrossRef]
174. Maslow, A.H. A theory of human motivation. *Psychol. Rev.* **1943**, *50*, 370. [CrossRef]
175. Heylighen, F. A cognitive-systemic reconstruction of Maslow's theory of self-actualization. *Behav. Sci.* **1992**, *37*, 39–58. [CrossRef]
176. MacIntyre, A. *After Virtue: A study in Moral Theory*; University of Notre Dame Press: Notre Dame, India, 1984.
177. Heyes, C. Rethinking Norm Psychology. *Perspect. Psychol. Sci.* **2022**. [CrossRef] [PubMed]
178. Drucker, P. *The Practice of Management*; Routledge: Oxford, UK, 2012.
179. Burns, J.M. *Transforming Leadership: A New Pursuit of Happiness*; Grove Press: New York, NY, USA, 2004.
180. Burns, J.M. *Leadership*; Harper Classics: New York, NY, USA, 2010.
181. Mohr, L.B. The concept of an organisational goal. *Am. Political Sci. Rev.* **1973**, *67*, 470–481. [CrossRef]
182. Simon, H.A. *Administrative Behavior*; Simon and Schuster: New York, NY, USA, 2013.
183. Etzioni, A. *Moral Dimension: Toward a New Economics*; Simon and Schuster: New York, NY, USA, 2010.
184. Dennett, D.C. *Elbow Room, New Edition: The Varieties of Free Will Worth Wanting*; MIT Press: Cambridge, MA, USA, 2015.
185. Ismael, J. *How Physics Makes Us Free*; Oxford University Press: Oxford, UK, 2016.
186. List, C. *Why Free Will Is Real*; Harvard: Cambridge, MA, USA, 2019.
187. Potter, H.D.; Mitchell, K.J. Naturalising agent causation. *Entropy* **2022**, *24*, 472. [CrossRef] [PubMed]
188. Noble, R.; Noble, D. Harnessing stochasticity: How organisms make choices. *Chaos* **2018**, *28*, 106309. [CrossRef] [PubMed]
189. Brown, A.I.; Sivak, D.A. Theory of nonequilibrium free energy transduction by molecular machines. *Chem. Rev.* **2019**, *120*, 434–459. [CrossRef] [PubMed]
190. Ball, P. *Organisms as Agents of Evolution*; John Templeton Foundation: West Conshohocken, PA, USA, 2023.
191. Ellis, G. Physics, determinism, and the brain. In *Top-Down Causation and Emergence*; Vooshholz, J., Gabriel, M., Eds.; Springer: Cham, Germany, 2021.
192. Carroll, S.M. The Quantum Field Theory on Which the Everyday World Supervenes. In *Levels of Reality in Science and Philosophy: Re-Examining the Multi-Level Structure of Reality*; Springer International Publishing: Cham, Germany, 2022; pp. 27–46.
193. Mayer, C. *Prosperity: Better Business Makes the Greater Good*; Oxford University Press: Oxford, UK, 2018.
194. Mossio, M.; Moreno, A. Organisational closure in biological organisms. Hist. Philos. *Life Sci.* **2010**, *32*, 269–288.
195. Ellis, G. Physics, complexity and causality. *Nature* **2005**, *435*, 743. [CrossRef]
196. Grasso, M.; Albantakis, L.; Lang, J.P.; Tononi, G. Causal reductionism and causal structures. *Nat. Neurosci.* **2021**, *24*, 1348–1355. [CrossRef]
197. Horgan, J. The Delusion of Scientific Omniscience. *Crosscheck*. 2023. Available online: https://blogs.scientificamerican.com/cross-check/the-delusion-of-scientific-omniscience/ (accessed on 11 June 2023).

entropy

MDPI

Article

Flickering Emergences: The Question of Locality in Information-Theoretic Approaches to Emergence

Thomas F. Varley [1,2]

[1] Department of Psychological and Brain Sciences, Indiana University Bloomington, Bloomington, IN 47405, USA; tvarley@iu.edu
[2] School of Informatics, Computing, & Engineering, Indiana University Bloomington, Bloomington, IN 47405, USA

Abstract: "Emergence", the phenomenon where a complex system displays properties, behaviours, or dynamics not trivially reducible to its constituent elements, is one of the defining properties of complex systems. Recently, there has been a concerted effort to formally define emergence using the mathematical framework of information theory, which proposes that emergence can be understood in terms of how the states of wholes and parts collectively disclose information about the system's collective future. In this paper, we show how a common, foundational component of information-theoretic approaches to emergence implies an inherent instability to emergent properties, which we call *flickering emergence*. A system may, on average, display a meaningful emergent property (be it an informative coarse-graining, or higher-order synergy), but for particular configurations, that emergent property falls apart and becomes misinformative. We show existence proofs that flickering emergence occurs in two different frameworks (one based on coarse-graining and another based on multivariate information decomposition) and argue that any approach based on temporal mutual information will display it. Finally, we argue that flickering emergence should not be a disqualifying property of any model of emergence, but that it should be accounted for when attempting to theorize about how emergence relates to practical models of the natural world.

Keywords: emergence; causality; higher-order interaction; partial information decomposition; synergy; networks; neuroscience

1. Introduction

Despite the ubiquity of "emergence" in the natural world, a satisfying and broadly accepted formal definition of emergence has remained an outstanding problem in the field of complex systems. In the last decade, there has been a concerted push by multiple groups of theorists to develop a formal, mathematical approach to the question of emergence [1–4]. Many (although not all) of these approaches have used information theory [5] as the *lingua franca* on which to build their formal systems. We argue, however, that the specific applications of information to emergence bring with them curious consequences that have gone largely un-discussed and may have implications for how we think about emergent dynamics.

Essentially, every information-theoretic approach to emergence starts with the question of how the structure of a system in the present informs on the structure of the system in the future. There is an intuitive sense that, for very emergent systems, the "whole" somehow takes on a "life of its own" that is not trivially reducible to the dynamics of each element (in contrast to the way that the behaviour of an ideal gas can be trivially reduced to all of its elements, for example). There are a large number of ways to formalize this intuition: for example, Hoel et al. take a renormalization-based approach, comparing the full system to some coarse-grained micro-scale [6,7]. In contrast, Mediano, Rosas et al. consider joint-versus-marginal mereological relationships [8], and Chang et al. consider agent/environment distinctions and autopoetic notions of information closure [3]. These different approaches show how rich the space of putative "emergences" might be, even when starting from an apparently simple common starting point.

In addition to the common focus on how the present informs the future, another key, but rarely discussed commonality is that they are average measures, summarizing the expected value of a whole ensemble of possibilities in a single scalar value. This is a real limitation, as complex systems can hide a considerable amount of variability around the long-term mean (at the risk of being glib, the long-term, expected state of the Universe is one of bleak desolation and entropic void, but there's quite a bit happening this week).

If, instead of considering the expected value over a whole distribution of configurations, one considers the local information contained in individual moments, they will see that the scalar, summary statistic can elide a large amount of variability. Sometimes, unexpected events can occur that break from the average behaviour of a system. For example, consider a flock of of starlings: on average, the dynamics of the flock show a strong, emergent structure, but when the birds unexpectedly scatter (perhaps in response to a predator), that emergence temporarily "breaks down" and must reform again in the future.

Written out in the language of information theory, these transient moments when the emergent dynamics break down can be understood as local instances of "misinformation" [9]—when knowing the present transiently stops helping you better predict the future (and sometimes can actually make your predictions worse). I call this *flickering emergence*: when the emergent structure "flickers" and the system briefly stops being a "whole" and becomes more like a collection of "parts". As we will see, this possibility is an unavoidable consequence of any formal approach based on time-delayed mutual information. This phenomenon has not been discussed much in prior literature: one of the few instances was in the context of integrated information theory, where Hoel et al. showed that, for some systems, the integrated information could be greater at the macro-scale for some transitions, but not others [6]. The state-dependent nature of integrated information in this context could be seen as an early example of flickering emergence, although it relied on the specific (and somewhat baroque) mathematical machinery of integrated information theory and was not discussed as a general phenomenon. Similarly, Comolatti and Hoel [10] described a large number of state-dependent definitions of "causation" in the context of causal emergence, although the question of the stability of local emergence is not discussed.

2. Information Theory and Emergence

2.1. A Note on Notation

The information theoretic formalisms around emergence unfortunately require notation to represent a number of overlapping, and potentially confusing, concepts. In general, one-dimensional random variables will be represented with italicized uppercase letters (e.g., X). Specific realizations of that variable will be denoted with lower-case, italicized letters (e.g., $X = x$). The support set of X (i.e., the set of all states X can adopt) will be denoted with Fraktur font: $\mathfrak{X}$. We would read: $\sum_{x \in \mathfrak{X}} \mathcal{P}(x)$ as "the sum of the probabilities of every state x that our random variable X can adopt". Multidimensional variables will be denoted with boldface uppercase (e.g., $\mathbf{X}$), their specific realizations as $\mathbf{x}$, and their support sets in Fraktur font ($\boldsymbol{\mathfrak{X}}$).

In addition to general and specific variables, there is also a need to differentiate between micro-scales and macro-scales. We will say that the *macro-scale* (after coarse-graining) of $\mathbf{X}$ is $\tilde{\mathbf{X}}$, and the specific realizations are $\mathbf{x}$ and $\tilde{\mathbf{x}}$ respectively. Only multivariate systems can be coarse-grained, and for our purposes, coarse-grained systems will always have at least two elements making them up. The expected value of a function will be denoted with calligraphic font (e.g., the expected mutual information between X and Y is $\mathcal{I}(X;Y)$), while specific, local functions will be in italicized lowercase (e.g., the local mutual information between $X = x$ and $Y = y$ is $i(x;y)$). Finally, following [11], we will denote time with subscript indexing (i.e., X_t is the random variable X at time t), and set membership with superscript indexing (i.e., X^k is the kth element of $\mathbf{X}$). Both kinds of indexing may be used simultaneously.

2.2. Expected and Local Mutual Information

The core of almost all information-theoretic approaches to emergence has been to start with the *mutual information* between the past state of a system and its own future (sometimes called the *excess entropy* [12]). The mutual information is a fundamental measure of the (statistical) interaction between two variables [5]. For two variables X and Y with states drawn from support sets $\mathfrak{X}$ and $\mathfrak{Y}$ according to $\mathcal{P}(X)$ and $\mathcal{P}(Y)$:

$$\mathcal{I}(X,Y) = \sum_{\substack{x\in\mathfrak{X} \\ y\in\mathfrak{Y}}} \mathcal{P}(x,y)\log\left(\frac{\mathcal{P}(x,y)}{\mathcal{P}(x)\mathcal{P}(y)}\right) \tag{1}$$

$$= \mathcal{H}(X) - \mathcal{H}(X|Y) \tag{2}$$

where $\mathcal{H}$ is the Shannon entropy function. $\mathcal{I}(X;Y)$ quantifies how much knowing the state of X reduces our uncertainty about the state of Y on average (and vice versa, as it is a symmetric measure). Consequently, the mutual information is fundamentally about our ability as observers to make inferences about objects of study under conditions of uncertainty. Unlike more standard correlation measures, mutual information is non-parametric, sensitive to non-linear relationships, and strictly non-negative (i.e., knowing the state of X can never make us more uncertain about the state of Y). Being an average measure, $\mathcal{I}$ can also be understood as the *expected value* over a distribution of particular configurations:

$$\mathcal{I}(X;Y) = \mathbb{E}_{X,Y}\left[\log\left(\frac{\mathcal{P}(x,y)}{\mathcal{P}(x)\mathcal{P}(y)}\right)\right] \tag{3}$$

We can "unroll" this expected value to get a *local* mutual information for every combination of realizations $X = x, Y = y$ (sometimes referred to as the pointwise mutual information):

$$i(x;y) = \log\left(\frac{\mathcal{P}(x,y)}{\mathcal{P}(x)\mathcal{P}(y)}\right) \tag{4}$$

$$= h(x) - h(x|y) \tag{5}$$

Unlike the average mutual information, the local mutual information can be negative: if $\mathcal{P}(x,y) < \mathcal{P}(x)\mathcal{P}(y)$ then $i(x;y) < 0$. To build intuition, consider the case where $\mathcal{I}(X;Y) > 0$. On average, if we know that $X = x$, we will be better at correctly inferring the state of Y than if we were basing our prediction on Y's statistics alone (and vice versa). Now, suppose we observe the particular configuration (x,y). What does it mean to say that $i(x;y) < 0$ when $\mathcal{I}(X;Y) > 0$? It means that the particular configuration (x,y) that we are observing would be more likely if $X \perp Y$ then if they are actually coupled (which we know, *a priori* that they are). Said differently, we would be more surprised to see $X = x$ if we knew that $Y = y$ than vice versa (see Equation (5)). *Local mutual information is negative when a system is transiently breaking from its own average, long-term behaviour.*

2.3. Temporal Mutual Information and Emergence

As mentioned above, a common starting point to assess formal theories of emergence is the time-delayed mutual information: information about the future that is disclosed by knowledge of the past. The total amount of information the entire past discloses about the entire future is the *excess entropy* [12]:

$$\mathcal{E}(X) = \mathcal{I}(X_{0:t-1}; X_{t:\infty}) \tag{6}$$

where $X_{0:t-1}$ refers to the joint state of the entire past (from time $t = 0$ to the immediate past) and $X_{t:\infty}$ refers to the entire future, from the present on. $\mathcal{E}(X)$ then provides a measure of the total dynamical "structure" of X (although it does not reveal how that structure is apportioned out over elements, see [11] for further discussion). Given the practical difficulties associated with infinitely long time series, it is common to assume that the system under study is Markovian and only "remembers" information from one time-step to the next. In this case, we would say that the constrained excess entropy is just:

$$\mathcal{E}(X) = \mathcal{I}(X_{t-1}; X_t) \tag{7}$$

For a discrete system that can only adopt a finite number of states from the support set $\mathfrak{X}$, the temporal structure of the whole system can be represented in a *transition probability matrix* (Figure 1), which gives the conditional probability $P(x_t|x_{t-1})$ for every $x \in \mathfrak{X}$. Being a special case of the bivariate mutual information, the excess entropy can also be localized in the same way (and can also be either positive or negative):

$$e(x) = i(x_{t-1}; x_t) \tag{8}$$

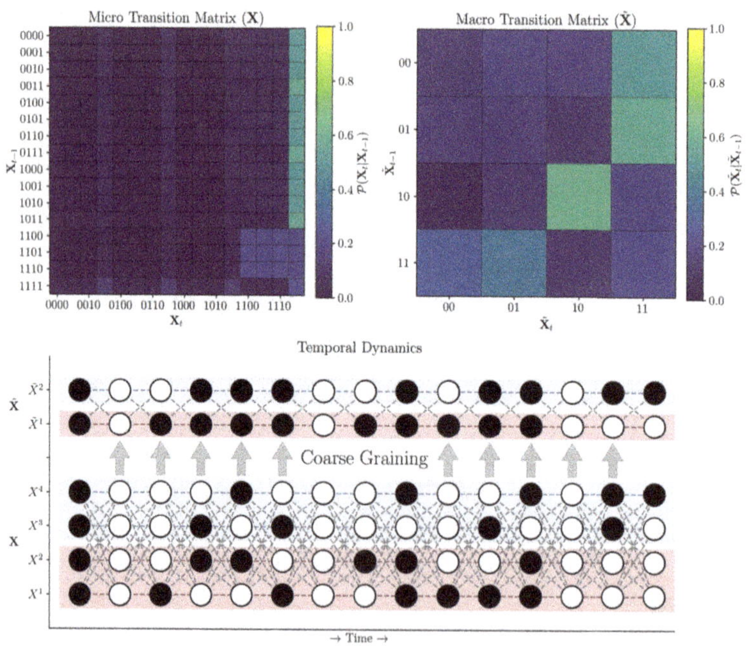

Figure 1. Transition probability matrices for a micro- and macro-scale system. Top Left: The transition probability matrix for the micro-scale view of system **X**. Each row corresponds to a possible past state $\mathbf{X}_{t-1}$, and each columns corresponds to a possible future state $\mathbf{X}_t$. The value of each cell TPM$_{ij}$ gives the conditional probability of transitioning to future state $\mathbf{x}_t$ given that the system is in state $\mathbf{x}_{t-1}$. **Top Right:** The transition probability matrix for the macro-scale of **X** (denoted as $\tilde{\mathbf{X}}$). **Bottom:** A cartoon showing the coarse-graining procedure. The micro-scale boolean network model **X** has four, binary, interconnected elements (X^{1-4}), which update their states according to the micro-scale TPM as the system evolves through time (each "column" corresponds to the state of every element in **X** at a given moment in time). When coarse graining, pairs of nodes are grouped together using a logical-AND gate. The two micro-scale nodes X^1 and X^2 get mapped to macro-scale node $\tilde{X}^2$, as indicated by the blue colour, and likewise for the red-labelled nodes. The state-transition dynamics of the macro-scale system is governed by the macro-scale TPM.

When $e(x) < 0$, the particular transition $(x_{t-1}; x_t)$ would be more likely to occur if subsequent moments were being drawn at random from some distribution $\mathcal{P}(X)$, rather than showing a temporal structure. If $\mathcal{P}(x_t|x_{t-1}) < \mathcal{P}(x_t)$, then you would be less likely to guess the correct x_t if you knew the state x_{t-1} then you would be if x_t was being randomly selected from a 0-memory process. You would be more surprised to see $x_t|x_{t-1}$ than you otherwise would be. Your prediction of the future has been misinformed by the statistics of the evolving system. For formal theories of emergence that rely on the excess entropy, this kind of breakage from the system's long-term expected statistics may represent a kind of failure mode whereby whatever "higher-order" dependency we are tracking is "interrupted". The past transiently ceases to inform of the future and instead misinforms.

2.4. *Two Formal Approaches to Emergence*

Here we focus on two formal approaches to emergence: the coarse-graining approach first proposed by Hoel et al. [1], and an integrated information approach, from Mediano, Rosas et al. [13]. We chose these two since, despite using much of the same mathematical machinery to answer a common question, they lead to very different interpretations of what emergence is. We should briefly note, however, that these are not the only information-theoretic formal approaches to emergence, for example Barnett and Seth have a proposal based on dynamical independence between micro- and macro-scales [4], and Chang et al. proposed a theory based on scale-specific information closure [3,14]. Both of these frameworks are based on excess entropy, or slight modifications thereof (Barnett and Seth consider the temporal conditional mutual information, for example). Based on the use of temporal mutual information, we anticipate that incongruous dynamics and flickering emergence are likely to appear in local formulations of both approaches (barring an unexpected mathematical result).

2.4.1. Coarse-Graining Approaches to Emergence

This framework was one of the first explicit, formal information-theoretic approaches to emergence, and remains one of the most well-developed. The coarse-graining approach compares the informational properties of a system $\mathbf{X}$ with the properties of a dimensionally reduced model $\tilde{\mathbf{X}}$. The core measure is the effective information, which is the excess entropy with a maximum-entropy distribution forced on the distribution of past states:

$$\mathcal{F}(\mathbf{X}) = \mathcal{E}(\mathbf{X})_{|\mathcal{H}(\mathbf{X}_{t-1})=\mathcal{H}^{\max}} \tag{9}$$

$$= \mathcal{I}(\mathbf{X}_{t-1}^{\mathcal{H}_{\max}}; \mathbf{X}_t) \tag{10}$$

The effective information quantifies how much knowing the past reduces your uncertainty about the future if all past states are equally likely. Consequently, it is a statistical approximation of experimental intervention: by forcing the prior distribution to be flat, $\mathcal{F}(\mathbf{X})$ is not confounded by the potential for biases introduced by an inhomogeneous distribution $\mathcal{P}(\mathbf{X}_{t-1})$. $\mathcal{F}$ is bounded from above by $\log(N)$ (where $N = |\mathfrak{X}|$): if $\mathcal{F}(\mathbf{X}) = \log(N)$, then knowing $\mathbf{X}_{t-1}$ completely resolves all uncertainty about the future (every x_{t-1} deterministically leads to a unique x_t). In contrast, if $\mathcal{F}(\mathbf{X}) = 0$, then knowing the past reduces no uncertainty about the future. This bound allows to normalize $\mathcal{F}$ to the interval $[0,1]$, which we refer to as the *effectiveness* ($\bar{\mathcal{F}}(\mathbf{X})$):

$$\bar{\mathcal{F}}(\mathbf{X}) = \frac{\mathcal{F}(\mathbf{X})}{\log(N)} \tag{11}$$

Hoel et al. [1] claim that "emergence" occurs when, for system $\mathbf{X}$, there exists some coarse-graining $\tilde{\mathbf{X}}$ such that:

$$\log\left(\frac{\bar{\mathcal{F}}(\tilde{\mathbf{X}})}{\bar{\mathcal{F}}(\mathbf{X})}\right) > 0 \tag{12}$$

In this case, the macro-scale is more effective than the micro-scale: knowing the past of the macro-scale resolves a greater proportion of the uncertainty about the future of the macro-scale than it would when using the "full", micro-scale model.

Consider the example system displayed in Figure 1: here, a 4-element, Boolean network evolves according to the micro-scale transition probability matrix. The system is then bipartitioned and each pair of elements (indicated by colour) is aggregated into a macro-scale with a lossy logical function (logical-AND), resulting in the 2-element system. Crucially, $\mathbf{X}$ is a system that displays non-trivial emergence upon coarse-graining into $\tilde{\mathbf{X}}$: $\log(\bar{\mathcal{F}}(\tilde{\mathbf{X}})/\bar{\mathcal{F}}(\mathbf{X})) \approx 0.202$.

2.4.2. Synergy-Based Approaches to Emergence

The synergy-based approach to emergence takes a different tack when looking for emergent phenomena in multi-element, dynamical systems. Where the coarse-graining emergence considers the relationship between scales, the integrated emergence looks at the relationships between "wholes" and "parts" at a single scale. Once again, the primary measure is the excess entropy (a maximum entropy prior is not explicitly assumed, although it is an option [13]). We begin with the insight that, for a multivariate system $\mathbf{X}$, $\mathcal{E}(\mathbf{X})$ gives a measure of the total temporal information structure of the whole, but it says nothing about how that information flow is apportioned out over various elements of $\mathbf{X}$. For example, if every element of $\mathbf{X}$ is independent of every other the excess entropy can still be greater than zero if the excess entropy of each part is greater than zero:

$$\mathcal{E}(\mathbf{X}) = \sum_{i=1}^{|\mathbf{X}|} \mathcal{E}(X^i) \iff X^i \perp X^j \forall X^i, X^j \in \mathbf{X} \tag{13}$$

In this case of a totally disintegrated system, then $\mathcal{E}(\mathbf{X}) - \sum_{i=1}^{|\mathbf{X}|} \mathcal{E}(X^i) = 0$: the problem of predicting the future of the "whole" trivially reduces to predicting the futures of each of the "parts" considered individually. This insight prompted Balduzzi and Tononi to propose a heuristic measure of "integration" (the degree to which the whole is greater than the sum of its parts), which we refer to as $\Phi(\mathbf{X})$:

$$\Phi(\mathbf{X}) = \mathcal{E}(\mathbf{X}) - \sum_{i=1}^{|\mathbf{X}|} \mathcal{E}(X_i) \tag{14}$$

If $\Phi(\mathbf{X}) > 0$, then there is some predictive information in the joint state of the whole $\mathbf{X}$ that is not accessible when considering all of the parts individually. This is a rough definition of "integrated emergence": when the future of the whole can only be predicted by considering the whole qua itself and not any of its constituent parts.

$\Phi(\mathbf{X})$ is only a rough heuristic though, and it can be negative if a large amount of redundant information swamps the synergistic part [15]. Recently, Mediano, Rosas, et al. introduced a complete decomposition of the excess entropy for a multivariate system. Based on the partial information decomposition framework [16,17], the *integrated information decomposition* (ΦID) [13,15] reveals how all of the elements of $\mathbf{X}$ (and ensembles of elements) collectively disclose temporal information about each-other. A rigorous derivation of the framework is beyond the scope of this paper, but intuitively the ΦID works by decomposing $\mathcal{E}(\mathbf{X})$ into an additive set of non-overlapping values called "integrated information atoms", each of which describes a particular dependency between elements (or ensembles of elements) at time $t-1$ and time t. For example, the atom $\{X^1\} \to \{X^1\}$ refers to the information that X^1 and only X^1 communicates to itself and only itself through time ("information storage"). Similarly, $\{X^1\} \to \{X^2\}$ is the information that X^1 uniquely transfers to X^2 alone. More exotic combinations also exist, for example $\{X^1\}\{X^2\} \to \{X^2\}$ which is the information redundantly present in X^1 and X^2 simultaneously that is "pruned" from X^1 and left in X^2.

The ΦID framework allows us to refine the original heuristic $\Phi(\mathbf{X})$ and construct a more rigorous metric for emergence: for a two-element system, the atom $\{X^1, X^2\} \to$

$\{X^1, X^2\}$ is the synergistic information that the whole (and only the whole) discloses about its own future (Mediano et al. refer to this as "causal decoupling", although we will refer to it simply as temporal synergy). It can be thought of as measuring the persistence of the whole qua itself without making reference to any simpler combinations of constituent elements. The ΦID framework also provides another emergence-related metric "for free:" Mediano et al. claim that "downward causation" [18,19] is revealed by atoms such as $\{X^1, X^2\} \to \{X^1\}$, where the synergistic past of the whole informs on the future of one of its individual constituent atoms. In this paper we focus on the temporal synergy, but all of the same technical concerns (localization, incongruous dynamics, etc) also applies to the downward causation atoms.

For a two-variable system evolving through time (such as our example macro-scale $\tilde{\mathbf{X}}$), it turns out that there are only sixteen unique integrated information atoms, and they are conveniently structured into an elegant lattice (see Figure 2). This means that given some "double-redundancy" function that can solve for the bottom of the lattice ($\{X^1\}\{X^2\} \to \{X^1\}\{X^2\}$), it is possible to bootstrap all the other atoms via Mobius inversion. For the given lattice $\mathfrak{A}$, the value of every atom ($\Phi_\partial(\boldsymbol{A})$) can be calculated recursively by:

$$\Phi_\partial(\boldsymbol{A} \to \boldsymbol{B}) = I_{\tau sx}(\boldsymbol{A} \to \boldsymbol{B}) - \sum_{\substack{\boldsymbol{A}' \to \boldsymbol{B}' \\ \preceq \\ \boldsymbol{A} \to \boldsymbol{B}}} \Phi_\partial(\boldsymbol{A}' \to \boldsymbol{B}') \tag{15}$$

where $I_{\tau sx}$ is the double redundancy function proposed by Varley in [11], which quantifies the shared information across time (for a more detailed discussion, see the above citation). The Mobius inversion framework provides an intuitive understanding of the double synergy atom $\{X^1, X^2\} \to \{X^1, X^2\}$: it is that portion of $\mathcal{E}(\mathbf{X})$ that is not disclosed by any simpler combination of elements in $\mathbf{X}$ then $\mathbf{X}$ itself. The system $\tilde{\mathbf{X}}$ shown in Figure 3 (upper right) shows non-trivial integrated emergence, with a value of $\Phi_\partial(\{X^1, X^2\} \to \{X^1, X^2\}) \approx 0.031$ bit.

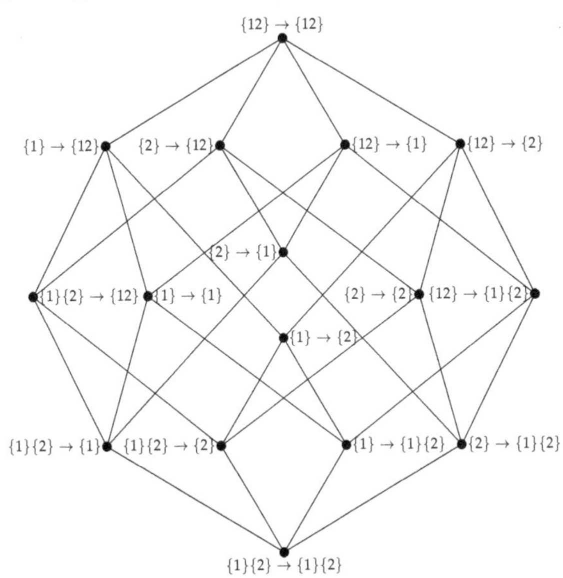

Figure 2. The double-redundancy lattice for a system $\mathbf{X} = \{X^1, X^2\}$. Every vertex of the lattice corresponds to a specific dependency between information in one element (or ensemble of elements) $t-1$ and another at time t. We use index-only notation following Williams and Beer [13,16] for notational compactness.

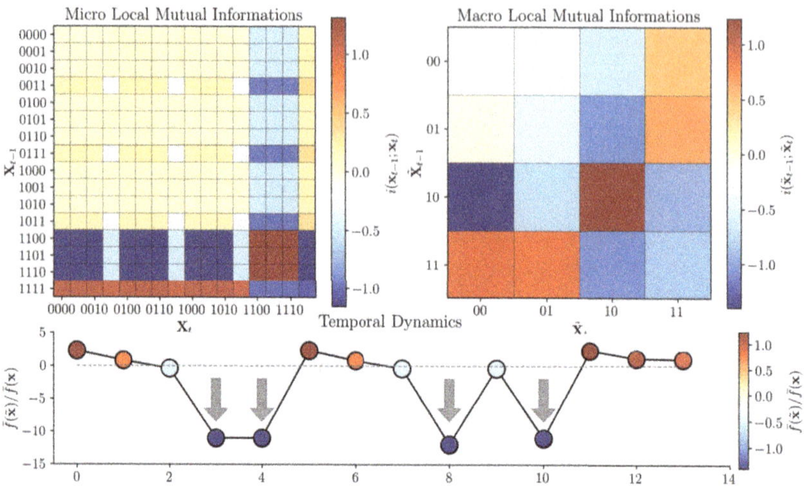

Figure 3. Local information of transitions at macro- and micro-scales. Top Left: The local mutual informations associated with every transition at the macro scale. We can see a mixture of informative and misinformative transitions distributed over the matrix. **Top Right:** The local mutual informations associated with every transition at the micro-scale. We can see that a very large number of weakly informative transitions at the micro-scale (upper left-hand square) get mapped to misinformative transitions at the macro-scale (upper left-hand square of the macro-scale matrix). **Bottom:** A time series generated by a weighted random walk on the micro-scale transition matrix. We plot the ratio of the local mutual information of each transition at the micro-scale to the associated transition at the macro-scale. If the microscale is informative and the macroscale is misinformative, we say that that transition displays "incongruous dynamics". This "incongruous dynamics" shows that, while on average the macro-scale may be more informative than the micro-scale, there are a large number of micro-scale transitions that become not only less informative, but actively misinformative!

3. Incongruous Emergence Appears in Multiple Frameworks

Having described how both formal approaches to emergence choose to define it, we are equipped to discuss local *incongruous* emergence. As mentioned above, incongruous dynamics occurs when, locally, the information structure of a system is the opposite of the expected tendency. Even if the system on average displays some emergent dynamic, it does not necessarily follow that it displays emergent properties at every moment. Below, we will show how the localizability of excess entropy implies incongruous dynamics can occur in both coarse-graining and synergy-based emergence frameworks.

3.1. Flickering Emergence in Coarse-Graining Approaches to Emergence

We say that a system $\mathbf{X}$ admits an emergent macro-scale $\tilde{\mathbf{X}}$ if $\log(\bar{\mathcal{F}}(\tilde{\mathbf{X}})/\bar{\mathcal{F}}(\mathbf{X})) > 0$, where $\bar{\mathcal{F}}(\mathbf{X})$ is the effectiveness of $\mathbf{X}$ (Equation (11)). In the context of the local excess entropy, the normalization by $\log(N)$ does not necessarily make sense (the inequality that $\mathcal{E}(\mathbf{X}) \leq \log(N)$ only holds in the average case: the local mutual information is unbounded), however, we can instead consider the signs of the relevant local excess entropies. When a change in sign occurs, information that may have been informative at one scale (i.e., helps us make better predictions about the future) may be misinformative at another (i.e., pushes us towards the wrong prediction).

We say that incongruous dynamics occurs when $e(\tilde{\mathbf{x}}) < 0$ and $e(\mathbf{x}) > 0$. That is, when a transition that is informative at the micro-scale gets mapped to a transition that is misinformative at the macro-scale. From the perspective of a scientist attempting to understand a complex system, this would occur if, on average more predictive power (or controllability) is accessible at the macro-scale, but there exist a subset of transitions at the micro-scale that actually do worse when coarse-grained. When considering the system in Figure 1 and its associated macro-scale, we can construct the local excess entropy for every transition (visualized in Figure 3).

It is visually apparent that the large number of weakly informative transitions at the micro-scale are getting mapped to weakly misinformative transitions at the macro-scale. In fact, ≈52.73% of informative micro-scale edges map to misinformative macro-scale edges! This means that, even though our toy system $\mathbf{X}$ displays non-zero emergence on average, over half of all informative micro-scale transitions are mapped to misinformative macro-scale transitions during coarse-graining. These are generally lower-probability transitions however, which accounts for the overall display of emergence. By running a random walk on $\mathbf{X}$ and computing the ratio $e(\tilde{\mathbf{x}}_t)/e(\mathbf{x}_t)$ we can see a number of instances where the sign is negative because incongruous dynamics have occurred (indicated with grey arrows). This is an example of what we call "flickering emergence", where the emergent quality transiently falls apart, like a candle sputtering.

Application to Networks

The phenomenon of incongruous dynamics is also relevant to extensions to other domains, such as network science. Klein, Griebenow, and Hoel showed that applying the same framework to the dynamics of random walkers on complex networks could reveal informative higher scales in the network structure, which in turn could be linked to many aspects of graph theory and network science [20,21]. In this approach, nodes in a network are aggregated into "macro-nodes" (analogous to communities), and those macro-nodes collapsed into a simpler network. From there, the effectiveness of the micro-scale network can be compared to the effectiveness of the macro-scale network in the usual way. This topological emergence has been found in a variety of biological networks and associated with evolutionary drives towards robust, fault-tolerant structures [21].

In keeping with prior work, Klein et al. focused on the average information structure over the entire network, however, we can do the same kind of localized analysis on the network that we do on the Markov chains. In Figure 4 (left panel), we can see a structural connectivity matrix taken from a random subject in the Human Connectome Project data set [22] (previously studied in [23]) from which we have computed the local excess entropy associated with each edge. We then used the Infomap algorithm [24,25] on the raw structural connectivity network and coarse-grained the communities into macro-nodes. When considering the macro-scale transition probability matrix, we can see that the main diagonal (corresponding to a walker staying put) are overwhelmingly informative, while off-diagonal transitions are generally misinformative (Figure 4, centre panel). This is consistent with the intuition that, in state-transition networks, Infomap finds shallow, metastable transient attractors in the landscape [26].

While the effectiveness of the macro-scale was barely lager than the effectiveness of the micro-scale (≈0.37 bit at the micro-scale vs. ≈0.38 bit at the macro-scale), we find that incongruous dynamics is quite common in this particular network: ≈22.47% of informative micro-scale edges are mapped to macro-scale edges that are misinformative. To assess whether the distribution of informative and misinformative micro-scale edges related to the overall macro-scale structure of the network, we examined the distribution of informative and misinformative edges within and between communities/macro-nodes. We found that informative edges were roughly just as likely to link within-community nodes (≈52.3%) as between community nodes (≈47.7%), however, misinformative edges where overwhelmingly more likely to link disparate communities (≈80.4%) as opposed to fall within a single community (≈19.6%). To ensure that these results held generally and were not an artifact of the Infomap algorithm, we replicated these results using a spinglass [27,28] and a leading eigenvector community detection algorithm and found that the results were consistent (see Supplementary Material). All analyses were done using the Python-iGraph package [29]. These results collectively show that, in much the same way expected effective information and emergence relate in fundamental ways to network topology, so do their local counterparts.

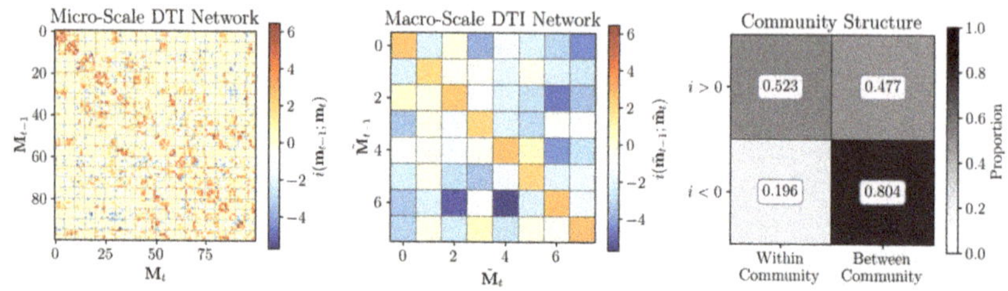

Figure 4. Incongruous dynamics in complex networks. Left: A single structural connectivity matrix taken from the Human Connectome Project [22], coloured according to the local excess entropy associated with a random walker on each edge. **Middle:** The same transition probability matrix after renormalizing the micro-scale community structure with Infomap [24,25]. **Right:** The proportion of informative and misinformative micro-scale nodes that sit within, or between, a macro-scale community.

3.2. Flickering Emergence in ΦID-Based Approaches to Emergence

In the ΦID-based framework, emergence is associated with information about the future of the "whole" that can only be learned by observing the whole itself and none of its simpler constituent components. This value can be computed using an decomposition of the excess entropy [11,13]. Like the coarse-graining framework, the decomposition of the excess entropy can be localized to particular moments in time. For a given transitions $((x^1_{t-1}, x^2_{t-1}) \to (x^1_t, x^2_t))$ with local excess entropy $e(\mathbf{x})$, we can construct a local redundancy lattice $\boldsymbol{\alpha}$ and solve it with the same Mobius inversion. All that is required is that the redundancy function is localizable in time. The function used above, $I_{\tau sx}$ is localizable and can be used to construct a local integrated information lattice for any configuration of $\mathbf{X}$ [11].

Once again, we take advantage of the distinction between informative and misinformative local mutual information for our indicator of incongruity. Here we say that incongruous dynamics occurs when the expected synergistic flow $(\{X^1, X^2\} \to \{X^1, X^2\})$ is informative (positive), but the local value of the same atom is negative. Intuitively, this is the case when, on average, the future of the whole can be meaningful predicted from its own past; however, there are some configurations where the current global state would lean an observer to make the wrong prediction about the future global state.

When considering the example macro-scale system (Figure 3), we found that 31.25% of the sixteen possible transitions had a negative value for the double-synergy atom. In Figure 5, we can see the global integrated information lattice for two different transitions, both landing in the universal-off state ((0,0)). It is clear that these two transitions have radically different local information structures, including opposite-signed double-synergy, double redundancy, and "downward causation", atoms: the expected value of any given atom elides a considerable amount of variability in the instantaneous dependencies. We can see this manifesting as flickering emergence when we run a random walk on the system and perform the ΦID for every time-step (Figure 5, Bottom): the system transiently moves through periods of informative, and misinformative emergence depending on the specific transitions occurring.

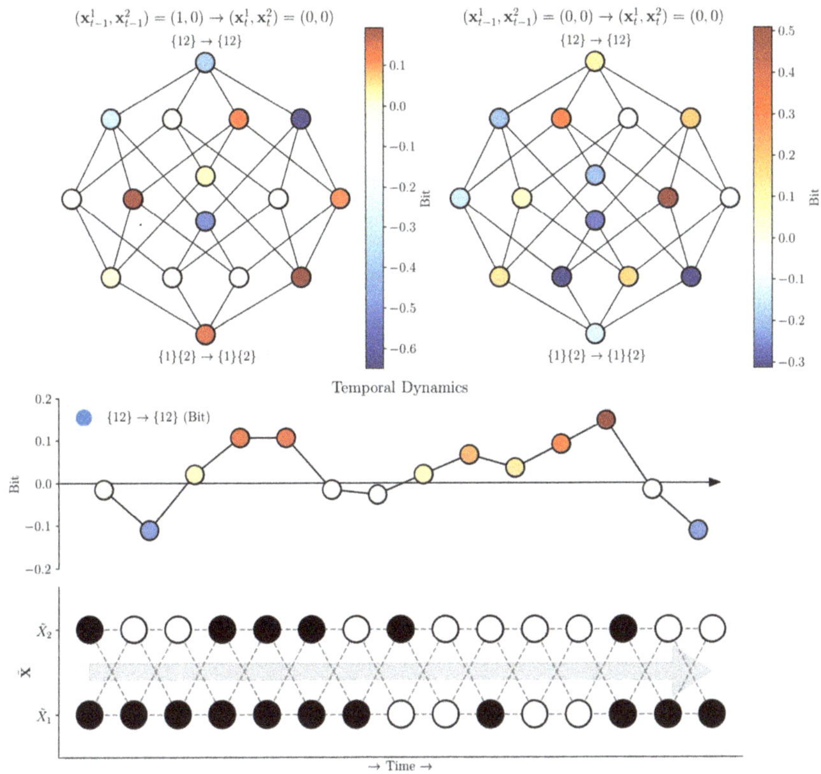

Figure 5. The structure of temporal mutual information varies across time. Top: The two double-redundancy lattices show the local integrated information decompositions for two distinct transitions ($(0,1) \to (0,0)$ and $(0,0) \to (0,0)$). Despite having the same end-state, the information structure of these two transitions is completely different. One transition has an informative causal decoupling, while the other has a misinformative one. As well as opposite-signed double-redundancy ($\{1\}\{2\} \to \{1\}\{2\}$) and a number of other discrepancies. **Bottom:** A visualization of the phenomenon of "flickering emergence" in the context of ΦID. As the system $\tilde{\mathbf{X}}$ evolves over time, it cycles through states (lower plot), and for each of those transitions, we can calculate the instantaneous causal decoupling (upper plot). We can see that incongruous dynamics can occur at different times, interspersed between congruent emergence.

4. Discussion

In this work, we have introduced the notion of "flickering emergence", which describes how a system can, on average, admit a meaningful emergent dynamic that falls apart locally when considering particular transitions. We argue that this is likely a feature of any formal approach that is built on the Shannon mutual information between the past and the future (excess entropy [12]). To demonstrate this phenomenon, we assess two approaches which share the same core feature of excess entropy, but define "emergence" in very different ways. The first takes a coarse-graining approach, comparing micro- and macro-scales [1,6,7,20], while the second takes a synergy-based approach and looks for information in the "whole" that is not accessible when considering any of the "parts [2,8].

The purpose of this paper is not to "poke holes" in, or critique, either approach to emergence. Instead, our aim has been to highlight how the particular mathematical formalism one commits to can produce intriguing new properties that may not have been obvious from the outset. In this case, the commitment to a temporal mutual information-based approach necessarily raises the question how to think about local instances and what it might mean for a measure of emergence to be locally negative.

How we interpret incongruous dynamics and flickering emergence depends largely on how we interpret "emergence" as a concept. If emergence refers solely to an observer's ability to model some process (as in [30]), then incongruous dynamics may just reflect the limitations inherent in modelling: no model makes perfect predictions in all contexts. For example, one can use a coarse-grained model of the heart as an oscillating pump very successfully and generally ignore the particular myocardial cells *when the heart is healthy*, however pathological states, such as ventricular fibrillation, can cause the predictions of the heart-as-a-pump model to diverge dangerously from the micro-scale model. In this case, the predictions of the macro-scale model fail and the apparent "emergent" structure of the pump falls apart.

If, instead of being a reflection of a modellers perspective, "emergence" is treated as an ontologically "real" process, and mapped to other observable phenomena, the situation may get more complicated. Consider the recent proposal from Luppi et al. [31], who suggest a link between integrated emergence and the persistent sense of one's conscious self as an unitary agent (also discussed in [32]). If there is an identity between temporal mutual information and the sense of self (an observable phenomena), then we are forced to wrangle with the question of temporal locality. The flickering of emergent synergy would imply some kind of associated flickering of the sense of self, or conscious awareness, which should be an observable (or at least reportable) process amenable to study.

Part of the difficulty with interpreting flickering emergence comes from the fact that it does not necessarily define *why* a particular moment breaks from the long-term behaviour. In some cases, it may merely be statistical fluctuations about the mean, while in others it might be reflective of an underlying change in the causal structure of the system. Any interpretation must be done in the context of the particular system under study and leverage domain expertise beyond what is accessible just from the statistics alone.

In addition to the main question about local information dynamics, a second aim of this paper was to bring the two frameworks into more explicit dialogue. Both approaches have developed largely in parallel (despite having a common intellectual heritage in integrated information theory) and propose different notions of what it means to be emergent. As we have seen however, they share significant commonalities in spite of their differences. While "emergence" is typically discussed as a single phenomena in complex systems, there is a strong argument to be made for the "pragmatic pluralist" approach [33,34], in which many different "kinds" of emergence are recognized in parallel. Under such a framework, both frameworks discussed here would both be considered valid kinds of emergent dynamics: similar enough to belong to a common category of phenomena, but distinct enough to be considered separate. This is very similar to how the question of defining "complexity" has practically been resolved: historically, there has been considerable debate on how we might define "complexity" in "complex systems", and various measures have been proposed over the years, including algorithmic compressibility [35], entropy rate [36], and integration/segregation balance [37]. Despite the considerable ink spilled on the question, Feldman and Crutchfield argued that there likely is not a single measure of what it means to be "complex" and that mathematical attempts at a universally intuitive measure were misguided [38]. Instead, the field has largely moved towards an understanding that different notions of "complexity" are appropriate in different contexts and can illuminate different aspects of system dynamics, all of which may be considered "complex" in their own way (for example, see [26], which proposes the notion of a "dynamical morphospace" to characterize systems along different axes complex dynamics). A similar resolution may end the perennial conflict between what is and is not a valid measure or kind of emergence. The multi-scale framework may turn out to be useful when attempting to think about how cells can be coarse grained into tissues (where there is a natural distinction of scales), while the integrated information framework may turn to be useful when considering the computational properties of ensembles of neurons [11] or flocking objects [8], but not vice-versa. Both of these may be instances where reductionism fails to provide the crucial insight into a collective process, but importantly, reductionism may fail *for different reasons in different contexts.*

Finally, we should note that there are other mathematical frameworks for tackling emergence in dynamical systems that are not based on classical information theory, and do not necessarily assume a fundamentally stochastic dynamical system (see [39] and associated papers). While stochastic models are ubiquitous in science due to the uncertainty inherent in modelling data, if the generative processes are actually deterministic, probabilistic, entropy-based models may be misleading about the causal structure of the system under study [40]. In such cases, measures of emergence based on algorithmic complexity may be more appropriate, such as the proposed measure given in [41]. There, Abrahao et al. describe an algorithmic approach to understanding emergence in finite, deterministic, dynamical systems based on trajectories through a state-space and the effects of perturbation on individual updates. The possibility of update-specific analysis implies that time-resolved analysis of emergent dynamics may not be restricted to frameworks based on Shannon information theory and expected values. Future work comparing and contrasting frameworks based on Shannon information theory and frameworks based on algorithmic information theory will help further our understanding of causal emergence in complex systems.

In summary, we feel that the problem of information-based approaches to emergence remains a rich area of research, with considerable territory remaining to be explored. Unexpected phenomena, such as flickering emergence may force us to challenge how we think about emergent properties in complex systems and potentially inform future research directions. The richness and variability of different measures is, to our mind, a feature, rather than a bug, with intriguing commonalities and differences.

5. Conclusions

Regardless of whether one prefers coarse graining-based or synergy-based approaches to emergence, and whether one chooses to think of emergence purely as a question of modelling, or of truly novel physical properties, any approach based on excess entropy is likely to display both incongruous dynamics and flickering emergence. The localizability of mutual information and related measures (such as the transfer entropy) shows us that, even when emergence (however defined) occurs on average, there can still be complex and unexpected moment-to-moment deviations from that average. Some of those deviations can run in express opposition to the expected behaviour (signified by negative local mutual information). These deviations from the long-term norm may have profound implications for how we think about emergent properties in nature, and suggest new avenues of research for scientists interested in the role emergence plays in the natural world.

Supplementary Materials: The following supporting information can be downloaded at: https://www.mdpi.com/article/10.3390/e25010054/s1, Figure S1: Replicating the network emergence results using community-detection algorithms not based on random walkers. Top: Spinglass [27,28], Bottom: Leading eigenvector community detection.

Funding: T.F.V. is supported by NSF-NRT grant 1735095, Interdisciplinary Training in Complex Networks and Systems.

Institutional Review Board Statement: Not applicable.

Data Availability Statement: No data was collected for this study. Python scripts are available from the author upon request.

Acknowledgments: I would like to thank Erik Hoel for helpful feedback on this manuscript, and Olaf Sporns for giving me the space to pursue this project when I should be focusing on finishing up my PhD.

Conflicts of Interest: The author declares no conflict of interest.

References

1. Hoel, E.P.; Albantakis, L.; Tononi, G. Quantifying causal emergence shows that macro can beat micro. *Proc. Natl. Acad. Sci. USA* **2013**, *110*, 19790–19795. [CrossRef] [PubMed]
2. Mediano, P.A.M.; Rosas, F.E.; Luppi, A.I.; Jensen, H.J.; Seth, A.K.; Barrett, A.B.; Carhart-Harris, R.L.; Bor, D. Greater than the parts: A review of the information decomposition approach to causal emergence. *Philos. Trans. R. Soc. A Math. Eng. Sci.* **2022**, *380*, 20210246. [CrossRef] [PubMed]
3. Chang, A.Y.; Biehl, M.; Yu, Y.; Kanai, R. Information Closure Theory of Consciousness. *Front. Psychol.* **2020**, *11*, 1504. [CrossRef] [PubMed]
4. Barnett, L.; Seth, A.K. Dynamical independence: Discovering emergent macroscopic processes in complex dynamical systems. *arXiv* **2021**, arXiv:2106.06511.
5. Cover, T.M.; Thomas, J.A. *Elements of Information Theory*; John Wiley & Sons: Hoboken, NJ, USA, 2012.
6. Hoel, E.P.; Albantakis, L.; Marshall, W.; Tononi, G. Can the macro beat the micro? Integrated information across spatiotemporal scales. *Neurosci. Conscious.* **2016**, *2016*, niw012. [CrossRef]
7. ErikPHoel, When the Map Is Better Than the Territory. *Entropy* **2017**, *19*, 188. [CrossRef]
8. Rosas, F.E.; Mediano, P.A.M.; Jensen, H.J.; Seth, A.K.; Barrett, A.B.; Carhart-Harris, R.L.; Bor, D. Reconciling emergences: An information-theoretic approach to identify causal emergence in multivariate data. *PLoS Comput. Biol.* **2020**, *16*, e1008289. [CrossRef]
9. Lizier, J.T. *The Local Information Dynamics of Distributed Computation in Complex Systems*; Springer Theses; Springer: Berlin/Heidelberg, Germany, 2013.
10. Renzo, Comolatti, Erik, Hoel, Causal emergence is widespread across measures of causation. *arXiv* **2022**, arXiv:2202.01854.
11. Varley, T.F. Decomposing past and future: Integrated information decomposition based on shared probability mass exclusions. *arXiv* **2022**, arXiv:2202.12992.
12. James, R.G.; Ellison, C.J.; Crutchfield, J.P. Anatomy of a bit: Information in a time series observation. *Chaos Interdiscip. J. Nonlinear Sci.* **2011**, *21*, 037109. [CrossRef]
13. Mediano, P.A.M.; Rosas, F.; Carhart-Harris, R.L.; Seth, A.K.; Barrett, A.B. Beyond integrated information: A taxonomy of information dynamics phenomena. *arXiv* **2019**, arXiv:1909.02297.
14. Bertschinger, N.; Olbrich, E.; Ay, N. Information and closure in systems theory. In *Explorations in the Complexity of Possible Life, Proceedings of the 7th German Workshop of Artificial Life, Jena, Germany, 26–28 July 2006*; IOS Press: Amsterdam, The Netherlands, 2006; pp. 9–19.
15. Mediano, P.A.M.; Rosas, F.E.; Luppi, A.I.; Carhart-Harris, R.L.; Bor, D.; Seth, A.K.; Barrett, A.B. Towards an extended taxonomy of information dynamics via Integrated Information Decomposition. *arXiv* **2021**, arXiv:2109.13186.
16. Williams, P.L.; Beer, R.D. Nonnegative Decomposition of Multivariate Information. *arXiv* **2010**, arXiv:1004.2515.
17. Gutknecht, A.J.; Wibral, M.; Makkeh, A. Bits and pieces: Understanding information decomposition from part-whole relationships and formal logic. *Proc. R. Soc. A Math. Phys. Eng. Sci.* **2021**, *477*, 20210110. [CrossRef]
18. Galaaen, Ø.S. The Disturbing Matter of Downward Causation. Ph.D. Thesis, University of Oslo, Oslo, Norway, 2006.
19. Davies, P.C.W. The Physics of Downward Causation. In *The Re-Emergence of Emergence*; Oxford University Press: Oxford, UK, 2008.
20. Klein, B.; Hoel, E. The Emergence of Informative Higher Scales in Complex Networks. *Complexity* **2020**, *2020*, e8932526. [CrossRef]
21. Klein, B.; Hoel, E.; Swain, A.; Griebenow, R.; Levin, M. Evolution and emergence: Higher order information structure in protein interactomes across the tree of life. *Integr. Biol.* **2021**, *13*, 283–294. [CrossRef]
22. Van Essen, D.C.; Smith, S.M.; Barch, D.M.; Behrens, T.E.J.; Yacoub, E.; Ugurbil, K. The WU-Minn Human Connectome Project: An overview. *NeuroImage* **2013**, *80*, 62–79. [CrossRef]
23. Pope, M.; Fukushima, M.; Betzel, R.F.; Sporns, O. Modular origins of high-amplitude cofluctuations in fine-scale functional connectivity dynamics. *Proc. Natl. Acad. Sci. USA* **2021**, *118*, e2109380118. [CrossRef]
24. Rosvall, M.; Bergstrom, C.T. Maps of random walks on complex networks reveal community structure. *Proc. Natl. Acad. Sci. USA* **2008**, *105*, 1118–1123. [CrossRef]
25. Rosvall, M.; Axelsson, D.; Bergstrom, C.T. The map equation. *Eur. Phys. J. Spec. Top.* **2009**, *178*, 13–23. [CrossRef]
26. Varley, T.F.; Denny, V.; Sporns, O.; Patania, A. Topological analysis of differential effects of ketamine and propofol anaesthesia on brain dynamics. *R. Soc. Open Sci.* **2021**, *8*, 201971. [CrossRef] [PubMed]
27. Reichardt, J.; Bornholdt, S. Statistical mechanics of community detection. *Phys. Rev. E* **2006**, *74*, 016110. [CrossRef] [PubMed]
28. Traag, V.A.; Bruggeman, J. Community detection in networks with positive and negative links. *Phys. Rev. E* **2009**, *80*, 036115. [CrossRef]
29. Csardi, G.; Nepusz, T. The igraph software package for complex network research. *InterJournal* **2006**, *1695*, 1–9.
30. Varley, T.F.; Hoel, E. Emergence as the conversion of information: A unifying theory. *Philos. Trans. R. Soc. A Math. Eng. Sci.* **2022**, *380*, 20210150. [CrossRef] [PubMed]
31. Luppi, A.I.; Mediano, P.A.M.; Rosas, F.E.; Harrison, D.J.; L Carhart-Harris, R.; Bor, D.; Stamatakis, E.A. What it is like to be a bit: An integrated information decomposition account of emergent mental phenomena. *Neurosci. Conscious.* **2021**, *2021*, niab027. [CrossRef]
32. Krakauer, D.; Bertschinger, N.; Olbrich, E.; Flack, J.C.; Ay, N. The information theory of individuality. *Theory Biosci.* **2020**, *139*, 209–223. [CrossRef] [PubMed]

33. Bedau, M.A. Weak Emergence and Context-Sensitive Reduction. In *Emergence in Science and Philosophy*; Routledge: London, UK, 2010; p. 18.
34. Bedau, M. Weak Emergence and Computer Simulation. In *Models, Simulations, and Representations*; Humphreys, P., Imbert, C., Eds.; Routledge: London, UK, 2011.
35. Ziv, J.; Lempel, A. Compression of individual sequences via variable-rate coding. *IEEE Trans. Inf. Theory* **1978**, *24*, 530–536. [CrossRef]
36. Richman, J.S.; Moorman, J.R. Physiological time-series analysis using approximate entropy and sample entropy. *Am. J. Physiol. Heart Circ.* **2000**, *278*, H2039–H2049. [CrossRef]
37. Tononi, G.; Sporns, O.; Edelman, G.M. A measure for brain complexity: Relating functional segregation and integration in the nervous system. *Proc. Natl. Acad. Sci. USA* **1994**, *91*, 5033–5037. [CrossRef]
38. Feldman, D.P.; Crutchfield, J.P. Measures of statistical complexity: Why? *Phys. Lett. A* **1998**, *238*, 244–252. [CrossRef]
39. Artime, O.; De Domenico, M. From the origin of life to pandemics: Emergent phenomena in complex systems. *Philos. Trans. R. Soc. A Math. Eng. Sci.* **2022**, *380*, 20200410. [CrossRef] [PubMed]
40. Zenil, H.; Kiani, N.A.; Tegnér, J. Low-algorithmic-complexity entropy-deceiving graphs. *Phys. Rev. E* **2017**, *96*, 012308. [CrossRef] [PubMed]
41. Abrahão, F.S.; Zenil, H. Emergence and algorithmic information dynamics of systems and observers. *Philos. Trans. R. Soc. A Math. Eng. Sci.* **2022**, *380*, 20200429. [CrossRef]

entropy

MDPI

Article

Neural Information Squeezer for Causal Emergence

Jiang Zhang [1,2,*] and Kaiwei Liu [1]

[1] School of Systems Sciences, Beijing Normal University, Beijing 100875, China
[2] Swarma Research, Beijing 100085, China
* Correspondence: zhangjiang@bnu.edu.cn

Abstract: Conventional studies of causal emergence have revealed that stronger causality can be obtained on the macro-level than the micro-level of the same Markovian dynamical systems if an appropriate coarse-graining strategy has been conducted on the micro-states. However, identifying this emergent causality from data is still a difficult problem that has not been solved because the appropriate coarse-graining strategy can not be found easily. This paper proposes a general machine learning framework called Neural Information Squeezer to automatically extract the effective coarse-graining strategy and the macro-level dynamics, as well as identify causal emergence directly from time series data. By using invertible neural network, we can decompose any coarse-graining strategy into two separate procedures: information conversion and information discarding. In this way, we can not only exactly control the width of the information channel, but also can derive some important properties analytically. We also show how our framework can extract the coarse-graining functions and the dynamics on different levels, as well as identify causal emergence from the data on several exampled systems.

Keywords: causal emergence; coarse-graining; invertible neural network

1. Introduction

Emergence, as one of the most important concepts in complex systems, describes the phenomenon that some overall properties of a system cannot be reduced to the parts [1,2]. Causality, as another significant concept, characterises the connection between cause and effect events through time [3,4] for a dynamical system. As pointed out by Hoel et al. [5,6], causality could be emergent, which means that the events of a system on the macro level may have stronger causal connections than the micro level, where the strength of causality could be measured by effective information (EI) [5,7]. This theoretical framework of causal emergence provides us a new way to understand emergence and other important conceptions in a quantitative way [8–11]. Previous works have shown that causal emergence can be applied in wide areas including studies on ant colony [12], protein interactomes [13], brain [14], and biological networks [15].

Although many concrete examples of causal emergence across different temporal and spatial scales have been shown in [5], a method to identify causal emergence merely from data is needed. This problem is hard because a method to search all possible coarse-graining strategies (functions, mappings) in a systematic and automatic way, in which the causal emergence can be shown [10], is needed.

The problem is difficult because the search space is all possible mapping functions between micro and macro, which is huge. To solve this problem, Klein et al. focuses on the complex systems with network structures [15,16], and converted the problem of coarse-graining into node clustering. That is, to find a way to group nodes into clusters such that the connections on the cluster level has larger EI than the original network. This method has been widely applied in various areas [12–14], nevertheless, it assumes that the underlying node dynamic is diffusion (random walks). Meanwhile, real complex systems have much richer node dynamics. For a general dynamic, even if the node grouping is given, the coarse-grained strategy still needs to consider how to map the micro-states of all nodes in a cluster to the macro-state of the cluster [5]. The tedious searching on a huge functional space of coarse-graining strategies is also needed.

When we consider all possible mappings, another difficulty is trivial coarse-graining strategies avoiding. An exampled trivial method is to map all the micro-states into an identical value as the macro-state. In this way, the macroscopic dynamics is only an identical mapping that will have large effective information (EI) measure. However, this can not be called causal emergence because all the information is eliminated by the coarse-graining method itself. Thus, we must find a way to exclude such trivial strategies.

An alternative way to identify causal emergence from data is based on partial information decomposition given by [10,17]. Although the methods based on information decomposition can avoid the discussion on coarse-graining strategies, a time consuming search on subsets of the system state space is also needed if we want to obtain the exact value. In addition, the reported numeric approximate method can only provide sufficient condition. Further, the method can not give the explicit coarse-graining strategy and the corresponding macro-dynamics which are useful in practice. Another common shortage shared by the two mentioned methods is that an explicit Markov transition matrix for both macro- and micro-dynamics are needed, and the transitional probabilities should be estimated from data. As a result, large bias on rare events can hardly be avoided, particularly for continuous data.

On the other hand, machine learning methods empowered by neural networks have been developed in recent years, and many cross-disciplinary applications have been made [18–21]. Equipped with this method, automated discovery of causal relationships and even dynamics of complex systems in a data driven way becomes possible [22–29]. Machine learning and neural networks can also help us to find good coarse-graining strategies [30–34]. If we treat a coarse-graining mapping as a function from micro-states to macro-states, then we can certainly approximate this function by a parameterized neural network. For example, Refs. [31,33] used normalized flow model equipped with invertible neural network to learn how to renormalize a multi-dimensional field (quantum field, images or joint probability distributions), and how to generate the field from Gaussian noise. Therefore, both the coarse-graining strategy and the generative model can be learned from data automatically.

These techniques can also help us to reveal causality on macro-level from data. Causal representation learning aims to use unsupervised representation learning to extract causal latent variables behind the observational data [35,36]. The encoding process from the original data to the latent causal variables can be understood as a kind of coarse-graining. This shows the similarity between causal emergence identification and causal representation learning; however, their basic objectives are different. Causal representation learning aims to extract the causality hidden in data, whereas causal emergence identification aims to find a good strategy of coarse-graining to reduce the given micro-level dynamics. Furthermore, introducing multi-scale modeling and coarse-graining operations into causal models brings some new theoretical problems [37–39]. For example, Refs. [38,39] discuss the basic requirements of the model abstraction (coarse-graining). However, these studies only care about static random variables and structural causal models but not Markovian dynamics.

In this paper, we formulate the problem of causal emergence identification as a maximization problem of the effective information (EI) for the macro-dynamics under the constraint of precise prediction of micro-dynamics. We then propose a general machine learning framework called Neural Information Squeezer (NIS) to solve the problem. By using invertible neural network to model the coarse-graining strategy, we can decompose any mapping from $\mathcal{R}^p$ to $\mathcal{R}^q$ ($q \leq p$) into a series of information conversions invertible processes and information discarding processes. In this way, the framework can not only allow us to control information conversion and discarding in a precise way but also enable us to mathematically analyze the whole framework in theory. We prove a series of mathematical theorems to reveal the properties of NIS. At last, we show how NIS can learn effective coarse-graining strategies and macro-state dynamics numerically on a set of examples.

2. Basic Notions and Problems Formulation

First, we will formulate our problems under a general setting, and layout our framework to solve the problems.

2.1. Background

Suppose the dynamics of the complex system that we consider can be described by a set of differential equations.

$$\frac{d\mathbf{x}}{dt} = g(\mathbf{x}(t), \xi), \tag{1}$$

where $\mathbf{x}(t) \in \mathcal{R}^p$ is the state of the system and $p \in \mathcal{Z}^+$ is a positive integer, ξ is a gaussian random noise. Normally, micro-dynamic g is always Markovian which means it could be also modeled as a conditional probability $Pr(\mathbf{x}(t+dt)|\mathbf{x}(t))$ equivalently.

However, we cannot directly obtain the evolution of the system but the discrete samples of the states, and we define these states as micro-states.

Definition 1. *(Micro-states): Each sample of the state of the dynamical system (Equation* (1)*)* $\mathbf{x}_t$ *is called a micro-state at time step* t*. In addition, the multi-variate time series* $\mathbf{x}_1, \mathbf{x}_2, \cdots, \mathbf{x}_T$ *which are sampled with equal intervals and a finite time step* T*, forms a micro-state time series.*

We always want to reconstruct g according to the observable micro-states. However, an informative dynamical mechanism g with strong causal connections is always hard to be reconstructed from the micro-states when noise ξ is strong. Meanwhile, we can ignore some information in the micro-state data and convert it into macro-state time series. In this way, we may reconstruct a macro-dynamic with stronger causality to describe the evolution of the system. This is the basic idea behind causal emergence [5,6]. We formalize the information ignoring process as a coarse-graining strategy (or mapping, method).

Definition 2. *(q dimensional coarse-graining strategy): Suppose the dimension of the macro-states is* $0 < q < p \in \mathcal{Z}^+$*, a* q *dimensional coarse-graining strategy is a continuous and differential function to map the micro-state* $\mathbf{x}_t \in \mathcal{R}^p$ *to a macro-state* $\mathbf{y}_t \in \mathcal{R}^q$*. The coarse-graining is denoted as* ϕ_q*.*

After coarse-graining, we obtain a new time series data of macro-states denoted by $\mathbf{y}_1 = \phi_q(\mathbf{x}_1), \mathbf{y}_2 = \phi_q(\mathbf{x}_2), \cdots, \mathbf{y}_T = \phi_q(\mathbf{x}_T)$. We then try to find another dynamical model (or a Markov chain) $\hat{f}_{\phi_q}$ to describe the evolution of $\mathbf{y}_t$:

Definition 3. *(macro-state dynamics): For the given time series of macro-states* $\mathbf{y}_1, \mathbf{y}_2, \cdots, \mathbf{y}_T$*, the macro-state dynamics are a set of differential equations*

$$\frac{d\mathbf{y}}{dt} = \hat{f}_{\phi_q}(\mathbf{y}, \xi'), \tag{2}$$

where $\mathbf{y} \in \mathcal{R}^q$*,* $\xi' \in \mathcal{R}^q$ *is the gaussian noise in the macro-state dynamics, and* $\hat{f}_{\phi_q}$ *is a continuous and differential function such that the solution of Equation* (2)*,* $\mathbf{y}(t)$*, can minimize:*

$$\langle ||\mathbf{y}_t - \mathbf{y}(t)|| \rangle_{\xi'} \tag{3}$$

for any given time step $t \in [1, T]$ *and given vector form* $||\cdot||$*.*

However, this formulation cannot reject some trivial strategies. For example, suppose a $q = 1$ dimensional ϕ_q is defined as $\phi_q(\mathbf{x}_t) = 1$ for $\forall \mathbf{y}_t \in \mathcal{R}^p$. Thus, the corresponding macro-dynamic is simply $d\mathbf{y}/dt = 0$ and $\mathbf{y}(0) = 1$. However, this is meaningless because the macro-state dynamic is trivial and coarse-graining mapping is too arbitrary.

Therefore, we must set limitations on coarse-graining strategies and macro-dynamics so that such trivial strategies and dynamics could be avoided.

2.2. Effective Coarse-Graining Strategy and Macro-Dynamics

We define an effective coarse-graining strategy to be a compressed map such that the macro-states may preserve the information of micro-states as much as it can. Formally,

Definition 4. *(ϵ-effective q coarse-graining strategy and macro-dynamcis): A q coarse-graining strategy $\phi_q : \mathcal{R}^p \to \mathcal{R}^q$ is ϵ-effective (or abbreviate as effective) if there exists a function $\phi_q^\dagger : \mathcal{R}^q \to \mathcal{R}^p$, such that the following inequality holds for a given small real number ϵ and given vector norm $||\cdot||$:*

$$||\phi_q^\dagger(\mathbf{y}(t)) - \mathbf{x}_t|| < \epsilon, \tag{4}$$

and the derived macro-dynamic $\hat{f}_{\phi_q}$ is also ϵ-effective, where $\mathbf{y}(t)$ is the solution of Equation (2), that is:

$$\mathbf{y}(t) = \phi_q(\mathbf{x}_{t-1}) + \int_{t-1}^{t} \hat{f}_{\phi_q}(\mathbf{y}(\tau), \xi')d\tau \tag{5}$$

for all $t = 1, 2, ..., T$. Thus, we can reconstruct the micro-state time series by $\phi_q^\dagger$ such that the macro-state variables contain the information of micro-states as much as they can.

Notice that this definition is in accordance with the approximate causal model abstraction [40].

2.3. Problem Formulation

Our final objective is to find a most informative macro-dynamic. Therefore, we need to optimize the coarse-graining strategy and the macro-dynamic among all possible effective strategies and dynamics. Therefore, our problem can be formulated as:

$$\max_{\phi_q, \hat{f}_{\phi_q}, \phi_q^\dagger, q} \mathcal{I}(\hat{f}_{\phi_q}), \tag{6}$$

under the constraint Equations (4) and (5), where $\mathcal{I}$ is a measure of effective information, it could be EI, Eff, or dimension averaged EI which is mainly used in this paper and is denoted as dEI (will mention in Section 3.3.3). ϕ_q is an effective coarse-graining strategy, and $\hat{f}_{\phi_q}$ is an effective macro-dynamic.

3. Methods

The problem (Equations (6) and (4)) is hard to solve because the objects that we will optimize are functions: $\phi_q, \hat{f}_{\phi_q}, \phi_q^\dagger$ but not numbers. Thus, we use neural networks to parameterize the functions and convert the function optimization problem into a parameter optimization problem.

3.1. Neural Information Squeezer Model

We propose a new machine learning framework called neural information squeezer (NIS) which is based on invertible neural network to solve the problem (Equation (6)). NIS is composed of three components: encoder, dynamics learner, and decoder. They are represented by neural networks ψ_α, f_β, and ψ_α^{-1} with the parameters α, β, and α respectively. The entire framework is shown in Figure 1. Next, we will describe each module separately.

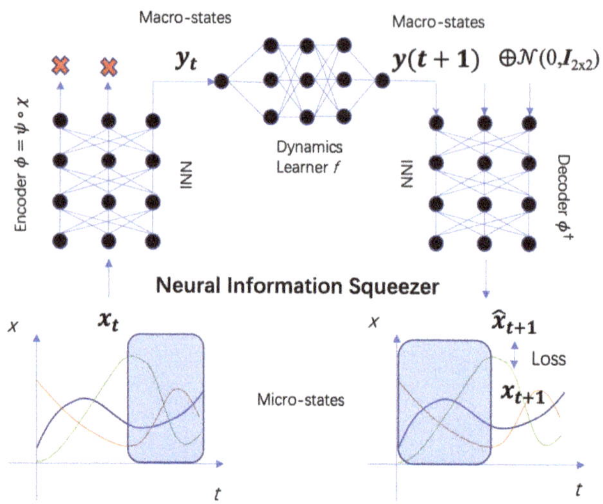

Figure 1. The workflow and the framework of the neural information squeezer. x_t is the data at time t. Encoder ψ_α is an invertible neural network (INN), from which the coarse-grained data y_t can be generated. The dynamics learner f_β is a common feed-forward neural network with parameters β. Through it the evolution from y_t to $y(t+1)$ can be conducted. The decoder converts the predicted macro-state of the next time step $\mathbf{y}(t+1)$ into the prediction of the micro-state at the next time step $\hat{\mathbf{x}}_{t+1}$.

Encoder

To be noticed, ψ_α is an invertible neural network (INN), therefore ψ and ψ^{-1} share the parameters α. However, invertible function has no information loss, we must introduce a new operator, projection.

Definition 5. *(Projection operator): A projection operator $\chi_{p,q}$ is a function from $\mathcal{R}^p$ to $\mathcal{R}^q$, such that:*

$$\chi_{p,q}(\mathbf{x}_q \bigoplus \mathbf{x}_{p-q}) = \mathbf{x}_q, \tag{7}$$

where $\bigoplus$ is the operation of vector concatenation, and $\mathbf{x}_q \in \mathcal{R}^q, \mathbf{x}_{p-q} \in \mathcal{R}^{p-q}$. Sometimes, we abbreviate $\chi_{p,q}$ as χ_q if there is no ambiguity.

Thus, the encoder (ϕ) maps the micro-state $\mathbf{x}_t$ to the macro-state $\mathbf{y}_t$, and this mapping can be separated into two steps. That is,

$$\phi_q = \chi_q \circ \psi_\alpha, \tag{8}$$

where $\circ$ represents the operation of function composition.

The first step is a bijective (invertible) mapping $\psi_\alpha : \mathcal{R}^p \to \mathcal{R}^p$ from $\mathbf{x}_t \in \mathcal{R}^p$ to $\mathbf{x}'_t \in \mathcal{R}^p$ without information lose and is realized by an invertible neural network, the second step is to project the resulting vector to q dimension by mapping $\mathbf{x}'_t \in \mathcal{R}^p$ into $\mathbf{y}_t \in \mathcal{R}^q$ by discarding the information on $p-q$ dimension.

There are several ways to realize an invertible neural network [41,42]. Meanwhile, we select RealNVP module [43] as shown in Figure 2 to concretely implement the invertible computation.

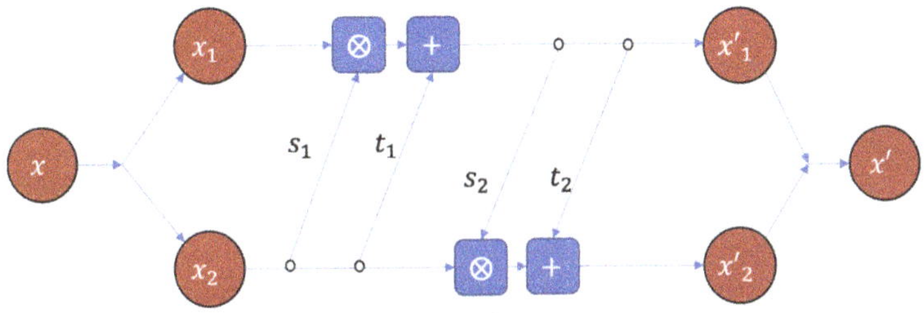

Figure 2. The RealNVP neural network implementation of the basic module of the bijector ψ, where s_1, s_2 and t_1, t_2 are all feed-forward neural networks with three layers, 64 hidden neurons, and ReLU active function. s_is and t_is share parameters, respectively. $\otimes$ and $+$ represent element-wised product and addition, respectively. $\mathbf{x} = \mathbf{x}_1 \bigoplus \mathbf{x}_2$ and $\mathbf{x}' = \mathbf{x}'_1 \bigoplus \mathbf{x}'_2$.

In the module, the input vector $\mathbf{x}$ can be separated into two parts, both vectors will be scaled, translated and merged again. The magnitude of the scaling and translation operations will be adjusted by the corresponding feed-forward neural networks. s_1, s_2 are the same neural networks shared parameters for scaling, $\otimes$ represents element-wised product. In addition, t_1, t_2 are the neural networks shared parameters for translation. In this way, an invertible computation from $\mathbf{x}$ to $\mathbf{y}$ can be realized. The same module can be repeated for multiple times (three times in this paper) to realize complex invertible computation, the details can be referred to Appendix A.

The reasons why we use invertible neural network are: (1) INN can reduce the complexity of the model by multiplexing the structure and the parameters in the encoder to the decoder because we can simply reverse the running direction of the encoder to implement decoding; (2) the encoder equipped with INN can separate out the information conversion process and information discarding process; (3) this enables us to do mathematical analysis on the whole framework, and several theorems reflecting the basic properties can be proved.

3.2. Decoder

The decoder converts the predicted macro-state of the next time step $\mathbf{y}(t+1)$ into the prediction of the micro-state at the next time step $\hat{\mathbf{x}}_{t+1}$. In our framework, because the coarse-graining strategy ϕ_q can be decomposed as a bijector ψ_α and a projector χ_q, we can simply reverse ψ_α to become ψ_α^{-1} as the decoder. However, because the dimension of the macro-state is q and the input dimension of ψ_α is $p > q$, we need to fill the remaining $p-q$ dimensions by a $p-q$ dimensional Gaussian random vector. That is, for any ϕ_q, the decoding mapping can be defined as:

$$\phi_q^\dagger = \psi_\alpha^{-1} \circ \chi_q^\dagger, \tag{9}$$

where ψ_α^{-1} is the inverse function of ψ_α, and $\chi_q^\dagger : \mathcal{R}^q \to \mathcal{R}^p$ is a function defined as follow: for any $\mathbf{x}_q \in \mathcal{R}^p$

$$\chi_q^\dagger(\mathbf{x}_q) = \mathbf{x}_q \bigoplus \mathbf{z}_{p-q}, \tag{10}$$

where $\mathbf{z}_{p-q} \sim \mathcal{N}(0, \mathcal{I}_{p-q})$ is a random Gaussian noise with $p-q$ dimension, and $\mathcal{I}_{p-q}$ is an identity matrix with the same dimension. That is, we can generate a micro-state by composing $\mathbf{x}_q$ and a random sample $\mathbf{z}_{p-q}$ from a $p-q$ dimensional standard normal distribution.

According to the point view of [31,33], the decoder can be regarded as a generative model of the conditional probability $Pr(\hat{\mathbf{x}}_{t+1}|\mathbf{y}(t+1))$, and the encoder just performs a renormalization process.

Dynamics Learner

The dynamics learner f_β is a common feed-forward neural network with parameters β, it will learn the effective Markov dynamic on the macro-level. Concretely, we at first use

f_β to replace $\hat{f}_{\phi_q}$ in Equation (2), and second we use Euler method with $dt = 1$ to solve the Equation (2), and suppose the noise is a additive Gaussian (or Laplacian) [44], therefore we can reduce Equation (5) as:

$$\mathbf{y}(t+1) = \mathbf{y}_t + \int_t^{t+1} f_\beta(\mathbf{y}(\tau), \xi')d\tau \approx \mathbf{y}_t + f_\beta(\mathbf{y}_t) + \xi' \tag{11}$$

where $\xi' \sim \mathcal{N}(0, \Sigma)$ or $Laplacian(0, \Sigma)$, $\Sigma = diag(\sigma_1^2, \sigma_2^2, \cdots, \sigma_q^2)$ is the covariance matrix, and σ_i is the standard deviation in the ith dimension which could be learned or fixed. Thus, the transitional probability of this dynamics can be written as

$$P(\mathbf{y}(t+1)|\mathbf{y}_t) = \mathcal{D}(\mu(\mathbf{y}_t), \Sigma), \tag{12}$$

where $\mathcal{D}$ represents the PDF of Gaussian distribution or Laplace distribution, $\mu(\mathbf{y}_t) \equiv \mathbf{y}_t + f_\beta(\mathbf{y}_t)$ is the mean vector of the distribution.

By training the dynamics learner in an end-to-end manner, we can avoid estimating the Markov transitional probabilities from the data to reduce biases because neural networks always have much better ability to fit the data and generalize to unseen cases.

3.3. *Two Stage Optimization*

Although the functions that will be optimized have been parameterized by neural networks, Equation (6) is still hard to be optimized directly because the objective function and the constraint condition must be combined together to be considered and q as a hyper-parameter can affect the structure of neural networks. Thus, in this paper, we propose a two-stage optimization method. In the first stage, we fix the hyper-parameter q and optimize the difference between the predicted micro-state and the observed data $|\phi_q^\dagger(\mathbf{y}(t)) - \mathbf{x}_t|$, that is Equation (4), to let the coarse-graining strategy ϕ_q and macro-dynamics $\hat{f}_q$ to be effective. Then, we search for all possible q values to find the optimal one such that $\mathcal{I}$ can be maximized.

3.3.1. Stage 1: Training a Predictor

In the first stage, we can use likelihood maximization and stochastic gradient descend techniques to obtain the effective q coarse-graining strategy and the effective predictor of the macro-state dynamics. The objective function is defined on the likelihood of micro-state prediction.

We can understand a feed-forward neural network as a machine to model a conditional probability with Gaussian or Laplacian distribution [44]. Thus, the entire NIS framework can be understood as a model of $P(\hat{\mathbf{x}}_{t+dt}|\mathbf{x}_t)$ with the output $\hat{\mathbf{x}}_{t+1}$ is just the mean value. In addition, the objective function Equation (14) is just the log-likelihood or cross-entropy of the observed data under the given form of the distribution.

$$\mathcal{L} = \sum_t \ln P(\hat{\mathbf{x}}_{t+1} = \mathbf{x}_{t+1}|\mathbf{x}_t), \tag{13}$$

where $P(\hat{\mathbf{x}}_{t+1} = \mathbf{x}_{t+1}|\mathbf{x}_t) \equiv \mathcal{N}(\hat{\mathbf{x}}_{t+1}, \Sigma)$ when $l = 2$ or $Laplace(\hat{\mathbf{x}}_{t+1}, \Sigma)$ when $l = 1$, where Σ is the covariance matrix which is always be a diagonal matrix and the magnitude can be calculated as the mean square error for $l = 2$ or mean absolute value for $l = 1$.

If we take the concrete form of Gaussian or Laplacian distribution into the conditional probability, we will see to maximize the log-likelihood is equivalent to minimize the l-norm objective function:

$$\mathcal{L} = \sum_t ||\hat{\mathbf{x}}_{t+1} - \mathbf{x}_{t+1}||_l \tag{14}$$

where $l = 1$ or 2.

Then, we can use stochastic gradient descend technique to optimize Equation (14).

3.3.2. Stage 2: Search for the Optimal Scale

In the previous step, we can obtain the effective q coarse graining strategy and the macro-state dynamics after a large number of training epochs, but the results are dependent on q.

To select the optimized q, we can compare the measure of effective information $\mathcal{I}$ for different q coarse-graining macro-dynamics. Because the parameter q only has one dimension, and its value range is also limited ($0 < q < p$), we can simply iterate all q to find out the optimal q^* and the optimal effective strategy.

3.3.3. About Effective Information

In the second stage, to compare coarse-graining strategies and macro-dynamics, we need to compute the important indicator: effective information (EI); however, the conventional computations of EIs are all for discrete Markov dynamics in most of previous works [5,6], and we may confront difficulties when we apply EI on continuous dynamics [9].

First, the conventional methods on mutual information computation for discrete variables cannot be used here, new methods for continuous variables and mappings especially for high dimensional space must be invented. To solve the problem, we treat the mapping of the dynamics learner neural network as an conditional Gaussian distribution, thereafter, we can calculate EI for this Gaussian distribution. Concretely, we have the following theorem:

Theorem 1. *(EI for feed-forward neural networks) In general, if the input of a neural network is $X = (x_1, x_2, \cdots, x_n) \in [-L, L]^n$, which means X is defined on a hyper-cube with size L, where L is a very large integer. The output is $Y = (y_1, y_2, \cdots, y_m)$, and $Y = \mu(X)$. Here μ is the deterministic mapping implemented by the neural network: $\mu : \mathcal{R}^n \to \mathcal{R}^m$, and its Jacobian matrix at X is $\partial_{X'}\mu(X) \equiv \left\{ \frac{\partial \mu_i(X')}{\partial X'_j}|_{X'=X} \right\}_{nm}$. If the neural network can be regarded as a Gaussian distribution conditional on given X:*

$$p(Y|X) = \frac{1}{\sqrt{(2\pi)^m|\Sigma|}} \exp\left(-\frac{1}{2}(Y-\mu(X))^T\Sigma^{-1}(Y-\mu(X))\right) \tag{15}$$

where $\Sigma = diag(\sigma_1^2, \sigma_2^2, \cdots, \sigma_m^2)$ is the co-variance matrix, and σ_i is the standard deviation of the output y_i which can be estimated by the mean square error of y_i, then the effective information (EI) of the neural network can be calculated in the following way:

(i) If there exists X such that $\det(\partial_{X'}\mu(X)) \neq 0$, then the effective information (EI) can be calculated as:

$$\begin{aligned} EI_L(\mu) = I(do(X \sim U([-L,L]^n;Y) \approx -\frac{m + m\ln(2\pi) + \sum_{i=1}^m \sigma_i^2}{2} \\ + n\ln(2L) + \mathbb{E}_{X\sim U([-L,L]^n}(\ln|\det(\partial_{X'}\mu(X))|). \end{aligned} \tag{16}$$

where $U([-L,L]^n)$ is the uniform distribution on $[-L,L]^n$, and $|\cdot|$ is absolute value, and det *is determinant.*

(ii) If $\det(\partial_{X'}\mu(X)) \equiv 0$ for all X, then $EI \approx 0$.

Although Theorem 1 can solve the problem of EI computation for continuous variables and functions, new problems must be confronted which are: (1) EI will be affected by the output dimension m easily, this may trouble the comparison of EI for different dimensional dynamics, and (2) EI is dependent on L, and will be divergent when L is very large.

To solve the first problem, we define a new indicator which is called dimension averaged effective information or effective information per dimension. Formally,

Definition 6. *(Dimension Averaged Effective Information (dEI)): For a dynamic f with n dimensional state space, then the dimension averaged effective information is defined as:*

$$dEI(f) = \frac{EI(f)}{n} \tag{17}$$

Therefore, if the dynamic f is continuous and can be regarded as a conditional Gaussian distribution, then according to Theorem 1, the dimension averaged EI can be calculated as ($m = n$):

$$dEI_L(f) = -\frac{1 + \ln(2\pi) + \sum_{i=1}^{n} \sigma_i^2/n}{2} + \ln(2L) + \frac{1}{n}\mathbb{E}_{X\sim U([-L,L]^n}(\ln|\det(\partial_{X'} f(X))|). \tag{18}$$

It is easy to see that all the terms related with dimension n in Equation (18) is eliminated. However, there is still L in the equation which may cause divergent when L is very large.

Therefore, to solve this problem, we can calculate the dimension averaged causal emergence (dCE) to eliminate the influence of L.

Definition 7. *(Dimension averaged causal emergence (dCE)): for macro-dynamics f_M with dimension n_M and micro-dynamics f_m with dimension n_m, we define dimension averaged causal emergence as:*

$$dCE(f_M, f_m) = dEI(f_M) - dEI(f_m) = \frac{EI(f_M)}{n_M} - \frac{EI(f_m)}{n_m}. \tag{19}$$

Thus, if the dynamics f_M and f_m are continuous and can be regarded as conditional Gaussian distributions, then according to Definition 7 and Equation (18), the dimension averaged causal emergence can be calculated as:

$$\begin{aligned} dCE(f_M, f_m) =& \left(\frac{1}{n_M}\mathbb{E}_{X_M} \ln|\det \partial_{X_M} f_M| - \frac{1}{n_m}\mathbb{E}_{X_m} \ln|\det \partial_{X_m} f_m|\right) \\ &- \left(\frac{1}{n_M}\sum_{i=1}^{n_M} \ln \sigma_{i,M}^2 - \frac{1}{n_m}\sum_{i=1}^{n_m} \ln \sigma_{i,m}^2\right) \end{aligned} \tag{20}$$

Therefore, all the effects of dimension n and L have been eliminated in Equation (20), and the result is only influenced by the relative values of the variances and the logarithmic values of the determinant of the jacobian matrices. In the following numeric computations, we will mainly use Equation (20). The reason why we not use Eff is also because it contains L.

4. Results

In this section, we will layout several theoretic properties of NIS at first; then, we will apply it on some numeric examples.

4.1. Theoretical Analysis

To understand why the neural information squeezer framework can find out the most informative macro-dynamics and how the effective strategy and dynamics change with q, we at first layout some major theoretical results through mathematical analysis. Notice that although all of the theorems are about mutual information, these conclusions are also suitable for effective information because all the theoretical results are irrelevant to the distribution of input data.

4.1.1. Squeezed Information Channel

First, we notice that the framework (Figure 1) can be regarded as an information channel as shown in Figure 3, and due to the existence of the projection operation, the channel is squeezed in the middle. Therefore, we call that a squeezed information channel (see also Appendix B for formal definition for the sqeezed information channel).

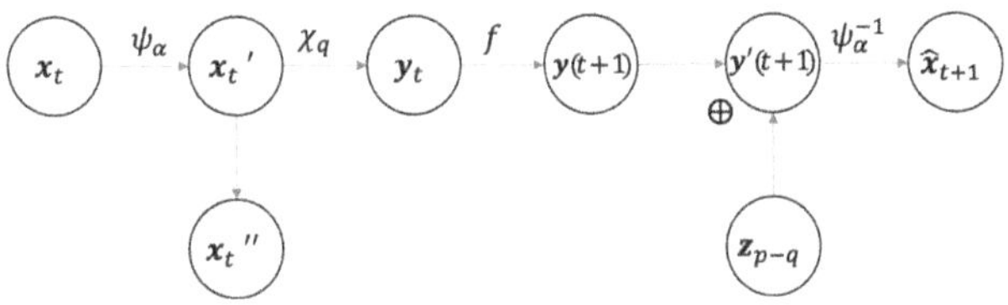

Figure 3. The graphic model of the neural information squeezer as a squeezed information channel.

As proved in Appendix B, we have a theorem for the squeezed information channel:

Theorem 2. *(Information bottleneck of Information Squeezer): For the squeezed information channel as shown in Figure 3 and for any bijector ψ, projector χ_q, macro-dynamics f, and the random noise $\mathbf{z}_{p-q} \sim \mathcal{N}(0, \mathcal{I}_{p-q})$, we have:*

$$I(\mathbf{y}_t; \mathbf{y}(t+1)) = I(\mathbf{x}_t; \hat{\mathbf{x}}_{t+1}), \tag{21}$$

where $\hat{\mathbf{x}}_{t+1}$ is the prediction of NIS, and $\mathbf{y}(t+1)$ follows Equation (2).

That is, for any neural network that implements the general framework as shown in Figure 3, the mutual information of macro-dynamic f_{ϕ_q} is identical to the entire dynamical model, i.e., the mapping from $\mathbf{x}_t$ to $\hat{\mathbf{x}}_{t+1}$ for any time. Theorem 2 is fundamental for NIS. Actually, the macro-dynamics f is the information bottleneck of the entire channel [45].

4.1.2. What Happens during Training

With Theorem 2, we can understand what happens when the neural squeezer framework is trained by data in an intuitive way.

First, we know as the neural networks are trained, the output of the entire framework $\hat{\mathbf{x}}_{t+1}$ is closed to the real data $\mathbf{x}_{t+1}$ under any given $\mathbf{x}_t$, so do the mutual information, that is the following theorem:

Theorem 3. *(Mutual information of the model will be closed to the data for a well trained framework): If the neural networks in NIS framework are well-trained (which means for any $t \in [1, T]$, the Kullback-Leibler divergence between $Pr_\tau(\hat{\mathbf{x}}_{t+1}|\mathbf{x}_t)$ and $Pr(\mathbf{x}_{t+1}|\mathbf{x}_t)$ approaches 0 when the training epoch $\tau \to \infty$), then:*

$$I(\hat{\mathbf{x}}_{t+1}; \mathbf{x}_t) \simeq I(\mathbf{x}_{t+1}; \mathbf{x}_t) \tag{22}$$

for any $t \in [1, T]$, where $\simeq$ means asymptotic equivalence when $\tau \to \infty$.

The proof is in the Appendix C.

Second, we suppose that the mutual information $I(\mathbf{x}_t, \mathbf{x}_{t+1})$ is always large because the time series of micro-states $\mathbf{x}_t$ contains information. Otherwise, we may not be interested in $\{\mathbf{x}_t\}$. Therefore, as the neural network is trained, $I(\mathbf{x}_t; \hat{\mathbf{x}}_{t+1})$ will increase to be closed to $I(\mathbf{x}_t; \mathbf{x}_{t+1})$.

Third, according to Theorem 2, $I(\mathbf{y}_t; \mathbf{y}(t+1)) = I(\mathbf{x}_t, \hat{\mathbf{x}}_{t+1})$ will also be increased such that it can be closed to $I(\mathbf{x}_t; \mathbf{x}_{t+1})$.

Because the macro-dynamics is the information bottleneck of the entire channel, therefore its information must be increased as training. At the same time, the determinant of the Jacobian of ψ_α and the entropy of $\mathbf{y}_t$ will also be increased in a general case. This conclusion is implied in Theorem 4.

Theorem 4. *(Information on bottleneck is the lower bound of the encoder): For the squeezed information channel shown in Figure 3, the determinant of the Jacobian matrix of ψ_α and the Shannon entropy of $\mathbf{y}_t$ are lower bounded by the information of the entire channel:*

$$H(\mathbf{x}_t) + \mathbb{E}(\ln|\det(J_{\psi_\alpha}(\mathbf{x}_t))|) \geq H(\mathbf{y}_t) + \mathbb{E}(\ln|\det(J_{\psi_\alpha,\mathbf{y}_t}(\mathbf{x}_t))|) \geq I(\mathbf{x}_t;\hat{\mathbf{x}}_{t+1}), \tag{23}$$

where H is the Shannon entropy measure, $J_{\psi_\alpha}(\mathbf{x}_t)$ is the Jacobian matrix of the bijector ψ_α at the input $\mathbf{x}_t$, and $J_{\psi_\alpha,\mathbf{y}_t}(\mathbf{x}_t)$ is the sub-matrix of $J_{\psi_\alpha}(\mathbf{x}_t)$ on the projection $\mathbf{y}_t$ of $\mathbf{x}'_t$.

The proof is also given in Appendix D.

Because the distribution of $\mathbf{x}_t$ and its Shannon entropy are given, thus, Theorem 4 states that the expectation of the logrithim of $|\det(J_{\psi_\alpha}(\mathbf{x}_t))|$ and the entropy of $\mathbf{y}_t$ must be larger than the information of the entire information channel.

Therefore, once the initial values of $\mathbb{E}|\det(J_{\psi_\alpha}(\mathbf{x}_t))|$ and $\mathbf{y}_t$ are small, as the model is trained, the mutual information of the entire channel increases, the determinant of the Jacobian must also be increased, and the distribution of the macro-state $\mathbf{y}_t$ must be more disperse. However, these may not happen if the information $I(\mathbf{x}_t;\hat{\mathbf{x}}_{t+1})$ has been closed to $I(\mathbf{x}_t;\mathbf{x}_{t+1})$ or $\mathbb{E}|\det(J_{\psi_\alpha}(\mathbf{x}_t))|$ and $H(\mathbf{y}_t)$ have been already large enough.

4.1.3. The Effective Information Is Mainly Determined by the Bijector

The previous analysis is about the mutual information but not the effective information of the macro-dynamic which is the key ingredients about causal emergence. Actually, with the good properties of the squeezed information channel, we can write down an expression of the EI for the macro-dynamic but without the explicit form of it. Accordingly, we find the major ingredient to determine causal emergence is the bijector ψ_α.

The proof is detailed in Appendix D.

Theorem 5. *(The mathematical expression for effective information of the macro-dynamics): Suppose the probability density of $\mathbf{x}_{t+1}$ under given $\mathbf{x}_t$ can be described by a function $Pr(\mathbf{x}_{t+1}|\mathbf{x}_t) \equiv G(\mathbf{x}_{t+1},\mathbf{x}_t)$, and the Neural Information Squeezer framework is well trained, then the effective information of the macro-dynamics of f_β can be calculated by:*

$$EI_L(f_\beta) = \frac{1}{(2L)^p} \cdot \int_\sigma \int_{\mathcal{R}^p} G(\mathbf{y},\psi_\alpha^{-1}(\mathbf{x})) \ln \frac{(2L)^p G(\mathbf{y},\psi_\alpha^{-1}(\mathbf{x}))}{\int_\sigma G(\mathbf{y},\psi_\alpha^{-1}(\mathbf{x}'))d\mathbf{x}'} d\mathbf{y}d\mathbf{x}, \tag{24}$$

where $\sigma \equiv [-L, L]^p$ is the integration region for $\mathbf{x}$ and $\mathbf{x}'$.

4.1.4. Change with the Scale (Q)

According to Theorems 2 and 3, we have the following Corollary 1:

Corollary 1. *(The mutual information of macro-dynamics will not change if the model is well trained): For the well trained NIS model, the Mutual Information of the macro-dynamics f_β will be irrelevant of all the parameters, including the scale q.*

If the neural networks are well-trained, the mutual information on the macro-dynamics will approach to the information in the data $\{\mathbf{x}_t\}$. Therefore, no matter how small q is (or how large is the scale), the mutual information of the macro-dynamics f_β will keep constant.

It seems that the scale q is an irrelevant parameter on causal emergence. However, according to Theorem 6, smaller q will lead to the encoder carrying more effective information.

Theorem 6. *(Narrower is Harder): If the dimension of $\mathbf{x}_t$ is p, then for $0 < q_1 < q_2 < p$:*

$$I(\mathbf{x}_t;\hat{\mathbf{x}}_{t+1}) \leq I(\mathbf{x}_t;\mathbf{y}_t^{q_1}) \leq I(\mathbf{x}_t;\mathbf{y}_t^{q_2}), \tag{25}$$

where $\mathbf{y}_t^q$ denotes the q-dimensional vector $\mathbf{y}_t$.

The mutual information in Theorem 6 is about the encoder, i.e., the micro-state $\mathbf{x}_t$ and the macro-state $\mathbf{y}_t$ in different dimension q. The theorem states that as q decreases, the mutual information of the encoder part must also decrease and more closed to the information limitation $I(\mathbf{x}_t; \hat{\mathbf{x}}_{t+1}) \simeq I(\mathbf{x}_t; \mathbf{x}_{t+1})$. Therefore, the entire information channel becomes narrower, the encoder must carry more useful and effective information to transfer to the macro-dynamics. In addition, the prediction becomes harder.

4.2. Empirical Results

We test our model on several data sets. All the data are generated by the simulated dynamical models. In addition, the models include continuous dynamics and discrete Markovian dynamics.

4.2.1. Spring Oscillator with Measurement Noise

The first experiment to test our model is a simple spring oscillator following the dynamical equations:

$$\begin{cases} dz/dt = v \\ dv/dt = -z \end{cases} \tag{26}$$

where z and v are position and velocity of the oscillator in one dimension, respectively. The states of the system can be represented as $\mathbf{x} = (z, v)$.

However, we can only observe the state from two sensors with measurement errors. Suppose the observational model is

$$\begin{cases} \tilde{\mathbf{x}}_1 = \mathbf{x} + \zeta \\ \tilde{\mathbf{x}}_2 = \mathbf{x} - \zeta \end{cases} \tag{27}$$

where $\zeta \sim \mathcal{N}(0, \sigma)$ is a random number following two dimensional Gaussian distribution, and σ is the vector of the standard deviations for position and velocity. In this example, we can understand the states $\mathbf{x}$ as latent macro-states and the measurements $\tilde{\mathbf{x}}_1, \tilde{\mathbf{x}}_2$ are micro-states. What the NIS will do is recover the latent macro-state $\mathbf{x}$ from the measurements.

According to Equation (27), although there is noise to disturb the measurement of the state, it can be easily eliminated by adding the measurements on the two channels together. Therefore, if NIS can discover a macro-state which is the addition of the two measurements, then it can easily obtain the correct dynamics. We sample the data for 10,000 batches (with Euler method and $dt = 1$), and in each batch, we randomly generate 100 random initial states and perform one step dynamic to obtain the state at the next time step. We use these data to train the neural network. To compare, we also use the same data set to train an ordinary feed-forward neural network with the same number of parameters.

The results are shown in Figure 4. To test if NIS can learn the real latent macro state, we directly plot the predicted and the real latent states. As shown in Figure 4a, the predicted and the real curves collapse together which means NIS can recover the macro state in the data although it is unknown. As a comparison, the feed-forward neural network cannot recover the macro state. We can also check if the NIS can learn the dynamic of the macro states by plotting the derivatives of the states $(dz/dt, dv/dt)$ against the macro state variables (v, z). If the learned dynamics follows Equation (26), then two cross-over lines for $dz/dt = v$ and $dv/dt = -z$ can be observed as shown in Figure 4c. However, the same pattern cannot be reproduced on the common feed-forward network as shown in Figure 4d. We also test the well-trained NIS by multiple-step prediction as shown in Figure 4e. Although there are larger and larger deviation from the prediction and the real data, the general trends can be captured by NIS model. We further study how the dimension averaged causal emergence dCE changes with the scale q which is measured by the number of effective information channels on the well-trained NIS model as shown in Figure 4f. dCE peaks at $q = 2$ which is exactly same as in the ground truth.

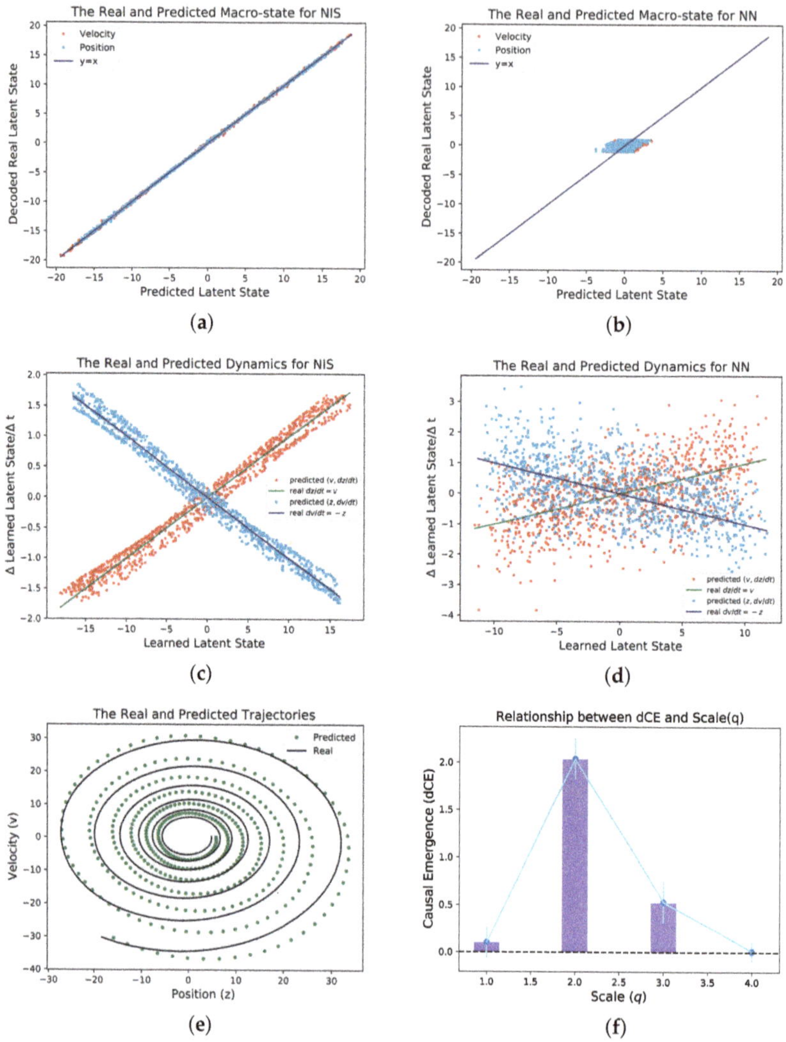

Figure 4. Experimental Results for the Simple Spring Oscillator with Measurement Noise. We sample data from Equations (26) and (27), and we use Euler method to simulate by taking $dt = 0.1$. (**a**,**b**) show the real macro-state versus the predicted ones both for NIS and the ordinary feed-forward neural network, respectively; (**c**,**d**) show the real and predicted dynamics, i.e., the dependence between dz/dt and v, and dv/dt with z for both neural networks for comparison; (**e**) shows the real and predicted trajectories with 400 time steps starting from the same latent state; (**f**) shows the dependence of the dimension averaged of *Causal Emergence* (dCE) on q (the number of effective channels).

Further, we use experimental results to verify the theorems mentioned in the previous section and the theory of information bottleneck [45]. First, we show how the mutual information of $I(\mathbf{x}_t, \mathbf{x}_{t+1})$, $I(\mathbf{y}_t, \mathbf{y}(t+1))$, and $I(\mathbf{x}_t, \hat{\mathbf{x}}_{t+1})$ change with time (epoch) when q takes different values as shown in Figure 5c,d. The results show that all the mutual information converge as predicted by Theorems 2 and 3. We also plot the mutual information between $\mathbf{x}_t$ and $\mathbf{y}_t$ with different q to test Theorem 6, and the results show that the mutual information increases when q increases as shown in Figure 5a.

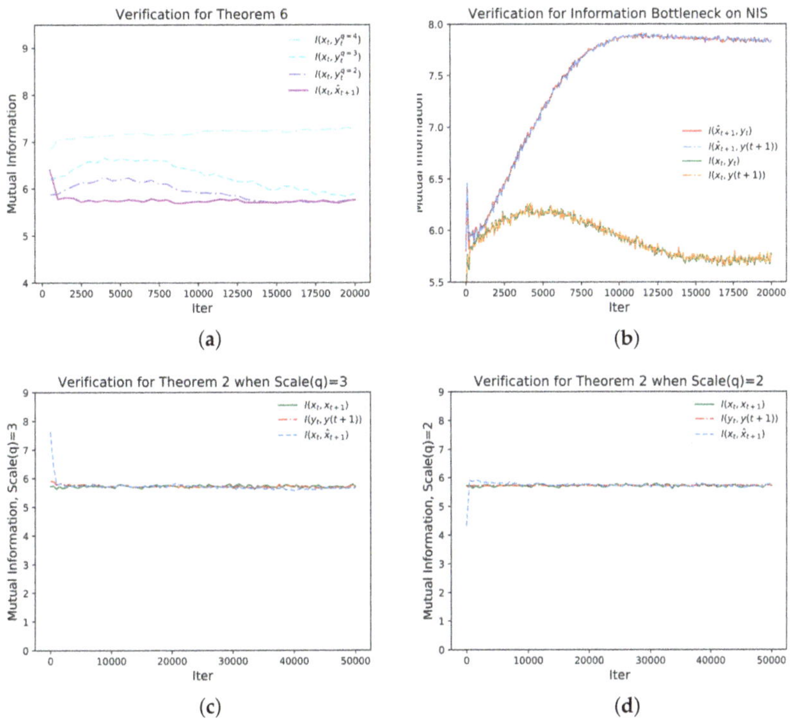

Figure 5. Various mutual information between variables change with training iterations. (**a**) shows the change of mutual information $I(x_t, y_t^{q=4})$, $I(x_t, y_t^{q=3})$, $I(x_t, y_t^{q=2})$ and $I(x_t, \hat{x}_t)$ with the increase of the number of iterations. From the figure, we can see that within the specified number of iterations, $I(x_t, \hat{x}_t) \leq I(x_t, y_t^{q=2}) \leq I(x_t, y_t^{q=3}) \leq I(x_t, y_t^{q=4})$. Among them, q is the dimension of the coarse-grained system. (**b**) verifies the theory of information bottleneck on NIS when Scale (q) = 2. (**c**,**d**) show the change of mutual information $I(x_t, x_{t+1})$, $I(y_t, y_{t+1})$ and $I(x_t, \hat{x}_t)$ with the increase of the number of iterations. It can be seen that under different scales, the three mutual information values are close to each other. The standard deviations of the three variables gradually decrease with iteration. Therefore, $I(x_t, x_{t+1}) \approx I(y_t, y_{t+1}) = I(x_t, \hat{x}_t)$ is reflected.

According to the information bottleneck theory [45], the mutual information between latent variable and output may increase while the information between input and latent variable should increase in the early stage and then decrease as training process proceed. As shown in Figure 5b, this conclusion is confirmed by the NIS model where the macro-states $\mathbf{y_t}$ and the prediction $\mathbf{y(t+1)}$ are all latent variables. Although the same conclusion is obtained, the information bottleneck can be reflected by the architecture in NIS model much clearer than the general neural networks because $\mathbf{y}_t$ and $\mathbf{y}(t+1)$ is the bottleneck and all other irrelevant information is discarded by the variable $\mathbf{x}_t''$ as shown in Figure 3.

4.2.2. Simple Markov Chain

In the second example, we show NIS can work on discrete Markov chain, and the coarse-graining strategy can work on state space. The Markov chain to generate the data is the following probability transition matrix:

$$\begin{pmatrix} 1/7 & 1/7 & 1/7 & 1/7 & 1/7 & 1/7 & 1/7 & 0 \\ 1/7 & 1/7 & 1/7 & 1/7 & 1/7 & 1/7 & 1/7 & 0 \\ 1/7 & 1/7 & 1/7 & 1/7 & 1/7 & 1/7 & 1/7 & 0 \\ 1/7 & 1/7 & 1/7 & 1/7 & 1/7 & 1/7 & 1/7 & 0 \\ 1/7 & 1/7 & 1/7 & 1/7 & 1/7 & 1/7 & 1/7 & 0 \\ 1/7 & 1/7 & 1/7 & 1/7 & 1/7 & 1/7 & 1/7 & 0 \\ 1/7 & 1/7 & 1/7 & 1/7 & 1/7 & 1/7 & 1/7 & 0 \\ 0 & 0 & 0 & 0 & 0 & 0 & 0 & 1 \end{pmatrix} \tag{28}$$

The system has 8 states, and seven of them can transfer each other. The last state is standalone. We use a one-hot vector to encode the states. Therefore, for example, state 2 will be represented as $(0, 1, 0, 0, 0, 0, 0, 0)$. We sample the initial state for 50,000 batches to generate data. We then feed these one-hot vectors into the NIS framework, after training for 50,000 epochs, we can obtain an effective model. The results are shown in Figure 6.

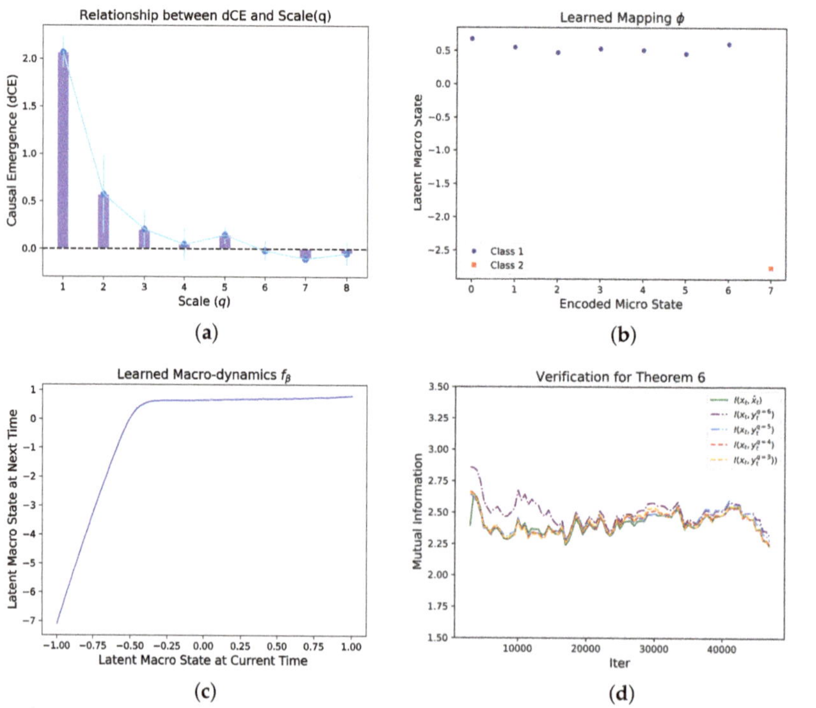

Figure 6. The dependence of the dimension averaged *Causal Emergence* (dCE) on different scales (q) of the Markov dynamics (**a**), the learned mapping between micro states and macro states on the optimal scale (q) (**b**), and the learned macro-dynamics the mapping from $\mathbf{y}_t$ to $\mathbf{y}(t+1)$ (**c**). There are two clear separated clusters on the y-axis in (**b**) which means the macro states are discrete. We found that the two discrete macro states and the mapping between micro and discrete macro states are identical as the example in Ref. [6] which means the correct coarse-graining strategy can be discovered by our algorithm automatically under the condition without any prior information. In (**d**), $I(x_t, \hat{x}_t) \le I(x_t, y_t^{q=3}) \le I(x_t, y_t^{q=4}) \le I(x_t, y_t^{q=5}) \le I(x_t, y_t^{q=6})$ is reflected. In order to make the data clearer, we have taken a moving average for each group of data. This result can be regarded as the verification of Theorem 6.

By systematically search for different q, we found that the dimension averaged causal emergence (dCE) peaks at $q = 1$ as shown in Figure 6a. On the optimal scale, we can visualize the coarse-graining strategy by Figure 6b, in which the x-coordinate is the decimal coding for different states, and the y-coordinate represents the coding for the macro-states. We find that the coarse-graining mapping successfully classifies the first seven states into a one macro-state, and leaves the last state stay alone. This learned coarse-graining strategy is identical as the example shown in [6].

We also visualize the learned macro-dynamics as shown in Figure 6c. This is a linear mapping when $y_t < 0$ and almost a constant for $y_t > 0$. Therefore, the dynamics can guarantee that all the first seven micro-states can be separated with the last state. We also verify Theorem 2 in Figure 6d.

4.2.3. Simple Boolean Network

Our framework can not only work on continuous time series and Markov chain, but also can work on a networked system in which each node follows a discrete micro mechanism.

For example, boolean network is a typical discrete dynamical system in which the node contains two possible states (0 or 1), and the state of each node is affected by the state of the neighbors connected to it. We follow the example in [5]. Figure 7 shows an exampled boolean network with four nodes, and each node follows the same micro mechanism as shown in the table of Figure 7. In the table, each entry is the probability of each node's state conditions on the state combination of its neighbors. For example, if the current node is A, then the first entry is $Pr(x_A^{t+1} = 0 | x_C^t = 0, x_D^t = 0) = 0.7$, which means that A will take value 0 with probability 0.7 when the state combination of C and D is 00. By taking all the single node mechanisms together, we can obtain a large Markovian transition matrix with $2^4 = 16$ states which is the complete micro mechanism of the whole network.

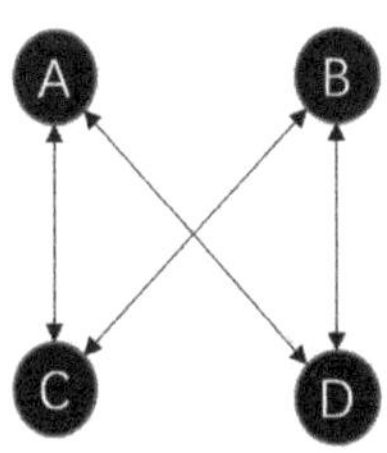

Micro mechanisms

t-1\t	0	1
00	0.7	0.3
01	0.7	0.3
10	0.7	0.3
11	0	1

Figure 7. An exampled Boolean network (**left**) and its micro mechanisms on nodes (**right**). Each node's state on the next time step is affected by its neighboring nodes' state combination randomly. The transition probabilities (micro mechanisms) on each case are shown in the table.

We sample the one step state transition of the entire network for 50,000 batches and each batch contains 100 different initial conditions which are randomly sampled from the possible state space evenly, and we then feed these data to the NIS model. By systematically search for different q, we found that the dimension averaged causal emergence peaks at $q = 1$ as shown in Figure 8a. Under this condition, we can visualize the coarse-graining strategy by Figure 8b, in which the x-coordinate is the decimal coding for the binary micro-states (e.g., 5 denotes for the state 0101), and the y-coordinate represents the codes for macro-states. The data points can be clearly classified into four clusters according to their y-coordinate. This means the NIS network found four discrete macro-states although the states are continuous real numbers. Interestingly, we found that the mapping between the 16 micro states and four macro states are identical as the coarse-graining strategy shown in the example in Ref. [5]. However, any prior information neither the method on how to group the nodes nor the coarse graining strategy, nor the dynamics are known by our algorithm. Finally, Theorems 2 and 6 are verified in this example as shown in Figure 8c,d.

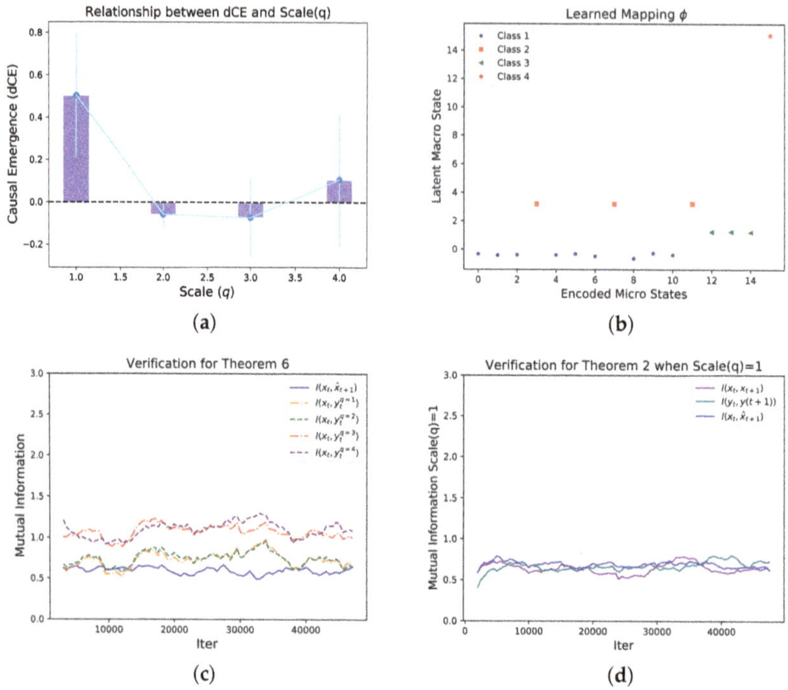

Figure 8. Experimentsl Results for the Boolean Network. The dependence of the dimension averaged *Causal Emergence* (dCE) on different scales (q) (**a**) and the learned mapping between micro states and macro states on the optimal scale (q) (**b**). There are four clear separated clusters on the y-axis in (**b**) which means the macro states are discrete. We found that the four discrete macro states and the mapping between micro and discrete macro states are identical as the example in Ref. [5] which means the correct coarse-graining strategy can be discovered by our algorithm automatically under the condition without any prior information. (**c**) shows the change of mutual information $I(x_t, y_t^{q=4})$, $I(x_t, y_t^{q=3})$, $I(x_t, y_t^{q=2})$,$I(x_t, y_t^{q=1})$ and $I(x_t, \hat{x}_t)$ with the increase of the number of iterations. From the figure, we can see approximately that within the specified number of iterations, $I(x_t, \hat{x}_t) \leq I(x_t, y_t^{q=1}) \leq I(x_t, y_t^{q=2}) \leq I(x_t, y_t^{q=3}) \leq I(x_t, y_t^{q=4})$. (**d**) shows the change of mutual information $I(x_t, x_{t+1})$, $I(y_t, y_{t+1})$ and $I(x_t, \hat{x}_t)$ with the increase of the number of iterations. In order to easily observe the trend of data changes, we added a moving average curve for each group of data. It can be seen that under different scales, the three mutual information values are close to each other. $I(x_t, x_{t+1}) \approx I(y_t, y_{t+1}) = I(x_t, \hat{x}_t)$ is reflected. Considering the experimental error, the overall trend of the data still conforms to the theorem.

5. Concluding Remarks

In this paper, we propose a novel neural network framework, Neural Information Squeezer, for discovering coarse-graining strategy, macro-dynamic and emergent causality in time series data. We first define effective coarse-graining strategy and macro-dynamic by constraining the coarse-graining strategies to predict the future micro-state with a precision threshold. Then, the causal emergence identification problem can be understood as a maximization problem for effective information under the constraint.

We then use an invertible neural network incorporating with the projection operation to realize the coarse-graining strategy. The usage of invertible neural network can not only allow us to reduce the number of parameters by sharing them between the encoder and the decoder but also can facilitate us to analyze the mathematical properties of the whole NIS architecture.

By treating the framework as a squeezed information channel, we can prove four important theorems. The results show that if the causal connection in the data is strong, then as we train the neural networks, the macro-dynamics will increase its informativeness. In addition, during this process, the determinant of the Jacobian of the bijector will increase at the same time. We also found a mathematical expression for the effective information of the macro-dynamics without the explicit dependence on the macro-dynamics, and it is determined solely by the bijector and the data when the whole framework is well trained. Furthermore, if the framework has been trained in a sufficient time, the mutual information of the macro-dynamics will keep a constant no matter the scale q is. However, as q decreases, the mutual information or the bandwidth on the encoder part also decreases and closed to the information limitation on the entire channel such that it can make correct prediction for the future micro-states. Thus, the task becomes harder for the encoder because more effective information must be encoded and pass to the dynamics learner such that it can make correct prediction with less information. Numerical experiments show that our framework can reconstruct the dynamics in different scales and also can discover emergent causality in data on several classic causal emergence examples.

There are several weak points in our framework. First, it can only work on small data set. The major reason is the invertible neural network is very difficult to train on large data set. Therefore, we will use some special techniques to optimize the architecture in future. Second, the framework is still lack of explainability, the grouping method for variables is implicitly encoded in the invertible neural network although we can illustrate what the coarse-graining mapping is, and decompose it into information conversion and information discarding parts clearly. A more transparent neural network framework with more explanatory power is deserved for future studies. Third, the conditional distribution that the model can predict actually is limited as Gaussian or Laplacian, and it should be extended to more general distributional forms in future studies.

There are several theoretical problems left for future studies. For example, we conjecture that all coarse-graining strategies can be decompose into a bijection and a projection, but this needs strict mathematical proof. Second, although an explicit expression for EI on macro-dynamics has been derived under NIS, we still cannot directly predict the causal emergence in the data. We believe that a more concise analytic results on the EI should be derived by setting some constraints on the data. Furthermore, we think the meaning and the usage of the discarding variable $\mathbf{x}_t''$ should be further explored since that it may relate with the redundant information of a pair of variables toward a target [46]. Therefore, we guess more deep connections between the framework of NIS and the mutual information decomposition may exist and NIS may work as a numeric tool to decompose the mutual information.

Author Contributions: Conceptualization and methodology, J.Z.; coding, J.Z. and K.L.; writing, J.Z. and K.L. All authors have read and agreed to the published version of the manuscript.

Funding: This research was funded by by the National Natural Science Foundation of China (NSFC) under Grant No. 61673070 at https://www.nsfc.gov.cn/, accessed on 24 October 2022.

Data Availability Statement: All the codes and data are available at: https://github.com/jakezj/NIS_for_Causal_Emergence, accessed on 24 October 2022.

Acknowledgments: J.Z. acknowledge the discussion in the reading group on "Causal Emergence" organized by Swarma Club, particularly for Yanbo Zhang, Everrete You and Erik Hoel. We thank the support from Causal Emergence Reading Group supported by the Save 2050 Programme jointly sponsored by Swarma Club and X-Order; We thank the support from Swarma Research.

Conflicts of Interest: The authors declare no conflict of interest.

Appendix A. RealNVP Implementation of Invertible Neural Network

In the main text, we mentioned that the invertible neural network can be realized by a RealNVP module. The architecture of a RealNVP module can be visualized by Figure 2.

Concretely, if the input of the module is $\mathbf{x}$ with dimension n and the output is $\mathbf{x}'$ with the same dimension, then the RealNVP module can perform the following computation steps:

$$\begin{cases} \mathbf{x_1} = \mathbf{x}_{1:m} \\ \mathbf{x_2} = \mathbf{x}_{m:n} \end{cases} \tag{A1}$$

where m is an integer in between 1 and n.

$$\begin{cases} \mathbf{x_1'} = \mathbf{x_1} \bigotimes s_1(\mathbf{x_2}) + t_1(\mathbf{x_2}) \\ \mathbf{x_2'} = \mathbf{x_2} \bigotimes s_2(\mathbf{x_1'}) + t_2(\mathbf{x_1'}) \end{cases} \tag{A2}$$

where s_1, s_2, t_1 and t_2 are feed-forward neural networks with arbitrary architectures, while their input-output dimensions must match with the data. In practice, s_1 or s_2 always do an exponential operation on the output of the feed-forward neural network [43] to facilitate the inverse computation.

Finally,

$$\mathbf{x}' = \mathbf{x_1'} \bigoplus \mathbf{x_2'} \tag{A3}$$

It is not difficult to verify that all three steps are invertible. Equation (A2) is invertible because the same form but with negative signs can be obtained by solving the expressions of $\mathbf{x_1}$ and $\mathbf{x_2}$ with $\mathbf{x_1'}$ and $\mathbf{x_2'}$ from Equation (A2).

To simulate more complex invertible functions, we always duplex the basic RealNVP modules by stacking them together. In the main text, we use duplex the basic RealNVP module by three times.

Appendix B. Approximated Calculation of Effective Information for Neural Networks

In this paper, we propose an approximated method to calculate EI for a neural network. Conventional methods usually coarse-grain the input and output spaces into small regions, and estimate the probability of each region by the frequency. However, this estimation is inaccurate especially for the regions with small probability.

To avoid this problem, we propose a new method to estimate the mutual information of a neural network. The key idea is to treat a Neural Network as a conditional probability with a Gaussian (or Laplacian) distribution in which the mean value is the output vector of the neural network, and the standard deviation takes the Mean Square Error of the prediction. The concrete distributional form (Gaussian or Laplacian) is determined by the types of Loss function. If MSE (Mean Square Error) is taken then Gaussian distribution is considered, otherwise if MAE (Mean Absolute Error) is considered then Laplacian distribution is considered. Without lose genarlity, here, we take the distributional form as Gaussian.

We restate Theorem 1:

Theorem 1: In general, if the input of a neural network is $X = (x_1, x_2, \cdots, x_n) \in [-L, L]^n$, where L is a big integer, the output is $Y = (y_1, y_2, \cdots, y_m)$, and $Y = \mu(X)$. Here μ is the deterministic mapping implemented by the neural network: $\mu : \mathcal{R}^n \to \mathcal{R}^m$, and its Jacobian matrix at X is $\partial_{X'}\mu(X) \equiv \left\{ \frac{\partial \mu_i(X')}{\partial X_j'} |_{X'=X} \right\}_{nm}$, and if the neural network can be regarded as an Gaussian distribution conditional on given X:

$$p(Y|X) = \frac{1}{\sqrt{(2\pi)^m |\Sigma|}} \exp\left(-\frac{1}{2}(Y - \mu(X))^T \Sigma^{-1} (Y - \mu(X)) \right) \tag{A4}$$

where $\Sigma = diag(\sigma_1^2, \sigma_2^2, \cdots, \sigma_m^2)$ is the co-variance matrix, and σ_i is the standard deviation of the output y_i which can be estimated by the mean square error of y_i. Then the effective information (EI) of the neural network can be calculated in the following way:

(i) If there exists X such that $\det(\partial_{X'}\mu(X)) \neq 0$, then the effective mutual information (EI) can be calculated as:

$$EI_L(\mu) = I(do(X \sim U([-L,L]^n;Y) \approx -\frac{m + m\ln(2\pi) + \Sigma_{i=1}^m \ln\det(\sigma_i^2)}{2} + n\ln(2L) + \mathbb{E}_{X\sim U([-L,L]^n}(\ln|\det(\partial_{X'}\mu(X))|). \tag{A5}$$

where $U([-L,L]^n)$ is the uniform distribution on $[-L,L]^n$, and $|\cdot|$ is absolute value, and det is determinant.

(ii) If $\det(\partial_{X'}\mu(X)) \equiv 0$ for all X, then $EI \approx 0$.

Proof. Because the calculation of mutual information can be separated into two parts:

$$\begin{aligned} I(X;Y) &= \int_{XY} p(X,Y)\ln\frac{p(X,Y)}{p(X)p(Y)}dXdY = \int_{XY} p(X)p(Y|X)\ln\frac{p(Y|X)}{p(Y)}dYdX \\ &= \int_X p(X)\left(\int_Y p(Y|X)\ln p(Y|X)dY\right)dX \\ &- \int_X p(X)\left(\int_Y p(Y|X)\ln p(Y)dY\right)dX \end{aligned} \tag{A6}$$

By inserting Equation (A4) into Equation (A6), the first term becomes (the Shannon entropy of the Gaussian Distribution):

$$\int_Y p(Y|X)\ln p(Y|X)dY = -\frac{m + m\ln(2\pi) + \ln\det(\Sigma)}{2} \tag{A7}$$

However, it is hard to derive an explicit expression of the second term in Equation (A6) because it contains integration. Therefore, we can expand $\mu(X')$ into Taylor series on the point X and keep only the first order term:

$$\mu(X') \approx \mu(X) + \partial_{X'}\mu(X)(X'-X), \tag{A8}$$

where $\partial_{X'}\mu(X) \equiv \frac{\partial\mu(X')}{\partial X'}|_{X'=X} = \left(\frac{\partial\mu_i(X)}{\partial X'_j}\right)_{m,n}$.

(i) If there exists X: $|\det(\partial_{X'}\mu(X))| \neq 0$, thus:

$$\begin{aligned} p(Y) &= \int_{X'} p(X',Y)dX' = \int_{X'} p(X')p(Y|X')dX' = \int_{X'} \rho p(Y|X')dX' \\ &\approx \rho\frac{1}{\sqrt{|\Sigma|}}\frac{1}{\sqrt{|\det(\partial_{X'}\mu(X)^T\cdot\Sigma^{-1}\cdot\partial_{X'}\mu(X))|}} = \frac{\rho}{|\det(\partial_{X'}\mu(X))|}, \end{aligned} \tag{A9}$$

where $\rho = (2L)^{-n}$. This is the multivariate Gaussian integral. Therefore:

$$\begin{aligned} \int_X p(X)\left(\int_Y p(Y|X)\ln p(Y)dY\right)dX &\approx \ln\rho - \rho\int_X \ln|\det(\partial_{X'}\mu(X))|dX \\ &\approx \ln\rho - \mathbb{E}_{X\sim U([-L,L]^n)}\ln|\det(\partial_{X'}\mu(X))| \end{aligned} \tag{A10}$$

Thus, EI can be derived by combining the two terms together:

$$EI_L \approx -\frac{m + m\ln(2\pi) + \ln|\det(\Sigma)|}{2} - \ln\rho + \mathbb{E}_{X\sim U([-L,L]^n)}\ln|\det(\partial_{X'}\mu(X))| \tag{A11}$$

To insert $\rho = (2L)^{-n}$ and $\det(\Sigma) = \prod_{i=1}^m \sigma_i$ into Equation (A11), we obtain Equation (A5).

(ii) If $\det(\partial_{X'}\mu(X)) = 0$ for all X, which means $\mu(X) \equiv \mu_0$ where μ_0 is a constant, then:

$$p(Y) \approx \frac{\exp\left(-\frac{1}{2}(Y-\mu_0)^T\Sigma^{-1}(Y-\mu_0)\right)}{\sqrt{(2\pi)^m|\det(\Sigma)|}}, \tag{A12}$$

so,

$$\int_Y p(Y|X)\ln p(Y)dY \approx -\frac{m + m\ln(2\pi) + \ln|\det(\Sigma)|}{2}, \tag{A13}$$

Combining with Equation (A7), we have:

$$EI_L \approx 0 \tag{A14}$$

□

With this theorem, we can numerically calculate the EI of a neural network in an approximate way. The mathematical expectation can be approximated by averaging the logarithm of the determinant of the Jacobian on the samples of X drawn on the hyper-cube $[-L, L]^n$ uniformly. This method can avoid partitioning intervals and counting frequencies which are very difficult when the dimension is large.

Lemma A1. *(Bijection mapping does not affect mutual information): For any given continuous random variables X and Z, if there is a bijection (one to one) mapping f and another random variable Y such that for any $x \in Dom(X)$ there is a $y = f(x) \in Dom(Y)$, and vice versa, where $Dom(X)$ denotes the domain of the variable X, then the mutual information between X and Z is equal to the information between Y and Z, that is:*

$$I(X;Z) = I(Y;Z). \tag{A15}$$

Proof. Because there is a one to one mapping $f : X \to Y$, we have:

$$p_X(x) = p_Y(y)|\det J|, \tag{A16}$$

where p_Y and p_X are the density functions of X, Y, $J = \frac{\partial f}{\partial X}|_x$ is the Jacobian matrix of f, and if we insert Equation (A16) into the expression of the mutual information of $I(X;Z)$, and replace the integration for x with the one for y, we have:

$$\begin{aligned}
I(X;Z) &= \int_X \int_Z p_{XZ}(x,z) \cdot \ln \frac{p_{XZ}(x,z)}{p_X(x)p_Z(z)} \cdot dz \cdot dx \\
&= \int_X \int_Z p_X(x)p_{Z|X}(z|x) \cdot \ln \frac{p_X(x)p_{Z|X}(z|x)}{p_X(x)p_Z(z)} \cdot dz \cdot dx \\
&= \int_Y \int_Z |\det(J)| \cdot p_Y(y) \cdot p_{Z|Y}(z|y) \cdot \ln \frac{p_{Z|Y}(z|y)}{p_Z(z)} \\
&\quad \cdot |\det(J^{-1})| \cdot dz \cdot dy \\
&= I(Y;Z).
\end{aligned} \tag{A17}$$

And Equation (A17) can also be proved because of the commutativeness of the mutual information. □

Lemma A2. *(Projection does not affect mutual information): Suppose $X \in \mathcal{R}^{p+q}$ and $Y \in Dom(Y)$, where $p, q \in \mathcal{Z}^+$. In addition, X can be decomposed as two components $U \in \mathcal{R}^p, V \in \mathcal{R}^q$, that is:*

$$X = U \bigoplus V, \tag{A18}$$

where ⊕ represents vector concatenation. We call that U and V are X's projections on p or q dimensional sub spaces, respectively. If U and Y form a Markov chain $U \to Y$, and V is independent on Y, then we have:

$$I(X;Y) = I(U;Y) \tag{A19}$$

Proof. Notice that the joint distribution of X and Y can be written as:

$$p(X,Y) \equiv p(U \bigoplus V, Y) \equiv p(U,V,Y) \tag{A20}$$

Further, because $X \to U$ forms a Markov chain, but V is not, thus:

$$p(V,Y|U) = p(V|U)p(Y|U,V) = p(V|U)p(Y|U), \tag{A21}$$

thus, we have:

$$p(X,Y) = p(U,V,Y) = p(U)p(V,Y|U) = p(U)p(V|U)p(Y|U) \tag{A22}$$

Therefore:

$$\begin{aligned} I(X;Y) &= \int_{X,Y} p(X,Y) \ln \frac{p(X,Y)}{p(X)p(Y)} dXdY \\ &= \int_{U,V,Z} p(U)p(V|U)p(Y|U) \ln \frac{p(U)p(V|U)p(Y|U)}{p(U)p(V|U)p(Y)} dUdVdZ \\ &= \int_{U,Y} p(U)p(Y|U) \ln \frac{p(U)p(Y|U)}{p(U)p(Y)} dUdY \\ &= I(U;Y) \end{aligned} \tag{A23}$$

□

Lemma A3. *(Mutual information will not be affected by concatenating independent variables): If $X \in Dom(X)$ and $Y \in Dom(Y)$ form a Markov chain $X \to Y$, and $Z \in Dom(Z)$ is a random variable which is independent on both X and Y, then:*

$$I(X;Y) = I(X; Y \bigoplus Z) \tag{A24}$$

Proof. Because:

$$p(X, Y \bigoplus Z) = p(X,Y,Z) = p(X)p(Y,Z|X), \tag{A25}$$

furthermore, because $X \to Y$ and Z is independent on both X and Y, therefore:

$$p(Y,Z|X) = p(Y|X)p(Z). \tag{A26}$$

Thus:

$$\begin{aligned} I(X;Y \bigoplus Z) = I(X;Y,Z) &= \int_{XYZ} p(X,Y,Z) \log \frac{p(X,Y,Z)}{p(X)p(Y,Z)} dXdYdZ \\ &= \int_{XYZ} p(X)p(Y,Z|X) \ln \frac{p(X)p(Y,Z|X)}{p(X)p(Y)p(Z)} dXdYdZ \\ &= \int_{XYZ} p(X)p(Y|X)p(Z) \ln \frac{p(X)p(Y|X)}{p(X)p(Y)} dXdYdZ \\ &= \int_{XY} p(X,Y) \ln \frac{p(X,Y)}{p(X)p(Y)} dXdY = I(X;Y) \end{aligned} \tag{A27}$$

□

Definition A1. *(Squeezed Information Channel): A squeezed information channel is a graphic model as shown in Figure A1 which also satisfies the following requirements: (1) the mapping ψ from X to X' is a bijection; (2) χ_q is a q dimensional projector, that is U is a q dimensional projection of X'; (3) U and V form a Markov chain $U \to V$, and f is the conditional probability $P(V|U)$; (3) $\mathcal{N}$ is a random noise which is independent on all other variables; (4) $Y = V \bigoplus N$.*

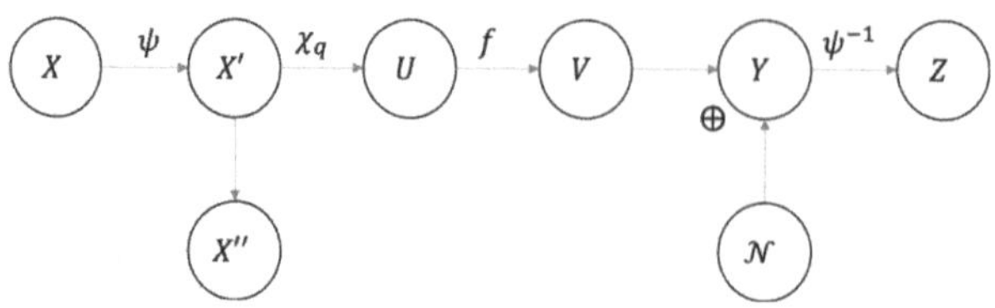

Figure A1. The graphic model of a squeezed information channel.

It is not hard to know that Figure 1 is actually a special case of the squeezed information channel, where $\mathbf{y}_t$, $\mathbf{y}(t+1)$, and $\hat{\mathbf{x}}_{t+1}$ correspond to U, V, and Z respectively.

For this general graphic model, we can prove Theorem 2:

Theorem 2 (Information bottleneck of the Squeezed Information Channel): For the squeezed information channel as shown in Figure A1 and for any ψ, f and $\mathcal{N}$, we have:

$$I(X;Z) = I(U;V) \tag{A28}$$

Proof. Because ψ and ψ^{-1} are all one to one mappings, thus, according to Lemmas A2–A4:

$$I(X;Z) = I(X';Z) = I(X';Y) = I(U;Y) = I(U;V) \tag{A29}$$

□

Therefore, the information of the whole squeezed channel is determined only by the Markov chain f, i.e., the macro-dynamics. Thus f is the bottleneck of the whole squeezed channel.

The Neural Information Squeezer framework can be converted as a Squeezed Information Channel as shown in Figure 3, in which, $\mathbf{x}_t, \mathbf{x}'_t, \mathbf{y}_t, \mathbf{y}(t+1), \mathbf{y}(t+1)', \hat{\mathbf{x}}_{t+1}$, and $\mathbf{z}_{p-q}$ correspond to X, X', U, V, Y, Z, and $\mathcal{N}$, respectively. Therefore,

$$I(\mathbf{y}_t; \mathbf{y}(t+1)) = I(\mathbf{x}_t; \hat{\mathbf{x}}_{t+1}) \tag{A30}$$

We can further extend Theorem 2 to the case of stacked neural information squeezer by the following corollary:

Corollary A1. *Theorem 2 can be extended to stacked neural information squeezer models.*

Proof. Because Equation (A30) holds for any neural information squeezer model whose encoder and decoder are composed by basic units of NIS, therefore, Theorem 2 holds for stacked neural information squeezer models. □

Appendix C. Proof of Theorem 3

At first, we restate Theorem 3 as follow:

Theorem 3 (Mutual information of the model will be closed to the data for a well trained framework): If the neural networks in NIS framework are well-trained, which means

$$p(\hat{\mathbf{x}}_{t+1}|\mathbf{x}_t) \simeq p(\mathbf{x}_{t+1}|\mathbf{x}_t) \tag{A31}$$

where $p \simeq q$ means $D_{KL}(p,q) \to 0$ when the training epoch $\tau \to \infty$, then:

$$I(\hat{\mathbf{x}}_{t+1};\mathbf{x}_t) \simeq I(\mathbf{x}_{t+1};\mathbf{x}_t) \tag{A32}$$

where $\simeq$ means asymptotic equivalence when $\tau \to \infty$.

Proof. According to the objective function, i.e., Equations (13) and (14), we know that if the neural networks in NIS framework are well-trained, Equation (A31) is hold. Therefore:

$$p(\mathbf{x}_t, \hat{\mathbf{x}}_{t+1}) = p(\mathbf{x}_t) \cdot p(\hat{\mathbf{x}_{t+1}}|\mathbf{x}_t) \simeq p(\mathbf{x}_t) \cdot p(\mathbf{x}_{t+1}|\mathbf{x}_t) = p(\mathbf{x}_t, \mathbf{x}_{t+1}), \tag{A33}$$

and also:

$$p(\hat{\mathbf{x}}_{t+1}) = \int_{\mathbf{x}_t} p(\mathbf{x}_t, \hat{\mathbf{x}}_{t+1}) d\mathbf{x}_t \simeq \int_{\mathbf{x}_t} p(\mathbf{x}_t, \mathbf{x}_{t+1}) d\mathbf{x}_t = p(\mathbf{x}_{t+1}), \tag{A34}$$

so,

$$I(\hat{\mathbf{x}}_{t+1}; \mathbf{x}_t)) \simeq I(\mathbf{x}_{t+1}; \mathbf{x}_t) \tag{A35}$$

□

Corollary A2. *(The mutual information of macro-dynamics will not change if the model is well trained): For the well trained NIS model, the Mutual Information of the macro-dynamics f_β will be irrelevant on all the parameters, including the scale q.*

Proof. According to Theorems 2 and 3:

$$I(\mathbf{y}_t; \mathbf{y}(t+1)) = I(\mathbf{x}_t; \hat{\mathbf{x}}_{t+1}) \approx I(\mathbf{x}_t; \mathbf{x}_{t+1}). \tag{A36}$$

This equality is irrelevant with all parameters in neural network and q. □

Appendix D. Proof for Theorem 4

Lemma A4. *For any continuous random variable X and Y, we have:*

$$I(X;Y) = H(Y) + \mathbb{E}_X(\ln|\det(\frac{\partial Y}{\partial X})|), \tag{A37}$$

where $\frac{\partial Y}{\partial X}$ is the Jacobian matrix.

Proof. According to the computation of the mutual information by a continuous mapping:

$$I(X;Y) = H(Y) - H(Y|X), \tag{A38}$$

and:

$$H(Y|X) = -\mathbb{E}_X(\ln|\det(\frac{\partial Y}{\partial X})| \tag{A39}$$

according to [47], thus:

$$I(X;Y) = H(Y) + \mathbb{E}_X(\ln|\det(\frac{\partial Y}{\partial X})|). \tag{A40}$$

□

Theorem 4 (Information on bottleneck is the lower bound of the encoder): For squeezed information chain shown in Figure A1, the information of $U \to V$ is bounded by:

$$I(U;V) \leq I(X;U) = H(U) + \mathbb{E}_X(\ln|\det(\frac{\partial U}{\partial X})|) \leq I(X;X') = H(X) + \mathbb{E}_X(\ln|\det(\frac{\partial X'}{\partial X})|)). \tag{A41}$$

Proof. Because both ψ, χ_q, and f are Markovian, so $X \to X' \to U \to V$ forms a Markov chain. Thus the data processing inequality holds:

$$I(U;V) = I(X;Z) \leq I(X;U) \leq I(X;X'), \tag{A42}$$

and according to Lemma A4:

$$I(U;V) \leq H(U) + \mathbb{E}_X(\ln|\det(\frac{\partial U}{\partial X})|) \leq H(X) + \mathbb{E}_X(\ln|\det(\frac{\partial X'}{\partial X})|)). \tag{A43}$$

□

Applying this theorem in the information squeezed channel (Figure A1), we can obtain the form of Equation (23).

Proof for Theorem 5

We re-state Theorem 5:

Theorem 5 (The mathematical expression for effective information of macro-dynamics): Suppose the probability density of $\mathbf{x}_{t+1}$ under given $\mathbf{x}_t$ can be described by a function $p(\mathbf{x}_{t+1}|\mathbf{x}_t) \equiv G(\mathbf{x}_{t+1}, \mathbf{x}_t)$, and the Neural Information Squeezer framework is well trained, then the effective information of the macro-dynamics of f_β can be calculated by:

$$EI_L(f_\beta) = \frac{1}{(2L)^p} \cdot \int_\sigma \int_{\mathcal{R}^p} G(\mathbf{y}, \psi_\alpha^{-1}(\mathbf{x})) \ln \frac{(2L)^p G(\mathbf{y}, \psi_\alpha^{-1}(\mathbf{x}))}{\int_\sigma G(\mathbf{y}, \psi_\alpha^{-1}(\mathbf{x}'))d\mathbf{x}'} d\mathbf{y}d\mathbf{x}, \tag{A44}$$

where $\sigma \equiv [-L, L]^p$ is the integration region for $\mathbf{x}$ and $\mathbf{x}'$.

Proof. According to Definition of effective information (EI),

$$EI_L(f_{\phi_q}) \equiv I(do(\mathbf{y}_t \equiv \mathbf{u} \sim U([-L, L]^q)); \mathbf{y}(t+1)). \tag{A45}$$

The effect of the do operator can be understood by another graphic model which is shown in Figure A2a.

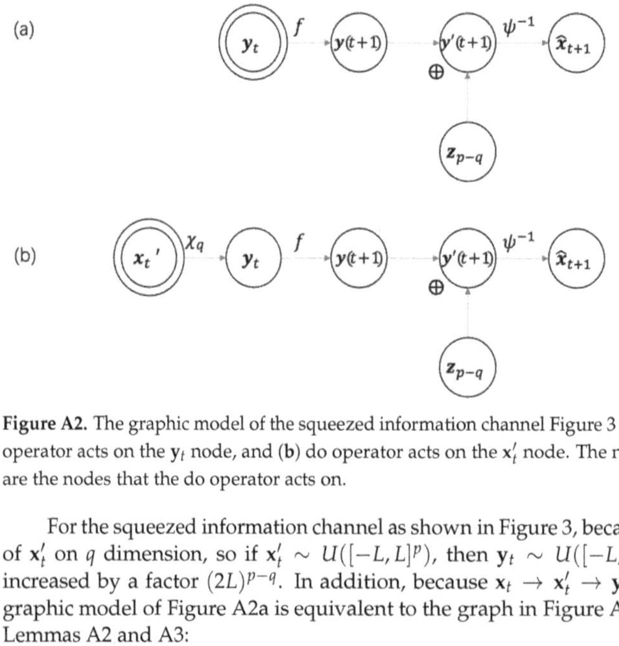

Figure A2. The graphic model of the squeezed information channel Figure 3 after do operation. (**a**) do operator acts on the $\mathbf{y}_t$ node, and (**b**) do operator acts on the $\mathbf{x}_t'$ node. The nodes with double circles are the nodes that the do operator acts on.

For the squeezed information channel as shown in Figure 3, because $\mathbf{y}_t$ is the projection of $\mathbf{x}_t'$ on q dimension, so if $\mathbf{x}_t' \sim U([-L, L]^p)$, then $\mathbf{y}_t \sim U([-L, L]^q)$, but the density increased by a factor $(2L)^{p-q}$. In addition, because $\mathbf{x}_t \to \mathbf{x}_t' \to \mathbf{y}_t \to \mathbf{y}(t+1)$, So, the graphic model of Figure A2a is equivalent to the graph in Figure A2b. And according to Lemmas A2 and A3:

$$I(\mathbf{y}_t; \mathbf{y}(t+1)) = I(\mathbf{x}_t'; \mathbf{y}(t+1)), = I(\mathbf{x}_t'; \hat{\mathbf{x}}_{t+1}) \tag{A46}$$

therefore,

$$\begin{aligned} EI_L(f_{\phi_q}) &\equiv I(do(\mathbf{y}_t \sim U([-L, L]^q)); \mathbf{y}(t+1)) \\ &= I(do(\mathbf{x}_t' \sim U([-L, L]^p)); \mathbf{y}(t+1)) \\ &= I(do(\mathbf{x}_t' \sim U([-L, L]^p)); \hat{\mathbf{x}}_{t+1}). \end{aligned} \tag{A47}$$

And,

$$\begin{aligned} &I(do(\mathbf{x}_t' \sim U([-L, L]^p)); \hat{\mathbf{x}}_{t+1}) \\ &= \int_\sigma \rho \cdot \left(\int_{\hat{\mathbf{x}}_{t+1} \in \mathcal{R}^q} p(\hat{\mathbf{x}}_{t+1}|\mathbf{x}_t') \ln \frac{p(\hat{\mathbf{x}}_{t+1}|\mathbf{x}_t')}{\rho \int_\sigma p(\hat{\mathbf{x}}_{t+1}|\mathbf{x}_t')d\mathbf{x}_t'} \cdot d\hat{\mathbf{x}}_{t+1} \right) d\mathbf{x}_t' \end{aligned} \tag{A48}$$

where $\sigma = [-L, L]^p$ is the integration region, and $\rho = (2L)^{-p}$. Meanwhile, the conditional probability of $\hat{\mathbf{x}}_{t+1}$ under given $\mathbf{x}_t$ is a function $p(\hat{\mathbf{x}}_{t+1} = y|\mathbf{x}_t = x) \equiv F(y, x)$, so:

$$p(\hat{\mathbf{x}}_{t+1}|\mathbf{x}'_t) = p(\hat{\mathbf{x}}_{t+1}|\mathbf{x}_t = \psi^{-1}(\mathbf{x}'_t)) = F(\hat{\mathbf{x}}_{t+1}, \psi^{-1}(\mathbf{x}'_t)) \tag{A49}$$

and according to Theorem 3, if the NIS framework is well trained, we have:

$$p(\hat{\mathbf{x}}_{t+1}|\mathbf{x}_t) = F(\hat{\mathbf{x}}_{t+1}, \mathbf{x}_t) \approx G(\mathbf{x}_{t+1}, \mathbf{x}_t) \tag{A50}$$

Therefore:

$$\begin{aligned} &I(do(\mathbf{x}'_t \sim U([-L, L]^p)); \hat{\mathbf{x}}_{t+1}) \\ &= \int_\sigma \rho \cdot \left(\int_{\hat{\mathbf{x}}_{t+1} \in \mathcal{R}^q} F(\hat{\mathbf{x}}_{t+1}, \psi^{-1}(\mathbf{x}'_t)) \ln \frac{F(\hat{\mathbf{x}}_{t+1}, \psi^{-1}(\mathbf{x}'_t))}{\rho \int_\sigma F(\hat{\mathbf{x}}_{t+1}, \psi^{-1}(\mathbf{x}'_t)) d\mathbf{x}'_t} \cdot d\hat{\mathbf{x}}_{t+1} \right) d\mathbf{x}'_t \\ &\approx \int_\sigma \rho \cdot \left(\int_{\mathbf{x}_{t+1} \in \mathcal{R}^q} G(\mathbf{x}_{t+1}, \psi^{-1}(\mathbf{x}'_t)) \ln \frac{G(\mathbf{x}_{t+1}, \psi^{-1}(\mathbf{x}'_t))}{\rho \int_\sigma G(\mathbf{x}_{t+1}, \psi^{-1}(\mathbf{x}'_t)) d\mathbf{x}'_t} \cdot d\mathbf{x}_{t+1} \right) d\mathbf{x}'_t \end{aligned} \tag{A51}$$

We then use $\mathbf{x}$ or $\mathbf{x}'$ to replace $\mathbf{x}_t{}'$ and use $\mathbf{y}$ to replace $\mathbf{x}_{t+1}$ in the integrations; then, we have:

$$EI_L(f_\beta) \approx \frac{1}{(2L)^p} \int_\sigma \left(\int_{\mathbf{y} \in \mathcal{R}^q} G(\mathbf{y}, \psi^{-1}(\mathbf{x})) \ln \frac{G(\mathbf{y}, \psi^{-1}(\mathbf{x}))}{\rho \int_\sigma G(\mathbf{y}, \psi^{-1}(\mathbf{x}')) d\mathbf{x}'} \cdot d\mathbf{y} \right) d\mathbf{x} \tag{A52}$$

□

Appendix E. Proof for Theorem 6

Theorem 6 (Narrower is Harder): If X is random variable with dimension p, and if the q_1 dimensional random variable U_{q_1} is the projection of a q_2 dimensional variable U_{q_2}, and $0 < q_1 < q_2 < p$, then:

$$I(X; U_{q_1}) \le I(X; U_{q_2}). \tag{A53}$$

Proof. Because $q_1 < q_2$, therefore, U_{q_2} contains U_{q_1} as the component, thus, there exists a $q_2 - q_1$ dimensional random variable $U'_{q_2-q_1}$ such that:

$$U_{q_2} = U_{q_1} \bigoplus U'_{q_2-q_1} \tag{A54}$$

Therefore:

$$H(U_{q_2}) = H(U_{q_1}, U'_{q_2-q_1}) = H(U_{q_1}) + H(U'_{q_2-q_1}|U_{q_1}) \ge H(U_{q_1}) \tag{A55}$$

because $H(U'_{q_2-q_1}|U_{q_1}) \ge 0$, and:

$$\mathbb{E}_X(\ln|\det(\frac{\partial U_{q_2}}{\partial X})| \ge \mathbb{E}_X(\ln|\det(\frac{\partial U_{q_1}}{\partial X})| \tag{A56}$$

because the matrices of $\frac{\partial U_{q_2}}{\partial X}$ and $\frac{\partial U_{q_2}}{\partial X}$ are all sub-matrices of $\frac{\partial \psi}{\partial X}$ and the former contains the latter. Thus, according to Lemma A4:

$$I(X; U_{q_2}) = H(U_{q_2}) + \mathbb{E}_X(\ln|\det(\frac{\partial U_{q_2}}{\partial X})| \ge H(U_{q_1}) + \mathbb{E}_X(\ln|\det(\frac{\partial U_{q_1}}{\partial X}) = I(X; U_{q_1}) \tag{A57}$$

□

Thus, if the number of dimension is smaller, the mutual information between X and U will also be smaller. That means, narrower channel is harder to transfer information.

Combined with Theorems 2 and 4, we have the following inequalities for the squeezed information channel of Figure 3:

$$I(\mathbf{x}_t; \hat{\mathbf{x}}_{t+1}) \leq I(\mathbf{x}_t; \mathbf{y}_t^{q_1}) \leq I(\mathbf{x}_t; \mathbf{y}_t^{q_2}). \tag{A58}$$

This is the form of Theorem 6 in the main text.

References

1. Holland, J.H. *Emergence: From Chaos To Order*; Illustrated edition; Basic Books: New York, NY, USA, 1999.
2. Bedau, M.A. Weak Emergence. *Philos. Perspect.* **1997**, *11*, 375–399. [CrossRef]
3. Pearl, J. *Causality: Models of Reasoning and Inference*, 2nd ed.; Cambridge University Press: Cambridge, UK, 2009.
4. Granger, C.W.J. Investigating Causal Relations by Econometric Models and Cross-spectral Methods. *Econometrica* **1969**, *37*, 424–438. [CrossRef]
5. Hoel, E.P.; Albantakis, L.; Tononi, G. Quantifying causal emergence shows that macro can beat micro. *Proc. Natl. Acad. Sci. USA* **2013**, *110*, 19790–19795. [CrossRef] [PubMed]
6. Hoel, E.P. When the Map Is Better Than the Territory. *Entropy* **2017**, *19*, 188. [CrossRef]
7. Tononi, G.; Sporns, O. Measuring information integration. *BMC Neurosci.* **2003**, *4*, 31. [CrossRef] [PubMed]
8. Varley, T.; Hoel, E. Emergence as the conversion of information: A unifying theory. *arXiv* **2021**, arXiv:2104.13368.
9. Chvykov, P.; Hoel, E. Causal Geometry. *Entropy* **2021**, *23*, 24. [CrossRef]
10. Rosas, F.E.; Mediano, P.A.M.; Jensen, H.J.; Seth, A.K.; Barrett, A.B.; Carhart-Harris, R.L.; Bor, D. Reconciling emergences: An information-theoretic approach to identify causal emergence in multivariate data. *PLoS Comput. Biol.* **2020**, *16*, e1008289. [CrossRef]
11. Varley, T.F. Flickering emergences: The question of locality in information-theoretic approaches to emergence. *arXiv* **2022**, arXiv:2208.14502.
12. Swain, A.; Williams, S.D.; Di Felice, L.J.; Hobson, E.A. Interactions and information: Exploring task allocation in ant colonies using network analysis. *Anim. Behav.* **2022**, *189*, 69–81. [CrossRef]
13. Klein, B.; Hoel, E.; Swain, A.; Griebenow, R.; Levin, M. Evolution and emergence: Higher order information structure in protein interactomes across the tree of life. *Integr. Biol.* **2021**, *13*, 283–294. [CrossRef] [PubMed]
14. Ravi, D.; Hamilton, J.L.; Winfield, E.C.; Lalta, N.; Chen, R.H.; Cole, M.W. Causal emergence of task information from dynamic network interactions in the human brain. *Rev. Neurosci.* **2022**, *31*, 25–46.
15. Klein, B.; Swain, A.; Byrum, T.; Scarpino, S.V.; Fagan, W.F. Exploring noise, degeneracy and determinism in biological networks with the einet package. *Methods Ecol. Evol.* **2022**, *13*, 799–804. [CrossRef]
16. Klein, B.; Hoel, E. The Emergence of Informative Higher Scales in Complex Networks. *Complexity* **2020**, *2020*, 8932526. [CrossRef]
17. Varley, T.; Hoel, E. Emergence as the conversion of information: A unifying theory. *Philos. Trans. R. Soc. A* **2022**, *380*, 20210150. [CrossRef] [PubMed]
18. Silver, D.; Schrittwieser, J.; Simonyan, K.; Antonoglou, I.; Huang, A.; Guez, A.; Hubert, T.; Baker, L.; Lai, M.; Bolton, A.; et al. Mastering the game of Go without human knowledge. *Nature* **2017**, *550*, 354–359. [CrossRef]
19. LeCun, Y.; Bengio, Y.; Hinton, G. Deep learning. *Nature* **2015**, *521*, 436–444. [CrossRef]
20. Reichstein, M.; Camps-Valls, G.; Stevens, B.; Jung, M.; Denzler, J.; Carvalhais, N. Deep learning and process understanding for data-driven Earth system science. *Nature* **2019**, *566*, 195–204. [CrossRef]
21. Senior, A.W.; Evans, R.; Jumper, J.; Kirkpatrick, J.; Sifre, L.; Green, T.; Qin, C.; Žídek, A.; Nelson, A.W.R.; Bridgland, A.; et al. Improved protein structure prediction using potentials from deep learning. *Nature* **2020**, *577*, 706–710. [CrossRef]
22. Tank, A.; Covert, I.; Foti, N.; Shojaie, A.; Fox, E. Neural Granger Causality. *arXiv* **2018**, arXiv:1802.05842.
23. Löwe, S.; Madras, D.; Zemel, R.; Welling, M. Amortized causal discovery: Learning to infer causal graphs from time-series data. *arXiv* **2020**, arXiv:2006.10833.
24. Glymour, C.; Zhang, K.; Spirtes, P. Review of Causal Discovery Methods Based on Graphical Models. *Front. Genet.* **2019**, *10*, 524. [CrossRef] [PubMed]
25. Casadiego, J.; Nitzan, M.; Hallerberg, S.; Timme, M. Model-free inference of direct network interactions from nonlinear collective dynamics. *Nat. Commun.* **2017**, *8*, 1–10. [CrossRef] [PubMed]
26. Sanchez-Gonzalez, A.; Heess, N.; Springenberg, J.T.; Merel, J.; Riedmiller, M.; Hadsell, R.; Battaglia, P. Graph networks as learnable physics engines for inference and control. In Proceedings of the International Conference on Machine Learning, Stockholm, Sweden, 10–15 July 2018 ; pp. 4470–4479.
27. Zhang, Z.; Zhao, Y.; Liu, J.; Wang, S.; Tao, R.; Xin, R.; Zhang, J. A general deep learning framework for network reconstruction and dynamics learning. *Appl. Netw. Sci.* **2019**, *4*, 1–17. [CrossRef]
28. Kipf, T.; Fetaya, E.; Wang, K.C.; Welling, M.; Zemel, R. Neural relational inference for interacting systems. In Proceedings of the International Conference on Machine Learning, Stockholm, Sweden, 10–15 July 2018; pp. 2688–2697.
29. Chen, B.; Huang, K.; Raghupathi, S.; Chandratreya, I.; Du, Q.; Lipson, H. Discovering State Variables Hidden in Experimental Data. *arXiv* **2021**, arXiv:2112.10755.

30. Koch-Janusz, M.; Ringel, Z. Mutual information, neural networks and the renormalization group. *Nat. Phys.* **2018**, *14*, 578–582. [CrossRef]
31. Li, S.H.; Wang, L. Neural Network Renormalization Group. *Phys. Rev. Lett.* **2018**, *121*, 260601. [CrossRef]
32. Hu, H.Y.; Li, S.H.; Wang, L.; You, Y.Z. Machine learning holographic mapping by neural network renormalization group. *Phys. Rev. Res.* **2020**, *2*, 023369. [CrossRef]
33. Hu, H.; Wu, D.; You, Y.Z.; Olshausen, B.; Chen, Y. RG-Flow: A hierarchical and explainable flow model based on renormalization group and sparse prior. *Mach. Learn. Sci. Technol.* **2022**, *3*, 035009. [CrossRef]
34. Gökmen, D.E.; Ringel, Z.; Huber, S.D.; Koch-Janusz, M. Statistical physics through the lens of real-space mutual information. *Phys. Rev. Lett.* **2021**, *127*, 240603. [CrossRef]
35. Chalupka, K.; Eberhardt, F.; Perona, P. Causal feature learning: An overview. *Behaviormetrika* **2017**, *44*, 137–164. [CrossRef]
36. Schölkopf, B.; Locatello, F.; Bauer, S.; Ke, N.R.; Kalchbrenner, N.; Goyal, A.; Bengio, Y. Toward causal representation learning. *Proc. IEEE* **2021**, *109*, 612–634. [CrossRef]
37. Iwasaki, Y.; Simon, H.A. Causality and model abstraction. *Artif. Intell.* **1994**, *67*, 143–194. [CrossRef]
38. Rubenstein, P.K.; Weichwald, S.; Bongers, S.; Mooij, J.; Janzing, D.; Grosse-Wentrup, M.; Schölkopf, B. Causal consistency of structural equation models. *arXiv* **2017**, arXiv:1707.00819.
39. Beckers, S.; Eberhardt, F.; Halpern, J.Y. Approximate causal abstractions. In Proceedings of the Uncertainty in Artificial Intelligence, Virtual, 3–6 August 2020; pp. 606–615.
40. Beckers, S.; Eberhardt, F.; Halpern, J.Y. Approximate Causal Abstraction. *arXiv* **2019**, arXiv:1906.11583v2.
41. Teshima, T.; Ishikawa, I.; Tojo, K.; Oono, K.; Ikeda, M.; Sugiyama, M. Coupling-based invertible neural networks are universal diffeomorphism approximators. *Adv. Neural Inf. Process. Syst.* **2020**, *33*, 3362–3373.
42. Teshima, T.; Tojo, K.; Ikeda, M.; Ishikawa, I.; Oono, K. Universal approximation property of neural ordinary differential equations. *arXiv* **2017**, arXiv:2012.02414.
43. Dinh, L.; Sohl-Dickstein, J.; Bengio, S. Density estimation using real nvp. *arXiv* **2016**, arXiv:1605.08803.
44. Kingma, D.P.; Welling, M. Auto-encoding variational bayes. *arXiv* **2013**, arXiv:1312.6114.
45. Shwartz-Ziv, R.; Tishby, N. Opening the black box of deep neural networks via information. *arXiv* **2017**, arXiv:1703.00810.
46. Williams, P.L.; Beer., R.D. Nonnegative decomposition of multivariate information. *arXiv* **2017**, arXiv:1004.2515.
47. Geiger, B.C.; Kubin, G. On the information loss in memoryless systems: The multivariate case. *arXiv* **2011**, arXiv:1109.4856.

entropy

MDPI

Article

An Exact Theory of Causal Emergence for Linear Stochastic Iteration Systems

Kaiwei Liu [1], Bing Yuan [2] and Jiang Zhang [1,2,*]

[1] School of Systems Science, Beijing Normal University, Beijing 100875, China; 202221250005@mail.bnu.edu.cn
[2] Swarma Research, Beijing 102300, China; yuanbing_cn@hotmail.com
* Correspondence: zhangjiang@bnu.edu.cn

Abstract: After coarse-graining a complex system, the dynamics of its macro-state may exhibit more pronounced causal effects than those of its micro-state. This phenomenon, known as causal emergence, is quantified by the indicator of effective information. However, two challenges confront this theory: the absence of well-developed frameworks in continuous stochastic dynamical systems and the reliance on coarse-graining methodologies. In this study, we introduce an exact theoretic framework for causal emergence within linear stochastic iteration systems featuring continuous state spaces and Gaussian noise. Building upon this foundation, we derive an analytical expression for effective information across general dynamics and identify optimal linear coarse-graining strategies that maximize the degree of causal emergence when the dimension averaged uncertainty eliminated by coarse-graining has an upper bound. Our investigation reveals that the maximal causal emergence and the optimal coarse-graining methods are primarily determined by the principal eigenvalues and eigenvectors of the dynamic system's parameter matrix, with the latter not being unique. To validate our propositions, we apply our analytical models to three simplified physical systems, comparing the outcomes with numerical simulations, and consistently achieve congruent results.

Keywords: causal emergence; effective information; linear stochastic iteration system; coarse-graining

1. Introduction

Many complex systems [1] in reality, such as cities [2–4], companies [5–7], bird flocks [8,9], perception systems [10–12], brains [13–15], cells [16,17], molecules, etc., all exhibit emergent behaviors or statistical laws on a macro-level that cannot be simply derived from micro-level properties or dynamics. However, how to quantitatively characterize emergence has only recently garnered widespread attention [18–24]. The theories of causal emergence attempt to capture the conception of emergence from the point of view of causality. Intuitively, causal emergence refers to the phenomenon in dynamical systems where stronger causal effects can be obtained on macro-states by coarse-graining the micro-states [25]. There are three different ways to quantify the idea of causal emergence, which are based on effective information [22,23], partial information decomposition [15,21,24,26,27], and dynamical independence [10,14,20], respectively. In this paper, we mainly focus on the first way.

Erik Hoel introduced the initial quantitative theory for causal emergence, founded on Effective Information (EI) [22,23,25]. Nevertheless, the original framework is limited to quantifying discrete Markov chains in both the time domain and state space [28,29], overlooking continuous state spaces. To extend the causal emergence theory in continuous spaces, P. Chvykov and E. Hoel put forth the theory of causal geometry [30], wherein they devised a method for calculating EI in functional mappings across continuous state spaces [6,31]. Nonetheless, this theory solely explores general functional mappings and neglects the multi-step dynamical evolution, rendering it inapplicable to dynamical systems in continuous state spaces. Furthermore, all of Hoel's theories [22,23,25,30,32,33] necessitate a predefined coarse-graining strategy to discern instances of causal emergence. While this coarse-graining strategy can be derived by maximizing EI for macro-dynamics, solving the optimization problem for continuous variables proves challenging [6,34,35].

There exist various approaches to coarse-grain the micro-states of complex systems, including manually designed renormalization methods [36], traditional dimensionality reduction techniques [37–41], and machine-learning-based methods for coarse-graining or renormalization [6,34,42]. To automatically discover coarse-graining strategies that optimize causal emergence, J. Zhang and K. Liu introduced a machine-learning framework known as the Neural Information Squeezer (NIS) [43], employing reversible neural networks. This framework facilitates the automatic extraction of effective coarse-graining strategies and macro-state dynamics, enabling the direct identification of causal emergence from diverse time series data. Subsequently, the research team proposed the enhanced NIS+ framework [35], which integrates the optimization of coarse-graining through EI maximization into machine learning. NIS and NIS+ have successfully addressed the challenge of identifying causal emergence in data by optimizing coarse-graining techniques and macro-dynamics within continuous stochastic dynamical systems through EI maximization. Nonetheless, machine-learning-based methods [44–46] rely heavily on data adequacy and the level of neural network training. While they can provide numerical solutions, they lack a ground truth for assessing the quality of model training and the reliability of outcome indicators.

To overcome the limitations identified in previous studies, this paper will first derive analytical solutions for EI and causal emergence in linear stochastic iterative systems. It will then determine the explicit expression for maximal causal emergence and the corresponding optimal coarse-graining strategies, under the condition that the dimension-averaged uncertainty eliminated by coarse-graining is constrained by a specified threshold. Subsequent to this, numerical simulation experiments will be conducted on simplified physical systems to validate the theoretical findings. Additionally, we will explore challenges such as maximizing causal emergence under an alternative condition involving constructing the coarse-graining map through a combination of dimensionality reduction projection and rotation, showcasing the interplay between determinism and non-degeneracy, examining the connection between maximizing causal emergence and minimizing prediction errors in dynamics, and addressing nonlinear dynamics. The primary objective of this research is to address deficiencies in EI related to Transitional Probability Matrices (TPM) [22,25] and causal geometry within a toy model context [30]. Furthermore, it aims to lay a theoretical groundwork to enhance the identification of causal emergence through machine learning [35,43].

2. Basic Notions and Problems Formulation

2.1. Continuous Linear Stochastic Iteration System

A stochastic iteration system [47] is a sequence of random variables, x_t, at different times, t, which usually represent the dynamic evolution of a certain quantity, such as stock prices, temperature changes, traffic flows, etc. This paper mainly focuses on linear high-dimensional stochastic iteration systems [48] to reduce our calculation.

For variable $x_t \in \mathcal{R}^n$ at time t in the stochastic iteration system, the evolution of x_t follows the stochastic iterative equation

$$x_{t+1} = Ax_t + \varepsilon_t. \tag{1}$$

We define matrix $A \in \mathcal{R}^{n\times n}$ as a dynamical parameter matrix. In Equation (1), $\varepsilon_t \sim \mathcal{N}(0,\Sigma)$ represents Gaussian noises with zero means and the covariance matrix $\Sigma \in \mathcal{R}^{n\times n}$. We specify the ranks of matrices $\text{rk}(A) = \text{rk}(\Sigma) = n$. $\text{rk}(\cdot)$ means the rank of a matrix. We can easily observe that the probability of x_{t+1} falling in a region centered with Ax_t.

2.2. Coarse-Graining

In the realm of linear stochastic iterative systems, we confine coarse-graining strategies to linear maps. Therefore, a direct approach entails employing the relatively straightforward projection matrix coarse-graining method.

Generally, the coarse-graining strategy can be represented as $\phi(x_t) : \mathcal{R}^n \to \mathcal{R}^k, k < n$. It is designed to map micro-states to a lower-dimensional space and to convert micro-states into macro-states.

Definition 1. *(Coarse-graining strategy): For variable x_t at time t in the linear stochastic iteration system, we define linear mapping*

$$\phi(x_t) = Wx_t, \tag{2}$$

where $W \in \mathcal{R}^{k\times n}$, $\mathrm{rk}(W) = k$, to map x_t in high-dimensional space $\mathcal{R}^n$ to y_t in low-dimensional space $\mathcal{R}^k$, achieving coarse-graining of variables

$$y_t = \phi(x_t) = Wx_t \tag{3}$$

in the stochastic iteration system.

2.3. Macro Dynamical System

The coarse-graining strategy can map a set of micro-states to specific macro-states, and thus can naturally derive the expressions from micro-state parameter matrices A and Σ for dynamical models on macro-state space, which can be described by macro-state parameter matrices A_M and Σ_M. Since $W \in \mathcal{R}^{k\times n}$ in the linear coarse-graining strategy is irreversible, we need the Moore–Penrose generalized inverse matrix [49] $W^\dagger$ in matrix theory [50] to derive A_M.

According to Equations (1) and (3), we can get that

$$y_{t+1} = Wx_{t+1} = WAx_t + W\varepsilon_t. \tag{4}$$

Due to the fact that both the micro-dynamical model itself and the coarse-graining strategies are linear transformations, and based on the properties of linear algebra, there is also a set of equations for the macro-dynamics. Thus, we hope that there is a matrix A_M satisfying the following equation:

$$y_{t+1} = A_M y_t + \varepsilon_{M,t}. \tag{5}$$

According to Equations (4) and (5) and $y_t = Wx_t$, we can get that

$$\begin{cases} WA = A_M W \\ W\varepsilon_t = \varepsilon_{M,t} \end{cases}. \tag{6}$$

Since $\varepsilon_t \sim \mathcal{N}(0,\Sigma)$, $\varepsilon_{M,t} = W\varepsilon_t \sim \mathcal{N}(0,\Sigma_M)$ and $W \in \mathcal{R}^{k\times n}$ is irreversible, we require the Moore–Penrose generalized inverse matrix $W^\dagger \in \mathcal{R}^{n\times k}$, $WW^\dagger = I_k$ to solve Equation (6). By multiplying both sides of the first equation of Equation (6) by $W^\dagger$, we can obtain the macro-state parameter matrix,

$$A_M = WAW^\dagger, \tag{7}$$

and the macro dynamics in the Definition 2 as follows.

Definition 2. *(Macro dynamics): For the linear stochastic iteration system in Equation (1), the variables $x_t \in \mathcal{R}^n, t = 0, 1, \ldots,$ are mapped to macro state variables $y_t \in \mathcal{R}^k, t = 0, 1, \ldots,$*

and there exists a new evolutionary dynamics between macro state variables, which we call macro dynamics. Macro dynamics can be represented by macro iterative equations,

$$y_{t+1} = A_M y_t + \varepsilon_{M,t}, \quad (8)$$

in which $A_M = WAW^\dagger \in \mathcal{R}^{k\times k}, \varepsilon_{M,t} \sim \mathcal{N}(0,\Sigma_M), \Sigma_M = W\Sigma W^T$. $W^\dagger$ *is the Moore–Penrose generalized inverse matrix of* W.

2.4. Inverse-Coarse-Graining

To evaluate the information loss caused by coarse-graining and derive macro dynamics, we also need to transform the macro-state back to the micro-state, which is called inverse-coarse-graining. Due to the difference in dimensions n and k of the vectors before and after transformation, coarse-graining is not a reversible process. For linear transformations, irreversibility is manifested as $W \in \mathcal{R}^{k\times n}$ in linear coarse-graining.

Definition 3. *(Inverse-coarse-graining): As* $W^\dagger$ *is the Moore–Penrose generalized inverse matrix of* W*, we define*

$$\phi^\dagger(y_t) = W^\dagger y_t, \quad (9)$$

$W^\dagger \in \mathcal{R}^{n\times k}$, $\mathrm{rk}(W^\dagger) = k$ *as the inverse-coarse-graining mapping of variables in the stochastic iteration system. By applying the inverse-coarse-graining*

$$\hat{x}_t = W^\dagger y_t, \quad (10)$$

we can map the variable $y_t \in \mathcal{R}^k$ *after dimensionality reduction back to a high-dimensional space,* $\mathcal{R}^n$.

With inverse-coarse-graining, we can then estimate the prediction loss function of the dynamics after coarse-graining.

3. Effective Information and Causal Emergence

With the definitions and expressions of micro dynamics and macro dynamics, we can study the phenomenon of causal emergence. We start with the calculation of effective information and then use the method of difference of effective information between micro-dynamics and macro-dynamics to calculate the degree of causal emergence.

3.1. Effective Information

We refer to Hoel's Effective Information (EI) metric to measure the magnitude of causal effects in dynamical systems. In general, EI can be understood as the mutual information between the probability distributions of the states of variables at two different time points when the state at the earlier time is intervened artificially and keeps the causal mechanism, i.e., the transitional probability $Pr(x_{t+1}|x_t)$, unchanged, which is

$$EI = I(\tilde{x}_{t+1}, x_t | do(x_t \sim U(X))), \quad (11)$$

where $x_t \in X$, and $U(X)$ means the uniform distribution or maximum entropy distribution on X. The intervention is formalized using Judea Pearl's theory [51] of causality, particularly through $do(\cdot)$ operations, which means artificially defining the probability distribution space of a variable. Consequently, the distribution of x_{t+1} will be indirectly altered by the intervention on x_t through the causal mechanism $Pr(x_{t+1}|x_t)$. Therefore, $\tilde{x}_{t+1}$ denotes the random variable representing x_{t+1} following the intervention on x_t. It should be noted that Equation (11) is only an operational definition and the intervention of the $do(\cdot)$ operator is just an imaginary operation to calculate EI but has no real physical meaning.

The most classic applications of EI are in the analysis of Transitional Probability Matrices (TPM) for Markov chains. Assuming our probability transition matrix is $M = (M_{ij})_{n\times n} = (M_1^T, \ldots, M_i^T, \ldots, M_n^T)^T \in \mathcal{R}^{n\times n}$, $M_i = (M_{i1}, \ldots, M_{ij}, \ldots, M_{in}) \in \mathcal{R}^{1\times n}$, $1 \leq i, j \leq n$, for the intervention on the Markov transition matrix at t, let $P(X_t = x_t) = 1/n$, then the state at $t+1$ will follow the effect distribution $E_D = (\sum_i M_{i1}/n, \ldots, \sum_i M_{ij}/n, \ldots, \sum_i M_{in}/n) \in \mathcal{R}^{1\times n}$. So, EI is [18]:

$$EI(M) = \frac{1}{n}\sum_{i=1}^{n} D_{KL}(M_i||E_D) = \frac{1}{n}\sum_{i,j} M_{ij}\log_2\left(\frac{nM_{ij}}{\sum_l M_{lj}}\right), \tag{12}$$

where $D_{KL}(\cdot||\cdot)$ is the KL-divergence between two probability distributions. The benefit of expressing Equation (11) to the new form of Equation (12) is to stress that EI is only the function of the dynamics (M) and independent of the distribution of x_t. This calculation method requires both variable time and state space to be discrete.

According to previous works [22,25,29], effective information, $EI(M)$, can be divided into two parts, determinism $-\langle H(M_i)\rangle_i$ and non-degeneracy $H(E_D)$, as

$$\begin{aligned} EI(M) &= -\langle H(M_i)\rangle_i + H(E_D) \\ &= \underbrace{\frac{1}{n}\sum_{i,j} M_{ij}\log_2(M_{ij})}_{Determinism} + \underbrace{\sum_j\left[-\frac{\sum_l M_{lj}}{n}\log_2\left(\frac{\sum_l M_{lj}}{n}\right)\right]}_{Non-degeneracy}. \end{aligned} \tag{13}$$

Determinism measures how reliably x_t leads to the future state x_{t+1} of the system. Non-degeneracy is the opposite of degeneracy. Degeneracy measures to what degree there is deterministic convergence (not due to noise) from other states onto the future states x_{t+1} specified by x_t; degeneracy refers to multiple ways of deterministically achieving the same effect and non-degeneracy is opposite to it. We optimized Hoel's method [22] in which $EI = determinism - degeneracy$ by replacing subtracting degeneracy with adding non-degeneracy, making the calculation commutative. Then, determinism and non-degeneracy can be calculated separately and added together to obtain EI.

Further, we can generalize EI to a continuous state space. We should replace summations with integrals and change the intervened distribution of x_t from a discrete equal probability distribution $P(x_t) = 1/n$ to a continuous uniform distribution $U([-L/2, L/2]^n)$ in which the probability density function is $p(x_t) = 1/L^n$. Since the intervened distribution cannot be defined on an infinite space such as $\mathcal{R}^n$, we set the intervention on a limited sub-region of $\mathcal{R}^n$, which is $[-L/2, L/2]^n$, where L is a hyperparameter with a value being at least larger than the maximum of x_t within finite time steps. Barnett and colleagues introduced a direct link between linear modeling and all the information theoretic measures [52]. Although their model is similar to a stochastic iterative system, it is based on Granger causality and there is no intervention.

We can refer to Hoel's framework [22,32] to derive an expression for the effective information of a linear stochastic iteration system (Equation (1)). Actually, according to Equation (1), the conditional distribution of x_{t+1} under given x_t is a Gaussian distribution, $p(x_{t+1}|x_t) = \mathcal{N}(Ax_t, \Sigma)$. Therefore, we can compute the EI for this Gaussian distribution [43] as $EI = I(x_{t+1}, x_t|do(x_t \sim U))$, drawing an analogy to mutual information and information entropy within a Gaussian distribution [53] as

$$EI(A, \Sigma) = \ln\frac{|\det(A)|L^n}{(2\pi e)^{\frac{n}{2}}\det(\Sigma)^{\frac{1}{2}}}. \tag{14}$$

It is particularly emphasized that when $n = 1$, $A = a, \Sigma = \sigma^2$ and $\mathcal{J}(a,\sigma^2) = EI(a,\sigma^2)$, the effective information can be expressed as

$$EI(a,\sigma^2) = \ln \frac{aL}{\sqrt{2\pi e}\sigma}, \tag{15}$$

which is the simplest form of the effective information of within a Gaussian distribution.

Similar to $EI(M)$ of discrete systems, $EI(A,\Sigma)$ of continuous systems can also be decomposed into two terms, determinism $-\langle H(p(x_{t+1}|x_t))\rangle_{x_t}$ and non-degeneracy $H(E_D(x_{t+1}))$ as

$$\begin{aligned} EI(A,\Sigma) &= -\langle H(p(x_{t+1}|x_t))\rangle_{x_t} + H(E_D(x_{t+1})) \\ &= \underbrace{-\ln\left[(2\pi e)^{\frac{n}{2}} \det(\Sigma)^{\frac{1}{2}}\right]}_{Determinism} + \underbrace{\ln(|det(A)|L^n)}_{Non-degeneracy}. \end{aligned} \tag{16}$$

The higher the determinism or the non-degeneracy, the stronger the causal effect of the stochastic iteration system [22]. The specific derivation process can refer to the calculation process in Appendix A.

Since the calculation of EI involves multiple integrals, L^n appears in the expression of EI. When the value of L is high, the value of EI becomes higher after n powers of L. Therefore, we stipulate that when calculating causal emergence, the EI in different dimensions is dimensionally averaged to eliminate the impact of power growth of L. Another reason for taking the average on the dimension is that, for the comparison of EI from different dimensions, dimension averaged EI can eliminate L, which is shown in Section 3.2. Here, in Theorem 4, we define a new index that is effective information for stochastic iterating systems ($\mathcal{J}$).

Definition 4. *(Effective information for stochastic iterating systems): For the linear stochastic iteration systems like Equation (1), the effective information of the dynamical system is calculated as*

$$\mathcal{J}(A,\Sigma) \equiv \frac{EI(A,\Sigma)}{n} = \frac{1}{n}\ln\frac{|\det(A)|L^n}{(2\pi e)^{\frac{n}{2}}\det(\Sigma)^{\frac{1}{2}}} = \ln\frac{|\det(A)|^{\frac{1}{n}}L}{(2\pi e)^{\frac{1}{2}}\det(\Sigma)^{\frac{1}{2n}}} \tag{17}$$

where $\det(\cdot)$ *represents the determinant value corresponding to a matrix* $\cdot$, $|\cdot|$ *represents the absolute value of* $\cdot$, *and L represents the interval size of the* $do(\cdot)$ *intervention.*

The effective information $\mathcal{J}$ *can also be decomposed into two parts, determinism and non-degeneracy, as*

$$\mathcal{J}(A,\Sigma) = \underbrace{-\ln\left[(2\pi e)^{\frac{1}{2}}\det(\Sigma)^{\frac{1}{2n}}\right]}_{Determinism} + \underbrace{\ln\left(|det(A)|^{\frac{1}{n}}L\right)}_{Non-degeneracy}. \tag{18}$$

For calculation process of Difinition 4, refer to Appendix A. $\mathcal{J}(A,\Sigma)$ can be used to measure the causal effects of micro dynamics and macro dynamics and then be used to calculate causal emergence. It should be noted that the scope L of *do* intervention in macro-state dynamics EI is related to $W \in \mathcal{R}^{n\times k}$. Therefore, we need to limit the range of W to ensure the *do* intervention range of macro-state $y_t \in \mathcal{R}^k$ and micro-state $x_t \in \mathcal{R}^n$ as $do(y_t) \sim U([-L/2, L/2]^k)$ and $do(x_t) \sim U([-L/2, L/2]^n)$, on which we will conduct more analysis in Section 3.4.

3.2. Causal Emergence

After obtaining effective information for stochastic iterating systems $\mathcal{J}$ at different dimensions k of variables x_t, we still have a problem to solve. Except for the influence of indices, the value of hyperparameter L itself, which is artificially assumed, also has a great influence on the results of $\mathcal{J}$. This hyperparameter can be eliminated by calculating causal emergence for stochastic iterating systems as Definition 5.

Definition 5. *(Causal emergence for stochastic iterating systems) Hyperparameter L can be eliminated by subtraction as*

$$\Delta\mathcal{J} = \mathcal{J}_M - \mathcal{J}_m, \tag{19}$$

where $\mathcal{J}_m \equiv \mathcal{J}(A, \Sigma)$ is the EI for the micro-dynamics (Equation (1), $\mathcal{J}_M \equiv \mathcal{J}(A_M, \Sigma_M)$ is the EI for the macro-dynamics (Equation (8)), and $\Delta\mathcal{J}$ is the degree of causal emergence for stochastic iterating systems.

Through the calculations in Appendix A, we obtain the following theorem. In this theorem, we not only calculate the analytical solution for causal emergence but also ensure that the degree of the analytical solution is only related to the parameters of stochastic iterating systems without the influence of L.

Theorem 1. *(Analytical solution for causal emergence): For the linear stochastic iteration systems like Equation (1), causal emergence of the system after coarse-graining $y_t = \phi(x_t) = Wx_t$, $W \in \mathcal{R}^{k\times n}$, is calculated as*

$$\Delta\mathcal{J} = \underbrace{\ln\frac{|\det(WAW^{\dagger})|^{\frac{1}{k}}}{|\det(A)|^{\frac{1}{n}}}}_{Non-degeneracy Emergence} + \underbrace{\ln\frac{|\det(\Sigma)|^{\frac{1}{2n}}}{|\det(W\Sigma W^T)|^{\frac{1}{2k}}}}_{Determinism Emergence} \tag{20}$$

$W \in \mathcal{R}^{k\times n}$, $x_t \in \mathcal{R}^n$, $y_t \in \mathcal{R}^k$. Causal Emergence can also be divided into two terms, and we name them as non-degeneracy emergence and determinism emergence separately. Both terms depend on the coarse-grained results of the overall derivative and noise indicators, respectively.

The premise for Theorem 1 to hold is that both macro and micro states can be represented by L as the range of values, and the premise is that the two cannot differ by too much order of magnitude. When the intervention interval size for each dimension of micro- and macro-variables is consistent and equal to L, L can be directly eliminated when calculating causal emergence, so $\Delta\mathcal{J}$ is independent with L.

3.3. Some Bounds Related with Causal Emergence

After inferring the calculation method of $\Delta\mathcal{J}$, we can determine whether there is causal emergence in the macro states after coarse-graining. Next, we will find an optimal matrix W to maximize the degree of causal emergence $\Delta\mathcal{J}$ [22,43]. To solve this problem, we will firstly discuss the upper bounds related with the two terms, the determinism emergence and non-degeneracy emergence, in Equation (20) separately. Here we have the lemmas below.

The first lemma is to analyze non-degeneracy emergence by optimizing $A_M = WAW^{\dagger}$.

Lemma 1. *For matrix A, its eigenvalues can be real numbers or complex numbers, while the range of absolute values (modulus) for $|\det(WAW^{\dagger})|$ is bounded:*

$$0 \leq \left|\det(WAW^{\dagger})\right| \leq \prod_{i=1}^{k}|\lambda_i|, \tag{21}$$

where $A \in \mathcal{R}^{n\times n}$, $W \in \mathcal{R}^{k\times n}$, $W^{\dagger} \in \mathcal{R}^{n\times k}$ is the Moore–Penrose generalized inverse matrix of W, and k is the rank of the matrix W.

(1) When the eigenvalues are all real numbers, $|\lambda_1| \geq |\lambda_2| \geq \cdots \geq |\lambda_n| \geq 0$ are n absolute values of eigenvalues of matrix A, sorted from largest to smallest, $\lambda_1, \lambda_2, \ldots, \lambda_n \in R$.

(2) When the eigenvalues contain imaginary numbers, $|\cdot|$ represents the modulus of complex numbers. Note that since the eigenvalues of imaginary numbers appear together with their conjugate complex numbers, both eigenvalues must have equal moduli and must be discarded or retained simultaneously.

(3) *When A is a symmetric matrix and $A > 0$ is a positive definite matrix, since $\lambda_1 \geq \lambda_2 \geq \cdots \geq \lambda_n \geq 0$, we can just write the equation as*

$$\prod_{i=n-k+1}^{n} \lambda_i \leq \det(WAW^{\dagger}) \leq \prod_{i=1}^{k} \lambda_i. \tag{22}$$

For proof of the lemma, refer to in Appendix B. In addition, we can verify this lemma through numerical simulations. For example, for matrix A with eigenvalues of $\lambda_1 = 2.540, \lambda_2 = 1.380, \lambda_3 = -0.4899, \lambda_4 = 0.1149$, we randomly generate the elements of the matrix W. From Figure 1a, we can see that there is an upper bound $\lambda_1\lambda_2$ on the corresponding $\det(A_M)$ value of each W. If A is also randomly generated, we can see that all the scatter points are below the diagonal line $y = x$ in Figure 1b, which means Lemma 1 is satisfied.

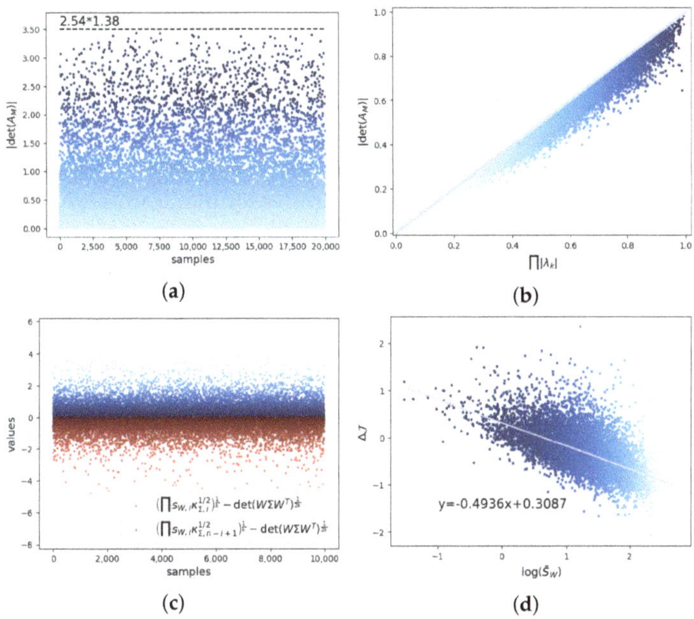

Figure 1. Experimental results of the simulation of the lemma and the theorem presented in Section 3. (**a**) For matrix A with eigenvalues of $\lambda_1 = 2.540, \lambda_2 = 1.380, \lambda_3 = -0.4899, \lambda_4 = 0.1149$, we randomly generate matrix W. We can see that there is an upper bound $\lambda_1\lambda_2$ on the corresponding $\det(A_M)$ value of each W. (**b**) If A is also randomly generated, we can see the scatter plot that conforms to Lemma 1. (**c**) We validate the inequality using randomly generated Σ and W. We can control the range of $\det(W\Sigma W^T)$ by adjusting the magnitude of the singular value of W. (**d**) The smaller the mean singular value of W we generate, the greater the degree of causal emergence $\Delta\mathcal{J}$.

After the lemma regarding $|\det(A_M)| = |\det(WAW^{\dagger})|$, the next lemma regards $\det(\Sigma_M) = \det(W\Sigma W^T)$, which is related to the determinism emergence.

Lemma 2. *We define the singular values of W as $s_{W,1} \geq s_{W,2} \geq \cdots \geq s_{W,k}$, then $\det(W\Sigma W^T)$ satisfies*

$$\left(\prod_{i=1}^{k} s_{W,i}\kappa_{n-i+1}^{\frac{1}{2}}\right)^{\frac{1}{k}} \leq \det(W\Sigma W^T)^{\frac{1}{2k}} \leq \left(\prod_{i=1}^{k} s_{W,i}\kappa_i^{\frac{1}{2}}\right)^{\frac{1}{k}}, \tag{23}$$

where $\kappa_1 \geq \kappa_2 \geq \cdots \geq \kappa_n$ are the eigenvalues of Σ. When $\Sigma = \sigma^2 I$, the equal sign holds and

$$\det(W\Sigma W^T)^{\frac{1}{2k}} = \sigma\left(\prod_{i=1}^{k} s_{W,i}\right)^{\frac{1}{k}}. \tag{24}$$

In Figure 1c, we validate the inequalities using randomly generated Σ and W. Therefore, we can control the range of $\det(W\Sigma W^T)$ by adjusting the magnitude of the singular values of W. We further can adjust the magnitude of the singular value of W to weaken the noise and enhance the causal emergence, as we can see in Lemma 2. As shown in Figure 1d, the smaller the mean singular values of W we generate, the greater the degree of causal emergence $\Delta\mathcal{J}$.

3.4. Causal Emergence Maximization under Given Information Loss

In this subsection, we will officially discuss the problem of causal emergence maximization. Before proceeding, we will introduce a condition on uncertainty elimination to constrain W, such that zeros in the denominator are excluded.

3.4.1. The Constraint on the Uncertainty Elimination by Coarse-Graining

According to Lemma 2, when the singular value of W, $s_{W,1} \to 0$, $\det(W\Sigma W^T) \to 0$. This means if $\phi(x_t) = Wx_t$ is a completely unconstrained map, as $do(y_t) \sim \mathcal{U}([-L/2, L/2]^k)$ and $do(x_t) \sim \mathcal{U}([-L/2, L/2]^n)$, the values of x_t and the noise ϵ_t may be scaled in an unbounded manner and the information entropy $H(p(y_{t+1}|y_t)) \to -\infty$, leading to y_{t+1} having an excessively narrow range. To prevent the macro variables from being excessively compressed by the coarse-graining map, which may result in excessive information content, it is essential to impose the following restriction,

$$\frac{1}{n}H(p(x_{t+1}|x_t)) - \frac{1}{k}H(p(y_{t+1}|y_t)) \leq \eta, \tag{25}$$

where n and k are the dimensionalities of micro- and macro-variables, and $\eta > 0$ is a given constant, and $H(p(x_{t+1}|x_t)) = (n/2)\ln(2\pi e) + (1/2)\ln(\det(\Sigma))$ and $H(p(y_{t+1}|y_t)) = (k/2)\ln(2\pi e) + (1/2)\ln(\det(W\Sigma W^T))$. The inequality can be understood as the dimension averaged uncertainty eliminated (or information gained) by the coarse-graining strategy under a given threshold η. According to the inequality (25), we can further get that

$$\det(W\Sigma W^T)^{\frac{1}{k}} \geq \epsilon \det(\Sigma)^{\frac{1}{n}}, \tag{26}$$

where W^T represents the transpose matrix of matrix W and $\epsilon = \exp(-2\eta)$. The covariance matrix affects the range of values of random variables; the limitations here can also ensure the effectiveness of the *do* intervention scope L mentioned in Section 3.1. It will be clear in the subsequent sections that this constraint could also significantly influence the scope of causal emergence.

With the help of Lemmas 1 and 2, we can obtain the optimal solution for causal emergence $\Delta\mathcal{J}^*$.

Theorem 2. *For linear stochastic iteration systems like Equation (1), after coarse-graining $y_t = \phi(x_t) = Wx_t$, $W \in \mathcal{R}^{k\times n}$, under the constraint of Equation (26), the maximum of the degree of causal emergence that the system can achieve is*

$$\Delta\mathcal{J}^* = \frac{1}{k}\sum_{i=1}^{k}\ln|\lambda_i| - \frac{1}{n}\sum_{i=1}^{n}\ln|\lambda_i| + \eta, \tag{27}$$

where $|\lambda_1| \geq |\lambda_2| \geq \cdots \geq |\lambda_n| \geq 0$ are n modulus of eigenvalues of matrix A sorted from the largest to the smallest, $\lambda_1, \lambda_2, \ldots, \lambda_n \in C$.

Proof. We will discuss the maximization of causal emergence from determinism emergence and non-degeneracy emergence separately.

(1) Non-degeneracy emergence ($\Delta\mathcal{J}_1$)
Based on Theorem 1, we know that

$$\Delta\mathcal{J}_1 = \ln \frac{|\det(WAW^\dagger)|^{\frac{1}{k}}}{|\det(A)|^{\frac{1}{n}}} \leq \ln \frac{\left(\prod_{i=1}^{k}|\lambda_i|\right)^{\frac{1}{k}}}{\left(\prod_{i=1}^{n}|\lambda_i|\right)^{\frac{1}{n}}} = \frac{1}{k}\sum_{i=1}^{k}\ln|\lambda_i| - \frac{1}{n}\sum_{i=1}^{n}\ln|\lambda_i|. \tag{28}$$

If and only if the maximum k eigenvalues are preserved, the equality holds. At this point, $A_M = WAW^\dagger = (WV)\Lambda(WV)^\dagger = \tilde{W}\Lambda\tilde{W}^\dagger$, $\Lambda = \mathrm{diag}(\lambda_1, \ldots, \lambda_n) \in \mathcal{R}^{n\times n}$; it is satisfied that $\tilde{W} = (\tilde{W}_k, O_{k\times(n-k)})$, $\tilde{W}_k \in \mathcal{R}^{k\times k}$ can be any invertible matrix. $V = (v_1, \ldots, v_n)$; v_i is the eigenvector corresponding to the eigenvalues λ_i of matrix A, $i = 1, \ldots, n$, $|\lambda_1| \geq \cdots \geq |\lambda_n|$. Since $\tilde{W} = WV$, we can obtain the expression for W as

$$W = (\tilde{W}_k, O_{k\times(n-k)})V^{-1}. \tag{29}$$

(2) Determinism emergence ($\Delta\mathcal{J}_2$)
Based on Equation (20) and the inequalities (23), (25), and (26), we know that

$$\begin{aligned}\Delta\mathcal{J}_2 &= \ln \frac{|\det(\Sigma)|^{\frac{1}{2n}}}{|\det(W\Sigma W^T)|^{\frac{1}{2k}}} = \frac{1}{2}\ln \frac{|\det(\Sigma)|^{\frac{1}{n}}}{|\det(W\Sigma W^T)|^{\frac{1}{k}}} \\ &\leq \frac{1}{2}\ln \frac{|\det(\Sigma)|^{\frac{1}{n}}}{|\det(\Sigma)|^{\frac{1}{n}}\epsilon} = \frac{1}{2}\ln\frac{1}{\epsilon} = \eta\end{aligned}. \tag{30}$$

When the information loss reaches the upper bound, the determinism emergence reaches the maximum. Determinism is enhanced while ensuring that randomness is not excessively reduced.

By taking the maximum value of $\Delta\mathcal{J}_1$ and $\Delta\mathcal{J}_2$, we can obtain

$$\Delta\mathcal{J}^* = \Delta\mathcal{J}_1^* + \Delta\mathcal{J}_2^* = \ln \frac{\left(\prod_{i=1}^{k}|\lambda_i|\right)^{\frac{1}{k}}}{\left(\prod_{i=1}^{n}|\lambda_i|\right)^{\frac{1}{n}}} + \frac{1}{2}\ln\frac{1}{\epsilon} = \frac{1}{k}\sum_{i=1}^{k}\ln|\lambda_i| - \frac{1}{n}\sum_{i=1}^{n}\ln|\lambda_i| + \eta \quad . \tag{31}$$

□

Suppose the solution set of the optimal coarse-grained matrix W^*, which satisfies $\Delta\mathcal{J}(W^*) = \Delta\mathcal{J}^*$, is $\mathcal{W}^*$. Although it is difficult for us to find all the elements in set $\mathcal{W}^*$, we will provide methods for calculating special solutions for different types of matrices in later sections.

3.4.2. Optimal Solution Set $\mathcal{W}^*$

After optimizing determinism emergence and non-degeneracy emergence, we can find two solution sets corresponding to the optimal solutions. Thus, the intersection of the two solution sets is the solution set of W corresponding to the maximum degree of causal emergence.

Corollary 1. *When $\varepsilon_t \sim \mathcal{N}(0,\Sigma)$ and the degree of causal emergence reaches its maximum value, W needs to satisfy*

$$\begin{cases} WV = (\tilde{W}_k, O_{k\times(n-k)}), \\ \det(W\Sigma W^T)^{\frac{1}{k}} = \epsilon \det(\Sigma)^{\frac{1}{n}}, \end{cases} \tag{32}$$

in which $V = (v_1, \ldots, v_n)$; v_i is the eigenvector corresponding to the eigenvalues λ_i of matrix A, $i = 1, \ldots, n$, $|\lambda_1| \geq \cdots \geq |\lambda_n|$. $\tilde{W}_k \in \mathcal{R}^{k\times k}$ can be any invertible matrix. The solution set of the optimal coarse-grained matrix W^* satisfying $\Delta\mathcal{J}(W^*) = \Delta\mathcal{J}^*$ as $\epsilon = \exp(-2\eta)$ is

$$\mathcal{W}^* = \left\{ W \middle| W = (\tilde{W}_k, O_{k\times(n-k)})V^{-1}, \det(W\Sigma W^T) = \epsilon \det(\Sigma)^{\frac{k}{n}} \right\}. \tag{33}$$

We can find the proof process in the previous Section 3.4.

3.4.3. A Case Study of $\mathcal{W}^*$

To understand the physical meaning of the solution set, we can use a simple example in the three-dimensional space to visualize our optimal solution set. In specific cases, when $k = 2, n = 3$, the projection of W in three-dimensional space is a circle. In this case, matrix $W = (w_1^T, w_2^T)^T \in \mathcal{R}^{2\times 3}$ can be split into two row-vectors, $w_i = (w_{i1}, w_{i2}, w_{i3}), i = 1, 2$, in $\mathcal{R}^3$, The eigenvector matrix $V = (v_1, v_2, v_3) \in \mathcal{R}^{3\times 3}$ can be regarded as the combining of three vectors, $v_j = (v_{1j}, v_{2j}, v_{3j})^T \in \mathcal{R}^3, j = 1, 2, 3$. To visualize the solution set of W, we introduce the following case as $\epsilon = \exp(-2\eta)$.

Example 1. *In order to present the results more intuitively, we specify $w_1 w_2^T = 0$, $\Sigma = \sigma^2 I_3$. According to Equation (33), we can get*

$$\begin{cases} w_1 v_3 = 0, \\ w_2 v_3 = 0, \\ (w_1 w_1^T)(w_2 w_2^T) = \epsilon \end{cases} . \tag{34}$$

Although $W \in \mathcal{R}^{2\times 3}$ is in a six-dimensional space, we can obtain the solution set of w_1 for specified w_2,

$$\begin{cases} w_{11}v_{13} + w_{12}v_{23} + w_{13}v_{33} = 0 \\ w_{11}^2 + w_{12}^2 + w_{13}^2 = R^2 \end{cases} , \tag{35}$$

in which $R^2 = \epsilon/(w_2 w_2^T)$; R is the radius of the sphere. Similarly, we can also obtain the range of values for w_2.

Proof. To meet the conditions $WV = (Wv_1, Wv_2, Wv_3) = (\tilde{W}_k, O_{k\times(n-k)})$, we only need to specify $w_1 v_3 = w2v_3 = 0$. This means that w_1 and w_2 are contained in the plane perpendicular to v_3 and passing through the origin, which is $w_{11}v_{13} + w_{12}v_{23} + w_{13}v_{33} = 0$. When w_1 and w_2 are in this plane, the non-degeneracy emergence $\Delta\mathcal{J}_1$ reaches its minimum value.

For determinism emergence $\Delta\mathcal{J}_2$,

$$\begin{aligned} \det(W\Sigma W^T) &= (w_1\Sigma w_1^T)(w_2\Sigma w_2^T) - (w_1\Sigma w_2^T)(w_2\Sigma w_1^T) \\ {}_{(\Sigma=\sigma^2 I_3)} &= \sigma^4\left[(w_1 w_1^T)(w_2 w_2^T) - (w_1 w_2^T)(w_2 w_1^T)\right] \\ {}_{w_1 w_2^T = 0} &= \sigma^4\left[(w_1 w_1^T)(w_2 w_2^T)\right] = \epsilon \det(\Sigma)^{\frac{k}{n}} \\ &= \epsilon\sigma^4 \end{aligned} . \tag{36}$$

When w_2 is fixed, the solution set of w_1 is a sphere in three-dimensional space, $w_{11}^2 + w_{12}^2 + w_{13}^2 = \mathcal{R}^2, \mathcal{R}^2 = \epsilon/(w_2 w_2^T)$. If we fix w_1, the result is the same. □

From this example, we can derive the following proposition:

Proposition 1. *In three-dimensional space $\mathcal{R}^3$, if the noise is a white noise sequence $\Sigma = \sigma^2 I_3$ and w_1 and w_2 are perpendicular to each other, when causal emergence $\Delta\mathcal{J}(W^*) = \Delta\mathcal{J}^*$, the solution set of w_i for $i = 1, 2$ is the intersection of a plane and a sphere in the space, which is a circle.*

In Figure 2, we visualize the solution set of $w_1 = (w_{11}, w_{12}, w_{13})$. At the same time, we can extend the scope of application of Example 1 for the general form of covariance matrix Σ; the solution set becomes an ellipsoid. If $w_1 w_2^T \neq 0$, then the spherical or ellipsoidal surface undergoes translation. Therefore, the final solution sets for w_1 and w_2 are the intersection lines of ellipsoids or spheres with planes. Two spatial curves form the solution set of W. Therefore, we can obtain the proposition below.

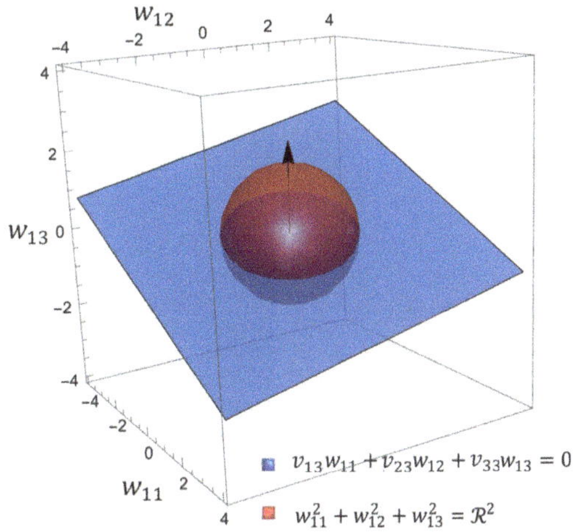

Figure 2. The visualization of the set for the optimal solutions of the coarse-graining strategy W. When $w_1 w_2^T = 0, \Sigma = \sigma^2 I_3$. Although $W \in \mathcal{R}^{2\times 3}$ is in a six-dimensional space, we can draw the range of values for w_1 while limiting w_2, $w_{11}v_{13} + w_{12}v_{23} + w_{13}v_{33} = 0$ and $w_{11}^2 + w_{12}^2 + w_{13}^2 = R^2$, in which $R^2 = \epsilon/(w_2 w_2^T)$. When causal emergence $\Delta\mathcal{J}(W^*) = \Delta\mathcal{J}^*$, the solution set of w_i is the intersection of a plane (blue) and a sphere (red) in 3D space $\mathcal{R}^3$, which is a circle.

Proposition 2. *In three-dimensional space $\mathcal{R}^3, \Sigma > 0$ the coarse-graining parameter matrix W can be regarded as composed of k row vectors w_i, $k = 1, 2, 3$, $i = 1, \ldots, k$; the solution space of each vector w_i is the intersection of a plane and an ellipsoid, which is an ellipse.*

With a visualized solution set in three-dimensional space, we can infer the optimal solution of W in high-dimensional space.

Proposition 3. *For any $n > 1$, a coarse-graining matrix $W \in \mathcal{R}^{k\times n}$ can be split into k row vectors $w_i \in \mathcal{R}^n$ in the same way, and the solution set of $\mathcal{W}^*$ can be understood as the intersection of hyperplanes and hyperellipsoids in an $\mathcal{R}^n$.*

Therefore, after obtaining the relevant parameters of dynamics, we first derive the expression for a high-dimensional ellipse, where any point on the high-dimensional ellipse can maximize the causal emergence. At the same time, when the model is more complex, we can also choose to find points close to the ellipse, even if it is not the optimal solution, which can increase the likelihood of causal emergence.

3.5. The Conditions for Causal Emergence

After understanding the solution method for the maximum causal emergence of the system, we need to analyze the conditions under which causal emergence occurs as $\Delta\mathcal{J} > 0$. Two scenarios are being examined: the presence of causal emergence in typical situations and its manifestation under optimized conditions.

First, in general cases, causal emergence $\Delta\mathcal{J}$ is determined by two factors: non-degeneracy $\Delta\mathcal{J}_1$ and determinism $\Delta\mathcal{J}_2$. The sufficient condition for $\Delta\mathcal{J} > 0$ is that $\Delta\mathcal{J}_1, \Delta\mathcal{J}_2 > 0$ at the same time.

The prerequisite for $\Delta\mathcal{J}_1 > 0$ is that there is a significant difference between the eigenvalues $\lambda_1 \geq \cdots \geq \lambda_n$ of parameter matrix $A \in \mathcal{R}^{n\times n}$. Assuming the macro-state $y_t \in \mathcal{R}^k$, the greater the difference between $\lambda_1, \ldots, \lambda_k$ and $\lambda_{k+1}, \ldots, \lambda_n$, the more obvious the causal emergence. The best condition is that $\lambda_k \gg \lambda_{k+1}$; if the latter $n-k$ term is discarded, there will be a significant causal emergence.

The condition for $\Delta\mathcal{J}_2 > 0$ is that there is significant randomness in the system as Σ is a positive definite matrix and $H(p(x_{t+1}|x_t)) > -\infty$ when $do(y_t) \sim U([-L/2, L/2]^k)$ and $do(x_t) \sim U([-L/2, L/2]^n)$. If $\Sigma = 0$ and $H(p(x_{t+1}|x_t)) = -\infty$, as there is no random noise in the system, effective information is also invalid. In theory, the larger the system noise, the larger the space that can be compressed during coarse-graining, and the stronger the causal emergence can appear.

Second, when causal emergence reaches its optimal solution, we can also determine the condition for $\Delta\mathcal{J} > 0$ based on the result of $\Delta\mathcal{J}^*$. From Equation (31), we can see that when

$$\frac{1}{n}\sum_{i=1}^{n}\ln|\lambda_i| - \frac{1}{k}\sum_{i=1}^{k}\ln|\lambda_i| < \eta \tag{37}$$

as the difference of the average singular value of A to the average singular value of A_M after taking the logarithm can be smaller than the bound of the information entropy η we specify, $\Delta\mathcal{J}^* > 0$. If this result holds, we can assert that there must exist a W to make $\Delta\mathcal{J} > 0$.

4. Results

After understanding how to optimize causal emergence, we can use the theorems we derived to analyze several cases of linear stochastic iteration systems. We will attempt to search for the maximum of causal emergence in systems with known dynamics. We provide three cases, focusing on the applications of determinism emergence, non-degeneracy emergence, and the manifestation of causal emergence in $\mathcal{R}^3$ space.

4.1. Random Walk

Our first case is random walk [54], and our analysis focuses on the noise ε_t and the covariance matrix Σ, which mainly impact determinism emergence. The random walk model is a mathematical model used to describe the random movement of objects in a specific space in which a walker moves between a series of locations, with the direction and distance of each movement being random. This model can study various phenomena, such as changes in asset prices in financial markets, the diffusion of particles in fluids, etc. In the random walk model, the walker can only move a certain distance to the left or right each time, and the distance obeys a normal distribution. When multiple wanderers coexist, a changing parameter matrix can be formed as an identity matrix, $A = I_n$,

$$x_{t+1} = x_t + \varepsilon_t, \varepsilon_t \sim \mathcal{N}(0, \Sigma), \tag{38}$$

which forms a linear stochastic series mainly affected by noise sequences ε_t.

We set an example as $n = 4, k = 1$, while

$$\Sigma = \begin{pmatrix} 0.4782 & -0.1967 & -0.0287 & 0.0419 \\ -0.1967 & 0.6711 & 0.0233 & -0.1067 \\ -0.0287 & 0.0233 & 0.3154 & 0.0738 \\ 0.0419 & -0.1067 & 0.0738 & 0.4211 \end{pmatrix}. \tag{39}$$

The motion trend of each dimension of x_t is shown in Figure 3a. From Equation (26), we already know that the ratio between $\det(W\Sigma W^T)^{1/k}$ and $\det(\Sigma)^{1/n}$ should be greater than the lower bound ϵ. The constant for uncertainty loss is $\eta = 0.3466$ and the corresponding $\epsilon = 0.5$. This value being selected guarantees that when the singular values of W are all 1, the determinism emergence $\Delta\mathcal{J}_2 = 0.2439 > 0$ as $W = (-0.0819, 0.1432, -0.8421, 0.5135)$ satisfies $\det(W\Sigma W^T)^{\frac{1}{k}} / \det(\Sigma)^{\frac{1}{n}} = 0.614 > \epsilon$.

We have plotted probability density graphs for the four dimensions of micro-state noise ε_t and macro-state noise $\varepsilon_{M,t}$ in Figure 3b, respectively. We can see that the variance of macro-state is smaller than that of micro-state, so the determinism emergence of macro-state dynamical systems is larger. Meanwhile, in Figure 3c we can see that under the condition that the singular values of W are all 1, the higher k, the stronger the uncertainty of the system, and the smaller the degree of causal emergence.

Reducing the average noise of the system and increasing its determinism is an important condition for the occurrence of causal emergence. The main reason for this is that we can reduce the dimensions with weaker determinism. The premise for this phenomenon is that there are significant differences in noise between different dimensions. As shown in Figure 3d, we randomly generate Σ and W and calculate the value of $\Delta\mathcal{J}$. We found that the larger the variance of the eigenvalues κ_i of Σ, $i = 1, \ldots, n$, the more likely the occurrence of causal emergence.

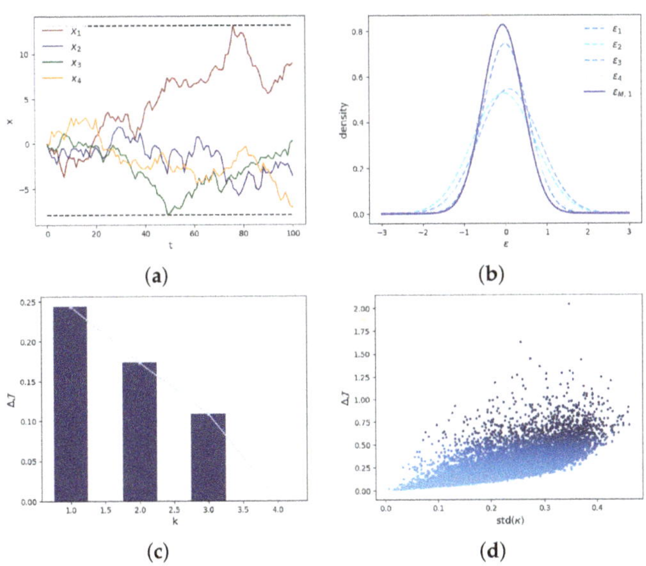

Figure 3. Experimental results for random walks model. (**a**) The trajectories x_t of a random walker in different dimensions. (**b**) The probability density functions for the four dimensions of micro-state noises ε_t and the macro-state noise $\varepsilon_{M,t}$. (**c**) The degree of causal emergence under different macro-state dimensions k. Under the condition that the singular values of W are all 1, the higher k, the stronger the uncertainty of the system, and the smaller the degree of causal emergence. (**d**) $\Delta\mathcal{J}$ and $std(\kappa)$. The larger the variance of the eigenvalues κ_i of Σ, $i = 1, \ldots, n$, the more likely the occurrences of causal emergence with higher degrees.

4.2. Heat Dissipation

The first case focuses on determinism and noise, while the second case focuses on non-degeneracy and parameter matrix A. This case is called the discretized [55] heat conduction model [56,57]. In this discretized case, the conduction of heat is mainly reflected in the temperature changes over time [58] at the corresponding observation nodes [59]. We can use matrix A to represent the changes in temperature, which includes information on the rate of change. This matrix usually corresponds to a positive definite sparse matrix, which can be used to describe a system's temperature change process. For example,

$$x_{t+1} = Ax_t + \varepsilon_t, \varepsilon_t \sim \mathcal{N}(0, \sigma^2 I_n), \sigma = 0.01 \tag{40}$$

describes the variation of temperature x_t over time t. When $n = 4$, $x_t = (x_{1,t}, x_{2,t}, x_{3,t}, x_{4,t})^T$, $x_{1,t}$, $x_{2,t}$, $x_{3,t}$, and $x_{4,t}$ represent the temperatures at four nodes at time t, as shown in Figure 4b. The parameter matrix is

$$A = \begin{pmatrix} 0.6 & 0.2 & 0 & 0 \\ 0.2 & 0.7 & 0.1 & 0 \\ 0 & 0.1 & 0.4 & 0.1 \\ 0 & 0 & 0.1 & 0.3 \end{pmatrix}, \tag{41}$$

where diagonal elements represent the rates of heat conservation at each node, and the off-diagonals represent the energy transfer between different nodes, as shown in Figure 4a. Assuming $\epsilon = 1$ as $\eta = 0$, then the uncertainties in both the dynamics at micro- and macro-levels are the same according to Equation (25). As a result, only the effect of non-degeneracy emergence can influence the causal emergence according to Equation (31).

We can simulate the diffusion process by setting the initial state to $x_0 = (10, 10, 10, 10)^T$, and we iterate the equation $x_{t+1} = Ax_t + \varepsilon_t$ for $t = 1, 2, \ldots$. The results are shown in Figure 4b. We can directly coarse-grain the micro-state data to obtain $y_t = Wx_t$ for $t = 0, 1, 2, \ldots$. At the same time, we can use the macro-state dynamics to iterate the initial macro-state y_0. In order to distinguish from the previous y_t data, we use $\hat{y}_t$ to represent the data generated by macro-state dynamical iterations. $\hat{y}_0 = y_0$ and $\hat{y}_{t+1} = WAW^{\dagger}\hat{y}_t + W\varepsilon_t$ for $t = 0, 1, 2, \ldots$. By comparison in Figure 4c, we can see that the dynamics of y_t and $\hat{y}_t$ are close to each other; macro-state dynamics can represent the dynamic evolution law of data after the coarse-graining.

By reducing the low correlation and dimensions that are difficult to reverse between x_t and x_{t+1}, non-degeneracy can be increased, resulting in stronger causal emergence. For example, in the case shown in Figure 4d, when $k = 1$, $\sigma = 0.01$, and $\eta = 0$ as Shannon entropy of x_t and y_t remains stable, causal emergence occurs with the degree $\Delta\mathcal{J} = 0.6656$, and it is greater than the case when $k > 1$. We can take any element from $\mathcal{W}^*$; for example, $W = (0.5856, 0.7910, 0.1748, 0.03065) \in \mathcal{R}^{1\times k}$, which satisfies our condition of W in Equation (32). The macro-state dynamic parameter matrix is $A_M \in \mathcal{R}^{1\times 1}$ with an eigenvalue $\lambda_{M,1} = 0.8702$. The eigenvalues of the micro-state matrix A are $\lambda_1 = 0.8702, \lambda_2 = 0.5000, \lambda_3 = 0.4000$, and $\lambda_4 = 0.2298$. It can be seen that retaining the maximum eigenvalue will result in significant causal emergence. In physical terms, it can be understood as a region with slower dissipation, and the causal relationship between the temperature at time $t+1$ and time t is stronger, making it more suitable for analyzing the temperature evolution law of the entire system.

To verify our theoretic result about the exact expression for causal emergence, we can compare the obtained analytical solution in Equation (27) with the numerical results, which can be obtained by the following steps. We first randomly generate numeric samples of $x_t \sim U([-1,1]^n)$ and $y_t \sim U([-1,1]^k)$, then perform a one-step iteration for micro- and macro-dynamics as $x_{t+1} = Ax_t + \varepsilon_t$ and $y_{t+1} = A_M y_t + \varepsilon_{M,t}$, $\varepsilon_t \sim \mathcal{N}_n(0, \sigma^2 I_n)$ and $\varepsilon_{M,t} \sim \mathcal{N}_k(0, \sigma^2 I_k)$. We then directly calculate the mutual information $I(x_{t+1}, x_t | do(x_t) \sim U([-1,1]^n))$ for micro-dynamics and $I(y_{t+1}, y_t | do(y_t) \sim U([-1,1]^k))$

between the generated samples of x_{t+1} at time $t+1$ and the samples of x_t at time t to obtain the numerical solution of effective information and calculate causal emergence as

$$\Delta\mathcal{I} = \frac{I(y_{t+1}, y_t | do(y_t) \sim U([-1,1]^k))}{k} - \frac{I(x_{t+1}, x_t | do(x_t) \sim U([-1,1]^n))}{n}. \quad (42)$$

To distinguish from analytical solutions $\Delta\mathcal{J}$, we use $\Delta\mathcal{I}$ to represent the causal emergence computed by the mentioned numeric method. From Figure 4e, we found that when $n = 4, k = 1$, and $\sigma^2 = 0.01$, as the sample size increases, the numerical solutions for causal emergence gradually approach the analytical solutions.

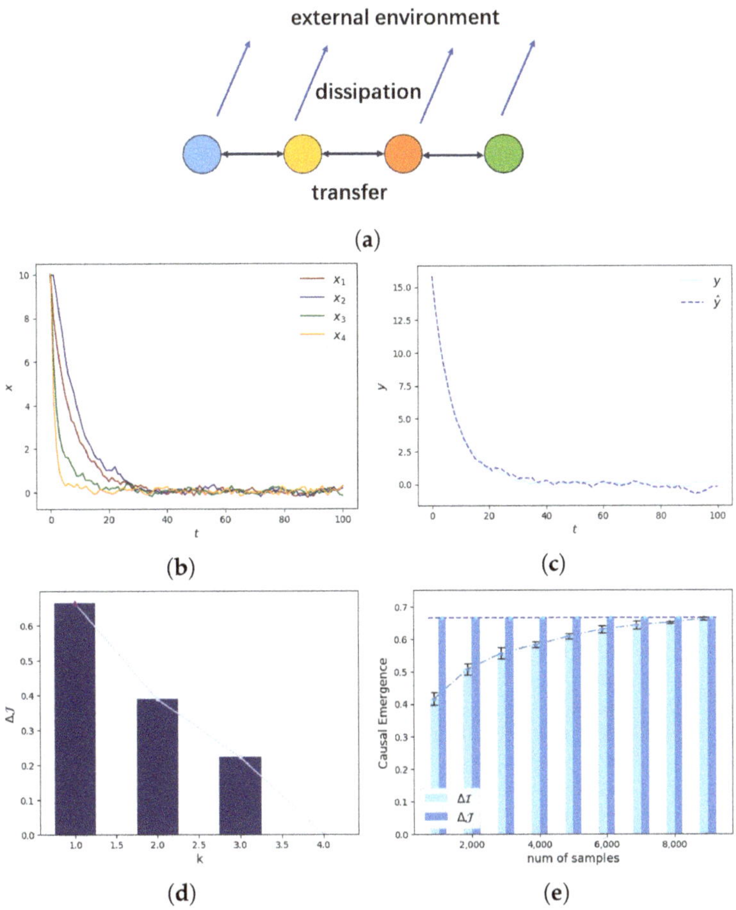

Figure 4. Experimental results for heat dissipation model. (**a**) The illustration of heat transfer and dissipation for a one-dimensional chain with four vertices. (**b**) The micro-state data of temperature at different times t for 4 nodes. (**c**) The comparison between the macro-state data directly obtained by coarsening the micro-state data, y_t, to obtain $y_t = Wx_t$ for $t = 0, 1, 2, \ldots$, and $\hat{y}_t$, which is generated by the macro-state dynamics to iterate the initial macro-state y_0. (**d**) The comparisons for the degrees of causal emergence under different dimensions of macro-states k. when $k = 1$ and $\epsilon = 1$, a maximized degree of causal emergence occurs as $\Delta\mathcal{J} = 0.6656$. (**e**) The comparison between $\Delta\mathcal{I}$ and $\Delta\mathcal{J}$. As the sample size increases, the numerical solutions for causal emergence $\Delta\mathcal{I}$ gradually approach the analytical solutions $\Delta\mathcal{J}$.

4.3. Spiral Rotating

In addition to the results obtained for specific models in Sections 4.1 and 4.2, we need a more intuitive understanding of the meaning of coarse-graining and causal emergence. Here, we take a spiral rotating model [60] from analytical geometry [61,62] as an example to visualize our model system in $\mathcal{R}^3$ space and analyze how causal emergence is reflected.

A common example is a model in which a rigid body rotates about an axis. Suppose we have a vector in three-dimensional space that represents the position of a point $x_0 \in \mathcal{R}^3$, and we want to rotate it around some straight line through the origin. This operation can be represented by the rotation matrix R. For rotation around the straight line represented by the unit vector $u = (a,b,c)$, $||u|| = \sqrt{a^2+b^2+c^2} = 1$, a rotation matrix can be used to describe the rotation operation:

$$R = \begin{pmatrix} \cos\theta + a^2(1-\cos\theta) & ab(1-\cos\theta) - c\sin\theta & ac(1-\cos\theta) + b\sin\theta \\ ab(1-\cos\theta) + c\sin\theta & \cos\theta + b^2(1-\cos\theta) & bc(1-\cos\theta) - a\sin\theta \\ ac(1-\cos\theta) - b\sin\theta & bc(1-\cos\theta) + a\sin\theta & \cos\theta + c^2(1-\cos\theta) \end{pmatrix}, \tag{43}$$

where θ represents the angle of the rotation. This matrix describes a rotation about the straight line represented by the unit vector u. Multiply the vector x_t by the matrix R to obtain the new rotated vector x_{t+1}. This rotation matrix describes a model of rotation around a certain straight line and can be used to describe rotation operations around a specified axis in three-dimensional space. Since R does not change the modulus of x_t, we can add an adjustment matrix $\Psi = \mathrm{diag}(\psi_1, \psi_2, \psi_3)$ to adjust the modulus of the variable x_t. Then, the linear stochastic iteration systems in $\mathcal{R}^3$ is

$$x_{t+1} = Ax_t + \varepsilon_t, A = R\Psi, \varepsilon_t \sim \mathcal{N}(0, \sigma^2 I_n), \sigma = 0.01, \tag{44}$$

When $\psi_i < 1, i = 1,2,3$, the model is attenuated. Adjusting ψ_i can cause the system to produce different values of causal emergence at different macro-state dimensions.

Assuming the direction vector of the rotation axis is $u_0 = (0, 0.1, 1)^T$, after normalization as $u = u_0/||u_0||$, the rotation axis u can be obtained. At the same time, we specify the rotation angle $\theta = \pi/16$ and $\eta = 0$ because the dimension averaged Shannon entropy of both x_t and y_t remains the same. Through θ and u, we can obtain the rotation matrix R. By changing Ψ, we will obtain causal emergence in different forms.

The occurrence of causal emergence in three-dimensional space can be understood as the stronger causal effect of system evolution when the path of x_t is projected onto a plane or a straight line. As shown in Figure 5a, when $\Psi = \mathrm{diag}(0.94, 0.94, 0.99)$ and $x_0 = (1,1,3)^T$, x_t contracts towards the axis of rotation. In Figure 5b, the causal emergence reaches its maximum value as $\Delta\mathcal{J} = 0.0341$ when $k = 1$. The eigenvalues of the micro-state matrix A are $\lambda_1 = 0.9895$,$\lambda_2 = 0.9222 + 0.1834i$, and $\lambda_3 = 0.9222 - 0.1834i$; the macro-state parameter matrix A_M only retains the eigenvalues with the maximum modulus $\lambda_1 = 0.9895$. This result is obtained by setting the coarse-graining mapping W to compress the rotation trajectory into a one-dimensional straight line as the macro-states.

In the second scenario in Figure 5c, when $\Psi = \mathrm{diag}(0.99, 0.97, 0.2)$ and $x_0 = (1,1,1)^T$, the path of x_t will first shrink to a plane perpendicular to u. In Figure 5d, we project x_t onto the plane as the macro-state, where $k = 2$, $\Delta\mathcal{J} = 0.5295$. We retain the two eigenvalues $\lambda_1 = 0.9612 + 0.1900i$ and $\lambda_2 = 0.9612 - 0.1900i$ with the largest and identical module lengths. The reason why we do not take $k = 1$ here is that the more dimensionality we reduce, the greater the information loss and $|\lambda_1| = |\lambda_2|$. Therefore, in the absence of further improvement in causal emergence, we do not need to continue the dimensionality reduction of the system.

As well as Ψ, rotation angle θ also significantly impacts causal emergence. In Figure 5f, when θ approaches π, the degree of causal emergence is smaller, while when it approaches 0 or 2π, it is larger. This is because, when $\pi/2 < \theta < 3\pi/2$, x_t tends to oscillate more than rotate, as shown in Figure 5e. The correlation between $x_t + 1$ and x_t in the model is relatively small, leading to a weakening of causal emergence.

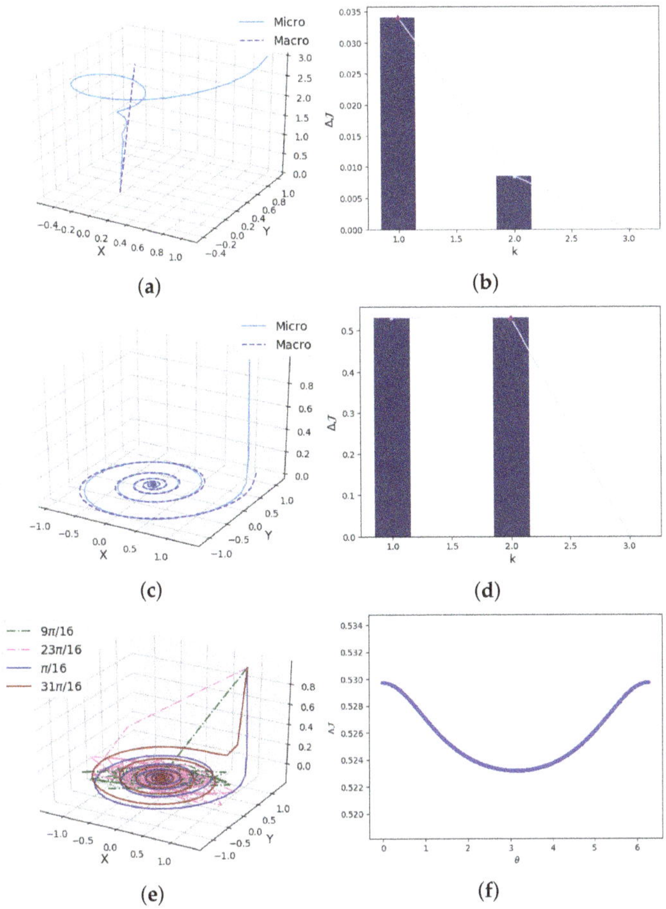

Figure 5. Experimental results of spiral rotating. (**a**) When $\Psi = \mathrm{diag}(0.94, 0.94, 0.99)$ and $x_0 = (1,1,3)^T$, x_t represents a point in space that rotates around the axis of rotation and contracts towards the axis of rotation. By the optimal coarse-graining W^*, we can obtain macro-states that move along the axis of rotation. (**b**) The degree of causal emergence and its dependence on the dimension of macro-states for the example in (**a**), which reaches its maximum value as $\Delta\mathcal{J} = 0.0341$ when $k = 1$. (**c**) The spiral curve when $\Psi = \mathrm{diag}(0.99, 0.97, 0.2)$ and $x_0 = (1,1,1)^T$; the trajectory of x_t is compressed to a plane perpendicular to u at the initial stage. (**d**) We can project x_t onto the plane as a macro-state, where $k = 2$, $\Delta\mathcal{J} = 0.5295$. (**e**) When $\pi/2 < \theta < 3\pi/2$, x_t tends to oscillate more than rotate, while $\theta < \pi/2$ or $\theta > 3\pi/2$ x_t tends to be a rotate model. (**f**) When θ approaches π, the degree of causal emergence is smaller, while when it approaches 0 or 2π, the degree of causal emergence is larger.

5. Discussion

5.1. Optimal Causal Emergence When $W^\dagger = W^T$

In previous sections, we have obtained the explicit expression for the maximum causal emergence and the optimal coarse-graining under the condition that the dimension averaged uncertainty loss by coarse-graining is bounded. However, under this condition, the competition between the non-degeneracy term, which is solely determined by A, and the determinism term, which is determined by A and Σ in the optimal causal emergence, cannot be observed, as shown in Equation (31).

Therefore, we will discuss the maximization of causal emergence under a different condition, which is

$$W^{\dagger} = W^{T} \tag{45}$$

in this section. Equation (45) means the coarse-graining map W can be decomposed as a projection by discarding the information in $n-k$ dimensions and a rotation in a k-dimensional space without information loss. This also means the k first singular values are units, and the norm of W and Σ will not be excessively enlarged or reduced. In this case, as $W^{\dagger} = W^{T}$, the coarse-graining strategy will simultaneously filter the eigenvalues of A and Σ. According to Equations (17) and (20), we can get that $|\det(A)|/\det(\Sigma)^{1/2} = |\det(A\Sigma^{-1/2})|$. Therefore, $A\Sigma^{-1/2}$ determines the causal emergence of the system and it is necessary for it to be analyzed below.

Theorem 3. *When $W^{\dagger} = W^{T}$, the causal emergence of linear stochastic iterative systems satisfies*

$$\Delta\mathcal{J} \leq \frac{1}{k}\sum_{i=1}^{k}\ln|\tilde{d}_i| - \frac{1}{n}\sum_{i=1}^{n}\ln|\tilde{d}_i|, \tag{46}$$

where $|\tilde{d}_1| \geq \cdots \geq |\tilde{d}_n|$ are n eigenvalues of $A\Sigma^{-1/2}$. The equal sign holds when A and Σ share the same n eigenvectors as

$$A\Sigma^{-1/2} = V\Lambda K^{-1/2}V^{T} = V\tilde{D}V^{T}, \tag{47}$$

where $\tilde{D} = \Lambda K^{-1/2} = \mathrm{diag}(\tilde{d}_1, \ldots, \tilde{d}_n)$ is also a diagonal matrix, in which $|\tilde{d}_1| \geq \cdots \geq |\tilde{d}_n|$, and V is the matrix formed by the shared eigenvectors of A and Σ.

When A and Σ do not share the eigenvector matrix, we cannot directly calculate the correlation between the eigenvalue matrix of $A\Sigma^{-1/2}$ and K or Λ within the current framework of matrix theory, so it is difficult to find an analytical solution for causal emergence. However, we can still obtain numerical solutions through optimization of W and confirm that the upper bound of causal emergence is to retain the maximum k eigenvalues of $A\Sigma^{-1/2}$. We have the inequality (46) in Theorem 3. To verify this inequality, we randomly generate matrices A, Σ, and W with a singular value of 1 when $n = 4, k = 2$; we can see that the upper bound of $|\det(WAW^{\dagger})|/\det(W\Sigma W^{T})^{1/2}$ is $\tilde{d}_1\tilde{d}_2$ in Figure 6b. Unlimited, the singular value of W means that it can reduce the macro-state noise and information entropy in the system. This also means that the locally effective information we retain can be adjusted arbitrarily by adjusting W. This is also a balance point between determinism and non-degeneracy.

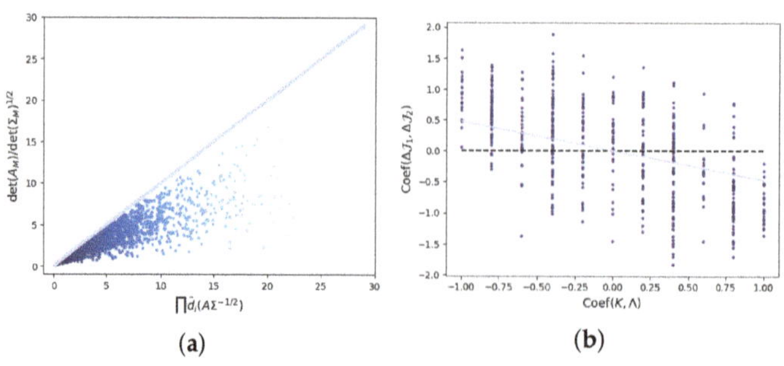

Figure 6. (**a**) We randomly generate matrices A, Σ, and W with a singular value of 1 when $n = 4, k = 2$; we can see that the upper bound of $|\det(WAW^{\dagger})|/\det(W\Sigma W^{T})^{1/2}$ is $\tilde{d}_1\tilde{d}_2$. The steel blue straight line is $|\det(WAW^{\dagger})|/\det(W\Sigma W^{T})^{1/2} = \tilde{d}_1\tilde{d}_2$. (**b**) When $\lambda_1 = 0.8, \lambda_1 = 0.2, \lambda_3 = 0.4, \lambda_4 = 0.2$, and we randomly arrange $(0.2, 0.4, 0.6, 0.8)$ to generate $(\kappa_1, \ldots, \kappa_n)$. $C(\Delta\mathcal{J}_1, \Delta\mathcal{J}_2)$ and $C(\kappa, \lambda)$ show a negative slope after drawing the scatter plot.

Then, we can derive an analytical expression for the maximized causal emergence when A and Σ share the same n eigenvectors; that is to say, $\Sigma = VKV^T$ and $A = V\Lambda V^T$, and Equation (47) holds. Rearranging the order of $\tilde{d}_i$ can result in diagonal matrix $\tilde{D} = \text{diag}(\tilde{d}_1, \ldots, \tilde{d}_n)$, in which $|\tilde{d}_1| \geq \cdots \geq |\tilde{d}_n|$. Then, according to Equation (20), we can obtain an analytical solution for the maximized causal emergence, which is also the case where Equation (46) takes the equal sign. The above proof process can refer to Appendix B.

Next, we will study when the relationship between the determinism ($\Delta\mathcal{J}_2$) and the non-degeneracy ($\Delta\mathcal{J}_1$) is cooperative, such that the causal emergence can be maximized under the condition of the simultaneous diagonalization for A and Σ. This problem is equivalent to asking when the quantity expressed in Equation (46), which is determined by the eigenvalues of $A\Sigma^{-1/2}$, will be maximized if the eigenvalues in A and Σ are unchanged. We found that the orders of the eigenvalues in both A and Σ, which can be characterized by the correlation between $\kappa = (\kappa_1, \ldots, \kappa_n)$ and $\lambda = (\lambda_1, \ldots, \lambda_n)$, denoted as $C(\kappa, \lambda)$, play an important role. If λ and κ are positively correlated, the effects of determinism and non-degeneracy contributed to the causal emergence cancel each other out. For example, when $\lambda = (0.8, 0.6, 0.4, 0.2)$, $\kappa = (0.8, 0.6, 0.4, 0.2)$, and $k = 2$, the optimal coarse-graining strategy for $\Delta\mathcal{J}_1$ should retain the largest $k = 2$ eigenvalues $\lambda_1 = 0.8, \lambda_2 = 0.6$ of A according to Equation (28), but for κ, the largest k eigenvalues $\kappa_1 = 0.8, \kappa_2 = 0.6$ are also retained, which implies small determinism and large non-degeneracy. We can see that the determinism and the non-degeneracy are mutually inhibiting, leading to a small causal emergence: $\Delta\mathcal{J} = 0$.

On the other hand, if λ and κ are negatively correlated, then causal emergence can be increased because determinism and non-degeneracy reinforce each other. For example, when $\lambda = (0.8, 0.6, 0.4, 0.2)$ and $\kappa = (0.2, 0.4, 0.6, 0.8)$, the optimal coarse-graining strategy for $\Delta\mathcal{J}_1$ should retain the largest $k = 2$ eigenvalues $\lambda_1 = 0.8, \lambda_2 = 0.6$ of A; this also means retaining the smallest k eigenvalues of Σ, then determinism and non-degeneracy are mutually reinforced, and a larger causal emergence can be obtained: $\Delta\mathcal{J} = 0.8959$.

In Figure 6a, we visualize how the correlation between λ and κ can influence the cooperative relationship between determinism and non-degeneracy, which can be characterized by the correlation between $\Delta\mathcal{J}_1$ and $\Delta\mathcal{J}_2$, denoted as $C(\Delta\mathcal{J}_1, \Delta\mathcal{J}_2)$ in a small example. First, we fix the values and the orders of Λ as $\lambda_1 = 0.8, \lambda_1 = 0.2, \lambda_3 = 0.4$, and $\lambda_4 = 0.2$. Second, we randomly permute $(0.2, 0.4, 0.6, 0.8)$ to generate κ. Finally, we randomly sample the invertible matrix V such that A and Σ can be obtained. The results are shown in Figure 6a; $C(\Delta\mathcal{J}_1, \Delta\mathcal{J}_2)$ and $C(\kappa, \lambda)$ show a negative slope after drawing the scatter plot. This means that the two values are negatively correlated. In general, maximizing causal emergence $\Delta\mathcal{J}$ is also a process of finding optimal orders to arrange λ_i and κ_i for all i to achieve a balance between determinism $\Delta\mathcal{J}_2$ and non-degeneracy $\Delta\mathcal{J}_1$.

5.2. About the Information Loss in Dynamics Prediction

Our entire paper discusses the changes in the causal emergence of systems after coarse-graining. For linear stochastic iteration systems, deleting smaller eigenvalues in the parameter matrix A or larger eigenvalues in Σ can both increase the value of causal emergence. Coarse graining and data dimensionality reduction [37–41] are intricately linked. Once data dimensionality is reduced, it will be accompanied by information loss, and the transformation from micro-states to macro-states is no exception. Therefore, we also need to briefly analyze the relationship between the loss function in dynamics prediction and the effective information of the dynamics. For linear stochastic iteration systems, we define the dynamical loss in the following way:

Definition 6. *(Dynamical loss): For the variable x_t at time t, we define the dynamical loss as*

$$L_D = ||x_{t+1} - \tilde{x}_{t+1}||, \tag{48}$$

in which $x_{t+1} = Ax_t + \varepsilon_t$, $\tilde{x}_{t+1} = \phi^{\dagger}(y_{t+1}) = W^{\dagger}y_{t+1}$.

In Definition 6, y_{t+1} is derived from y_t and the macro iterative Equation (8) and $y_t = Wx_t$. Therefore,

$$\tilde{x}_{t+1} = W^{\dagger}WAW^{\dagger}Wx_t + W^{\dagger}W\varepsilon_t, \tag{49}$$

the dynamical loss then should be:

$$L_D = ||(W^{\dagger}WAW^{\dagger}W - A)x_t + (W^{\dagger}W - I)\varepsilon_t||. \tag{50}$$

This is the difference between the micro-state variables $x_t \in \mathcal{R}^n$ that are then mapped into micro-states after one iteration in the macro dynamics and the actual micro-state x_{t+1}, which reflects the information loss caused by coarse-graining on dynamics.

Due to the dependence between L_D and variables x_t and ε_t, in order to directly analyze the relationship between the causal emergence of the system $\Delta\mathcal{J}$ and the dynamical loss, we consider the upper bound of L_D to eliminate the influence of random variables.

Lemma 3. *(Supremum of dynamical loss): For the variable* x_t *at time t, when* $||x_t||^* = \sup_t ||x_t|| < \infty$, *we define the supremum of dynamical loss* L_D *as*

$$L_D \leq S_D = \underbrace{||A - \hat{A}||_F||x_t||^*}_{Non-degeneracySupremum} + \underbrace{(n-k)||\varepsilon_t||}_{DeterminismSupremum}, \tag{51}$$

in which $\hat{A} = W^{\dagger}WAW^{\dagger}W$. S_D *can be decomposed into determinism supremum and non-degeneracy supremum.* $||\cdot||_F$ *is the Frobenius norm of matrix* $\cdot$.

We can directly determine the relationship between the upper bound and $\Delta\mathcal{J}_1$. When k is a constant, the minimum value of S_D is equivalent to the maximum value of non-degeneracy emergence, $\Delta\mathcal{J}_1$.

Theorem 4. *(*$\Delta\mathcal{J}_1$ *and* S_D*): For the known variables* x_t, *the micro-state parameter matrix A and the noise* ε_t, $t = 0, 1, ...,$

$$\arg\max_W \Delta\mathcal{J}_1 = \arg\min_W S_D = \mathcal{W}^*. \tag{52}$$

The proof of this theorem is referred to in Appendix C. After obtaining the relationship between the supremum S_D and the non-degeneracy emergence $\Delta\mathcal{J}_1$, it can be observed that after minimizing S_D, the solution set of W, $\mathcal{W}_L$, satisfies $\mathcal{W}_L \in \mathcal{W}^*$. It can be seen that reducing loss can only increase the non-degeneracy of the system, but a further search for W is needed for determinism. This explains why we still need to train for a few steps to find the maximum causal emergence after the loss function converges in machine learning for causal emergence identification [35,43].

Through this indicator, we can easily see that there are two situations that can ensure that the system is under control. One is that the model is a decay model, that is,

$$|\lambda_n| < \cdots < |\lambda_1| < 1, \tag{53}$$

where λ_i are eigenvalues of matrix A. The cases in Sections 4.2 and 4.3 all meet this condition, ensuring the validity of the analysis.

The second possible situation is that we specify the time range of evolution,

$$\exists \tau < \infty, s.t. \forall t > \tau, x_t = 0. \tag{54}$$

In this way, even if the system is divergent and will grow infinitely over time, it will become 0 after time τ, making $x_t < \infty$. We used this method in Section 4.1 to make our evolution controllable within the specified time $0 \leq t \leq 100$. Although the future cannot be measured, as shown by the black dashed line in Figure 3a, we can confirm that the data is bounded within the specified time range.

5.3. Nonlinear Form

Although the effective information and causal emergence in this paper are based on linear stochastic iterative systems, we can still apply them to nonlinear models under certain conditions. Nonlinear stochastic iterative systems like $x_{t+1} = f(x_t) + \varepsilon_t$ do not have the same known parameter matrix A as linear stochastic iterative systems. However, when $f : \mathcal{R}^n \to \mathcal{R}^n$, we can replace A with the gradient matrix of $\nabla f(x_t) \in \mathcal{R}^{n\times n}$ at x_t.

Therefore, near x_t, when the noise ε_t and the length of intervention space L are small, we can obtain an expression for the effective information of the nonlinear iterative system,

$$\begin{aligned}\mathcal{J}(f(x_t),\Sigma) &= \ln\left(\frac{L}{(2\pi e)^{1/2}}\right) + \frac{1}{L^n}\int_{[-\frac{L}{2},\frac{L}{2}]^n} \ln\left|\frac{\det(\nabla f(x_t))}{\det(\Sigma)^{\frac{1}{2}}}\right|^{\frac{1}{n}} dx_t \\ &= \ln\frac{|\det(\nabla f(x_t'))|^{\frac{1}{n}} L}{(2\pi e)^{\frac{1}{2}}\det(\Sigma)^{\frac{1}{2n}}} \approx \ln\frac{|\det(\nabla f(x_t))|^{\frac{1}{n}} L}{(2\pi e)^{\frac{1}{2}}\det(\Sigma)^{\frac{1}{2n}}}\end{aligned}, \tag{55}$$

as $x_t \approx x_t' \in [-L/2, L/2]^n$; x_t' is the differential mean value in the Lagrange mean value theorem.

Analogous to linear iterative systems, we can infer the macro-state expression of nonlinear iterative systems,

$$f_M(y_t) = \phi(f(\phi^\dagger(y_t))), \tag{56}$$

as $y_t = \phi(x_t)$ and $\phi : \mathcal{R}^n \to \mathcal{R}^k, k < n$. $\phi^\dagger : \mathcal{R}^k \to \mathcal{R}^n, \phi(\phi^\dagger(y_t)) = y_t$.

In this way, we can obtain the expression of causal emergence as

$$\Delta\mathcal{J} = \ln\frac{|\det(\nabla f_M(y_t)|^{\frac{1}{k}}}{|\det(\nabla f(x_t)|^{\frac{1}{n}}} + \ln\frac{|\det(\Sigma)|^{\frac{1}{2n}}}{|\det(\Sigma_M)|^{\frac{1}{2k}}}. \tag{57}$$

For some simple differentiable nonlinear functions $f(x_t)$, we can use this method to calculate the magnitude of causal emergence.

6. Conclusions

In this article, we first propose the coarse-graining strategy $y_t = Wx_t$ of linear stochastic iterative systems like $x_{t+1} = Ax_t + \varepsilon_t, \varepsilon_t \sim \mathcal{N}(0,\Sigma)$, which map micro-states $x_t \in \mathcal{R}^n$ into macro-states $y_t \in \mathcal{R}^k, k < n$. Coarse-graining can naturally derive macro dynamical models $y_{t+1} = A_M y_t + \varepsilon_{M,t}$ for $y_t \in \mathcal{R}^k$, $A_M = WAW^\dagger$, $\varepsilon_{M,t} \sim \mathcal{N}(0,\Sigma_M)$, $\Sigma_M = W\Sigma W^T$. For $x_{t+1} = Ax_t + \varepsilon_t$, we can use $\mathcal{J}$ and $\Delta\mathcal{J}$ to represent the effective information of the system and causal emergence in different dimensions k and n. To ensure that the macro dynamical information entropy $H(p(y_{t+1}|y_t))$ is not excessively reduced during coarse-graining, we need to ensure that $\frac{H(p(x_{t+1}|x_t))}{n} - \frac{H(p(y_{t+1}|y_t))}{k}$ is bounded by η when $do(y_t) \sim U([-L/2, L/2]^k)$ and $do(x_t) \sim U([-L/2, L/2]^n)$.

To directly determine the causal emergence in the system without being affected by coarse-graining parameter matrix W, we optimize W to obtain the maximum causal emergence $\Delta\mathcal{J}^*$ that the system can achieve. When obtaining the optimal solution, the iterative parameter matrix A_M only retains the maximum k eigenvalues of A, and the determinant value of Σ_M is compressed to the lowest allowed lower limit $\epsilon\det(\Sigma)^{\frac{k}{n}}$. The obtained solution set can be understood as the intersection of k hyperplanes and hyperellipsoids, an ellipse in three-dimensional space. We search for causal emergence in three systems that are known models, focusing on the application of determinism, non-degeneracy, and the manifestation of causal emergence in $\mathcal{R}^3$ space. In random walks, energy dissipation, and accurate selection models, varying degrees of causal emergence can be detected.

We conclude that there are two influencing factors for causal emergence; one is the iterative parameter matrix A and the other is the covariance matrix Σ of random noise, which respectively affect the non-degeneracy and determinism of the system. Smaller eigenvalues in the parameter matrix indicate weak causal relationships between variables in certain dimensions. Suppose the coarse-grained strategy precisely discards these dimensions. In that case, the causal effect of the macro-state dynamics is stronger than that of the micro-state, and the optimal causal emergence will occur.

The causal emergence calculation method in this article has several advantages. Firstly, we present the causal emergence of a known model in a linear stochastic iterative system as an analytical solution. This is also the first time that causal emergence has been calculated as an analytical solution in a continuous-state dynamic system. Secondly, in maximizing causal emergence, we found the solution set of the coarse-graining strategy. We found that the eigenvalues of the parameter matrix in a linear system determine the value of causal emergence. The third is the final result we obtain, which is only related to the system itself and not to specific data. This, to some extent, solves the problem of numerical solutions relying on data and the need for artificial search for coarse-graining strategies.

However, our model still has many shortcomings. One is that the current model is only applicable to linear systems, and there is still a lack of unified analysis and judgment for nonlinear systems. On the other hand, the time of the linear stochastic iterative system we study is discrete, and the calculation method of causal emergence is not applicable to continuous time dynamic systems. Combing EI with relevant work about the dynamic interaction between neural spike trains [63] could be a possible direction to solve the problem.

There are three important research directions in the future. One is to consider how to correctly calculate causal emergence for continuous-time Markov processes with discrete probability space, such as birth and death processes or queuing processes. The other direction concerns the causal emergence of stochastic differential equations or Fokker–Plank equations [64,65], such as option pricing equations and Langevin equations. The third direction is to quantify and explore the causal relationship between EI and unknown models, such as Granger causality [52] or the causal effect of neural spike trains [63]. We will continue to conduct in-depth research on these contents in the future.

Author Contributions: Methodology, B.Y.; writing—original draft, K.L.; writing—review and editing, J.Z. All authors have read and agreed to the published version of the manuscript.

Funding: This research received no external funding.

Institutional Review Board Statement: Not applicable.

Data Availability Statement: All the codes and data are available at: https://github.com/kilovoltage/An_Exact_Causal_Emergence_Theory (accessed on 21 May 2024).

Acknowledgments: This work is inspired by the insightful discussions held in the "Causal Emergence" series reading groups organized by Swarma Club and the "Swarma–Kaifeng" Workshop. Sincere thanks to Jing Xu, Mingzhe Yang, Zhipeng Wang, Ruyi Tao, Muyun Mou, Yue He, and Zhihan Gao for their suggestions and support on theory, methods, and writing. We would also like to extend our sincere gratitude to Yizhuang You, Peng Cui, Jing He, Chaochao Lu, and Yanbo Zhang for their invaluable contributions and insightful discussions. We express our appreciation for the support from the Save 2050 Programme, a joint initiative of Swarma Club and X-OrderSwarma Research. Additionally, we are grateful for the support received from Swarma Research.

Conflicts of Interest: The authors declare no conflicts of interest.

Appendix A. Calculation Effective Information and Causal Emergence

In this appendix, we will prove the theorems related to effective information and causal emergence and demonstrate the specific process of formula derivation. The first process to be demonstrated is the inference of effective information related to linear stochastic iterative systems $\mathcal{J}$.

Proof (Calculation process of Definition 4). For the linear stochastic iteration system like Equation (1), x_{t+1} follows a normal distribution about x_t, so $x_{t+1} \sim \mathcal{N}(Ax_t, \Sigma)$,

$$p(x_{t+1}|x_t) = \frac{1}{\det(\Sigma)^{\frac{1}{2}}(2\pi)^{\frac{n}{2}}} \exp\left\{-\frac{1}{2}(x_{t+1} - Ax_t)'\Sigma^{-1}(x_{t+1} - Ax_t)\right\} \tag{A1}$$

Following the calculation method of causal geometry, assuming ε_t is small, $do(x_t \sim U([-L/2, L/2]^n)) \equiv do(x_t \sim U)$, then $p(x_t) = 1/L^n, L > 0$, we can calculate the effect distribution.

$$\begin{aligned}
E_D(x_{t+1}) &= \int_U p(x_{t+1}|x_t)p(x_t)d^n x_t \\
&= \int_U \frac{1}{\det(\Sigma)^{\frac{1}{2}}(2\pi)^{\frac{n}{2}}} \exp\left\{-\frac{1}{2}(x_{t+1} - Ax_t)'\Sigma^{-1}(x_{t+1} - Ax_t)\right\}\frac{1}{L^n}d^n x_t \\
{\scriptstyle (x_t\approx A^{-1}x_{t+1})} &\approx \int_{\mathcal{X}} \frac{1}{\det(\Sigma)^{\frac{1}{2}}(2\pi)^{\frac{n}{2}}} \exp\left\{-\frac{1}{2}(x_{t+1} - Ax_t)'\Sigma^{-1}(x_{t+1} - Ax_t)\right\}\frac{|\det(A^{-1})|}{L^n}d^n x_{t+1} \\
&= \frac{1}{|\det(A)|L^n}
\end{aligned} \tag{A2}$$

Afterward, as $\mathcal{X} = [-\infty, \infty]^n$ is domain of x_{t+1}, we can calculate the effective information as

$$\begin{aligned}
EI &= \int_{\mathcal{X}} D_{KL}[p(x_{t+1}|x_t)|E_D(x_{t+1})]d^n x_{t+1} \\
&= \int_U \frac{d^n x_t}{L^n} \int_{\mathcal{X}} \frac{1}{\det(\Sigma)^{\frac{1}{2}}(2\pi)^{\frac{n}{2}}} \exp\left\{-\frac{1}{2}(x_{t+1} - Ax_t)'\Sigma^{-1}(x_{t+1} - Ax_t)\right\} \\
&\left[-\ln\left(\det(\Sigma)^{\frac{1}{2}}(2\pi)^{\frac{n}{2}}\right) - \frac{1}{2}(x_{t+1} - Ax_t)'\Sigma^{-1}(x_{t+1} - Ax_t) - \ln\frac{1}{|\det(A)|L^n}\right]d^n x_{t+1} \\
&= -\frac{1}{2}\ln(\det(\Sigma)(2\pi)^n) - \frac{n}{2} - \ln\frac{1}{|\det(A)|L^n} \\
&= \ln\frac{|\det(A)|L^n}{\det(\Sigma)^{\frac{1}{2}}(2\pi e)^{\frac{n}{2}}}.
\end{aligned} \tag{A3}$$

According to the properties of information entropy, we use determinism information,

$$\begin{aligned}
-\langle H(p(x_{t+1}|x_t))\rangle_{x_t} &= -\left\langle -\int_{\mathcal{X}} p(x_{t+1}|x_t)\ln(p(x_{t+1}|x_t))d^n x_{t+1}\right\rangle_{x_t} \\
&= \int_U \frac{d^n x_t}{L^n} \int_{\mathcal{X}} \frac{1}{\det(\Sigma)^{\frac{1}{2}}(2\pi)^{\frac{n}{2}}} \exp\left\{-\frac{1}{2}(x_{t+1} - Ax_t)'\Sigma^{-1}(x_{t+1} - Ax_t)\right\} \\
&\left[-\ln\left(\det(\Sigma)^{\frac{1}{2}}(2\pi)^{\frac{n}{2}}\right) - \frac{1}{2}(x_{t+1} - Ax_t)'\Sigma^{-1}(x_{t+1} - Ax_t)\right]d^n x_{t+1} \quad , \\
&= \left[-\ln\left(\det(\Sigma)^{\frac{1}{2}}(2\pi)^{\frac{n}{2}}\right) - \frac{n}{2}\right] \\
&= \ln\frac{1}{\det(\Sigma)^{\frac{1}{2}}(2\pi e)^{\frac{n}{2}}}
\end{aligned} \tag{A4}$$

and non-degeneracy information,

$$\begin{aligned} H(E_D(x_{t+1})) &= -\int_{\mathcal{X}} E_D(x_{t+1}) \ln(E_D(x_{t+1})) d^n x_{t+1} \\ (x_t \approx A^{-1}x_{t+1}) &\approx -\int_{\mathcal{X}} E_D(x_{t+1}) \ln \frac{1}{|det(A)|L^n} d^n x_{t+1}. \\ &= \ln(|det(A)|L^n) \end{aligned} \tag{A5}$$

It is obvious that

$$-\langle H(p(x_{t+1}|x_t)) \rangle_{x_t} + H(E_D(x_{t+1})) = \ln \frac{|\det(A)|L^n}{\det(\Sigma)^{\frac{1}{2}} (2\pi e)^{\frac{n}{2}}} = EI. \tag{A6}$$

Then, we can easily get

$$\mathcal{J} \equiv \frac{EI}{n} = \frac{1}{n} \ln \frac{|\det(A)|L^n}{(2\pi e)^{\frac{n}{2}} \det(\Sigma)^{\frac{1}{2}}} = \ln \frac{|\det(A)|^{\frac{1}{n}} L}{(2\pi e)^{\frac{1}{2}} \det(\Sigma)^{\frac{1}{2n}}}. \tag{A7}$$

If the system is nonlinear, it can be understood that $A = \nabla f(x_t)$ will change with x_t. Then, Equations (55) and (57) can also be proven. □

After obtaining effective information, we can calculate causal emergence.

Proof of Theorem 1. For the micro dynamical systems like Equation (1) and macro dynamical systems like Equation (8) after coarse-graining, we can calculate the micro effective information $\mathcal{J}_m$ and macro effective information $\mathcal{J}_M$ of two kinds of dynamical systems separately. In this way, causal emergence is

$$\begin{aligned} \Delta\mathcal{J} = \mathcal{J}_M - \mathcal{J}_m &= \frac{EI_M}{k} - \frac{EI_m}{n} \\ &= \frac{1}{k} \ln \frac{|\det(A_M)|L^k}{\det(\Sigma_M)^{\frac{1}{2}} (2\pi e)^{\frac{k}{2}}} - \frac{1}{n} \ln \frac{|\det(A)|L^n}{\det(\Sigma)^{\frac{1}{2}} (2\pi e)^{\frac{n}{2}}} \\ &= \frac{1}{k} \Bigg(\underbrace{\ln \frac{1}{\det(\Sigma_M)^{\frac{1}{2}} (2\pi e)^{\frac{k}{2}}}}_{Determinism Information} + \underbrace{\ln\left(|\det(A_M)| L^k \right)}_{Non-degeneracy Information} \Bigg) \\ &- \frac{1}{n} \left(\ln \frac{1}{\det(\Sigma)^{\frac{1}{2}} (2\pi e)^{\frac{n}{2}}} + \ln(|\det(A)|L^n) \right) \\ &= \underbrace{\ln \frac{|\det(WAW^{\dagger})|^{\frac{1}{k}}}{|\det(A)|^{\frac{1}{n}}}}_{Non-degeneracy Emergence} + \underbrace{\ln \frac{|\det(\Sigma)|^{\frac{1}{2n}}}{|\det(W\Sigma W^T)|^{\frac{1}{2k}}}}_{Determinism Emergence}. \end{aligned} \tag{A8}$$

□

Appendix B. Optimization of Macrodynamic Parameter Matrix

To maximize causal emergence, we need to use relevant content from matrix theory to optimize coarse-graining strategies.

Proof of Lemma 1. Perform eigendecomposition on matrix A, $A = V\Lambda V^{-1}$, $\Lambda = \mathrm{diag}(\lambda_1, \ldots, \lambda_n) \in \mathcal{R}^{n\times n}$ is the diagonal matrix of eigenvalues, $V \in \mathcal{R}^{n\times n}$ is the eigenvector matrix corresponding to the eigenvalue matrix. Determinant

$$\det(WAW^{\dagger}) = \det(WV\Lambda V^{-1}W^{\dagger}) = \det(\tilde{W}\Lambda\tilde{W}^{\dagger}) = \sum_m \left(\gamma_m \prod_{\lambda_i \in L_m} \lambda_i \right), \tag{A9}$$

in which $L_m = \{\lambda_{N_{m,1}}, \lambda_{N_{m,2}}, \ldots, \lambda_{N_{m,k}}\} \subseteq \{\lambda_1, \ldots, \lambda_n\}$ are new sets formed by arbitrarily choosing k eigenvalues from n eigenvalues of A. The sorting of these sets is based on the sum of the elements in the set, in descending order. $N_m \subseteq \{1, \ldots, n\}$, the number of elements in sets $|N_m|, |L_m| = k$, $m = 1, 2, \ldots, C_n^k$. γ_m are coefficients determined by W, $\gamma_m > 0$, $\sum_m \gamma_m = 1$. It is not difficult to find that when $\gamma_m = 1$, matrix A only retains the eigenvalues in L_m after transformation.

The calculation of $\gamma_1, \ldots, \gamma_{C_n^k}$ is as follows. Set $WV = \tilde{W} = (w_{ij})_{k\times n}$, then $W^\dagger V^{-1} = \tilde{W}^\dagger = (v_{ij})_{n\times k}$. According to the principle of determinant calculation, we can divide γ_m into two parts,

$$\gamma_m = \gamma_{m,1} - \gamma_{m,2}, \tag{A10}$$

where $\gamma_{m,1}, \gamma_{m,2}$ correspond to the sum of terms with coefficients of 1 and -1 in the determinant calculation, respectively. Therefore,

$$\gamma_{m,1} = \sum_{l=0}^{k-1}\left[\sum_{s\in\{s\}_m}\left(\prod_{i=1}^{k} w_{i,s_i} v_{s_i,j}\right)\right], j = \begin{cases} i+l, i+l & \leq k \\ i+l-k, i+l & > k \end{cases}, \tag{A11}$$

$$\gamma_{m,2} = \sum_{l=2}^{k+1}\left[\sum_{s\in\{s\}_m}\left(\prod_{i=1}^{k} w_{i,s_i} v_{s_i,j}\right)\right], j = \begin{cases} l-i, l-i & > 0 \\ l-i+k, l-i & \geq 0 \end{cases}. \tag{A12}$$

where $s = \{s_1, s_2, \ldots s_k\}$ is a new sequence formed by randomly arranging all elements in N_m; $\{s\}_m$ is a set composed of such elements s. Number of elements in the set $|\{s\}_m| = k!$.

If all eigenvalues of A satisfy $\lambda_1 \geq \lambda_2 \geq \cdots \geq \lambda_n$, we can simultaneously find the maximum and minimum values of $\det(WAW^\dagger)$. When $\gamma_1 = 1$, only the maximum k eigenvalues are retained, and $\det(WAW^\dagger)$ takes the maximum value $\prod_{i=1}^{k}\lambda_i$. On the contrary, when $\gamma_m = 1$, only the smallest k eigenvalues are retained, and the $\det(WAW^\dagger)$ takes the minimum value $\prod_{i=n-k+1}^{n}\lambda_i$. Therefore,

$$\prod_{i=n-k+1}^{n}\lambda_i \leq \det(WAW^\dagger) \leq \prod_{i=1}^{k}\lambda_i. \tag{A13}$$

From the proof of (A13), we know that γ_m are coefficients determined by W and when $\gamma_m = 1$, matrix A only retains the eigenvalues in L_m. Therefore, when the eigenvalues of matrix A are not specified to be all positive real numbers, the modulus length satisfies $|\lambda_1| \geq |\lambda_2| \geq \cdots \geq |\lambda_n|$, then

$$|\det(WAW^\dagger)| = \left|\sum_m\left(\gamma_m \prod_{\lambda_i\in L_m}\lambda_i\right)\right| \leq \sum_m \gamma_m \left|\prod_{\lambda_i\in L_m}\lambda_i\right| = \sum_m \gamma_m \left(\prod_{\lambda_i\in L_m}|\lambda_i|\right) \leq \prod_{i=1}^{k}|\lambda_i|. \tag{A14}$$

We directly study the situation of eigenvalues in the complex field. When $L_m = \lambda_1, \ldots, \lambda_k$, the determinant $|\det(WAW^\dagger)|$ reaches its maximum value. The decrease of γ_m and the intervention of smaller absolute values of eigenvalues $|\lambda_i|, i \geq k$ lead to the decrease of $|\det(WAW^\dagger)|$. □

Proof of Theorem 3. According to (A9) and Jensen's inequality, we can obtain inequalities

$$|\det(W\Sigma W^\dagger)|^{-\frac{1}{2}} = \left[\sum(\gamma_m \prod \kappa_i)\right]^{-\frac{1}{2}} \leq \left[\sum \gamma_m \left(\prod \kappa_i\right)^{-\frac{1}{2}}\right] = |\det(W\Sigma^{-\frac{1}{2}}W^\dagger)|, \tag{A15}$$

if and only if the eigenvalues are equal; the equal sign holds. By utilizing this inequality and combining it with the relevant properties of linear algebra, we can conclude that

$$
\begin{aligned}
\Delta\mathcal{J} &= \ln\frac{|\det(WAW^{\dagger})|^{\frac{1}{k}}}{|\det(W\Sigma W^{\dagger})|^{\frac{1}{2k}}} - \ln\frac{|\det(A)|^{\frac{1}{n}}}{|\det(\Sigma)|^{\frac{1}{2n}}} \\
&= \frac{1}{k}\ln(|\det(W\Sigma W^{\dagger})|^{-\frac{1}{2}}|\det(WAW^{\dagger})|) - \frac{1}{n}\ln|\Sigma^{-\frac{1}{2}}A| \\
&\leq \frac{1}{k}\ln(|\det(W\Sigma^{-\frac{1}{2}}W^{\dagger})||\det(WAW^{\dagger})|) - \frac{1}{n}\ln|\Sigma^{-\frac{1}{2}}A| \\
&= \frac{1}{k}\ln|\det(W\Sigma^{-\frac{1}{2}}W^{\dagger}WAW^{\dagger})| - \frac{1}{n}\ln|\Sigma^{-\frac{1}{2}}A| \\
{\scriptstyle(\Sigma=VKV^T, A=V\Lambda V^T)} &\leq \frac{1}{k}\ln|\det(W\Sigma^{-\frac{1}{2}}AW^{\dagger})| - \frac{1}{n}\ln|\Sigma^{-\frac{1}{2}}A| \\
{\scriptstyle(W=(\tilde{W}_k, O_{k\times(n-k)})V^T)} &\leq \frac{1}{k}\sum_{i=1}^{k}\ln|\tilde{d}_i| - \frac{1}{n}\sum_{i=1}^{n}\ln|\tilde{d}_i|
\end{aligned}
\tag{A16}
$$

When A and Σ share the same n eigenvectors, that is to say, $\Sigma = VKV^T$ and $A = V\Lambda V^T$, where V is the matrix formed by the shared eigenvectors and K and Λ are the eigenvalues for A and Σ, respectively, the eigenvalues of $\Sigma^{-1/2}A$ are equal to the product of the eigenvalues of A and $\Sigma^{-1/2}$. $W = (\tilde{W}_k, O_{k\times(n-k)})V^T$ represents that both A and $\Sigma^{-1/2}$ retain the eigenvalues with the highest norm; the second and third unequal signs can also be taken as equal signs. □

Appendix C. Loss Function and Causal Emergence

In this section, we first prove that S_D is the supremum of L_D.

Proof of Lemma 3. Based on the theory of matrix modules, when $||x_t||^* = \sup_t ||x_t|| < \infty$,

$$
\begin{aligned}
L_D &= ||Ax_t + \varepsilon_t - (W^{\dagger}WAW^{\dagger}Wx_t + W^{\dagger}W\varepsilon_t)|| \\
&= ||(A - W^{\dagger}WAW^{\dagger}W)x_t + (I_n - W^{\dagger}W)\varepsilon_t|| \\
&\leq ||(A - W^{\dagger}WAW^{\dagger}W)x_t|| + ||(I_n - W^{\dagger}W)\varepsilon_t|| \\
&\leq ||(A - W^{\dagger}WAW^{\dagger}W)||_F||x_t|| + ||(I_n - W^{\dagger}W)||_F||\varepsilon_t|| \\
&= ||(A - W^{\dagger}WAW^{\dagger}W)||_F||x_t|| + (n-k)||\varepsilon_t|| \\
&\leq ||(A - W^{\dagger}WAW^{\dagger}W)||_F||x_t||^* + (n-k)||\varepsilon_t|| = S_D
\end{aligned}
\tag{A17}
$$

□

Next, we prove that W at the minimum value of the supremum S_D can maximize the non-degeneracy emergence.

Proof of Lemma 4. $|\lambda_1| \geq |\lambda_2| \geq \cdots \geq |\lambda_n| \geq 0$ are n modulus of eigenvalues of matrix A sorted from largest to smallest. $\Lambda = \mathrm{diag}(\lambda_1, \ldots, \lambda_n) \in \mathcal{R}^{n\times n}$. $\tilde{W} = WV$, $\tilde{W}^{\dagger}\tilde{W}$ and $I - \tilde{W}^{\dagger}\tilde{W}$ are both symmetric idempotent matrices. $rk(\tilde{W}^{\dagger}\tilde{W}) = k$, $I - \tilde{W}^{\dagger}\tilde{W} = (r_{ij})_{n\times n}$ has the following properties:

(1) $\sum_{l=1}^{n} r_{il}r_{lj} = r_{ij}$.

(2) $||I - \tilde{W}^{\dagger}\tilde{W}||_F = \sqrt{\sum_{i,j=1}^{n,n} r_{ij}^2} = k$.

(3) $\forall l, 0 < l \leq n, \sqrt{\sum_{i,j=1}^{n,n} (r_{il}r_{lj})^2} = 1$

Based on the theory of matrix modules,

$$
\begin{aligned}
S_D &= ||(A - W^{\dagger}WAW^{\dagger}W)||_F||x_t|| + (n-k)||\varepsilon_t|| \\
\overset{(\tilde{W}=WV)}{} &= ||V(\Lambda - \tilde{W}^{\dagger}\tilde{W}\Lambda\tilde{W}^{\dagger}\tilde{W})V^{-1}||_F||x_t|| + (n-k)||\varepsilon_t|| \\
&= ||\Lambda - \tilde{W}^{\dagger}\tilde{W}\Lambda\tilde{W}^{\dagger}\tilde{W}||_F||x_t|| + (n-k)||\varepsilon_t|| \\
&= ||(I_n - \tilde{W}^{\dagger}\tilde{W})\Lambda(I_n - \tilde{W}^{\dagger}\tilde{W}) + 2(I_n - \tilde{W}^{\dagger}\tilde{W})\Lambda\tilde{W}^{\dagger}\tilde{W}||_F||x_t|| + (n-k)||\varepsilon_t|| \\
&\geq ||(I_n - \tilde{W}^{\dagger}\tilde{W})\Lambda(I_n - \tilde{W}^{\dagger}\tilde{W})||_F||x_t|| + (n-k)||\varepsilon_t|| \\
&= \sqrt{\sum_{0<i,j\leq n}\left|\sum_{l=1}^{n} r_{il}r_{lj}\lambda_l\right|^2}||x_t|| + (n-k)||\varepsilon_t|| \\
&\geq \sqrt{\sum_{0<i,j\leq n}\sum_{l=1}^{n}\left|r_{il}r_{lj}\lambda_l\right|^2}||x_t|| + (n-k)||\varepsilon_t|| \\
&\geq \sqrt{\sum_{0<i,j\leq n}\sum_{l=k+1}^{n}\left|r_{il}r_{lj}\lambda_l\right|^2}||x_t|| + (n-k)||\varepsilon_t|| \\
&\geq \sqrt{\sum_{l=k+1}^{n}|\lambda_l|^2}||x_t|| + (n-k)||\varepsilon_t||
\end{aligned}
\quad , \qquad \text{(A18)}
$$

if and only if the maximum k eigenvalues are preserved in $\hat{A}$, only the $n-k$ eigenvalues with the smallest modulus are retained, S_D; the equal sign holds. $W = (\tilde{W}_k, O_{k\times(n-k)})V^{-1}$ is exactly the same solution set as the non-degeneracy emergence at its maximum $\Delta\mathcal{J}_1^*$. □

References

1. Holland, J.H. *Emergence: From Chaos to Order*; OUP: Oxford, UK, 2000.
2. West, G. *Scale: The Universal Laws of Life, Growth, and Death in Organisms, Cities, and Companies*; Penguin: London, UK, 2018.
3. Li, R.; Dong, L.; Zhang, J.; Wang, X.; Wang, W.X.; Di, Z.; Stanley, H.E. Simple spatial scaling rules behind complex cities. *Nat. Commun.* **2017**, *8*, 1841. [CrossRef] [PubMed]
4. Dong, L.; Huang, Z.; Zhang, J.; Liu, Y. Understanding the mesoscopic scaling patterns within cities. *Sci. Rep.* **2020**, *10*, 21201. [CrossRef] [PubMed]
5. Zhang, J.; Kempes, C.P.; Hamilton, M.J.; Tao, R.; West, G.B. Scaling laws and a general theory for the growth of public companies. *arXiv* **2021**, arXiv:2109.10379.
6. Zhang, Y.; Liu, K.; Gui, W. Bayesian and e-bayesian estimations of bathtub-shaped distribution under generalized type-i hybrid censoring. *Entropy* **2021**, *23*, 934. [CrossRef] [PubMed]
7. Xu, J.; Chen, X.; Wen, L.; Zhang, J. Company scaling and its deviations: New indicators for enterprise evaluation and bankruptcy prediction. *PLoS ONE* **2023**, *18*, e0287105. [CrossRef] [PubMed]
8. Wicks, R.T.; Chapman, S.C.; Dendy, R. Mutual information as a tool for identifying phase transitions in dynamical complex systems with limited data. *Phys. Rev. E* **2007**, *75*, 051125. [CrossRef] [PubMed]
9. Hartman, C.; Benes, B. Autonomous boids. *Comput. Animat. Virtual Worlds* **2006**, *17*, 199–206. [CrossRef]
10. Liu, D.; Liu, W.; Yuan, X.; Jiang, Y. Conscious and unconscious processing of ensemble statistics oppositely modulate perceptual decision-making. *Am. Psychol.* **2023**, *78*, 346. [CrossRef] [PubMed]
11. Wang, L.; Jiang, Y. Action observation network: Domain-specific or domain-general? *Trends Cogn. Sci.* **2023**, *27*, 981–982. [CrossRef]
12. Wang, R.; Gates, V.; Shen, Y.; Tino, P.; Kourtzi, Z. Flexible Structure Learning Under Uncertainty. *SSRN Electron. J.* **2022** . [CrossRef]
13. Jingnan, S.; He, J.; Gao, X. Neurofeedback training of control network improves SSVEP-based BCI performance in children. 2021, *preprint*. [CrossRef]
14. Sporns, O.; Faskowitz, J.; Teixeira, A.S.; Cutts, S.A.; Betzel, R.F. Dynamic expression of brain functional systems disclosed by fine-scale analysis of edge time series. *Netw. Neurosci.* **2021**, *5*, 405–433. [CrossRef] [PubMed]
15. Varley, T.F. *Uncovering Higher-Order Structures in Complex Systems with Multivariate Information Theory*; Indiana University: Bloomington, Indiana, 2023.
16. Zhao, Z.; Zhou, Y.; Liu, B.; He, J.; Zhao, J.; Cai, Y.; Fan, J.; Li, X.; Wang, Z.; Lu, Z.; et al. Two-photon synthetic aperture microscopy for minimally invasive fast 3D imaging of native subcellular behaviors in deep tissue. *Cell* **2023**, *186*, 2475–2491. [CrossRef] [PubMed]

17. Dong, T.; He, J.; Wang, S.; Wang, L.; Cheng, Y.; Zhong, Y. Inability to activate Rac1-dependent forgetting contributes to behavioral inflexibility in mutants of multiple autism-risk genes. *Proc. Natl. Acad. Sci. USA* **2016**, *113*, 7644–7649. [CrossRef] [PubMed]
18. Yuan, B.; Zhang, J.; Lyu, A.; Wu, J.; Wang, Z.; Yang, M.; Liu, K.; Mou, M.; Cui, P. Emergence and Causality in Complex Systems: A Survey of Causal Emergence and Related Quantitative Studies. *Entropy* **2024**, *26*, 108. [CrossRef] [PubMed]
19. Oden, J.T.; Belytschko, T.; Babuska, I.; Hughes, T. Research directions in computational mechanics. *Comput. Methods Appl. Mech. Eng.* **2003**, *192*, 913–922. [CrossRef]
20. Seth, A.K. Measuring emergence via nonlinear Granger causality. *alife* **2008**, *2008*, 545–552.
21. Rosas, F.E.; Mediano, P.A.M.; Jensen, H.J.; Seth, A.K.; Barrett, A.B.; Carhart-Harris, R.L.; Bor, D. Reconciling emergences: An information-theoretic approach to identify causal emergence in multivariate data. *PLoS Comput. Biol.* **2020**, *16*, e1008289. [CrossRef] [PubMed]
22. Hoel, E.P.; Albantakis, L.; Tononi, G. Quantifying causal emergence shows that macro can beat micro. *Proc. Natl. Acad. Sci. USA* **2013**, *110*, 19790–19795. [CrossRef] [PubMed]
23. Hoel, E.P.; Albantakis, L.; Marshall, W.; Tononi, G. Can the macro beat the micro? Integrated information across spatiotemporal scales. *Neurosci. Conscious* **2016**, *2016*, niw012. [CrossRef] [PubMed]
24. Rosas, F.E.; Geiger, B.C.; Luppi, A.I.; Seth, A.K.; Polani, D.; Gastpar, M.; Mediano, P.A. Software in the natural world: A computational approach to emergence in complex multi-level systems. *arXiv* **2024**, arXiv:2402.09090.
25. Hoel, E.P. When the map is better than the territory. *Entropy* **2017**, *19*, 188. [CrossRef]
26. Williams, P.L.; Beer, R.D. Nonnegative decomposition of multivariate information. *arXiv* **2010**, arXiv:1004.2515.
27. Rassouli, B.; Rosas, F.E.; Gündüz, D. Data disclosure under perfect sample privacy. *IEEE Trans. Inf. Forensics Secur.* **2019**, *15*, 2012–2025. [CrossRef]
28. Liu, K.; Lü, X.; Gao, F.; Zhang, J. Expectation-maximizing network reconstruction and most applicable network types based on binary time series data. *Phys. D Nonlinear Phenom.* **2023**, *454*, 133834. [CrossRef]
29. Zhang, J.; Tao, R.; Yuan, B. Dynamical Reversibility and A New Theory of Causal Emergence. *arXiv* **2024**, arXiv:2402.15054.
30. Chvykov, P.; Hoel, E. Causal geometry. *Entropy* **2020**, *23*, 24. [CrossRef] [PubMed]
31. Transtrum, M.K.; Machta, B.B.; Brown, K.S.; Daniels, B.C.; Myers, C.R.; Sethna, J.P. Perspective: Sloppiness and emergent theories in physics, biology, and beyond. *J. Chem. Phys.* **2015**, *143*, 010901. [CrossRef] [PubMed]
32. Klein, B.; Hoel, E. The emergence of informative higher scales in complex networks. *Complexity* **2020**, *2020*, 8932526. [CrossRef]
33. Comolatti, R.; Hoel, E. Causal emergence is widespread across measures of causation. *arXiv* **2022**, arXiv:2202.01854.
34. Liu, K.; Zhang, Y. The E-bayesian estimation for Lomax distribution based on generalized type-I hybrid censoring scheme. *Math. Probl. Eng.* **2021**, *2021*, 5570320. [CrossRef]
35. Yang, M.; Wang, Z.; Liu, K.; Rong, Y.; Yuan, B.; Zhang, J. Finding emergence in data: Causal emergence inspired dynamics learning. *arXiv* **2023**, arXiv:2308.09952.
36. Kadanoff, L.P. Scaling laws for Ising models near Tc. *Phys. Phys. Fiz.* **1966**, *2*, 263. [CrossRef]
37. Villemagne, C.d.; Skelton, R.E. Model reductions using a projection formulation. *Int. J. Control* **1987**, *46*, 2141–2169. [CrossRef]
38. Boley, D.L. Krylov space methods on state-space control models. *Circuits Syst. Signal Process.* **1994**, *13*, 733–758. [CrossRef]
39. Gallivan, K.; Grimme, E.; Van Dooren, P. Asymptotic waveform evaluation via a Lanczos method. *Appl. Math. Lett.* **1994**, *7*, 75–80. [CrossRef]
40. Gugercin, S. An iterative SVD-Krylov based method for model reduction of large-scale dynamical systems. *Linear Algebra Its Appl.* **2008**, *428*, 1964–1986. [CrossRef]
41. Antoulas, A.C. An overview of approximation methods for large-scale dynamical systems. *Annu. Rev. Control* **2005**, *29*, 181–190. [CrossRef]
42. Hu, H.Y.; Li, S.H.; Wang, L.; You, Y.Z. Machine learning holographic mapping by neural network renormalization group. *Phys. Rev. Res.* **2020**, *2*, 023369. [CrossRef]
43. Zhang, J.; Liu, K. Neural information squeezer for causal emergence. *Entropy* **2022**, *25*, 26. [CrossRef] [PubMed]
44. Schölkopf, B.; Locatello, F.; Bauer, S.; Ke, N.R.; Kalchbrenner, N.; Goyal, A.; Bengio, Y. Toward causal representation learning. *Proc. IEEE* **2021**, *109*, 612–634. [CrossRef]
45. Murphy, K.A.; Bassett, D.S. Information decomposition to identify relevant variation in complex systems with machine learning. *arXiv* **2023**, arXiv:2307.04755.
46. Murphy, K.A.; Bassett, D.S. Information decomposition in complex systems via machine learning. *Proc. Natl. Acad. Sci. USA* **2024**, *121*, e2312988121. [CrossRef] [PubMed]
47. Dunsmuir, W.; Hannan, E.J. Vector linear time series models. *Adv. Appl. Probab.* **1976**, *8*, 339–364. [CrossRef]
48. Hannan, E.J.; Kavalieris, L. Multivariate linear time series models. *Adv. Appl. Probab.* **1984**, *16*, 492–561. [CrossRef]
49. Barata, J.C.A.; Hussein, M.S. The Moore–Penrose pseudoinverse: A tutorial review of the theory. *Braz. J. Phys.* **2012**, *42*, 146–165. [CrossRef]
50. Horn, R.A.; Johnson, C.R. *Matrix Analysis*; Cambridge University Press: Cambridge, UK, 2012.
51. Pearl, J. Causal inference in statistics: An overview. *Stat. Surv.* **2009**, *3*, 96–146. [CrossRef]
52. Barnett, L.; Barrett, A. B.; Seth, A.K. Granger causality and transfer entropy are equivalent for gaussian variables. *Phys. Rev. Lett.* **2009**, *103*, 238701. [CrossRef] [PubMed]

53. Venkatesh, P.; Bennett, C.; Gale, S.; Ramirez, T.; Heller, G.; Durand, S.; Olsen, S.; Mihalas, S. Gaussian Partial Information Decomposition: Bias Correction and Application to High-dimensional Data. In Proceedings of the Advances in Neural Information Processing Systems 36 (NeurIPS 2023), New Orleans, LA, USA, 10–16 December 2023.
54. Lawler, G.F.; Limic, V. *Random Walk: A Modern Introduction*; Cambridge University Press: Cambridge, UK, 2010; Volume 123.
55. Peaceman, D.W.; Rachford, H.H., Jr. The numerical solution of parabolic and elliptic differential equations. *J. Soc. Ind. Appl. Math.* **1955**, *3*, 28–41. [CrossRef]
56. Bergman, T.L. *Fundamentals of Heat and Mass Transfer*; John Wiley & Sons: Hoboken, NJ, USA, 2011.
57. Patankar, S. *Numerical Heat Transfer and Fluid Flow*; CRC Press: Boca Raton, FL, USA, 2018.
58. LeVeque, R.J. *Finite Difference Methods for Ordinary and Partial Differential Equations: Steady-State and Time-Dependent Problems*; SIAM: Philadelphia, PA, USA, 2007.
59. Roy, N.R.; Chandra, P. Energy dissipation model for wireless sensor networks: A survey. *Int. J. Inf. Technol.* **2020**, *12*, 1343–1353. [CrossRef]
60. Weisstein, E.W. Rotation Matrix. 2003. Available online: https://mathworld.wolfram.com/RotationMatrix.html (accessed on 30 March 2024).
61. Qiu, W. *Analytic Geometry*; Peking University Press: Beijing, China, 1996.
62. Boyer, C.B. *History of Analytic Geometry*; Courier Corporation: Chelmsford, MA, USA, 2012.
63. Mijatovic, G.; Antonacci, Y.; Loncar-Turukalo, T.; Minati, L.; Faes, L. An information-theoretic framework to measure the dynamic interaction between neural spike trains. *IEEE Trans. Biomed. Eng.* **2021**, *68*, 3471–3481. [CrossRef] [PubMed]
64. Maoutsa, D.; Reich, S.; Opper, M. Interacting Particle Solutions of Fokker–Planck Equations Through Gradient–Log–Density Estimation. *Entropy* **2020**, *22*, 802. [CrossRef] [PubMed]
65. Boffi, N.M.; Vanden-Eijnden, E. Probability flow solution of the fokker–planck equation. *Mach. Learn. Sci. Technol.* **2023**, *4*, 035012. [CrossRef]

entropy
MDPI

Article

A Synergistic Perspective on Multivariate Computation and Causality in Complex Systems

Thomas F. Varley

Vermont Complex Systems Center, University of Vermont, Burlington, VT 05405, USA; tfvarley@uvm.edu

Abstract: What does it mean for a complex system to "compute" or perform "computations"? Intuitively, we can understand complex "computation" as occurring when a system's state is a function of multiple inputs (potentially including its own past state). Here, we discuss how computational processes in complex systems can be generally studied using the concept of statistical synergy, which is information about an output that can *only* be learned when the joint state of all inputs is known. Building on prior work, we show that this approach naturally leads to a link between multivariate information theory and topics in causal inference, specifically, the phenomenon of causal colliders. We begin by showing how Berkson's paradox implies a higher-order, synergistic interaction between multidimensional inputs and outputs. We then discuss how causal structure learning can refine and orient analyses of synergies in empirical data, and when empirical synergies meaningfully reflect computation versus when they may be spurious. We end by proposing that this conceptual link between synergy, causal colliders, and computation can serve as a foundation on which to build a mathematically rich general theory of computation in complex systems.

Keywords: Berkson's paradox; synergy; multivariate information theory; higher-order interactions; partial information decomposition

1. Introduction

What does it mean to say that a complex system, such as the brain, "computes"? The metaphor of computation is a canonical one throughout the field of complex systems [1,2] although unlike digital and analog computers designed by engineers, complex systems are self-organizing, noisy, and often continuous. While early cyberneticians made use of concepts like Turing machines and Boolean logic gates as analogies [3], as the field has progressed, it has become increasingly clear that complex systems are not merely elaborate Turing machines. Formal theories that rely on mathematical notions of well-defined, computable functions are often too rigid for the noisy, multifaceted, ill-defined, and non-deterministic world of complex systems. As a result, like many other topics in the field of complex systems, applying the concept of computation often relies on the intuition of researchers rather than objective quantification.

Despite this, it is also clear that many systems *do* seem to do something very much like the most general theories of computation. Consider a neuron: it is well known that neurons receive inputs from pre-synaptic parent neurons (in the form of excitatory and inhibitory neurotransmitters) and account for those inputs when "deciding" (computing) their behavior in the immediate future (whether to fire an action potential or not). Here, we suggest a relaxed and pragmatic definition of computation, in the spirit of the simple mapping account [4,5], that incorporates these basic features. In the context of complex systems, we operationalize computation as occurring when a system, or subset of a system, accounts for the state of multiple exogenous or endogenous inputs when deciding its next state. While this definition is very general, this may ultimately be a virtue; it does not require that the process of accounting for inputs be mathematically well defined, nor does it assume a discrete, finite state machine, and it works just as well for continuous systems as discrete ones. For instance, an economist might say that a business computes the optimal price of its products as some nebulous function of inputs (costs of material, competitors' pricing, etc).

The specific mechanisms and physical implementations of these computations are all different, but they share a common high-level feature: information about the states of many elements, possibly including the past state of the computer itself, is integrated to "decide" on a given next state, out of some space of possibilities. We might call this the "integrated information" account of computation (note that "integrated information" in this context is not necessarily the same as integrated information theory, which is a proposed theory of consciousness).

Here, we show that this definition of computation is particularly useful in the context of multivariate information theory [6–8], which concerns itself with the interactions between three or more variables (higher-order interactions). For such an account to be useful, particularly one as general as this, it would be useful if it pointed to some analytic tools that scientists could use to try and understand the computational structure of whatever system they are interested in. Based on the integrated information account of computation, we would expect that an observer attempting to model a putative computational process would find that predicting the output requires knowing the joint state of all of the inputs simultaneously. This notion is formalized by the concept of *synergy*: information about a target that is only disclosed by the joint state of all of the inputs and no simpler combination of sources [9].

Much of this work is inspired by the developments of Lizier et al. [10], who proposed that "non-trivial" computation could be recognized by multivariate dependencies that were "greater than the sum of their parts". This approach was further refined by Lizier, Flecker, and Williams in 2013 [11], who combined their method with the recently proposed approach using the partial information decomposition (explained in Section 2.2.1) as a principled measure of synergy. Subsequently, Timme et al. proposed using synergy as a measure of computation in neocortical circuits [12], an approach that has led to a series of studies in the area of computational neuroscience [13–16]. While highly productive, many instances of this approach have relied on intuitive arguments relating synergy to computation, and the formal connections have been largely unexplored. In this paper, we propose to refine the mathematical links between synergy and the integrated information account of computation, showing that the two can be linked to another set of fundamental concepts in complex systems science: collider bias and causal inference.

2. Berkson's Paradox, Colliders, and "Computation"

Berkson's paradox is one of the most well-known veridical paradoxes in statistics and is often used to demonstrate the effects of non-random sampling of data [17]. The usual presentation is as follows:

> Alice is a social psychologist who is interested in how desirable traits (intelligence, attractiveness, etc.) are distributed over the U.S. population. Her data include information from a large number of Hollywood actors (a convenience sample; talent scores can be inferred from movie reviews and attractiveness from tabloids). Using movie reviews and tabloids, every actor is assigned a score for both talent and attractiveness. When Alice plots acting talent against attractiveness, she finds a statistically significant negative correlation. With a p-value ≤ 0.05 in hand, Alice rushes off to publish a paper about how attractiveness and acting talent are anticorrelated and then writes a grant proposing a research program into how the genes that code for acting talent and facial attractiveness are antagonistic.

When phrased in this somewhat cartoonish way, Alice's mistake is fairly obvious: she has an extremely biased sample (indeed, Berkson's paradox is sometimes called selection bias [18]). Hollywood celebrity is fickle; however, it is generally true that to reach the status of celebrity, one must be either unusually attractive or unusually talented. Ugly and untalented people do not (typically) make it to the silver screen, and so Alice's data are fatally compromised from the outset. Thinking in terms of computation, we might say that "the media system" is "computing" whether a person reaches some threshold baseline of joint talent and attractiveness to be allowed onto the red carpet (and, by extension, onto Alice's list). For a geometric visualization of Berkson's paradox, see Figure 1. In the next section, we will discuss the usual interpretation of Berkson's paradox in the context of collider bias and causal inference, before moving on to an alternative interpretation that relates collider bias and Berkson's paradox to higher-order information sharing and synergy.

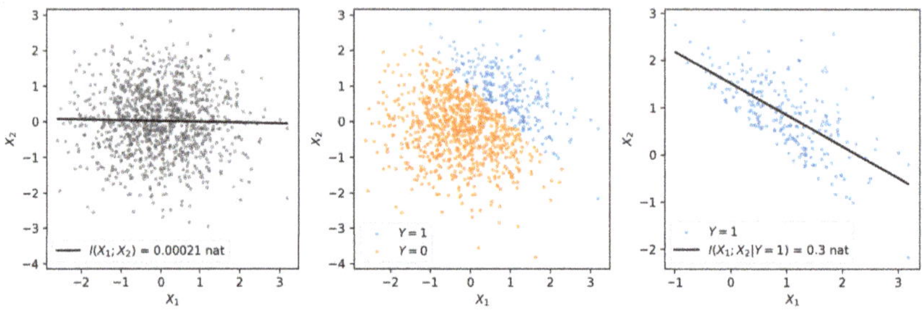

Figure 1. Left: Two random, normally distributed variables X_1 and X_2 with zero mean, unit variance, and $X_1 \perp X_2$. There is no mutual information between them. In the example of movie stars, X_1 and X_2 might be analogous to attractiveness and talent. **Center:** we can define a third random variable as a threshold function: $Y = (X_1 + X_2) > 1$, analogous to the "selection" criteria that define who will be a movie star as a function of whether they reach some minimal threshold of attractiveness and/or talent. **Right:** If we then compute the mutual information between X_1 and X_2 conditional on $Y = 1$, we see a spurious correlation, suggesting that X_1 and X_2 are anticorrelated, when they are actually independent. This is Berkson's paradox.

2.1. The Usual Interpretation: Collider Bias

Berkson's paradox appears to be about two variables (such as attractiveness and acting talent) but is, in fact, actually about a higher-order interaction between three variables (one of which is "hidden"). This third variable is whether a given member of the population is selected to be in Alice's dataset or not. Importantly, the state of this hidden variable, Y, is itself a function of the two other variables we are interested in. Both talent and attractiveness causally influence an actor's success. In the case of Alice's study, the inclusion criteria could be a threshold function that computes whether someone is talented enough or attractive enough to make it to Hollywood stardom.

Written out in the language of causal diagrams (directed, acyclic graphs, or DAGs), we can represent our system of three variables as a *collider*:

$$X_1 \rightarrow Y \leftarrow X_2 \tag{1}$$

Colliders are something of a bugbear in modern causal inference and multivariate statistics [19]. We will discuss the problem of causal structure inference in more detail below, but briefly, when attempting to understand the structure of a system, the presence of colliders makes it difficult to understand when there is real dependence between two variables, or if they are actually ("causally") independent and the empirical dependence is illusory. Much has been written on the problem of collider bias, but from an intuitive perspective, the source of the bias is fairly simple. When we sample data from a system with a collider, we are unwittingly creating an unbiased sample. If we then try and learn correlations between features, we are actually computing the conditional mutual information $I(X_1;X_2|Y)$ when we might believe that we are computing the bivariate mutual information $I(X_1;X_2)$. The subtlety emerges when we realize that conditioning the mutual information is not a purely subtractive operation (which it is commonly believed to be). It is entirely possible for the conditional mutual information to be greater than the unconditioned mutual information. In the language of causal diagrams, Pearl might say that conditioning on the collider opens a path between X_1 and X_2 [20]: an illusion of dependency has been created, one that may not be there in the original dataset.

2.2. The Synergistic Interpretation

In the example of Alice and the movie stars, the two input variables (talent and attractiveness) are a priori independent (i.e., $I(X_1;X_2) = 0$ bit), but when conditioned on the third variable (whether they are attractive enough, or talented enough, to make it in Hollywood), a significant dependency appears (i.e., $I(X_1;X_2|Y) >> 0$ bit). A very natural question to ask might be how different is the true dependency between X_1 and X_2 from the conditional dependency? We can compute the simple difference as follows: $I(X_1;X_2) - I(X_1;X_2|Y)$.

For readers already familiar with information theory, this relationship should be recognizable. It defines the *co-information* [21], one of three proposed multivariate generalizations of the classic, bivariate, Shannon mutual information:

$$\begin{aligned} Co(X_1;X_2;Y) &= I(X_1;X_2) - I(X_1;X_2|Y) \\ &= I(X_1;Y) - I(X_1;Y|X_2) \\ &= I(X_2;Y) - I(X_2;Y|X_1) \end{aligned} \tag{2}$$

As a generalized mutual information, co-information is interesting because it does not obey the non-negativity of either the bivariate mutual information or the two other generalizations (both the total correlation [22] and the dual total correlation [23] are strictly non-negative). Let us first imagine the case where $Co(X_1;X_2;Y) > 0$ bit. If the co-information is positive, then $I(X_1;X_2) > I(X_1;X_2|Y)$. In this case, learning the state of Y "explains away" the dependency between X_1 and X_2. There must be some uncertainty that is "triply redundant" between all three variables, such that learning the state of any individual variable accounts for correlations between the other two (consider the symmetry of the three equations in Equation (2)). The case of the negative co-information is a little bit harder. Clearly, this occurs when $I(X_1;X_2) < I(X_1;X_2|Y)$, which implies that learning Y somehow "illuminates" (or perhaps "hallucinates") a dependency between X_1 and X_2 that is not visible when the two are considered on their own. Interpreting this phenomenon (which is widespread in empirical data [24]) has been a standing puzzle in information theory since co-information was introduced in the 1950s. Various information theorists have proposed a variety of interpretations and decompositions, including in terms of joint and conditional mutual information, sums and differences of entropies [25], or lattice structures [26]. However, it was not until the development of the partial information decomposition (PID) by Williams and Beer in 2010 that the negativity of the co-information was finally interpreted in terms of purely higher-order interactions [9].

The PID (explained below) reveals that the co-information is negative (and by extension, Berkson's paradox occurs) when there is information about Y that is only learnable when the state of the rest of the system (i.e., X_1 and X_2) is known jointly. We will argue below that, in the context of a collider where Y is causally influenced by both X_1 and X_2, this is indicative of a "computational process" happening in Y, where multiple streams of information are integrated as part of Y's "choice" of what state to adopt.

2.2.1. Explaining Partial Information Decomposition

The partial information decomposition (PID) is a framework for assessing how the interaction of many "input" variables reveals information about the state of a target variable [9,27]. As previously mentioned, the PID was not the first attempt to study different orders of information sharing in the case of multiple sources and a single target (see [25] for an early example), but the PID is unique in that it revealed the entire structure of multivariate information and formalized the notion of multiple "kinds" of higher-order interaction. For two inputs and the target, it is straightforward to compute the joint mutual information that both sources provide about the target as follows:

$$I(X_1, X_2; Y) = H(Y) - H(Y|X_1, X_2) \tag{3}$$

However, this scalar value does not reveal the structure of the information: What information about Y could only be learned by observing X_1? Or only by observing X_2? What information could be learned by observing either X_1 alone or X_2 alone? What "synergistic" information can only be learned by observing X_1 and X_2 jointly (and no simpler combination of elements)? The PID was proposed in a seminal paper by Williams and Beer [9] and decomposes the joint mutual information into a set of non-overlapping "partial information atoms":

$$I(X_1, X_2; Y) = Red(X_1, X_2; Y) + Syn(X_1, X_2; Y) + \tag{4}$$
$$Unq(X_1; Y/X_2) + Unq(X_2; Y/X_1) \tag{5}$$

In the two-variable case, these four terms describe every possible dependency between inputs and the target. The redundant information $Red(X_1, X_2; Y)$ is the information that is duplicated over X_1 and X_2 such that it could be learned by observing either X_1 alone or X_2 alone. The unique information term $Unq(X_i; Y/X_j)$ is the information about Y that could only be learned by observing X_i. Finally, the synergistic information $Syn(X_1, X_2; Y)$ is the information about Y that can only be learned when the states of X_1 and X_2 are observed together and, crucially, cannot be learned by any simpler set of sources.

The marginals' mutual information can be similarly decomposed as follows:

$$I(X_1; Y) = Red(X_1, X_2; Y) + Unq(X_1; Y/X_2) \tag{6}$$
$$I(X_2; Y) = Red(X_1, X_2; Y) + Unq(X_2; Y/X_1) \tag{7}$$

Note here that context is important: since we are analyzing the bivariate relationship $X_i - Y$ in the context of the collider $\{X_1, X_2\} \rightarrow Y$, the redundant information $Red(X_1, X_2; Y)$ still counts toward $I(X_i; Y)$. For a visualization of the PID using Venn diagrams, see Figure 2.

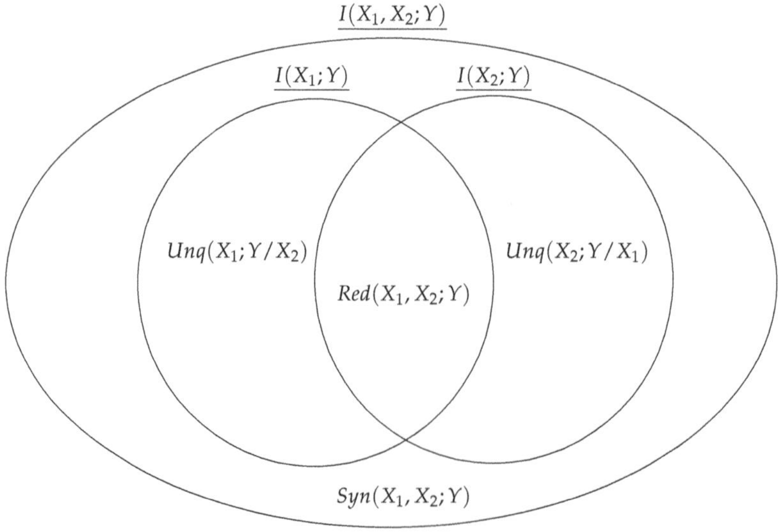

Figure 2. Visual intuition behind the bivariate PID.

There remains an active debate about the best way to define redundancy. Unlike the Shannon entropy, which is uniquely specified by Shannon's original axioms, many different possible redundancy functions can be shown to satisfy the initial Williams and Beer axioms. These functions can return meaningfully different results (for further discussion, see [28,29]); thus, in any given analysis of empirical data, care should be taken when choosing one or another. By and large, however, the arguments made in this paper do not require operationalizing a specific measure. In cases where we want to compute a PID for didactic purposes (see Section 2.3), we use the minimum mutual information [30]:

$$Red(X_1, X_2; Y) := \min_i I(X_i; Y) \tag{8}$$

Intuitively, we can understand the minimum mutual information and estimate how much uncertainty, on average, about Y would be resolved regardless of whether we learn X_1 alone or X_2 alone. Once again, this is not the only viable measure and has a number of limitations; however, it is also conceptually the simplest, which suits our purposes here. One significant benefit of this redundancy function is that it is known to be analytically correct for multivariate Gaussian variables [31] and has the nice property that it only depends on the pairwise, marginal relationship between X_i and Y (for more, see [32,33]).

2.2.2. Decomposing Conditional Mutual Information and Co-Information

With the PID established, it is possible to gain new insights into measures like co-information and conditional mutual information. For example, consider the following identity:

$$I(X_1; X_2|Y) = I(X_1; X_2, Y) - I(X_1; Y) \tag{9}$$

If we substitute in Equations (4) and (6), we find

$$\begin{aligned} I(X_1; X_2|Y) &= Unq(X_1; X_2/Y) + Syn(X_1, Y; X_2) && (10) \\ &= Unq(X_1; X_2/Y) + Syn(X_2, Y; X_1) && (11) \end{aligned}$$

where $Unq(X_1; X_2/Y)$ refers to the unique information about X_2 disclosed by X_1 *in the context of* Y.

We can see that the effect of conditioning on the collider is to make visible the higher-order interaction between all three variables: $Syn(X_1, Y; X_2)$ is the synergistic information about X_2 that is only learnable when X_1 and Y are known together (and likewise for $Syn(X_2, Y; X_1)$). This provides the crux of why conditioning on a collider can cause dependencies to appear: the observer suddenly gains access to higher-order information (in the form of the synergistic dependency) that they can only "see" when only considering X_1, X_2, and Y together.

We can further refine this intuition by considering the following co-information:

$$Co(X_1; X_2; Y) = I(X_1; X_2) - I(X_1; X_2|Y) \tag{12}$$

Decomposing the co-information with respect to the target, Y reveals that

$$Co(X_1; X_2; Y) = Red(X_1, X_2; Y) - Syn(X_1, X_2; Y) \tag{13}$$

We can see that, whenever Berkson's paradox occurs and $Co(X_1; X_2; Y) < 0$, synergy outweighs redundancy. Said differently, information about the state of Y is dominated by an "integrated" interaction between multiple sources. Y is "choosing" its state as a function of multiple inputs. Accordingly, we say that synergy is reflecting this high-order computation. This link between Berkson's paradox and synergy was first noted by Rosas et al. [34] in an excellent study of higher-order information sharing. Here, we elaborate on this crucial insight by extending it using the PID, as well as discussing how it may be applied in empirical contexts.

2.3. Case Study I: Summing Dice

To demonstrate the proposed link between synergy and computation, it helps to go through a simple example. Here, we have (arguably) the simplest "computation" possible: addition. To model it, consider two fair, six-sided dice, D_1 and D_2, with $D_1 \perp D_2$. We will create a third variable S, such that $S = D_1 + D_2$. We hope it is not controversial to say that S implements a computation (in this case, addition). While the distributions of D_1 and D_2 are maximally entropic, this is not the case for S: the probability that $S = 2$ is $1/36$ (since there is only one combination of inputs that leads to that outcome). In contrast, the probability that $S = 6$ is $1/6$ since there are six possible combinations of inputs that sum to 6.

By construction, we know that $I(D_1; D_2) = 0$ bit. However, $I(D_1; D_2|S) \approx 1.896$ bit, and so $Co(X_1; X_2; Y) \approx -1.896$ bit. The synergistic component of the information dominates and so the co-information is negative and Berkson's paradox has occurred!

If we compute the actual PID using the minimum mutual information function for redundancy, we find that $Red(D_1, D_2; S) \approx 0.689$ bit and $Syn(D_1, D_2; Y) \approx 2.585$ bit (and both unique terms are 0 bit exactly since the dice are identical). Where do these numbers come from? Intuitively, we can understand the non-zero redundancy by noticing that, even though $D_1 \perp D_2$, learning the state of either die alone is enough to "rule out" some possible states of S. For example, learning that $D_1 = 1$ or $D_2 = 1$ is sufficient to exclude all possible values of $S > 7$, since to achieve such a value requires that at least one die be greater than or equal to two. This is what Harder refers to as "mechanistic redundancy", in contrast to "source redundancy", which is attributable to correlations between the inputs [35].

The remaining information about S is synergistic. This is because completely resolving all the uncertainty about the state of S requires knowing both inputs. Learning that $D_1 = 1$ is sufficient to rule out any $S > 7$; however, it is not enough to specify the value of S any further. Doing so requires knowing both inputs, and this is the nature of computation. We should note that we are not saying that synergistic information *is* computation in any fundamental sense. Whatever physical process that reads the value of the individual dice and computes the sum is what is performing the computation. The synergistic information is merely a kind of statistical fingerprint, indicating that information has been integrated in some higher-order fashion.

2.4. Case Study II: Transfer Entropy

The perspective that synergistic information represents some putative notion of "computation" can help us make sense of difficult-to-interpret phenomena in complex systems research. As a second case study, let us consider the transfer entropy [36,37]. The transfer entropy from some variable X to another variable Y is defined as follows:

$$TE(X \to Y) = I(X_{past}; Y_t|Y_{past}) \tag{14}$$

where X_{past} refers to the (potentially multivariate) embedded past of X, Y_{past} refers to the (potentially multivariate) embedded past of Y, and Y_t refers to the state of Y at time t. The logic behind the transfer entropy is to capture that information about Y's next state disclosed by X's past that is above and beyond the information disclosed by Y's own past (hence the conditioning).

As we have already established, conditioning mutual information is not a purely subtractive manipulation. Generally, the tacit assumption implicit in applications of the transfer entropy is that conditioning on Y_{past} will reduce the apparent correlation between X_{past} and Y_t. However, this is not always the case: how do we interpret the case of $I(X_{past}; Y_t) < I(X_{past}; Y_t|Y_{past})$?

Williams and Beer [38] showed that the transfer entropy can be decomposed into

$$TE(X \to Y) = Unq(X_{past}; Y_t/Y_{past}) + Syn(X_{past}, Y_{past}; Y_t) \tag{15}$$

The first term, $Unq(X_{past}; Y_t / Y_{past})$, is generally understood to refer to the true bivariate information transfer and was termed the "state-independent transfer entropy" (SITE) by Williams and Beer, as it does not depend on the past state of the target. The second term, $Syn(X_{past}, Y_{past}; Y_t)$, is less clear: it refers to the information about Y_t that can only be learned when both X's past and Y's past are known together. Williams and Beer termed it the "state-dependent information transfer" (SDTE) since it does depend on the past state of the target.

This decomposition shows that the putatively bivariate transfer entropy actually conflates pairwise and higher-order dependencies (this is also generally true of any conditional mutual information). This discovery prompted intense criticism of the transfer entropy as a technique for complex network inference by James and Crutchfield [39], as it obviously challenges the interpretation that $TE(X \rightarrow Y)$ measures unidirectional information "flow". Consequently, they argue that the transfer entropy cannot be properly localized to a single source. Since the critique, however, this facet of the bivariate transfer entropy has received little attention, despite its significance. Recently, Daube et al. [40] showed that the SDTE contributes to the estimation of transfer entropy from simulated data. Furthermore, contra Barrett [31], who suggested stripping the SDTE and using only the "true" bivariate SITE transfer, Daube et al. argued that the SITE actually does worse than the SDTE.

Based on both empirical findings and theoretical arguments presented here, it seems implausible to continue to treat the transfer entropy as a measure of conveniently bivariate information flow. However, none of the existing treatments meditate on how to best intuitively understand what kinds of dynamics are represented by the SDTE. Formally, the synergy is well understood and easy to derive. However, a unifying interpretative framework has largely been lacking. If we take that synergy refers to integrative computation, then the SDTE starts to become a little bit less mysterious: any process that "decides" its next state as a function of some combinations of memory and external perturbation can be modeled as performing a "computation" on two inputs: one is the state of its own past, and one is the value of the input it receives. State-dependent transfer entropy could be thought of as reporting that part of the transfer entropy reflects the computation that the target element performs in deciding its next state as a function of what is stored in its memory and what input it receives from another part of the system.

3. Computation and Causality in Complex Systems

So far, we have assumed that the causal model of the collider is known, and notions such as "inputs" and "outputs" are well specified. In the case of summing the values of the dice, the inputs (D_is) are obviously the individual dice, and the output (or target, S) is the sum of the input. In this context, it is obvious that the relevant information decomposition is of $I(D_1, D_2; S)$, and the notion of synergy makes intuitive sense. Now suppose that we have three new variables, A_1, A_2 and B, and that rather than being related by a collider motif, they are related by a broadcasting motif as follows:

$$A_1 \leftarrow B \rightarrow A_2 \tag{16}$$

where B broadcasts its state to each A_i. In this case, Berkson's paradox will not hold: if A_1 and A_2 are otherwise independent, when conditioning on B, we would expect $I(A_1; A_2|B) = 0$ bit. Given the definition of the co-information given in Equation (12), it is easy to see that $Co(A_1; A_2; B) = I(A_1; A_2)$. Since $Co(A_1; A_2; B) >> 0$ bit, we can infer that the information structure of the triad is, overall, dominated by redundancy. This is consistent with the intuition that a broadcaster is duplicating information over both A_1 and A_2 (as well as representing it in itself).

There is, however, an apparent problem. From Equation (13), we know that

$$Co(A_1; A_2; B) = Red(A_1, A_2; B) - Syn(A_1, A_2; B) \tag{17}$$

If $Co(A_1; A_2; B) >> 0$, then how might we interpret the possibility of non-zero synergy in this context? From a mathematical perspective, it is straightforward: there is uncertainty about the state of B that can only be resolved when A_1 and A_2 are both known. Unfortunately, this seems to complicate our argument that synergy is a statistical fingerprint of computation; the broadcaster motif does not seem to be performing any meaningful "computation". It is merely duplicating information over downstream elements.

To resolve this uncertainty, it is important to remember that the PID is an inherently directed analysis, dividing the system into inputs and targets. As previously mentioned in the case of the collider, the inputs and targets map neatly onto the causal model of the collider itself. In the case of the broadcaster motif, this is not the case. While it is numerically possible to compute $Syn(A_1, A_2; B)$, doing so is running "against the causal flow" and, consequently, appears to be meaningless from a directed perspective. It could be said that the map and territory are in conflict: the orientation of the PID is misaligned with the causal structure of the system. This is important to highlight, as it shows that not all computable synergies are necessarily meaningful: the structure of the underlying causal model is a key consideration, and researchers interested in applying these analyses should be mindful of the different contextual factors that might change the interpretation of the numerical value.

What about in cases where the causal ground truth is not known? It is easy to construct tractable toy models in theoretical contexts, but in natural sciences, rarely is a blueprint handed to us by God. Instead, it must be inferred. Suppose we have some triad, $\{X, Y, Z\}$, which could be either a collider or a broadcaster and we do not know which. Furthermore, we lack any domain expertise that can be leveraged to assume a structure. In the material we have covered so far, disambiguating these two cases is difficult. We could look for Berkson's paradox, assuming that if $X \rightarrow Z \leftarrow Y$ then $Co(X; Y; Z) < 0$, but even if the structure is a collider, if X and Y are correlated, we may still find that redundancy outweighs synergy. In systems that have a large synchronous component to their dynamics (for example, the nervous system), this is a real concern.

If a scientist has a dataset from which synergies can be computed, how could they disambiguate between those synergies that represent some kind of computational process (as in the collider) and those that do not (as in the broadcaster)? We argue that, ultimately, this is a question of causal inference [20] and leveraging both domain expertise, as well as more refined techniques for structure learning in complex systems [41,42] must be incorporated into the analysis. If, given some dataset, it is possible to construct a causal (or merely effective) scaffold of the system, then colliders can be identified as putative sites of computation. This approach has been leveraged in computational neuroscience: given finely resolved, temporally ordered spiking data, it is possible to infer effective connectivity networks using measures like the bivariate or multivariate transfer entropy [15,16], from which colliders can be sampled.

Alternately, if one has strong priors on the structure of the system under study, then those may be leveraged. For example, in a quantitative study of intersectionality in social systems, Varley and Kaminski studied how demographic factors such as race and sex synergistically disclose information about outcomes such as incomes [43]. In this context, there is ample prior evidence to assume a collider-like structure, while a broadcaster-like structure can be ruled out because there is no plausible way that income could causally impact features like race or sex.

Recently, considerable work has involved the problem of inferring directed models that account for higher-order interactions. It has long been known that strictly pairwise approaches to structure learning fail in the presence of higher-order interactions [8], and finding optimal ways to account for higher-order redundancies and synergies remains an open problem. One popular approach is the multivariate transfer entropy [44,45], which takes a serial conditioning approach to account for higher-order information in transfer entropy, although other approaches include the framework proposed by Mijatovic et al., which introduced a balance index (B-index) that quantified whether the interaction between two elements was redundancy-dominated or synergy-dominated in the context of the rest of the system. Beyond the pairwise network approach, representing higher-order information with hypergraphs has been recently explored [46,47] as well. Similarly, generalizations of the partial information decomposition to stochastic processes [48] can reveal time-directed higher-order information in dynamical systems.

Assuming that one is able to construct a plausible causal (or effective) model of the system under study, there is still the issue that the joint mutual information itself is not a causal measure. Previous work has established that even time-directed measures of information flow, such as temporal mutual information or transfer entropy, poorly reflect causal dependencies [49,50]. The link between information flow, causality, and structure inference is a rich field that we cannot completely survey (for further discussion, see [51–53]), and the problem of true causal information decomposition remains an outstanding issue. Ultimately, the question of attributing higher-order, synergistic causation may not have a unique solution but, like the question of redundancy, may depend on the specific way one operationalizes the notion of "causality" (interventional, counterfactual, etc). In the short term, however, we propose that a small modification of the joint mutual information may be useful here. In 2003, Tononi and Sporns proposed a measure they termed "effective information", which is the mutual information from a source to a target when the entropy of the sources is maximal [54]:

$$EI(\mathbf{X} \to Y) = I(\mathbf{X}^{H_{\max}}; Y) \tag{18}$$

By forcing a maximum entropy distribution on the inputs, the effective information attempts to simulate random assignment in interventional approaches to causality. Later, Hoel et al. [52] argued that the effective information could be understood as an instance of Pearl's do-calculus applied to mutual information: $EI(\mathbf{X} \to Y) = I(Y; do(\mathbf{X}))$. Being modified mutual information, effective information can be decomposed using the PID, lending a more causal flavor to the synergy than is usually the case (as well as removing any possible source redundancy [35]). For an example of this approach to discrete data, see [43]. We should be very clear, however, that while effective information and do-calculus approximate a causal inference (and by extension, causal computation), they are still ultimately based on correlational analyses, which can break down in certain contexts. It is known that the Shannon entropy can misrepresent structures in complex systems [55]. For researchers interested in applying these methods, considering the appropriateness of a an information-theoretic model should be seen as a necessary first step in experimental design. Future work considering other notions of information structure (such as algorithmic information theory and algorithmic information dynamics [56]) will complement this work.

4. Discussion

Since the notion of synergy was formalized in the context of the PID, it has been widely applied to a number of different fields. Each of these applications brings with it distinct interpretations, and there is not much cross-talk between disciplines as to the general meaning of synergistic information. For example, when considering sociological identities, synergy is equated with the sociological concept of "intersectionality" [43]. In the context of biological neural networks, synergy has been associated with information processing in the nervous system [12,13,15,16,57,58], while in artificial neural networks, synergy has been associated with the complexity of representations [59] or multi-task learning [60]. Synergy has been identified in the cardiovascular system as well [48]. When considering econometric data, synergy has been associated with economic sophistication [61], and synergy has been found to correlate with the level of consciousness in patients who have been anesthetized or are comatose [58,62]. In climatological data, synergy has been identified, although its significance remains unclear [57,63,64], and in theoretical biology, synergy has been associated with notions of "individuality" or organismic autonomy [65].

This list is non-exhaustive, but it is sufficient to indicate that synergy is ubiquitous in the natural world; far from being some kind of strange or exotic dependency that only occurs in constructed models, synergy has been found in complex systems at almost every scale. Despite this ubiquity, the variety of different, context-dependent interpretations shows that science in general lacks a unified framework for understanding the significance of synergy generally. Here, we propose that synergy can be understood as a kind of fingerprint of computation in complex systems: when an element of a system "chooses" its next state based on some multi-argument function that accounts for multiple inputs, synergistic information will almost certainly exist. By showing that synergistic dynamics are intimately related to the notion of colliders in causal inference, we hope to ground future studies of synergistic dynamics in complex systems in a common framework.

Since the groundbreaking work of Williams and Beer first formalized the notion of synergy in the context of the PID over a decade ago [9], the majority of the focus of the field has been on solving the problem of how to recognize it in data. This has included work on a plethora of redundancy functions (for review, see [28,29]), extensions of the PID (such as the multi-target integrated information decomposition [66,67] and the partial entropy decomposition [68,69]), and the generalized information decomposition [70], as well as non-PID-based heuristics such as the O-information [71], the O-information rate O-information rate [48] (a derivative of the O-information specifically designed for dynamical system), or the α-synergy decomposition [72].

At this point, the problem of recognizing synergistic dependencies in data is, if not totally solved, well studied enough that the field has a rich toolkit of measures to apply to any given dataset. This puts us in the position of being able to move beyond asking merely "is there synergy?" or "where is the synergy?" Instead, we must begin asking "what is synergy for?"

Conclusions

In this paper, we explored the idea that modeling "computation" in complex systems is related to the information-theoretic notion of statistical synergy. Synergy occurs when there is information about the state of an output variable that can only be learned when the joint state of all of its input variables is known and proposed that this is a statistical "fingerprint" reflecting some physical process by which an output element "chooses" its next state as a function of multiple inputs (rather than merely propagating information forward). To further formalize this notion, we related this process to the collider motif studied in the field of causal inference, where a single variable is causally influenced by multiple inputs simultaneously. We showed that the well-known collider bias (also known as Berkson's paradox) occurs because of a synergistic interaction between the inputs and output, providing a mathematical link between the world of multivariate information theory and causal inference or structure learning. We further proposed that this link deepens our understanding of both statistical synergy as a concept and the phenomenon of computation in complex systems.

Funding: This research received no external funding.

Institutional Review Board Statement: Not applicable.

Informed Consent Statement: Not applicable.

Data Availability Statement: No new data were created for this article.

Acknowledgments: I would like to thank Maria Pope for extensive discussions around the links between synergy and Berkson's paradox and Olaf Sporns for support.

Conflicts of Interest: The author declares no conflicts of interest.

References

1. Flake, G.W. *The Computational Beauty of Nature: Computer Explorations of Fractals, Chaos, Complex Systems, and Adaptation*; MIT Press: Cambridge, MA, USA, 2000.
2. Mitchell, M. *Complexity: A Guided Tour*; Oxford University Press: Oxford, UK, 2009.

3. McCulloch, W.S.; Pitts, W. A logical calculus of the ideas immanent in nervous activity. *Bull. Math. Biophys.* **1943**, *5*, 115–133. [CrossRef]
4. Piccinini, G. Mapping Accounts. In *Physical Computation: A Mechanistic Account*; Piccinini, G., Ed.; Oxford University Press: Oxford, UK, 2015. [CrossRef]
5. Schweizer, P. Computation in Physical Systems: A Normative Mapping Account. In *On the Cognitive, Ethical, and Scientific Dimensions of Artificial Intelligence*; Berkich, D., d'Alfonso, M.V., Eds.; Series Title: Philosophical Studies Series; Springer International Publishing: Cham, Switzerland, 2019; Volume 134, pp. 27–47. [CrossRef]
6. Lizier, J.T. *The Local Information Dynamics of Distributed Computation in Complex Systems*; Springer Theses; Springer: Berlin/Heidelberg, Germany, 2013. [CrossRef]
7. Cover, T.M.; Thomas, J.A. *Elements of Information Theory*; John Wiley & Sons: Hoboken, NJ, USA, 2012.
8. Varley, T.F. Information Theory for Complex Systems Scientists. *arXiv* **2023**, arXiv:2304.12482. [CrossRef]
9. Williams, P.L.; Beer, R.D. Nonnegative Decomposition of Multivariate Information. *arXiv* **2010**, arXiv:1004.2515.
10. Lizier, J.T.; Prokopenko, M.; Zomaya, A.Y. Detecting Non-trivial Computation in Complex Dynamics. In *Proceedings of the Advances in Artificial Life*; Almeida e Costa, F., Rocha, L.M., Costa, E., Harvey, I., Coutinho, A., Eds.; Lecture Notes in Computer Science; Springer: Berlin/Heidelberg, Germany, 2007; pp. 895–904. [CrossRef]
11. Lizier, J.T.; Flecker, B.; Williams, P.L. Towards a Synergy-based Approach to Measuring Information Modification. *arXiv* **2013**, arXiv:1303.3440. [CrossRef]
12. Timme, N.M.; Ito, S.; Myroshnychenko, M.; Nigam, S.; Shimono, M.; Yeh, F.C.; Hottowy, P.; Litke, A.M.; Beggs, J.M. High-Degree Neurons Feed Cortical Computations. *PLoS Comput. Biol.* **2016**, *12*, e1004858. [CrossRef]
13. Faber, S.P.; Timme, N.M.; Beggs, J.M.; Newman, E.L. Computation is concentrated in rich clubs of local cortical networks. *Netw. Neurosci.* **2018**, *3*, 1–21. [CrossRef]
14. Sherrill, S.P.; Timme, N.M.; Beggs, J.M.; Newman, E.L. Correlated activity favors synergistic processing in local cortical networks in vitro at synaptically relevant timescales. *Netw. Neurosci.* **2020**, *4*, 678–697. [CrossRef]
15. Newman, E.L.; Varley, T.F.; Parakkattu, V.K.; Sherrill, S.P.; Beggs, J.M. Revealing the Dynamics of Neural Information Processing with Multivariate Information Decomposition. *Entropy* **2022**, *24*, 930. [CrossRef]
16. Varley, T.F.; Sporns, O.; Schaffelhofer, S.; Scherberger, H.; Dann, B. Information-processing dynamics in neural networks of macaque cerebral cortex reflect cognitive state and behavior. *Proc. Natl. Acad. Sci. USA* **2023**, *120*, e2207677120. [CrossRef]
17. Berkson, J. Limitations of the Application of Fourfold Table Analysis to Hospital Data. *Biom. Bull.* **1946**, *2*, 47–53. [CrossRef]
18. Westreich, D. Berkson's bias, selection bias, and missing data. *Epidemiology* **2012**, *23*, 159–164. [CrossRef] [PubMed]
19. Holmberg, M.J.; Andersen, L.W. Collider Bias. *JAMA* **2022**, *327*, 1282–1283. [CrossRef] [PubMed]
20. Pearl, J.; Glymour, M.; Jewell, N.P. *Causal Inference in Statistics: A Primer*; John Wiley & Sons: Hoboken, NJ, USA, 2016.
21. Matsuda, H. Physical nature of higher-order mutual information: Intrinsic correlations and frustration. *Phys. Rev. E* **2000**, *62*, 3096–3102. [CrossRef] [PubMed]
22. Watanabe, S. Information Theoretical Analysis of Multivariate Correlation. *IBM J. Res. Dev.* **1960**, *4*, 66–82. [CrossRef]
23. Abdallah, S.A.; Plumbley, M.D. A measure of statistical complexity based on predictive information with application to finite spin systems. *Phys. Lett. A* **2012**, *376*, 275–281. [CrossRef]
24. Varley, T.F.; Pope, M.; Faskowitz, J.; Sporns, O. Multivariate information theory uncovers synergistic subsystems of the human cerebral cortex. *Commun. Biol.* **2023**, *6*, 1–12. [CrossRef]
25. McGill, W.J. Multivariate information transmission. *Psychometrika* **1954**, *19*, 97–116. [CrossRef]
26. Bell, A.J. The co-information lattice, Nara, Japan, 2003. In Proceedings of the 4th International Symposium on Independent Component Analysis and Blind Signal Separation (ICA 2003), Nara, Japan, 1–4 April 2003.
27. Gutknecht, A.J.; Wibral, M.; Makkeh, A. Bits and pieces: Understanding information decomposition from part-whole relationships and formal logic. *Proc. R. Soc. A Math. Phys. Eng. Sci.* **2021**, *477*, 20210110. [CrossRef]
28. Kolchinsky, A. A Novel Approach to the Partial Information Decomposition. *Entropy* **2022**, *24*, 403. [CrossRef]
29. Kay, J.W.; Schulz, J.M.; Phillips, W.A. A Comparison of Partial Information Decompositions Using Data from Real and Simulated Layer 5b Pyramidal Cells. *Entropy* **2022**, *24*, 1021. [CrossRef]
30. Bertschinger, N.; Rauh, J.; Olbrich, E.; Jost, J. Shared Information–New Insights and Problems in Decomposing Information in Complex Systems. *arXiv* **2013**, arXiv:1210.5902. [CrossRef]
31. Barrett, A.B. Exploration of synergistic and redundant information sharing in static and dynamical Gaussian systems. *Phys. Rev. E* **2015**, *91*, 052802. [CrossRef] [PubMed]
32. Bertschinger, N.; Rauh, J.; Olbrich, E.; Jost, J.; Ay, N. Quantifying Unique Information. *Entropy* **2014**, *16*, 2161–2183. [CrossRef]
33. Rauh, J.; Bertschinger, N.; Olbrich, E.; Jost, J. Reconsidering unique information: Towards a multivariate information decomposition. In Proceedings of the 2014 IEEE International Symposium on Information Theory, Honolulu, HI, USA, 29 June–4 July 2014; pp. 2232–2236. [CrossRef]
34. Rosas, F.; Ntranos, V.; Ellison, C.J.; Pollin, S.; Verhelst, M. Understanding Interdependency Through Complex Information Sharing. *Entropy* **2016**, *18*, 38. [CrossRef]
35. Harder, M.; Salge, C.; Polani, D. Bivariate measure of redundant information. *Phys. Rev. E Stat. Nonlinear Soft Matter Phys.* **2013**, *87*, 012130. [CrossRef]
36. Schreiber, T. Measuring Information Transfer. *Phys. Rev. Lett.* **2000**, *85*, 461–464. [CrossRef]

37. Bossomaier, T.; Barnett, L.; Harré, M.; Lizier, J.T. *An Introduction to Transfer Entropy: Information Flow in Complex Systems*; Springer: Berlin/Heidelberg, Germany, 2016.
38. Williams, P.L.; Beer, R.D. Generalized Measures of Information Transfer. *arXiv* **2011**, arXiv:1102.1507.
39. James, R.G.; Barnett, N.; Crutchfield, J.P. Information Flows? A Critique of Transfer Entropies. *Phys. Rev. Lett.* **2016**, *116*, 238701. [CrossRef]
40. Daube, C.; Gross, J.; Ince, R.A.A. A whitening approach for Transfer Entropy permits the application to narrow-band signals. *arXiv* **2022**, arXiv:2201.02461.
41. Scanagatta, M.; Salmerón, A.; Stella, F. A survey on Bayesian network structure learning from data. *Prog. Artif. Intell.* **2019**, *8*, 425–439. [CrossRef]
42. Kitson, N.K.; Constantinou, A.C.; Guo, Z.; Liu, Y.; Chobtham, K. A survey of Bayesian Network structure learning. *Artif. Intell. Rev.* **2023**, *56*, 8721–8814. [CrossRef]
43. Varley, T.F.; Kaminski, P. Untangling Synergistic Effects of Intersecting Social Identities with Partial Information Decomposition. *Entropy* **2022**, *24*, 1387. [CrossRef] [PubMed]
44. Novelli, L.; Lizier, J.T. Inferring network properties from time series using transfer entropy and mutual information: Validation of multivariate versus bivariate approaches. *Netw. Neurosci.* **2021**, *5*, 373–404. [CrossRef] [PubMed]
45. Wollstadt, P.; Lizier, J.T.; Vicente, R.; Finn, C.; Martinez-Zarzuela, M.; Mediano, P.; Novelli, L.; Wibral, M. IDTxl: The Information Dynamics Toolkit xl: A Python package for the efficient analysis of multivariate information dynamics in networks. *J. Open Source Softw.* **2019**, *4*, 1081. [CrossRef]
46. Varley, T.F.; Pope, M.; Puxeddu, M.G.; Faskowitz, J.; Sporns, O. Partial entropy decomposition reveals higher-order structures in human brain activity. *arXiv* **2023**, arXiv:2301.05307. [CrossRef]
47. Marinazzo, D.; Van Roozendaal, J.; Rosas, F.E.; Stella, M.; Comolatti, R.; Colenbier, N.; Stramaglia, S.; Rosseel, Y. An information-theoretic approach to build hypergraphs in psychometrics. *Behav. Res. Methods* **2024**, *56*, 8057–8079. [CrossRef]
48. Faes, L.; Mijatovic, G.; Antonacci, Y.; Pernice, R.; Barà, C.; Sparacino, L.; Sammartino, M.; Porta, A.; Marinazzo, D.; Stramaglia, S. A New Framework for the Time- and Frequency-Domain Assessment of High-Order Interactions in Networks of Random Processes. *IEEE Trans. Signal Process.* **2022**, *70*, 5766–5777. [CrossRef]
49. Lizier, J.T.; Prokopenko, M. Differentiating information transfer and causal effect. *Eur. Phys. J. B* **2010**, *73*, 605–615. [CrossRef]
50. Eldhose, E.; Chauhan, T.; Chandel, V.; Ghosh, S.; Ganguly, A.R. Robust Causality and False Attribution in Data-Driven Earth Science Discoveries. *arXiv* **2022**, arXiv:2209.12580. [CrossRef]
51. Ay, N.; Polani, D. Information flows in causal networks. *Adv. Complex Syst.* **2008**, *11*, 17–41. [CrossRef]
52. Hoel, E.P.; Albantakis, L.; Tononi, G. Quantifying causal emergence shows that macro can beat micro. *Proc. Natl. Acad. Sci. USA* **2013**, *110*, 19790–19795. [CrossRef] [PubMed]
53. Goodwell, A.E.; Jiang, P.; Ruddell, B.L.; Kumar, P. Debates—Does Information Theory Provide a New Paradigm for Earth Science? Causality, Interaction, and Feedback. *Water Resour. Res.* **2020**, *56*, e2019WR024940. [CrossRef]
54. Tononi, G.; Sporns, O. Measuring information integration. *BMC Neurosci.* **2003**, *4*, 31. [CrossRef] [PubMed]
55. Zenil, H.; Kiani, N.A.; Tegnér, J. Low-algorithmic-complexity entropy-deceiving graphs. *Phys. Rev. E* **2017**, *96*, 012308. [CrossRef]
56. Zenil, H.; Kiani, N.A.; Tegnér, J. *Algorithmic Information Dynamics: A Computational Approach to Causality with Applications to Living Systems*; Cambridge University Press: Cambridge, UK, 2023. [CrossRef]
57. Antonacci, Y.; Minati, L.; Nuzzi, D.; Mijatovic, G.; Pernice, R.; Marinazzo, D.; Stramaglia, S.; Faes, L. Measuring High-Order Interactions in Rhythmic Processes Through Multivariate Spectral Information Decomposition. *IEEE Access* **2021**, *9*, 149486–149505. [CrossRef]
58. Luppi, A.I.; Mediano, P.A.M.; Rosas, F.E.; Allanson, J.; Pickard, J.D.; Carhart-Harris, R.L.; Williams, G.B.; Craig, M.M.; Finoia, P.; Owen, A.M.; et al. A Synergistic Workspace for Human Consciousness Revealed by Integrated Information Decomposition. *eLife* **2023**, *12*, RP88173. [CrossRef]
59. Ehrlich, D.A.; Schneider, A.C.; Priesemann, V.; Wibral, M.; Makkeh, A. A Measure of the Complexity of Neural Representations based on Partial Information Decomposition. *arXiv* **2023**, arXiv:2209.10438.
60. Proca, A.M.; Rosas, F.E.; Luppi, A.I.; Bor, D.; Crosby, M.; Mediano, P.A.M. Synergistic information supports modality integration and flexible learning in neural networks solving multiple tasks. *arXiv* **2022**, arXiv:2210.02996. [CrossRef]
61. Rajpal, H.; Guerrero, O.A. Quantifying the Technological Foundations of Economic Complexity. *arXiv* **2023**, arXiv:2301.04579. [CrossRef]
62. Luppi, A.I.; Mediano, P.A.M.; Rosas, F.E.; Allanson, J.; Pickard, J.D.; Williams, G.B.; Craig, M.M.; Finoia, P.; Peattie, A.R.D.; Coppola, P.; et al. Reduced emergent character of neural dynamics in patients with a disrupted connectome. *NeuroImage* **2023**, *269*, 119926. [CrossRef]
63. Goodwell, A.E.; Kumar, P. Temporal information partitioning: Characterizing synergy, uniqueness, and redundancy in interacting environmental variables. *Water Resour. Res.* **2017**, *53*, 5920–5942. [CrossRef]
64. Goodwell, A.E.; Kumar, P. Temporal Information Partitioning Networks (TIPNets): A process network approach to infer ecohydrologic shifts. *Water Resour. Res.* **2017**, *53*, 5899–5919. [CrossRef]
65. Krakauer, D.; Bertschinger, N.; Olbrich, E.; Flack, J.C.; Ay, N. The information theory of individuality. *Theory Biosci.* **2020**, *139*, 209–223. [CrossRef]

66. Mediano, P.A.M.; Rosas, F.E.; Luppi, A.I.; Carhart-Harris, R.L.; Bor, D.; Seth, A.K.; Barrett, A.B. Towards an extended taxonomy of information dynamics via Integrated Information Decomposition. *arXiv* **2021**, arXiv:2109.13186.
67. Varley, T.F. Decomposing past and future: Integrated information decomposition based on shared probability mass exclusions. *PLoS ONE* **2023**, *18*, e0282950. [CrossRef]
68. Ince, R.A.A. The Partial Entropy Decomposition: Decomposing multivariate entropy and mutual information via pointwise common surprisal. *arXiv* **2017**, arXiv:1702.01591.
69. Finn, C.; Lizier, J.T. Generalised Measures of Multivariate Information Content. *Entropy* **2020**, *22*, 216. [CrossRef]
70. Varley, T.F. Generalized decomposition of multivariate information. *PLoS ONE* **2024**, *19*, e0297128. [CrossRef]
71. Rosas, F.; Mediano, P.A.M.; Gastpar, M.; Jensen, H.J. Quantifying High-order Interdependencies via Multivariate Extensions of the Mutual Information. *Phys. Rev. E* **2019**, *100*, 032305. [CrossRef]
72. Varley, T.F. A scalable synergy-first backbone decomposition of higher-order structures in complex systems. *Npj Complex.* **2024**, *1*, 1–11. [CrossRef]

entropy

MDPI

Article

Causality Analysis with Information Geometry: A Comparison

Heng Jie Choong [1,*], Eun-jin Kim [1] and Fei He [2]

1 Centre for Fluid and Complex Systems, Coventry University, Coventry CV1 5FB, UK; ejk92122@gmail.com
2 Centre for Computational Science and Mathematical Modelling, Coventry University, Coventry CV1 5FB, UK; fei.he@coventry.ac.uk
* Correspondence: choongh2@uni.coventry.ac.uk

Abstract: The quantification of causality is vital for understanding various important phenomena in nature and laboratories, such as brain networks, environmental dynamics, and pathologies. The two most widely used methods for measuring causality are Granger Causality (GC) and Transfer Entropy (TE), which rely on measuring the improvement in the prediction of one process based on the knowledge of another process at an earlier time. However, they have their own limitations, e.g., in applications to nonlinear, non-stationary data, or non-parametric models. In this study, we propose an alternative approach to quantify causality through information geometry that overcomes such limitations. Specifically, based on the information rate that measures the rate of change of the time-dependent distribution, we develop a model-free approach called information rate causality that captures the occurrence of the causality based on the change in the distribution of one process caused by another. This measurement is suitable for analyzing numerically generated non-stationary, nonlinear data. The latter are generated by simulating different types of discrete autoregressive models which contain linear and nonlinear interactions in unidirectional and bidirectional time-series signals. Our results show that information rate causalitycan capture the coupling of both linear and nonlinear data better than GC and TE in the several examples explored in the paper.

Keywords: causality; information geometry; Transfer Entropy; Granger Causality; information causal rate; signal processing; nonlinear models; non-stationary; probability distribution

1. Introduction

The study of causality aims to explore cause-and-effect relationships between processes. In general, causality can be investigated in two categories: causal discovery and causal analysis. Causal discovery shows the inherent causal relationship within the dataset by analyzing and creating causal models based on graph theory. The construction of these models can be achieved via algorithmic dynamics and evaluating the algorithms against the observed data [1–3]. Generally, the complexity of the models' networks is characterized and measured using graph-theoretic measures. A recent approach using classical information theory, such as Shannon entropy, has been considered as an alternative measurement, but its high dependence on the distribution can lead to spurious disparate values for the same complexity, as shown in [4].

Alternatively, causal analysis, which is the focus of this paper, studies the potential changes in a system caused by another. In practical terms, causal discovery requires more detailed background information about the provided dataset to accurately conduct the study. However, the causal analysis does not require detailed underlying knowledge of the connectivity embedded within the dataset [3,5]. Among the various analysis methods used to quantify causality, Granger causality (GC) and Transfer Entropy (TE) are extensively used in various fields, including economics, climate, education, meteorology, neuroscience, and more [5–16]. For instance, Rebecca M. Pullon et al. utilized GC to demonstrate the decrease in cortical information flow throughout the brain as the subject loses responsiveness [10]; Yunyuan Gao et al. used TE to investigate the coupling strength of the brain between the motor and sensory areas [15]. Both of these methods are derived from the same notion of examining the reliability of a present process towards the past process(es). Despite sharing the same notion, their approaches to quantifying causality are completely different. GC evaluates the dependency based on signal models, which means modelling the signals incorrectly can lead to the wrong conclusion about the causality [11,17,18]. On the other hand, TE is model-free and employs the statistical dependency approach to access causality. However, it is subject to the estimation of the probability distribution, such as the number of bin size and the high dimensionality in the distribution due to the number of lags [19,20].

More specifically, inspired by Norbert Wiener, Clive Granger introduced GC [6,21], which suggested that the causality of two stochastic processes ($x_1(t)$ and $x_2(t)$) exists if and only if one of the processes is able to predict another. For instance, if including the past observation of $x_1(t)$ along with $x_2(t)$ improves the prediction of the current state of $x_2(t)$ compared to using only past information of $x_2(t)$, then this would suggest that $x_1(t)$ is Granger-causing $x_2(t)$. This predictivity is quantitatively studied by comparing the errors of the autoregressive model (linear regressive model) that is used in modelling the signals [6,18]. As natural time series such as electroencephalogram (EEG) often exhibit oscillatory aspects, it is interesting to study the spectrum of the GC. John Geweke has discussed the evaluation of GC in the frequency domain instead of the time domain [17,22,23]. Additionally, the time-varying frequency domain of the GC that is studied in [18,24,25] is able to show both the spectrum of the GC and the period of causation occurrence. The frequency domain of GC is the spectral of GC which shows the amplitude of GC correlated to a specific frequency of the entire signals, while the time-varying frequency of GC shows when the coupling of the signals occurs alongside the spectral of GC.

When utilizing the GC, it is necessary to model the provided signals using a linear autoregressive model [17,18]. However, this linear model cannot accommodate possible nonlinear and non-stationary effects within real-world signals, such as the brain EEG signals [26,27]. Therefore, instead of studying the causality through deterministic or parametric linear models, causality can be statistically quantified using information-theoretic measures like TE [19]. In the event of two stochastic processes, TE measures the additional information required from one process to achieve the current realization of another process [28]. Therefore, TE is not limited to any specific model or linearity assumption. Although TE uses a different approach in evaluating the causality, it can yield similar results to GC for a Gaussian process, as discussed analytically by Lionel Barnett et al. [29].

Alternatively, the causality can be investigated by examining the changes in the probability distribution that are caused by the inclusion of the other variables [30]. In a statistical space, the change in distribution is known as distance and can be quantified via Kullback–Leibler (KL) divergence. However, KL divergence cannot be well-defined as a distance, as it is not symmetrical and not path-dependent. Hence, information rate and information length are used with the intention to have the symmetrical and path-dependent measurement of the distance [30–33]. Information rate quantifies the rate of the temporal change in distributions, while information length measures the total statistical change in the process along the time [30,32]. Refs. [30,31] proposed an information-geometric causality measure, the so-called *information rate causality* based on the information rate, by quantifying causality through the effects of the information rate (see also [34]) and applied it to a solvable, linear Gaussian process (Kramer model) which has an exact time-dependent distribution.

In this paper, we will further develop this information rate causality for analyzing the numerically generated time-series signals that are in general time-varying and nonlinear and compare it with the GC and TE. Specifically, we will generate the signals by simulating the (discrete) autoregressive equations which contain unidirectional or bidirectional interactions. For the GC, both the frequency domain and time varying of GC will be presented. For the TE, the signals are evaluated as a whole at different lags. Next, the net TE is calculated by taking the difference in the TE from both directions. For instance, $T^{net}_{1,2} = T_{1\to2} - T_{2\to1}$

represents the net TE of signals 1 and 2. The net TE enables us to identify the appropriate lag(s) that yield significant results in TE. Using the knowledge of the appropriate lag(s) from the net TE, the TE is calculated through the window sliding approach, with each small window of the signals evaluating TE at the designated lag. Similarly, information rate causality will be evaluated through the window sliding approach with the information rate calculated within each window. In the scenario where the signals are coupled, it is expected that there will be spikes in the information rate causality, indicating changes in the distribution of one signal caused by another. Note that the methodology and concepts of the analyses used in this paper are mainly from the previous works [17–19,28,30,32].

The remainder of this paper is organized as follows. In Section 2, we briefly review the concepts for GC, TE, and information rate causality along with their implementation. The three different types of autoregressive models—unidirectional, interchange unidirectional, and bidirectional models—are introduced and analyzed in Sections 3 to 5, respectively. Section 6 contains our conclusions. Appendices A–C contain some background theory to make the paper self-contained. As a reference, the basic model of continuous coupling is studied and analyzed in Appendix D.

2. Methodologies

2.1. Granger Causality

The general idea behind GC is to evaluate the dependency of one process on another process [17,18]. This dependency is calculated by comparing the errors/noises of the modelled signals through the autoregressive model. Consider two stochastic processes, namely $x_1(t)$ and $x_2(t)$, which can be modelled using the information from their respective signals (as shown in Equations (1) and (2)) or including some information from each other (as shown in Equations (3) and (4)).

$$x_1(t) = \sum_{i=1}^{n} a_i x_1(t-i) + \epsilon_1(t), \tag{1}$$

$$x_2(t) = \sum_{i=1}^{n} c_i x_2(t-i) + \epsilon_2(t), \tag{2}$$

$$x_1(t) = \sum_{i=1}^{n} a_i^* x_1(t-i) + \sum_{i=1}^{n} b_i^* x_2(t-i) + \epsilon_1^*(t), \tag{3}$$

$$x_2(t) = \sum_{i=1}^{n} c_i^* x_1(t-i) + \sum_{i=1}^{n} d_i^* x_2(t-i) + \epsilon_2^*(t). \tag{4}$$

Here, $\{a_i, c_i, a_i^*, b_i^*, c_i^*, d_i^*\} \in \mathbb{R}$ are the constant parameters that represent the fractions of contribution from the past observations towards $x_1(t)$ and $x_2(t)$. $\epsilon_{i\in[1,2]}$ is the uncorrelated external additive noise needed for modelling the processes with variance $\Sigma_{ii,i\in[1,2]}$. $\epsilon^*_{i\in[1,2]}$ is the correlated noise with the variance $\Sigma^*_{ij,(i,j)\in[1,2]}$, which can be represented by the covariance matrix $\mathbf{\Sigma} = \begin{bmatrix} \Sigma_{11}^* & \Sigma_{12}^* \\ \Sigma_{21}^* & \Sigma_{22}^* \end{bmatrix}$.

The total interdependence or total causality index ($F_{x_1 \cdot x_2}$) between $x_1(t)$ and $x_2(t)$ is composed of two directional causalities ($F_{x_1\to x_2}$ and $F_{x_2\to x_1}$) and one instantaneous causality ($F_{x_1\leftrightarrow x_2}$). These are defined in Equations (5) to (8).

$$F_{x_1 \cdot x_2} = \log \frac{\Sigma_{11}\Sigma_{22}}{|\mathbf{\Sigma}|} = \log \frac{\Sigma_{11}\Sigma_{22}}{\Sigma_{11}^*\Sigma_{22}^* - (\Sigma_{12}^*)^2} = F_{x_1\to x_2} + F_{x_2\to x_1} + F_{x_1\leftrightarrow x_2}, \tag{5}$$

$$F_{x_1\to x_2} = \log \frac{\Sigma_{11}}{\Sigma_{11}^*}, \tag{6}$$

$$F_{x_2 \to x_1} = \log \frac{\Sigma_{22}}{\Sigma_{22}^*}, \tag{7}$$

$$F_{x_1 \leftrightarrow x_2} = \log \frac{\Sigma_{11}^* \Sigma_{22}^*}{|\boldsymbol{\Sigma}|}. \tag{8}$$

In conjunction, the spectral of the GC can be evaluated in the frequency domain ($\omega = 2\pi f$, $f \equiv$ frequency) using the spectral matrix $\boldsymbol{S}(\omega)$, transfer matrix $\boldsymbol{H}(\omega)$, and the covariance matrix $\boldsymbol{\Sigma}$. They are related according to Equation (9).

$$\boldsymbol{S}(\omega) = \begin{bmatrix} S_{11}(\omega) & S_{12}(\omega) \\ S_{21}(\omega) & S_{22}(\omega) \end{bmatrix} = \left\langle \boldsymbol{x}(\omega)\boldsymbol{x}^{\dagger}(\omega) \right\rangle = \boldsymbol{H}(\omega)\boldsymbol{\Sigma}\boldsymbol{H}^{\dagger}(\omega). \tag{9}$$

Here, $\boldsymbol{x}(\omega) = \begin{bmatrix} x_1(\omega) \\ x_2(\omega) \end{bmatrix}$, $\boldsymbol{H}(\omega) = \begin{bmatrix} H_{11}(\omega) & H_{12}(\omega) \\ H_{21}(\omega) & H_{22}(\omega) \end{bmatrix} = \begin{bmatrix} 1 - \sum_{i=1}^{n} a_i^* e^{-j\omega i} & -\sum_{i=1}^{n} b_i^* e^{-j\omega i} \\ -\sum_{i=1}^{n} c_i^* e^{-j\omega i} & 1 - \sum_{i=1}^{n} d_i^* e^{-j\omega i} \end{bmatrix}$; $\langle \cdot \rangle$ is defined as an ensemble average and $\dagger$ is denoted as the complex conjugate transpose of a matrix.

Similar to the analysis in the time domain, the total independence in the frequency domain between $x_1(\omega)$ and $x_2(\omega)$ ($I_{x_1 \cdot x_2}$) also consists of two directional causalities ($I_{x_1 \to x_2}$ and $I_{x_2 \to x_1}$) and one instantaneous causality ($I_{x_1 \leftrightarrow x_2}$). They are expressed as Equations (10) to (13).

$$I_{x_1 \cdot x_2} = \log \frac{S_{11}(\omega) S_{22}(\omega)}{|\boldsymbol{S}(\omega)|} = I_{x_1 \to x_2} + I_{x_2 \to x_1} + I_{x_1 \leftrightarrow x_2}. \tag{10}$$

$$I_{x_1 \to x_2} = \log \frac{S_{22}(\omega)}{\hat{H}_{22}(\omega)\Sigma_{22}\overline{\hat{H}_{22}(\omega)}}, \tag{11}$$

$$I_{x_2 \to x_1} = \log \frac{S_{11}(\omega)}{\tilde{H}_{11}(\omega)\Sigma_{11}\overline{\tilde{H}_{11}(\omega)}}, \tag{12}$$

$$I_{x_1 \leftrightarrow x_2} = \log \frac{\left(\tilde{H}_{11}(\omega)\Sigma_{11}\overline{\tilde{H}_{11}(\omega)}\right)\left(\hat{H}_{22}(\omega)\Sigma_{22}\overline{\hat{H}_{22}(\omega)}\right)}{|\boldsymbol{S}(\omega)|}. \tag{13}$$

Here, $\hat{H}_{22}(\omega) = H_{22}(\omega) + \frac{\Sigma_{12}^*}{\Sigma_{22}^*} H_{21}(\omega)$ and $\tilde{H}_{11}(\omega) = H_{11}(\omega) + \frac{\Sigma_{12}^*}{\Sigma_{11}^*} H_{12}(\omega)$; $\overline{[\cdot]}$ is denoted as the complex conjugate of the element.

In this paper, the frequency domain and the time-varying frequency domain of GC will be calculated through the non-parametric method. The general idea of this method is to decompose the spectral matrix $\boldsymbol{S}(\omega)$ into the transfer matrix $\boldsymbol{H}(\omega)$ and the covariance of the noises $\boldsymbol{\Sigma}$. This decomposition can be achieved using Wilson's algorithm [18,24,25,35,36]. The spectral matrices for the frequency domain and the time-varying frequency domain are expressed as Equations (14) and (15), respectively.

$$\boldsymbol{S}(\omega) = \frac{\left\langle x_i(\omega)\overline{x_j(\omega)} \right\rangle}{T}, \; i, j \in \mathbb{R}, \tag{14}$$

$$\boldsymbol{S}(t, \omega) = \frac{\left\langle s_i(t,\omega)\overline{s_j(t,\omega)} \right\rangle}{T}, \; i, j \in \mathbb{R}. \tag{15}$$

Here, T denotes the total period of the signal. $x(\omega)_{n|n \in [i,j]}$ is the discrete Fourier transform of the signal and $s_{n|n \in [i,j]}(t, \omega)$ is the short-time Fourier transform of the signal $x(t)_{n|n \in [i,j]}$. Note that $\overline{[\cdot]}$ denotes the complex conjugate. The Hann function window is used when evaluating the short-time Fourier transform. The window will move through the whole series with half of the data points being overlapped. The general flow of the procedure is shown in Figure 1a.

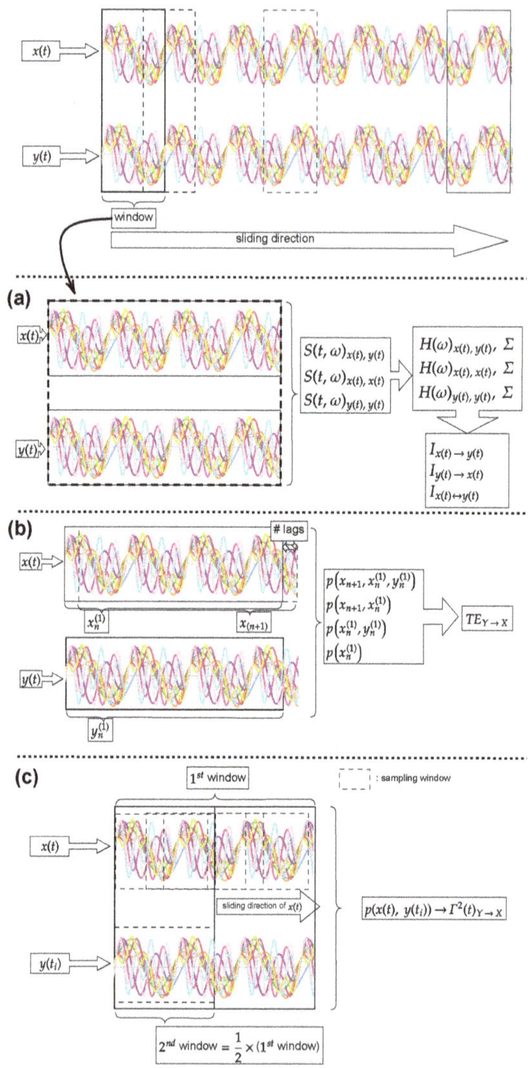

Figure 1. The procedure of implementing the causality analyses used in this paper , each colour of the lines in the image represents a different simulation. In this study, each window contains 0.5 s of data points and overlaps with the previous window by 0.25 s. The causality analyses are conducted within each window. (**a**) illustrates the components ($S(\ldots)$, $H(\ldots)$) calculated within the windows for the non-parametric GC analysis. Refer to Section 2.1 to know the corresponding components. (**b**) shows the estimation of distributions $p(\ldots)$ for TE evaluation. The distributions $p(\ldots)$ are estimated based on the samples $x_n^{(1)}$, x_{n+1}, and $y_n^{(1)}$. Refer to Section 2.2 for the definition of TE. (**c**) demonstrates the evaluation of information rate causality. Each window (labelled as 1st window) is divided into two windows with the first half labelled as 2nd window. The distribution $p(x(t), y(t_i))$ estimates the evolution of distribution $x(t)$ while $y(t_i)$ is fixed at the 2nd window. Refer to Section 2.3 for the definition of information rate causality.

2.2. Transfer Entropy

TE is a model-free approach used to calculate causality by evaluating the dependency between processes. The general expression of TE is given by Equation (17), which measures the additional information required for the realization of one state of the process ($x_1(t)$) depending on the past states of the processes (e.g., $x_1(t-1)$ and $x_2(t-1)$) [19,28,37].

$$TE_{x_2(t)\to x_1(t)} = \sum_{x\in x_1(t), y\in x_2(t)} p(x_{n+1}, x_n^{(k)}, y_n^{(l)}) \log_2 \frac{p(x_{n+1}|x_n^{(k)}, y_n^{(l)})}{p(x_{n+1}|x_n^{(k)})} \tag{16}$$

$$= \sum_{x\in x_1(t), y\in x_2(t)} p(x_{n+1}, x_n^{(k)}, y_n^{(l)}) \log_2 \frac{p(x_{n+1}, x_n^{(k)}, y_n^{(l)})p(x_n^{(k)})}{p(x_{n+1}, x_n^{(k)})p(x_n^{(k)}, y_n^{(l)})}. \tag{17}$$

Here, x_{n+1} represents the state of $x_1(t)$ at the $(n+1)$-th moment, $x_n^{(k)}$ represents the state at n-th moment of $x_1(t)$ consisting of k previous states of $x_1(t)$, $y_n^{(l)}$ represents the state at n-th moment of $x_2(t)$ consisting of l previous states. Note that the previous states of k and l are arbitrary depending on the interest of the study. For instance, in a collective observed stochastic process $X = (x_1, x_2, \ldots, x_{10})$, $x_8^{(2)} = (x_n, x_m)\ |n, m \in [1,8] \to (x_1, x_2)$ or (x_3, x_8), etc. Thus, TE quantifies the additional information needed for the realization of $x_1(t)$ at $(n+1)$ from $x_2(t)$ with the assumption that $x_1(t)$ is independent of $x_2(t)$. If $x_2(t)$ has no impact on the future evolution of $x_1(t)$, and hence $p(x_{n+1}|x_n^{(k)}, y_n^{(l)}) = p(x_{n+1}|x_n^{(k)})$, then $T_{Y\to X} = 0$.

For the TE calculation, the probability distribution $p(\ldots)$ will be estimated via histogram with the bin size of 5, as this bin size is determined by the cubic root of Rice's rule to accommodate the 3-dimensional of joint probability within TE ($p(x_{n+1}, x_n^{(1)}, y_n^{(1)})$). Using a larger number of bin sizes will not be able to properly depict the distribution and it will bring a spurious result in calculating the TE. To simplify the analysis, the number of past values of k and l is set to 1 ($k = l = 1$) in this paper. Two different evaluations will be conducted for TE. First, assuming that the processes are stationary, the net TE ($TE_{x_1(t),x_2(t)} = TE_{x_1(t)\to x_2(t)} - TE_{x_2(t)\to x_1(t)}$) is evaluated on the entire processes at different lags. This will enable us to choose the appropriate past value(s)/lag(s) in evaluating the TE based on the significance of the net TE. Second, using the knowledge of the appropriate lag from the net TE, the TE is next evaluated via a sliding window approach. This sliding window approach is used to calculate the TE at each instance of the interested window. In this sliding window approach, a small number of data points of the stochastic processes is sampled within the window and the TE is calculated. These calculations are sketched in Figure 1b.

2.3. Information Rate Causality

In a dimensionless statistical manifold, the distance between two probability distributions is defined by their statistical difference. One commonly used measure of this difference is the KL divergence/relative entropy, but this measure is not symmetrical and not path-dependent. For the time-dependent probability distribution, the changes in the distribution along with time can be measured through the information rate and information length. The information rate ($\Gamma(t)$) quantifies the rate of change of the distribution, while information length ($\mathcal{L}$) measures the total change of the distribution. These measures are defined and expressed as Equations (18) and (19) [30–32].

$$\Gamma^2(t) = \int dx\, p(x,t)[\partial_t \ln p(x,t)]^2 = 4\int dx \left[\partial_t \sqrt{p(x,t)}\right]^2, \tag{18}$$

$$\mathcal{L} = \int dt\, \Gamma(t). \tag{19}$$

Here $p(x,t)$ is the probability distribution of a stochastic process x at the time t.

For studying causality, we consider two stochastic processes ($x_1(t)$ and $x_2(t)$) and the information rate for a joint probability distribution is evaluated. The causality between these processes can be quantified by the changes in the information rate (statistical changes or the changes in distribution) while having another process remain static. For instance, the information rate of $x_2(t)$ causing $x_1(t)$ is defined as Equation (21) and called information rate causality in this paper.

$$\Gamma^2(t)_{x_2(t)\to x_1(t)} = \int dx_1\, dx_2\, p(x_1(t), x_2(t_i))[\partial_t \ln p(x_1(t), x_2(t_i))]^2 \tag{20}$$

$$= 4\int dx_1\, dx_2 \left[\partial_t \sqrt{p(x_1(t), x_2(t_i))}\right]^2. \tag{21}$$

Referring to Figure 1c, here t_i is denoted as the reference time that remains static in the process. Therefore, $p(x_1(t), x_2(t_i))$ is a probability distribution that is sampled by having the process $x_2(t)$ remain static at time t_i while the process $x_1(t)$ evolves along the time t. Since information rate can only quantify the changes in the distribution, therefore the *information rate causality* is evaluated within each window of interest instead of the whole process of the time series to determine whether the coupling of the processes is still persists. To accommodate the calculation, a discretized version of Equation (21) is used and it is expressed as Equation (22).

$$\Gamma^2(t)_{x_2\to x_1} = 4 \sum_{x_1\in X_1, x_2\in X_2} \frac{\Delta x_1 \Delta x_2}{[\Delta t]^2}\left[\sqrt{p(x_1(t+\Delta t), x_2(t_i))} - \sqrt{p(x_1(t), x_2(t_i))}\right]^2 \tag{22}$$

For calculating the information rate, the joint probability distribution for two processes is estimated via the histogram with the bin size (b) determined by the square root of Rice's rule, as expressed in Equation (23). Rice's rule is used because it is able to appropriately determines the bin size to sample the obtained data [38,39] for 1-dimensional distribution. Hence, the square root of Rice's rule is to accommodate the 2-dimensional distribution in this case.

$$b = \sqrt{\lceil 2\sqrt[3]{n} \rceil},\ n = \text{number of sampled data}. \tag{23}$$

In this paper, we evaluate the information rate causality by employing Equation (22) to examine the impact of one process, which remains static in time, on the distribution of another process within a specific time window. To estimate the joint probability distribution utilized in Equation (22), a histogram is employed with a bin size determined by Equation (23). Figure 1c illustrates the overall procedure of this evaluation.

2.4. Summary of the Procedure: Data And Analysis

We further develop *information rate causality* (refer to Section 2.3) for the analysis of our numerically generated data and compare it with the non-parametric GC (refer to Section 2.1) and window sliding TE (refer to Section 2.2). Our numerical data are generated by simulating different discrete autoregressive models covering both linear and nonlinear models. The simulation is conducted for 10,000 trials with each trial running for 25 s (physical time) at 200 Hz (physical sampling frequency). Different coupling/causal relationships between the signals are considered in this paper, such as unidirectional (refer to Section 3), interchanging unidirectional (refer to Section 4), and bidirectional (refer to Section 5). Note that the noncoupling cases are also considered in this paper to check the robustness of the causality analyses; specifically, we refer to the uncoupling of $x_1(t)$ towards $x_2(t)$ after the physical time 10 s. Using simulated signals, the causality analyses (GC, TE, *information rate causaltiy*) are conducted according to the sketch shown in Figure 1.

To be consistent with the data points used for each window, each sampling window will contain 0.5 s of data points with an overlap of 0.25 s (0.5 × 0.5 s), which is equivalent to 100 data points for one simulation. Since the models are simulated for 10,000 trials, each window will consist of 1×10^6 sample points (100 points $\times$ 10,000 trials). Note that this window is not applied to the frequency domain of GC and the net TE as both are calculated based on the whole series.

2.5. Summary of the Different Models and Key Results

Prior to the discussion of different models in Sections 3 to 5 with the implementation of different analysis methods, we provide the key results/findings in Table 1.

Table 1. Summary of the performance of GC, TE, and information rate causality for different models discussed in Sections 3 to 5. In general, GC performs well for linear and stationary signals; TE performs well only if the lags are chosen correctly; information rate causality performs well and can recover the underlying lags of the signals.

Method	Unidirectional (Section 3)		Interchange (Section 4)		Bidirectional (Section 5)	
	Linear	Nonlinear	Linear	Nonlinear	Linear	Nonlinear
GC	performs well	fails in nonstationary signals	performs well		fails to capture the bidirectional coupling of signals	
TE	performs well if correct lags are chosen or else produces spurious results					
Information rate causality	performs well and able to recover the underlying lags of coupling					

3. Unidirectional Model

In this part, unidirectional causality, where the first process ($x_1(t)$) influencing the second process ($x_2(t)$), is considered for both linear and nonlinear autoregressive models given by Equations (24) and (25), respectively. The causality between the processes occurs as the processes are coupled with each other through the Heaviside step function ($H(\ldots)$).
Linear model:

$$\begin{aligned} x_1(t) &= 0.55x_1(t-1) + \epsilon_1(t), \\ x_2(t) &= H(\tau - 10)x_1(t-2) + \epsilon_2(t). \end{aligned} \tag{24}$$

Nonlinear model:

$$\begin{aligned} x_1(t) &= 0.55x_1(t-1)e^{1-|x_1(t-1)|} + \epsilon_1(t), \\ x_2(t) &= H(\tau - 10)x_1(t-2) + \epsilon_2(t). \end{aligned} \tag{25}$$

Here, t is the time steps and τ is the physical time. Both t and τ are related as $\tau = [\text{physical frequency}] \times t$. $H(\tau - 10)$ is a Heaviside step function that allows the coupling to occur starting at the physical time of 10 s. $\epsilon_{n|n\in[1,2]}$ is the Gaussian noise that perturbates the systems. In this study, the noises are set to have zero mean ($\langle\epsilon_n\rangle = 0|n \in [1,2]$) along with specific covariance/variance ($\Sigma_{nm} = \langle(\epsilon_n - \langle\epsilon_n\rangle)(\epsilon_m - \langle\epsilon_m\rangle)\rangle|n,m \in [1,2]$), which will be expressed in covariance matrix ($\begin{bmatrix}\Sigma_{11} & \Sigma_{12} \\ \Sigma_{21} & \Sigma_{22}\end{bmatrix}$). Due to the exponential term in the nonlinear model, the process will have non-stationary oscillation when the power of the exponential term becomes positive ($e^{\mathbb{R}} \to$ diverge). Hence, two different values of noise covariance will be considered to study the stationary and non-stationary oscillation of the processes. They are labelled as large noise and small noise with the respective matrices expressed as $\begin{bmatrix}\Sigma_{11} & \Sigma_{12} \\ \Sigma_{21} & \Sigma_{22}\end{bmatrix} = \begin{bmatrix}1.0 & 0.0 \\ 0.0 & 1.0\end{bmatrix}$ and $\begin{bmatrix}\Sigma_{11} & \Sigma_{12} \\ \Sigma_{21} & \Sigma_{22}\end{bmatrix} = \begin{bmatrix}0.005 & 0.0 \\ 0.0 & 0.005\end{bmatrix}$. Note that the cross-covariance of the noises is set to zero ($\Sigma_{12} = \Sigma_{21} = 0.0$) to ensure the coupling is purely due to the intrinsic interaction in the model but not through the mutual noises. The linear model will have stationary oscillation for either large or small noises, and hence only one noise will be used to simulate the linear model and large noise is chosen. The general structure of the models is shown in Figure 2.

To explore all possible combinations of cases, we investigate the coupling and noncoupling cases for both linear and nonlinear models. To this end, we investigate the following six difference cases: [linear: couple], [linear: noncouple], [nonlinear: large noise, coupling], [nonlinear: large noise, noncoupling], [nonlinear: small noise, coupling], and [nonlinear: small noise, noncoupling].

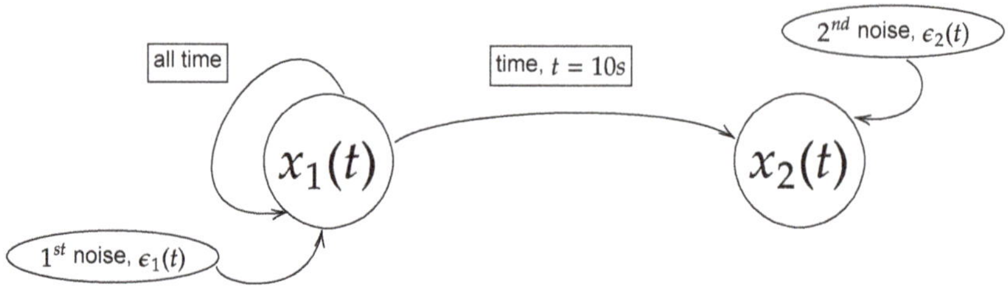

Figure 2. Model of the flow of information of the processes $x_1(t)$ and $x_2(t)$ for Equations (24) and (25). In this paper, the equations are simulated with the physical time of 25 s and sampling frequency of 200 Hz (5000 realizations) with either large noise or small noise. The coupling between the processes occurs at physical time of 10 s.

The result of the simulation for the Equations (24) and (25) is shown in Figure 3. Notice that the signals for the nonlinear model exhibit non-stationary oscillation when the perturbating noise is small, as shown in Figure 3e,f. This is due to the divergence of the positive power of the exponential term of Equation (25) ($e^{1-|x_1(t-1)|} = e^{\mathbb{R}} \rightarrow$ diverge $|\epsilon_1(t) \equiv$ small noise) and the influences of the previous state towards the current state ($x_1(t) \leftarrow 0.55x_1(t-1)$). The rest of the simulated signals have stationary oscillation, as shown in the phase space where the observed states are localized around $(x_1, x_2) = (0, 0)$.

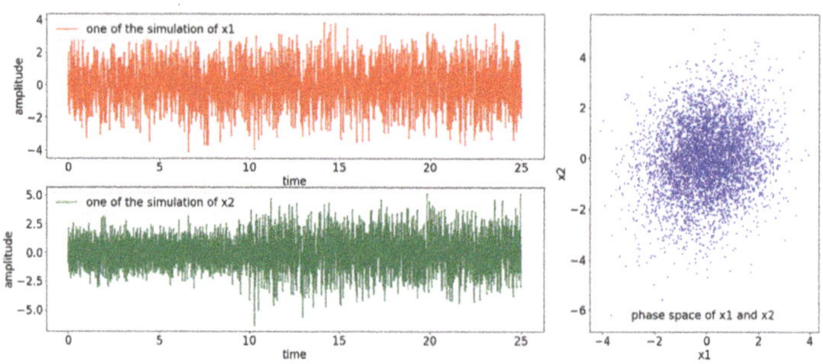

(**a**) linear: coupling

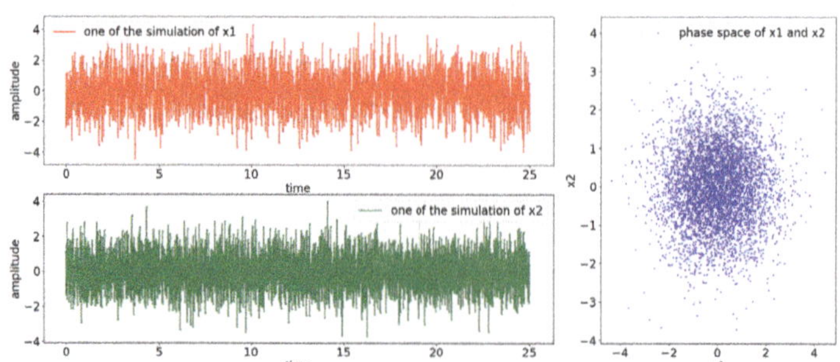

(**b**) linear: noncouple

Figure 3. *Cont.*

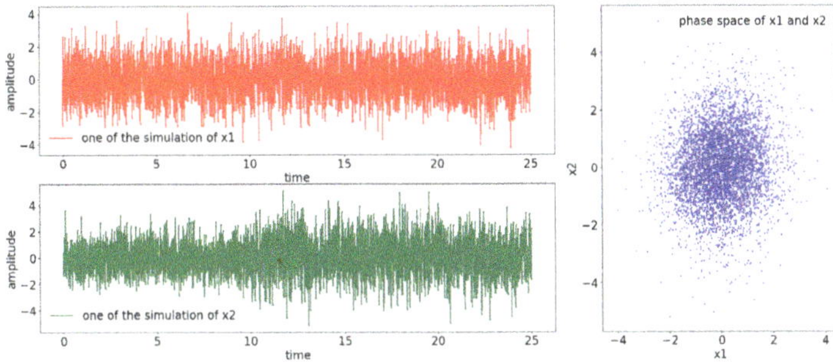

(**c**) nonlinear: large noise, couple

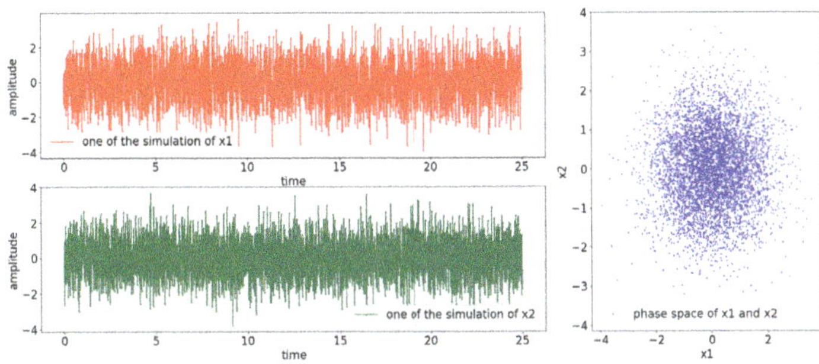

(**d**) nonlinear: large noise, noncouple

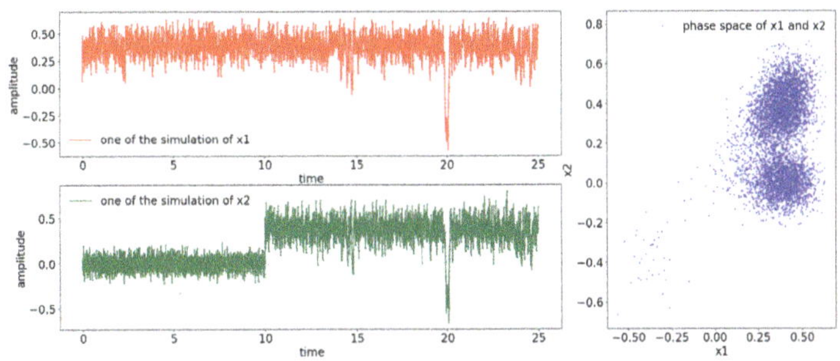

(**e**) nonlinear: small noise, couple

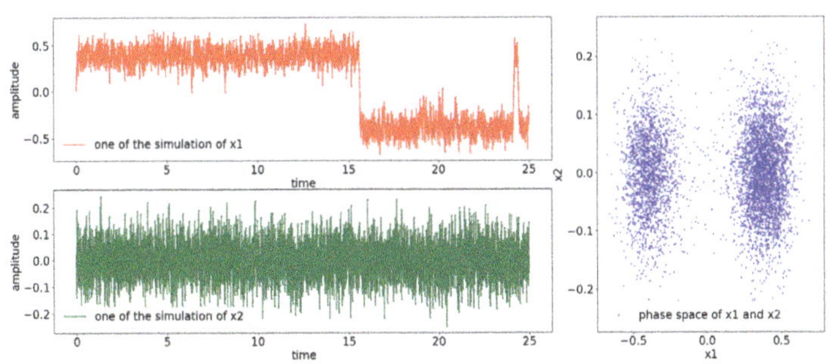

(**f**) nonlinear: small noise, noncouple

Figure 3. Result of the simulation based on Equations (24) and (25) (refer to Figure 2 for graphical explanation of the process). The [top left, red] is the result of x_1 and [bottom, green] is the result of x_2; [right blue] is the phase space of x_1 and x_2. Note that the coupling of the processes occurs at 10 s.

3.1. Granger Causality

As shown in Figure 4, the coupling of x_1 to x_2 can be captured well through nonparametric GC analysis for stationary linear signals, as shown in Figure 4a. Concurrently, the detection of the causality works well for stationary nonlinear signals, as shown in Figure 4c. This is because the nonlinear exponential term is well-approximated to a constant value as the spectral matrix decomposed to the transfer matrix and covariance matrix of noise via Wilson's algorithm. Note that the amplitude of the GC decreases for this nonlinear stationary signal. This is due to the contribution of the exponential term ($e^{-\mathbb{R}}$) that eventually affects the $S_{22}(\omega)$ element of the spectral matrix (refer to Equation (11)) and hence the amplitude of the causality ($I_{x_1 \to x_2}$). For non-stationary signals, the frequency domain of GC is still able to show the causality within the signals, but the time-varying frequency of GC cannot represent well the period of causation, as shown in Figure 4e. From the figure, we can see that the nonparametric GC gives a false result, as it suggests that the coupling between the processes occurs throughout the time. Similarly, the nonparametric GC analysis works fine in evaluating the non-causality cases for stationary cases but not so well for the non-stationary case (refer to Figure 4b,d,f. GC analysis fails to work on the signals oscillating non-stationary, as the signals cannot be modelled well via the linear autoregressive equations (refer to Equations (3) and (4)).

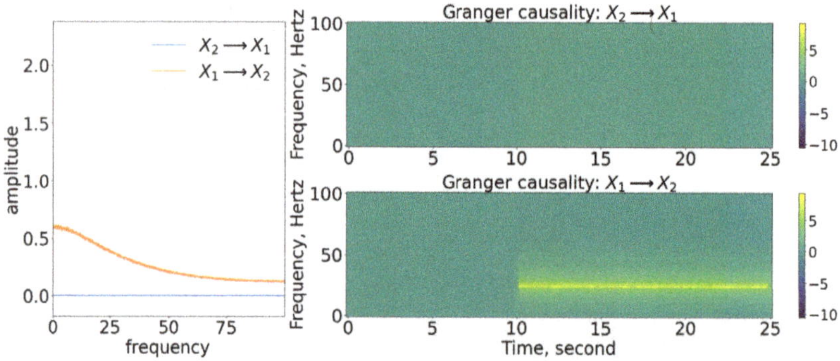

(**a**) linear: couple

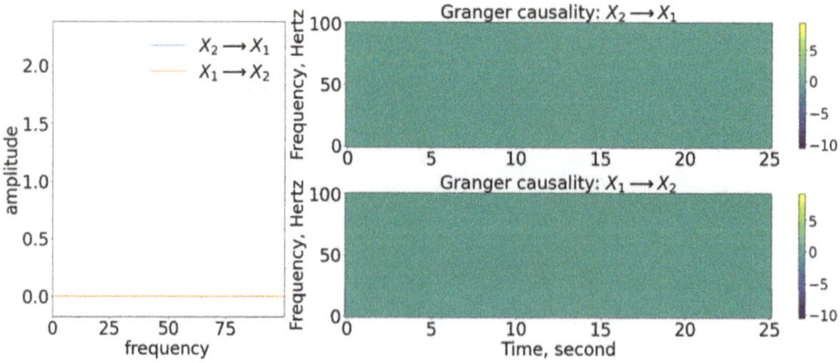

(**b**) linear: noncouple

Figure 4. *Cont.*

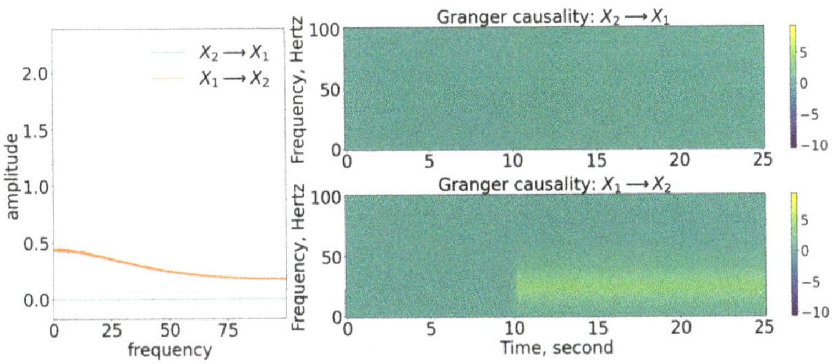

(**c**) nonlinear: large noise, couple

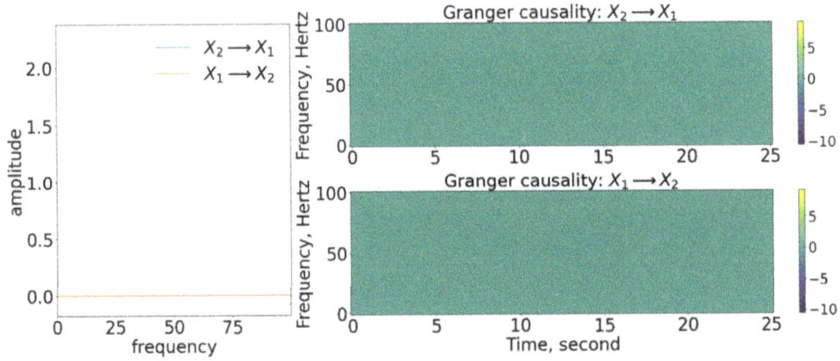

(**d**) nonlinear: large noise, noncouple

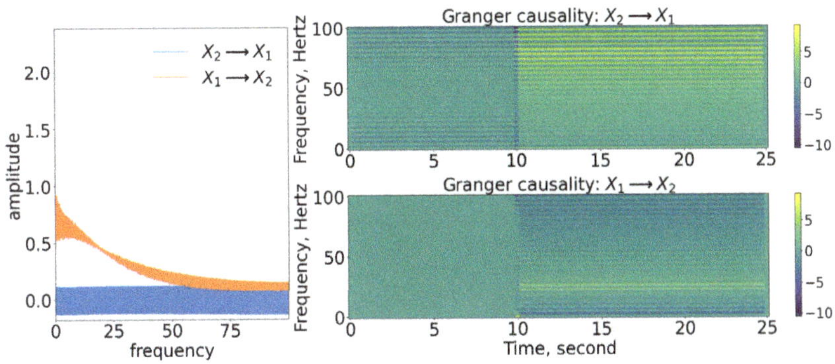

(**e**) nonlinear: small noise, couple

Figure 4. *Cont.*

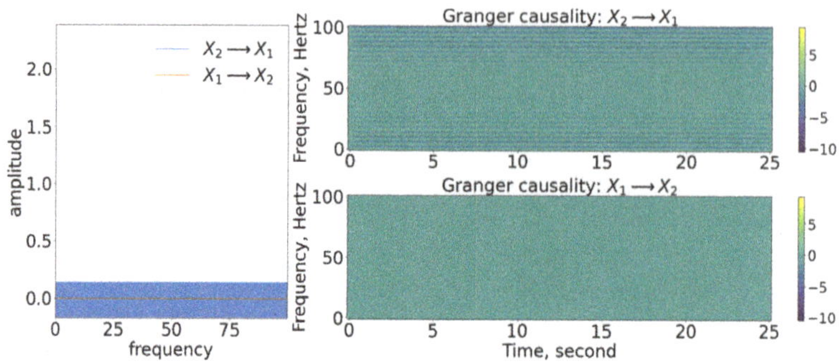

(f) nonlinear: small noise, noncouple

Figure 4. Result of the spectral and time-varying frequency of GC. Note that for each subfigure, the [left] shows the spectral (frequency domain) of GC, [blue] indicates x_2 causes x_1, while [orange] indicates x_1 causes x_2; [top, right] shows the time-varying frequency of GC of x_2 to x_1; [bottom, right] shows the time-varying frequency of GC of x_1 to x_2. The results shown are based on the processes in Equations (24) and (25). Refer to Figure 2 for the graphical explanation of the process.

3.2. Transfer Entropy

The results from TE analysis are shown in Figure 5. By first assuming that the signals are stationary, the net TE ($TE_{X,Y} = TE_{X \to Y} - TE_{Y \to X}$) is first calculated to find the suitable lag for evaluating the sliding window TE later. Figure 5a,c,e show that the net TE between the signals is significant at the lag of 1. This is because the simulated models (Equations (24) and (25)) have the coupling occurring at one lag (compares $x_1(t) := x_1(t-1)$ and $x_2(t) := x_1(t-2)$). Next, the window sliding TE is conducted through the conditional probability (multidimensional probability) that contains the data from one previous lag (refer to Equation (17)) at each window of the evaluation of TE. As shown in Figure 5a,c,e, the window sliding TE is able to show the time (10 s physical time) when the causality occurs. Similarly, the TE is also able to capture the non-causality situation well for all the cases, as shown in Figure 5b,d,f. Even though TE is able to detect the causality between the signals for either linear stationary or nonlinear non-stationary cases, it requires extra inputs/assumptions (such as bin sizes, number of lags, and the dimension of the multidimensional probability) to work properly/accurately. The failure of TE in capturing the causality for the linear model (Equation (24)) is shown in Figure 6 when the lag is set to 9 instead of 1 when evaluating the TE.

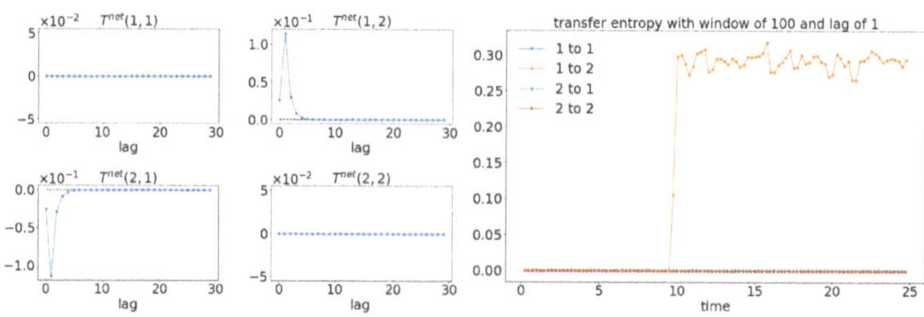

(a) linear: couple

Figure 5. *Cont.*

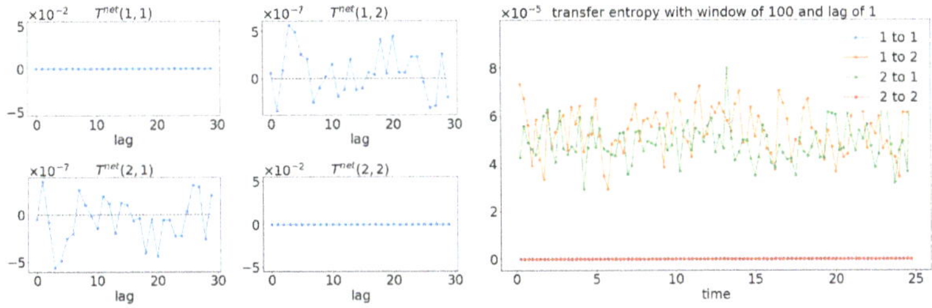

(**b**) linear: noncouple

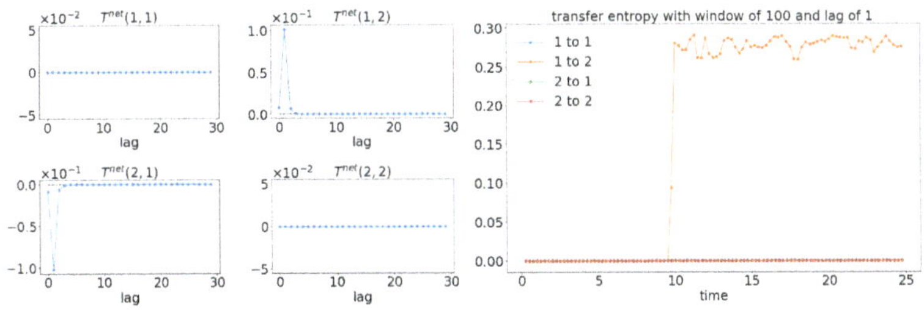

(**c**) nonlinear: large noise, couple

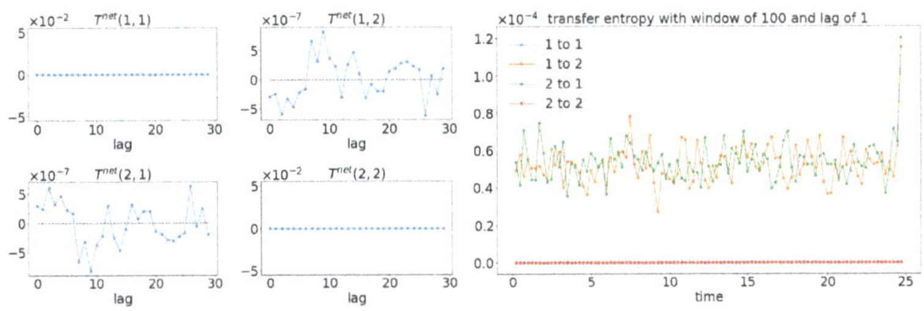

(**d**) nonlinear: large noise, noncouple

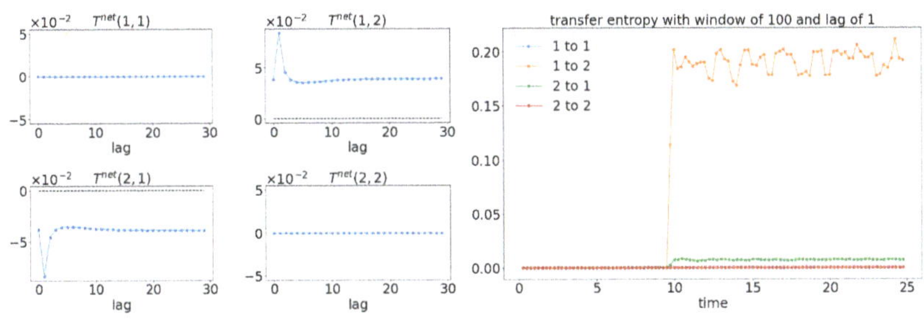

(**e**) nonlinear: small noise, couple

Figure 5. *Cont.*

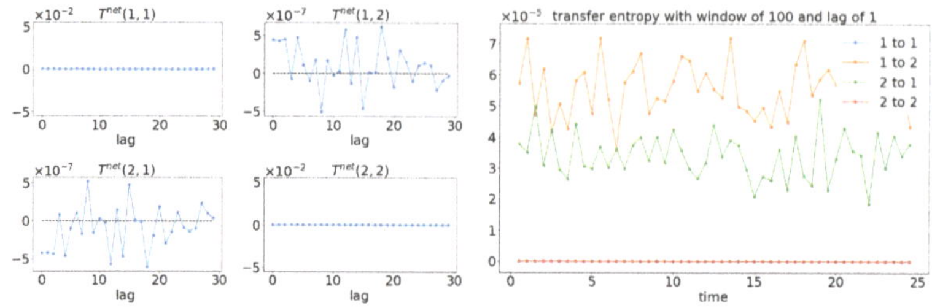

(f) nonlinear: small noise, noncouple

Figure 5. Result of the net TE and window sliding TE. Note that for each subfigure, [left, 4×4] depicts the net TE for the whole signals; while the [right] shows the window sliding TE. The results shown are based on the processes in Equations (24) and (25). Refer to Figure 2 for the graphical explanation of the process.

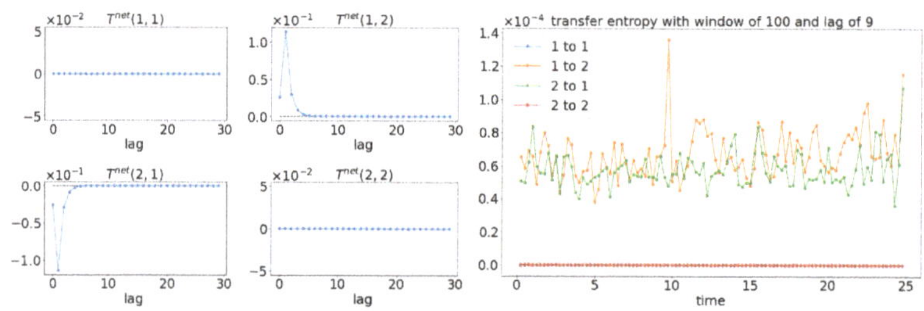

Figure 6. Failure of TE in capturing the causality between the signals x_1 and x_2 for [linear: couple] (refer to Equation (24)) when lag 9 is used for evaluation, as compared to Figure 5a, where the TE accurately shows that the coupling occurs after 10 s.

3.3. Information Rate Causality

Both GC and TE detect causality by examining the increase in the predictability of the stochastic processes (measured by the inverse of entropy) when the past information is included. In comparison, information rate causality evaluates causality by quantifying the rate of change of the probability distribution of one variable conditioned on another, as noted previously. The results are shown in Figures 7 and 8 where the changes of the distribution due to the causality between the processes are well-reflected via the changes in the information rate (Γ). For the cases of noncoupling, the information rate is not changing and remains constant, which would suggest that none of the signals cause the changes to the joint distribution (refer to Figure 7b,d,f). Hence, no causality occurs between the signals. Similarly, prior to the coupling of the signals, the causality is not seen, and hence the information rate again remains constant. Notice that the information rate does not stay at zero when no causality happens, it is due to the noises/spikes of the estimated distribution, as shown in Figure S1.

In the presence of the couplings, the changes in the distribution due to the causality among the signals can be observed via the changes in the information rate. For instance, the changes in the information rate due to the causality of $x_1(t)$ to $x_2(t)$ can be observed in Figure 7a,c,e (zoom-in: Figure 8a,c,e). Referring to the models, the signals are coupled with the lag difference of one ($x_1(t) = x_1(t-1)$ and $x_2(t) = x_1(t-2)$), and hence the peak of the information rate is observed after one lag. From Figure 8a,c,e, the changes in the information rate prior to the coupling (at physical time 10 s) are observed as the evaluation window of [9.75 s to 10.25 s] picks up the causality of the signals from [10 s to 10.25 s]. Referring to the starting time (near 0 s) of Figure 7e,f, there is the presence of a sharp difference in information rate. This is due to the non-stationary oscillation of $x_1(t)$ that causes the high disturbance of the distribution.

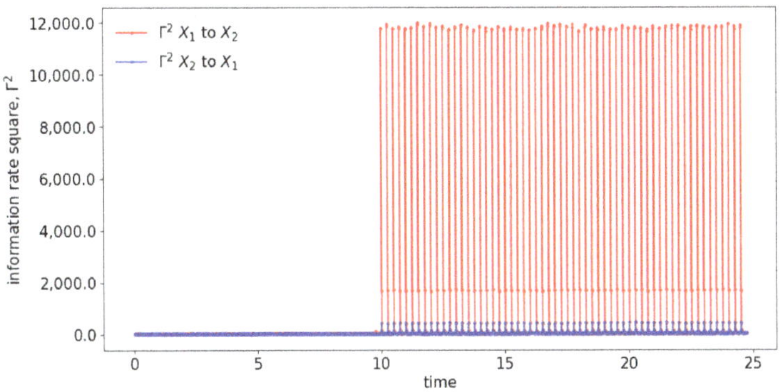

(**a**) linear: couple

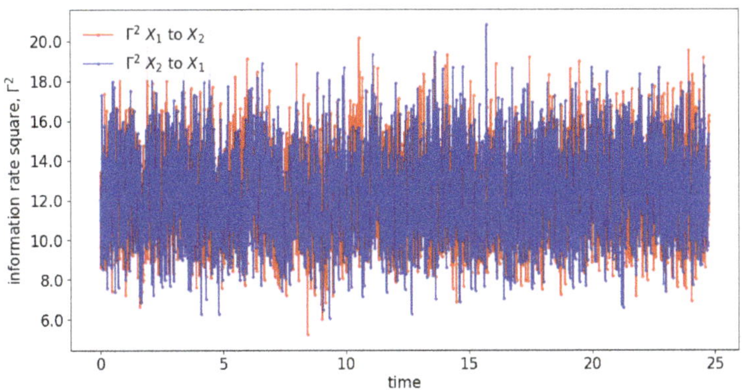

(**b**) linear: noncouple

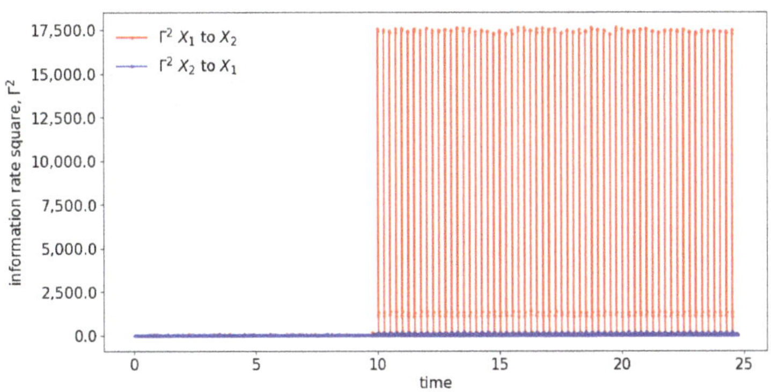

(**c**) nonlinear: large noise, couple

Figure 7. *Cont.*

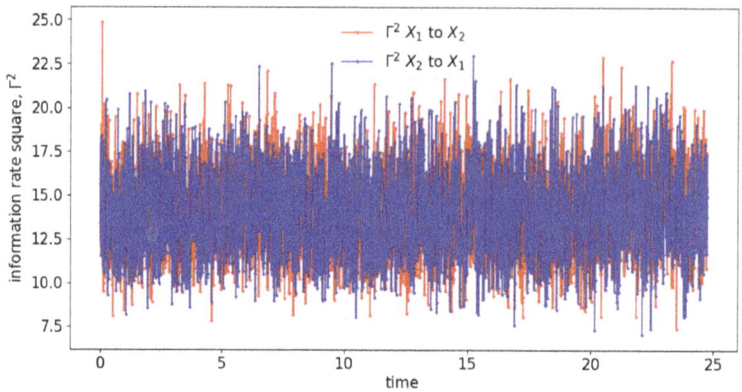

(**d**) nonlinear: large noise, noncouple

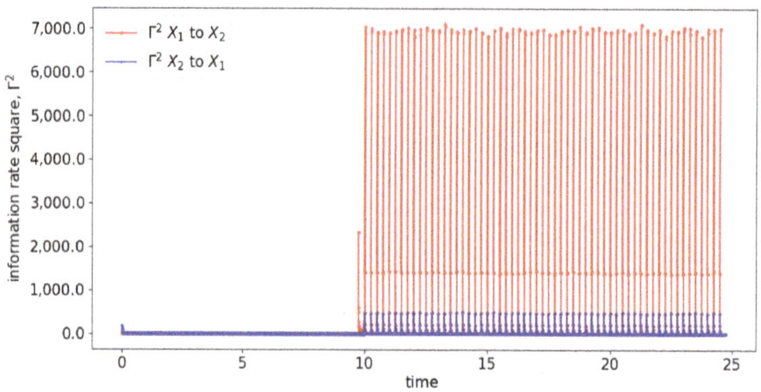

(**e**) nonlinear: small noise, couple

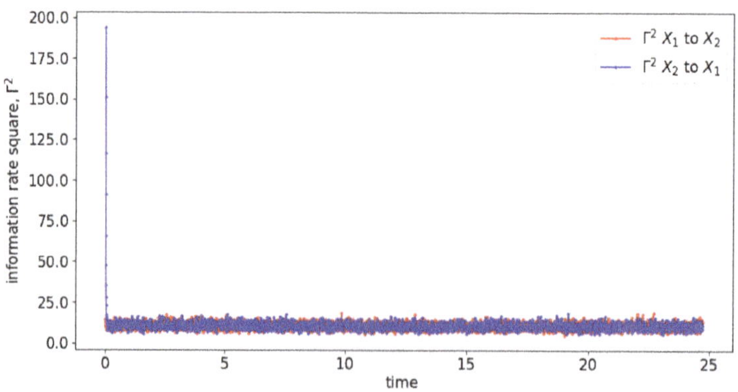

(**f**) nonlinear: small noise, noncouple

Figure 7. Result of information rate causality for Equations (24) and (25).

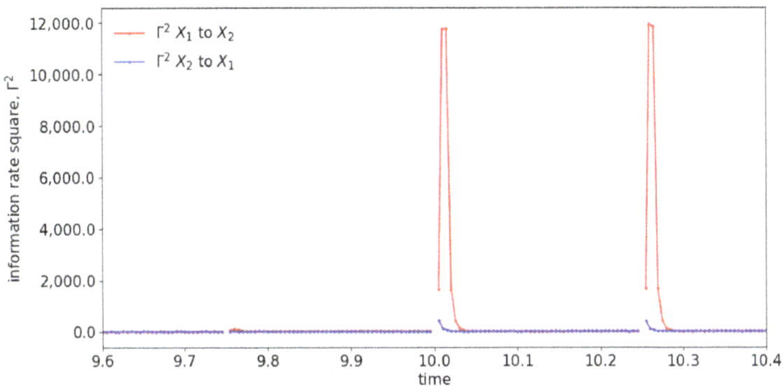

(**a**) linear: couple

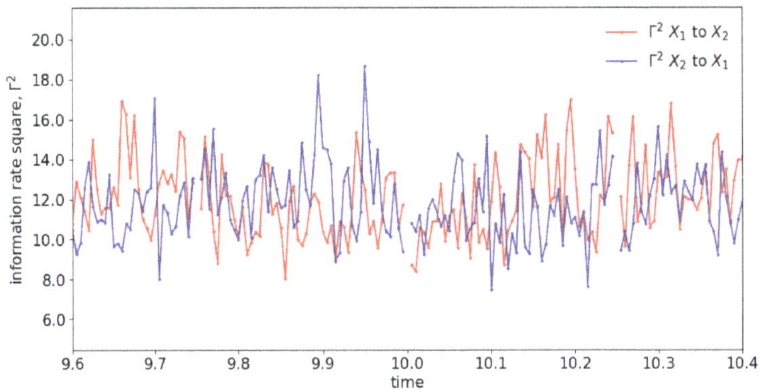

(**b**) linear: noncouple

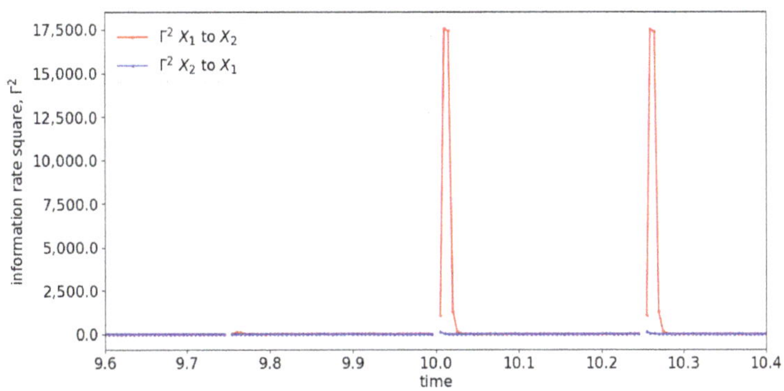

(**c**) nonlinear: large noise, couple

Figure 8. *Cont.*

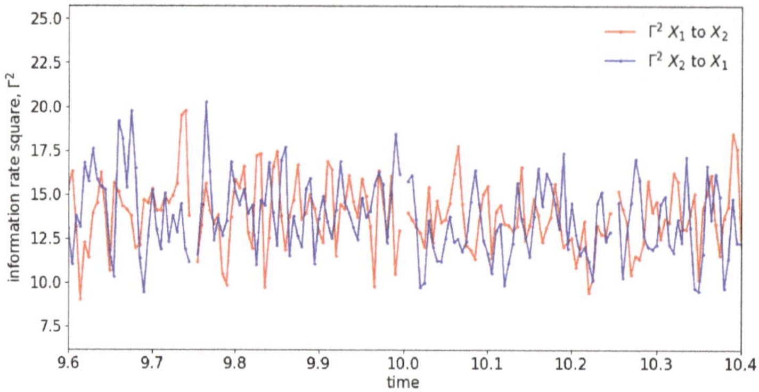

(**d**) nonlinear: large noise, noncouple

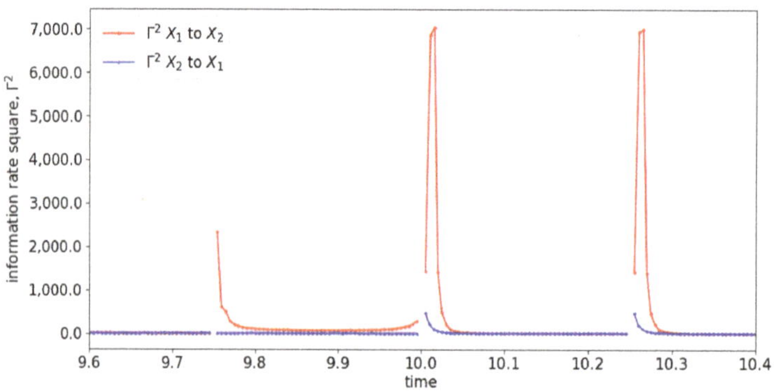

(**e**) nonlinear: small noise, couple

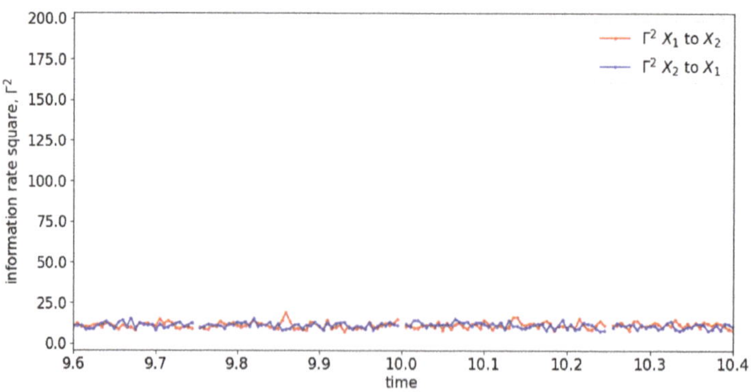

(**f**) nonlinear: small noise, noncouple

Figure 8. Zoom-in of Figure 7 for the information rate causality between 9.6 s and 10.4 s. Note that the change in the causality occurs at 10 s.

To demonstrate the capability of information rate causality to detect lag differences within a signal, we simulated and analyzed Equation (26), which has the coupling starting at 10 s with a lag difference of 9 (compares $x_1 = x_1(t-1)$ and $x_2 = x_1(t-10)$). Figure 9 shows the section of the information rate from 9.6 s to 10.4 s. The figure reveals that the peak of the information rate appears at the 9th time step (0.045 s) at every window of evaluation, which accurately reflects the lag difference specified in Equation (26). This result suggests that information rate causality can effectively capture the underlying causality of the signals at each evaluation window.

$$x_1(t) = 0.55x_1(t-1) + \epsilon_1(t),$$
$$x_2(t) = H(\tau-10)x_1(t-10) + \epsilon_2(t). \quad (26)$$

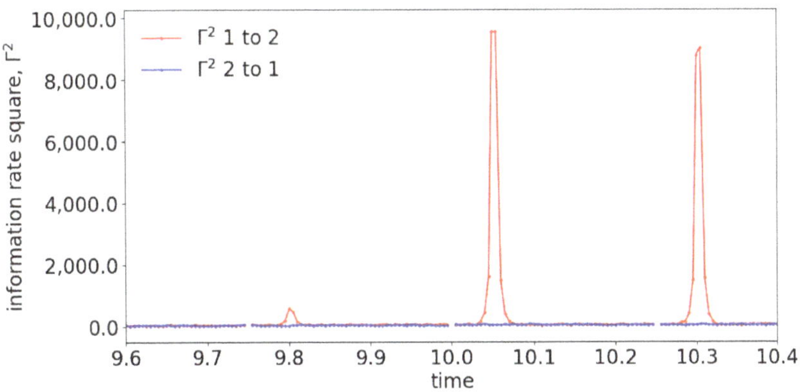

Figure 9. The information rate causality of Equation (26) between 9.6 s and 10.4 s where the causality occurs at 10 s.

4. Interchange of Unidirectional Model

In this part, similar models from Section 3 are used with slight modifications to study the interchange of the unidirectional causality. The models are modified to Equations (27) and (28) for linear and nonlinear models, respectively. The modification with the Heaviside step functions ($H(\ldots)$) in the models portrays that the signal $x_2(t)$ causing $x_1(t)$ occurs prior to physical time (τ) 10 s, while the signal $x_1(t)$ causes $x_2(t)$ after 10 s. The general structure of Equations (27) and (28) is illustrated in Figure 10.

Linear model:

$$x_1(t) = H(10-\tau)0.55x_2(t-1) + \epsilon_1(t),$$
$$x_2(t) = H(\tau-10)x_1(t-2) + \epsilon_2(t). \quad (27)$$

Nonlinear model:

$$x_1(t) = H(10-\tau)0.55x_2(t-1)e^{1-|x_2(t-1)|} + \epsilon_1(t),$$
$$x_2(t) = H(\tau-10)x_1(t-2) + \epsilon_2(t). \quad (28)$$

Here t is the time-step and τ is the physical time. The Heaviside step functions are used with $H(10-\tau)$ suggesting the coupling occurs from the beginning of the simulation till the physical time 10 s conversely $H(\tau-10)$, suggesting the coupling occurs after 10 s. Similar to Section 3, 6 possible cases are simulated based on Equations (27) and (28). The simulated signals will be evaluated by GC, TE, and information rate causality.

The result of the simulations is shown in Figure 11, which suggests that all the signals oscillate stationary. Unlike Equation (25), in which the signal $x_1(t)$ is perturbated by its previous state by a factor of 0.55 ($0.55x_1(t-1)$) and the small noise ($\epsilon_1(t)$), Equation (28) is perturbated by the past state of $x_2(t)$ ($x_2(t-2)$) instead. Hence, the power of the exponential will always be negative; consequently, all the simulated signals have stationary oscillations. Note that the noncoupling is referring to the decoupling of $x_1(t)$ to $x_2(t)$ ($H(\tau-10) = 0$).

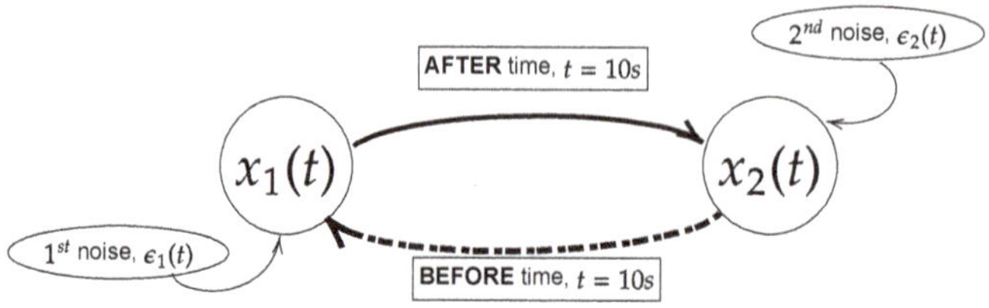

Figure 10. Model of the flow of information of the processes $x_1(t)$ and $x_2(t)$ for Equations (27) and (28). In this paper, the equations are simulated with the physical time of 25 s and sampling frequency of 200 Hertz (5000 realizations) with either large noise or small noise. Note that the process $x_2(t)$ coupling with $x_1(t)$ occurs before 10 s and the interchange of coupling occurs after 10 s. In the context of noncoupling, it is referring to $H(\tau - 10) = 0$.

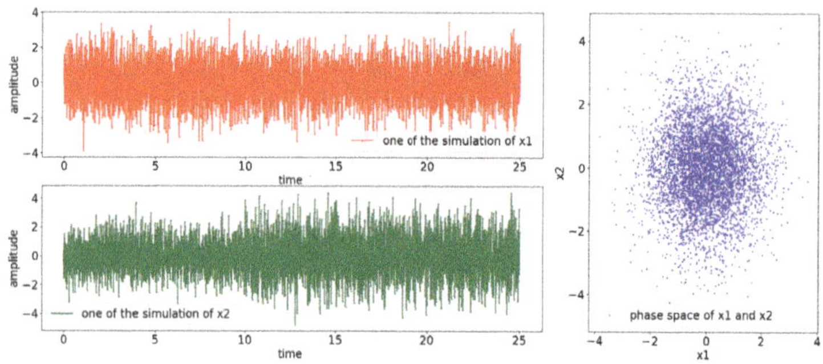

(**a**) linear: couple

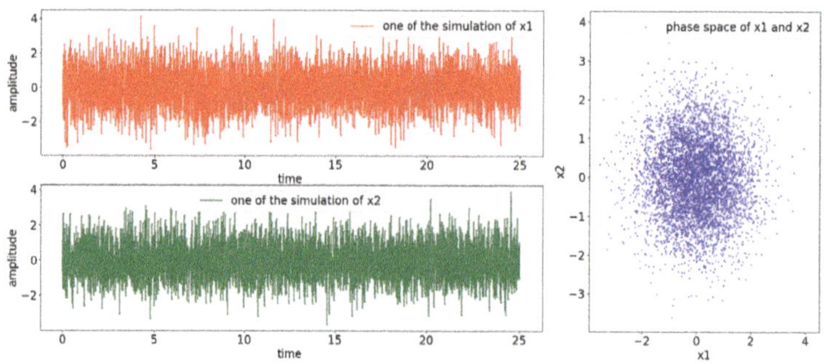

(**b**) linear: noncouple

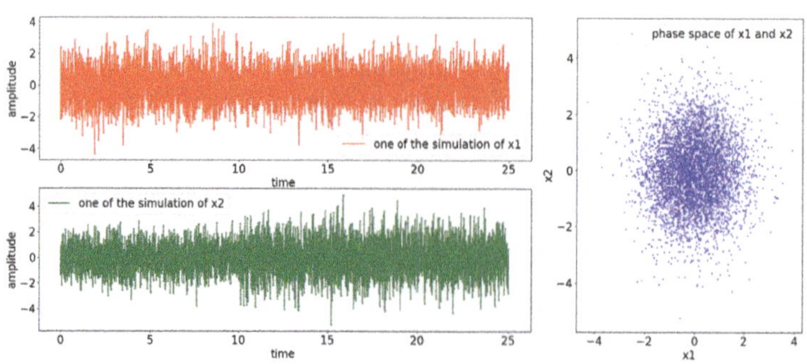

(**c**) nonlinear: large noise, couple

Figure 11. *Cont.*

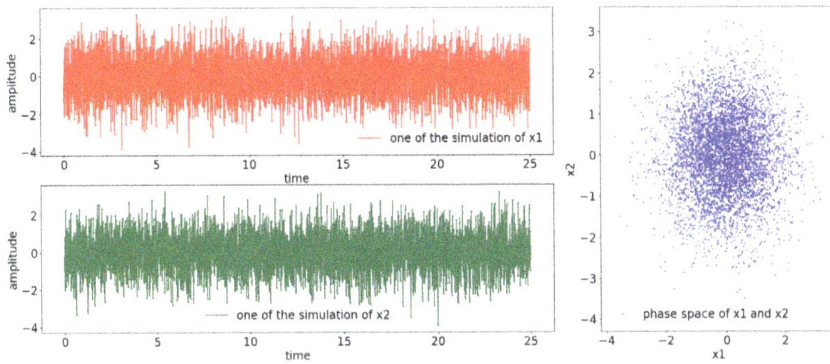

(**d**) nonlinear: large noise, noncouple

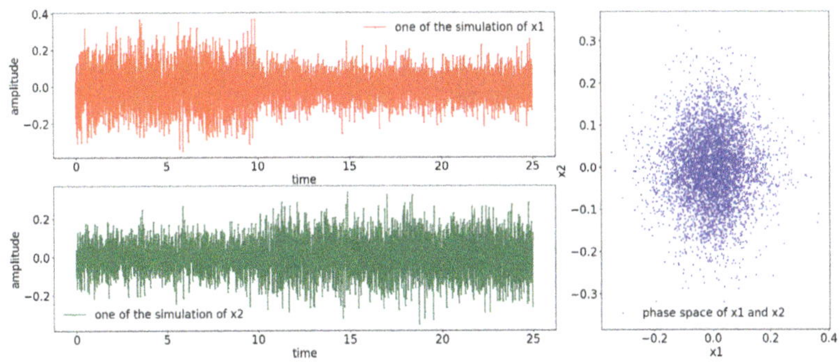

(**e**) nonlinear: small noise, couple

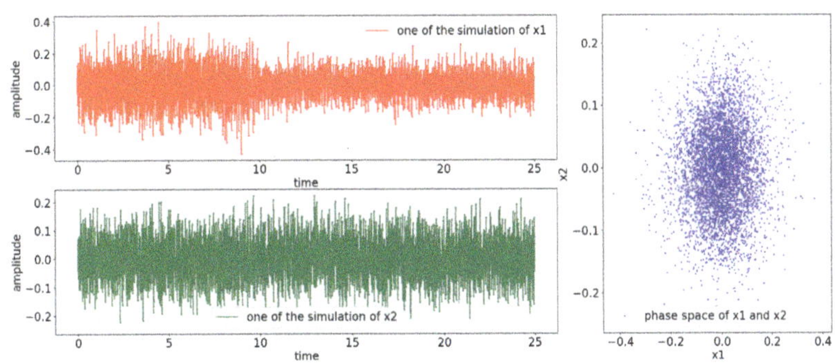

(**f**) nonlinear: small noise, noncouple

Figure 11. Result of simulation based on Equations (27) and (28) (refer to Figure 10 for graphical explanation of the process). The [top left, red] is the result of x_1 and [bottom, green] is the result of x_2; [right, blue] is the phase space of x_1 and x_2. Note that in the context of noncoupling, it is referring to $H(\tau - 10) = 0$.

4.1. Granger Causality

Based on the models, the signal $x_2(t)$ will first cause $x_1(t)$ for the beginning of the process until the physical time of 10 s, and $x_1(t)$ causes $x_2(t)$ after the 10 s. This pattern is captured in the time-varying frequency of GC, as shown in Figure 12 for all the cases. Prior to 10 s, the $x_1(t)$ is caused by $x_2(t)$ by a factor of 0.55, and hence a similar factor of GC is shown in the time-varying frequency domain. Similarly, the coupling between the signals can also be observed in the frequency domain of GC. Notice that the [nonlinear:

small noise] cases are able to show the significance of $x_2(t)$ causing $x_1(t)$ prior to 10 s because the small noise and the exponential term had $x_2(t)$ causing $x_1(t)$ increased to about 1.5 ($e^1 \times 0.55 \approx 1.5$).

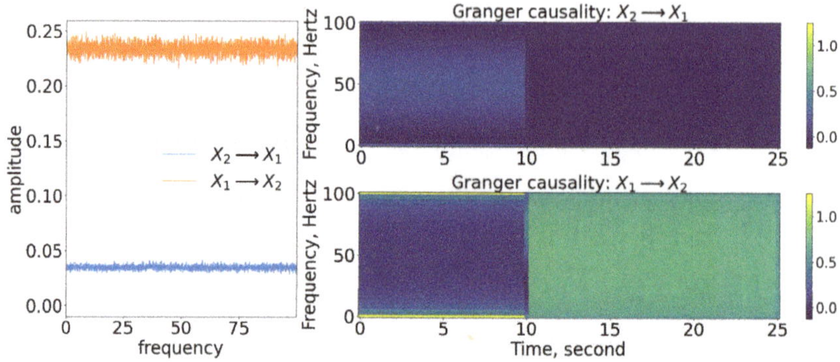

(**a**) linear: couple

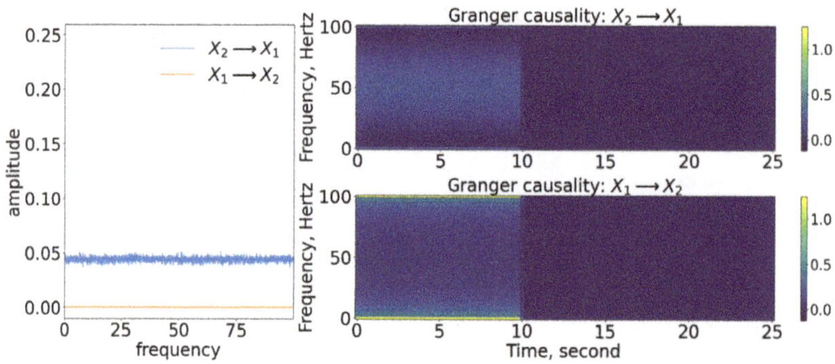

(**b**) linear: noncouple

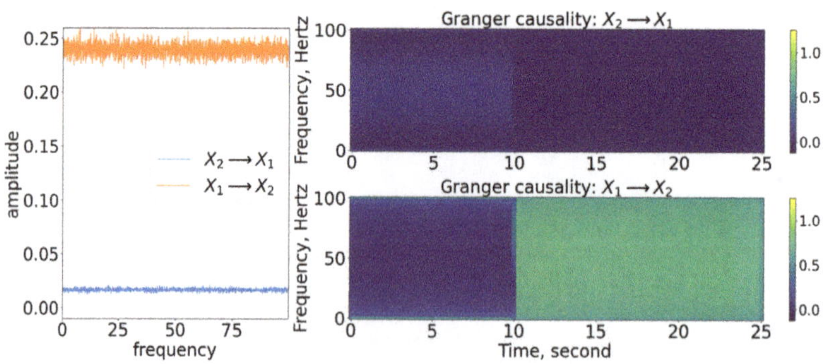

(**c**) nonlinear: large noise, couple

Figure 12. *Cont.*

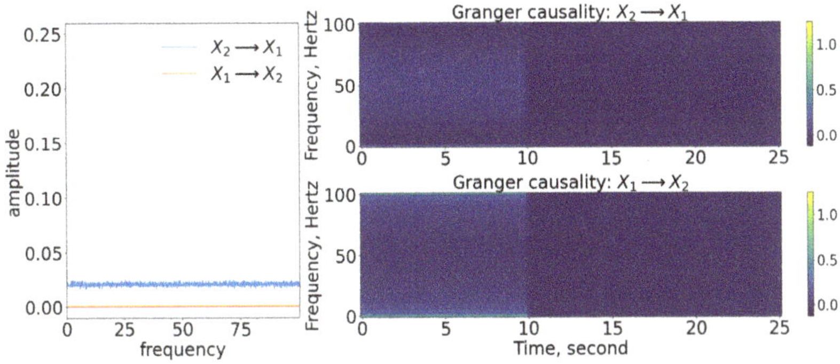

(**d**) nonlinear: large noise, noncouple

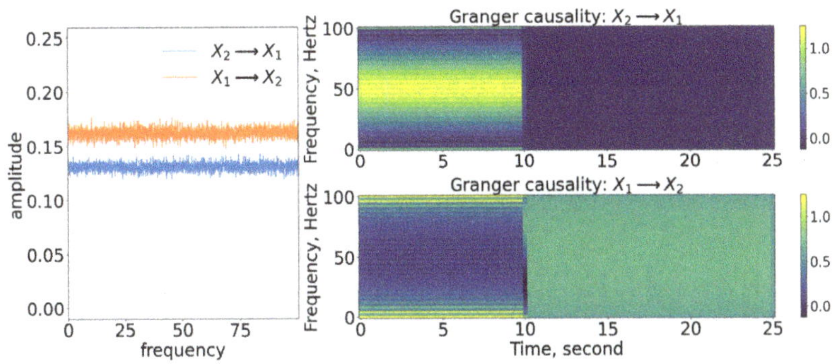

(**e**) nonlinear: small noise, couple

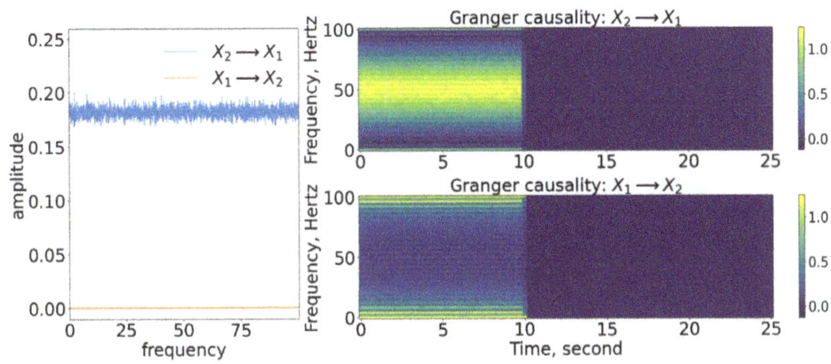

(**f**) nonlinear: small noise, noncouple

Figure 12. Result of the spectral and time-varying frequency of GC. Note that for each subfigure, the [left] shows the spectral (frequency domain) of GC, [blue] indicates x_2 causes x_1, while [orange] indicates x_1 causes x_2; [top, right] shows the time-varying frequency of GC of x_2 to x_1; [bottom, right] shows the time-varying frequency of GC of x_1 to x_2. The results shown are based on the processes in Equations (27) and (28). Refer to Figure 10 for the graphical explanation of the process. Note that the noncoupling is referring to $H(\tau - 10) = 0$ for all the cases.

4.2. Transfer Entropy

TE is able to show the correction direction of the causality between the signals if the correct lag is chosen. Therefore, having models (like Equations (27) and (28)) with the coupling occurring at different time lags cannot properly show the direction of the causality via the window sliding TE. For instance, the window sliding TE shows that $x_2(t)$ is causing the $x_1(t)$ when lag 0 is chosen, while the reverse is shown when lag 1 is used, as shown in Figure 13 (for lag 0) and Figure 14 (for lag 1). This is depicted well in the underlining models (Equations (27) and (28)), in which $x_1(t)$ causes $x_2(t)$ one lag later. As a result, TE cannot show the whole causality of the signals by just one lag.

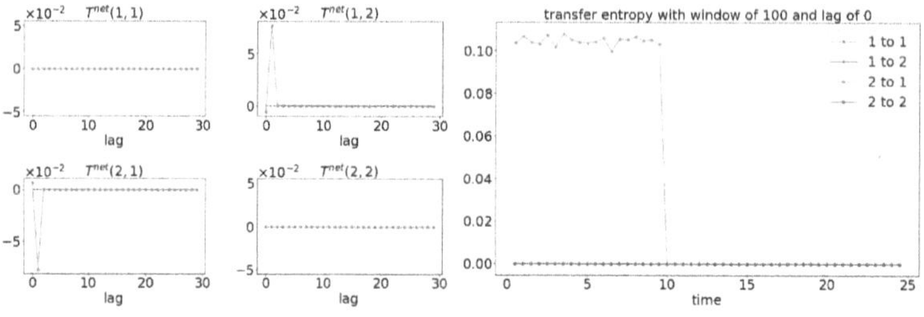

(**a**) linear: couple

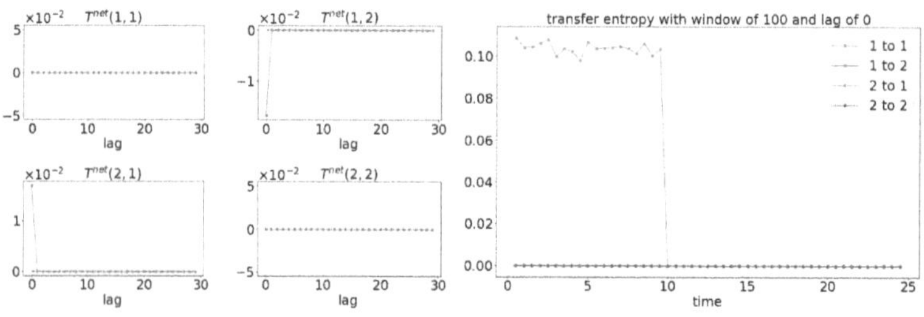

(**b**) linear: noncouple

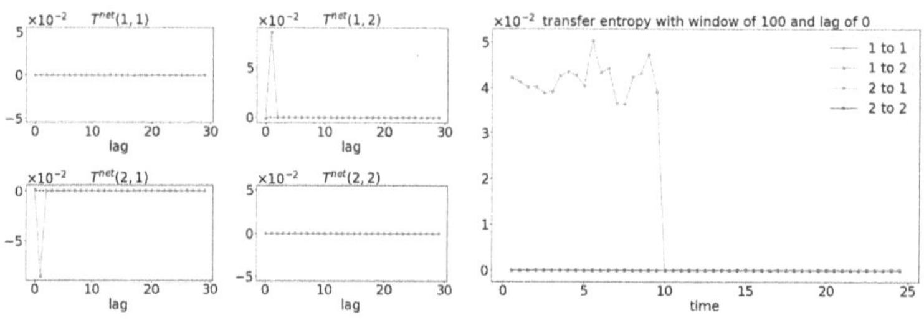

(**c**) nonlinear: large noise, couple

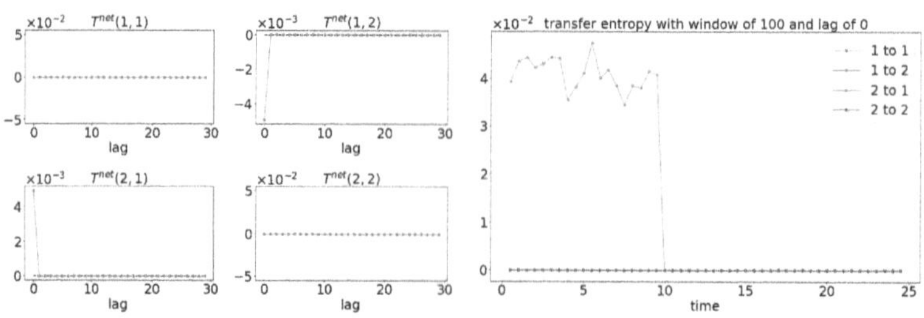

(**d**) nonlinear: large noise, noncouple

Figure 13. *Cont.*

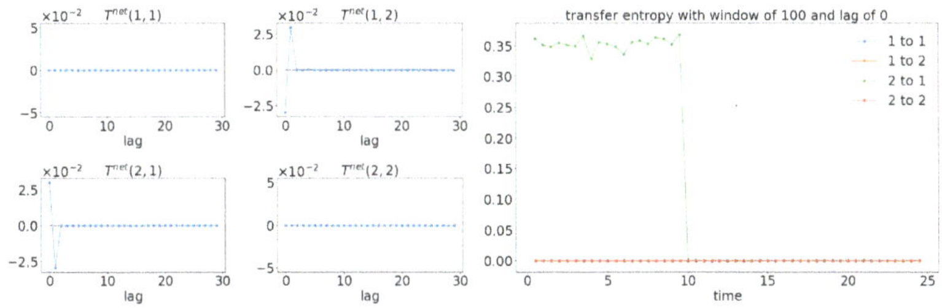

(e) nonlinear: small noise, couple

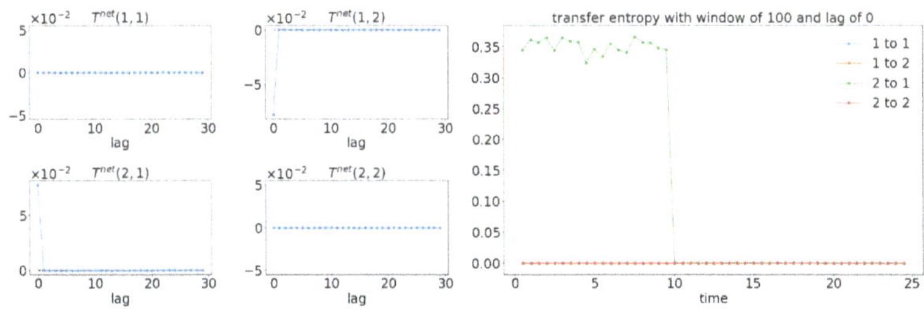

(f) nonlinear: small noise, noncouple

Figure 13. Result of the net TE and window sliding TE with the lag of 0. Note that for each subfigure, [left, 4 × 4] depicts the net TE for the whole signals, while the [right] shows the window sliding TE. The results shown are based on the processes in Equations (27) and (28). Refer to Figure 10 for the graphical explanation of the process. Note that the noncoupling is referring to $H(\tau - 10) = 0$ for all the cases.

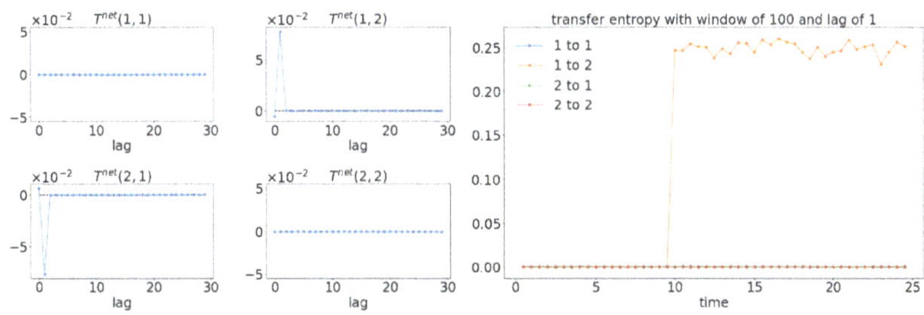

(a) linear: couple

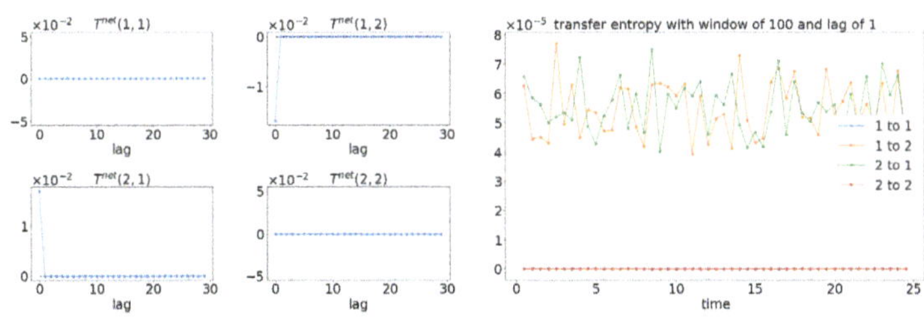

(b) linear: noncouple

Figure 14. *Cont.*

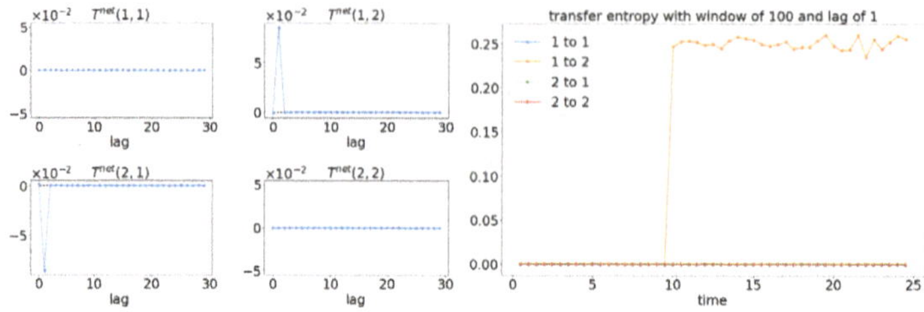

(**c**) nonlinear: large noise, couple

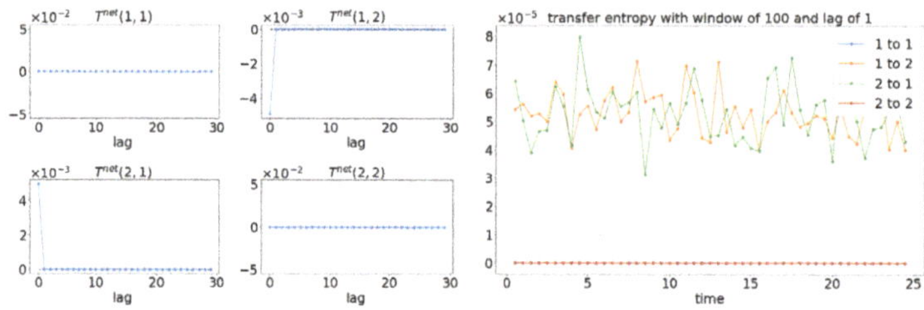

(**d**) nonlinear: large noise, noncouple

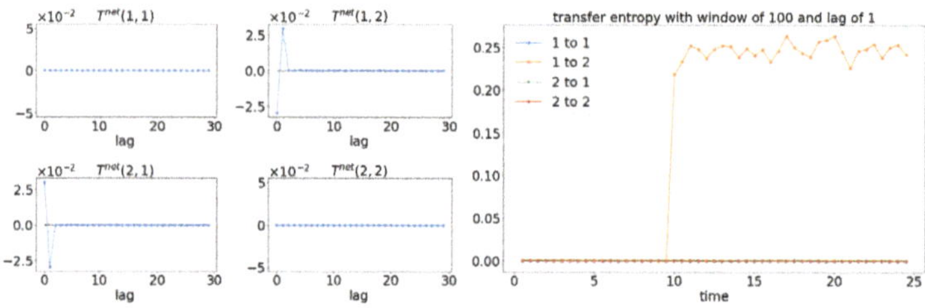

(**e**) nonlinear: small noise, couple

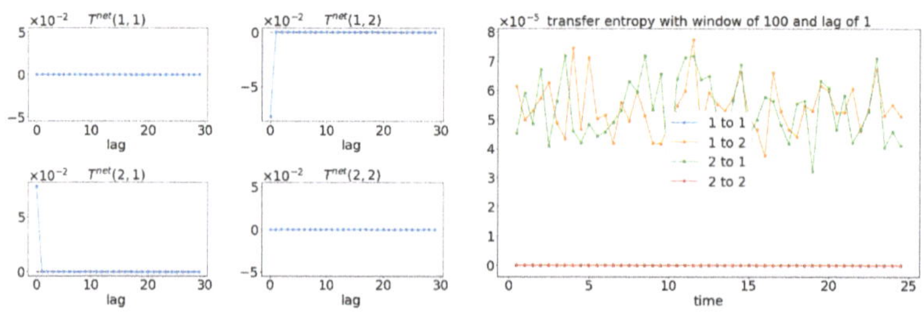

(**f**) nonlinear: small noise, noncouple

Figure 14. Result of the net TE and window sliding TE with the lag of 1. Note that for each subfigure, [left, 4×4] depicts the net TE for the whole signals, while the [right] shows the window sliding TE. The results shown are based on the processes in Equations (27) and (28). Refer to Figure 10 for the graphical explanation of the process. Note that the noncoupling is referring to $H(\tau - 10) = 0$ for all the cases.

4.3. Information Rate Causality

Alternatively, the information rate causality is able to show the coupling of the signals along with the lag of coupling in each window of the evaluation. As discussed, the information rate causality evaluates the causality by observing the changes in the probability distribution of one signal after it is influenced by another signal. As shown in Figures 15 and 16, the information rate causality can captures the interchange of the coupling among the signals of the simulated models (Equations (27) and (28)). As discussed in TE, signal $x_2(t)$ is causing $x_1(t)$ at a lag of 0, and $x_1(t)$ causes $x_2(t)$ at a lag of 1. These lags can be observed at each window of the information rate evaluation. For instance, as shown in Figure 16, the information rate of 2 to 1 (Γ^2 2 to 1) has a spike at the beginning of the time, while the information rate of 1 to 2 (Γ^2 1 to 2) has a spike after one time step (one lag). Hence, the information rate causality is capable of showing the underlying causality of the signals.

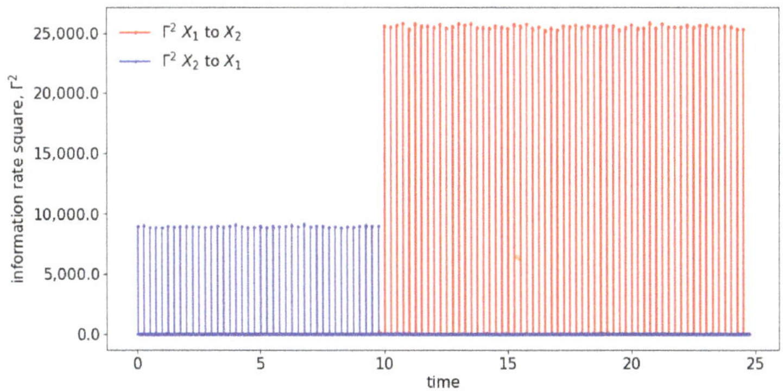

(**a**) linear: couple

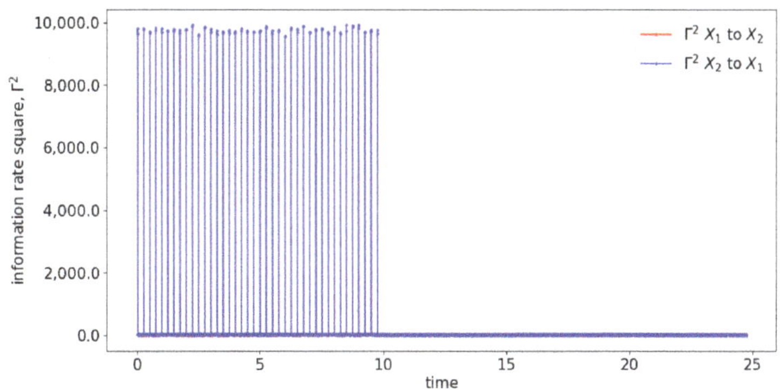

(**b**) linear: noncouple

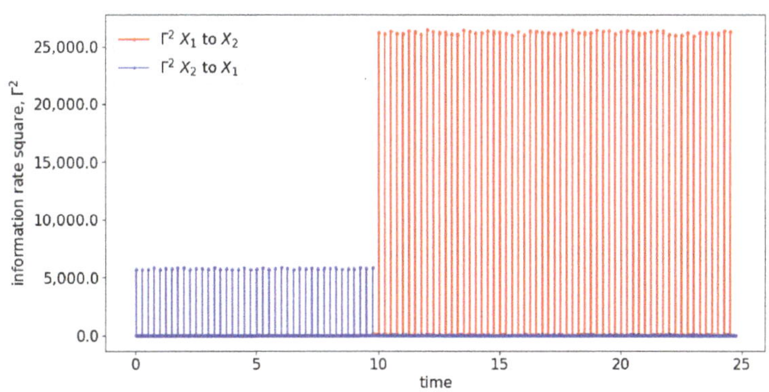

(**c**) nonlinear: large noise, couple

Figure 15. *Cont.*

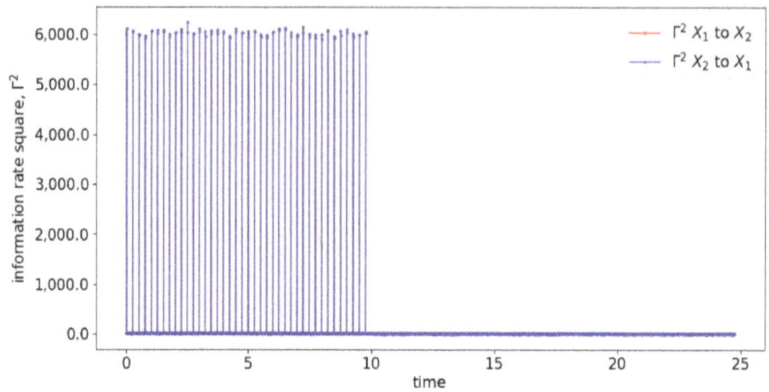

(**d**) nonlinear: large noise, noncouple

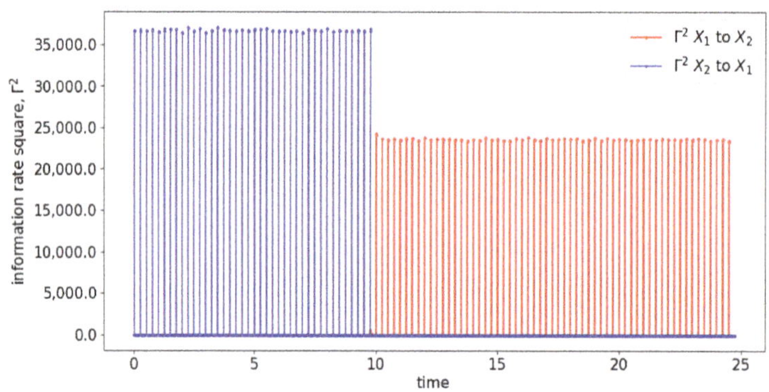

(**e**) nonlinear: small noise, couple

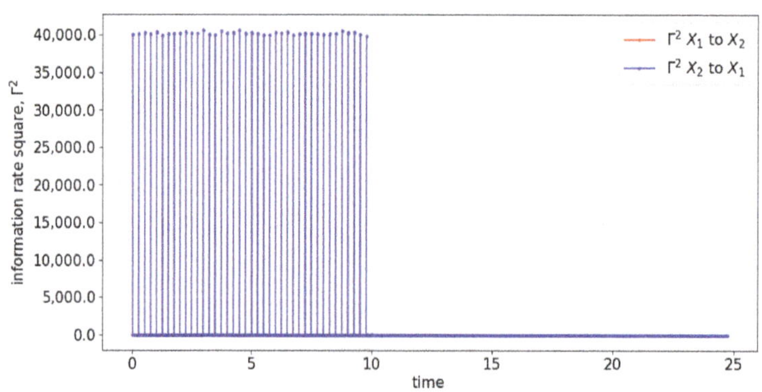

(**f**) nonlinear: small noise, noncouple

Figure 15. Result of information rate causality for Equations (27) and (28). Note that the interchange of the causality occurs at 10 s.

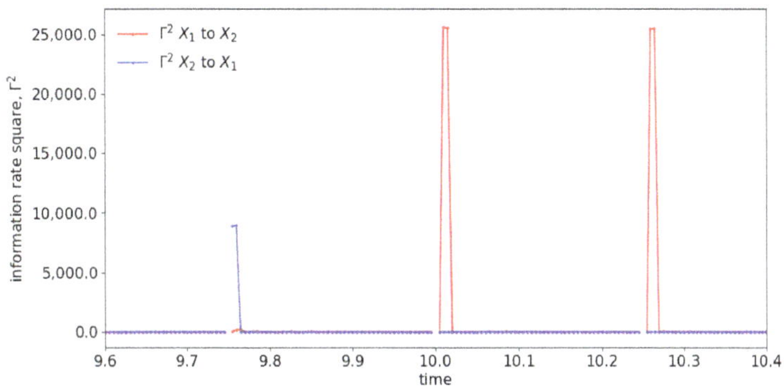

(**a**) linear: couple

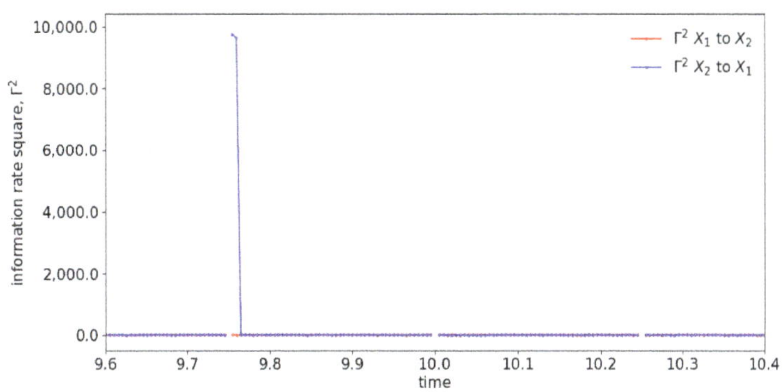

(**b**) linear: noncouple

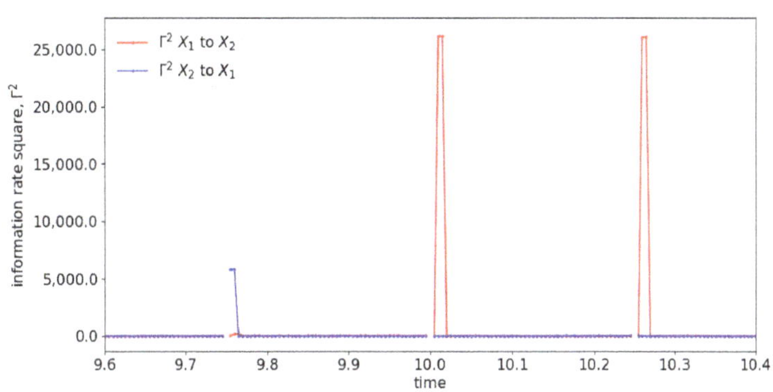

(**c**) nonlinear: large noise, couple

Figure 16. *Cont.*

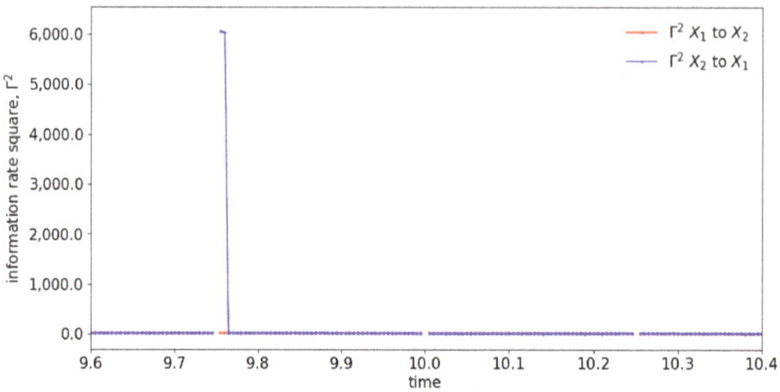

(**d**) nonlinear: large noise, noncouple

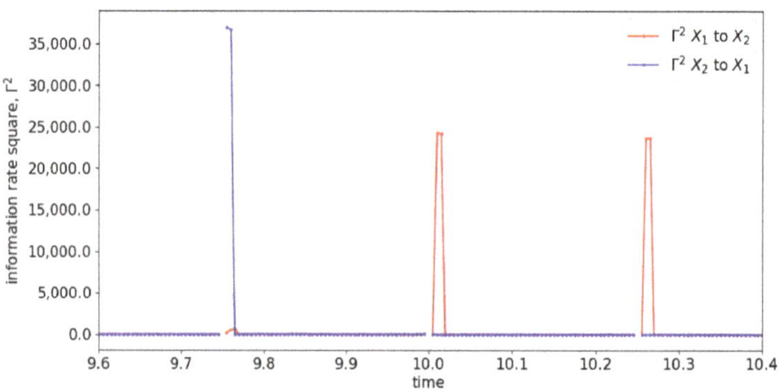

(**e**) nonlinear: small noise, couple

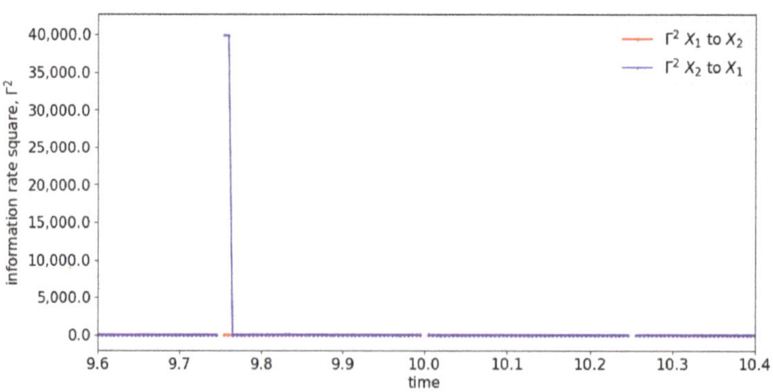

(**f**) nonlinear: small noise, noncouple

Figure 16. Zoom-in of Figure 15 for the information rate causality between 9.6 s and 10.4 s. Note that the interchange of the causality occurs at 10 s.

5. Bidirectional Model

In this section, the bidirectional causality is studied by modifying the linear and nonlinear models from Section 3 as Equations (29) and (30), respectively. These modified models have the signals $x_2(t)$ continuously influencing $x_1(t)$ at all times $t \geq 1$. In addition, at time 10 s, the Heaviside step function $(H(\tau - 10))$ enables the coupling of $x_1(t)$ and

$x_2(t)$, which allows $x_1(t)$ to influence $x_2(t)$ while the previous coupling remains intact. The general structure of the Equations (29) and (30) is illustrated in Figure 17.
Linear model:

$$x_1(t) = 0.55x_2(t-1) + \epsilon_1(t),$$
$$x_2(t) = H(\tau - 10)x_1(t-2) + \epsilon_2(t). \tag{29}$$

Nonlinear model:

$$x_1(t) = 0.55x_2(t-1)e^{1-|x_2(t-1)|} + \epsilon_1(t),$$
$$x_2(t) = H(\tau - 10)x_1(t-2) + \epsilon_2(t). \tag{30}$$

Here, t is the time step and τ is the physical time; $H(\tau - 10)$ is the Heaviside step function that allows the coupling of the signal starting at a physical time of 10 s. Similar to the previous model, 6 cases are simulated and the signals are used to evaluate through GC, TE, and information rate causality. Recall that the noncoupling cases here are referring to the decoupling of $x_1(t)$ to $x_2(t)$ ($H(\tau - 10) = 0$).

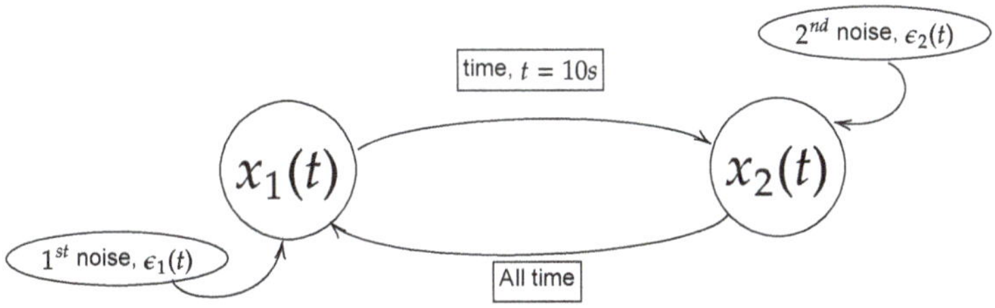

Figure 17. Model of the flow of information of the processes $x_1(t)$ and $x_2(t)$ for Equations (29) and (30). In this paper, the equations are simulated with physical time of 25 s and sampling frequency of 200 Hz (5000 realizations) with either large noise or small noise. Note that the $x_2(t)$ coupled with $x_1(t)$ throughout the process and the occurrence of bidirectional causality happens after 10 s. In the context of noncoupling, it is referring to $H(\tau - 10) = 0$.

The simulation result from all aforementioned cases is shown in Figure 18. From the observation of the individual signal and the phase space, the scenario of [nonlinear: small noise, couple] has non-stationary oscillation after the coupling, as shown in Figure 18e. This is due to the divergence caused by the nonlinear exponential term embedded within the simulated equation ($e^{1-|x_2(t-1)|} = e^{\mathbb{R}}$) along with the factor of 0.55 of the previous state of $x_2(t)$ ($0.55x_2(t-1)\ldots$). On the other hand, [nonlinear: small noise, noncouple] has a stationary oscillation, as shown in Figure 18f; this is because $x_1(t)$ only receives the input from $x_2(t)$, which keeps the power of the exponential term negative and hence results in a stationary oscillation.

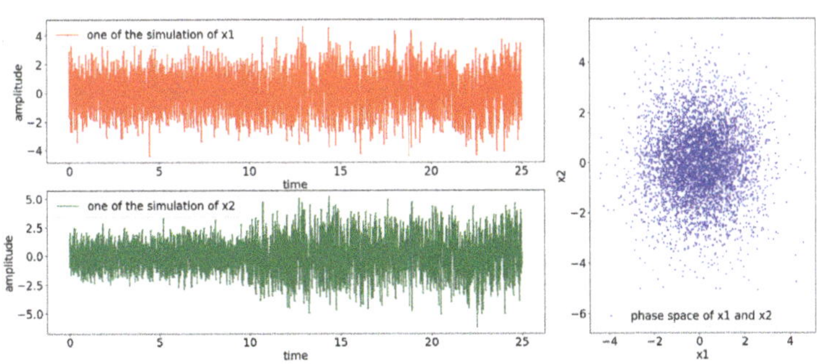

(**a**) linear: couple

Figure 18. *Cont.*

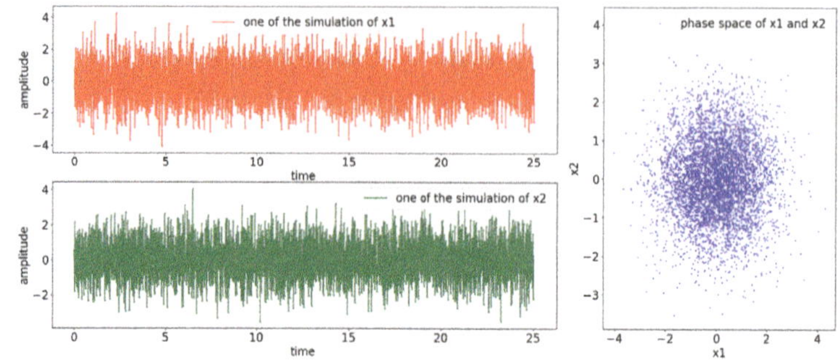

(**b**) linear: noncouple

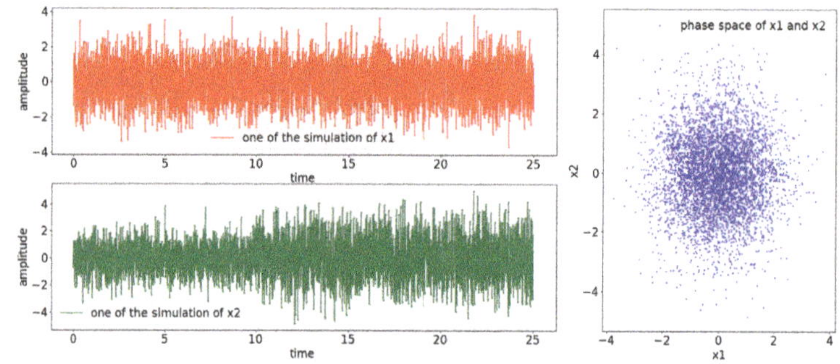

(**c**) nonlinear: large noise, couple

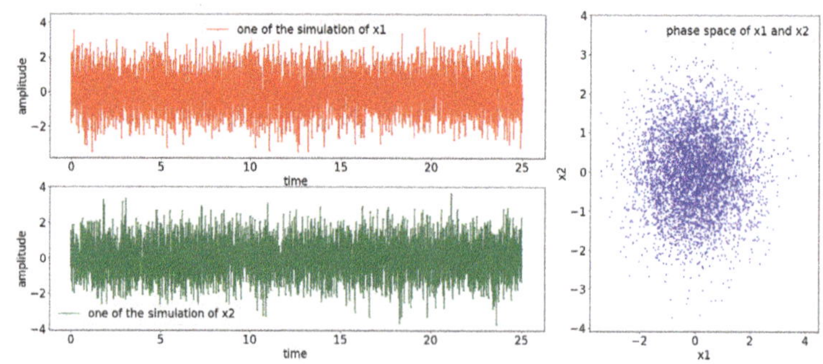

(**d**) nonlinear: large noise, noncouple

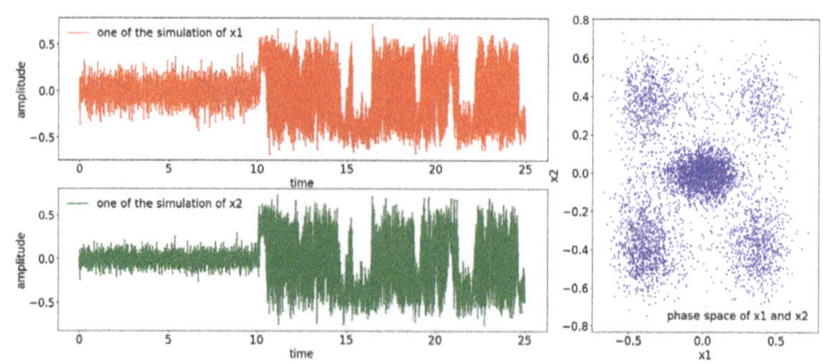

(**e**) nonlinear: small noise, couple

Figure 18. *Cont.*

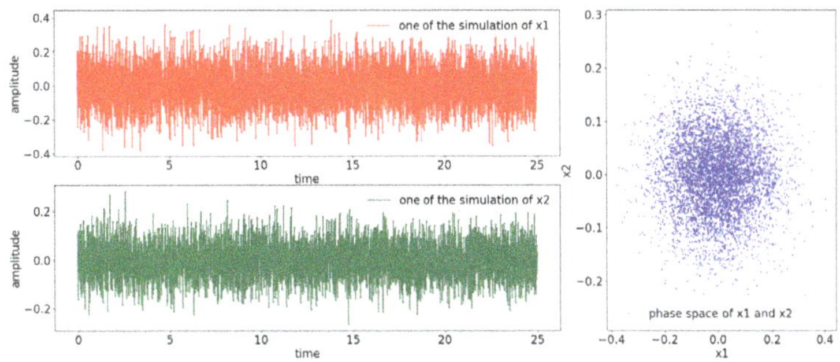

(**f**) nonlinear: small noise, noncouple

Figure 18. Result of simulation based on Equations (29) and (30) (refer to Figure 17 for graphical explanation of the process). The [top left, red] is the result of x_1; [bottom, green] shows the result of x_2; [right, blue] shows the phase space of x_1 and x_2. Note that the noncoupling in the context is referring to $H(\tau - 10) = 0$.

5.1. Granger Causality

From the GC analysis, the coupling from $x_2(t)$ to $x_1(t)$ cannot be captured well in it except for the [nonlinear: small noise] cases. This result is due to a similar reason as discussed in Section 4, i.e., the coupling between the signals is affected by a factor of 1.5 ($e^1 \times 0.55 \approx 1.5$). Therefore, the rest of the cases cannot show the significant contrast of the causality from [$x_2(t)$ to $x_1(t)$] as shown in Figure 19. Furthermore, referring to the time-varying GC, the bidirectional coupling/causality between $x_1(t)$ and $x_2(t)$ that occurs after 10 s are not able to capture all the coupling cases.

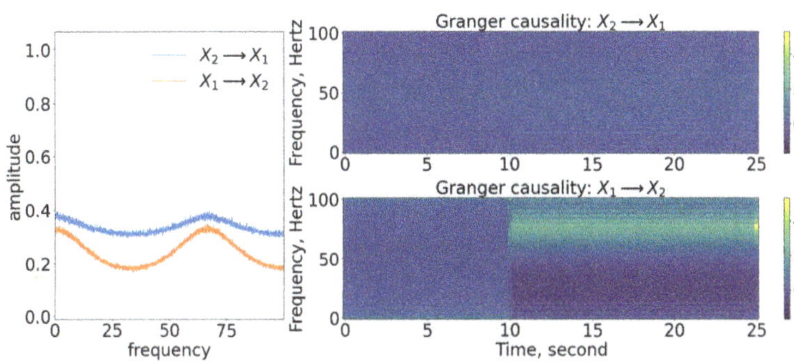

(**a**) linear: couple

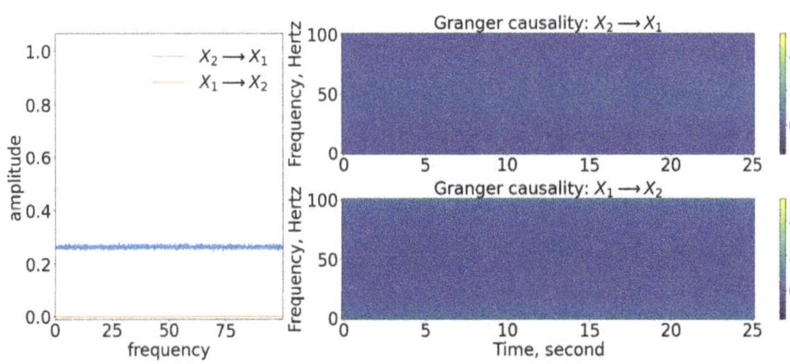

(**b**) linear: noncouple

Figure 19. *Cont.*

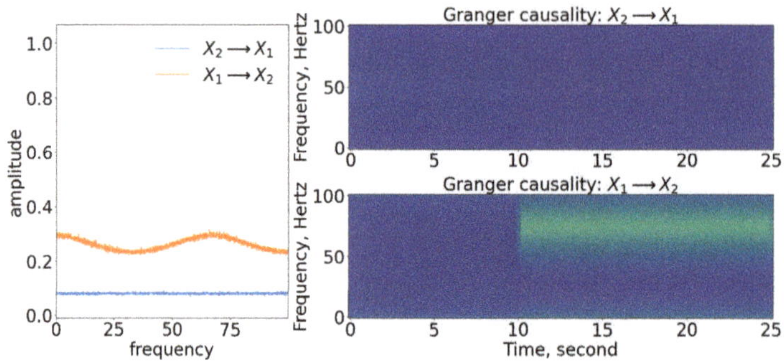

(**c**) nonlinear: large noise, couple

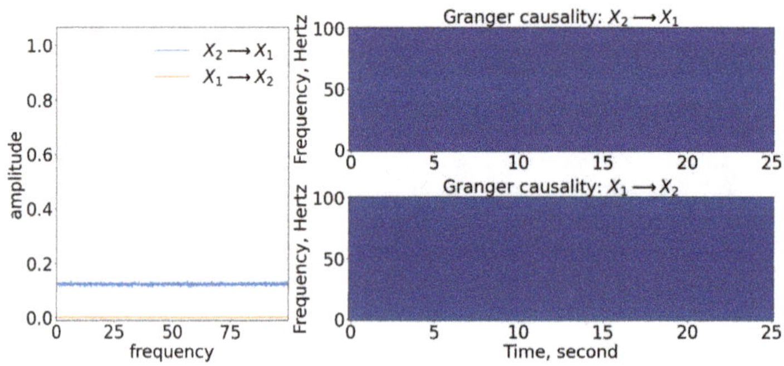

(**d**) nonlinear: large noise, noncouple

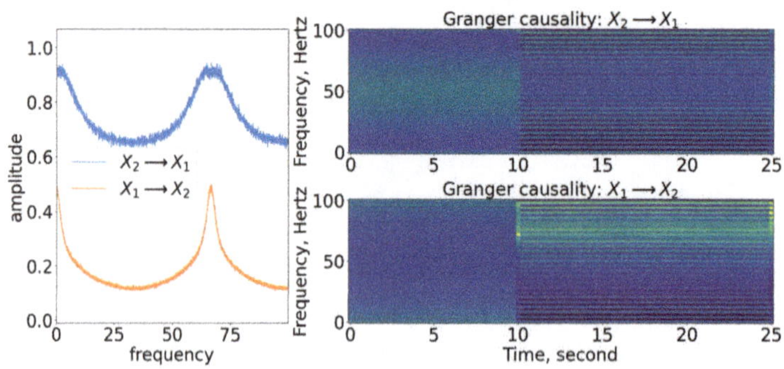

(**e**) nonlinear: small noise, couple

Figure 19. *Cont.*

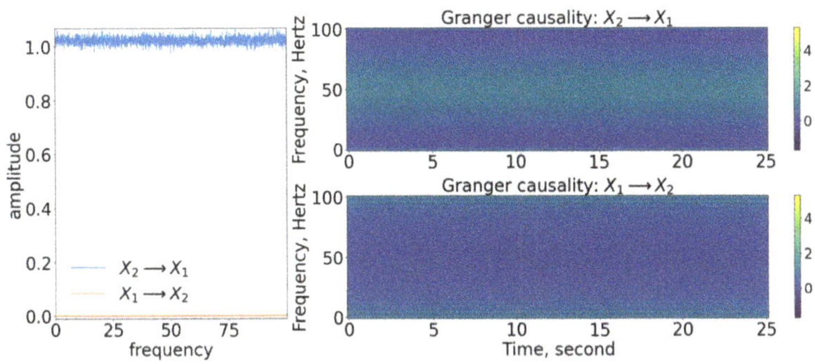

(**f**) nonlinear: small noise, noncouple

Figure 19. Result of the spectral and time-varying frequency of GC. Within each subfigure, the [left] shows the spectral (frequency domain) of GC, with [blue] showing that x_2 causes x_1 ($I_{x_2 \to x_1}$) and [orange] indicating that x_1 causes x_2 ($I_{x_1 \to x_2}$). The [top, right] figure shows that the time-varying frequency of GC of x_2 causes x_1 and [bottom, right] shows that x_1 causes x_2. The results shown are based on the expression in Equations (29) and (30). Refer to Figure 17 for the graphical explanation of the process. Note that the noncoupling is referring to $H(\tau - 10) = 0$ for all the cases.

5.2. Transfer Entropy

The results of TE shown in Figures 20 and 21 once again are quite similar to those shown in Section 4. The window sliding TE, evaluated with lag 0, shows that signal $x_2(t)$ causes $x_1(t)$ throughout the time, as shown in Figure 20. For the coupling cases, the amplitude of the TE changes when $x_1(t)$ feedbacks to $x_2(t)$ (after time 10 s). Similar to Section 4, the window sliding TE only shows that signal $x_1(t)$ is causing $x_2(t)$ when evaluated at lag 1 for the coupling cases shown in Figure 21. Hence, TE cannot fully capture the causality between the signals with just one lag.

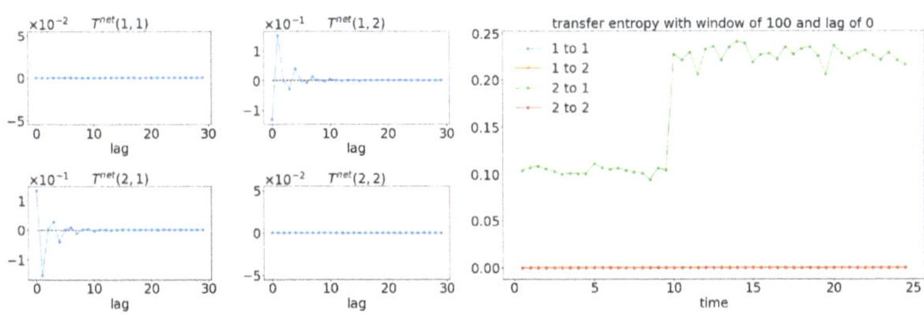

(**a**) linear: couple

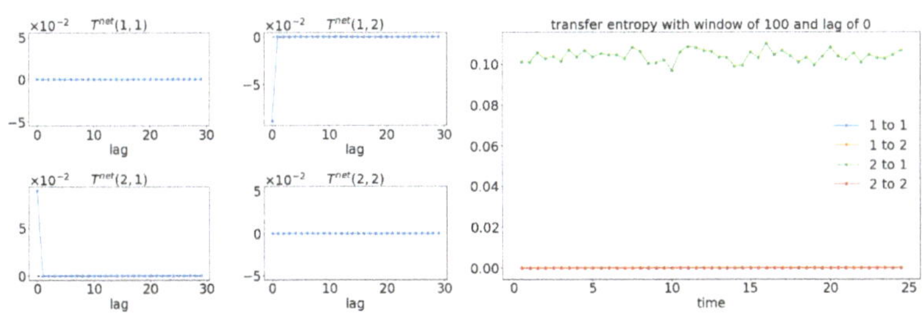

(**b**) linear: noncouple

Figure 20. *Cont.*

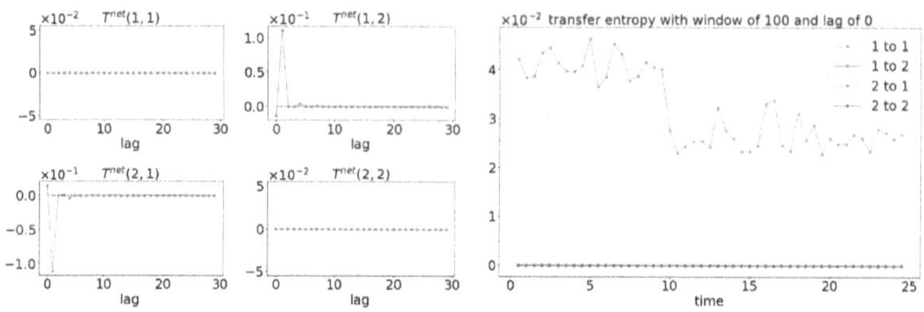

(c) nonlinear: large noise, couple

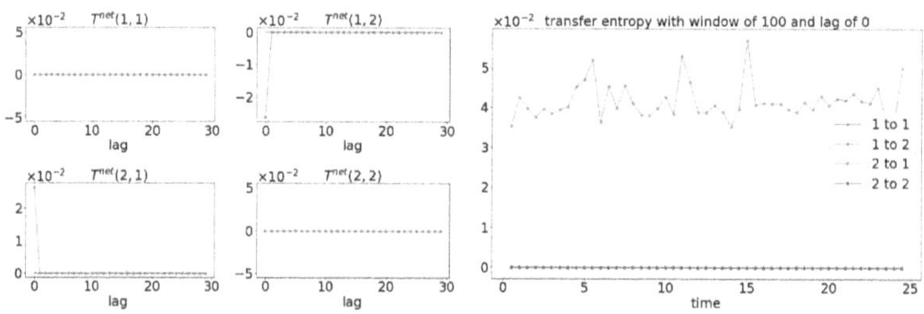

(d) nonlinear: large noise, noncouple

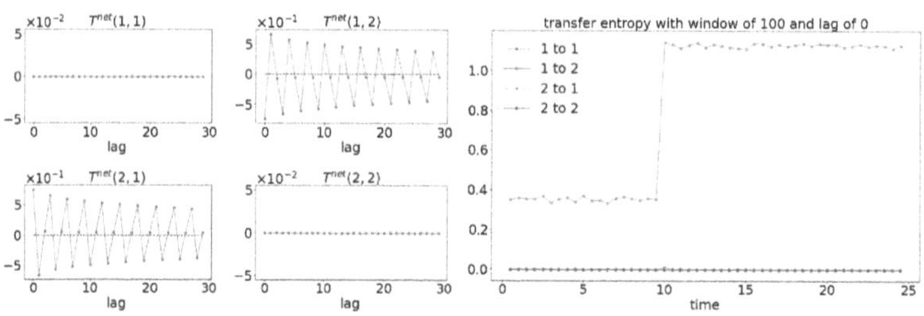

(e) nonlinear: small noise, couple

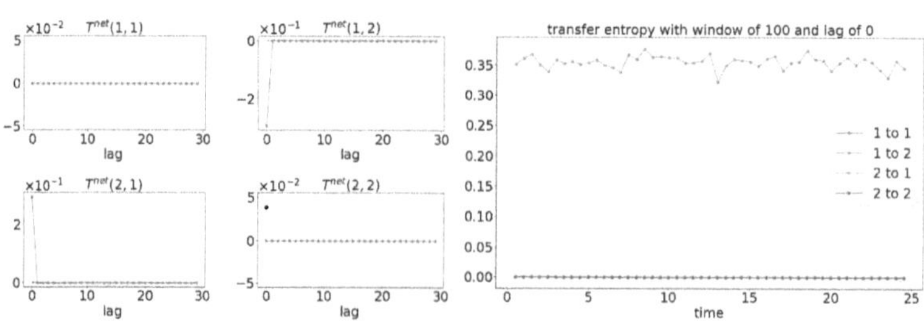

(f) nonlinear: small noise, noncouple

Figure 20. Result of the net TE and window sliding TE with the lag at 0. Within each subfigure, the [left, 4×4] figures show the net TE for the whole signals, while the [right] shows the window sliding TE. The results shown are based on the expression in Equations (29) and (30). Refer to Figure 17 for the graphical explanation of the process. Note that the noncoupling is referring to $H(\tau - 10) = 0$ for all the cases.

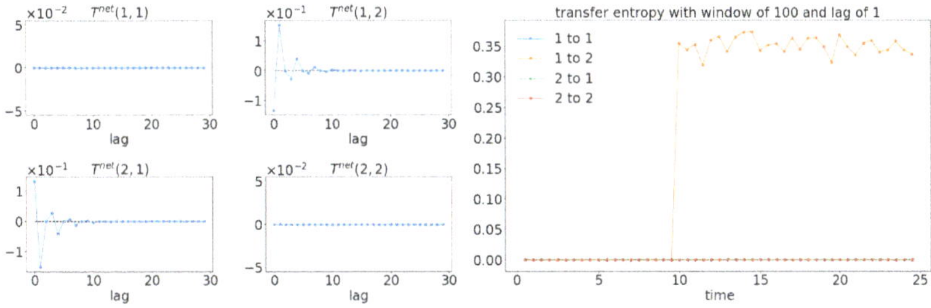

(**a**) linear: couple

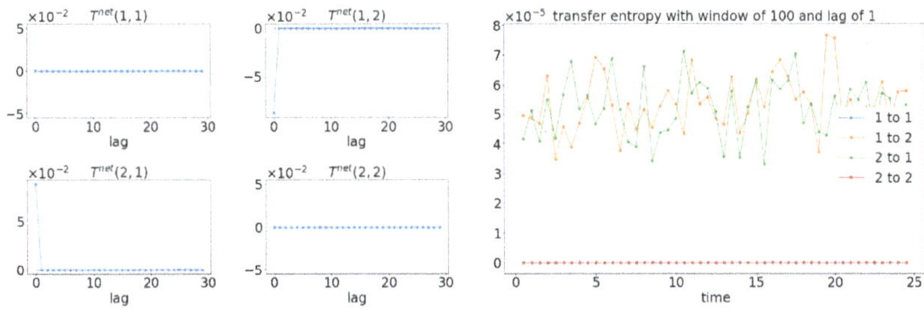

(**b**) linear: noncouple

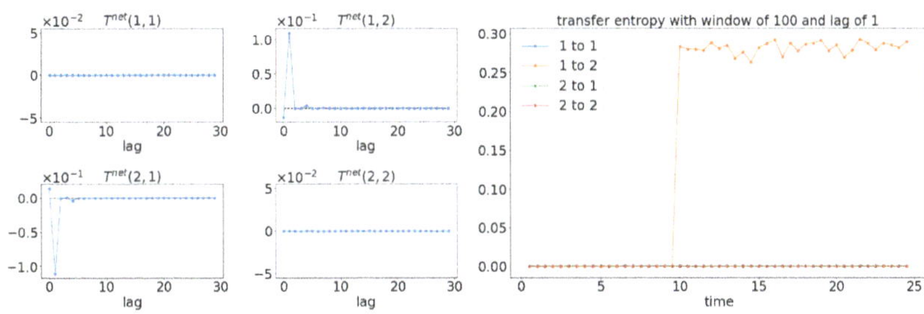

(**c**) nonlinear: large noise, couple

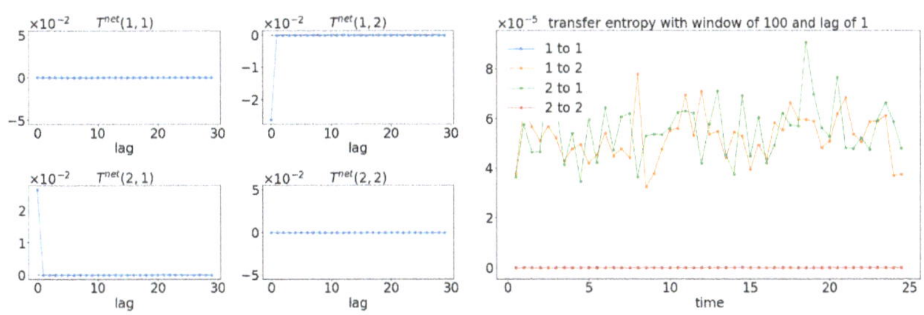

(**d**) nonlinear: large noise, noncouple

Figure 21. *Cont.*

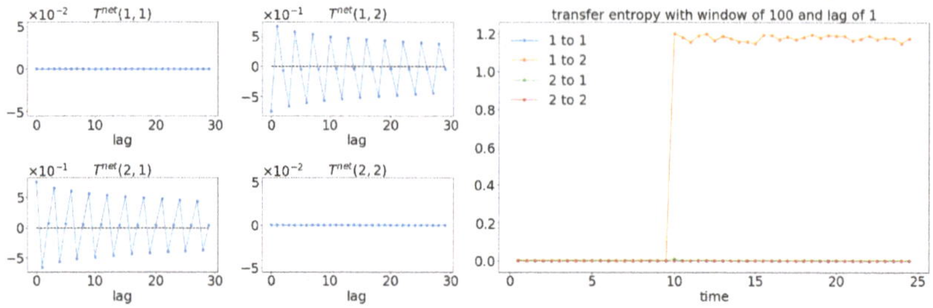

(**e**) nonlinear: small noise, couple

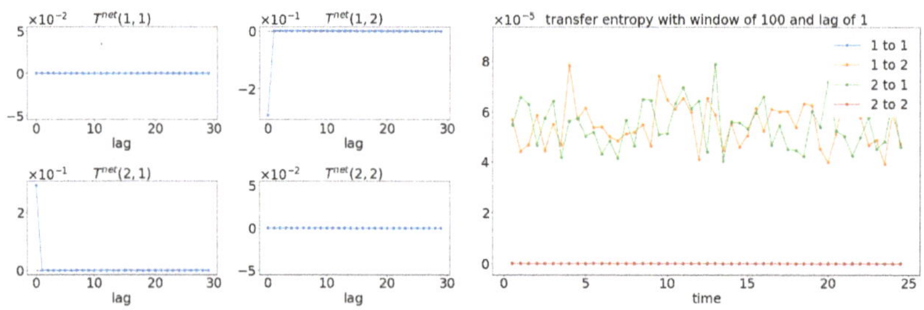

(**f**) nonlinear: small noise, noncouple

Figure 21. Result of the net TE and window sliding TE with the lag at 1. Within each subfigure, the [left, 4×4] figures show the net TE for the whole signals, while the [right] shows the window sliding TE. The results shown are based on the expression in Equations (29) and (30). Refer to Figure 17 for the graphical explanation of the process. Note that the noncoupling is referring to $H(\tau - 10) = 0$ for all the cases.

5.3. Information Rate Causality

The information rate causality analysis evaluates the causality through the change in probability distribution of an original signal after including another signal assuming it causes the original signal. The information rate causality is able to show the coupling among the signals well, as shown in Figures 22 and 23. Similar to Section 4, prior to time 10 s, the causality from signal $x_2(t)$ to $x_1(t)$ can be depicted with the presence of the peak of Γ^2 2 to 1. The peak presented at the beginning of the evaluation window suggests that the coupling occurs at lag 0. After 10 s, the mutual feedback between the signals is shown within the evaluation window of the information rate causality. This mutual causality between the signals is observed through the alternating oscillations of the peak occurrence in the information rate within the window. Hence, this can reflect well the underlying model of the signals. Note that this is different than Section 4, which is an interchange of unidirectional causality that has the feedback solely from one signal to the other without retaining information from itself.

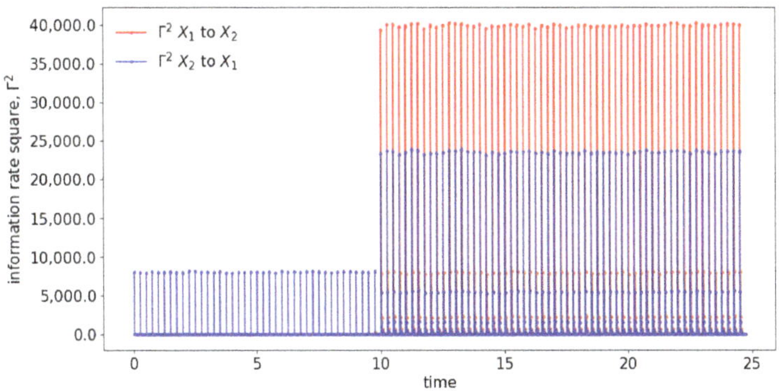

(**a**) linear: couple

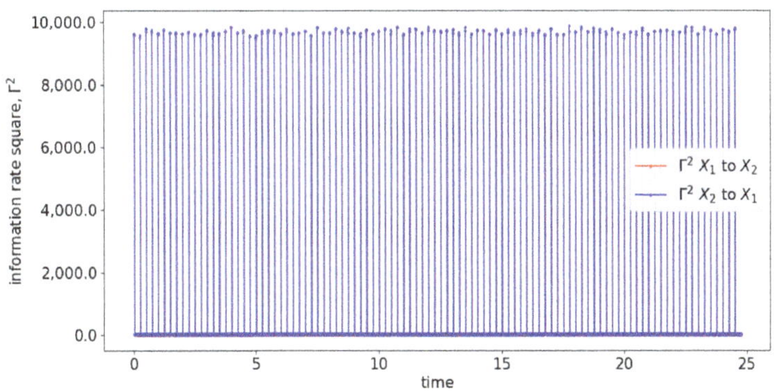

(**b**) linear: noncouple

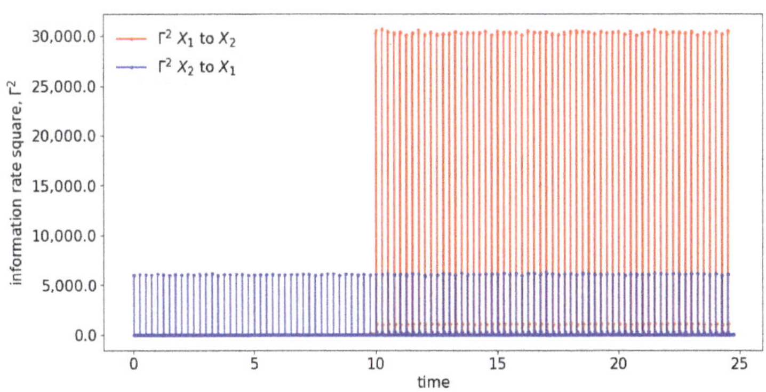

(**c**) nonlinear: large noise, couple

Figure 22. *Cont.*

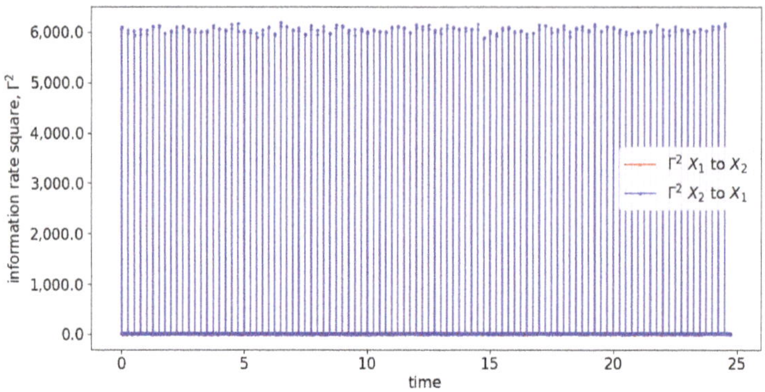

(**d**) nonlinear: large noise, noncouple

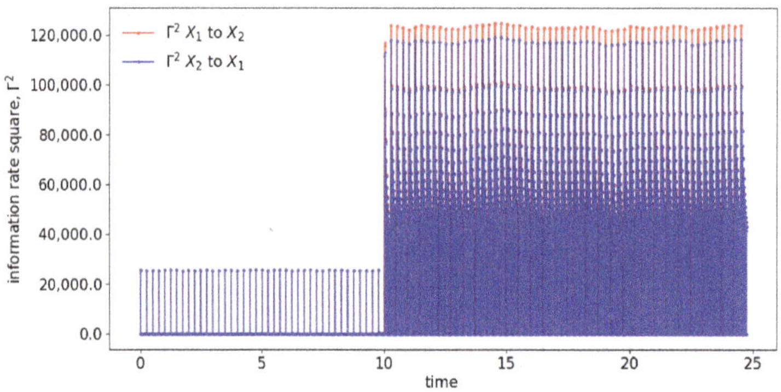

(**e**) nonlinear: small noise, couple

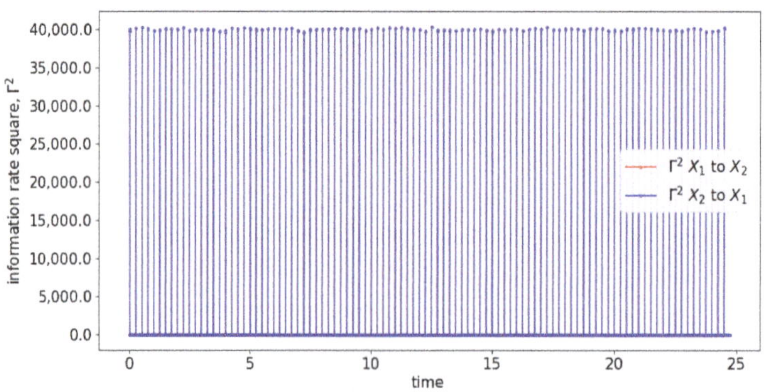

(**f**) nonlinear: small noise, noncouple

Figure 22. Result of information rate causality for Equations (29) and (30). Note that the bidirectional causation begins at 10 s. The results shown are based on the expression in Equations (29) and (30). Refer to Figure 17 for the graphical explanation of the process. Note that the noncoupling is referring to $H(\tau - 10) = 0$ for all the cases.

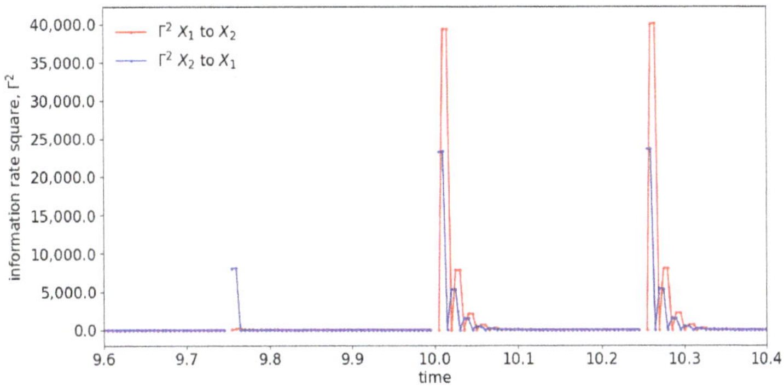

(**a**) linear: couple

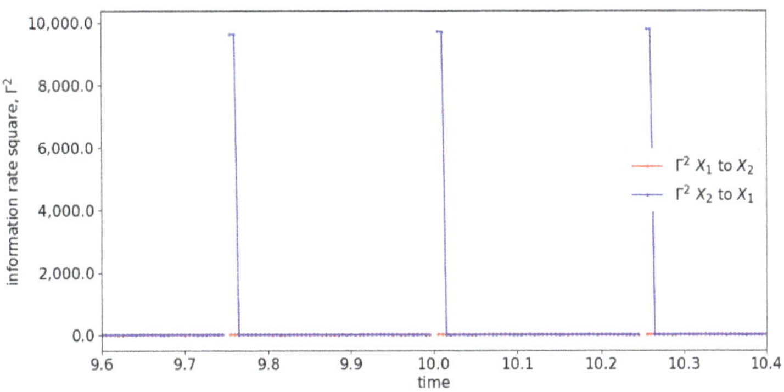

(**b**) linear: noncouple

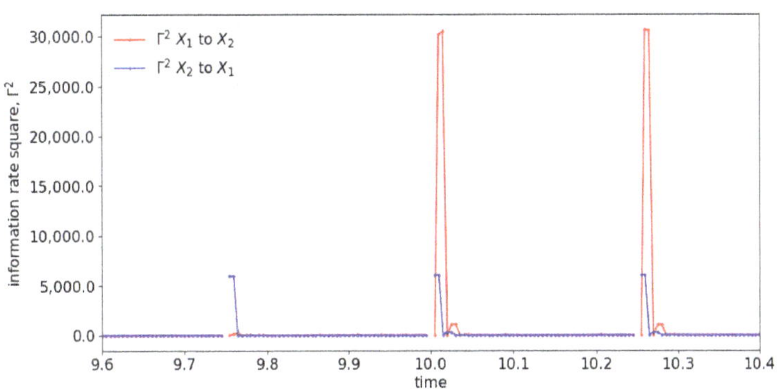

(**c**) nonlinear: large noise, couple

Figure 23. *Cont.*

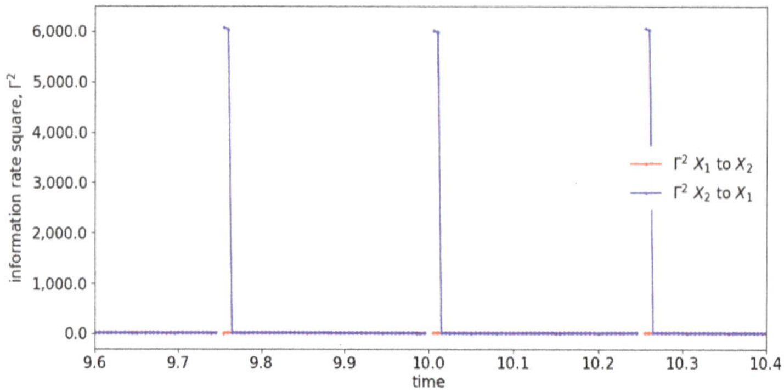

(**d**) nonlinear: large noise, noncouple

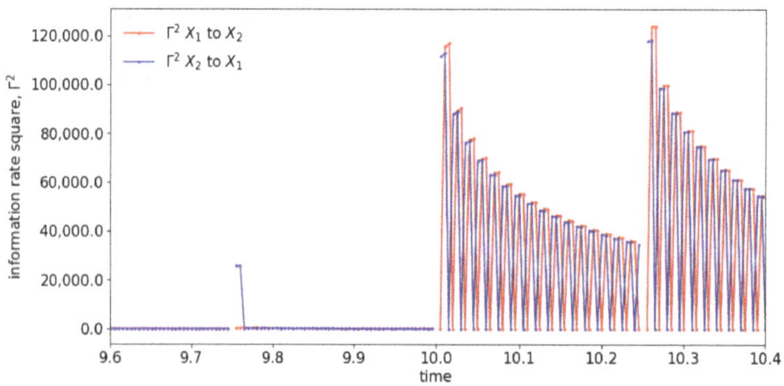

(**e**) nonlinear: small noise, couple

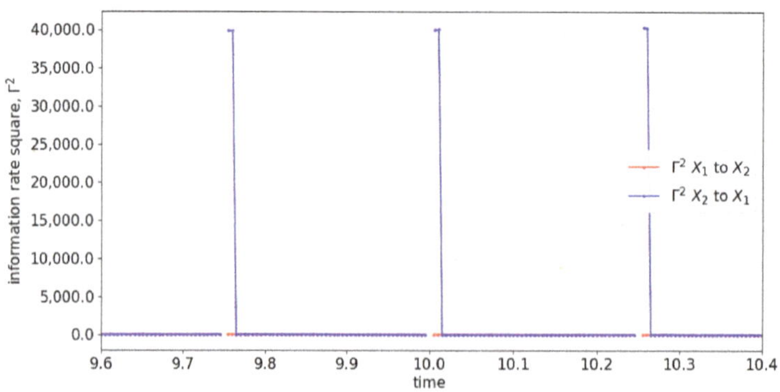

(**f**) nonlinear: small noise, noncouple

Figure 23. Zoom-in of Figure 22 for the information rate causality between 9.6 s and 10.4 s. Note that the bidirectional causation begins at 10 s. The results shown are based on the expression in Equations (29) and (30). Refer to Figure 17 for the graphical explanation of the process. Note that the noncoupling is referring to $H(\tau - 10) = 0$ for all the cases.

6. Conclusions

In this paper, we proposed an alternative causal analysis method to the popular GC and TE for causality quantification. Specifically, based on information rate, which measures the rate of temporal change in the time-dependent distribution, we developed a model-free, information-geometric measure of causality—information rate causality—that is suitable for analyzing numerically generated non-stationary, nonlinear data. To compare the GC, TE, and information rate causality, we applied the methods to numerical data generated by simulating different types of discrete autoregressive models which contain linear and nonlinear interactions. In Section 3, we showed that information rate causality performs equally well compared to GC in the standard linear stationary signals. Later, we showed that the GC did not perform well for non-stationary and/or nonlinear signals. Furthermore, it failed to capture mutual feedback between the signals, as shown specifically in Section 5 in all the coupling cases. TE performed slightly better than GC, since it is model-independent. However, the information on the lag is needed to properly evaluate the TE, as shown in Sections 4 and 5. In comparison with GC and TE, information rate causality has shown to be able to uncover the underlying mechanism of causality in the signals, such as the interchanging oscillatory feedback between the signals that is discussed in Section 5, which was not captured by either GC or TE.

While our results in this paper were obtained based on the interaction of two time series of different types of (non)linearity and (non)stationary, they have at least pointed out some limitations of GC and TE that can be resolved by employing information rate causality. It remains as future work to extend this work and to investigate a larger class of time series data, including real data such as EEG signals.

Supplementary Materials: The following supporting information can be downloaded at: https://www.mdpi.com/article/10.3390/e25050806/s1, Figure S1: Estimation of the joint probability distribution via histogram.

Author Contributions: Conceptualization, E.-j.K.; Methodology; E.-j.K., F.H. and H.J.C.; software, H.J.C.; Writing–original draft, H.J.C.; Writing–review & editing, E.-j.K.; Supervision, E.-j.K. and F.H. All authors have read and agreed to the published version of the manuscript.

Funding: E.-j.K.and F.H. are partly supported by EPSRC Grant EP/W036770/1.

Institutional Review Board Statement: Not applicable.

Data Availability Statement: The data that support the findings of this study are available from the corresponding author upon reasonable request.

Conflicts of Interest: The authors declare no conflict of interest.

Appendix A. Granger Causality

Appendix A.1. Autoregressive Process

Given a stochastic process ($x(t)$), it can be modelled through an autoregressive (AR) model with available/appropriate n number of observations from the process (e.g., AR(n) known as autoregressive of nth order). The general expression of the AR(n) model is expressed as Equation (A1).

$$x(t) = \sum_{i=1}^{n} \alpha_i x(t-i) + \epsilon(t), \tag{A1}$$

such that t is the time step, and α_i is the constant coefficient which suggested the weight of contribution from the ith past observation towards the process $x(t)$. $\epsilon(t)$ is the additive noise that has the variance Σ, which indicated the proportion of the external influence towards the process. Hence, a process that is strongly related to past observations will have small noise (e.g., small Σ).

Appendix A.2. Granger Causality: Time Domain

Given two stochastic processes ($x_1(t)$ and $x_2(t)$), they can be modelled independently, as shown in Equation (A1) and expressed as Equations (A2) and (A3).

$$x_1(t) = \sum_{i=1}^{n} a_i x_1(t-i) + \epsilon_1(t); \quad \text{(A2)}$$

$$x_2(t) = \sum_{i=1}^{n} c_i x_2(t-i) + \epsilon_2(t), \quad \text{(A3)}$$

such that $\epsilon_1(t)$ and $\epsilon_2(t)$ are the noises with variances of Σ_{11} and Σ_{22}, respectively; a_i and c_i are the constant parameters that suggested the fractions of the contribution from the past observations towards $x_1(t)$ and $x_2(t)$, respectively.

If there is a present causal relationship between two processes, they can be modelled with the past values from each other, as shown in Equations (A4) and (A5).

$$x_1(t) = \sum_{i=1}^{n} a_i x_1(t-i) + \sum_{i=1}^{n} b_i x_2(t-i) + \epsilon_1^*(t), \quad \text{(A4)}$$

$$x_2(t) = \sum_{i=1}^{n} c_i x_1(t-i) + \sum_{i=1}^{n} d_i x_2(t-i) + \epsilon_2^*(t). \quad \text{(A5)}$$

Here a_i, b_i, c_i, and d_i are the constants parameters. The noises ($\epsilon_1^*(t)$ and $\epsilon_2^*(t)$) would have the variance presented as the covariance matrix $\mathbf{\Sigma}$ shown in Equation (A6):

$$\mathbf{\Sigma} = \begin{bmatrix} \Sigma_{11}^* & \Sigma_{12}^* \\ \Sigma_{21}^* & \Sigma_{22}^* \end{bmatrix}. \quad \text{(A6)}$$

Similar to Equations (A2) and (A3), Σ_{11}^* and Σ_{22}^* are the variance of the $\epsilon_1^*(t)$ and $\epsilon_2^*(t)$, respectively, while $\Sigma_{12}^* = \Sigma_{21}^*$ is the covariance of the noises ($\epsilon_1^*(t)$ and $\epsilon_2^*(t)$).

The causal relationship between $x_1(t)$ and $x_2(t)$ can determined by evaluating the noises from Equations (A2) to (A5). For instance, $\Sigma_{11}^* < \Sigma_{11}$ would indicate that the predictability of $x_1(t)$ increases as the past information of $x_2(t)$ is included. Hence, this would suggest that there is a causal relationship from $x_2(t)$ to $x_1(t)$ which is known as GC ($x_2(t)$ Granger-causes $x_1(t)$, $F_{x_2 \to x_1}$). Similarly, $\Sigma_{22}^* < \Sigma_{22}$ would suggest $x_1(t)$ Granger-causes $x_2(t)$, $F_{x_1 \to x_2}$. The covariance of the noises $\Sigma_{12}^* = \Sigma_{21}^*$ would suggest that the processes are correlated by one another via a common external force that drives the processes; consequently, it shows an instantaneous causality ($F_{x_1 \leftrightarrow x_2}$).

The idea behind GC is to evaluate the total interdependence (also known as total causality index) between $x_1(t)$ and $x_2(t)$, which consists of two directional causalities ($F_{x_1 \to x_2}$ and $F_{x_2 \to x_1}$) and one instantaneous causality ($F_{x_1 \leftrightarrow x_2}$). The total interdependence between $x_1(t)$ and $x_2(t)$ is defined as Equation (A7).

$$F_{x_1 \cdot x_2} = \log \frac{\Sigma_{11}\Sigma_{22}}{|\mathbf{\Sigma}|} = \log \frac{\Sigma_{11}\Sigma_{22}}{\Sigma_{11}^*\Sigma_{22}^* - (\Sigma_{12}^*)^2} = F_{x_1 \to x_2} + F_{x_2 \to x_1} + F_{x_1 \leftrightarrow x_2}, \quad \text{(A7)}$$

such that $|\mathbf{\Sigma}|$ is the determinant of the covariance matrix $\mathbf{\Sigma}$. If either one of the signals Granger-causes or correlates to one another, the value of $F_{x_1 \cdot x_2} > 0$ because the $\Sigma_{11}^* < \Sigma_{11}$, $\Sigma_{22}^* < \Sigma_{22}$, or $\Sigma_{12}^* \neq 0$. On the contrary, $F_{x_1 \cdot x_2} = 0$ indicates there is no GC relationship and correlation between the signals.

The directional causalities and instantaneous causality are defined as Equations (A8) to (A10).

$$F_{x_1 \to x_2} = \log \frac{\Sigma_{11}}{\Sigma_{11}^*}, \quad \text{(A8)}$$

$$F_{x_2 \to x_1} = \log \frac{\Sigma_{22}}{\Sigma_{22}^*}, \quad \text{(A9)}$$

$$F_{x_1 \leftrightarrow x_2} = \log \frac{\Sigma_{11}^*\Sigma_{22}^*}{|\mathbf{\Sigma}|}. \quad \text{(A10)}$$

Similar to Equation (A7), the individual causalities from Equations (A8) to (A10) have the range of $[0, \infty)$, with $F_{(\ldots)} = 0$ indicating the absence of causality relationship.

Appendix A.3. Granger Causality: Frequency Domain

The spectral of the GC is studied at the frequency domain of the AR model. Unlike the time domain, the frequency domain of GC required both the constant parameters and the variance of the noises for the evaluation. To understand the formulation, the lag operator (L^k) is used and defined as Equation (A11).

$$L^k x(t) = x(t-k). \tag{A11}$$

Hence, by applying the lag operator expressed in Equation (A11) to Equations (A4) and (A5), they can be rewritten as

$$\begin{cases} x_1(t) &= (\sum_{i=1}^{n} a_i L^i)x_1(t) + (\sum_{i=1}^{n} b_i L^i)x_2(t) + \epsilon_1^*(t), \\ x_2(t) &= (\sum_{i=1}^{n} c_i L^i)x_1(t) + (\sum_{i=1}^{n} d_i L^i)x_2(t) + \epsilon_2^*(t), \end{cases} \tag{A12}$$

$$\begin{cases} (1 - \sum_{i=1}^{n} a_i L^i)x_1(t) + (-\sum_{i=1}^{n} b_i L^i)x_2(t) = \epsilon_1^*(t), \\ (-\sum_{i=1}^{n} c_i L^i)x_1(t) + (1 - \sum_{i=1}^{n} d_i L^i)x_2(t) = \epsilon_2^*(t), \end{cases} \tag{A13}$$

$$\begin{cases} \begin{bmatrix} a(L) & b(L) \\ c(L) & d(L) \end{bmatrix} \begin{bmatrix} x_1(t) \\ x_2(t) \end{bmatrix} = \begin{bmatrix} \epsilon_1^*(t) \\ \epsilon_2^*(t) \end{bmatrix}, \end{cases} \tag{A14}$$

$$\text{Fourier transform} \rightarrow \begin{cases} \begin{bmatrix} a(\omega) & b(\omega) \\ c(\omega) & d(\omega) \end{bmatrix} \begin{bmatrix} x_1(\omega) \\ x_2(\omega) \end{bmatrix} = \begin{bmatrix} \epsilon_1^*(\omega) \\ \epsilon_2^*(\omega) \end{bmatrix} \end{cases} \equiv \boldsymbol{A}(\omega)\boldsymbol{x}(\omega) = \boldsymbol{\epsilon}^*(\omega), \tag{A15}$$

$$\begin{cases} \begin{bmatrix} x_1(\omega) \\ x_2(\omega) \end{bmatrix} = \begin{bmatrix} a(\omega) & b(\omega) \\ c(\omega) & d(\omega) \end{bmatrix}^{-1} \begin{bmatrix} \epsilon_1^*(\omega) \\ \epsilon_2^*(\omega) \end{bmatrix} = \begin{bmatrix} H_{11}(\omega) & H_{12}(\omega) \\ H_{21}(\omega) & H_{22}(\omega) \end{bmatrix} \begin{bmatrix} \epsilon_1^*(\omega) \\ \epsilon_2^*(\omega) \end{bmatrix}, \end{cases} \tag{A16}$$

$$\begin{cases} \boldsymbol{x}(\omega) = \boldsymbol{H}(\omega)\boldsymbol{\epsilon}^*(\omega), \end{cases} \tag{A17}$$

such that $\boldsymbol{A}(\omega)$ is known as the coefficient matrix. The elements in the coefficient matrix are expressed as

$$a(\omega) = 1 - \sum_{i=1}^{n} a_i e^{-j\omega i}, \tag{A18}$$

$$b(\omega) = -\sum_{i=1}^{n} b_i e^{-j\omega i}, \tag{A19}$$

$$c(\omega) = -\sum_{i=1}^{n} c_i e^{-j\omega i}, \tag{A20}$$

$$d(\omega) = 1 - \sum_{i=1}^{n} d_i e^{-j\omega i}, \tag{A21}$$

which is obtained via the Fourier transform from the time domain to the frequency domain. Note that j is the imaginary unit while ω is the angular frequency that is defined as $\omega = 2\pi f, f =$ frequency. The matrix $\boldsymbol{H}(\omega)$ is known as the transfer matrix. The spectral matrix ($\boldsymbol{S}(\omega)$) can be obtained by proper ensemble averaging of Equation (A17), which is expressed as Equation (A22):

$$\boldsymbol{S}(\omega) = \begin{bmatrix} S_{11}(\omega) & S_{12}(\omega) \\ S_{21}(\omega) & S_{22}(\omega) \end{bmatrix} = \left\langle \boldsymbol{x}(\omega)\boldsymbol{x}^\dagger(\omega) \right\rangle = \boldsymbol{H}(\omega)\boldsymbol{\Sigma}\boldsymbol{H}^\dagger(\omega), \tag{A22}$$

such that $\langle\cdot\rangle$ is defined as an ensemble average, and $\dagger$ is denoted as the complex conjugate transpose of a matrix. The element $S_{nm|n=m}$ is known as auto spectra and $S_{nm|n\neq m}$ is known as cross spectra. Similar to Equation (A7), the total interdependence between $x_1(\omega)$ and $x_2(\omega)$ is defined as Equation (A23), which consists of two directional causalities ($I_{x_1\rightarrow x_2}$ and $I_{x_2\rightarrow x_1}$) and one instantaneous causality ($I_{x_1\leftrightarrow x_2}$).

$$I_{x_1\cdot x_2} = \log\frac{S_{11}(\omega)S_{22}(\omega)}{|\boldsymbol{S}(\boldsymbol{\omega})|} = I_{x_1\rightarrow x_2} + I_{x_2\rightarrow x_1} + I_{x_1\leftrightarrow x_2}, \tag{A23}$$

such that $|\boldsymbol{S}(\boldsymbol{\omega})|$ is the determinant of spectral matrix $\boldsymbol{S}(\boldsymbol{\omega})$. The individual causalities are defined as

$$I_{x_1\rightarrow x_2} = \log\frac{S_{22}(\omega)}{\hat{H}_{22}(\omega)\Sigma_{22}\hat{H}^*_{22}(\omega)}, \tag{A24}$$

$$I_{x_2\rightarrow x_1} = \log\frac{S_{11}(\omega)}{\tilde{H}_{11}(\omega)\Sigma_{11}\tilde{H}^*_{11}(\omega)}, \tag{A25}$$

$$I_{x_1\leftrightarrow x_2} = \log\frac{\left(\tilde{H}_{11}(\omega)\Sigma_{11}\tilde{H}^*_{11}(\omega)\right)\left(\hat{H}_{22}(\omega)\Sigma_{22}\hat{H}^*_{22}(\omega)\right)}{|\boldsymbol{S}(\boldsymbol{\omega})|}. \tag{A26}$$

Here $\hat{H}_{22}(\omega) = H_{22}(\omega) + \frac{\Sigma_{12}}{\Sigma_{22}}H_{21}(\omega)$ and $\tilde{H}_{11}(\omega) = H_{11}(\omega) + \frac{\Sigma_{12}}{\Sigma_{11}}H_{12}(\omega)$; $*$ is denoted as the complex conjugate of the element [17].

As shown in Equations (A23) to (A26), the elements from the transfer matrix and covariance matrix of the noises are needed to evaluate the GC in the frequency domain. The elements can be obtained via the constant parameters of Equations (A4) and (A5), which can be estimated via Yule–Walker equations [18,40]. This approach of evaluating GC through the knowledge of constant parameters is known as the parametric method; it has the disadvantage that the information of lags (number of past values) is needed when estimating the constant parameters. Alternatively, the non-parametric method conducts the GC analysis by directly decomposing the spectral matrix ($\boldsymbol{S}(\boldsymbol{\omega})$) into the transfer matrix ($\boldsymbol{H}(\boldsymbol{\omega})$) and the covariance matrix of the noises ($\boldsymbol{\Sigma}$). The decomposition is conducted via a recursive algorithm known as the Wilson algorithm [18,35]. The derivation of the Wilson algorithm will be discussed in the next section.

Appendix A.4. Wilson Algorithm

The spectral matrix $\boldsymbol{S}(\boldsymbol{\omega})$ that is defined in the range $[-\pi,\pi]$ is known as the spectral density function. It can be expressed as Equation (A27).

$$\boldsymbol{S}(\boldsymbol{\omega}) = \sum_{i=-\infty}^{\infty} C_i e^{j\omega i}, \tag{A27}$$

$$C_i = \frac{1}{2\pi}\int_{-\pi}^{\pi} \boldsymbol{S}(\boldsymbol{\omega})e^{-j\omega i}\, d\omega, \tag{A28}$$

such that the C_k is known as the correlation coefficient obtained via inverse Fourier transform Equation (A28).

Following Wilson's factorization theorem (theorem 1.1 in [35]), the spectral density function is the product of generating function $\psi(e^{j\omega})$ with its complex conjugate transpose that is defined on a unit circle $|z| = 1$:

$$\boldsymbol{S}(\boldsymbol{\omega}) = \psi(e^{j\omega})\psi(e^{j\omega})^{\dagger}, \tag{A29}$$

$$\psi(e^{j\omega}) = \sum_{i=0}^{\infty} A_i e^{j\omega i}, \tag{A30}$$

$$A_i = \frac{1}{2\pi}\int_{-\pi}^{\pi} \psi(e^{j\omega})e^{-j\omega i}\, d\omega. \tag{A31}$$

Here A_k is the moving average coefficient, which can be obtained by inverse Fourier transform as expressed in Equation (A31). With Equation (A30) being holomorphic extended to the inner of the unit circle ($|z| < 1$), it can be rewritten as Equation (A32).

$$\psi(e^{j\omega}) = \psi(z) = \sum_{i=0}^{\infty} A_i z^i = A_0 + \sum_{i=1}^{\infty} A_i z^i. \tag{A32}$$

$$\therefore S(z) = \psi(z)\psi(z)^\dagger = \left(\sum_{i=0}^{\infty} A_i z^i\right)\left(\sum_{i'=0}^{\infty} {A_{i'}}^\top z^{-i'}\right) = \sum_{i=0}^{\infty}\sum_{i'=0}^{\infty} A_i {A_{i'}}^\top z^{i-i'}. \tag{A33}$$

Comparing Equations (A22) and (A33) when $z = e^{j\omega} = 0$:

$$S(0) = \psi(0)\psi(0)^\dagger = H(0)\Sigma H^\dagger(0) = I\Sigma I^\top = \Sigma = A_0 {A_0}^\top, \tag{A34}$$

such that I is the identity matrix, and $[\cdot]^\top$ indicates the transpose of the matrix. Since ${A_0}^{-1} A_0 {A_0}^\top {A_0}^{-\top} = I$, the transfer matrix $H(\omega)$ can be obtained via

$$S(z) = \psi(z) I \psi(z)^\dagger = \psi(z) {A_0}^{-1} A_0 {A_0}^\top {A_0}^{-\top} \psi(z)^\dagger = \psi(z) {A_0}^{-1} \Sigma {A_0}^{-\top} \psi(z)^\dagger, \tag{A35}$$

$$\therefore H(\omega) = \psi(e^{j\omega}) {A_0}^{-1},\ H(\omega)^\dagger = {A_0}^{-\top} \psi(e^{j\omega})^\dagger. \tag{A36}$$

As shown, the transfer matrix $H(\omega)$ and covariance matrix of the noises Σ can be obtained once the generating function $\psi(e^{j\omega})$ is known. G.T. Wilson introduces the solution of $\psi(e^{j\omega})$ by iteration along with the plus operator ($[\cdot]^+$) of a given spectral density function $f(\omega)$, as expressed in Equations (A37) to (A39).

$$f(\omega) = \sum_{i=\infty}^{\infty} \beta_i e^{j\omega i},\ \beta_i = \frac{1}{2\pi}\int_{-\pi}^{\pi} f(\omega) e^{-j\omega i} d\omega, \tag{A37}$$

$$[f(\omega)]^+ = 0.5\beta_0 + \sum_{i=1}^{\infty} \beta_i e^{j\omega i}, \tag{A38}$$

$$\psi_{i+1} = \psi_i \underbrace{\left[\psi_i^{-1} S\left(\psi_i^{-1}\right)^\dagger + I\right]^+}_{[f(\omega)]^+}. \tag{A39}$$

From the previous work [35], it has been shown that the iteration of Equation (A39) will be uniquely converged if the initial generating function (ψ_0) is an upper triangle of the matrix which can be obtained via Cholesky factorization.

Appendix B. Transfer Entropy

Given a stochastic process (X), the average information/uncertainty needed to describe the process can be defined by Shannon entropy (I_X) and expressed as Equation (A40).

$$I_X = -\sum_{x\in X} p(x)\log_2 p(x), \tag{A40}$$

such that $p(x)$ is the discrete probability distribution at state x. The unit of the Shannon entropy varies with the base of the logarithm (i.e., the unit is bits when the logarithm is based 2) [28,41,42].

For the situation of two stochastic processes (X and Y), the statistical dependency of these two processes can be evaluated via Mutual Information (MI) and defined as Equation (A41).

$$MI = \sum_{x\in X, y\in Y} p(x,y)\log_2 \frac{p(x,y)}{p(x)p(y)}. \tag{A41}$$

The definition of MI is derived from the Kullback–Leibler (KL) divergence. KL divergence measures the differences between two probability distributions ($p(x)$ and $q(x)$) non-symmetrically; it is defined as Equation (A42) [37].

$$D_{KL}(P||Q) = \sum_{x \in X} p(x) \log_2 \frac{p(x)}{q(x)}. \tag{A42}$$

Hence, MI measures the difference between the marginal probability distribution ($p(x)p(y)$) and joint probability distribution ($p(x,y)$) that quantifies the common information shared between the processes. Therefore, the MI will be zero when both processes are statistically independent and no common information is presented between the processes as the joint probability distribution will be equal to the product of marginal probability distribution ($p(x,y) = p(x)p(y) \rightarrow MI = \sum_{x \in X, y \in Y} p(x,y) \log_2 1 = 0$) [19,37].

As discussed above, MI only measured the commonly shared information, which subsequently does not indicate the directional flow of information. On the contrary, Transfer Entropy (TE) is able to reveal the directional flow of information by considering the conditional probability $p(\cdot|\cdot)$ and is defined as Equation (A43).

$$TE_{Y \rightarrow X} = \sum_{x \in X, y \in Y} p(x_{n+1}, x_n^{(k)}, y_n^{(l)}) \log_2 \frac{p(x_{n+1}|x_n^{(k)}, y_n^{(l)})}{p(x_{n+1}|x_n^{(k)})}, \tag{A43}$$

such that x_{n+1} is the state of X at the $(n+1)$-th moment; $x_n^{(k)}$ is the state at n-th moment of X consists of k previous states of X; $y_n^{(l)}$ is the state at n-th moment of Y consisting of l previous states. Note that the previous states of k and l are arbitrary and depend on the interest of the study. For instance, given a collective observed stochastic process $X = (x_1, x_2, \ldots, x_{10})$, $x_8^{(2)} = (x_n, x_m) \; |n,m \in [1,8] \rightarrow (x_1, x_2)$ or (x_3, x_8), etc. Hence, TE measures the additional information needed for the realization of X at $(n+1)$ from Y with the assumption that X is independent of Y. If Y does not affect the future evolution of X, then $p(x_{n+1}|x_n^{(k)}, y_n^{(l)}) = p(x_{n+1}|x_n^{(k)})$ and subsequently $T_{Y \rightarrow X} = 0$. Using the general definition of conditional probability distribution ($p(x|y) = \frac{p(x,y)}{p(y)}$), Equation (A43) can be rewritten as Equation (A44) [19].

$$TE_{Y \rightarrow X} = \sum_{x \in X, y \in Y} p(x_{n+1}, x_n^{(k)}, y_n^{(l)}) \log_2 \frac{p(x_{n+1}, x_n^{(k)}, y_n^{(l)}) p(x_n^{(k)})}{p(x_{n+1}, x_n^{(k)}) p(x_n^{(k)}, y_n^{(l)})}. \tag{A44}$$

Appendix C. Information Rate, Information Length, and Information Rate Causality

In a dimensionless statistical manifold, the distance of two probability distributions is defined by their differences. One of the distances is discussed in Appendix B; this is KL divergence/relative entropy with the expression as Equation (A42). As mentioned, the KL divergence measured the differences non-symmetrically, and hence it is hardly considered as a metric distance because it does not satisfy the triangle inequality [32]. The symmetric version of KL divergence is introduced as Jensen divergence and expressed as Equation (A45). The square root of Jensen divergence has shown to be a metric distance that satisfies triangle inequality [32,43,44].

$$D_{JS} = \frac{1}{2}[D_{KL}(P||Q) + D_{KL}(Q||P)]. \tag{A45}$$

As depicted in Equations (A42) and (A45), the distance is measured at the ending points (e.g., initial and final probabilities), and hence it is not path-dependent. The path-dependent distance can be evaluated with the *information length* ($\mathcal{L}$), which is computed through the knowledge of *information rate* (Γ). The detailed discussion and derivation are shown in [32]. An essential brief discussion and derivation of Γ and $\mathcal{L}$ are shown in the next part.

Consider a time-dependent probability distribution ($p(x,t)$) that evolves over time. For instance, $p(x,t)$ changes to $p(x,t+dt)$ with the small time step of $dt \rightarrow 0$. This evolution of difference can be expressed as Equation (A46) with the dt as the leading order.

$$\lim_{dt\rightarrow 0} \frac{1}{(dt)^2} D_{KL}(p(x,t+dt)||p(x,t)) = \lim_{dt\rightarrow 0} \frac{1}{(dt)^2} D_{KL}(p(x,t)||p(x,t+dt)) = \lim_{dt\rightarrow 0} \frac{1}{(dt)^2} D_{JS}, \tag{A46}$$

$$\lim_{dt\rightarrow 0} \frac{1}{(dt)^2} \int dx\, p(x,t+dt) \ln \frac{p(x,t+dt)}{p(x,t)}, \tag{A47}$$

$$\lim_{dt\rightarrow 0} \frac{1}{(dt)^2} \int dx \left[p(x,t) + (dt)\partial_t p + \frac{1}{2}(dt)^2(\partial_{tt} p) + \mathcal{O}((dt)^3)\right]$$

$$\ln\left[1 + \frac{(dt)\partial_t p}{p(x,t)} + \frac{1}{2}\frac{(dt)^2(\partial_{tt} p)}{p(x,t)} + \mathcal{O}((dt)^3)\right], \tag{A48}$$

$$\lim_{dt\rightarrow 0} \frac{1}{(dt)^2} \int dx \left[p(x,t) + (dt)\partial_t p\right]\left[\frac{(dt)\partial_t p}{p(x,t)} - \frac{1}{2}\left[\frac{(dt)\partial_t p}{p(x,t)}\right]^2\right], \tag{A49}$$

$$\lim_{dt\rightarrow 0} \frac{1}{(dt)^2} \int dx \left[p(x,t)\frac{(dt)\partial_t p}{p(x,t)} - \frac{1}{2}\left[\frac{(dt)\partial_t p}{p(x,t)}\right]^2 p(x,t) + (dt)\partial_t p\frac{(dt)\partial_t p}{p(x,t)} - \frac{1}{2}\left[\frac{(dt)\partial_t p}{p(x,t)}\right]^2 (dt)\partial_t p\right], \tag{A50}$$

$$\lim_{dt\rightarrow 0} \frac{1}{(dt)^2} \int dx \left[(dt)\partial_t p - \frac{1}{2}\frac{(dt)^2(\partial_t p)^2}{p(x,t)} + \frac{(dt)^2(\partial_t p)^2}{p(x,t)} - \frac{1}{2}\frac{(dt)^3(\partial_t p)^3}{(p(x,t))^2}\right], \tag{A51}$$

$$\lim_{dt\rightarrow 0} \frac{1}{(dt)^2} \int dx \left[(dt)\partial_t p + \frac{1}{2}\frac{(dt)^2(\partial_t p)^2}{p(x,t)} - \frac{1}{2}\frac{(dt)^3(\partial_t p)^3}{(p(x,t))^2}\right], \tag{A52}$$

$$\lim_{dt\rightarrow 0} 0 \int dx \frac{\partial_t p}{dt} + \int dx \frac{1}{2}\frac{(\partial_t p)^2}{p(x,t)} - 0 \int dx \frac{1}{2}\frac{(dt)(\partial_t p)^3}{(p(x,t))^2}, \tag{A53}$$

$$\therefore \lim_{dt\rightarrow 0} \frac{1}{(dt)^2} D_{JS} = \frac{1}{2}\int dx\, p(x,t)(\partial_t \ln p(x,t))^2 \equiv \frac{1}{2}\Gamma^2(t), \tag{A54}$$

$$\because \int dx\, \partial_t p(x,t) = \int dx\, \partial_{tt} p(x,t) = 0 \because \int dx\, p(x,t) = 1, \tag{A55}$$

$$\therefore \Gamma^2(t) = \int dx\, p(x,t)[\partial_t \ln p(x,t)]^2 = 4\int dx \left[\partial_t \sqrt{p(x,t)}\right]^2 \tag{A56}$$

Note that Taylor series is implemented in Equation (A48) and Mercator series is used in Equation (A49). The final result $\Gamma(t)$ is defined as the information rate which measures the rate of the statistical change (e.g., due to the new input of information) from one state to another. Hence, the total statistical change in $p(x,t)$ or the total path-dependent distance of $p(x,t)$ that evolves through the time is expressed as Equation (A57) and defined as information length ($\mathcal{L}$).

$$\mathcal{L} = \int dt\, \Gamma(t). \tag{A57}$$

To accommodate the computation, the continuous differentiation ($\frac{df(t)}{dt}$, $\frac{\partial f(x,t)}{\partial t}$) and integration ($\int dt\, f(t)$, $\int \partial t\, f(x,t)$) are discretized, as shown in Equations (A58) to (A61).

$$\frac{df(t)}{dt} = \frac{f(t+\Delta t) - f(t)}{\Delta t}, \tag{A58}$$

$$\frac{\partial f(x,t)}{\partial t} = \frac{f(x,t+\Delta t) - f(x,t)}{\Delta t}, \tag{A59}$$

$$\int dt\, f(t) = \sum_{t_i=0}^{N} \Delta t\, f(t_i),\ \Delta t = t_{i+1} - t_i,\ N \in \mathbb{R} \tag{A60}$$

$$\int \partial t\, f(x,t) = \sum_{t_i=0}^{N} \Delta t\, f(x,t_i),\ \Delta t = t_{i+1} - t_i,\ N \in \mathbb{R}. \tag{A61}$$

Hence, the discretized version of information rate (Γ), information length ($\mathcal{L}$), and information rate causality ($\Gamma_{x_n \to x_m \mid n \neq m \& (n,m) \in [1,2]}$), shown in Equations (A62) to (A64), are used when computing the results that are included in the paper.

$$\Gamma^2 = 4 \sum_{x \in X} \frac{\Delta x}{[\Delta t]^2} \left[\sqrt{p(x,t+\Delta t)} - \sqrt{p(x,t)} \right]^2, \tag{A62}$$

$$\mathcal{L} = \sum_{t \in T} \Delta t\, \Gamma(t), \tag{A63}$$

$$\Gamma^2_{x_2 \to x_1} = 4 \sum_{x_1 \in X_1, x_2 \in X_2} \frac{\Delta x_1 \Delta x_2}{[\Delta t]^2} \left[\sqrt{p(x_1(t+\Delta t), x_2(t_i))} - \sqrt{p(x_1(t), x_2(t_i))} \right]^2. \tag{A64}$$

Appendix D. Basic Model—Stationary and Continuous Coupling

In this part, we investigate the coupling between two processes, namely $x_1(t)$ and $x_2(t)$, where the first process ($x_1(t)$) influences the second process ($x_2(t)$) throughout the entire process. We consider both linear and nonlinear cases, which are represented by Equations (A65) and (A66), respectively.

Linear model:

$$\begin{aligned} x_1(t) &= 0.55 x_1(t-1) + \epsilon_1(t), \\ x_2(t) &= x_1(t-2) + \epsilon_2(t). \end{aligned} \tag{A65}$$

Nonlinear model:

$$\begin{aligned} x_1(t) &= 0.55 x_1(t-1) e^{1-|x_1(t-1)|} + \epsilon_1(t), \\ x_2(t) &= x_1(t-2) + \epsilon_2(t). \end{aligned} \tag{A66}$$

Here, t is the time steps and $\epsilon_{n|n \in [1,2]}$ is the Gaussian white noise. The white noise has zero mean ($\langle \epsilon_n \rangle = 0 | n \in [1,2]$) with unit variance ($\begin{bmatrix} \Sigma_{11} & \Sigma_{12} \\ \Sigma_{21} & \Sigma_{22} \end{bmatrix} = \begin{bmatrix} 1.0 & 0.0 \\ 0.0 & 1.0 \end{bmatrix}, \Sigma_{nm} = \langle (\epsilon_n - \langle \epsilon_n \rangle)(\epsilon_m - \langle \epsilon_m \rangle) \rangle | n,m \in [1,2]$). Additionally, we also consider the noncoupling scenario where the process $x_2(t)$ solely depends on the noise $\epsilon_2(t)$ ($x_2(t) = \epsilon_2(t) \because x_1(t-2) = 0$).

The simulation results for Equations (A65) and (A66) are presented in Figure A1. From the figures, it can be observed that both the linear and nonlinear processes exhibit stationary oscillation, regardless of whether they are coupled or noncoupled.

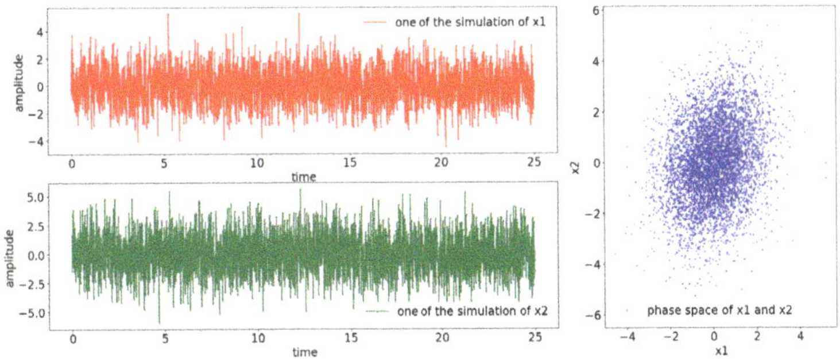

(**a**) linear: coupling

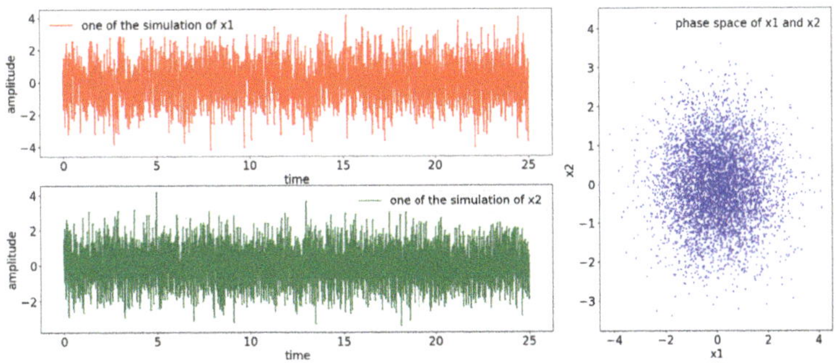

(**b**) linear: noncoupling

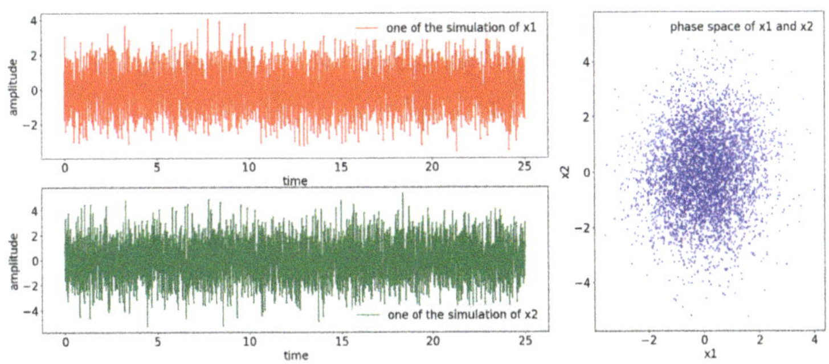

(**c**) nonlinear: coupling

Figure A1. *Cont.*

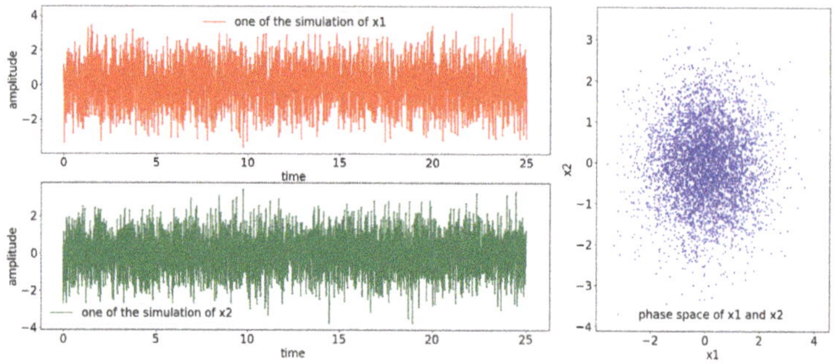

(**d**) nonlinear: noncoupling

Figure A1. Result of the simulation based on Equations (A65) and (A66). The [top left, red] is the result of x_1, while the [bottom left, green] shows the result of x_2. The phase space of x_1 and x_2 is shown in [right blue] figure. Note that the noncoupling here refers to the processes oscillating by themselves without sharing any information with each other.

Appendix D.1. Granger Causality

The results of the GC are shown in Figure A2 for all the cases. Based on the results, both the coupling and noncoupling cases can be depicted well via the nonparametric GC approach (refer to Section 2.1). The continuous causality from x_1 to x_2 can be depicted well in Figure A2a,c. Similarly, the noncoupling between the signals is shown well in Figure A2b,d.

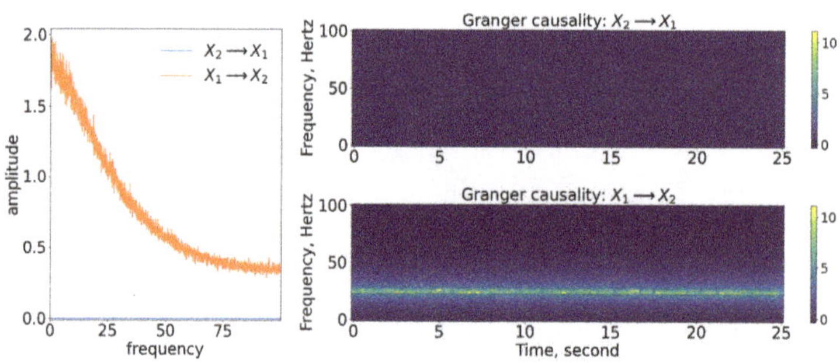

(**a**) linear: coupling

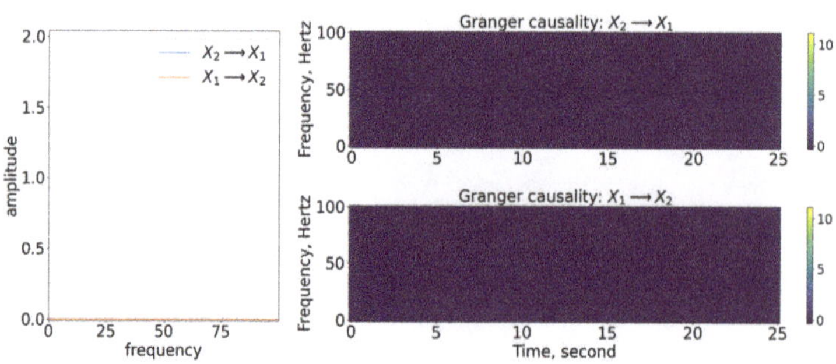

(**b**) linear: noncoupling

Figure A2. *Cont.*

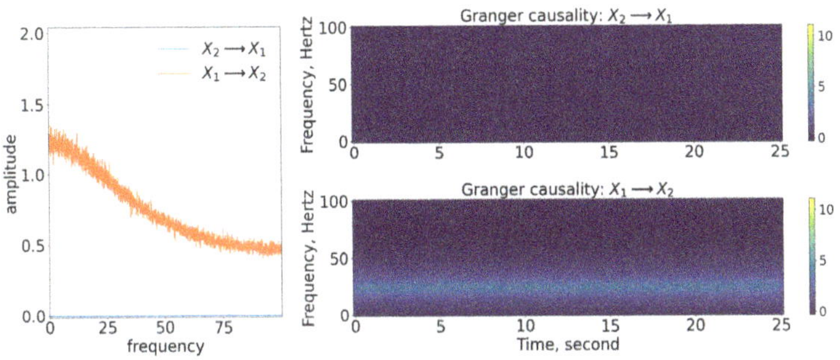

(**c**) nonlinear: coupling

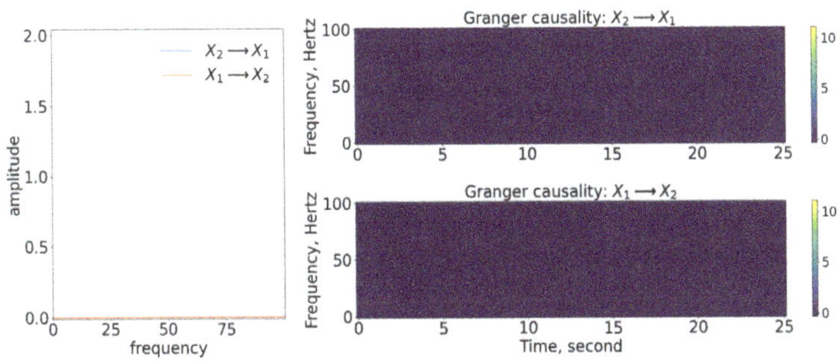

(**d**) nonlinear: noncoupling

Figure A2. Result of the spectral and time-varying frequency of GC. In each subfigure, the [left panel] shows the spectral (frequency domain) of GC with [blue line] indicating that x_2 causes x_1, while [orange line] indicates that x_1 causes x_2. The [top, right] subfigure illustrates the time-varying frequency of GC of x_2 to x_1, while [bottom, right] shows x_1 to x_2. The results are based on Equations (A65) and (A66).

Appendix D.2. Transfer Entropy

The results of TE shown in Figure A3 also show similar findings as GC for both coupling and noncoupling of the signals. As depicted in Figure A3a,c, TE can effectively capture the coupling from x_1 to x_2 when appropriate lag is selected. The suitable lag can be determined by observing the peak of Net TE ($TE_{x_1,x_2} = TE_{x_1 \to x_2} - TE_{x_2 \to x_1}$), as it indicates the lag at which a significant result can be expected. Similarly, the noncoupling cases are depicted well in Figure A3b,d, where the TE between the two signals is extremely low, in the order of magnitude of $\times 10^{-4}$.

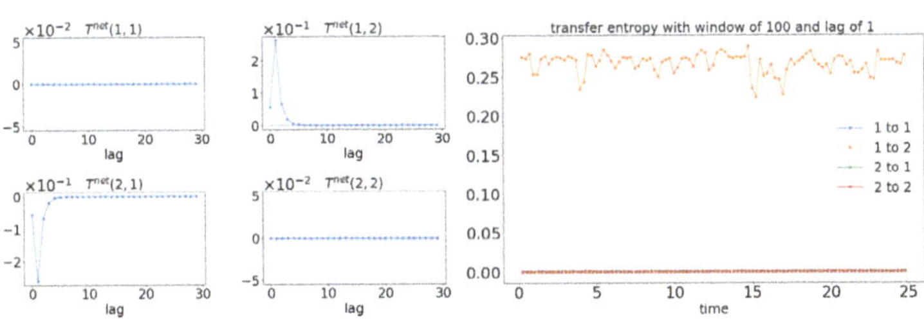

(**a**) linear: coupling

Figure A3. *Cont.*

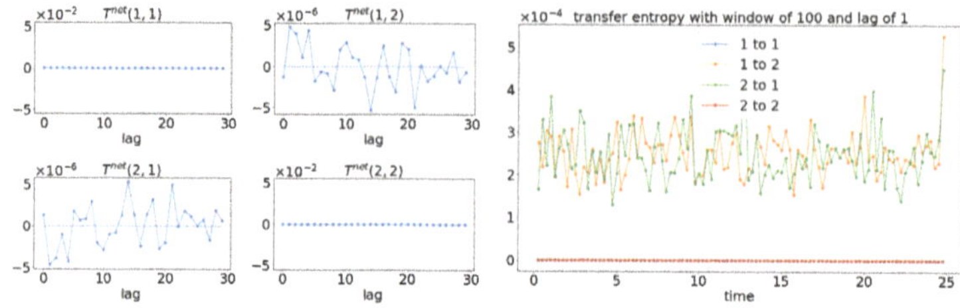

(**b**) linear: noncoupling

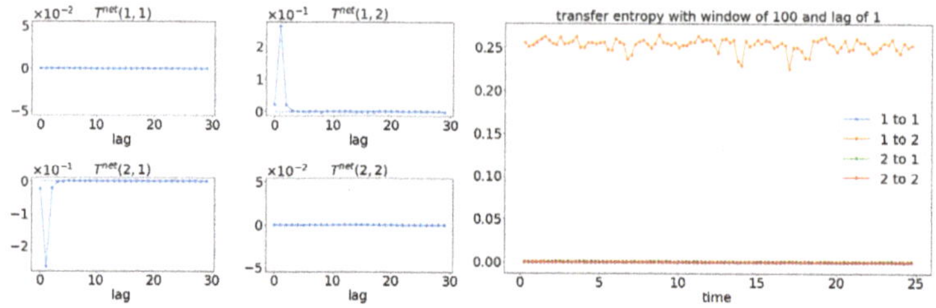

(**c**) nonlinear: coupling

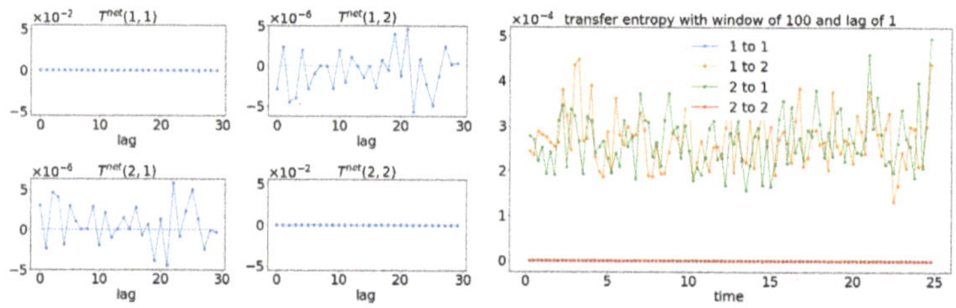

(**d**) nonlinear: noncoupling

Figure A3. Result of the net TE and window sliding TE. Note that for each subfigure, [left, 4×4] depicts the net TE for the whole signals. The [right] subfigure shows the window sliding TE. The results shown are based on Equations (A65) and (A66).

Appendix D.3. Information Rate Causality

Information rate causality is a quantitative measure of the changes in probability distribution caused by one signal influencing another. In the cases of coupling, a high peak is expected to indicate a significant change in the distribution due to the causal relationship between the signals, as depicted in Figure A4a,c. The magnification of these figures is shown in Figure A5a,c. In this scenario, the causation from $x_1(t)$ to $x_2(t)$ is represented well by the peaks at an order of magnitude of $\times 10^4$. In noncoupling cases, as shown in Figure A4b,d (with magnification shown in Figure A5b,d), information rate causality does not reduce to zero due to the noise present in the estimation of the probability distribution (refer to Figure S1). However, this noise does not affect the evaluation, as it does not result in a high order of peaks observed in coupling cases.

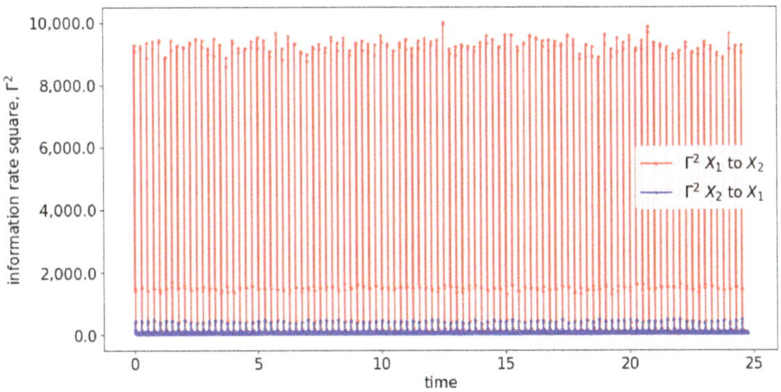

(**a**) linear: coupling

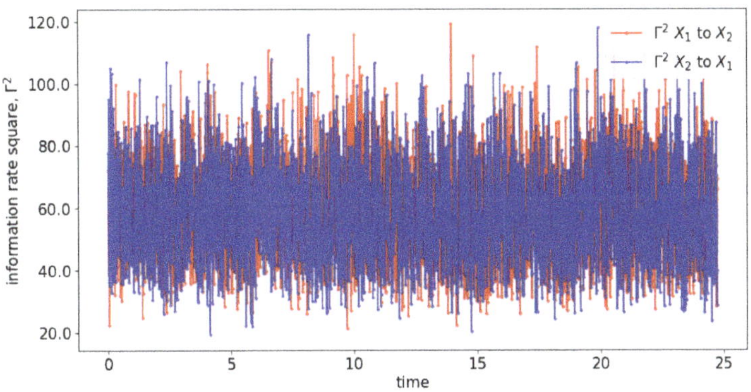

(**b**) linear: noncoupling

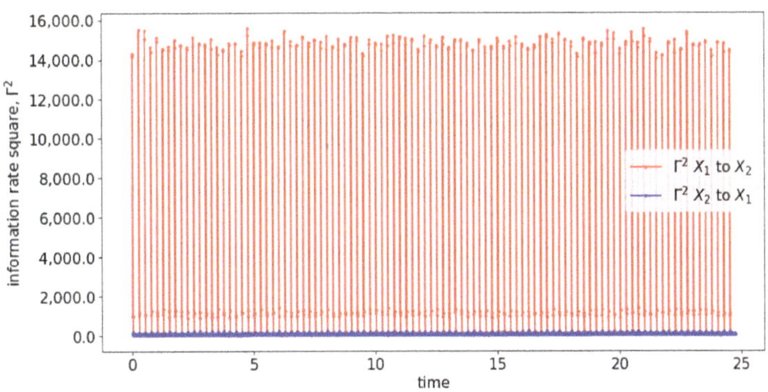

(**c**) nonlinear: coupling

Figure A4. *Cont.*

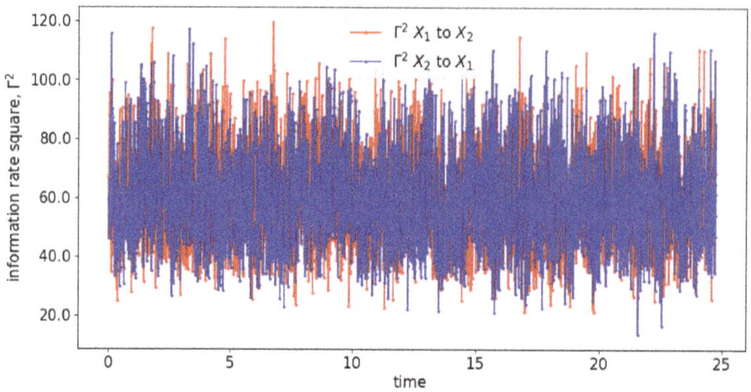

(**d**) nonlinear: noncoupling

Figure A4. Result of information rate causality for Equations (A65) and (A66).

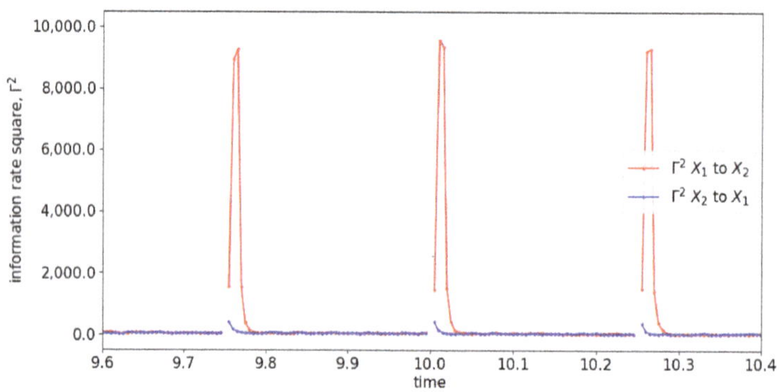

(**a**) linear: coupling

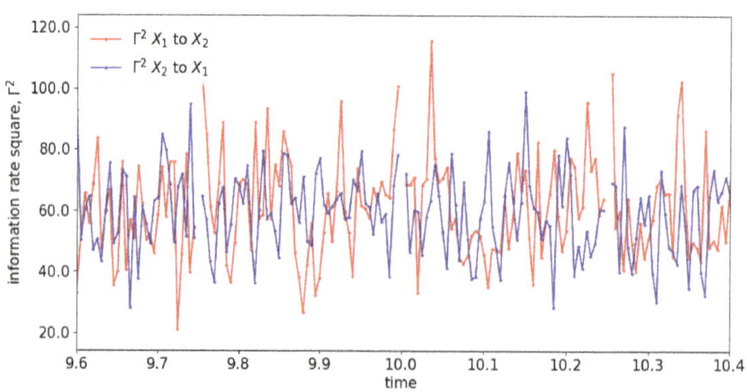

(**b**) linear: noncoupling

Figure A5. *Cont.*

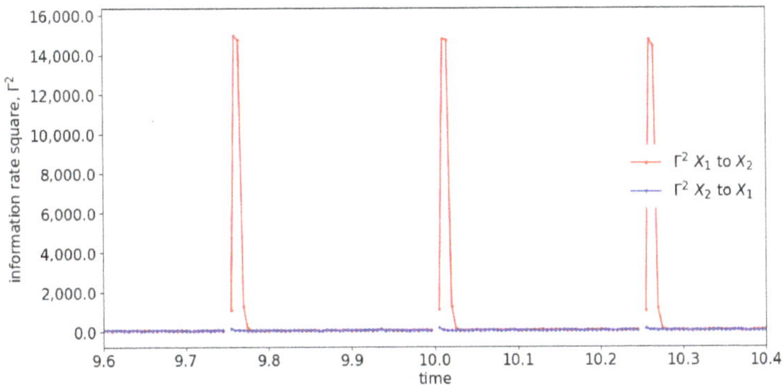

(**c**) nonlinear: coupling

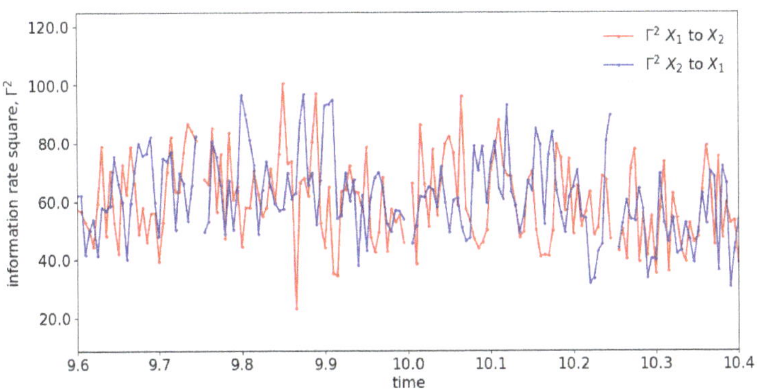

(**d**) nonlinear: noncoupling

Figure A5. Zoom-in of Figure A4 for the information rate causality between 9.6 s and 10.4 s.

Reference

1. Zenil, H.; Kiani, N.A.; Marabita, F.; Deng, Y.; Elias, S.; Schmidt, A.; Ball, G.; Tegnér, J. An Algorithmic Information Calculus for Causal Discovery and Reprogramming Systems. *iScience* **2019**, *19*, 1160–1172. [CrossRef] [PubMed]
2. Zenil, H.; Kiani, N.A.; Zea, A.A.; Tegnér, J. Causal deconvolution by algorithmic generative models. *Nat. Mach. Intell.* **2019**, *1*, 58–66. [CrossRef]
3. Nogueira, A.R.; Pugnana, A.; Ruggieri, S.; Pedreschi, D.; Gama, J. Methods and tools for causal discovery and causal inference. *Wiley Interdiscip. Rev. Data Min. Knowl. Discov.* **2022**, *12*, e1449. [CrossRef]
4. Zenil, H.; Kiani, N.A.; Tegnér, J. Low-algorithmic-complexity entropy-deceiving graphs. *Phys. Rev. E* **2017**, *96*, 012308. [CrossRef] [PubMed]
5. Danks, D.; Davis, I. Causal inference in cognitive neuroscience. *WIRES Cogn. Sci.* **2023**, e1650 . [CrossRef]
6. Granger, C.W.J. Investigating Causal Relations by Econometric Models and Cross-spectral Methods. *Econom. J. Econom. Soc.* **1969**, *37*, 424–438. [CrossRef]
7. Guo, R.; Cheng, L.; Li, J.; Hahn, P.R.; Liu, H. A Survey of Learning Causality with Data: Problems and Methods. *ACM Comput. Surv. (CSUR)* **2020**, *53*, 1–37. [CrossRef]
8. Kaufmann, R.K.; Stern, D.I. Evidence for human influence on climate from hemispheric temperature relations. *Nature* **1997**, *388*, 39–44. [CrossRef]
9. Imbens, G.W. Nonparametric Estimation of Average Treatment Effects under Exogeneity: A Review*. *Rev. Econ. Stat.* **2004**, *86*, 4–29. [CrossRef]
10. Pullon, R.M.; Yan, L.; Sleigh, J.W.; Warnaby, C.E. Granger causality of the electroencephalogram reveals abrupt global loss of cortical information flow during propofol-induced loss of responsiveness. *Anesthesiology* **2020**, *133*, 774–786. [CrossRef]
11. Zhao, Y.; Billings, S.A.; Wei, H.; He, F.; Sarrigiannis, P.G. A new NARX-based Granger linear and nonlinear casual influence detection method with applications to EEG data. *J. Neurosci. Methods* **2013**, *212*, 79–86. [CrossRef] [PubMed]
12. Ebert-Uphoff, I.; Deng, Y. Causal discovery for climate research using graphical models. *J. Clim.* **2012**, *25*, 5648–5665. [CrossRef]

13. Dehejia, R.H.; Wahba, S. Causal Effects in Nonexperimental Studies: Reevaluating the Evaluation of Training Programs. *J. Am. Stat. Assoc.* **1999**, *94*, 1053–1062. [CrossRef]
14. Shovon, M.H.I.; Nandagopal, N.; Vijayalakshmi, R.; Du, J.T.; Cocks, B. Directed Connectivity Analysis of Functional Brain Networks during Cognitive Activity Using Transfer Entropy. *Neural Process. Lett.* **2017**, *45*, 807–824. [CrossRef]
15. Gao, Y.; Su, H.; Li, R.; Zhang, Y. Synchronous analysis of brain regions based on multi-scale permutation transfer entropy. *Comput. Biol. Med.* **2019**, *109*, 272–279. [CrossRef]
16. Seth, A.K.; Barrett, A.B.; Barnett, L. Granger causality analysis in neuroscience and neuroimaging. *J. Neurosci.* **2015**, *35*, 3293–3297. [CrossRef]
17. Ding, M.; Chen, Y.; Bressler, S.L. Granger Causality: Basic Theory and Application to Neuroscience; In *Handbook of Time Series Analysis: Recent Theoretical Developments and Applications*; John Wiley & Sons: Hoboken, NJ, USA, 2006.
18. Lima, V.; Dellajustina, F.J.; Shimoura, R.O.; Girardi-Schappo, M.; Kamiji, N.L.; Pena, R.F.; Roque, A.C. Granger causality in the frequency domain: Derivation and applications. *Rev. Bras. Ensino Fis.* **2020**, *42* . [CrossRef]
19. van Milligen, B.P.; Birkenmeier, G.; Ramisch, M.; Estrada, T.; Hidalgo, C.; Alonso, A. Causality detection and turbulence in fusion plasmas. *Nucl. Fusion* **2014**, *54*, 023011. [CrossRef]
20. Sigtermans, D. Is Information Theory Inherently a Theory of Causation? *arXiv* **2020**, arXiv:2010.01932.
21. Bressler, S.L.; Seth, A.K. Wiener-Granger Causality: A well established methodology. *Neuroimage* **2011**, *58*, 323–329. [CrossRef]
22. Geweke, J. Measurement of Linear Dependence and Feedback Between Multiple Time Series Measurement of Linear Dependence and Feedback Betwveen Multiple Time Series. *J. Am. Stat. Assoc.* **1982**, *77*, 304–313. [CrossRef]
23. Geweke, J.F. Measures of Conditional Linear Dependence and Feedback Between Time Series. *J. Am. Stat. Assoc.* **1984**, *79*, 907–915. [CrossRef]
24. Dhamala, M.; Rangarajan, G.; Ding, M. Estimating granger causality from fourier and wavelet transforms of time series data. *Phys. Rev. Lett.* **2008**, *100*, 018701. [CrossRef]
25. Dhamala, M.; Rangarajan, G.; Ding, M. Analyzing information flow in brain networks with nonparametric Granger causality. *NeuroImage* **2008**, *41*, 354–362. [CrossRef] [PubMed]
26. Klonowski, W. Everything you wanted to ask about EEG but were afraid to get the right answer. *Nonlinear Biomed. Phys.* **2009**, *3*, 2. [CrossRef] [PubMed]
27. He, F.; Yang, Y. Nonlinear System Identification of Neural Systems from Neurophysiological Signals. *Neuroscience* **2021**, *458*, 213–228. [CrossRef]
28. Schreiber, T. Measuring Information Transfer. *Phys. Rev. Lett.* **2000**, *85*, 461–464. [CrossRef]
29. Barnett, L.; Barrett, A.B.; Seth, A.K. Granger causality and transfer entropy Are equivalent for gaussian variables. *Phys. Rev. Lett.* **2009**, *103*, 238701. [CrossRef] [PubMed]
30. Kim, E.J.; Guel-Cortez, A.J. Causal information rate. *Entropy* **2021**, *23*, 1087. [CrossRef]
31. Kim, E.J. Information geometry and non-equilibrium thermodynamic relations in the over-damped stochastic processes. *J. Stat. Mech. Theory Exp.* **2021**, *2021*, 93406. [CrossRef]
32. Kim, E.j. Information geometry, fluctuations, non-equilibrium thermodynamics, and geodesics in complex systems. *Entropy* **2021**, *23*, 1393. [CrossRef]
33. Ito, S.; Dechant, A. Stochastic Time Evolution, Information Geometry, and the Cramér-Rao Bound. *Phys. Rev. X* **2020**, *10*, 021056. [CrossRef]
34. O'donnell, R.T.; Korb, K.B.; Allison, L. Causal KL: Evaluating Causal Discovery. *arXiv* **2021**, arXiv:2111.06029.
35. Wilson, G.T. The Factorization of Matricial Spectral Densities. *SIAM J. Appl. Math.* **1972**, *23*, 420–426. [CrossRef]
36. Detto, M.; Molini, A.; Katul, G.; Stoy, P.; Palmroth, S.; Baldocchi, D. Causality and persistence in ecological systems: A nonparametric spectral Granger causality approach. *Am. Nat.* **2012**, *179*, 524–535. [CrossRef] [PubMed]
37. Gencaga, D.; Knuth, K.H.; Rossow, W.B. A recipe for the estimation of information flow in a dynamical system. *Entropy* **2015**, *17*, 438–470. [CrossRef]
38. Sahann, R.; Muller, T.; Schmidt, J. Histogram binning revisited with a focus on human perception. In Proceedings of the 2021 IEEE Visualization Conference (VIS), New Orleans, LA, USA, 24–29 October 2021. [CrossRef]
39. Terrell, G.R.; Scott, D.W. Oversmoothed nonparametric density estimates. *J. Am. Stat. Assoc.* **1985**, *80*, 209–214. [CrossRef]
40. Schelter, B.; Winterhalder, M.; Timmer, J. *Handbook of Time Series Analysis*; Wiley-VCH Verlag GmbH & Co KGaA: Weinheim, Germany, 2006; pp. 335–491.
41. Shannon, C.E. A Mathematical Theory of Communication PART III: MATHEMATICAL PRELIMINARIES. *Bell Syst. Tech. J.* **1948**, *27*, 623–656. [CrossRef]
42. Shannon, C.E. A Mathematical Theory of Communication. *Bell Syst. Tech. J.* **1948**, *27*, 379–423. [CrossRef]
43. Virosztek, D. The metric property of the quantum Jensen-Shannon divergence. *Adv. Math.* **2021**, *380*, 107595. [CrossRef]
44. Briët, J.; Harremoës, P. Properties of classical and quantum Jensen-Shannon divergence. *Phys. Rev. A—At. Mol. Opt. Phys.* **2009**, *79*, 052311. [CrossRef]

entropy

MDPI

Article

Kernel-Based Independence Tests for Causal Structure Learning on Functional Data

Felix Laumann [1,*], Julius von Kügelgen [2,3], Junhyung Park [2], Bernhard Schölkopf [2] and Mauricio Barahona [1,*]

1 Department of Mathematics, Imperial College London, London SW7 2BX, UK
2 Max Planck Institute for Intelligent Systems, 72076 Tübingen, Germany
3 Department of Engineering, University of Cambridge, Cambridge CB2 0QQ, UK
* Correspondence: f.laumann18@imperial.ac.uk (F.L.); m.barahona@imperial.ac.uk (M.B.)

Abstract: Measurements of systems taken along a continuous functional dimension, such as time or space, are ubiquitous in many fields, from the physical and biological sciences to economics and engineering. Such measurements can be viewed as realisations of an underlying smooth process sampled over the continuum. However, traditional methods for independence testing and causal learning are not directly applicable to such data, as they do not take into account the dependence along the functional dimension. By using specifically designed kernels, we introduce statistical tests for bivariate, joint, and conditional independence for functional variables. Our method not only extends the applicability to functional data of the Hilbert–Schmidt independence criterion (HSIC) and its d-variate version (*d*-HSIC), but also allows us to introduce a test for conditional independence by defining a novel statistic for the conditional permutation test (CPT) based on the Hilbert–Schmidt conditional independence criterion (HSCIC), with optimised regularisation strength estimated through an evaluation rejection rate. Our empirical results of the size and power of these tests on synthetic functional data show good performance, and we then exemplify their application to several constraint- and regression-based causal structure learning problems, including both synthetic examples and real socioeconomic data.

Keywords: causal discovery; independence tests; functional data analysis; kernel methods

1. Introduction

Uncovering the causal relationships between measured variables, a discipline known as *causal structure learning* or *causal discovery*, is of great importance across various scientific fields, such as climatology [1], economics [2], and biology [3]. Doing so from passively collected ('observational') data enables the inference of causal interactions between variables without performing experiments or randomised control trials, which are often expensive, unethical, or impossible to conduct [4]. Causal structure learning is the inference, under a given set of assumptions, of directed and undirected edges in graphs representing the data-generating process, where the nodes represent variables and the inferred edges capture causal (directed) or non-causal (undirected) relationships between them.

Research in various areas collates *functional* data consisting of multiple series of measurements observed conjointly over a given continuum (e.g., time, space, or frequency), where each series is assumed to be a realisation of an underlying *smooth* process ([5], §3). By viewing the series of measurements as discretisations of functions, the observations are not required to be collected over regular meshes of points along the continuum. If the variables are measured over time as the underlying continuum, then there is a long history of methods that have been developed to infer (time-based) causality between variables. Among those, the classic Granger causality [6] declares that variable 'X causes Y' ($X \to Y$) if predicting the future of Y becomes more accurate with, as compared to without, access to the past of X, conditional on all other relevant variables [7]. However, these methods assume that the observed time-series are stationary and the causal dependency of X on Y

is linear. More recently, Sugihara et al. [8] developed convergent cross mappings (CCMs), a method that relaxes the assumption of linearity and finds causal relationships based on time-embeddings of the (stationary) time-series at each point. While useful in many situations, Granger causality and CCM can perform weakly when the time-series for X and Y are nonlinearly related or nonstationary, respectively (see Appendix H).

Here, we present a method that uses kernel-based independence tests to detect statistically significant causal relationships by extending constraint- and regression-based causal structure learning to functional data. The key advantages over Granger causality and CCM are both the systematic consideration of confounders and the relaxation of assumptions around linear relationships or stationarity in the data, which can lead to different causal relationships between variables. As a motivating example, consider the relationship between two variables, 'corruption' and 'income inequality', as measured using the World Governance Indicators (WGIs) [9] and the World Bank [10], respectively. Using data for 48 African countries from 1996 to 2016, Sulemana and Kpienbaareh [2] investigated their cause–effect relationship and found that corruption 'Granger-causes' lead to income inequality. We have also confirmed independently that applying CCM to the same data leads to the same conclusion. However, by considering the time-series data as realisations of functions over time, and thus avoiding linearity and stationarity assumptions, our proposed kernel-based approach suggests the reverse result, i.e., causal influence of income inequality on corruption appears as the more statistically likely direction. Although a bidirectional causal dependency between these two variables might appear as more realistic, this conclusion is in agreement with other quantitative findings, which draw on different data sources [11–13]. We will return to this example in Section 4.2.2 where we analyse causal dependencies between all six WGIs.

Methodologically, our work extends the applicability of two popular paradigms in causal structure learning—*constraint-based* ([14], § 5) and *regression-based* methods [15]—to functional data. Independence tests play a crucial role in uncovering causal relationships in both paradigms, and kernels provide a powerful framework for such tests by embedding probability distributions in reproducing kernel Hilbert spaces (RKHSs) ([16], § 2.2). Until now, however, related methods for causal learning had only been applicable to univariate and multivariate data, but not to functional data. To address this limitation, we employ recently derived kernels over functions [17] to widen the applicability of kernel-based independence tests to functional data settings. To test for conditional independence, we can then compute HSCIC [18] in a conditional permutation test (CPT) [19], and we propose a straightforward search to determine the optimised regularisation rate in HSCIC.

We structure our paper as follows. Section 2 provides a brief overview of prior literature on functional data analysis, kernel-based independence tests, and causal structure learning methods. Section 3 presents the definition of a conditional independence test for functional data and its applicability to causal structure learning on such data. Then, we empirically analyse the performance of our independence tests and causal structure learning algorithms on synthetic and real-world data in Section 4. We conclude with a discussion in Section 5.

Our main contribution lies in Section 3, where we propose a conditional independence test for functional data that combines a novel test statistic based on HSCIC with CPT to generate samples under the null hypothesis. The algorithm also searches for the optimised regularisation strength λ^* required to compute HSCIC, by pre-test permutations to calculate an *evaluation rejection rate*. We also highlight the following secondary contributions:

- In Section 4.1.2, we extend the historical functional linear model [20] to the multivariate case $\{X_1, \ldots, X_i, \ldots, X_d\} \rightarrow Y$ for regression-based causal structure learning, and we show how a joint independence test can be used to verify candidate directed acyclic graphs (DAGs) ([21], § 5.2) that embed the causal structure of function-valued random variables. This model has been contributed to the Python package `scikit-fda` [22].
- On synthetic data, we show empirically that our bivariate, joint, and conditional independence tests achieve high test power, and that our causal structure learning algorithms outperform previously proposed methods.

- Using a real-world dataset (World Governance Indicators), we demonstrate how our method can yield insights into cause–effect relationships amongst socioeconomic variables measured in countries worldwide.
- Implementations of our algorithms are made available at https://github.com/felix-laumann/causal-fda/ (accessed on 10 October 2023) in an easily usable format that builds on top of `scikit-fda` and `causaldag` [23].

2. Background and Related Work

2.1. Functional Data Analysis

In functional data analysis [5], a variable X is described by a set of n samples (or realisations), $\mathbf{X} = \{x_i(s)\}_{i=1}^{n}$, where each functional sample $x_i(s)$ corresponds to a series of observations over the continuum s, also called the *functional dimension*. Typical functional dimensions are time or space. In practical settings, the observations are taken at a set of S discrete values $s_1, \ldots, s_S$ of the continuum variable s. Examples of functional datasets include the vertical position of the lower lip over time when speaking out a given word [20], the muscle soreness over the duration of a tennis match [24], or the ultrafine particle concentration in air measured over the distance to the nearest motorway [25].

In applications, the functional samples are usually represented as linear combinations of a finite set of M basis functions $\{\phi_m(s)\}_{m=1}^{M}$ (e.g., Fourier or monomial basis functions):

$$x_i(s) = \sum_{m=1}^{M} c_{i,m}\phi_m(s), \tag{1}$$

where the coefficients $C_i = (c_{i,1}, c_{i,2}, \ldots, c_{i,M})$ characterise each sample. If the number of basis functions is equal to the number of observations, $M = S$, then each observed value $x_i(s_k)$ can be fitted exactly by obtaining the coefficients C_i using standard nonlinear least squares fitting techniques (provided the $\phi_m(s)$ are valid basis functions), and Equation (1) allows us to interpolate between any two observations. When the number of basis functions is smaller than the number of observations, $M < S$, as it is commonly the case in practice, the basis function expansion (1) provides a smoothed approximation to the set of observations, $\hat{x}_i(s_k)$.

For the many applications where the continuum is time, historical functional linear models (HFLMs) [20] provides a comprehensive framework to map the relationship between two sets of functional samples. Let 0 and T be the initial and final time points for a set of samples $y_i(t)$. HFLMs describes the dependencies that can vary over time using the function $\beta(s,t)$, which encapsulates the influence of $x(s), s \in [0, S]$ on another variable $y(t), t \in [0, T]$ at any two points in time, s_k and t_k:

$$y_i(t) = \int_{s_0(t)}^{t} x_i(s)\, \beta(s,t)\, ds\,, \quad t \in [0, T] \tag{2}$$

where $s_0(t)$ is the maximum allowable lag for any influence of X on Y and $s_0(t) \leq s \leq t$. Typical choices for $\beta(s,t)$ are exponential decay and hyperbolic paraboloid (or "saddle") functions. The continuum is not required to be time but can also be space, frequency, or others (see Ramsay and Hooker [26] for an extensive collection of function-to-function models and applications).

2.2. Kernel Independence Tests

Let $\mathcal{H}_{k_1}$ and $\mathcal{H}_{k_2}$ be separable RKHSs with kernels $k_1 : \mathbb{R}^{\mathbf{X}} \times \mathbb{R}^{\mathbf{X}} \to \mathbb{R}$ and $k_2 : \mathbb{R}^{\mathbf{Y}} \times \mathbb{R}^{\mathbf{Y}} \to \mathbb{R}$ such that the tensor product kernel $(k_1 \otimes k_2)(x, y, x', y') = k_1(x, x') \cdot k_2(y, y')$ implies $(\mathbb{R}^{\mathbf{X}} \times \mathbb{R}^{\mathbf{Y}}) \times (\mathbb{R}^{\mathbf{X}} \times \mathbb{R}^{\mathbf{Y}}) \to \mathbb{R}$. If the kernel k_1 uniquely embeds a distribution $\mathbb{P}_{\mathbf{X}}$ in an RKHS by a mean embedding, then

$$\mu_{\mathbf{X}} := \int_{\mathcal{X}} k_1(\mathbf{x}, \cdot) d\mathbb{P}_{\mathbf{X}} \tag{3}$$

which captures any information about $\mathbb{P}_{\mathbf{X}}$; we call k_1 a characteristic kernel on $\mathbb{R}^{\mathbf{X}} \times \mathbb{R}^{\mathbf{Y}}$ [27]. Characteristic kernels have thus been extensively used in bivariate ($\mathbb{P}_{XY} = \mathbb{P}_X\mathbb{P}_Y$), joint ($\mathbb{P}_{XYZ} = \mathbb{P}_X\mathbb{P}_Y\mathbb{P}_Z$), and conditional ($\mathbb{P}_{XY|Z} = \mathbb{P}_{X|Z}\mathbb{P}_{Y|Z}$) independence tests (e.g., [21,28,29]).

For the bivariate independence test, let $\mathbb{P}_{\mathbf{XY}}$ denote the joint distribution of $\mathbf{X}$ and $\mathbf{Y}$. Then, HSIC is defined as

$$\text{HSIC}(\mathcal{H}_{k_1}, \mathcal{H}_{k_2}, \mathbb{P}_{\mathbf{XY}}) := \|\mu_{\mathbf{XY}} - \mu_{\mathbf{X}} \otimes \mu_{\mathbf{Y}}\|^2_{\mathcal{H}_{k_1} \otimes \mathcal{H}_{k_2}} \geq 0, \quad \text{with equality if and only if} \quad \mathbb{P}_{\mathbf{XY}} = \mathbb{P}_{\mathbf{X}}\mathbb{P}_{\mathbf{Y}}. \tag{4}$$

We refer to Gretton et al. [28] for the definition of an estimator for finite samples that constitutes the test statistic in the bivariate independence test with null hypothesis $H_0 : X \perp\!\!\!\perp Y$. The test statistic is then computed on the original data $(\mathbf{X}, \mathbf{Y})$ and statistically compared to random permutations $\{(\mathbf{X}, \mathbf{Y}_{p'})\}_{p'=1}^{P}$ under the null hypothesis.

For distributions with more than two variables, let $\mathbb{P}_{\mathbf{X}_1,\mathbf{X}_2,\ldots,\mathbf{X}_d}$ denote the joint distribution on $\mathbf{X}_1, \mathbf{X}_2, \ldots, \mathbf{X}_d$. To test for joint independence, we compute

$$d\text{-HSIC}(\mathcal{H}_{k_1}, \mathcal{H}_{k_2}, \ldots, \mathcal{H}_{k_d}, \mathbb{P}_{\mathbf{X}_1,\mathbf{X}_2,\ldots,\mathbf{X}_d}) := \|\mu_{\mathbf{X}_1,\mathbf{X}_2,\ldots,\mathbf{X}_d} - \mu_{\mathbf{X}_1} \otimes \mu_{\mathbf{X}_2} \otimes \cdots \otimes \mu_{\mathbf{X}_d}\|^2_{\mathcal{H}_{k_1} \otimes \mathcal{H}_{k_2} \otimes \cdots \otimes \mathcal{H}_{k_d}} \geq 0 \quad \text{with equality if and only if} \quad \mathbb{P}_{\mathbf{X}_1,\mathbf{X}_2,\ldots,\mathbf{X}_d} = \mathbb{P}_{\mathbf{X}_1}\mathbb{P}_{\mathbf{X}_2} \cdots \mathbb{P}_{\mathbf{X}_d}. \tag{5}$$

Pfister et al. [21] derive a numerical estimator, which serves as the basis for a joint independence test on finite samples. Here, the distribution under the null hypothesis of joint independence is generated by randomly permuting all sample sets in the same way as $\mathbf{Y}$ is in the bivariate independence test.

Lastly, the conditional independence test relies on accurately sampling from the distribution under the null hypothesis $H_0 : X \perp\!\!\!\perp Y | Z$. At the core of conditional permutation test [19] lies a randomisation procedure that generates permutations of $\mathbf{X}$, denoted $\{\mathbf{X}_{p'}\}_{p'=1}^{P}$, which are generated without altering the conditional distribution $\mathbb{P}_{\mathbf{X}|\mathbf{Z}}$, so that

$$\mathbb{P}_{\mathbf{X}_{p'},\mathbf{Y},\mathbf{Z}} = \mathbb{P}_{\mathbf{X},\mathbf{Y},\mathbf{Z}} \tag{6}$$

under H_0, while breaking any dependence between X and Y. The null distribution can therefore be generated by repeating this procedure multiple times, and we can decide whether H_0 should be rejected by comparing a test statistic on the original data against its results on the generated null distribution.

The existing literature on kernel-based independence tests is extensive, see, e.g., Berrett et al. [19] for a relevant review, but only a small part of those tests investigates independence among functional variables [30,31]. There have been particularly strong efforts in developing conditional independence tests and understanding their applicable settings. The authors of kernel conditional independence test (KCIT) [29], for example, gave promising results in use with univariate data but increasingly suffered when the number of conditional variables was large. In contrast, the authors of kernel conditional independence permutation test (KCIPT) [32] repurposed the well-established kernel two-sample test [33] to a conditional independence setting which delivered stable results for multiple conditional variables. However, Lee and Honavar [34] pointed out that, as the number of permutations increases, while its power increases, its calibration decreases. This issue was overcome by their proposed self-discrepancy conditional independence test (SDCIT), which is based on a modified unbiased estimate of the maximum mean discrepancy (MMD).

2.3. Causal Structure Learning

The aim of causal structure learning, or causal discovery, is to infer the qualitative causal relationships among a set of observed variables, typically in the form of a causal diagram or DAG. Once learnt, such a causal structure can then be used to construct a causal model such as a causal Bayesian network or a *structural causal model* (SCM) [35]. Causal models are endowed with a notion of manipulation and, unlike a statistical model, do not just describe a single distribution, but many distributions indexed by different interventions and counterfactuals. They can be used for causal reasoning, that is, to answer causal questions such as computing the average causal effect of a treatment on a given outcome variable. Such questions are of interest across many disciplines, and causal discovery is thus a highly topical area. We refer to Glymour et al. [4], Mooij et al. [36], Peters et al. [37], Schölkopf and von Kügelgen [38], Squires and Uhler [39], Vowels et al. [40] for comprehensive surveys and accounts of the main research concepts. In particular, we focus here on causal discovery methods for causally sufficient systems, for which there are no unobserved confounders influencing two or more of the observed variables. Existing causal discovery methods can roughly be categorised into three families:

- Score-based approaches assign a score, such as a penalised likelihood, to each candidate graph and then pick the highest scoring graph(s). A common drawback of score-based approaches is the need for a combinatorial enumeration of all DAGs in the optimisation, although greedy approaches have been proposed to alleviate such issues [41].
- Constraint-based methods start by characterising the set of *conditional independences* in the observed data [14]. They then determine the graph(s) consistent with the detected conditional independences by using a graphical criterion called d-separation, as well as the causal Markov and faithfulness assumptions, which establish a one-to-one connection between d-separation and conditional independence (see Appendix B for definitions). When only observational i.i.d. data are available, this yields a so-called Markov equivalence class, possibly containing multiple candidate graphs. For example, the graphs $X \to Y \to Z$, $X \leftarrow Y \leftarrow Z$, and $X \leftarrow Y \to Z$ are Markov equivalent, as they all imply $X \perp\!\!\!\perp Z|Y$ and no other conditional independence relations.
- Regression-based approaches directly fit the structural equations $X_i := f_i(\mathbf{PA}_i, U_i)$ of an underlying SCM for each X_i, where $\mathbf{PA}_i$ denote the parents of X_i in the causal DAG and $U = (U_1, ..., U_n)$ are *jointly independent* exogenous noise variables. Provided that the function class of the f_i is sufficiently restricted, e.g., by considering only linear relationships [42] or additive noise models [43], the true causal graph is identified as the unique choice of parents for each i such that the resulting residuals $\hat{U}_i = X_i - \hat{f}_i(\mathbf{PA}_i)$ are jointly independent.

As can be seen from these definitions, conditional, bivariate, and joint independence tests are an integral part of constraint- and regression-based causal discovery methods. Our main focus in the present work is therefore to extend the applicability of these causal discovery frameworks to functional data by generalising the underlying independence tests to such domains.

3. Methods

In all three of our independence tests (bivariate, joint, conditional), we employ kernels over functions, also known as squared-exponential T (SE-T) kernels [17]. Let $\mathcal{X}$ and $\mathcal{Y}$ be real, separable Hilbert spaces with norms $\|\cdot\|_{\mathcal{X}}$ and $\|\cdot\|_{\mathcal{Y}}$, respectively. Then, for $T : \mathcal{X} \to \mathcal{Y}$, SE-T kernels are defined as

$$k_T(x, y) = e^{-\frac{1}{2\sigma^2}\|T(x)-T(y)\|^2_{\mathcal{Y}}}. \tag{7}$$

where σ^2 is commonly defined as the median heuristic, $\sigma^2 = \text{Median}\{\|T(a) - T(b)\|^2_{\mathcal{Y}} : a, b \in \{x_i\}_{i=1}^n \cup \{y_i\}_{i=1}^n, a \neq b\}$. Replacing any characteristic kernel by the SE-T kernels for bivariate independence tests (based on HSIC) and for joint independence tests (based on d-variable Hilbert–Schmidt independence criterion ($d-$HSIC)) is straightforward and does not require further theoretical investigation besides evaluating numerically the validity and power of the tests (see Section 4). However, the application of SE-T kernels to conditional independence tests needs further theoretical results, as we discuss next.

3.1. Conditional Independence Test on Functional Data

We consider the conditional independence test, which generates samples under the null hypothesis based on the CPT, and uses the sum of HSCICs over all samples $z \in \mathbf{Z}$ as its test statistic. The CPT defines a permutation procedure that preserves the dependence of Z on both X and Y while resampling data for X that eliminates any potential dependence between X and Y. This procedure results in samples according to the null hypothesis, $X \perp\!\!\!\perp Y|Z$. We use this procedure whenever permutations are required as part of the conditional independence test. Given the computation of the HSCIC is based on a kernel ridge regression, it requires to set a regularisation strength λ, which has been manually chosen previously [18]. Generally, our aim is to have type-I error rates close to the allowable false-positive rate α. However, choosing λ inappropriately may result in an invalid test (type-I error rates exceed α if λ is chosen too large), or in a deflated test power (type-I error rates are well below α and type-II error rates are high if λ is chosen too small). Thus, we must define an algorithm that conducts a search over a range of potentially suitable values for λ and assesses each candidate value by—what we will call—an *evaluation rejection rate*.

The search proceeds by iterating over a range of values $\{\lambda_l\}_{l=1}^{L}$ to find the optimised value λ^*, as follows. For each λ_l, we start by producing one permutation of the samples $\mathbf{X}$, which we denote as $\mathbf{X}_b$, and we compute its corresponding *evaluation test statistic* given by the sum of HSCICs over all samples $z \in \mathbf{Z}$. Then, we apply the usual strategy for permutation-based statistical tests: we produce an additional set of P permuted sample sets of $\mathbf{X}$, which we denote $\{\mathbf{X}_\pi\}_{\pi=1}^{P}$, and for each $\mathbf{X}_\pi$, we determine the sum of HSCICs over $z \in \mathbf{Z}$ to generate a distribution over statistics under the null hypothesis, which we call the *evaluation null statistics*. Then, we compute the percentile where the evaluation test statistic on $\mathbf{X}_b$ falls within the distribution of evaluation null statistics on the permutation set $\{\mathbf{X}_\pi\}_{\pi=1}^{P}$. This results in an evaluation p-value which is compared to the allowable false-positive rate α to determine whether the hypothesis $H_0 : \mathbf{X}_b \not\perp\!\!\!\perp \mathbf{Y}|\mathbf{Z}$ can be rejected. Given that both the evaluation test statistic and the evaluation null statistics are computed on conditionally independent samples, we repeat this procedure for $b = 1, \ldots, B \geq 100$ times to estimate an *evaluation rejection rate* for each value of λ_l. Having completed this procedure over all values $\{\lambda_l\}_{l=1}^{L}$, we select the λ_l that produces an evaluation rejection rate closest to α as the optimised regularisation strength, λ^*. Finally, we apply a CPT-based conditional independence test using the optimised λ^* to test the null hypothesis $H_0 : X \not\perp\!\!\!\perp Y|Z$. This entire procedure is summarised in Algorithm 1.

The following Theorem 1 guarantees the consistency of the conditional independence test in Algorithm 1 with respect to the regularisation parameter λ.

Theorem 1. *Let $\mathcal{H}_{k_1}$ and $\mathcal{H}_{k_2}$ be separable RKHSs with kernels $k_1 : \mathbb{R}^{\mathbf{X}} \times \mathbb{R}^{\mathbf{X}} \to \mathbb{R}$ and $k_2 : \mathbb{R}^{\mathbf{Y}} \times \mathbb{R}^{\mathbf{Y}} \to \mathbb{R}$ such that the tensor product kernel $k_1 \otimes k_2 : (\mathbb{R}^{\mathbf{X}} \times \mathbb{R}^{\mathbf{Y}}) \times (\mathbb{R}^{\mathbf{X}} \times \mathbb{R}^{\mathbf{Y}}) \to \mathbb{R}$ is a characteristic kernel on $\mathbb{R}^{\mathbf{X}} \times \mathbb{R}^{\mathbf{Y}}$ [44]. If the regularisation parameter $\lambda = \lambda_n$ decays as $n \to \infty$ at a slower rate than $n^{-1/2}$, then the test based on the test statistic in Algorithm 1 (lines 19–27) is consistent.*

Proof. See Appendix A. □

Algorithm 1 Search for λ^* with subsequent conditional independence test

Require: Samples $(\mathbf{X}, \mathbf{Y}, \mathbf{Z})$, Range $\{\lambda_l\}_{l=1}^{L}$, Significance level α, Permutation iterations P, Rejection iterations B
Initialise: evaluation rejection rate$[\lambda^*] = 0$
for $1 \leq l \leq L$ **do** ▷ **Start:** Search for λ^*
  for $1 \leq b \leq B$ **do**
    Permute $\mathbf{X}$ by CPT, call them $\mathbf{X}_b$
    evaluation test statistic$[b] \leftarrow \sum_{z \in \mathbf{Z}} \text{HSCIC}(\mathbf{X}_b, \mathbf{Y}, \mathbf{Z}, \lambda_l)$
    for $1 \leq \pi \leq P$ **do**
      Permute $\mathbf{X}_b$ by CPT, call them $\mathbf{X}_{b,\pi}$
      evaluation null statistics$[b, \pi] \leftarrow \sum_{z \in \mathbf{Z}} \text{HSCIC}(\mathbf{X}_{b,\pi}, \mathbf{Y}, \mathbf{Z}, \lambda_l)$
    evaluation p-value $\leftarrow 1-$
        percentile(evaluation test statistic$[b]$, evaluation null statistics$[b, :]$)
    if evaluation p-value $\geq \alpha$ **then**
      Fail to reject $H_0 : \mathbf{X}_b \perp\!\!\!\perp \mathbf{Y} | \mathbf{Z}$
      rejects$[b] = 0$
    else
      Reject $H_0 : \mathbf{X}_b \not\perp\!\!\!\perp \mathbf{Y} | \mathbf{Z}$
      rejects$[b] = 1$
  evaluation rejection rate$[\lambda_l] \leftarrow \text{mean}_{1 \leq b \leq B}(\text{rejects})$
  if $|$evaluation rejection rate$[\lambda^*] - \alpha| \geq |$evaluation rejection rate$[\lambda_l] - \alpha|$ **then**
    $\lambda^* \leftarrow \lambda_l$
return λ^* ▷ **End:** Search for λ^*

test statistic $\leftarrow \sum_{z \in \mathbf{Z}} \text{HSCIC}(\mathbf{X}, \mathbf{Y}, \mathbf{Z}, \lambda^*)$ ▷ **Start:** Conditional independence test
for $1 \leq p' \leq P$ **do**
  Permute $\mathbf{X}$ by CPT, call them $\mathbf{X}_{p'}$
  null statistics$[p'] \leftarrow \sum_{z \in \mathbf{Z}} \text{HSCIC}(\mathbf{X}_{p'}, \mathbf{Y}, \mathbf{Z}, \lambda^*)$
p-value $\leftarrow 1 -$ percentile(test statistic, null statistics)
if p-value $\geq \alpha$ **then**
  Fail to reject $H_0 : X \perp\!\!\!\perp Y | Z$
else
  Reject $H_0 : X \not\perp\!\!\!\perp Y | Z$
▷ **End:** Conditional independence test

3.2. *Causal Structure Learning on Functional Data*

To infer the existence of (directed) edges in an underlying causal graph G based on the joint data distribution $\mathbb{P}$ over a set of observed variables, we must assume that G and $\mathbb{P}$ are intrinsically linked. The authors of (Spirtes et al. [14], § 2.3.3) define the *faithfulness* assumption, from which it follows that if two random variables are (conditionally) independent in the observed distribution $\mathbb{P}$, then they are d-separated in the underlying causal graph G ([35], § 1.2.3). Using this fact, constraint-based causal structure learning methods ([14], § 5) take advantage of bivariate and conditional independence tests to infer whether two nodes are d-separated in the underlying graph. These methods yield completed partially directed acyclic graphs (CPDAGs), which are graphs with undirected and/or directed edges. In contrast, regression-based methods [15] utilise the joint independence test to discover DAGs that have all edges oriented. Next, we describe both of these approaches in more detail.

3.2.1. Constraint-Based Causal Structure Learning

Constraint-based causal structure learning relies on performing conditional independence tests for each pair of variables, X and Y, conditioned on any possible subset of the remaining variables, that is, any subset within the power set of the $d \setminus \{X, Y\}$ remaining variables. Therefore, for d variables, we need to carry out 2^{d-2} conditional independence tests for every pair of variables, which results in $\binom{d}{2}2^{d-2}$ tests in total.

Conditional dependences found in the data can then be used to delete and orient edges in the graph G, as follows. We start with a complete graph with d nodes, where each node corresponds to one of the variables. The edge connecting X and Y is deleted if there exists a subset $\mathcal{Z}_1$ of the $d-2$ remaining variables such that $X \perp\!\!\!\perp Y|\mathcal{Z}_1$. If we then find another subset $\mathcal{Z}_2$, such that $Z_* \in \mathcal{Z}_2$, $\mathcal{Z}_1 = \mathcal{Z}_2 \setminus \{Z_*\}$, and for which $X \not\!\perp\!\!\!\perp Y|\mathcal{Z}_2$, we can orient the edges $X - Z_*$ and $Y - Z_*$ to form colliders (or v-structures), $X \rightarrow Z_* \leftarrow Y$.

Based on these oriented edges, 'Meek's orientation rules', defined in Meek [45] ([37], see, e.g., § 7.2.1) can be applied to direct additional edges based on certain graphical compositions, as shown in Appendix C. Briefly, these rules follow from the avoidance of cycles, which would violate the acyclicity of a DAG, and colliders, which violate the found conditional independence. Algorithms that implement these criteria are the SGS algorithm and the more efficient PC algorithm [14], which we summarise in Appendix C.

3.2.2. Regression-Based Causal Structure Learning

To carry out our regression-based causal learning, we choose additive noise models (ANMs), a special class of SCMs where the noise terms are assumed to be independent and additive. This assumption guarantees that the causal graph can be identified if the function f_i is nonlinear with Gaussian additive noise [43,46], a typical setting in functional data. Our model is set over the set of random variables $\{X\}_{i=1}^{d}$ is given by:

$$\mathbf{X}_i := f_i(\mathbf{PA}_i) + U_i\,, \tag{8}$$

where the additive noise terms U_i are jointly independent, i.e., any noise term U_i is independent of any intersection of the other noise terms,

$$\mathbb{P}(\cap_{j=1}^{k} U_{i_j}) = \prod_{j=1}^{k} \mathbb{P}(U_{i_j}), \quad \forall\, k \leq d.$$

Based on these assumptions, we follow RESIT (regression with subsequent independence testing; [15]), an approach to causal discovery that can be briefly described as follows. If we only have two variables X and Y, then we start by assuming that the samples in $\mathbf{Y}$ are the effect and the samples in $\mathbf{X}$ are the cause. Therefore we write $\mathbf{Y}$ as a function $\hat{f}_\mathbf{Y}$ of $\mathbf{X}$ plus some noise, and we run tests to determine whether the residual $r_\mathbf{Y} = \mathbf{Y} - \hat{f}_\mathbf{Y}(\mathbf{X})$ is independent of $\mathbf{X}$. Then, we exchange the roles of assumed effect and assumed cause to obtain the residual $r_\mathbf{X} = \mathbf{X} - \hat{f}_\mathbf{X}(\mathbf{Y})$, which is tested for independence from $\mathbf{Y}$. To overcome issues with finite samples and test power, Peters et al. [15] used the p-value of the independence tests as a measure of strength of independence, which we follow in our experiments in Section 4. Alternatively, one may determine the causal direction for this bivariate case by comparing both cause–effect directions with respect to a score defined by Bühlmann et al. [47].

For d variables, the joint independence test replaces the bivariate independence test. Firstly, we consider the set of candidate causal graphs, $\Gamma = \{G_1, \ldots, G_\gamma, \ldots, G_\Gamma\}$, which contains every potential DAG with d nodes. For each candidate DAG, G_γ, we regress each descendant $\mathbf{X}_i$ on its parents $\mathbf{PA}_i$:

$$\mathbf{X}_i := \sum_{k \in \mathbf{PA}_i} \hat{f}_{i,k}(\mathbf{X}_k) + U_i\,, \qquad i \in 1, \ldots, d\,, \tag{9}$$

and we compute the residuals $r_{\mathbf{X}_i} = \mathbf{X}_i - \sum_{k \in \mathbf{PA}_i} \hat{f}_{i,k}(\mathbf{X}_k)$. Then, we apply the joint independence test to all d residuals. The candidate DAG G_γ is accepted as the 'true' causal graph if the null hypothesis of joint independence amongst the residuals is not rejected. This process is repeated over all candidate causal graphs in the set Γ. Again, because in finite samples this procedure may not always lead to only one candidate DAG being accepted, the one with the highest p-value is chosen [15].

4. Experiments

In practice, functional data analysis requires samples of continuous functions evaluated over a mesh of discrete observations. In our synthetic data, we consider the interval $s = [0, 1]$ for our functional dimension and draw 100 equally spaced points over s to evaluate the functions. For real-world data, we map the space in which the data live (e.g., the years 1996 to 2020) to the interval $s = [0, 1]$ and interpolate over the discrete measurement points. Then, we use this interpolation to evaluate the functional samples on 100 equally spaced points. Unless otherwise mentioned, henceforth we use SE-T kernels with $T = I$, where I is the identity matrix and σ^2 as the median heuristic, as previously defined in Section 3.

4.1. Evaluation of Independence Tests for Functional Data

Before applying our proposed independence tests to causal structure learning problems, we use appropriate synthetic data to evaluate their type-I error rate (test size) and type-II error rate (test power). Type-I errors are made when the samples are independent (achieved by setting $a = 0$ in our experiments below) but the test concludes that they are dependent, i.e., the test falsely rejects the null hypothesis H_0. In contrast, type-II errors appear when the samples are dependent but the test fails to reject H_0 (achieved by setting $a > 0$). Specifically, we compute the error rates on 200 independent trials, which correspond to different random realisations of the datasets, i.e., synthetically generated datasets with random Fourier basis coefficients, random coefficients of the β-functions and random additive noise. We set the test significance level at $\alpha = 0.05$ and approximate the null hypothesis of independence by 1000 permutations using the CPT scheme described above. Note that although our synthetic data are designed to replicate typical behaviour in time-series, the independence tests are not limited to time as the functional dimension, and can be used more generally.

4.1.1. Bivariate Independence Test

We consider n functional samples $\{x_i(s)\}_{i=1}^n$ of a random variable X defined over the interval $s = [0, 1]$. To generate our samples, we sum $M = 3$ Fourier basis functions $\phi_{m,T}(s)$ with period $T = 0.1$ and coefficients $c_{i,m}$ randomly drawn from a standard normal distribution:

$$x_i(s) = \sum_{m=1}^{M} c_{i,m}\phi_{m,T}(s) \,, \tag{10}$$

where the Fourier functions are $\phi_{1,T}(s) = 1$, $\phi_{2,T}(s) = \sqrt{\frac{2}{T}}\sin(\frac{2\pi m}{T}s)$ and $\phi_{3,T}(s) = \sqrt{\frac{2}{T}}\cos(\frac{2\pi m}{T}s)$. To mimic real-world measurements, we draw each sample over a distinct, irregular mesh of evaluation points. Then, we interpolate them with splines, and generate realisations over a regular mesh of points. Multivariate random noise $\epsilon_i^X(s) \sim \mathcal{N}(0, I)$, where I is the identity matrix, is then added. The samples $\{y_i(t)\}_{i=1}^n$ of random variable Y are defined as a HFLM [20] over $t = [0, 1]$ by:

$$y_i(t) = a \int_0^t x_i(s)\ \beta(s, t)\ ds \,, \tag{11}$$

where $a \in [0, 1]$. The function $\beta(s, t)$ maps the dependence from x_i at any point s to y_i at any point t, and is defined here as a hyperbolic paraboloid function:

$$\beta(s, t) = 8(s - c_1)^2 - 8(t - c_2)^2, \tag{12}$$

with coefficients c_1 and c_2 drawn independently from a uniform distribution over the interval $[0.25, 0.75]$. Afterwards, the samples $y_i(t)$ are evaluated over a regular mesh of 100 points $t \in [0,1]$ and random noise $\epsilon_i^Y(t) \sim \mathcal{N}(0, I)$ is added. Clearly, for $a = 0$, our samples are independent, as the samples $y_i(t) = \epsilon_i^Y(t)$ are just random noise. As a increases, the dependence between the samples $x_i(s)$ and $y_i(t)$ becomes easier to detect. Figure 1a shows that our test stays within the allowable false-positive rate α and detects the dependence as soon as $a > 0$, even with a low number of samples.

4.1.2. Joint Independence Test

To produce the synthetic data for joint independence tests, we first generate random DAGs with d nodes using an Erdös-Rényi model with density 0.5 ([21], § 5.2). For each DAG, we first use Equation (10) to produce function-valued random samples for the variables X^i without parents. Then, we generate samples for other variables using a historical functional linear model:

$$x_i^j(t) = a \sum_{p \in \mathbf{PA}^j} \int_0^t x_i^p(s)\, \beta^p(s,t)\, ds\,, \tag{13}$$

where $\mathbf{PA}^j$ are the parents of node X^j, and the function $\beta^p(s,t)$ is given by Equation (12) with random coefficients c_1 and c_2 independently generated for each descendant-parent pair indexed by p. After being evaluated at a regular mesh of 100 points within $t \in [0,1]$, random noise $\epsilon_i^j(t) \sim \mathcal{N}(0, I)$ is added. Note that, again, an increase in the factor $a \in [0,1]$ should make the dependence structure of the DAG easier to detect. Figure 1b shows the test size where $a = 0$, resulting in independent variables, and test power where $a > 0$. We evaluate the joint independence test for $d = 4$ variables over various values of a and a range of sample sizes.

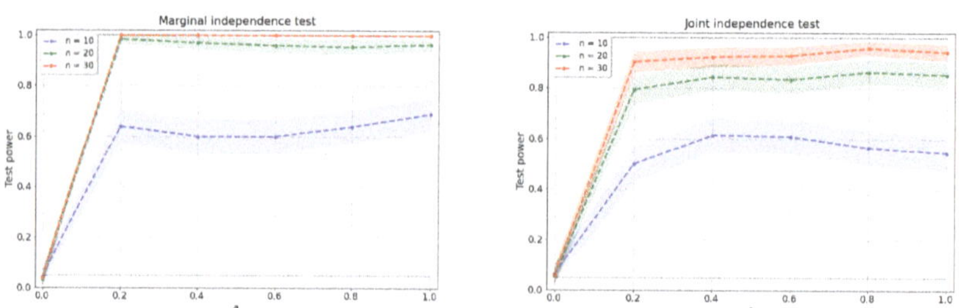

(a) (b)

Figure 1. (**a**) Bivariate and (**b**) joint independence tests over various values of the dependence factor a and sample size n. The joint independence test is conducted with $d = 4$ variables.

4.1.3. Conditional Independence Test

To evaluate whether X is independent of Y given $\mathcal{Z}$, where $\mathcal{Z}$ may be any subset within the power set of the $d \setminus \{X, Y\}$ remaining variables, we generate data samples according to:

$$\begin{aligned} z_i^j(u) &= \sum_{m=1}^{M} c_{i,m}^j \phi_{m,T}(u),\ j = 1, \ldots, |\mathcal{Z}| \\ x_i(s) &= \sum_{p \in \mathbf{PA}^X} \int_0^s z_i^p(u)\, \beta^p(u,s)\, du \\ y_i(t) &= \sum_{p \in \mathbf{PA}^Y} \int_0^t z_i^p(u)\, \beta^p(u,t)\, du + a' \int_0^t x_i(s)\, \beta^Y(s,t)\, ds\,, \end{aligned} \tag{14}$$

where $|\mathcal{Z}|$ is the cardinality of the set $\mathcal{Z}$, β's are given by Equation (12), and noise terms $\epsilon_i^{Zj}(u)$, $\epsilon_i^X(s)$ and $\epsilon_i^Y(t)$, are added to the discrete observation values.

Then, we apply Algorithm 1 to compute the statistics for our conditional independence test. Firstly, we find that the optimised regularisation strength λ^* is robust and reproducible for different random realisations with the same sample size and model parameters. Consequently, we search for one optimised λ^* (line 1–18 in Algorithm 1) for each sample size, and fix this value for all 200 independent trials. Figure 2 summarises the results for λ^* for $n \in \{100, 200, 300\}$ samples after conducting a grid search over a range of $L = 18$ possible values $10^{-4} \leq \lambda \leq 10^{-1}$, with $P = 1000$ permutations, and $B = 100$ rejection iterations. Note that the range of values for λ can be tuned in stages by the practitioner, e.g., starting with a coarse initial exploration followed by a more fine-grained range. We recommend to choose $B \geq 100$ for ease of comparison of the evaluation rejection rate to the acceptable false-positive rate, α. We find that the optimised λ^* exhibits a saturation as the number of conditional variables (the dimension of the conditional set) is increased. Given that we perform a kernel ridge regression, a larger number of samples n should result in lower requirements for regularisation—which aligns with our observations of a decreasing λ^* over the increase in number of samples n. Therefore, Algorithm 1 optimises the regularisation parameter λ^* such that the evaluation rejection rate of the test is closest to the allowable false-positive rate $\alpha = 0.05$.

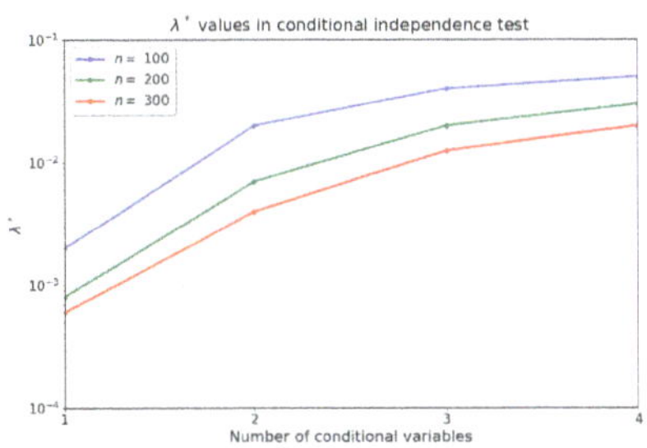

Figure 2. The optimised λ^* for increasing dimension d of the evaluated size of the conditional set and different sample sizes $n \in \{100, 200, 300\}$.

Figure 3a–d shows the results of the conditional independence test for increasing dimension d of the conditional set (i.e., number of conditional variables). We find that the test power is well preserved as d increases through a concomitant increase in λ^* that partly ameliorates the "curse of dimensionality" [48]. Furthermore, the values of the test power for $a' = 0$ correspond to the type-I error rates.

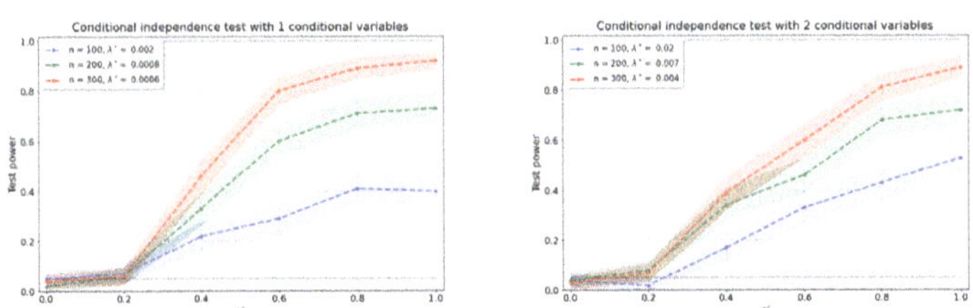

(a) (b)

Figure 3. *Cont.*

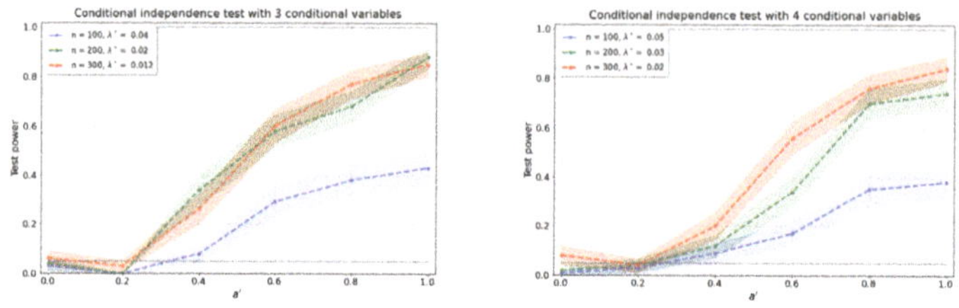

(c) (d)

Figure 3. The test power of the conditional independence tests over various values for a' and sample sizes n, from (**a–d**) 1–4 conditional variables. The regularisation parameter λ^* is given in the legend.

4.2. Causal Structure Learning

We use the three independence tests evaluated numerically in Section 4.1 to learn different causal structures among function-valued random variables. We start with regression-based methods for the bivariate case $X \to Y$ and extend to the multivariate case through regression-, constraint-based, and a combination of constraint- and regression-based causal structure learning approaches.

4.2.1. Synthetic Data

Regression-based causal discovery. We start by evaluating synthetic data for a bivariate system $X \to Y$ generated according to Equations (10) and (11) with $a = 1$. We generate 200 independent trials, and we score the performance of the method using the structural Hamming distance (SHD) (see Appendix D for its definition). As seen in Figure 4a, our regression-based algorithm using RESIT outperforms two well-known algorithms for causal discovery: Granger causality, which assumes linearity in the relationships [6], and CCM, which allows for nonlinearity through a time-series embedding [8].

Then, we evaluate how the regression-based approach performs in a system of three variables where data are generated according to random DAGs with three nodes that entail historical nonlinear dependence. One of the above methods (CCM) is commonly applied to bivariate problems only, hence we compare our method on a system with three variables to multivariate Granger causality [7] as well as to PC algorithm with momentary conditional independence (PCMCI), an algorithm where each time point is represented as a node in a graph [49] from which we extract a directed graph for the variables. Figure 4b shows substantially improved performance (lower SHD) of our regression-based algorithm with respect to both of these methods on three-variable systems. Details of all the methods are given in Appendix E.

Constraint-based causal discovery. The accuracy of our constraint-based approach is evaluated by computing three metrics: normalised SHD (SHD_{norm}), precision, and recall (see Appendix D for definitions). Figure 5 shows the accuracy of our algorithm when applied to $d \in \{3, 4, 5, 6\}$ variables. The normalised SHD in Figure 5a demonstrates consistent accuracy of the constraint-based causal structure learning method across sample sizes for all d. To complement this measure, we can examine jointly precision and recall in Figure 5b,c, where we find that the learnt edges are predominantly unoriented (low values of recall) but the oriented edges that are found are indeed correctly oriented (high values of precision).

Combined approach. To scale up our causal discovery techniques more efficiently to larger graphs, it is possible to combine constraint- and regression-based causal learning, yielding DAGs. In this "combined" approach we start with a constraint-based step through which we learn CPDAGs by applying conditional independence tests to any two variables conditioned on any subset of the remaining $d - 2$ variables and orient edges according to the Algorithm in Appendix C, which finds v-structures, applies Meek's orientation rules and returns the Markov equivalence class. Often, the Markov equivalence class entails undirected edges, but we can then take a second step using a regression-based approach, under a different set of assumptions, to orient edges by applying RESIT. This two-step process yields a DAG, i.e., every edge in the graph is oriented, in a more scalable manner than applying directly regression-based causal discovery. Then, we measure the accuracy of our approach computing the normalised SHD (A2) as above. Figure 6 shows that our results for $d = 3, 4, 5, 6$ variables compare favourably to PCMCI and to multivariate Granger causality with consistently lower SHD for all d.

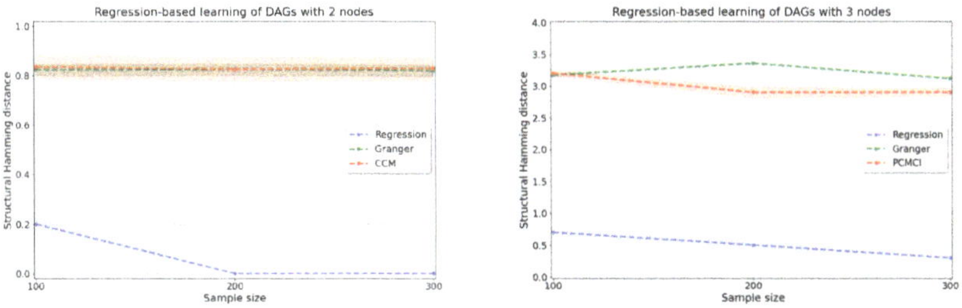

(**a**) (**b**)

Figure 4. Accuracy of the regression-based causal discovery using kernel-based joint independence tests among residuals for (**a**) two and (**b**) three variables. In the case of two variables (**a**), we compare our kernel-based method to Granger causality and CCM. In the case of three variables (**b**), we compare to multivariate Granger causality as well as using PCMCI to produce comparable results. Our method significantly outperforms both Granger causality and CCM in the bivariate setting, with just a few mistakes made for low sample numbers ($n = 100$) and no mistakes for higher sample sizes. For three variables, our method is substantially more accurate than PCMCI and Granger causality, with an average SHD of 0.3 at $n = 300$ versus 2.9 for PCMCI and 3.12 for Granger causality. The accuracy of the methods is measured in terms of the structural Hamming distance (SHD).

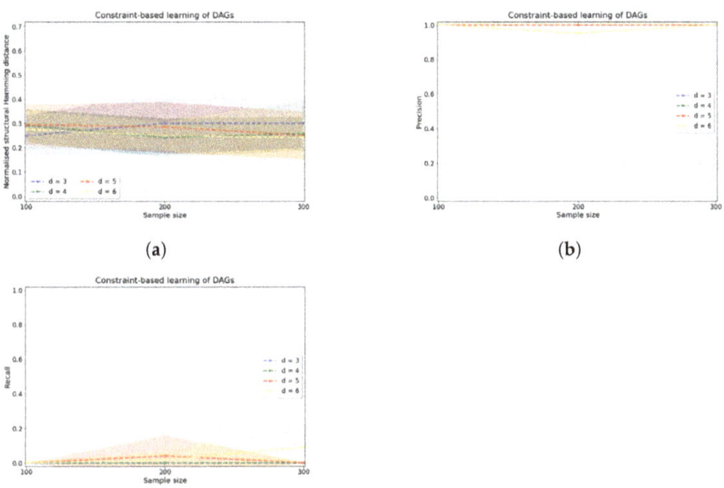

(**a**) (**b**) (**c**)

Figure 5. Constraint-based causal structure learning experiments. From left to right, we compute (**a**) the normalised SHD, (**b**) precision and (**c**) recall over $d \in \{3, 4, 5, 6\}$ variables and $n \in \{100, 200, 300\}$ samples with $a = 1$ as the dependence between any two variables in the data that are connected by an edge in the true DAG.

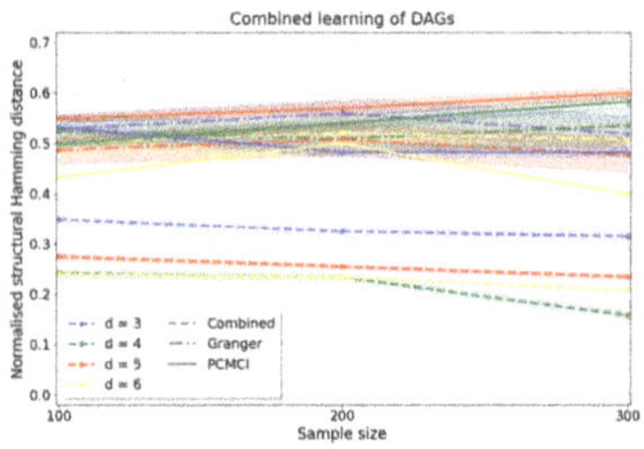

Figure 6. Causal structure learning with the "combined" approach, where we first apply the constraint-based method to find the Markov equivalence class, followed by the regression-based method to orient the undirected edges of the Markov equivalence class. We compute the normalised SHD over $d \in \{3,4,5,6\}$ variables and $n \in \{100,200,300\}$ samples with $a = 1$ as in Equation (13). Our results *(dashed lines)* have substantially lower normalised SHD than those obtained from Granger causality *(dash-dotted lines)* and PCMCI *(solid lines)*, applied as described in Appendix E.

4.2.2. Real-World Data

To showcase the application of our methods to real data, we return now to the motivating example on socioeconomic indicators mentioned in the Introduction (Section 1). Sulemana and Kpienbaareh [2] tested for the causal direction between *corruption* and *income inequality*, as measured using the Control of Corruption index [9] and Gini coefficient [50], respectively. They applied Granger causality with Wald-χ^2 tests, which statistically test the null hypothesis that an assumed explanatory variable does not have a (linear) influence on other considered variables. Each variable, *corruption* and *income inequality*, was tested against being the explanatory variable (i.e., the cause) in their bivariate relationship. Their findings showed that *income inequality* as the explanatory variable results in a p-value of 0.079, whereas *corruption* is more likely to be the cause with a p-value of 0.276. Analysing the same data using CCM, which does not assume linearity, we also find the same cause–effect direction: 70.9% of the sample pairs (x_i, y_i) validate corruption as the cause, against 29.7% of pairs which detect the opposite direction. However, using our proposed regression-based kernel approach, which does not assume linearity or stationarity, we find the opposite result, i.e., the causal dependence of *corruption* on *income inequality* is statistically more likely ($p = 0.0859$) than the reverse direction ($p = 0.0130$) when applying regression with subsequent independence test (RESIT) that rejects the null hypothesis of independence of the residuals after regression in the false causal directions.

Going beyond pairwise interactions, we have also applied our causal structure learning method to the set of World Governance Indicators (WGIs) [9]. The WGIs are a collection of six variables, which have been measured in 182 countries over 25 years from 1996 to 2020 (see Appendix I). We view the time-series of the countries as independent functional samples of each variable (so that $n = 182$ and the functional dimension is time), and we apply our methods as described above to establish the causal structure amongst the six WGIs. In this case, we use the "combined" approach by successively applying our constraint- and regression-based causal structure learning methods. We first learn an undirected causal skeleton from the WGIs (Figure 7a), and we find a triangle between Government Effectiveness (GE), Rule of Law (RL) and Control of Corruption (CC), and a separate link between Voice and Accountability (VA) and Regulatory Quality (RQ). Then, we orient these edges (Figure 7b) and find that Government Effectiveness (GE) causes both Rule of Law (RL) and Control of Corruption (CC), and Rule of Law (RL) causes Control of Corruption (CC). We also find that Voice and Accountability (VA) causes Regulatory Quality (RQ).

(a) (b)

Figure 7. Undirected (**a**) and directed (**b**) causal networks on the World Governance Indicators dataset to evaluate the results of the constraint-based approach alone (**a**) and the subsequent regression-based approach (**b**). The labels are abbreviations of the official names: Voice and Accountability (VA), Political Stability (PS), Government Effectiveness (GE), Regulatory Quality (RQ), Rule of Law (RL), and Control of Corruption (CC) (see Appendix I).

5. Discussion and Conclusions

We present a causal structure learning framework on functional data that utilises kernel-based independence tests to extend the applicability of the widely used regression- and constraint-based approaches. The foundation of the framework originates from the functional data analysis literature by interpreting any discrete-measured observations of a random variable as finite-dimensional realisations of functions.

Using synthetic data, we have demonstrated that our regression-based approach outperforms existing methods such as Granger causality, CCM and PCMCI when learning causal relationships between two and three variables. In the bivariate case, we have carried out a more detailed comparison to Granger causality and CCM to explore the robustness of our regression-based approach to nonlinearity and nonstationarity in the data (see Appendix H) We find that while Granger degrades under the introduction of nonlinearity in the data, and CCM degrades under the introduction of nonstationarity, our method remains robust in its performance under both nonlinearity and nonstationarity. In addition, as seen in Figure 4a, CCM can have difficulty in detecting strong unidirectional causal dependencies [8,51], where the cause variable X uniquely determines the state of the effect variable Y inducing "generalised synchrony" [52]. In such cases, CCM can predict samples of Y from X equally well as X from Y; hence, CCM finds $X \to Y$ and $X \leftarrow Y$ indistinctly. In contrast, our experiments (Section 4.2.1 and Appendix H) show that our regression-based method is unaffected by the presence of 'generalised synchrony' in the data.

Further, we show that our conditional independence test, which is the cornerstone of the constraint-based causal discovery approach, achieves type-I error rates close to the acceptable false-positive rate α and high type-II error rates, even when the number of variables in the conditional set increases. Shah et al. [48] rightly state that any conditional independence test can suffer from an undesirable test size or low test power in finite samples, and our method is obviously no exception. However, Figure 3 demonstrates the counterbalance of the "curse of dimensionality" through the optimised regularisation strength λ^*. Indeed, while with larger numbers of conditional variables, we would generally expect the test power to diminish, the optimisation of λ^* offsets this reduction, resulting in no significant decrease in test power with a growing number of conditional variables. Although our proposed method is computationally expensive and significantly benefits from high sample sizes, a suitable regularisation strength could be chosen for large conditional sets in principle.

Moreover, we demonstrate that constraint- and regression-based causal discovery methods can be combined to learn DAGs with large number of nodes, which would otherwise be computationally very expensive when relying on regression-based methods to yield DAGs. By comparing Figures 5a and 6 we see however that it does not necessarily result in a lower SHD. After learning the Markov equivalence class through the constraint-based approach, we apply RESIT to orient undirected edges in the "combined" approach. Here, mistakes in the orientation of undirected edges add 2 to the SHD whereas an undirected edge only adds 1 to the SHD. When applied to real-world data, we have utilised this approach to learn a causal graph of the WGIs, assuming each relationship between two variables is uni-directionally identifiable as suggested by several economic studies [11–13].

The presented work contributes to opening the field of causal discovery to functional data. Beyond the results presented here, we believe that more research needs to be conducted to (i) increase the efficiency of the independence tests, meaning smaller sample sets can achieve higher test power; (ii) learn about upper bounds of the regularisation strength λ^* with respect to the size of the sample and conditional sets; (iii) reduce the computational cost of the conditional independence test (see Appendices F and G for a comparison to other methods); and (iv) establish connections and investigate differences to causal structure learning approaches based on transfer entropy [53,54].

Author Contributions: Conceptualization: F.L., J.v.K. and J.P.; Methodology: F.L., J.v.K. and J.P.; Software: F.L.; Validation: F.L., B.S. and M.B.; Formal analysis: F.L.; Data curation: F.L.; Writing—original draft: F.L.; Writing—review and editing: J.v.K., B.S. and M.B.; Supervision: M.B. All authors have read and agreed to the published version of the manuscript.

Funding: F.L. and M.B. acknowledge support by EPSRC grant EP/N014529/1 funding the EPSRC Centre for Mathematics of Precision Healthcare at Imperial, and by the Nuffield Foundation under the project "The Future of Work and Well-being: The Pissarides Review". J.v.K., J.P. and B.S. acknowledge support by the Tübingen AI Center (FKZ: 01IS18039B) and by the Deutsche Forschungsgemeinschaft (DFG, German Research Foundation) under Germany's Excellence Strategy—EXC number 2064/1—Project number 390727645.

Data Availability Statement: Data are contained within the article.

Conflicts of Interest: The authors declare no conflict of interest.

Appendix A. Proof of Theorem 1

Proof. All norms $\|\cdot\|$ and inner products $\langle\cdot,\cdot\rangle$ in this proof are taken with respect to the RKHS in which the normand and the arguments of the inner product reside.

Denote by $\mathrm{HSCIC}(\mathbf{X},\mathbf{Y},\mathbf{Z})$ the *true* Hilbert–Schmidt conditional independence criterion between the random variables $\mathbf{X}$ and $\mathbf{Y}$ given $\mathbf{Z}$, i.e.,

$$\mathrm{HSCIC}(\mathbf{X},\mathbf{Y},\mathbf{Z}) = \|\mu_{\mathbf{XY}|\mathbf{Z}} - \mu_{\mathbf{X}|\mathbf{Z}} \otimes \mu_{\mathbf{Y}|\mathbf{Z}}\|,$$

and denote by $\widehat{\mathrm{HSCIC}}(\mathbf{X},\mathbf{Y},\mathbf{Z},\lambda_n)$ the empirical estimate of $\mathrm{HSCIC}(\mathbf{X},\mathbf{Y},\mathbf{Z})$ based on samples, i.e.,

$$\widehat{\mathrm{HSCIC}}(\mathbf{X},\mathbf{Y},\mathbf{Z},\lambda_n) = \|\hat{\mu}_{\mathbf{XY}|\mathbf{Z}} - \hat{\mu}_{\mathbf{X}|\mathbf{Z}} \otimes \hat{\mu}_{\mathbf{Y}|\mathbf{Z}}\|,$$

where $\hat{\mu}_{\mathbf{XY}|\mathbf{Z}}$, $\hat{\mu}_{\mathbf{X}|\mathbf{Z}}$ and $\hat{\mu}_{\mathbf{Y}|\mathbf{Z}}$ are the empirical estimates of the conditional mean embeddings $\mu_{\mathbf{XY}|\mathbf{Z}}$, $\mu_{\mathbf{X}|\mathbf{Z}}$ and $\mu_{\mathbf{Y}|\mathbf{Z}}$ obtained with the regularisation parameter λ_n.

Note that by the reverse triangle inequality, followed by the ordinary triangle inequality, we have

$$\begin{aligned}
\left|\mathrm{HSCIC}(\mathbf{X},\mathbf{Y},\mathbf{Z}) - \widehat{\mathrm{HSCIC}}(\mathbf{X},\mathbf{Y},\mathbf{Z},\lambda_n)\right| &= \left|\|\mu_{\mathbf{XY}|\mathbf{Z}} - \mu_{\mathbf{X}|\mathbf{Z}} \otimes \mu_{\mathbf{Y}|\mathbf{Z}}\| - \|\hat{\mu}_{\mathbf{XY}|\mathbf{Z}} - \hat{\mu}_{\mathbf{X}|\mathbf{Z}} \otimes \hat{\mu}_{\mathbf{Y}|\mathbf{Z}}\|\right| \\
&\leq \|\mu_{\mathbf{XY}|\mathbf{Z}} - \mu_{\mathbf{X}|\mathbf{Z}} \otimes \mu_{\mathbf{Y}|\mathbf{Z}} - \hat{\mu}_{\mathbf{XY}|\mathbf{Z}} + \hat{\mu}_{\mathbf{X}|\mathbf{Z}} \otimes \hat{\mu}_{\mathbf{Y}|\mathbf{Z}}\| \\
&\leq \|\mu_{\mathbf{XY}|\mathbf{Z}} - \hat{\mu}_{\mathbf{XY}|\mathbf{Z}}\| + \|\mu_{\mathbf{X}|\mathbf{Z}} \otimes \mu_{\mathbf{Y}|\mathbf{Z}} - \hat{\mu}_{\mathbf{X}|\mathbf{Z}} \otimes \hat{\mu}_{\mathbf{Y}|\mathbf{Z}}\|.
\end{aligned}$$

Here,

$$
\begin{aligned}
\|\mu_{\mathbf{X}|\mathbf{Z}} \otimes \mu_{\mathbf{Y}|\mathbf{Z}} - \hat{\mu}_{\mathbf{X}|\mathbf{Z}} \otimes \hat{\mu}_{\mathbf{Y}|\mathbf{Z}}\|^2 &= \langle \mu_{\mathbf{X}|\mathbf{Z}} \otimes \mu_{\mathbf{Y}|\mathbf{Z}}, \mu_{\mathbf{X}|\mathbf{Z}} \otimes \mu_{\mathbf{Y}|\mathbf{Z}} \rangle \\
&\quad - 2\langle \mu_{\mathbf{X}|\mathbf{Z}} \otimes \mu_{\mathbf{Y}|\mathbf{Z}}, \hat{\mu}_{\mathbf{X}|\mathbf{Z}} \otimes \hat{\mu}_{\mathbf{Y}|\mathbf{Z}} \rangle \\
&\quad + \langle \hat{\mu}_{\mathbf{X}|\mathbf{Z}} \otimes \hat{\mu}_{\mathbf{Y}|\mathbf{Z}}, \hat{\mu}_{\mathbf{X}|\mathbf{Z}} \otimes \hat{\mu}_{\mathbf{Y}|\mathbf{Z}} \rangle \\
&= \langle \mu_{\mathbf{X}|\mathbf{Z}}, \mu_{\mathbf{X}|\mathbf{Z}} \rangle \langle \mu_{\mathbf{Y}|\mathbf{Z}}, \mu_{\mathbf{Y}|\mathbf{Z}} \rangle \\
&\quad - 2\langle \mu_{\mathbf{X}|\mathbf{Z}}, \hat{\mu}_{\mathbf{X}|\mathbf{Z}} \rangle \langle \mu_{\mathbf{Y}|\mathbf{Z}}, \hat{\mu}_{\mathbf{Y}|\mathbf{Z}} \rangle \\
&\quad + \langle \hat{\mu}_{\mathbf{X}|\mathbf{Z}}, \hat{\mu}_{\mathbf{X}|\mathbf{Z}} \rangle \langle \hat{\mu}_{\mathbf{Y}|\mathbf{Z}}, \hat{\mu}_{\mathbf{Y}|\mathbf{Z}} \rangle \\
&= \langle \mu_{\mathbf{X}|\mathbf{Z}}, \mu_{\mathbf{X}|\mathbf{Z}} \rangle \langle \mu_{\mathbf{Y}|\mathbf{Z}}, \mu_{\mathbf{Y}|\mathbf{Z}} \rangle \\
&\quad - 2\langle \mu_{\mathbf{X}|\mathbf{Z}}, \mu_{\mathbf{X}|\mathbf{Z}} \rangle \langle \mu_{\mathbf{Y}|\mathbf{Z}}, \hat{\mu}_{\mathbf{Y}|\mathbf{Z}} \rangle + 2\langle \mu_{\mathbf{X}|\mathbf{Z}}, \mu_{\mathbf{X}|\mathbf{Z}} - \hat{\mu}_{\mathbf{X}|\mathbf{Z}} \rangle \langle \mu_{\mathbf{Y}|\mathbf{Z}}, \hat{\mu}_{\mathbf{Y}|\mathbf{Z}} \rangle \\
&\quad + \langle \mu_{\mathbf{X}|\mathbf{Z}}, \mu_{\mathbf{X}|\mathbf{Z}} \rangle \langle \hat{\mu}_{\mathbf{Y}|\mathbf{Z}}, \hat{\mu}_{\mathbf{Y}|\mathbf{Z}} \rangle \\
&\quad + \langle \hat{\mu}_{\mathbf{X}|\mathbf{Z}} - \mu_{\mathbf{X}|\mathbf{Z}}, \hat{\mu}_{\mathbf{X}|\mathbf{Z}} + \mu_{\mathbf{X}|\mathbf{Z}} \rangle \langle \hat{\mu}_{\mathbf{Y}|\mathbf{Z}}, \hat{\mu}_{\mathbf{Y}|\mathbf{Z}} \rangle \\
&= \langle \mu_{\mathbf{X}|\mathbf{Z}}, \mu_{\mathbf{X}|\mathbf{Z}} \rangle \|\mu_{\mathbf{Y}|\mathbf{Z}} - \hat{\mu}_{\mathbf{Y}|\mathbf{Z}}\|^2 + 2\langle \mu_{\mathbf{X}|\mathbf{Z}}, \mu_{\mathbf{X}|\mathbf{Z}} - \hat{\mu}_{\mathbf{X}|\mathbf{Z}} \rangle \langle \mu_{\mathbf{Y}|\mathbf{Z}}, \hat{\mu}_{\mathbf{Y}|\mathbf{Z}} \rangle \\
&\quad + \langle \hat{\mu}_{\mathbf{X}|\mathbf{Z}} - \mu_{\mathbf{X}|\mathbf{Z}}, \hat{\mu}_{\mathbf{X}|\mathbf{Z}} + \mu_{\mathbf{X}|\mathbf{Z}} \rangle \langle \hat{\mu}_{\mathbf{Y}|\mathbf{Z}}, \hat{\mu}_{\mathbf{Y}|\mathbf{Z}} \rangle \\
&\leq \|\mu_{\mathbf{X}|\mathbf{Z}}\|^2 \|\mu_{\mathbf{Y}|\mathbf{Z}} - \hat{\mu}_{\mathbf{Y}|\mathbf{Z}}\|^2 \\
&\quad + \|\mu_{\mathbf{X}|\mathbf{Z}} - \hat{\mu}_{\mathbf{X}|\mathbf{Z}}\| \Big(2\|\mu_{\mathbf{X}|\mathbf{Z}}\| \langle \mu_{\mathbf{Y}|\mathbf{Z}}, \hat{\mu}_{\mathbf{Y}|\mathbf{Z}} \rangle + \|\hat{\mu}_{\mathbf{X}|\mathbf{Z}} + \mu_{\mathbf{X}|\mathbf{Z}}\| \|\hat{\mu}_{\mathbf{Y}|\mathbf{Z}}\| \Big),
\end{aligned}
$$

where we used the Cauchy–Schwarz inequality in the last inequality. We note that (Park and Muandet [18], Theorem 4.4) ensures that each of $\|\mu_{\mathbf{XY}|\mathbf{Z}} - \hat{\mu}_{\mathbf{XY}|\mathbf{Z}}\|$, $\|\mu_{\mathbf{Y}|\mathbf{Z}} - \hat{\mu}_{\mathbf{Y}|\mathbf{Z}}\|$ and $\|\mu_{\mathbf{X}|\mathbf{Z}} - \hat{\mu}_{\mathbf{X}|\mathbf{Z}}\|$ converge to 0 in probability, hence $\widehat{\text{HSCIC}}(\mathbf{X}, \mathbf{Y}, \mathbf{Z}, \lambda_n) \to \text{HSCIC}(\mathbf{X}, \mathbf{Y}, \mathbf{Z})$ in probability with respect to the L_2-norm.

Now we show that the empirical average of the empirical HSCIC converges to the population integral of the population HSCIC. Writing $\widehat{\text{HSCIC}}$ as a shorthand for $\widehat{\text{HSCIC}}(\mathbf{X}, \mathbf{Y}, \mathbf{Z}, \lambda_n)$, we see that

$$
\begin{aligned}
\left| \frac{1}{n} \sum_{i=1}^{n} \widehat{\text{HSCIC}}(z_i) - \int \text{HSCIC}(z) d\mathbb{P}(z) \right| &\leq \left| \frac{1}{n} \sum_{i=1}^{n} \widehat{\text{HSCIC}}(z_i) - \int \widehat{\text{HSCIC}}(z) d\mathbb{P}(z) \right| \\
&\quad + \left| \int \widehat{\text{HSCIC}}(z) d\mathbb{P}(z) - \int \text{HSCIC}(z) d\mathbb{P}(z) \right| \\
&\leq \sup_{f \in \mathcal{F}} \left| \frac{1}{n} \sum_{i=1}^{n} f(z_i) - \int f(z) d\mathbb{P}(z) \right| \\
&\quad + \left| \int \widehat{\text{HSCIC}}(z) d\mathbb{P}(z) - \int \text{HSCIC}(z) d\mathbb{P}(z) \right|.
\end{aligned}
$$

Here, the first term converges to 0 thanks to the uniform law of large numbers over the function class $\mathcal{F}$ in which the empirical estimation of $\widehat{\text{HSCIC}}$ is carried out, and the second term converges to 0, as shown above.

Now, by (Park and Muandet [18], Theorem 5.4), since our kernel $k_1 \otimes k_2$ is characteristic, we have that $\text{HSCIC}(\mathbf{X}, \mathbf{Y}, \mathbf{Z})$ is the identically zero function if—and only if—$\mathbf{X} \perp \mathbf{Y} \mid \mathbf{Z}$. Hence, if the alternative hypothesis H_1 holds, then we have

$$
\int \text{HSCIC}(z) d\mathbb{P}(z) > 0.
$$

See that, for any $r > 0$, we have

$$\begin{aligned}\lim_{n\to\infty} \mathbb{P}\left(\frac{1}{\sqrt{n}}\sum_{i=1}^{n} \widehat{\text{HSCIC}}(z_i) \geq r\right) &= 1 - \lim_{n\to\infty} \mathbb{P}\left(\frac{1}{\sqrt{n}}\sum_{i=1}^{n} \widehat{\text{HSCIC}}(z_i) < r\right) \\ &= 1 - \lim_{n\to\infty} \mathbb{P}\left(\frac{1}{n}\sum_{i=1}^{n} \widehat{\text{HSCIC}}(z_i) - \frac{r}{\sqrt{n}} < 0\right) \\ &= 1 - \lim_{n\to\infty} \mathbb{P}\left(\int \text{HSCIC}(z) d\mathbb{P}(z) < 0\right) \\ &= 1,\end{aligned}$$

where we used Portmanteau's theorem ([55], p. 6, Lemma 2.2) to get from the second line to the third, using the convergence of $\frac{1}{n}\sum_{i=1}^{n} \widehat{\text{HSCIC}}(z_i)$ to $\int \text{HSCIC}(z)d\mathbb{P}(z)$ shown above. Hence, our test is consistent. □

Appendix B. Additional Definitions for Causal Learning

Appendix B.1. d-Separation

If X, Y, and Z are three pairwise disjoint (sets of) nodes in a DAG G, then Z d-separates X from Y in G if Z blocks every possible path between (any node in) X and (any node in) Y in G ([35], § 1.2.3). Then, we write $X \perp\!\!\!\perp_G Y|Z$. The symbol $\perp\!\!\!\perp_G$ is commonly used to denote d-separation.

Appendix B.2. Faithfulness Assumption

If two random variables are (conditionally) independent in the observed distribution $\mathbb{P}$, then they are d-separated in the underlying causal graph G ([37], Definition 6.33).

Appendix B.3. Causal Markov Assumption

The distribution $\mathbb{P}_{XYZ}$ is Markov with respect to a DAG G if $X \perp\!\!\!\perp_G Y|Z \implies X \perp\!\!\!\perp Y|Z$ for all disjoint (sets of) nodes X, Y, Z, where $\perp\!\!\!\perp_G$ denotes d-separation ([37], Definition 6.21).

Appendix C. Meek's Orientation Rules, the SGS and the PC Algorithms

In Figure A1, a node is placed at each end of the edges. Rule 1 states that if one directed edge (here the vertical edge) points towards another undirected edge (the horizontal edge) that is not further connected to any other edges, the undirected edge must point in the same direction as the adjacent edge, because the three vertices would otherwise form a v-structure (which are only formed with conditional dependence). Rule 2, in contrast, points the undirected edge in both adjacent vertices' direction because it would violate the acyclicity of a DAG otherwise. Rule 3 and 4 avoid new v-structures which would come into existence by applying Rule 2 twice if the oriented edges pointed in the opposite direction. These new v-structures would be in the left top corners of the rectangles.

Based on Meek's orientation rules, the SGS algorithm tests each pair of variables as follows ([14], § 5.4.1):

1. Form the complete undirected graph G from the set of vertices (or nodes) $\mathbf{V}$.
2. For each pair of vertices X and Y, if there exists a subset S of $\mathbf{V} \setminus \{X, Y\}$ such that X and Y are d-separated, i.e., conditionally independent (causal Markov condition), given Z, remove the edge between X and Y from G.
3. Let K be the undirected graph resulting from the previous step 2. For each triple of vertices X, Y, and Z such that the pair X and Y and the pair Y and Z are each adjacent in K (written as $X - Y - Z$) but the pair X and Z are not adjacent in K, orient $X - Y - Z$ as $X \to Y \leftarrow Z$ if—and only if—there is no subset S of Y that d-separates X and Z.
4. Repeat the following steps until no more edges can be oriented:

(a) If $X \rightarrow Y$, Y and Z are adjacent, X and Z are not adjacent, and there is no arrowhead of other vertices at Y, then orient $Y - Z$ as $Y \rightarrow Z$ (Rule 1 of Meek's orientation rules).

(b) If there is a directed path over some other vertices from X to Y, and an edge between X and Y, then orient $X - Y$ as $X \rightarrow Y$ (Rule 2 of Meek's orientation rules).

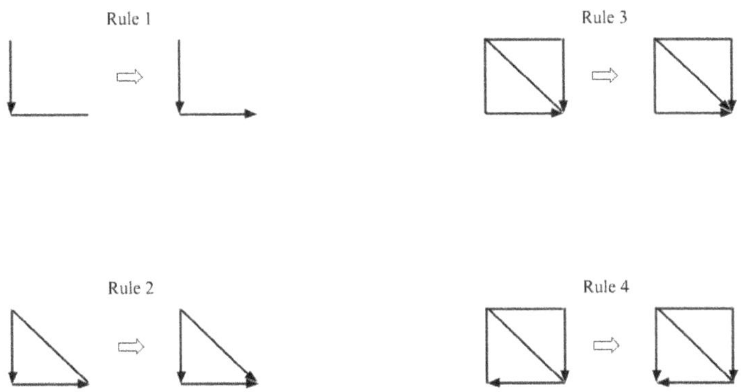

Figure A1. Meek rules to orient edges that remain in the graph after conditional independence tests and edges are oriented based on detected colliders. Proofs that edges cannot be oriented in the opposite direction without violating the acyclicity of the graph and found conditional independencies are given in Meek [45].

The large computational cost of applying the SGS algorithm (especially step 2) to data, due to the large number of combinations of variables as the potential conditional sets, opened the door for computationally more efficient methods. The PC algorithm ([14], § 5.4.2) is amongst the most popular alternatives and minimises the computational cost by searching for conditional independence in a structured manner, as opposed to step 2 of the SGS algorithm that iterates over all possible conditional subsets to any two variables A and B. Starting again with a fully connected undirected graph, the PC algorithm begins by testing for marginal independence between any two variables A and B and deletes the edge connecting A and B, $A - B$, if $A \perp\!\!\!\perp B$. Then, it proceeds with testing for $A \perp\!\!\!\perp B|C$ and erases $A - B$ if one conditional variable C is found that makes A and B independent given C. Afterwards, the conditional set is extended to two variables, $\{C, D\}$, and the edge $A - B$ is deleted if this conditional set makes A and B independent. The conditional set is extended, round after round, until no more conditional independencies are found, resulting in the sparse graph K. Step 3 and 4 are then pursued as in the SGS algorithm.

Appendix D. Definitions of Performance Metrics

Appendix D.1. SHD

For two graphs, G_1 and G_2, SHD is the sum of the element-wise absolute differences between the adjacency matrices A_1 and A_2 of G_1 and G_2, respectively:

$$\text{SHD} = \sum_{ij} |A_1^{ij} - A_2^{ij}| \,. \tag{A1}$$

Thus, when a learnt causal graph G_1 includes an edge $X \rightarrow Y$ oriented opposite to the corresponding edge in the true graph G_2 (i.e., $X \leftarrow Y$ is true), we add 2 to the SHD score ("double penalty"). Note that others (e.g., [56]) only penalise by 1 for a learnt edge being directed opposite to the true edge.

Appendix D.2. Normalised SHD

We also define the normalised SHD, where we divide SHD by the number of possible directed edges in a graph of size d, thus allowing comparison across graphs with different number of nodes:

$$\mathrm{SHD}_{\mathrm{norm}} = \frac{\mathrm{SHD}}{d(d-1)} \,. \tag{A2}$$

Appendix D.3. Precision

Let the total number of edges in a learnt graph G_1 be the sum of truly and falsely oriented edges, $e = e_t + e_f$ (the true-positives and false-positives, respectively). The truly oriented edges are the edges that correspond to the zero elements in the matrix containing the element-wise differences between the learnt A_1 and the true A_2. In contrast, the falsely oriented edges are the elements having a value of 2 ("double penalty"). Precision is the proportion of correctly oriented edges e_t in a learnt graph G_1 in comparison to a true graph G_2 out of all learnt edges e in G_1:

$$\mathrm{Precision} = \frac{e_t}{e} \,. \tag{A3}$$

Appendix D.4. Recall

We separate between oriented and unoriented edges, e_o and e_u, respectively, which can again be summed up to the total number of edges, $e = e_o + e_u$. Recall is the fraction of edges in the CPDAG that are oriented:

$$\mathrm{Recall} = \frac{e_o}{e} \,. \tag{A4}$$

Appendix E. Other Causal Methods Used for Comparison

Appendix E.1. Granger causality

We implement Granger causality through software provided by Seabold and Perktold [57] for $d = 2$ and by Runge et al. [49] for $d > 2$, and define the optimal lag as the first local minimum in the mutual information function over measurement points. Given that Granger causality is applied to a pair of samples, (x_i, y_i), we iterate over every pair and determine the percentage of pairs that result in $X \rightarrow Y$ against $X \leftarrow Y$. We follow a similar process for more than two variables.

Appendix E.2. CCM

We implement CCM through software provided by Javier [58] and define the optimal lag as for Granger causality. The embedding dimensionality is determined by a false nearest neighbour method [59]. As with Granger causality, CCM is also applied to a pair of samples, (x_i, y_i). We take the same summarising approach and iterate over every pair and determine the percentage of of pairs that result in $X \rightarrow Y$ against $X \leftarrow Y$.

Appendix E.3. PCMCI

Runge et al. [49] proposed PCMCI, a method that produces *time-series graphs* where each node represents a variable at a certain state in time. In our experiments, we estimate the maximum possible lag as the average of the first local minimum of mutual information of all considered data series. To test for the presence of an edge, we apply distance correlation-based independence tests [60] between the residuals of X and Y that remain after regressing out the influence of the remaining nodes in the graph through Gaussian processes. The distance correlation coefficients of the significant edges between two variables are summed up to measure the prevalence of a causal direction of edges connecting these two variables. The causal direction with the greater sum is considered to be the directed edge, and assessed against the edge between the same two variables in the true DAG.

Appendix F. Computational Complexity of Our Proposed Methods

Appendix F.1. Regression-Based Causal Discovery

One needs to iterate over all possible candidate DAGs to check the possibility that it was hte causal graph that generated the observed data. The total number of candidate DAGs κ_d of a graph with d nodes is given by

$$\kappa_d = \sum_{i=1}^{d} (-1)^{i+1} \binom{d}{i} 2^{i(d-i)} \kappa_{d-i} \,. \tag{A5}$$

Appendix F.2. Constraint-Based Approach

One needs to exhaustively test for conditional independence between any two nodes of the graph given any possible subset of the remaining nodes. Including the empty conditional set, this results in 2^{d-2} conditional independence tests for every pair of nodes in the graph. Then, the total number of conditional independence tests is:

$$\eta_d = \binom{d}{2} 2^{d-2} \,. \tag{A6}$$

Appendix G. Comparison of Running Times of Our Proposed Method and the Other Causal Methods

Table A1 shows the running times of the proposed and comparison methods for synthetic data in Section 4. Furthermore, for the bivariate real-world socioeconomic dataset of *corruption* and *income inequality* in Section 4.2.2, Granger causality completes the computation in 731 ms, CCM in 537 ms, and the regression-based approach in 19.2 s (according to our Python implementations).

Table A1. Running times for one trial with 100 samples for our three proposed methods (regression, constraint, combined) and the three comparison methods (Granger, CCM, PCMCI) over various graph sizes (number of variables $d \in \{2,3,4\}$). The dash "–" implies that the method was not applied in our experiments in Section 4.

d	Regression-Based	Constraint-Based	Combined	Granger Causality	CCM	PCMCI
2	1 min 57 s	–	–	998 ms	1.57 s	–
3	30 min 35 s	1 min 10 s	3 min 13 s	43 s	–	45.5 s
4	–	8 min 10 s	8 min 1 s	1 min 23 s	–	1 min 29 s
5	–	34 min 33 s	39 min 8 s	2 min 44 s	–	2 min 50 s
6	–	1 h 31 min 36 s	1 h 43 min 54 s	3 min 20 s	–	3 min 27 s

Appendix H. Influence of Nonlinearity and Nonstationarity on Granger Causality and CCM

Appendix H.1. Nonlinearity and Granger Causality:

To examine the increased robustness of our proposed algorithm to nonlinearity, we define a bivariate system with X as the cause and Y as the effect under the assumption of causal sufficiency, i.e., $X \to Y$. We consider n functional samples $\{x_i(s)\}_{i=1}^n$ of X defined over the interval $s = [0,1]$ generated as described in Equation (10), and the samples $\{y_i(t)\}_{i=1}^n$ of Y defined over $t = [0,1]$ by:

$$y_i(t) = (1-r) \int_0^t x_i(s)\, ds + r \int_0^t x_i(s)\, \beta(s,t)\, ds \,. \tag{A7}$$

By sweeping $r \in [0,1]$, we go from linear dependence between $x_i(s)$ and $y_i(t)$ at $r = 0$ to nonlinear dependence at $r = 1$, where we recover the model in Equation (11) with $a = 1$. We thus expect high accuracy from Granger causality at $r = 0$, where there is stationarity and linearity [6]. As r increases, we expect that our regression-based approach will achieve more accurate results, and the results of Granger will degrade as the assumption of linearity will not be met. As expected, Figure A2 shows the improved prediction accuracy (lower SHD) of our regression-based approach as r is increased, reaching SHD of 0.425 ± 0.1542 (versus 0.8 ± 0.092 for Granger causality) at $r = 1$.

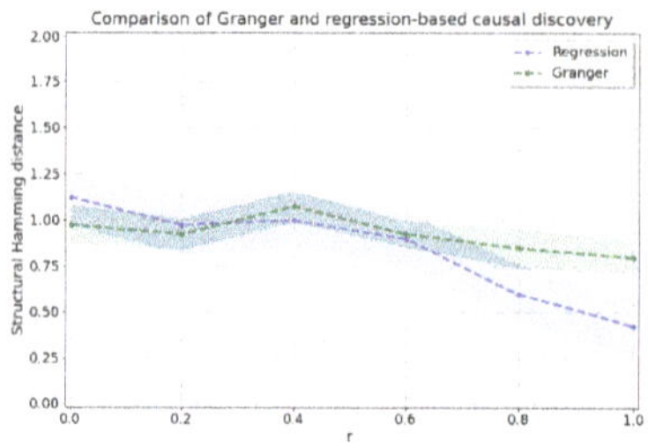

Figure A2. Comparison between Granger causality and our regression-based method for $n = 100$ and various values for r which influence the level of nonlinearity in the dependence from X to Y.

Appendix H.2. Nonstationarity and CCM:

To evaluate the importance of nonstationarity in causal learning, we compare our regression-based method against CCM [8], as a nonstationary component is introduced. We generate samples from a bivariate coupled nonlinear logistic map as defined in Sugihara et al. [8] such that X influences Y more strongly than vice versa and we add nonstationary trends $\nu_X(t)$ and $\nu_Y(t)$:

$$x_i(t+1) = x_i(t)\,[0.8 - 3.5x_i(t) - 0.02y_i(t)] + r\,\nu_X(t) \tag{A8}$$
$$y_i(t+1) = y_i(t)\,[0.2 - 3.2y_i(t) - 0.1x_i(t)] + r\,\nu_Y(t)\,, \tag{A9}$$

where $\nu_X(t) = \tanh\left(c_\nu t - \frac{c_\nu}{2}\right)$ with $c_\nu \sim \mathcal{N}(8,1)$, and similarly for $\nu_Y(t)$. The factor $r \in [0,1]$ controls the weight of the nonstationarity of the time-series as it is increased.

As shown in Figure A3, CCM is only able to capture the true causal direction $X \to Y$ for $r = 0$, as expected, but CCM loses its detection power as soon as the data become nonstationary ($r > 0$). In contrast, the regression-based maintains its detection power as the nonstationarity is increased.

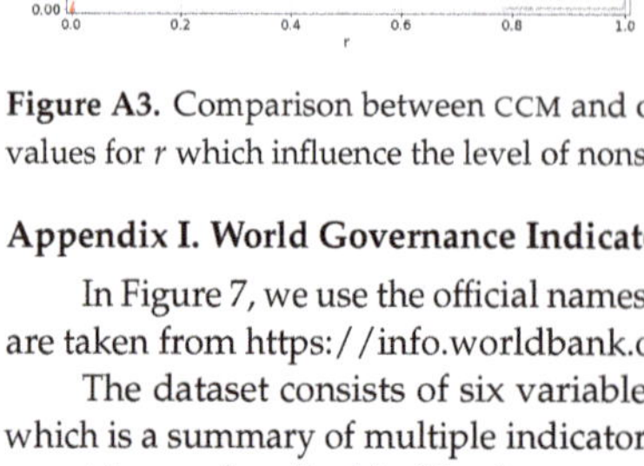

Figure A3. Comparison between CCM and our regression-based method for $n = 100$ and various values for r which influence the level of nonstationarity in the data for X and Y.

Appendix I. World Governance Indicators

In Figure 7, we use the official names, as mentioned in Table A2, where the descriptions are taken from https://info.worldbank.org/governance/wgi/ (accessed on 7 June 2023).

The dataset consists of six variables (normalised to a range from 0 to 100), each of which is a summary of multiple indicators measured over 25 years from 1996 to 2020 in 182 countries, as described in (Kaufmann et al. [9], §4).

Table A2. Abbreviations, official names and descriptions of the variables in the World Governance Indicators data set.

Abbreviation	Official Name	Description
VA	Voice and Accountability	Voice and accountability captures perceptions of the extent to which a country's citizens are able to participate in selecting their government, as well as freedom of expression, freedom of association, and a free media.
PS	Political Stability and No Violence	Political Stability and Absence of Violence/Terrorism measures perceptions of the likelihood of political instability and/or politically-motivated violence, including terrorism.
GE	Government Effectiveness	Government effectiveness captures perceptions of the quality of public services, the quality of the civil service and the degree of its independence from political pressures, the quality of policy formulation and implementation, and the credibility of the government's commitment to such policies.
RQ	Regulatory Quality	Regulatory quality captures perceptions of the ability of the government to formulate and implement sound policies and regulations that permit and promote private sector development.
RL	Rule of Law	Rule of law captures perceptions of the extent to which agents have confidence in and abide by the rules of society, and in particular the quality of contract enforcement, property rights, the police, and the courts, as well as the likelihood of crime and violence.
CC	Control of Corruption	Control of corruption captures perceptions of the extent to which public power is exercised for private gain, including both petty and grand forms of corruption, as well as "capture" of the state by elites and private interests.

References

1. Runge, J.; Bathiany, S.; Bollt, E.; Camps-Valls, G.; Coumou, D.; Deyle, E.; Glymour, C.; Kretschmer, M.; Mahecha, M.D.; Muñoz-Marí, J.; et al. Inferring causation from time series in Earth system sciences. *Nat. Commun.* **2019**, *10*, 2553. [CrossRef] [PubMed]
2. Sulemana, I.; Kpienbaareh, D. An empirical examination of the relationship between income inequality and corruption in Africa. *Econ. Anal. Policy* **2018**, *60*, 27–42. [CrossRef]
3. Finkle, J.D.; Wu, J.J.; Bagheri, N. Windowed granger causal inference strategy improves discovery of gene regulatory networks. *Proc. Natl. Acad. Sci. USA* **2018**, *115*, 2252–2257. [CrossRef]
4. Glymour, C.; Zhang, K.; Spirtes, P. Review of causal discovery methods based on graphical models. *Front. Genet.* **2019**, *10*, 524. [CrossRef]
5. Ramsay, J.O. *Functional Data Analysis*, 2nd ed.; Springer series in statistics; Springer: New York, NY, USA, 2005.
6. Granger, C.W. Investigating causal relations by econometric models and cross-spectral methods. *Econom. J. Econom. Soc.* **1969**, *37*, 424–438. [CrossRef]
7. Geweke, J. Measurement of linear dependence and feedback between multiple time series. *J. Am. Stat. Assoc.* **1982**, *77*, 304–313. [CrossRef]
8. Sugihara, G.; May, R.; Ye, H.; Hsieh, C.h.; Deyle, E.; Fogarty, M.; Munch, S. Detecting causality in complex ecosystems. *Science* **2012**, *338*, 496–500. [CrossRef]
9. Kaufmann, D.; Kraay, A.; Mastruzzi, M. The worldwide governance indicators: Methodology and analytical issues. *Hague J. Rule Law* **2011**, *3*, 220–246. [CrossRef]
10. World Bank. Gini Index. 2022. Available online: https://data.worldbank.org/indicator/SI.POV.GINI (accessed on 7 June 2023).
11. Jong-Sung, Y.; Khagram, S. A comparative study of inequality and corruption. *Am. Sociol. Rev.* **2005**, *70*, 136–157. [CrossRef]
12. Alesina, A.; Angeletos, G.M. Corruption, inequality, and fairness. *J. Monet. Econ.* **2005**, *52*, 1227–1244. [CrossRef]
13. Dobson, S.; Ramlogan-Dobson, C. Is there a trade-off between income inequality and corruption? Evidence from Latin America. *Econ. Lett.* **2010**, *107*, 102–104. [CrossRef]
14. Spirtes, P.; Glymour, C.N.; Scheines, R.; Heckerman, D. *Causation, Prediction, and Search*; MIT Press: Cambridge, MA, USA, 2000.
15. Peters, J.; Mooij, J.M.; Janzing, D.; Schölkopf, B. Causal discovery with continuous additive noise models. *J. Mach. Learn. Res.* **2014**, *15*, 2009–2053.
16. Muandet, K.; Fukumizu, K.; Sriperumbudur, B.; Schölkopf, B. Kernel mean embedding of distributions: A review and beyond. *Found. Trends Mach. Learn.* **2017**, *10*, 1–141. [CrossRef]
17. Wynne, G.; Duncan, A.B. A kernel two-sample test for functional data. *J. Mach. Learn. Res.* **2022**, *23*, 1–51.
18. Park, J.; Muandet, K. A measure-theoretic approach to kernel conditional mean embeddings. *Adv. Neural Inf. Process. Syst.* **2020**, *33*, 21247–21259.

19. Berrett, T.B.; Wang, Y.; Barber, R.F.; Samworth, R.J. The conditional permutation test for independence while controlling for confounders. *J. R. Stat. Soc. Ser. B Stat. Methodol.* **2020**, *82*, 175–197. [CrossRef]
20. Malfait, N.; Ramsay, J.O. The historical functional linear model. *Can. J. Stat.* **2003**, *31*, 115–128. [CrossRef]
21. Pfister, N.; Bühlmann, P.; Schölkopf, B.; Peters, J. Kernel-based tests for joint independence. *J. R. Stat. Soc. Ser. B Stat. Methodol.* **2018**, *80*, 5–31. [CrossRef]
22. Ramos-Carreño, C.; Suárez, A.; Torrecilla, J.L.; Carbajo Berrocal, M.; Marcos Manchón, P.; Pérez Manso, P.; Hernando Bernabé, A.; García Fernández, D.; Hong, Y.; Rodríguez-Ponga Eyriès, P.M.; et al. GAA-UAM/scikit-fda: Version 0.7.1, 2022. Available online: https://zenodo.org/records/5903557 (accessed on 7 June 2023). [CrossRef]
23. Squires, C. Causaldag: Creation, Manipulation, and Learning of Causal Models. 2018. Available online: https://github.com/uhlerlab/causaldag (accessed on 7 June 2023).
24. Girard, O.; Lattier, G.; Micallef, J.P.; Millet, G.P. Changes in exercise characteristics, maximal voluntary contraction, and explosive strength during prolonged tennis playing. *Br. J. Sport. Med.* **2006**, *40*, 521–526. [CrossRef]
25. Zhu, Y.; Kuhn, T.; Mayo, P.; Hinds, W.C. Comparison of daytime and nighttime concentration profiles and size distributions of ultrafine particles near a major highway. *Environ. Sci. Technol.* **2006**, *40*, 2531–2536. [CrossRef]
26. Ramsay, J.; Hooker, G. *Dynamic Data Analysis*; Springer: Berlin/Heidelberg, Germany, 2017.
27. Fukumizu, K.; Gretton, A.; Sun, X.; Schölkopf, B. Kernel measures of conditional dependence. In Proceedings of the 20th International Conference on Neural Information Processing Systems, Vancouver, BC, Canada, 3–6 December 2007.
28. Gretton, A.; Fukumizu, K.; Teo, C.H.; Song, L.; Schölkopf, B.; Smola, A.J. A kernel statistical test of independence. In Proceedings of the 20th International Conference on Neural Information Processing Systems, Vancouver, BC, Canada, 3–6 December 2007; pp. 585–592.
29. Zhang, K.; Peters, J.; Janzing, D.; Schölkopf, B. Kernel-based conditional independence test and application in causal discovery. *arXiv* **2012**, arXiv:1202.3775.
30. Lai, T.; Zhang, Z.; Wang, Y.; Kong, L. Testing independence of functional variables by angle covariance. *J. Multivar. Anal.* **2021**, *182*, 104711. [CrossRef]
31. Górecki, T.; Krzyśko, M.; Wołyński, W. Independence test and canonical correlation analysis based on the alignment between kernel matrices for multivariate functional data. *Artif. Intell. Rev.* **2020**, *53*, 475–499. [CrossRef]
32. Doran, G.; Muandet, K.; Zhang, K.; Schölkopf, B. A Permutation-Based Kernel Conditional Independence Test. In Proceedings of the Thirtieth Conference on Uncertainty in Artificial Intelligence, Quebec City, QC, Canada, 23–27 July 2014; pp. 132–141.
33. Gretton, A.; Borgwardt, K.M.; Rasch, M.J.; Schölkopf, B.; Smola, A. A kernel two-sample test. *J. Mach. Learn. Res.* **2012**, *13*, 723–773.
34. Lee, S.; Honavar, V.G. Self-discrepancy conditional independence test. In Proceedings of the 33rd Conference on Uncertainty in Artificial Intelligence, UAI 2017, Sydney, Australia, 11–15 August 2017; Volume 33.
35. Pearl, J. *Causality*; Cambridge University Press: Cambridge, UK, 2009.
36. Mooij, J.M.; Peters, J.; Janzing, D.; Zscheischler, J.; Schölkopf, B. Distinguishing cause from effect using observational data: Methods and benchmarks. *J. Mach. Learn. Res.* **2016**, *17*, 1103–1204.
37. Peters, J.; Janzing, D.; Schölkopf, B. *Elements of Causal Inference*; The MIT Press: Cambridge, MA, USA, 2017.
38. Schölkopf, B.; von Kügelgen, J. From statistical to causal learning. *arXiv* **2022**, arXiv:2204.00607.
39. Squires, C.; Uhler, C. Causal structure learning: A combinatorial perspective. *Found. Comput. Math.* **2023**, *23*, 1781–1815. [CrossRef]
40. Vowels, M.J.; Camgoz, N.C.; Bowden, R. D'ya like dags? A survey on structure learning and causal discovery. *ACM Comput. Surv.* **2022**, *55*, 1–36. [CrossRef]
41. Chickering, D.M. Optimal structure identification with greedy search. *J. Mach. Learn. Res.* **2002**, *3*, 507–554.
42. Shimizu, S.; Hoyer, P.O.; Hyvärinen, A.; Kerminen, A.; Jordan, M. A linear non-Gaussian acyclic model for causal discovery. *J. Mach. Learn. Res.* **2006**, *7*, 2003–2030.
43. Hoyer, P.; Janzing, D.; Mooij, J.M.; Peters, J.; Schölkopf, B. Nonlinear causal discovery with additive noise models. In Proceedings of the 21st International Conference on Neural Information Processing Systems, Vancouver, BC, Canada, 8–10 December 2008.
44. Szabó, Z.; Sriperumbudur, B.K. Characteristic and Universal Tensor Product Kernels. *J. Mach. Learn. Res.* **2017**, *18*, 1–29.
45. Meek, C. *Complete Orientation Rules for Patterns*; Carnegie Mellon, Department of Philosophy: Pittsburgh, PA, USA, 1995.
46. Peters, J.; Mooij, J.; Janzing, D.; Schölkopf, B. Identifiability of causal graphs using functional models. *arXiv* **2012**, arXiv:1202.3757.
47. Bühlmann, P.; Peters, J.; Ernest, J. CAM: Causal additive models, high-dimensional order search and penalized regression. *Ann. Statist.* **2014**, *42*, 2526–2556. [CrossRef]
48. Shah, R.D.; Peters, J. The hardness of conditional independence testing and the generalised covariance measure. *Ann. Stat.* **2020**, *48*, 1514–1538. [CrossRef]
49. Runge, J.; Nowack, P.; Kretschmer, M.; Flaxman, S.; Sejdinovic, D. Detecting and quantifying causal associations in large nonlinear time series datasets. *Sci. Adv.* **2019**, *5*, eaau4996. [CrossRef] [PubMed]
50. Gini, C. On the measure of concentration with special reference to income and statistics. *Colo. Coll. Publ. Gen. Ser.* **1936**, *208*, 73–79.
51. Ye, H.; Deyle, E.R.; Gilarranz, L.J.; Sugihara, G. Distinguishing time-delayed causal interactions using convergent cross mapping. *Sci. Rep.* **2015**, *5*, 14750. [CrossRef] [PubMed]

52. Rulkov, N.F.; Sushchik, M.M.; Tsimring, L.S.; Abarbanel, H.D. Generalized synchronization of chaos in directionally coupled chaotic systems. *Phys. Rev. E* **1995**, *51*, 980. [CrossRef]
53. Barnett, L.; Barrett, A.B.; Seth, A.K. Granger causality and transfer entropy are equivalent for Gaussian variables. *Phys. Rev. Lett.* **2009**, *103*, 238701. [CrossRef]
54. Porta, A.; Faes, L.; Nollo, G.; Bari, V.; Marchi, A.; De Maria, B.; Takahashi, A.C.; Catai, A.M. Conditional self-entropy and conditional joint transfer entropy in heart period variability during graded postural challenge. *PLoS ONE* **2015**, *10*, e0132851.
55. Van der Vaart, A.W. *Asymptotic Statistics*; Cambridge University Press: Cambridge, UK, 2000; Volume 3.
56. Peters, J.; Bühlmann, P. Structural intervention distance for evaluating causal graphs. *Neural Comput.* **2015**, *27*, 771–799. [CrossRef] [PubMed]
57. Seabold, S.; Perktold, J. Statsmodels: Econometric and statistical modeling with Python. In Proceedings of the 9th Python in Science Conference (SCIPY 2010), Austin, TX, USA, 28–30 June 2010.
58. Javier, P.J.E. Causal-ccm: A Python Implementation of Convergent Cross Mapping. 2021. Available online: https://github.com/PrinceJavier/causal_ccm (accessed on 12 July 2021).
59. Munch, E.; Khasawneh, F.; Myers, A.; Yesilli, M.; Tymochko, S.; Barnes, D.; Guzel, I.; Chumley, M. Teaspoon: Topological Signal Processing in Python. 2022. Available online: https://teaspoontda.github.io/teaspoon/ (accessed on 12 July 2022).
60. Székely, G.J.; Rizzo, M.L.; Bakirov, N.K. Measuring and testing dependence by correlation of distances. *Ann. Statist.* **2007**, *35*, 2769–2794. [CrossRef]

entropy

MDPI

Article

Neural Causal Information Extractor for Unobserved Causes

Keng-Hou Leong [1,2], Yuxuan Xiu [1,2], Bokui Chen [1,3,*] and Wai Kin (Victor) Chan [1,2,4,*]

1 Tsinghua Shenzhen International Graduate School, Tsinghua University, Shenzhen 518055, China; liangjh22@mails.tsinghua.edu.cn (K.-H.L.); xiuyx19@mails.tsinghua.edu.cn (Y.X.)
2 Tsinghua-Berkeley Shenzhen Institute, Tsinghua University, Shenzhen 518055, China
3 Peng Cheng Laboratory, Shenzhen 518055, China
4 International Science and Technology Information Center, Shenzhen 518055, China
* Correspondence: chen.bokui@sz.tsinghua.edu.cn (B.C.); chanw@sz.tsinghua.edu.cn (W.K.C.)

Abstract: Causal inference aims to faithfully depict the causal relationships between given variables. However, in many practical systems, variables are often partially observed, and some unobserved variables could carry significant information and induce causal effects on a target. Identifying these unobserved causes remains a challenge, and existing works have not considered extracting the unobserved causes while retaining the causes that have already been observed and included. In this work, we aim to construct the implicit variables with a generator–discriminator framework named the Neural Causal Information Extractor (NCIE), which can complement the information of unobserved causes and thus provide a complete set of causes with both observed causes and the representations of unobserved causes. By maximizing the mutual information between the targets and the union of observed causes and implicit variables, the implicit variables we generate could complement the information that the unobserved causes should have provided. The synthetic experiments show that the implicit variables preserve the information and dynamics of the unobserved causes. In addition, extensive real-world time series prediction tasks show improved precision after introducing implicit variables, thus indicating their causality to the targets.

Keywords: causal inference; maximizing mutual information; unobserved causes; complex system

1. Introduction

Identifying the complete and valid causes of a variable has been a significant pursuit in causal inference toward complex systems. A causal inference approach is called "causally faithful" [1] when it reveals the causal relationships shown in the observed variables, and it is "causally sufficient" [2] if it does not omit any of the hidden confounder or unobserved variables that should be included. To hold causal sufficiency when deriving faithful causal relationships, traditional causality inference methods [1–6] often assume the complete observability of the system, i.e., all of the variables and information within the system are collected and observed. In the perspective of [7,8], the information within the system flows from the causes to the targets; thus, the complete causes can provide most of the target's information and can describe it (except the noise terms) in detail, as shown in Figure 1a.

However, in practical scenarios, complex systems are often partially observable since only a subset of variables can be directly measured. For instance, in financial markets, the influence of media [9] and company-specific factors [10], which are hardly measurable, drive important causal effects in local tradings [9] and price reversals [10]. Another example can be shown in ecosystems, in which the dynamics are described by species populations, habitat quality, and threats; however, one can rarely acquire a perfect knowledge of the system states [11,12] to perform adequate management actions. The partial observability also induces analyzing challenges in domains such as monitoring biophysical objects [13], weather and climate forecasting [14], and industrial management [15]. While part of the causes are unobserved, the target's information that should be provided is unknown, as shown in Figure 1b. To describe the causal structures in such incomplete systems, causal sufficiency in traditional works is no longer guaranteed, and their results do not necessarily identify the real causes even when they are causally faithful [1,16].

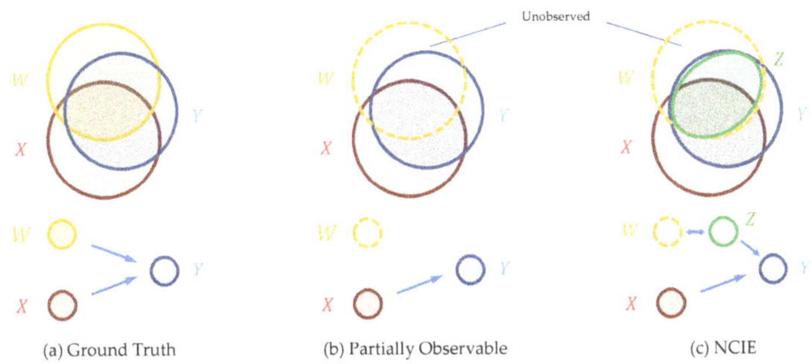

Figure 1. Illustration of the information in a Venn diagram, as well as the causal relationships of the (**a**) ground truth; (**b**) partially observable scenario in reality; and (**c**) an alternative representation of causal relationships with the implicit variables Z, which is generated by NCIE, where Y, X, and W denote the target, observed causes, and unobserved causes, respectively.

Therefore, to avoid identifying spurious causes, the common idea shared by most practices [17–28] is to introduce implicit variables that compensate for the missing causes. Most of them have applied neural networks as a powerful tool for generating variables, which could be categorized into two streams: either (i) employing neural networks with latent layers to uncover the significant features in observed variables that better formulate the targets, or (ii) utilizing the ability to preserve information in representation learning to extract unobserved or latent causes that provide significant information of the targets.

The works from the first approach adopt observed causes as the inputs to train a neural network that minimizes the fitting loss between the output and the target. The intermediate layers in the neural networks help to better fit the target in supervised learning [17], for example, by capturing the hidden long-/short-term dependencies in the dynamics [18,19]. Granger [29] suggested that we could consider these hidden variables as causes, since including them could perform a better regression of the targets. However, such methods are, in actuality, just recombining the neurons from the input to extract advanced features, and they cannot provide information beyond the input [30]. Therefore, they do not necessarily provide unobserved information; thus, we can hardly identify these hidden variables as those that are unobserved in the system.

The second stream aims to generate implicit variables that provide more information to the targets. This echoes another definition of causality [3,31], in which a cause should conditionally correlate with the target given any of the sets of other variables, or it could provide information that all the other variables could not provide to the target [32]. These methods [20–28] adopt the idea of representation learning, which inputs the target (and all the observed variables) into neural networks to project an embedding. This preserves the information while describing the prominent dynamics of the original data. Since these latent variables generate a cover of most of the targets' information, they could be referred to as the causes that drive the system. However, in general, the observed and unobserved causes are entangled and inseparable in the causal structure. While refs. [20–28] excluded all of the observed causes and only considered the generated latent variables as the targets' causes, their depiction does not necessarily reveal the real causal relationships.

Motivated by the aforementioned issues of either missing the unobserved information or giving up on the observed causes, this paper proposes a framework to complete the causal structure by extracting the unobserved variables while retaining the observed causes. We assume the existence of unobserved causes to the target variables; hence, the targets' information should be provided by both the observed and unobserved causes. Given the part of the information from the observed causes, our objective is to generate implicit variables from the observed variables that provide as much information to the target as possible, thus covering the information that should have been provided by the unobserved causes. As shown in Figure 1c, the implicit variables Z would cover the information of the target Y that should have been provided by the unobserved causes W, and hence it could provide an alternative representation ($\{X, Z\} \to Y$) of the information flow in the causal relationships $\{X, W\} \to Y$.

In detail, we employ a generator–discriminator architecture named the Neural Causal Information Extractor (NCIE) that extracts and embeds the targets' information into the implicit variables. The generator obtains implicit variables fromthe time series inputs, and the discriminator maximizes the mutual information between the targets and the union of explicit and implicit causes by constraining implicit variables to have diverse marginal and joint distributions. This results in a holistic causal structure that encompasses both observed and unobserved factors to the target. To highlight the ability of NCIE to complement unobserved information and recover unobserved dynamics, we generate implicit variables for three synthetic cases. To further demonstrate the efficacy of the generated implicit causes in improving time series predictions and to verify their causality, we perform extensive experiments on real-world time series data.

The contribution of our work can be highlighted as follows:

1. We propose a generator–discriminator architecture that generates implicit variables to complement the unobserved causes in the causal structures while retaining the observed causes.
2. The implicit variables we generate could carry information from the unobserved variables and reveal their dynamics.
3. Time series prediction tasks show that the combination of observed and implicit variables helps improve the prediction of targets, verifying that they are better candidates for causal inference.

This paper is organized as follows. Section 2 provides a comprehensive review of related works. Section 3 presents the basic theories in information theory and causal inference and states the objective of this work. Section 4 introduces the methodology of the proposed approach. Section 5 details the experimental setup and dataset descriptions, and then presents the results and discussion of our experiments. Finally, in Section 6, we provide a discussion on the implications of our work and present future possible advanced works.

2. Literature Review

In the scope of our work, we categorize the related works on causal inference into two parts, which cover the methods with and without considering unobserved variables.

2.1. Causal Inference without Considering Unobserved Variables

Assuming that the given observations are complete and thus sufficient, the objectives of traditional works often include drawing causal faithful graphs, in which nodes represent the variables of interest and edges indicate the existence of causal relationships between variables. The constrained-based methods, including the Peter–Clark (PC) algorithm [2] and its improvements [2,3,33], are graph algorithms that start with a fully connected graph and iteratively delete the edges between two variables if they are conditionally independent or d-separated [2]. They provide causal faithful graphs that satisfy the causal Markov condition [31], i.e., a variable is conditionally independent to all variables except its effects given its causes. On the other hand, score-based approaches present the causal structure with the Bayesian network with the highest score, measured by the Bayesian Dirichlet equivalent (BDe) score [4] and the K2 score [5]. Though the latter methods do not ensure faithfulness, they pursue a representation that shows the causal structure and, at the same time, the strength of cause-to-effect dependencies. Other approaches include those based on Granger causality [6], which also aim to identify the existence and magnitudes of the causal edges among variables.

2.2. Causal Inference Considering Unobserved Variables

There are plenty of works on causal inference that are aware of the existence of unobserved variables, and for clarity, we attempt to classify them into three groups. The first group refers to those that detect the existence of hidden confounders without knowing the effects, including Fast Casual Inference (FCI) [2] and Latent PCMCI (LPCMCI, where PCMCI [3] is a PC-based condition selection with the Momentary Conditional Independence (MCI) test) [34]. They are the modified versions of the PC algorithm [2] and PCMCI [3], respectively, which follow similar procedures but identify an extra kind of edge (relationship) between variables: bidirectional arrows. This indicates the conditional correlational relationship between two variables that could not be explained by any directional causal path from one to another, thus identifying the existence of a hidden confounder driving the two variables.

The second group attempts to explain the causal effects originating from unobserved variables toward the target variable. Assuming linear, additive, and first-order Markovian causal effects, ref. [16] constructs a linear regression model that describes the observed variables by past observed variables, unobserved causes, and noises. Based on this model, the effects of the unobserved causes, which refer to their coefficients, could be obtained by variational expectation maximization or by solving the autocovariance.

The third group [20–28] aims to identify the unobserved causes via latent representations. They assume that the observed signals are driven or caused by a set of unobserved latent signals, and there exists a latent dynamic that drives the latent variables from past to future. Therefore, given the observed dynamics, their objectives are to identify the posterior distributions of future latent signals given past latent signals, the posterior distributions of observed signals given the contemporaneous latent signals, and the latent signals themselves. They identify latent signals via different approaches, including Variational Autoencoder (VAE) [20,21,35,36], Dynamical Component Analysis [25–27], and maximizing the (conditional) mutual information [22,28].

While refs. [20–28] ensure the identifiability of implicit variables, their structures do not include the causes that are already observed, which might also be involved in the causal process. In our work, we express the causal structures containing both observed and implicit causes. Moreover, while refs. [20–28] could precisely identify the implicit variables, many of their generators, such as VAE [20,21,35,36], hold specific assumptions about the implicit variables. With a simple generator that holds comparably few assumptions about the distribution, our architecture can be applied to more general cases.

2.3. Mutual Information Estimator

$$
\begin{aligned}
H(Y) &= -\sum_{y \in Y} p(y) log(p(y)), \\
H(Y) &= -\int_Y p(y) log(p(y)) dy.
\end{aligned}
\tag{1}
$$

In Equation (1), Shannon provided an information theory-based definition for the entropy of random variables with known distributions. However, the distribution of variables in real-world time series remains unknown in many scenarios. To sample the unknown distributions, one of the fundamental methods is binning [37,38]. By partitioning the continuous variables into discrete bins and counting the sampled distributions, one can apply Equation (1) to estimate entropy. Provided the entropy of variables, one can calculate the mutual information between two variables, X and Y, with

$$\begin{aligned} I(X;Y) &= \sum_{x \in X} \sum_{y \in Y} p_{XY}(x,y) \log\left(\frac{p_{XY}(x,y)}{p_X(x)p_Y(y)}\right) \\ &= H(X) + H(Y) - H(X,Y). \end{aligned} \tag{2}$$

The Mutual Information Neural Estimator (MINE) [39] is another popular method that uses a neural network to estimate the KL Divergence of two random variables, which could then provide a tight lower bound for their mutual information. Deep InfoMax [22] provides a similar approach by estimating Jensen–Shannon (JS) Divergence. Under the Gaussian assumption, Refs. [25,26] measure entropy by $H(Z) = \frac{r1}{2} ln(2\pi e)^{dT} |\Sigma_T(Z)|$, and prove that the estimation is still tight if the assumption is violated. Refs. [40–42] provide other effective estimators for information based on classifiers and k-nearest neighbor (kNN).

3. Problem Statement

Suppose we have target variable Y_t at time t. First, we consider the case where Y_t is auto-correlated, and all the causes of Y_t are known, denoted by $\{X_t, Y_{<t}\}$, where $X_t = \{X^1, X^2, \dots, X^n\}_t$ and $Y_{<t} = \{Y_1, \dots, Y_{t-1}\}$. In this work, we assume a k-order Markovian property on auto-correlated causality, i.e., $Y_{<t} = \{Y_{t-k}, \dots, Y_{t-1}\}$.

For simplicity, we abbreviate Y_t as Y. While all the causes $\{X, Y_{<t}\}$ are known, we assume

$$H(Y) = I(Y;\ X,\ Y_{<t}), \tag{3}$$

where $H(Y)$ is the entropy of Y, a measure of uncertainty, and $I(Y;\ X,\ Y_{<t})$ is the mutual information (MI) between Y and $\{X,\ Y_{<t}\}$. MI is a measure of "information" or "reduction of entropy" that the two variables provide to each other. In Equation (3), the entropy reduction that X and $Y_{<t}$ provide to Y equals the entropy of Y. Hence, the causes of Y could eliminate all the uncertainty of Y, in other words, provide all the information of Y.

Now, we consider another case in which, besides some observed causes $X = \{X^1, X^2, \dots, X^n\}$, there are other unobserved causes W. Therefore, we assume

$$H(Y) = I(Y;\ X,\ Y_{<t},\ W). \tag{4}$$

The absence of information about W induces

$$H(Y) > I(Y;\ X,\ Y_{<t}). \tag{5}$$

As shown in Figure 2, X and $Y_{<t}$ could only provide a part (the red part) of the information to Y. Therefore, our objective is to generate some implicit variables $Z = \{Z^1, Z^2, \dots, Z^m\}$ to maximize $I(Y;\ X,\ Y_{<t},\ Z)$ (the yellow part), which attempts to approach its upper bound $H(Y)$ (the large black box).

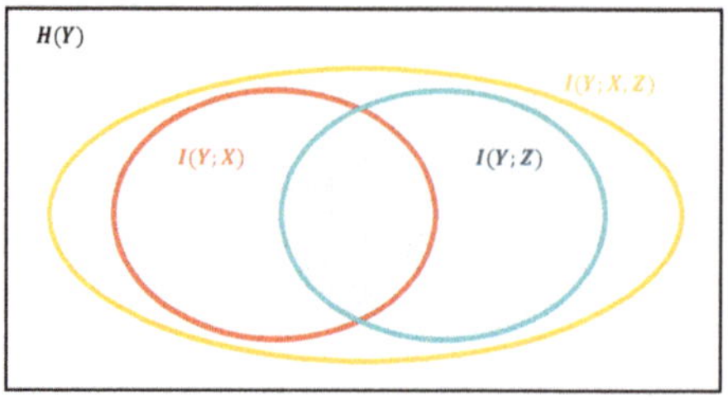

Figure 2. The Venn Diagram illustration of the information provided to Y by X (red), Z (blue), and $\{X, Z\}$ (yellow).

Hence, if we could search for a Z that could perfectly provide this information, we could say that Z somehow represents the unobserved causes W. More specifically, Z traces the information for Y from W.

While the upper bound of the MI equals the entropy of Y, i.e.,

$$\sup_{Z} I(Y;\, X,\, Y_{<t},\, Z) = H(Y), \tag{6}$$

the objective of our work is to generate Z which maximizes the MI and makes it approach $H(Y)$:

$$\max_{Z} I(Y;\, X,\, Y_{<t},\, Z), \tag{7}$$

which is equivalent to maximizing the conditional mutual information of Z and Y given X and $Y_{<t}$:

$$I(Y; Z|X,\, Y_{<t}) = I(Y;\, X,\, Y_{<t},\, Z) - I(Y;\, X,\, Y_{<t}). \tag{8}$$

Since the term without Z could be considered constant here,

$$\max_{Z} I(Y;\, X,\, Y_{<t},\, Z) = \max_{Z} I(Y; Z|X,\, Y_{<t}). \tag{9}$$

Objective (7) is maximized if Z covers all the conditional mutual information from W,

$$\sup_{Z} I(Y;\, Z|\, X,\, Y_{<t}) = I(Y;\, W|\, X,\, Y_{<t}) = H(Y|X), \tag{10}$$

and meanwhile $X, Y_{<t}, Z$ together cover all the entropy (Equation (6)) and provide all the information of Y.

There are some assumptions made on Z:

1. We focus on the unobserved variables that provide information to Y. Those without information of Y do not affect the distributions of Y.
2. In the case of time series, we denote $X_{<t}$, $Z_{<t}$ as the explicit and implicit causes of Y_t to uphold the assumption of temporal priority [1], i.e., causal relationships only move from past variables to future variables in time series. For simplicity, we denote $X_{<t}$ and $Z_{<t}$ as X and Z, and Y_t as Y.
3. We assume X_t, Y_t, and Z_t are in a closed system and there is a causal loop among them, i.e., $X_{<t}$ and $Z_{<t}$ may induce Y_t, and $X_{<t}$ and $Y_{<t}$ may induce Z_t.
4. While we are generating $Z_{<t}$, we do not necessarily obey temporal priority [1], which is a common practice in refs. [20–28,30]. Therefore, we employ $X_{<t}$ and Y_t to generate $Z_{<t}$. We note that we do not focus on finding the exact causes of Z here. Instead of finding causes of Z by applying the whole structures we use on Y, we just use a basic RNN to present Z from the explicit causes.

To better illustrate our problem and objective, we provide a simple numerical example as follows:

Example 1. *We consider a temporal Boolean network with three Boolean variables: Y_t, X_t, and W_t, where Y_t at time t is determined by*

$$Y_t = X_{t-1} \text{ AND } W_{t-1}. \tag{11}$$

At every time step t, X_t and W_t are sampled from a uniform binomial distribution, i.e., $P(X_t = 0) = P(X_t = 1) = P(W_t = 0) = P(W_t = 1) = 0.5$.

In this context, the time-varying variables Y_t, X_{t-1}, and W_{t-1} at a particular time t are considered as the static random variables generated by the random process [1–3,22,24,28]. We list all the possible circumstances of the truth table of these three variables.

$$\begin{aligned} P(X_{t-1} = 0, W_{t-1} = 0, Y_t = 0) = 1/4; \\ P(X_{t-1} = 0, W_{t-1} = 1, Y_t = 0) = 1/4; \\ P(X_{t-1} = 1, W_{t-1} = 0, Y_t = 0) = 1/4; \\ P(X_{t-1} = 1, W_{t-1} = 1, Y_t = 1) = 1/4. \end{aligned} \tag{12}$$

Then, we calculate $H(Y_t)$, $I(Y_t; X_{t-1})$, and $I(Y_t; X_{t-1}, W_{t-1})$ respectively:

$$\begin{aligned} H(Y_t) &= -\sum_{y \in Y_t} p(y) \log(p(y)) = 2 - \frac{3}{4} log3, \\ I(Y_t; X_{t-1}) &= \sum_{y \in Y_t} \sum_{x \in X_{t-1}} p(x,y) \log\left(\frac{p(x,y)}{p(x)p(y)}\right) = \frac{3}{2} - \frac{3}{4}\log 3, \\ I(Y_t; X_{t-1}, W_{t-1}) &= \sum_{y \in Y_t} \sum_{x \in X_{t-1}} \sum_{w \in W_{t-1}} p(w,x,y) \log\left(\frac{p(w,x,y)}{p(w,x)p(y)}\right) = 2 - \frac{3}{4}\log 3. \end{aligned} \tag{13}$$

We notice that $H(Y_t) = I(Y_t; X_{t-1}, W_{t-1}) > I(Y_t; X_{t-1})$, which means that the information of Y_t could be completely covered when X_{t-1}, W_{t-1} are known. When W_{t-1} is unobserved, the observed X_{t-1} can only provide part of the information of Y_t. This gap of information is described by the conditional mutual information, $I(Y_t; W_{t-1}|X_{t-1})$, where

$$I(Y_t; W_{t-1}|X_{t-1}) = I(Y_t; X_{t-1}, W_{t-1}) - I(Y_t; X_{t-1}) = \frac{1}{2}, \tag{14}$$

which quantifies the information that W_{t-1} provides to Y_t that X_{t-1} cannot provide.

Example 2. *Now, we consider the scenario in which we do not know Y_t is generated by Equation (11) or the distribution of W_{t-1}, but we are provided with X_{t-1} and Y_t, and we wish to generate Z_{t-1} to complement $I(W_{t-1}; Y_t|X_{t-1})$ and maximize the objective in Equation (7). The ideal case is to reverse the Markov chain $(W_{t-1}, X_{t-1} \rightarrow Y_t)$ to $(X_{t-1}, Y_t \rightarrow W_{t-1})$ and make the posterior distribution $p(Z_{t-1}|X_{t-1}, Y_t)$ equal to $p(W_{t-1}|X_{t-1}, Y_t)$, where the joint and posterior distributions are*

$$\begin{aligned} P(X_{t-1} = 0, Y_t = 0, Z_{t-1} = 0) = 1/4, \\ P(X_{t-1} = 0, Y_t = 0, Z_{t-1} = 1) = 1/4, \\ P(X_{t-1} = 1, Y_t = 0, Z_{t-1} = 1) = 1/4, \\ P(X_{t-1} = 1, Y_t = 1, Z_{t-1} = 0) = 1/4, \end{aligned} \tag{15}$$

$$p(Z_{t-1} = 1|X_{t-1}, Y_t) = p(W_{t-1} = 1|X_{t-1}, Y_t) = \begin{cases} 1, & X_{t-1} = 1, Y_t = 1 \\ 0, & X_{t-1} = 1, Y_t = 0. \\ \frac{1}{2}, & X_{t-1} = 0 \end{cases} \tag{16}$$

In such a case, we calculate that

$$\begin{aligned} I(Y_t; X_{t-1}, Z_{t-1}) = I(Y_t; X_{t-1}, W_{t-1}) = 2 - \frac{3}{4} log3, \\ I(Y_t; Z_{t-1}|X_{t-1}) = I(Y_t; W_{t-1}|X_{t-1}) = \frac{1}{2}. \end{aligned} \tag{17}$$

Example 3. *However, there actually exist more than one $p(Z_{t-1}|X_{t-1}, Y_t)$ that can maximize $I(Y_t; Z_{t-1}|X_{t-1})$. For example, we let*

$$Z_{t-1} = X_{t-1} \text{ XOR } Y_t, \tag{18}$$

and we can again list all the possible circumstances of the truth table of these three variables.

$$
\begin{aligned}
P(X_{t-1} = 0, Y_t = 0, Z_{t-1} = 0) = 1/2, \\
P(X_{t-1} = 1, Y_t = 0, Z_{t-1} = 1) = 1/4, \\
P(X_{t-1} = 1, Y_t = 1, Z_{t-1} = 0) = 1/4.
\end{aligned} \tag{19}
$$

In such a case, we can obtain the same result as that in Equation (17)*, which means a different* Z *from Equations* (16) *and* (18) *can achieve the optimal objective in* (7)*. This indicates that they are providing the same conditional information that* W *provides to* Y*. The value of* Y_t *is known when* $X_{t-1} = 0$*, but is uncertain when* $X_{t-1} = 1$*.* W *provides the conditional information by helping to eliminate this uncertainty (or conditional entropy* $H(Y|X)$*), which can also be eliminated by not including* W *but including* Z *from Equation* (16) *or* (18)*. Therefore,* Z *can express conditional information* $I(W; Y|X)$*.*

4. Methods

4.1. Neural Causal Information Extractor

We name our architecture the Neural Causal Information Extractor (NCIE), which is composed of a generator and a discriminator. The architecture is shown in Figure 3.

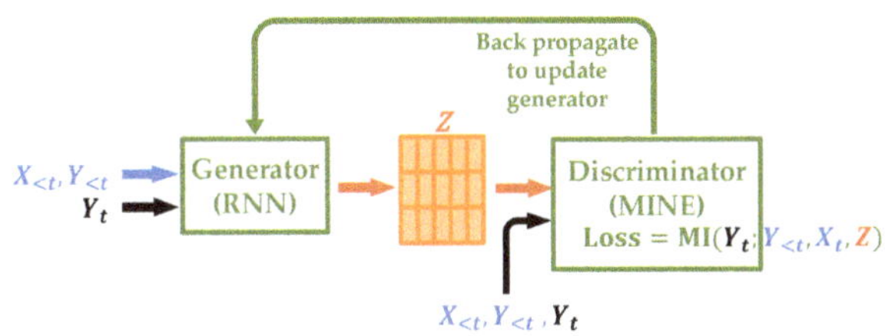

Figure 3. The architecture of the Neural Causal Information Extractor.

4.1.1. Generator

Although Z is not explicitly collected and observed from the system, we consider part of it to be involved in the system, specifically the part that provides information to Y. While we suppose that Y is generated by $\{X, Y_{<t}, Z\}$, reversely, the information of Z that we are interested in should be covered by (a part of) Y. Therefore, Z could be represented as a function of X, $Y_{<t}$, and Y. Other variables V besides $\{X, Y_{<t}, Y\}$ in the raw data should not be included to generate Z in case they have not provided information via path $V \to Z \to Y$ (or V should be detected as an observed direct cause before Z is included).

While finding the causes of Z is not the focus of this work (we only focus on finding the explicit and implicit causes of Y_t), we apply a basic RNN [18] to capture the lagged dependencies from X and Y to generate Z. The RNN consists of two neural networks to manipulate and propagate its hidden states. The first neural network, f_1, generates H_t from $X_{<t}$, $Y_{<t}$, Y_t, and H_{t-1} (Equation (20)), where H_t denotes the hidden states at time t. Then, the second neural network, f_2, reads H_t and generates the output Z (Equation (21)), while H_t is propagated to the next episode.

$$H_t = f_1(X_{t-1}, Y_{t-1}, H_{t-1}), \tag{20}$$

$$Z_t = f_2(H_t). \tag{21}$$

With the propagation of H_t, the memory of X and Y in previous episodes is also propagated. Furthermore, since Z is generated directly from H, the propagation of H also passes the memory and information of Z. It is worth noting here that Z is jointly generated by the explicit $\{X, Y\}$ and the implicit variables $Z_{<t}$. Suppose we employ another architecture that generates Z solely by explicit variables $\{X, Y\}$ (and without $Z_{<t}$); Z then

acts as an intermediate hidden layer in our architecture, which is equivalent to directly depicting Y by a neural network structure with $\{X, Y\}$ and without Z. In other words, Y would then be solely caused by explicit variables. This is why we apply RNN to generate Z jointly by implicits and explicits, which matches our assumption that Y is causally related to implicits and explicits.

4.1.2. Discriminator

The discriminator provides a measurement of $I(Y; X, Y_{<t}, Z)$, where Z is the output of the generator. Here, we consider Y and $\{X, Y_{<t}, Z\}$ as two sets of random variables, and their mutual information is equivalent to Kullback–Leibler (KL) divergence between their marginal and joint distributions,

$$\begin{aligned} I(Y; X, Y_{<t}, Z) &= D_{KL}(\mathbb{P}_{\mathbf{YXY_{<t}Z}} \,||\, \mathbb{P}_{\mathbf{Y}} \bigotimes \mathbb{P}_{\mathbf{XY_{<t}Z}}) \\ &= \sup_{T: Y \times \mathbf{X} \times \mathbf{Y_{<t}} \times \mathbf{Z} \to \mathbb{R}} \mathbb{E}_{\mathbb{P}_{YXY_{<t}Z}}[T] - \log(\mathbb{E}_{\mathbb{P}_Y \otimes \mathbb{P}_{XY_{<t}Z}}[e^T]), \end{aligned} \tag{22}$$

where D_{KL} denotes the KL divergence of two distributions and $\mathbb{P}_Y$ denotes the distribution of Y. The lower bound of KL divergence can be provided by Donsker–Varadhan representation (Equation (22)), where $T(Y, X, Y_{<t}, Z)$ is any class of function.

We follow MINE [39] to implement function T by a neural network with parameters Θ and maximize the lower bound of mutual information I_Θ by searching for optimized function T_θ:

$$I(Y; X, Y_{<t}, Z) \geq I_\Theta(Y; X, Y_{<t}, Z), \tag{23}$$

$$I_\theta(Y; X, Y_{<t}, Z) = \max_{\theta \in \Theta} \mathbb{E}_{\mathbb{P}_{YXY_{<t}Z}}[T_\theta] - \log(\mathbb{E}_{\mathbb{P}_Y \otimes \mathbb{P}_{XY_{<t}Z}}[e^{T_\theta}]). \tag{24}$$

Optimization is performed using stochastic gradient descent (SGD). However, a naive derivation of Equation (24) leads to biased gradient estimation. MINE [39] proposed addressing this bias by reformulating the loss function. For batch sample B, the gradient is

$$\widehat{G_B} = \mathbb{E}_B[\nabla_\theta T_\theta] - \frac{\mathbb{E}_B[\nabla_\theta T_\theta e^{T_\theta}]}{\mathbb{E}_B[e^{T_\theta}]}. \tag{25}$$

MINE suggests estimating the denominator of the second term using the moving average from previous epochs, while the other parts are the averaged gradient from the network parameters.

Among all (conditional) mutual information estimators, MINE estimates MI by stochastic gradient descent (some do not provide MI, and some are not trained by gradient descent). The available gradient is essential in our architecture because one of the inputs of MINE, Z, is exactly the output of the generator. Hence, the generator and discriminator are fused together by Z, which acts as the bridge to back-propagate the gradient from the discriminator to the generator and thus update the parameters in both neural networks.

4.1.3. NCIE: Maximizing Mutual Information

In Section 3, we claim that the objective of our architecture is to find implicit variables Z such that $I(Y; X, Y_{<t}, Z)$ is maximized. In this case, Z could represent the information provided by unobserved variables.

Since the generator and discriminator are fused together, they could be jointly considered as a whole neural network that trains both components simultaneously, where Z could be viewed as a layer in between that we are interested in. While training together by gradient descent, the generator is trained to provide better Z to push up I_θ, and the discriminator is trained to provide a better (higher) estimation of I_θ given the Z from the generator. Therefore, NCIE pursues objective

$$\max_{Z,\, \theta \in \Theta} I_\theta(Y; X, Y_{<t}, Z). \tag{26}$$

In an alternative view, the whole NCIE structure could be interpreted as a variant of an RNN that pursues to provide a maximized value of the Donsker–Varadhan representation given the batched inputs of X, $Y_{<t}$, and Y.

4.2. Verifying Causality from Z to Y by Time Series Prediction

4.2.1. Motivation and Architecture

To verify the capability of extracting effective implicit causes, we modify the NCIE in Section 4.1 and apply the architecture to perform multi-variate time series prediction in Section 5.2.2. To predict Y_t, we cannot use Y_t itself or any variables at time t or after t as the input; therefore, we have to find an alternative for the input of the generator. Here, we use a simple RNN to pre-train a $\hat{Y}_t$ that tries to estimate Y_t given all the explicit causes $\{X, Y_{<t}\}$ of Y_t. After the pre-training stage, $\hat{Y}_t$ is plugged into the input of the generator in the NCIE and replaces Y_t, to avoid the information leakage in the original architecture in Section 4.1.

The overall procedure is shown in Figure 4, which is summarized as follows:

1. We select the explicit causes X from the raw time series with a maximum lag of k using PCMCI [3], which is a framework that identifies the time-lagged causal relationship given the assumption of the completeness of the given data (no unobserved data). With its high precision, we assume the resulting X is the set of all the real causes of Y. Furthermore, we select the lagged $Y_{<t}$ from $t-k$ to $t-1$ as the autoregressive terms, together with X to be the set of observed causes;
2. We train the pre-training module and generate $\hat{Y}_t$ to estimate Y_t;
3. After finishing training the previous module, we use output $\hat{Y}_t$ as the input of this modified NCIE module and train the generator and discriminator (Section 4.1) together to generate Z;
4. We train neural network f_3 (Equation (27)) to generate $\hat{Y}_t{}'$, which is applied to examine the improvement of the prediction effect on Y given by Z.

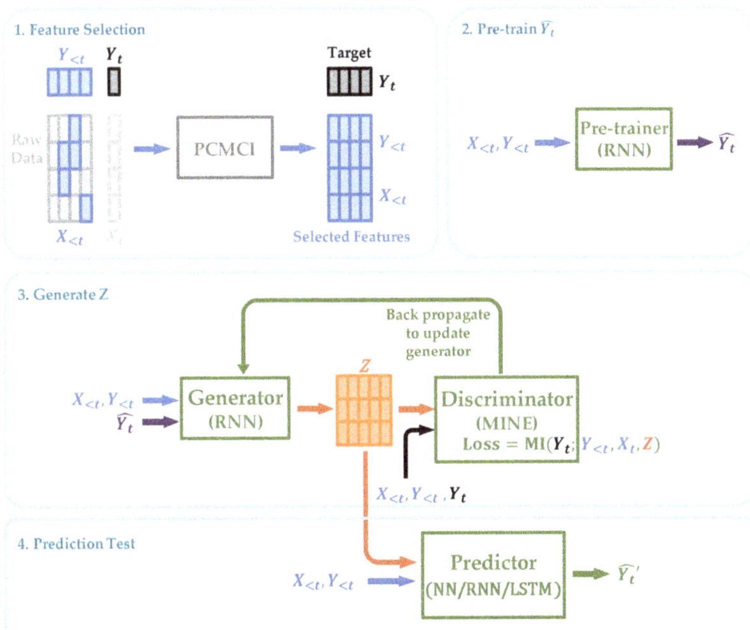

Figure 4. The architecture of Neural Causal Information Extractor to perform time series prediction.

We note that although there are four neural network architectures in Figure 4 and some of their inputs and outputs are connected, only the two networks in the third module train and update their parameters simultaneously. The framework in Figure 4 proceeds module by module, and the next one starts after the previous one finishes.

4.2.2. Prediction

We test whether the generated Z can help to improve the prediction of Y by comparing $\hat{Y}_t$ and $\hat{Y}_t{}'$. In Section 5.2.2, we employ different neural networks to implement f_3, which performs the prediction of Y by minimizing the mean squared error (MSE):

$$\hat{Y}_t{}' = f_3(X_t,\ Y_{t-1},\ Z_t). \tag{27}$$

5. Experiments

5.1. Synthetic Data Experiments: Dynamics of Z

In the following experiments on synthetic data, we demonstrate that the proposed NCIE framework can accurately extract the unobserved causal variables. We consider three synthetic systems (Figure 5) to compare the generated Z with the unobserved cause W that Z mimics. Targets Y in the synthetic systems are constructed with causes exhibiting long-term and short-term dynamics. We investigate the ability of NCIE in Section 4.1 to extract causes W from target Y when Y and the other causes X are given.

5.1.1. Case 1: A Linear System

We suppose the time-varying X and Y are observable while W is unobserved:

$$\begin{aligned} Y(t) &= X(t) + W(t), \\ X(t) &= \sin\frac{t}{10}, \\ W(t) &= \sin 10t. \end{aligned} \tag{28}$$

5.1.2. Case 2: A Non-Linear System

We suppose the time-varying X and Y are observable while W is unobserved:

$$\begin{aligned} Y(t) &= X(t) + W(t)(0.2 + X(t)), \\ X(t) &= 0.05t^3 - 15t^2 - 80t + 2, \\ W(t) &= \sin 10t. \end{aligned} \tag{29}$$

5.1.3. Case 3: A Non-Linear System

We suppose the time-varying X and Y are observable while W is unobserved:

$$\begin{aligned} Y(t) &= X(t) + 0.2W(t)(0.2 + X(t)), \\ X(t) &= 0.05t^3 - 15t^2 - 80t + 2, \\ W(t) &= \sin 10t. \end{aligned} \tag{30}$$

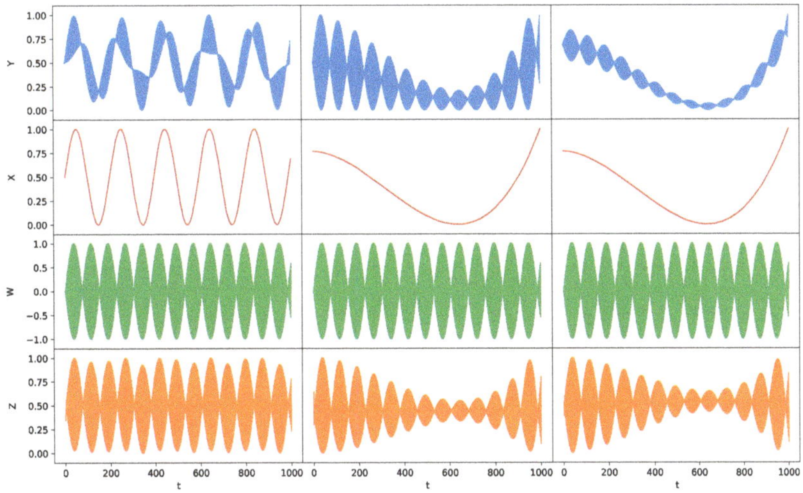

Figure 5. Dynamics of the normalized Y, X, W, and Z for Synthetic Case 1 (**Left**), Case 2 (**Middle**), Case 3 (**Right**).

5.1.4. Case 4: 1—Predator 2—Prey Model Where Prey Share the Same Food

We investigate our approach with the predator–prey model, which is a classical problem in ecology [43,44]. Specifically, we choose the model with 1 predator species, wolves, and 2 prey species, sheep and rabbits. The prey species share the same food source: grass. In total, there are four species in the ecosystem, and their populations grow according to the Lotka–Volterra model [45,46]:

$$\begin{aligned} \frac{dW(t)}{dt} &= W(t)(-a_0 + a_1 S(t) + a_2 R(t)), \\ \frac{dS(t)}{dt} &= S(t)(b_0 - b_1 W(t) + b_2 G(t)), \\ \frac{dR(t)}{dt} &= R(t)(c_0 - c_1 W(t) + c_2 G(t)), \\ \frac{dG(t)}{dt} &= G(t)(d_0 - d_1 S(t) - d_2 R(t)), \end{aligned} \tag{31}$$

where $W(t)$, $S(t)$, $R(t)$, and $G(t)$ represent the population of wolves, sheep, rabbits, and grass at time t, respectively. Because this dynamic system can lead to negative populations and we want to prevent extinction from halting our simulation, we add a modification that sets any population to 1 if it drops below 1.

We consider the scenario in which some intermediate species in the biological chain are unknown or unobserved. Therefore, we assume that $S(t)$ and $R(t)$ are unobserved. We set $W(t)$ as the target variable and $G(t-1)$ as the observed cause, and attempt to recover the information provided by the unobserved causes $S(t)$ and $R(t)$. It is worth noting that $G(t-1)$ is not a direct cause of $W(t)$ in this case. The absence of $S(t-1)$ and $R(t-1)$ makes $G(t-1)$ and $W(t)$ conditionally dependent, thus creating a spurious causal link. Since it is not the focus of our work, we do not discuss how to eliminate spurious links after recovering unobserved causes in this study.

The dynamics of the population of the four species and Z are shown in Figure 6. From this, we can observe that Z provides information about the unobserved variables $S(t)$ and $R(t)$.

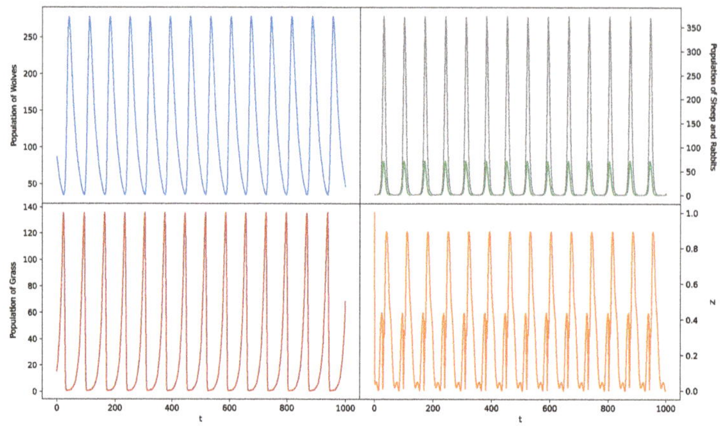

Figure 6. Dynamics of Z and the population of four species for Synthetic Case 4.

5.1.5. The Interpretation of Z

Our target is to generate Z that carries the unique information that unobserved causes provide to Y. However, in the three synthetic examples, instead of revealing the dynamic of W, Z exhibits a variable that tries to introduce Y while eliminating the information of X.

We try to explain the result using partial information decomposition theory [47], which suggests that we could decompose the Venn Diagram (Figure 2) of mutual information into the following parts shown in Figure 7:

$$\begin{aligned} H(Y) &= I(Y; X, Y_{<t}, W) \\ &= I_{\text{uni}}(Y; X, Y_{<t}) + I_{\text{uni}}(Y; W) \\ &\quad + I_{\text{red}}(Y; X, Y_{<t}, W) + I_{\text{syn}}(Y; X, Y_{<t}, W). \end{aligned} \tag{32}$$

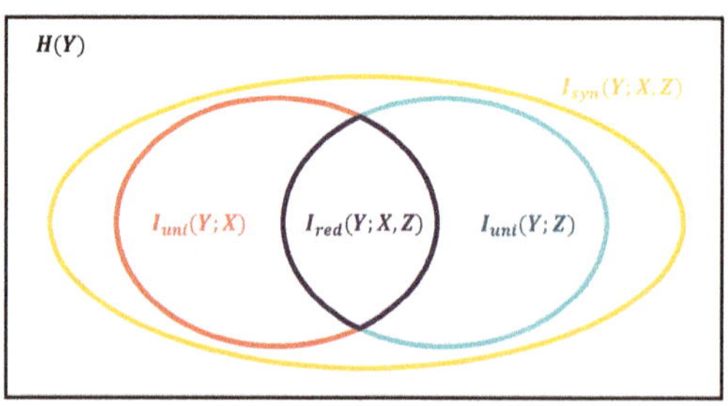

Figure 7. The Venn Diagram illustrates the partial information decomposition of Y into four discrete parts: the unique information from X (red), the unique information from Z (blue), the redundant information from X and Z (purple), and the synergistic information from X and Z (yellow).

The information to Y from all of its causes consists of four parts:

- $I_{\text{uni}}(Y; W)$, the unique information that could only be provided by W;
- $I_{\text{uni}}(Y; X, Y_{<t})$, the unique information that could only be provided by $\{X, Y_{<t}\}$;
- $I_{\text{syn}}(Y; X, Y_{<t}, W)$, the synergistic information provided only when both $\{X, Y_{<t}\}$ and W are present;

- $I_{\text{red}}(Y; X, Y_{<t}, W)$, the redundant information that could be provided by either $\{X, Y_{<t}\}$ or W.

If our objective is to recover W, Z should only contain the unique information $I_{\text{uni}}(Y; W)$ and the synergistic information $I_{\text{syn}}(Y; X, Y_{<t}, W)$, while the unique information $I_{\text{uni}}(Y; X, Y_{<t})$ and the redundant information $I_{\text{red}}(Y; X, Y_{<t}, W)$ are not present in this case. However, our objective in generating Z is not to exactly mimic W, but to maximize the information that the observed and unobserved causes provide to Y, so that we can acquire a better causal representation for Y.

Moreover, it is difficult to integrate different methods; therefore, our architecture does not measure the four components [48–50] separately but rather measures and maximizes the entire $I(Y; X, Y_{<t}, Z)$ at once. Thus, $I_{\text{uni}}(Y; Z)$, $I_{\text{syn}}(Y; X, Y_{<t}, Z)$, and $I_{\text{red}}(Y; X, Y_{<t}, Z)$ in Equation (32) are maximized. As a result, the implicit causes Z may contain all four components, which is the information from both the observed $\{X, Y_{<t}\}$ and the unobserved W.

Therefore, in the synthetic cases, we still observe the trend information from X that is not fully eliminated in Z. Still, in this case, we argue that Z carries significant information and reveals evident dynamics of W. As shown in Table 1, the observed causes X only provide very little information to the target Y in simple synthetic cases, where the mutual information of target Y provided by itself, $I(Y; Y)$, is equivalent to the entropy of Y, $H(Y)$, provided that we consider Y as a random variable. In contrast, after we add the implicit causes Z, all the causes together provide most of the information of target Y and thus complete the causal structure of Y.

Table 1. Mutual information provided to Y from different sets of variables.

Case	Explicit X	Explicit X + Implicit Z	Target Y
1	0.646	5.46	5.52
2	0.679	4.11	5.35
3	1.44	3.47	5.29
4	2.84	3.48	5.36

5.2. *Preformance Evaluation by Real-World Data Experiments*

5.2.1. Information Recovery

We first examine the ability of NCIE (Section 4.1) to extract implicit causes that recover unobserved information of the targets in several real-world datasets, including

- The Electricity Transformer (Oil) Temperature (ETT) [17], which includes four datasets sampled at different time intervals (1 min, 2 min, 1 h, and 2 h). The observed causes include useful and useless loads in different levels;
- The daily exchange rates [51] of eight countries, with one of them set as the target and the other seven as the observed causes for predicting the target;
- Minneapolis–St Paul interstate metro traffic volume [52], in which observed causes include temperature, weather, and holidays;
- The PM2.5 quantity in Beijing (https://www.kaggle.com/datasets/rupakroy/lstm-datasets-multivariate-univariate) (accessed on 6 November 2023), in which observed causes include dew, temperature, atmospheric pressure, weather, as well as wind direction and speed (all the codes and data are available at https://github.com/jh-liang/NeuralCausalInfoExtractor) (accessed on 6 November 2023).

These data provide partial observations of complete systems in industrial monitoring, financial markets, and urban operations. In the provided datasets, it is obvious that some causes, W, are unobserved. For example, exchange rates are influenced not only by foreign exchange rates but also by the domestic economy and complex international trade. Similarly, the PM2.5 datasets do not involve urban human activities and pollution emissions from power plants. We aim to recover conditional information $I(W; Y|X)$ using Z, which advances the precision of time series forecasting.

Table 2 shows the information provided by only observed causes and by the combination of observed and implicit causes. It illustrates that the generated Z can provide significant extra information besides the observed causes X in real-world scenarios. The Z in this table is generated by NCIE (Section 4.1). We do not discuss the dimensionality of Z in this paper. While the higher dimensionality of Z provides the wider information channel, we simply set the dimension of Z to be the dimension of $\{X, Y_{<t}\}$.

Table 2. Mutual information provided to Y from different sets of variables. The Z in this table is generated by the original NCIE (Section 4.1).

Datasets	Explicit	Explicit + Implicit Z	Target Y
ETTh1	2.78	5.54	6.75
ETTh2	3.55	5.55	6.66
ETTm1	3.12	5.46	6.33
ETTm2	4.278	5.36	6.27
ExcRat	3.63	6.24	7.31
Metro	2.66	5.68	7.37
PM2.5	1.80	4.59	5.52

5.2.2. Single-Step Time Series Forecasting

While we claim that our architecture helps to identify unobserved causes of the target variables, it holds massive potential for extracting useful information from the available features and for conducting time series forecasting. We evaluate our architecture by performing time series forecasting on the real-time series datasets and comparing our results with the baselines [18,19] listed in Table 3. To prevent future information leakage in time series prediction, we employ the modified NCIE architecture in Section 4.2 to generate Z.

In this work, we are considering one-dimensional targets Y with multiple features that are candidates for observed causes chosen by PCMCI. Additionally, our architecture focuses on single-step time series forecasting because our goal is to find the direct causes for Y, which could be X_{t-k} and Z_{t-k} with a small lag k. The results are shown in Table 3. For the three chosen time series analyzing tools, we compare the prediction results with and without Z. It is illustrated that including Z in most cases does outperform those predictions without implicit variables Z.

Table 3. Single-step time series forecasting with and without Z in three different architectures, where 'NN' denotes the result from a simple NN with input including only observed causes, and 'I-NN' denotes the result with input including both observed causes and implicit variables Z generated by modified NCIE. The better result in the comparison is underlined.

Datasets	NN	I-NN	RNN	I-RNN	LSTM	I-LSTM
ETTh1	1.97×10^{-4}	$\underline{1.89 \times 10^{-4}}$	$\underline{1.65 \times 10^{-4}}$	1.77×10^{-4}	2.05×10^{-4}	$\underline{2.01 \times 10^{-4}}$
ETTh2	1.81×10^{-4}	$\underline{1.45 \times 10^{-4}}$	2.05×10^{-4}	$\underline{1.28 \times 10^{-4}}$	2.62×10^{-4}	$\underline{1.64 \times 10^{-4}}$
ETTm1	4.19×10^{-5}	$\underline{4.16 \times 10^{-5}}$	4.35×10^{-5}	$\underline{4.24 \times 10^{-5}}$	7.57×10^{-5}	$\underline{5.12 \times 10^{-5}}$
ETTm2	2.22×10^{-5}	$\underline{1.68 \times 10^{-5}}$	4.59×10^{-5}	$\underline{3.37 \times 10^{-5}}$	1.45×10^{-4}	$\underline{8.17 \times 10^{-5}}$
ExcRat	9.90×10^{-5}	$\underline{9.84 \times 10^{-5}}$	2.01×10^{-4}	$\underline{1.99 \times 10^{-4}}$	4.25×10^{-4}	$\underline{3.57 \times 10^{-4}}$
Metro	3.33×10^{-3}	$\underline{2.91 \times 10^{-3}}$	4.09×10^{-3}	$\underline{4.03 \times 10^{-3}}$	4.36×10^{-3}	$\underline{3.94 \times 10^{-3}}$
PM2.5	5.50×10^{-4}	$\underline{5.46 \times 10^{-4}}$	5.87×10^{-4}	$\underline{5.78 \times 10^{-4}}$	5.87×10^{-4}	$\underline{5.70 \times 10^{-4}}$

Our problem could be considered a feature selection task. The Z we generate could be considered as a feature that helps to describe Y. We see that in a few cases, Z does not necessarily improve the prediction of Y. This could be due to two reasons. First, although we know there is a gap between the entropy of Y and the information that X and $Y_{<t}$ bring to Y, this gap might be too narrow for NCIE to generate a Z that brings sufficient information from it. Second, when the system is time-varying, the underlying causality

structure of the system could also vary with time. Z that acts as a significant cause in (part of) the training dataset may become a redundant variable that perturbs the prediction.

It is worth mentioning that RNN and LSTM do not outperform simple neural networks (NN) in all cases. Our explanation is that the features X that PCMCI chooses cover most of the (observed) direct causes of Y, and we also choose autoregressive features $Y_{<t}$ from $t-k$ to $t-1$ that already cover short- and long-term memories of Y. Therefore, the memories that RNN and LSTM extract could not significantly help the prediction, but, in contrast, overfit Y.

Table 4 shows the mutual information between different sets of variables and Y. For real data, the Z that NCIE generates can provide extra information to Y. It demonstrates NCIE's ability to extract part of the implicit causes in the system, although we find a gap between $I(Y; X, Y_{<t}, Z)$ and $I(Y; Y)$. It is unavoidable in cases in which the systems are open or noisy because external noises are not driven by variables within the system. Furthermore, for a large system with too many causes, some causes may carry very little unique information to the target, and it is difficult to express them with limited Z.

Table 4. Mutual information provided to Y from different sets of variables. The Z in this table is generated by the modified NCIE (Section 4.2).

Datasets	Pre-Trained $\hat{Y}$	Explicit	Explicit + Z	Y
ETTh1	1.46	3.59	3.60	6.31
ETTh2	2.56	3.65	3.90	6.69
ETTm1	2.51	3.05	2.94	5.58
ETTm2	3.39	4.36	4.37	6.23
ExcRat	2.87	2.98	4.14	6.88
Metro	1.06	3.42	3.45	7.60
PM2.5	0.96	2.32	2.34	6.53

The first column of Table 4 shows the mutual information between the pre-trained $\hat{Y}$ and the actual Y. We recall that the pre-trained $\hat{Y}$ is generated by an RNN architecture that minimizes the mean square error (MSE), given the explicit causes X and $Y_{<t}$. The gap from the first column to the others shows that RNN and other recurrent structures do not necessarily provide a regression result with sufficient information to the target. While it is not a key point to argue the effectiveness of different objectives in this work, it reminds us that NCIE provides more information than general neural architectures.

6. Conclusions

In this work, we propose NCIE to generate implicit variables that complement the unobserved information of the target not provided by the observed variables. We can complete the causal structure of the target with the implicit variables while retaining the observed causes, as they together provide most of the target's information. Furthermore, the generated implicit variables have similar dynamics to the unobserved causes in the synthetic experiments and help to predict the target in the real-world time series. These results provide sufficient evidence that the implicit variables can be an effective candidate to substitute the unobserved causes and complete the causal structure.

While this work only focuses on discovering unobserved causes for single targets, future attempts could be made to apply similar methods to construct a complete graph for multiple targets, in which all the causes provide complete information for all the targets. With such methods, we are able to depict the evolution of systems by the information flow among variables, which could contribute to the research of emergence in real-world complex systems.

Author Contributions: Conceptualization, K.-H.L. and Y.X.; Data curation, K.-H.L.; Formal analysis, K.-H.L.; Funding acquisition, B.C. and W.K.C.; Investigation, K.-H.L.; Methodology, K.-H.L. and Y.X.; Project administration, B.C. and W.K.C.; Resources, B.C. and W.K.C.; Software, K.-H.L. and Y.X.;

Supervision, B.C. and W.K.C.; Validation, K.-H.L., Y.X., B.C. and W.K.C.; Visualization, K.-H.L. and Y.X.; Writing—original draft, K.-H.L.; Writing—review and editing, K.-H.L., Y.X., B.C. and W.K.C. All authors have read and agreed to the published version of the manuscript.

Funding: This research was funded by the Science and Technology Innovation Commission of Shenzhen (JCYJ20210324135011030, JCYJ20210324115604012, WDZC20200818121348001), the National Natural Science Foundation of China (71971127), the Guangdong Pearl River Plan (2019QN01X890), the High-End Foreign Expert Talent Introduction Plan (G2021032022L), the Tsinghua Shenzhen International Graduate School Fund (JC2021004), and the Science and Technology Innovation Committee of Shenzhen-Platform and Carrier (International Science and Technology Information Center).

Institutional Review Board Statement: Not applicable.

Data Availability Statement: All the codes and data are available at https://github.com/jh-liang/NeuralCausalInfoExtractor (accessed on 6 November 2023)

Acknowledgments: We gratefully acknowledge Keqin Guan, Kexin Cao, Siyu Chen, and Chang-Yan Shih for their tremendous advice on ideas and academic writing. Likewise, we thank the support from the Causal Emergence Reading Group supported by the Save 2050 Programme jointly sponsored by Swarma Club and X-Order.

Conflicts of Interest: The authors declare no conflict of interest. The funders had no role in the design of the study; in the collection, analyses, or interpretation of data; in the writing of the manuscript; or in the decision to publish the results.

References

1. Gong, C.; Yao, D.; Zhang, C.; Li, W.; Bi, J. Causal discovery from temporal Data: An overview and new perspectives. *arXiv* **2023**, arXiv:2303.10112.
2. Spirtes, P.; Glymour, C.N.; Scheines, R. *Causation, Prediction, and Search*; MIT Press: Cambridge, MA, USA, 2000.
3. Runge, J.; Nowack, P.; Kretschmer, M.; Flaxman, S.; Sejdinovic, D. Detecting and quantifying causal associations in large nonlinear time series datasets. *Sci. Adv.* **2019**, *5*, eaau4996. [CrossRef]
4. Heckerman, D.; Geiger, D.; Chickering, D.M. Learning Bayesian networks: The combination of knowledge and statistical data. *Mach. Learn.* **1995**, *20*, 197–243. [CrossRef]
5. Kayaalp, M.; Cooper, G.F. A Bayesian network scoring metric that is based on globally uniform parameter priors. *arXiv* **2012**, arXiv:1301.0576.
6. Marcinkevičs, R.; Vogt, J.E. Interpretable models for Granger causality using self-explaining neural networks. *arXiv* **2021**, arXiv:2101.07600.
7. Jiang, P.; Kumar, P. Information transfer from causal history in complex system dynamics. *Phys. Rev. E* **2019**, *99*, 012306. [CrossRef] [PubMed]
8. Li, J.; Convertino, M. Inferring ecosystem networks as information flows. *Sci. Rep.* **2021**, *11*, 7094. [CrossRef]
9. Engelberg, J.E.; Parsons, C.A. The causal impact of media in financial markets. *J. Financ.* **2011**, *66*, 67–97. [CrossRef]
10. Farag, H.; Cressy, R. Do unobservable factors explain the disposition effect in emerging stock markets? *Appl. Financ. Econ.* **2010**, *20*, 1173–1183. [CrossRef]
11. Williams, B.K.; Brown, E.D. Partial observability and management of ecological systems. *Ecol. Evol.* **2022**, *12*, e9197. [CrossRef]
12. Chadès, I.; Pascal, L.V.; Nicol, S.; Fletcher, C.S.; Ferrer-Mestres, J. A primer on partially observable Markov decision processes (POMDPs). *Methods Ecol. Evol.* **2021**, *12*, 2058–2072. [CrossRef]
13. Singh, M.F.; Wang, A.; Braver, T.S.; Ching, S. Scalable surrogate deconvolution for identification of partially-observable systems and brain modeling. *J. Neural Eng.* **2020**, *17*, 046025. [CrossRef] [PubMed]
14. Gupta, V.; Li, L.K.; Chen, S.; Wan, M. Model-free forecasting of partially observable spatiotemporally chaotic systems. *Neural Netw.* **2023**, *160*, 297–305. [CrossRef]
15. Duan, C.; Jiang, Y.; Pu, H.; Luo, J.; Liu, F.; Tang, B. Health prediction of partially observable failing systems under varying environments. *ISA Trans.* **2023**, *137*, 379–392. [CrossRef] [PubMed]
16. Geiger, P.; Zhang, K.; Schoelkopf, B.; Gong, M.; Janzing, D. Causal inference by identification of vector autoregressive processes with hidden components. In Proceedings of the 32nd International Conference on Machine Learning, Lille, France, 6–11 July 2015; pp. 1917–1925.
17. Zhou, H.; Zhang, S.; Peng, J.; Zhang, S.; Li, J.; Xiong, H.; Zhang, W. Informer: Beyond efficient transformer for long sequence time-series forecasting. In Proceedings of the Thirty-Fifth AAAI Conference on Artificial Intelligence (AAAI-21), Virtual, 2–9 February 2021; Volume 35, pp. 11106–11115.
18. Lipton, Z.C.; Berkowitz, J.; Elkan, C. A critical review of recurrent neural networks for sequence learning. *arXiv* **2015**, arXiv:1506.00019.
19. Hochreiter, S.; Schmidhuber, J. Long short-term memory. *Neural Comput.* **1997**, *9*, 1735–1780. [CrossRef]

20. Yao, W.; Sun, Y.; Ho, A.; Sun, C.; Zhang, K. Learning temporally causal latent processes from general temporal data. *arXiv* **2021**, arXiv:2110.05428.
21. Klindt, D.; Schott, L.; Sharma, Y.; Ustyuzhaninov, I.; Brendel, W.; Bethge, M.; Paiton, D. Towards nonlinear disentanglement in natural data with temporal sparse coding. *arXiv* **2020**, arXiv:2007.10930.
22. Hjelm, R.D.; Fedorov, A.; Lavoie-Marchildon, S.; Grewal, K.; Bachman, P.; Trischler, A.; Bengio, Y. Learning deep representations by mutual information estimation and maximization. *arXiv* **2018**, arXiv:1808.06670.
23. Hyvärinen, A.; Shimizu, S.; Hoyer, P.O. Causal modelling combining instantaneous and lagged effects: An identifiable model based on non-Gaussianity. In Proceedings of the 25th International Conference on Machine Learning, Helsinki, Finland, 5–9 July 2008; pp. 424–431.
24. Hyvarinen, A.; Morioka, H. Nonlinear ICA of temporally dependent stationary sources. In *Proceedings of the 20th International Conference on Artificial Intelligence and Statistics*; Singh, A., Zhu, J., Eds.; MIT Press: Cambridge, MA, USA, 2017; Volume 54, pp. 460–469.
25. Clark, D.; Livezey, J.; Bouchard, K. Unsupervised discovery of temporal structure in noisy data with dynamical components analysis. In Proceedings of the 33rd International Conference on Neural Information Processing Systems, Vancouver, BC, Canada, 8–14 December 2019.
26. Bai, J.; Wang, W.; Zhou, Y.; Xiong, C. Representation learning for sequence data with deep autoencoding predictive components. *arXiv* **2020**, arXiv:2010.03135.
27. Meng, R.; Luo, T.; Bouchard, K. Compressed predictive information coding. *arXiv* **2022** arXiv:2203.02051.
28. Wu, H.; Gattami, A.; Flierl, M. Conditional mutual information-based contrastive loss for financial time series forecasting. In Proceedings of the First ACM International Conference on AI in Finance, New York, NY, USA, 15–16 October 2020; pp. 1–7.
29. Granger, C.W. Investigating causal relations by econometric models and cross-spectral methods. *Econom. J. Econom. Soc.* **1969**, *37*, 424–438. [CrossRef]
30. Tishby, N.; Zaslavsky, N. Deep learning and the information bottleneck principle. In Proceedings of the 2015 IEEE Information Theory Workshop (ITW), Jerusalem, Israel, 26 April–1 May 2015; pp. 1–5.
31. Pearl, J. *Causality*; Cambridge University Press: Cambridge, UK, 2009.
32. Rosas, F.E.; Mediano, P.A.; Jensen, H.J.; Seth, A.K.; Barrett, A.B.; Carhart-Harris, R.L.; Bor, D. Reconciling emergences: An information-theoretic approach to identify causal emergence in multivariate data. *PLoS Comput. Biol.* **2020**, *16*, e1008289. [CrossRef] [PubMed]
33. Malinsky, D.; Spirtes, P. Causal structure learning from multivariate time series in settings with unmeasured confounding. In Proceedings of the 2018 ACM SIGKDD Workshop on Causal Discovery, London, UK, 20 August 2018; pp. 23–47.
34. Gerhardus, A.; Runge, J. High-recall causal discovery for autocorrelated time series with latent confounders. *Adv. Neural Inf. Process. Syst.* **2020**, *33*, 12615–12625.
35. Kingma, D.P.; Welling, M. Auto-encoding variational bayes. *arXiv* **2013**, arXiv:1312.6114.
36. Louizos, C.; Shalit, U.; Mooij, J.M.; Sontag, D.; Zemel, R.; Welling, M. Causal effect inference with deep latent-variable models. In Proceedings of the 31st International Conference on Neural Information Processing Systems, Long Beach, CA, USA, 4–9 December 2017.
37. Kraskov, A.; Stögbauer, H.; Grassberger, P. Estimating mutual information. *Phys. Rev. E* **2004**, *69*, 066138. [CrossRef]
38. Xiu, Y.; Cao, K.; Ren, X.; Chen, B.; Chan, W.K. Self-similar growth and synergistic link prediction in technology-convergence networks: The case of intelligent transportation systems. *Fractal Fract.* **2023**, *7*, 109. [CrossRef]
39. Belghazi, M.I.; Baratin, A.; Rajeswar, S.; Ozair, S.; Bengio, Y.; Courville, A.; Hjelm, R.D. Mine: Mutual information neural estimation. *arXiv* **2018**, arXiv:1801.04062.
40. Mukherjee, S.; Asnani, H.; Kannan, S. CCMI: Classifier based conditional mutual information estimation. In Proceedings of the Uncertainty in Artificial Intelligence, Virtual, 3–6 August 2020; pp. 1083–1093.
41. Zhang, R.; Koyama, M.; Ishiguro, K. Learning structured latent factors from dependent data: A generative model framework from information-theoretic perspective. In Proceedings of the International Conference on Machine Learning, Virtual, 13–18 July 2020; pp. 11141–11152.
42. Zhu, H.; Wang, S. Learning fair models without sensitive attributes: A generative approach. *arXiv* **2022**, arXiv:2203.16413.
43. Diz-Pita, É.; Otero-Espinar, M.V. Predator–prey models: A review of some recent advances. *Mathematics* **2021**, *9*, 1783. [CrossRef]
44. Leeuwen, E.v.; Jansen, V.; Bright, P. How population dynamics shape the functional response in a one-predator–two-prey system. *Ecology* **2007**, *88*, 1571–1581. [CrossRef] [PubMed]
45. Lotka, A.J. *Elements of Physical Biology*; Williams & Wilkins: Philadelphia, PA, USA, 1925.
46. Volterra, V. Volume 2, Societá anonima tipografica "Leonardo da Vinci". In *Variazioni e Fluttuazioni del Numero d'Individui in Specie Animali Conviventi*; Accademia Nazionale dei Lincei: Roma, Italy, 1927.
47. Williams, P.L.; Beer, R.D. Nonnegative decomposition of multivariate information. *arXiv* **2010**, arXiv:1004.2515.
48. Bertschinger, N.; Rauh, J.; Olbrich, E.; Jost, J.; Ay, N. Quantifying unique information. *Entropy* **2014**, *16*, 2161–2183. [CrossRef]
49. Kleinman, M.; Achille, A.; Soatto, S.; Kao, J.C. Redundant information neural estimation. *Entropy* **2021**, *23*, 922. [CrossRef]
50. Quax, R.; Har-Shemesh, O.; Sloot, P.M. Quantifying synergistic information using intermediate stochastic variables. *Entropy* **2017**, *19*, 85. [CrossRef]

51. Lai, G.; Chang, W.C.; Yang, Y.; Liu, H. Modeling long-and short-term temporal patterns with deep neural networks. In Proceedings of the 41st International ACM SIGIR Conference on Research & Development in Information Retrieval, Ann Arbor, MI, USA, 8–12 July 2018; pp. 95–104.
52. Hogue, J. Metro Interstate Traffic Volume. *Uci Mach. Learn. Repos.* **2019**. (accessed on 21 December 2023). [CrossRef]

entropy

MDPI

Review

Comparison of Bootstrap Methods for Estimating Causality in Linear Dynamic Systems: A Review

Fumikazu Miwakeichi [1,2,*] and Andreas Galka [3]

1 Department of Statistical Modeling, The Institute of Statistical Mathematics, Tokyo 190-8562, Japan
2 Statistical Science Program, Graduate Institute for Advanced Studies, SOKENDAI, Tokyo 190-8562, Japan
3 Clinic for Pediatric and Adolescent Medicine II, University Clinic, University of Kiel, 24105 Kiel, Germany; a.galka@pedneuro.uni-kiel.de
* Correspondence: miwake1@ism.ac.jp

Abstract: In this study, we present a thorough comparison of the performance of four different bootstrap methods for assessing the significance of causal analysis in time series data. For this purpose, multivariate simulated data are generated by a linear feedback system. The methods investigated are uncorrelated Phase Randomization Bootstrap (uPRB), which generates surrogate data with no cross-correlation between variables by randomizing the phase in the frequency domain; Time Shift Bootstrap (TSB), which generates surrogate data by randomizing the phase in the time domain; Stationary Bootstrap (SB), which calculates standard errors and constructs confidence regions for weakly dependent stationary observations; and AR-Sieve Bootstrap (ARSB), a resampling method based on AutoRegressive (AR) models that approximates the underlying data-generating process. The uPRB method accurately identifies variable interactions but fails to detect self-feedback in some variables. The TSB method, despite performing worse than uPRB, is unable to detect feedback between certain variables. The SB method gives consistent causality results, although its ability to detect self-feedback decreases, as the mean block width increases. The ARSB method shows superior performance, accurately detecting both self-feedback and causality across all variables. Regarding the analysis of the Impulse Response Function (IRF), only the ARSB method succeeds in detecting both self-feedback and causality in all variables, aligning well with the connectivity diagram. Other methods, however, show considerable variations in detection performance, with some detecting false positives and others only detecting self-feedback.

Keywords: causal analysis; Granger causality; bootstrap methods; multivariate time series; impulse response function

1. Introduction

In many fields of scientific inquiry, the analysis of causal relationships in complex systems represents an important task, which depends on the synergistic interplay between theory and application. An important contribution in this area has been the proposal of Granger Causality (GC) [1], which tests the significance of dynamic influence between pairwise time series. Building upon this foundation, Geweke [2] expanded GC to encompass multivariate time series, introducing conditional Granger Causality (cGC). Bressler et al. [3] and Schiatti et al. [4] further refined cGC, enabling the estimation of causality among multivariate time series using Vector AutoRegressive (VAR) models.

Granger causality and its generalizations represent a statistical method that depends on the comparison of the residual variances resulting from applying different models to the same time series; a wide array of predictive models, including non-linear variants, may be employed. As an alternative approach to quantifying causality from predictive modeling, Impulse Response Function (IRF) analysis has been developed as a tool for examining variable responses to shocks within an identified model.

However, it is worth noting that Granger causality and IRF analysis always depend on the particular chosen model classes; they are not suitable for model discovery since they are lacking invariance theorems, as they exist for the more general concept of algorithmic complexity [5].

Conceptually, the statistical significance of numerically calculated cGC and IRF should be assessed using the asymptotic method. However, real-world data analysis may yield incorrect results due to potential distribution discrepancies. In cases where the distribution function is unknown, such as with partial Granger causality [6], the asymptotic method is inapplicable. The bootstrap strategy serves as a widely used alternative for cGC and IRF significance testing. However, with numerous bootstrap methods available, each with varying sensitivity and specificity, selecting the appropriate method remains a critical challenge when applying time series models to real data analysis.

In a causal analysis of time series data, failing to apply an appropriate bootstrap method can lead to several important issues. First, as causal analysis is based on the estimation of causal relationships, not using a suitable bootstrap method could potentially result in inaccuracies in estimating these relationships, thereby undermining the reliability of statistical inferences. Furthermore, bootstrap methods are often used for estimating confidence intervals, and if an unsuitable method is chosen, the confidence intervals could be under- or over-estimated, leading to inappropriate assessments of uncertainty. Additionally, bootstrap methods are used to estimate the magnitude of causal effects, and without a suitable method, the magnitude of these effects could be inaccurately estimated, which could affect the appropriateness of subsequent actions. Therefore, to avoid these problems, it is important to select and apply suitable bootstrap methods for causal analysis and choose methods based on understanding the characteristics of the time series data and the objectives of the causal analysis.

In this study, we thoroughly evaluate the performance of four bootstrap methods designed for time series analysis. The first method we present is an adaptation of the Phase Randomize Bootstrap (FRB), which generates surrogate data for hypothesis testing through phase randomization in the Fourier transform of original time series data. We propose a modification, the uncorrelated Phase-Randomized Bootstrap (uPRB), which randomizes phases for each variable in the spectral domain, for causality detection among variables. As a counterpart, we consider a technique based on Circular Block Bootstrap (CBB), a method for transfer randomization in the time domain [7]. This approach remedies the under-representation of the beginning and the end of the time series in surrogate data by creating a circular time series. Time-Shifted Surrogates (TSS) [8,9], another technique we discuss, ensures the preservation of all characteristics of the initial signal by maintaining the same stat–space trajectory. The Stationary Bootstrap (SB) [10] uses random block lengths for standard error calculations and confidence region construction in weakly dependent stationary observations. Last, we discuss the AR-Sieve Bootstrap (ARSB), a method that approximates the underlying data-generating process by fitting an AR model, useful for handling dependent data [11,12].

2. Causal Analysis

2.1. Conditional Granger Causality (cGC)

Let $\boldsymbol{Y}_t = \{y_t^1, \ldots, y_t^M\}^T$ denote the vector variables at time t, $1 \leq t \leq N$, where N denotes the length of the time series. The feedback system among the variables $\boldsymbol{Y}_t$ can be represented by a basic Vector AutoRegressive (VAR) model of order p, defined as

$$\boldsymbol{Y}_t = \sum_{k=1}^{p} \boldsymbol{A}_k \boldsymbol{Y}_{t-k} + \boldsymbol{E}_t, \tag{1}$$

where $\boldsymbol{A}_k$ denotes a set of $M \times M$-dimensional coefficient matrices, and $\boldsymbol{E}_t = \{e_t^1, \ldots, e_t^M\}^T$ denotes a series of shocks (disturbances), given by white noise vectors with zero means.

Extracting the lth variable of the VAR model gives

$$y_t^l = \sum_{k=1}^{p} \boldsymbol{A}_k^l \boldsymbol{Y}_{t-k} + e_t^l, \tag{2}$$

where $\boldsymbol{A}_k^l = \{a_k^{l1}, a_k^{l2}, \ldots, a_k^{lm}, \ldots, a_k^{lM}\}$ denotes the lth row of $\boldsymbol{A}_k$. Equation (2) represents an autoregressive model with exogenous input (ARX model) that consists of an endogenous part of the lth variable and an exogenous part of all other variables.

The ARX model, excluding the mth variable, is called the restricted ARX (rARX) model:

$$y_t^l = \sum_{k=1}^{p} \widetilde{\boldsymbol{A}}_k^l \boldsymbol{Y}_{t-k}^{(m)} + e_t^{lm}, \tag{3}$$

where $\boldsymbol{Y}_t^{(m)}$ denotes the vector $\boldsymbol{Y}_t$ with the mth element excluded (e.g., $\boldsymbol{Y}_t^{(1)} = \{y_t^2, \ldots, y_t^M\}^T$, $\boldsymbol{Y}_t^{(2)} = \{y_t^1, y_t^3, \ldots, y_t^M\}^T$ and so on) and $\widetilde{\boldsymbol{A}}_k^l$ denotes a set of re-estimated $(M-1)$-dimensional coefficient vectors. Suppose that the past values of the mth variable $\{y_{t-1}^m, y_{t-2}^m, \ldots, y_{t-p}^m\}$ contribute to the prediction of the lth variable $\{y_t^l\}$; then, the variances of the residuals should satisfy $\mathrm{var}(e_t^l) < \mathrm{var}(e_t^{lm})$. The significance of the difference in variances can be evaluated by a likelihood ratio test:

$$F_{m\to l} = \log \frac{\mathrm{var}\left(e_t^{lm}\right)}{\mathrm{var}\left(e_t^l\right)}. \tag{4}$$

The null hypothesis of absence of conditional Granger causality from the mth to the lth element given $Y_t^m = \{y_1^m, y_2^m, \ldots, y_p^m\}$ states that all a_k^{lm} were zero, i.e., $H_0 : a_1^{lm} = a_2^{lm} = \ldots = a_p^{lm} = 0$. This implies that past values of Y_t^m do not improve the prediction of y_t^l. On the contrary, the rejection of this null hypothesis suggests that Y_t^m in Granger causes y_t^l.

2.2. *Impulse Response Function (IRF)*

There is another representation of the VAR model of Equation (1) using a delay operator L, such that $L\boldsymbol{Y}_t = \boldsymbol{Y}_{t-1}$:

$$\boldsymbol{A}(L)\boldsymbol{Y}_t = \boldsymbol{E}_t, \tag{5}$$

$$\boldsymbol{A}(L) = \boldsymbol{I}_M - \boldsymbol{A}_1 L - \boldsymbol{A}_2 L^2 - \ldots - \boldsymbol{A}_p L^p. \tag{6}$$

where $\boldsymbol{I}_M$ denotes the $M \times M$-dimensional unity matrix. The roots (eigenvalues) λ_j of the polynomial $\boldsymbol{A}(L)$ need to fulfill $|\lambda_j| < 1$ for all j.

Further transformation of Equation (5) yields

$$\begin{aligned} \boldsymbol{Y}_t &= \boldsymbol{A}(L)^{-1}\boldsymbol{E}_t \\ &= \{\boldsymbol{I}_M + \boldsymbol{\Psi}_1 L + \boldsymbol{\Psi}_2 L^2 + \ldots\}\boldsymbol{E}_t. \end{aligned} \tag{7}$$

which demonstrates that a VAR model can be rewritten as

$$\boldsymbol{Y}_t = \sum_{k=0}^{\infty} \boldsymbol{\Psi}_k \boldsymbol{E}_{t-k} = \boldsymbol{\Psi}(L)\boldsymbol{E}_t, \tag{8}$$

where

$$\begin{aligned} \boldsymbol{\Psi}(L) &= \boldsymbol{A}(L)^{-1} \\ &= \{\boldsymbol{I}_M - \boldsymbol{A}_1 L - \boldsymbol{A}_2 L^2 - \ldots - \boldsymbol{A}_p L^p\}^{-1} \\ &= \boldsymbol{I}_M + \boldsymbol{\Psi}_1 L + \boldsymbol{\Psi}_2 L^2 + \ldots \end{aligned}$$

Equation (8) represents the Vector Moving Average (VMA) representation of the VAR model and can be denoted as VMA(∞).

Partial differentiation of the VMA(∞) model with respect to one particular shock (disturbance term) $\boldsymbol{E}_t$ yields a set of derivatives

$$\frac{\partial \boldsymbol{Y}_t}{\partial \boldsymbol{E}_t} = \boldsymbol{I}_M, \ \frac{\partial \boldsymbol{Y}_{t+1}}{\partial \boldsymbol{E}_t} = \boldsymbol{\Psi}_1, \cdots, \ \frac{\partial \boldsymbol{Y}_{t+s}}{\partial \boldsymbol{E}_t} = \boldsymbol{\Psi}_s. \tag{9}$$

The (l, m)th element of $\boldsymbol{\Psi}_s$ is given by $\frac{\partial y^l_{t+s}}{\partial e^m_t}$, which represents the marginal effect (influence) from the mth shock e^m_t to the lth variable y^l_{t+s}. The function defining the time series of such marginal effects is called the Impulse Response Function (IRF) and is denoted by IRF^{lm}_s.

The null hypothesis for the IRF states that a one-time shock to the mth variable has no impact on future values of the lth variable. This can be represented as: $H_0 : \mathrm{IRF}^{lm}_s = 0$ for all $s > 0$. The rejection of this null hypothesis suggests that a one-time shock to the mth variable significantly affects the lth variable at some future point in time.

3. Bootstrap Methods

3.1. *Uncorrelated Phase Randomization Bootstrap (uPRB)*

The Phase Randomization Bootstrap method has been proposed as a technique to generate surrogate time series data for hypothesis testing [13,14]. Using the Fourier transform, the method transforms the original time series data into the frequency domain. Then, the phase of each frequency component is randomized while preserving the original amplitude spectrum. Finally, the surrogate data are obtained by applying the inverse Fourier transform to the randomized frequency components.

This process generates surrogate time series data with the same power spectrum as the original data but with disrupted temporal correlations. By comparing the original data's non-linearity measures or other statistical properties to those of the surrogate data, researchers can test hypotheses and detect the presence of non-linear dynamics in the original time series data. This method has been applied in various fields, including the study of physiological signals [15], economics and finance [16], climate data [9], and so on.

In order to preserve all linear auto-correlations and cross-correlations, the Phase Randomization Bootstrap adds a common random sequence $\varphi(f)$ to the phases of all variables. Thus, since this method cannot detect causality among variables, we prepare random sequences independently for each variable. In this paper, we call this method uncorrelated Phase Randomization Bootstrap (uPRB).

The procedure for generating surrogate datasets by uPRB is as follows.

Step 1 Transform the original time series by applying Fourier transform to each variable as

$$\mathcal{Y}^l(f) = \mathcal{F}\{y^l_t\} = A^l(f)e^{i\phi^l(f)},$$

where l is the index of the variable, and $A^l(f)$ and $\phi^l(f)$ denote the amplitude and the phase, respectively.

Step 2 For each frequency f, add an independent random value $\varphi^l(f)$ following a uniform distribution throughout the interval $[0, 2\pi)$ to $\phi^l(f)$, while satisfying the symmetry property $\varphi^l(f) = -\varphi^l(-f)$. That is,

$$\tilde{\mathcal{Y}}^l(f) = A^l(f)e^{i[\phi^l(f)+\varphi^l(f)]}.$$

Step 3 Transform the spectral domain representation back to the time domain by applying the inverse Fourier transform to each variable as

$$y^{*l}_t = \mathcal{F}^{-1}\{\tilde{\mathcal{Y}}^l(f)\} = \mathcal{F}^{-1}\left\{\mathcal{Y}^l(f)e^{i\varphi^l(f)}\right\}.$$

Step 4 Repeat Steps 2–3 for all variables.

Step 5 Repeat Steps 2–4 a large number of times, thereby generating a set of surrogate datasets.

3.2. Stationary Bootstrap (SB)

The conventional Non-overlapping Block Bootstrap (NBB) has been proposed by Carlstein [17]. By improving this conventional method, Künsch [18] has proposed a Moving-Blocks Bootstrap (MBB). This method is useful, especially for small sample data having a wider range of blocks than the conventional method. However, in the process of random sampling, there is an edge effect of the uneven weighting of the selection at the beginning and end of the data. To compensate for this shortcoming, Politis and Romano [7] proposed a Circular Block Bootstrap (CBB) that concatenates the start and end points of the original data. In the block bootstrap method, the stationarity of the sample is an important assumption. However, surrogate data obtained by resampling using the above-mentioned method are not necessarily stationary. Therefore, the Stationary Bootstrap (SB) method has been proposed, in which the surrogate data are also stationary. This method is similar to the TSS method, except that the block width is not fixed but is resampled as a random variable following a geometric distribution [10]. The procedure for generating surrogate data by SB is as follows.

Step 1 Set the mean block width to w. Then, in the geometric distribution used in Step 3, we have $p = 1/w$.
Step 2 Duplicate the original data and merge it to the end of the original data such that $\mathbf{Y}_{N+1} = \mathbf{Y}_1, \mathbf{Y}_{N+2} = \mathbf{Y}_2, \ldots, \mathbf{Y}_{2N} = \mathbf{Y}_N$.
Step 3 Generate a sequence of natural random numbers $L_1^{*b}, \ldots, L_K^{*b}$ corresponding to each block width following a geometric distribution so that the probability of the event $L_l^{*b} = r$ is $(1-p)^{r-1}p$ for $r = 1, 2, \ldots$. Here, the value of K is determined to satisfy the condition $K = \min\{k : \sum_{l=1}^{k} L_l^{*b} \geq N\}$.
Step 4 Generate a sequence of natural random numbers $I_1^{*b}, \ldots, I_K^{*b}$, corresponding to the index of the starting point of the block, following a uniform distribution over the interval $[1, N]$.
Step 5 The blocks, $\left\{\xi^{*b}\left(I_1^{*b}, L_1^{*b}\right), \ldots, \xi^{*b}\left(I_K^{*b}, L_K^{*b}\right)\right\}$, constructed according to Steps 1 and 2, are arranged in the order in which they were extracted, and a pair of resamples is obtained with the first N elements as $Y_1^{*b}, \ldots, Y_N^{*b}$.
Step 6 Repeat Steps 3–5 a large number of times, thereby generating a set of surrogate datasets.

In the case of multivariate time series, there are two ways to perform Steps 3–5. One way is to use the same blocks $\left\{\xi^{*b}\left(I_1^{*b}, L_1^{*b}\right), \ldots, \xi^{*b}\left(I_K^{*b}, L_K^{*b}\right)\right\}$ for all variables for data shuffling, as described above, and the other is to perform Steps 3–5 for each variable independently. In this paper, we refer to the former as correlated SB (cSB) and to the latter as uncorrelated SB (ucSB).

3.3. Time Shift Surrogates (TSS)

While PRB is a method for generating surrogate datasets by randomizing the phases in the frequency domain, we evaluated the performance of TSS as a method of randomizing the phase in the time domain. This method corresponds to the special case of the CBB, where the number of blocks is limited to 1. The procedure for generating surrogate datasets by TSS is as follows.

Step 1 Duplicate the original data and merge it to the end of the original data such that $\mathbf{Y}_{N+1} = \mathbf{Y}_1, \mathbf{Y}_{N+2} = \mathbf{Y}_2, \ldots, \mathbf{Y}_{2N} = \mathbf{Y}_N$.
Step 2 Generate a natural random number s following a uniform distribution over the interval $[I_a, I_b]$, extract a sequence of the data $\{y_s^l, \ldots, y_{N+s}^l\}$, and use it as surrogate dataset for the lth variable.
Step 3 Repeat Step 2 for all variables.

Step 4 Repeat Steps 2–3 a large number of times, thereby generating a set of surrogate datasets.

3.4. AR-Sieve Bootstrap (ARSB)

The AR-Sieve Bootstrap (ARSB) method generates surrogate datasets by feeding a VAR model, which employs re-estimated parameters, with residuals from modeling [11,12].

The procedure for generating surrogate datasets using ARSB is as follows.

Step 1 Fit the VAR model of Equation (1) to the original time series, obtaining estimates for the parameters and the residuals $\hat{\boldsymbol{E}}_t$.

Step 2 Compute centered residuals $\hat{\boldsymbol{E}}_1 - \bar{\boldsymbol{E}}, \ldots, \hat{\boldsymbol{E}}_N - \bar{\boldsymbol{E}}$, where $\bar{\boldsymbol{E}} = N^{-1}\sum_{t=1}^{N} \hat{\boldsymbol{E}}_t$, and generate bootstrap residuals $\boldsymbol{E}_1^*, \ldots, \boldsymbol{E}_N^*$ by shuffling the indices according to a sequence of natural random numbers $\{J_1^{*b}, \ldots, J_N^{*b}\}$, which was drawn randomly with replacement from a uniform distribution over the interval $[1, N]$.

Step 3 Compute the surrogate time series recursively by

$$\boldsymbol{Y}_t^* = \sum_{k=1}^{p} \hat{\boldsymbol{A}}_k \boldsymbol{Y}_{t-k}^* + \boldsymbol{E}_t^*$$

where $\left(\boldsymbol{Y}_1^*, \ldots, \boldsymbol{Y}_p^*\right) = (\boldsymbol{Y}_1, \ldots, \boldsymbol{Y}_p)$.

Step 4 Re-estimate the VAR parameter matrices $\boldsymbol{A}_1, \ldots, \boldsymbol{A}_p$ based on the bootstrap time series.

Step 5 Repeat Steps 2–4 a large number of times, thereby generating a set of surrogate datasets.

Similar to the SB method, there are two ways to process Step 2 in the ARSB method. One is to use the same sequence of random values $\{J_1^{*b}, \ldots, J_N^{*b}\}$ for all variables for data shuffling, as mentioned above, and the other is to perform Step 2 independently for each variable. In this paper, we refer to the former as correlated ARSB (cARSB) and to the latter as uncorrelated ARSB (ucARSB).

4. Simulation

In order to verify the performance of the methods for causal analysis and of the bootstrap methods, as discussed above, we prepared a simulation model by modifying a model proposed by [19]. We set up seven oscillatory variables as depicted in Figure 1, five of which generated their stochastic oscillations locally from driving white noise via self-feedback; furthermore, the seven variables were coupled directly or indirectly within a global Vector AutoRegressive (VAR) process, such that a dynamic feedback system results. We fixed the frequency of each variable to 0.1 Hz and randomly selected a damping coefficient for each variable from a normal distribution. The sixth and seventh variables were isolated from the other five. For instance, the first and third variables were directly connected, while the first and fourth variables were indirectly connected through the third variable. The fourth and fifth variables were directly and bidirectionally connected.

The sixth variable generated a local oscillation at 0.1 Hz via self-feedback, like the other five, while the seventh variable did not have any self-feedback, but was driven only by the sixth variable. If causality would be detected between either the sixth or seventh variables and any of the first to fifth variables, this would represent a false positive.

We set the connectivity among variables as shown in Figure 1 and generate a simulated time series of length $N = 2000$ through the VAR process of Equation (1), with $p = 2$. The nominal sampling frequency was 10 Hz, and the series of shocks (disturbances) $\boldsymbol{E}_t$ was sampled from a 7-dimensional multivariate Gaussian noise distribution with zero mean and diagonal covariance matrix given by $\boldsymbol{\Sigma}_E = 0.1\boldsymbol{I}_7$.

Table 1 displays the parameters of the VAR model for the simulations. Figure 2 displays the simulated time series.

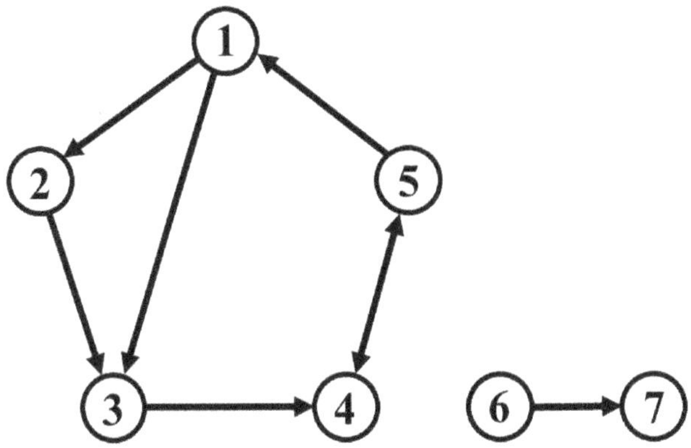

Figure 1. Connectivity diagram of the simulation model.

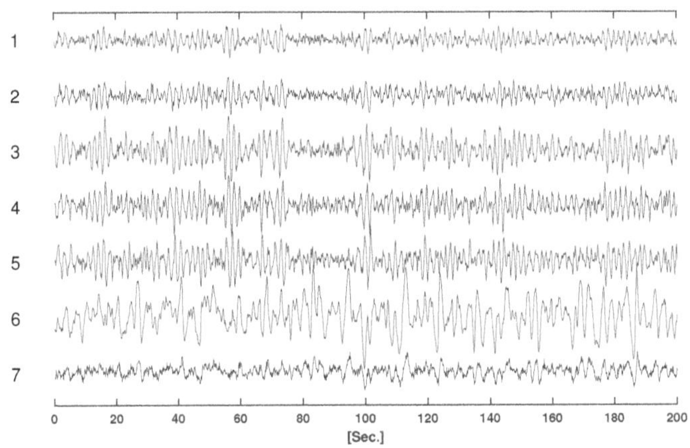

Figure 2. Simulated time series.

Table 1. VAR parameters for the simulation.

$$A_1 = \begin{pmatrix} 0.828 & 0 & 0 & 0 & 0 & 0 & 0 \\ 0.541 & 0.651 & 0 & 0 & 0 & 0 & 0 \\ 0.74 & 0 & 0.744 & 0 & 0 & 0 & 0 \\ 0 & 0 & 0.456 & 0.73 & 0.3 & 0 & 0 \\ 0 & 0 & 0 & -0.4 & 0.859 & 0 & 0 \\ 0 & 0 & 0 & 0 & 0 & 1.752 & 0 \\ 0 & 0 & 0 & 0 & 0 & -0.120 & 0 \end{pmatrix}$$

$$A_2 = \begin{pmatrix} -0.172 & 0 & 0 & 0 & 0.17 & 0 & 0 \\ 0 & -0.107 & 0 & 0 & 0 & 0 & 0 \\ 0 & 0.238 & -0.139 & 0 & 0 & 0 & 0 \\ 0 & 0 & 0 & -0.134 & 0 & 0 & 0 \\ 0 & 0 & 0 & 0 & -0.185 & 0 & 0 \\ 0 & 0 & 0 & 0 & 0 & -0.810 & 0 \\ 0 & 0 & 0 & 0 & 0 & 0.430 & 0 \end{pmatrix}$$

5. Results

In our pursuit of accurately estimating the 99% confidence intervals (CI) for both conditional Granger Causality (cGC) and Impulse Response Function (IRF) analyses, we generated 2000 surrogate datasets using each of the previously discussed bootstrap methods. For the SB method, we determined the optimal mean block width w, selecting values of 5, 10, 20, and 40. As illustrated in Figure 3a, the cSB method consistently yielded correct causality results, irrespective of the chosen mean block width. In contrast, the ucSB method produced correct causality results for $w = 5$, but the detection rate of self-feedback diminished as w increased (see Figure 3b,c).

While the uPRB method provided accurate causality results concerning variable interactions, it failed to detect the self-feedbacks of the first through fifth variables, yielding results akin to ucSB(20) and ucSB(40) (see Figure 3c). If the time shift s in the TSS method was excessively small or large, the data closely resembled the original data, consequently minimizing the phase randomization effect. The selection of interval $[I_a, I_b]$ in the Time Shift Surrogates (TSS) method has potential implications on the statistical characteristics of the generated surrogate data, particularly its correlation structure. For causality detection between variables, it is necessary to set the interval large enough beyond the lag where cross-correlation occurs. In this simulation, we set $[I_a, I_b] = [3/N, 0.9N]$.

Notably, the TSS method's detection performance is inferior to that of the ucSB(20) and ucSB(40) methods, failing to detect causality from the fifth to the first variable. Importantly, our study identified no false positives within any bootstrap method. Table 2 concisely summarizes the sensitivity and specificity for each combination of causal analysis and bootstrap methods.

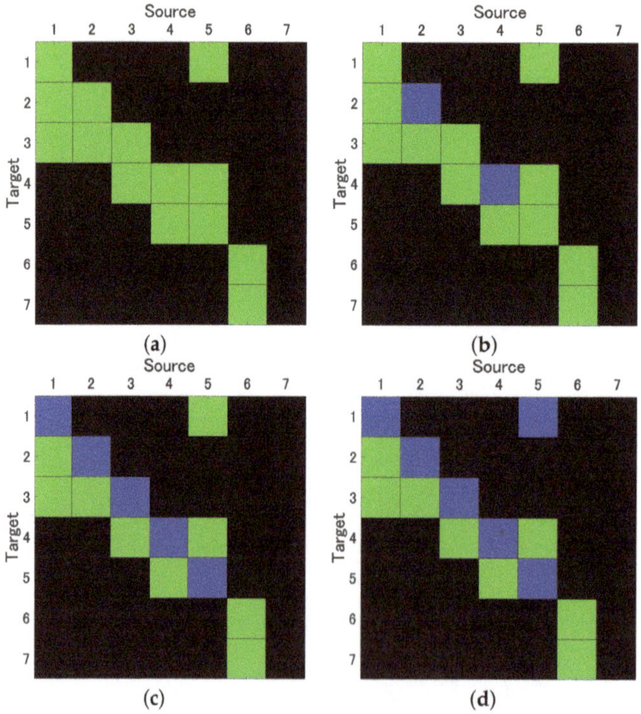

Figure 3. Results of evaluation of Granger Causality by correlated Stationary Bootstrap (cSB) with mean block width $w = 5$ (**a**), and uncorrelated Stationary Bootstrap (ucSB) with mean block width $w = 10$ (**b**) and $w = 40$ (**c**), and by Time Shift Surrogates (TSS) (**d**); variables in columns represent sources, variables in rows represent targets ($p < 0.01$); green: true positives, blue: false negatives.

Table 2. Sensitivity and specificity of detected causality by Granger Causality and Impulse response function, according to different bootstrap methods. Numbers in parentheses indicate mean block width w for correlated and uncorrelated Stationary Bootstrap (cSB and ucSB, respectively).

	Granger Causality		Impulse Response	
Bootstrap Method	**Sensitivity**	**Specificity**	**Sensitivity**	**Specificity**
cSB(5)	1.0	1.0	0.94	0.93
cSB(10)	1.0	1.0	1.0	0.89
cSB(20)	1.0	1.0	1.0	0.89
cSB(40)	1.0	1.0	1.0	0.93
ucSB(5)	1.0	1.0	0.41	1.0
ucSB(10)	0.86	1.0	0.41	1.0
ucSB(20)	0.64	1.0	0.41	1.0
ucSB(40)	0.64	1.0	0.41	1.0
uPRB	0.64	1.0	0.76	0.78
TSS	0.57	1.0	0.41	1.0
cARSB	1.0	1.0	1.0	1.0
cuARSB	1.0	1.0	1.0	1.0

As shown in Equation (9), the IRF is denoted as IRF_s^{lm}, which represents the impact of the mth shock e_t^m on the lth variable y_{t+s}^l at time s. We evaluated the significance of IRF_s^{lm} using each bootstrap method. Figure 4 provides a two-dimensional representation of significant IRF_s^{lm}.

In the IRF analysis, only the ARSB method, whether correlated or uncorrelated, successfully detects both self-feedback and causality among variables in their entirety. Figure 4a displays the IRFs for the impact assigned to each variable ($m = 1, \ldots, 7$), with ucARSB evaluating the significance. This outcome aligns with the connectivity diagram depicted in Figure 1. The cSB method demonstrates results were almost identical to the ARSB method for the first through fifth variables. However, it detects a response from the sixth to seventh variable, constituting a false positive, which was observed for all tested values of the mean block width. The uPRB method primarily detects causality between directly coupled variables (see Figure 4c). Additionally, false positives emerge where responses occur between uncoupled variables, such as the reciprocal response between the first and seventh variables and between the fifth and sixth variables. For all tested values of the mean block width, the ucSB method exhibits the weakest detection performance among the evaluated bootstrap methods, detecting only self-feedback (see Figure 4d).

To summarize the results of these IRFs, such as GC, we compared the true IRFs generated through the VAR parameters in Table 1 with the IRFs detected by the respective bootstrap methods and summarized the sensitivity and specificity in Table 2. The time interval of the IRFs used for comparison was the maximum time step before feedback occurs, i.e., the IRFs up to three time steps before the impact on the third variable propagates to the first variable to the fourth and fifth variables (see Figure 1).

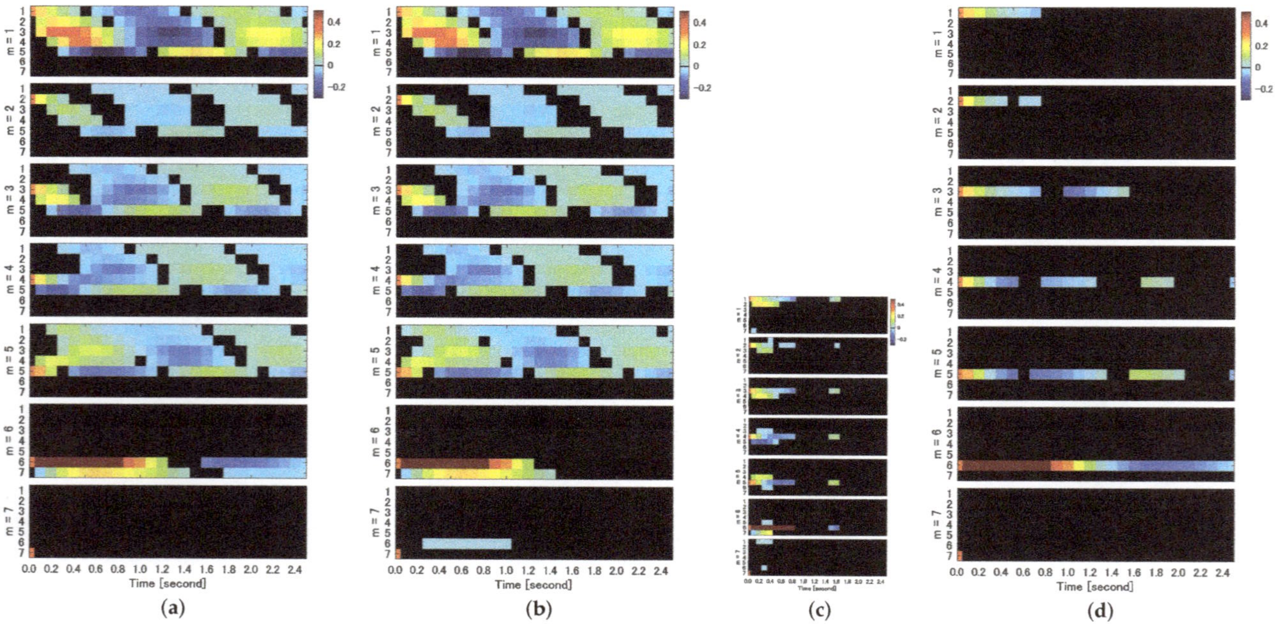

Figure 4. Significant impulse response function (IRF_s^{lm}) evaluated by uncorrelated AR-Sieve Bootstrap (ucARSB) (**a**), correlated Stationary Bootstrap (cSB) with mean block width $w = 40$ (**b**), uncorrelated Phase Randomization Bootstrap (uPRB) (**c**), and uncorrelated Stationary Bootstrap (ucSB) with mean block width $w = 40$ (**d**). Responses exceeding the significance level ($p < 0.01$) are displayed using color coding (see colorbars). Non-significant parts of impulse response functions remain black. Each column of subfigures displays IRF_s^{lm} for $m = 1, \ldots, 7$ (subfigures from top to bottom) and for each value of m for $l = 1, \ldots, 7$ (rows within each subfigure).

6. Discussion

In this study, we present a thorough comparison of the performance of four different bootstrap methods (encompassing twelve variations, including different values of mean block width, as well as correlated and uncorrelated derivations) to evaluate the results from causal analyses.

Our findings reveal that, for the cSB method, the Confidence Interval (CI) width decreases as the mean block width increases, which is particularly evident in Figure 5a,b. A possible explanation is that a shorter block width introduces more discontinuities in the surrogate time series, causing the dynamic properties to deviate further from those of the original time series due to the random shuffling of blocks disrupting temporal forward/backward relationships. This disruption may lead to falsely detecting causality from the seventh to sixth variables in the IRF analysis, as seen in Figure 4b. In contrast, the CI width for the ucSB method remains wider than that of the cSB method, irrespective of the mean block width (see Figure 5a,c), or even increases with the mean block width (Figure 5b). This stems from each block's starting point being determined independently for each variable, causing unnecessary destruction of causality among variables in the surrogate time series. Consequently, no causality among variables is detected in the corresponding IRF analysis (see Figure 4d).

The TSS method accurately detects significance for the Granger causality $F_{1\to3}$, but the CI widths for $F_{5\to1}$ and $F_{2\to2}$ are so large that they include zero, resulting in false negatives. This could be attributed to the $(1,5)$th element of A_2 having the smallest value among the VAR parameters corresponding to causality among variables, and the $(2,2)$th element of A_2 having the smallest value among the VAR parameters corresponding to the attenuation rate of self-feedback. A prime example is $F_{2\to5}$, which should be numerically ignorable since our simulation model does not contain causality from the second to fifth variable (see Table 1). Although the TSS method correctly assesses non-significance, the CI width is substantially larger than that estimated by the other bootstrap methods. These results suggest that the TSS method may not provide stable estimates of bootstrap statistics, compared to other methods, when the statistic value of the original time series is small.

In contrast to other methods, the uPRB method's algorithm does not require a priori tuning of parameters, such as a mean block width for the SB method. Upon providing the original time series, surrogate time series can be generated almost instantaneously. The uPRB method is characterized by its simplicity and the ability to generate surrogate time series devoid of discontinuous time points, while preserving stationarity. However, a limitation of this method is its inability to detect self-feedback (see Figure 5b). Although it accurately identifies causality among variables, some of the Confidence Intervals (CIs) have considerable width, which questions its reliability (see Figure 5a). By constraining the interval of phase randomization in Step 2, the CI width may be reduced, thereby enhancing performance; however, adjusting the degree of restriction remains arbitrary. A key distinction between the TSS and uPRB methods is that the former shifts the phases in all frequency bands simultaneously, while the latter does so for each frequency band. As the uPRB method can selectively disturb the phases corresponding to a specific frequency band, it may prove valuable for evaluating causality in the spectral domain.

For both cGC and IRF analyses, the ARSB method outperforms the other bootstrap methods, regarding detection performance. For this method, determining the VAR model order p is essential, which can be accomplished using the Akaike Information Criterion (AIC). As outlined in Section 3.4, there are two derivations: correlated ARSB (cARSB), which randomly shuffles the residuals across all variables synchronously, and uncorrelated ARSB (ucARSB), which shuffles the residuals independently for each variable. Our simulation study demonstrates that both derivatives yield nearly identical results. However, observational errors (artifacts) may be concurrently superimposed onto the data when analyzing actual time series, rendering ucARSB potentially more effective for canceling noise correlation among variables.

Finally, we emphasize that beyond Granger causality, as discussed in this paper, other approaches to causality estimation have been proposed; as an example, we mention Convergent Cross Mapping, which has been shown to be effective in deterministic nonlinear dynamical systems [20]. Furthermore, Transfer Entropy has been defined as an extension of mutual information, representing the causality from one random variable to another [21]. Moreover, Zenil et al. [22] have developed a very general framework for model discovery, which may overcome the inherent limitations of statistical methods based on predictive models and entropy-like measures; their method is based on algorithmic probability, i.e., on decomposing observations into the most likely algorithmic generative models. Future research should investigate whether this framework can compensate for or replace the incompleteness of Granger causality.

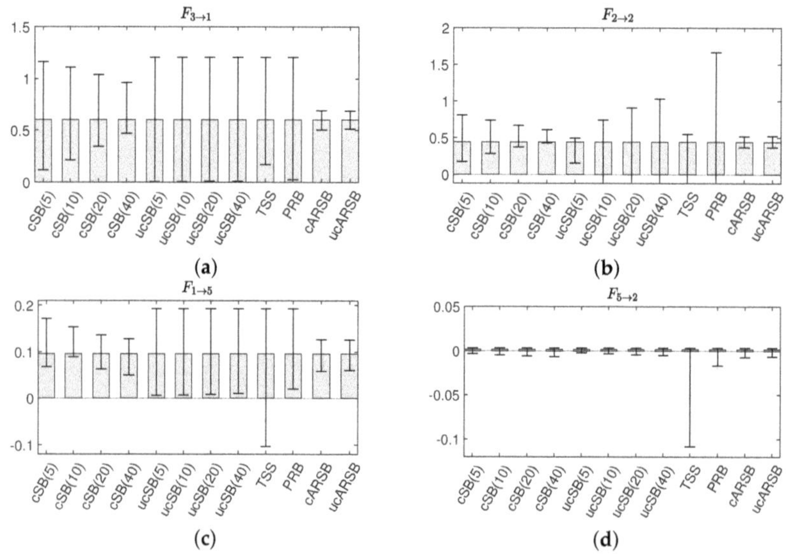

Figure 5. Representative examples of 99% confidence intervals of Granger Causality $F_{l \to m}$, estimated for each bootstrap method.

Author Contributions: Methodology, F.M. and A.G.; Investigation, F.M.; Writing—original draft, F.M.; Writing—review & editing, A.G.; Visualization, F.M.; Project administration, F.M. All authors have read and agreed to the published version of the manuscript.

Funding: This work was supported by JSPS KAKENHI Grant Numbers 19K12212 and 21H04874, and "Strategic Research Projects" grant from ROIS (Research Organization of Information and Systems).

Institutional Review Board Statement: Not applicable.

Data Availability Statement: Not applicable.

Conflicts of Interest: The authors declare no conflict of interest.

References

1. Granger, C.W.J. Investigating causal relations by econometric models and cross-spectral methods. *Econometrica* **1969**, *37*, 424–438. [CrossRef]
2. Geweke, J. Measures of conditional linear dependence and feedback between time series. *J. Am. Stat. Assoc.* **1984**, *79*, 907–915. [CrossRef]
3. Bressler, S.L.; Seth, A.K. Wiener-Granger causality: A well established methodology. *Neuroimage* **2011**, *58*, 323–329. [CrossRef] [PubMed]
4. Schiatti, L.; Nollo, G.; Rossato, G.; Faes, L. Extended Granger causality: A new tool to identify the structure of physiological networks. *Physiol. Meas.* **2015**, *36*, 827–843. [CrossRef] [PubMed]

5. Zenil, H.; Kiani, N.A.; Tegnér, J. Low-algorithmic-complexity entropy-deceiving graphs. *Phys. Rev. E* **2017**, *96*, 012308. [CrossRef] [PubMed]
6. Guo, S.; Seth, A.K.; Kendrick, K.M.; Zhou, C.; Feng, J. Partial Granger causality—Eliminating exogenous inputs and latent variables. *J. Neurosci. Methods* **2008**, *172*, 79–93. [CrossRef] [PubMed]
7. Politis, D.N.; Romano, J.P. A circular block resampling procedure for stationary data. In *Exploring the Limits of Bootstrap*; LePage, R., Billard, L., Eds.; John Wiley & Sons: New York, NY, USA, 1992; pp. 263–270.
8. Quiroga, R.Q.; Kraskov, A.; Kreuz, T.; Grassberger, P. Performance of different synchronization measures in real data: A case study on electroencephalographic signals. *Phys. Rev. E* **2002**, *65*, 041903. [CrossRef] [PubMed]
9. Ashkenazy, Y.; Baker, D.R.; Gildor, H.; Havlin, S. Nonlinearity and multifractality of climate change in the past 420,000 years. *Geophys. Res. Lett.* **2003**, *30*, 2146. [CrossRef]
10. Politis, D.N.; Romano, J.P. The stationary bootstrap. *J. Am. Stat. Assoc.* **1994**, *89*, 1303–1313. [CrossRef]
11. Bühlmann, P. Sieve bootstrap for time series. *Bernoulli* **1997**, *3*, 123–148. [CrossRef]
12. Berg, A.; Paparoditis, E.; Politis, D. A bootstrap test for times series linearity. *J. Stat. Plan. Inference* **2010**, *140*, 3841–3857. [CrossRef]
13. Theiler, J.; Eubank, S.; Longtin, A.; Galdrikian, B.; Farmer, J.D. Testing for nonlinearity in time series: The method of surrogate data. *Phys. D* **1992**, *58*, 77–94. [CrossRef]
14. Prichard, D.; Theiler, J. Generating surrogate data for time series with several simultaneously measured variables. *Phys. Rev. Lett.* **1994**, *73*, 951–954. [CrossRef] [PubMed]
15. Stam, C.J.; Breakspear, M.; van Walsum, A.M.v.C.; van Dijk, B.W. Nonlinear synchronization in EEG and whole-head MEG recordings of healthy subjects. *Hum. Brain Mapp.* **2003**, *19*, 63–78. [CrossRef] [PubMed]
16. Soofi, A.S.; Galka, A.; Li, Z.; Zhang, Y.; Hui, X. Applications of methods and algorithms of nonlinear dynamics in economics and finance. In *Complexity in Economics: Cutting Edge Research*; Faggini, M., Parziale, A., Eds.; Springer: Cham, Switzerland, 2014; pp. 1–30.
17. Carlstein, E. The use of subseries values for estimating the variance of a general statistic from a stationary sequence. *Ann. Stat.* **1986**, *14*, 1171–1179. [CrossRef]
18. Künsch, H.R. The jackknife and the bootstrap for general stationary observations. *Ann. Stat.* **1989**, *17*, 1217–1241. [CrossRef]
19. Baccalá, L.A.; Sameshima, K. Overcoming the limitations of correlation analysis for many simultaneously processed neural structures. *Prog. Brain Res.* **2001**, *130*, 33–47. [PubMed]
20. Sugihara, G.; May, R.; Ye, H.; Hsieh, C.h.; Deyle, E.; Fogarty, M.; Munch, S. Detecting causality in complex ecosystems. *Science* **2012**, *338*, 496–500. [CrossRef] [PubMed]
21. Schreiber, T. Measuring information transfer. *Phys. Rev. Lett.* **2000**, *85*, 461. [CrossRef] [PubMed]
22. Zenil, H.; Kiani, N.A.; Zea, A.A.; Tegnér, J. Causal deconvolution by algorithmic generative models. *Nat. Mach. Intell.* **2019**, *1*, 58–66. [CrossRef]

entropy

MDPI

Article

Inferring a Causal Relationship between Environmental Factors and Respiratory Infections Using Convergent Cross-Mapping

Daipeng Chen [1,2], Xiaodan Sun [1,*] and Robert A. Cheke [3]

[1] School of Mathematics and Statistics, Xi'an Jiaotong University, Xi'an 710049, China; chendaipeng@stu.xjtu.edu.cn
[2] Mathematical Institute, Leiden University, 2333 CA Leiden, The Netherlands
[3] Natural Resources Institute, University of Greenwich at Medway, Central Avenue, Chatham Maritime, Chatham ME4 4TB, Kent, UK; robert.cheke@btinternet.com
* Correspondence: xiaodansun@mail.xjtu.edu.cn

Abstract: The incidence of respiratory infections in the population is related to many factors, among which environmental factors such as air quality, temperature, and humidity have attracted much attention. In particular, air pollution has caused widespread discomfort and concern in developing countries. Although the correlation between respiratory infections and air pollution is well known, establishing causality between them remains elusive. In this study, by conducting theoretical analysis, we updated the procedure of performing the extended convergent cross-mapping (CCM, a method of causal inference) to infer the causality between periodic variables. Consistently, we validated this new procedure on the synthetic data generated by a mathematical model. For real data in Shaanxi province of China in the period of 1 January 2010 to 15 November 2016, we first confirmed that the refined method is applicable by investigating the periodicity of influenza-like illness cases, an air quality index, temperature, and humidity through wavelet analysis. We next illustrated that air quality (quantified by AQI), temperature, and humidity affect the daily influenza-like illness cases, and, in particular, the respiratory infection cases increased progressively with increased AQI with a time delay of 11 days.

Keywords: environmental factors; respiratory infection; nonlinear system; causality

1. Introduction

Understanding the driving force of infectious disease spread is critical to designing effective interventions curbing the threat of diseases transmission to public health around the world [1]. In tracking driving factors of infectious disease spread, examining the relationship between environmental changes and disease transmission is one of the most important topics [2–5]. Previous works have established that monsoon rains and temperature affect the epidemiology of cholera [6] and the life cycles of vectors such as mosquitoes, and the parasites that they transmit, so they are important environmental drivers of malaria [7], dengue [8] and Ross River fever [9]. Moreover, regional temperature and humidity are also related to influenza transmissibility [10,11]. Recently, there is an increasing recognition that poorer air quality is synchronized with a higher incidence of infectious diseases [12]. For example, air pollution is associated with an increased risk of tuberculosis [13,14], influenza [15–17], influenza-like illness [18,19] and COVID-19 [20,21]. Unlike the vector-transmitted diseases [7–9] with clear biological evidence, however, the driving effect of environments on respiratory infection is still controversial, at least partly because two unlinked variables in complex systems may have significant correlations [22]. To design interventions which can reduce infection risk effectively, it is of great importance to infer or falsify causal links between environmental factors and respiratory infection.

Recent studies have revealed a broad correlation between respiratory infections and environmental factors during climate change [23]. While correlation does not imply causality [24], correlated variables may potentially share information in a complex system and increase the complexity of this system. To address the issue that a system is too complex to be parameterized, researchers have developed a nonparametric framework called empirical dynamic modeling (EDM) that is designed to analyze complex systems using observed time series [25–29]. In the EDM methods, convergent cross-mapping (CCM) is specifically used to detect causal relationships in complex systems [28]. This approach is based on the mathematical theory of reconstructing attractor manifolds [30,31], that is, in the homeomorphic sense, the attractor of a dynamical system can be reconstructed from the time series of a single observed variable of this system. Therefore, the reconstructed manifolds of two bidirectionally coupled variables are homeomorphic [30]. For two unidirectionally coupled variables, the reconstructed manifold of the response variable is homeomorphic to the original attractor, while the reconstructed manifold of the driving variable is only a subset of the original attractor and is therefore a subset of the reconstructed manifold of the response variable [31]. Based on these consequences, Sugihara et al. [28] developed convergent cross-mapping (CCM) to predict the points in one reconstructed manifold using the points in another reconstructed manifold to then infer/falsify a causal relationship between two variables through the accuracy of predictions (CCM skill). To date, CCM has been used to analyze the causality involved in a prey–predator system [28], Earth system [32], locust abundance [33], and deep-sea biodiversity [34].

Although CCM has been widely applied to infer causality between variables with weak to moderate coupling strengths [28,32–34], Sugihara et al. [28,35] found that it is very easy to infer two variables with an unidirectionally strong coupling as having two-way causality because of the phenomenon of "generalized synchrony" [36]. To resolve this problem, Ye et al. [35] extended the CCM by considering the time delay between interacting variables. In contrast to the CCM where the predicted values of one of two variables is based on the values of another with the same time label, the extended CCM takes into account that the value of the driving variable should be more suitable for predicting the future values of the response variable and that the response variable is better at predicting the past values of the driving variable [35]. The time delay with optimal prediction suggests a causal relationship between two variables and gives an estimate of the interaction lag [35]. The biggest challenge for extended CCM is that the optimal time delay is not unique when the observation data present periodicity [37]. For respiratory infections such as influenza [38] and influenza-like illness (Figure 1a), an annual cycle is one of the most obvious characteristics. Thus, extended CCM appears to be limited by its potential inability to infer causality between respiratory infections and environmental factors.

Here, we theoretically demonstrated that while the time lags that make the CCM skill locally optimal are not unique, they occur periodically, and the period has a lower bound. This inspired the notion that the time delay with optimal prediction is unique in a narrow testing window whose width does not exceed the lower bound. The numerical analysis on a mathematical model is consistent with our theoretical analysis. For real data in Xi'an, our analysis shows that air quality, temperature, and humidity are driving factors of respiratory infection with different time delays, and suggests that the interventions such as improving air quality and appropriately increasing temperature as well as humidity could reduce the respiratory infection risk in the population.

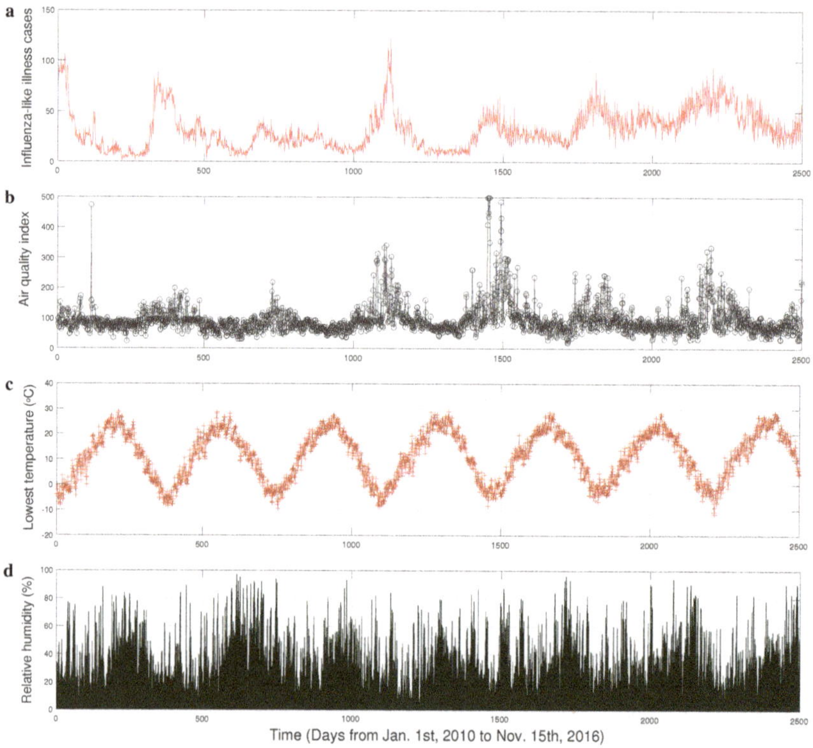

Figure 1. The time series of influenza-like illness (ILI) cases and experimental factors in Xi'an. (**a**) The influenza-like illness (ILI) cases collected from seven hospitals. (**b**) The real time air quality index (AQI). (**c**) The lowest daily temperature. (**d**) The relative humidity.

2. Materials and Methods

2.1. The Data

The data of respiratory infections (Figure 1a) we used consist of reports of daily cases who seek medical attention with influenza-like illness (ILI) (symptoms commonly include fever, shivering, chills, malaise, dry cough, loss of appetite, body aches, and nausea) in Xi'an from 1 January 2010 to 15 November 2016 [19]. Air pollution is a mixture of multiple pollutants, so an air quality index (AQI) is used by government agencies to communicate to the public the pollution levels of the air. [39]. The AQI in Xi'an (Figure 1b) was collected from the website [40] which is an open platform for weather data. The time series of temperature and relative humidity (Figure 1c,d) were downloaded from the shared portal [41] of the China Meteorological Administration.

An alternative test for causality is the Granger test [42], but this method is inappropriate for nonlinear dynamic systems [43], so the convergent cross-mapping was proposed by Sugihara et al. [28]. One of the limitations of CCM is that CCM is sensitive to high levels of process noise in the data [44]. In order to reduce the noise level, we split the time series of collected data into low-frequency series and residuals (Figure A1a) using Kalman filtering [45]. Since the standardized residuals follow the normal distribution (Figure A1b), we assumed that the main information in real time series was included in the filtered low-frequency series which is used in the following analysis.

2.2. The Method

The general dynamical system actually corresponds to a complex causal network of interlocking variables. We apply extended convergent cross-mapping (CCM) [28,35] to examine the causality and interaction delay between two variables. We let $x(t)$ and $y(t)$ be the observed time series corresponding to the variables x and y, respectively, and begin by reconstructing the lagged-coordinate vectors $X(t) = [x(t), x(t-s), \ldots, x(t-(\Pi-1)s)]$ and $Y(t) = [y(t), y(t-s), \ldots, y(t-(\Pi-1)s)]$ with dimension Π based on the Takens embedding theorem [30,31]. We denote the reconstructed manifolds as $M_x = \{X(t)\}$ and $M_y = \{Y(t)\}$. For any point $Y(t_*)$ in M_y, we mark the time label of its $\Pi+1$ nearest neighbors in M_y as $t_1, t_2, \ldots, t_{\Pi+1}$, and the estimated point $\overline{X}(t_* + \tau)$ with some delay τ on M_x is given by the simplex projection [25]:

$$\overline{X}(t_* + \tau) = \sum_{i=1}^{\Pi+1} \chi^i X(t_i + \tau), \tag{1}$$

where

$$\chi^i = \frac{exp(-\|(Y(t_i) - Y(t_*)\| / \|Y(t_1) - Y(t_*)\|)}{\sum_{i=1}^{\Pi+1} exp(-\|(Y(t_i) - Y(t_*)\| / \|Y(t_1) - Y(t_*)\|)}.$$

We denote $\bar{x}(t \mid \tau)$, the first coordinate of $\overline{X}(t)$, as the estimated value of time series $x(t)$ using this method. We use the Pearson correlation coefficient $\rho(\tau) = Corr(\bar{x}(t \mid \tau), x(t))$ between estimated values and observed values to quantify CCM skill. From the perspective of the extended CCM [35], the CCM skill $\rho(\tau)$ reaching its maximum at a negative τ means that there is a driving force from x to y with time delay $|\tau|$.

Given a T-periodic observed time series $x(t)$, the reconstructed manifold M_x is a closed orbit in the Π-dimensional space. According to the Whitney embedding theorem [46], $\Pi = 3$ is sufficient to ensure that all information of the original complex system is represented in the periodic orbit M_x. During any small period $[t, t+\Delta t]$, the length $\Delta l(t)$ of the corresponding small arc on M_x can be approximated by

$$\Delta l(t) = \sqrt{x'(t)^2 + x'(t-s)^2 + x'(t-2s)^2}\Delta t. \tag{2}$$

The prediction using simplex projection (1) mainly depends on the local distance between points [25] on the reconstructed manifold M_x. Therefore, the characters of $\Delta l(t)$ affect the evaluation accuracy of extended CCM. If s is very small (i.e., the data are collected densely), then $\Delta l(t) \approx \sqrt{3}\|x'(t)\|\Delta t$. To investigate the mathematical characters of $\Delta l(t)$ (i.e., $\|x'(t)\|$), as the first step, we give the following proposition.

Proposition 1. *A continuous, periodic, and nonconstant function $x(t)$ has a smallest (positive) period T. For any other period $\tilde{T}$ of $x(t)$, there is an integer n such that $\tilde{T} = nT$.*

Proof. Suppose there is no smallest (positive) period, then there is a decreasing (positive) sequence $T_1, T_2, \ldots, T_n, \ldots$ of periods such that $\lim_{n\to\infty} T_n = 0$. For any given t_0 and t_1 ($t_0 < t_1$), we define a sequence of integers:

$$z_1 = [\frac{t_1 - t_0}{T_1}], z_2 = [\frac{t_1 - t_0}{T_2}], \ldots, z_n = [\frac{t_1 - t_0}{T_n}], \ldots$$

then the sequence $t_1, t_{n+1} = t_n - z_n T_n$ ($n = 1, 2, \ldots$) such that

$$x(t_n) = x(t_{n+1}) \text{ and } \lim_{n\to\infty} t_n = t_0.$$

By continuity of $x(t)$, $x(t_1) = \lim_{n\to\infty} x(t_n) = x(t_0)$, which contradicts that $x(t)$ is a nonconstant function. Consequently, there is a smallest (positive) period T of $x(t)$.

For any other period $\tilde{T}$ of $x(t)$, there always is an integer k such that $kT < \tilde{T} \leq (k+1)T$. Consequently,

$$0 < \tilde{T} - kT \leq T.$$

If $\tilde{T} \neq (k+1)T$, then $\tilde{T} - kT$ is a new smallest (positive) period of $x(t)$ because

$$x(t + \tilde{T} - kT) = x(t).$$

Therefore, there is an integer $n = k + 1$ such that $\tilde{T} = nT$ for any other period $\tilde{T}$ of $x(t)$. □

Based on the result of Proposition 1, we further draw the following proposition about the derivative of a nonconstant periodic function.

Proposition 2. *For any smooth periodic function $x(t)$, the derivative $x'(t)$ is a periodic function and minimum period of $x'(t)$ is the minimum period T of the original function.*

Proof. On the one hand,

$$x'(t) = \lim_{\triangle t \to 0} \frac{x(t + \triangle t) - x(t)}{\triangle t} = \lim_{\triangle t \to 0} \frac{x(t + T + \triangle t) - x(t + T)}{\triangle t} = x'(t + T).$$

Therefore, $x'(t)$ is a periodic function. Suppose the minimum period of derivative $x'(t)$ is $\bar{T}$, and then Proposition 1 implies that there is a positive integer k_1 such that $T = k_1 \bar{T}$. On the other hand,

$$x'(t) = x'(t + \bar{T})$$

gives

$$\int_t x'(s)ds = \int_t x'(s + \bar{T})ds = \int_{t+\bar{T}} x'(s)ds.$$

Consequently, $x(t + \bar{T}) = x(t) + C$ for some constant C. Because function $x(t)$ is periodic, we must have $C = 0$. Therefore, there is a positive integer k_2 such that $\bar{T} = k_2 T$. Collectively, $k_1 = k_2 = 1$. □

Finally, we give a proposition which presents the mathematical characters of the length $\Delta l(t)$ (i.e., $\|x'(t)\|$) of the corresponding small arc on the reconstructed manifold M_x from time series $x(t)$.

Proposition 3. *Given a smooth function $x(t)$ with minimum period T, suppose that the function has at most k extreme points in a single period, then the function $\|x'(t)\|$ is periodic and the minimum period of $\|x'(t)\|$ is not less than T/k.*

Proof. The result of Proposition 2 yields that

$$\|x'(t + T)\| = \|x'(t)\|.$$

This shows that the function $\|x'(t)\|$ is periodic. Suppose the minimum period of function $\|x'(t)\|$ is $\ddot{T}$, and then by Proposition 1 that there is a positive integer n such that $T = n\ddot{T}$. For any period $[t, t + T]$, we have

$$\int_t^{t+T} x'(s)ds = x(t + T) - x(t) = 0.$$

Therefore, there is a $t_0 \in [t, t + T]$ such that $x'(t_0) = 0$, and then $\|x'(t_0)\| = 0$. Without loss of generality, we assume that $t_0 - t < \ddot{T}$. Consequently, we have t_0, $t_0 + \ddot{T}$, $t_0 + 2\ddot{T}, \ldots,$ $t_0 + (n-1)\ddot{T} \in [t, t + T]$ such that

$$\|x'(t_0)\| = \|x'(t_0 + \ddot{T})\| = \|x'(t_0 + 2\ddot{T})\| = \cdots = \|x'(t_0 + (n-1)\ddot{T})\| = 0.$$

Thus, $n \leq k$, which means that $\ddot{T} = T/n \geq T/k$. □

Simplex projection (1) means that the higher-density data points (i.e., smaller arc length $\Delta l(t)$) on manifold M_x corresponds to lower uncertainty of estimates [25], which is consistent with the tests on simulated data and real data [37]. The proposition 3 links the period of arc length $\Delta l(t)$ (2) to the period of time series $x(t)$ via the function $\|x'(t)\|$. For the time series $x(t)$ of common environmental infectious disease with period T, based on Proposition 3, the minimum positive period of $\|x'(t)\|$ is the heuristic $T/2$. In addition, an infectious disease such as hand–foot and mouth disease (HFMD) with multiple peaks [47], wavelet analysis [48] of corresponding time series estimates the periodicity of peaks. Collectively, for environmental infectious disease with estimated minimal period T, if the Pearson's correlation coefficient $\rho(\tau)$ reaches a local maximal at τ_*, $\rho(\tau)$ will not peak again in $(\tau_* - T/2, \tau_* + T/2)$. Thus, we provide a boundary $B = (-T/4, T/4)$ with width $T/2$ as the empirical testing window so that the extended CCM can be used to infer causality between periodic variables such as seasonal infectious diseases and environmental factors.

We next present the procedure to infer causality between variables $\boldsymbol{x}$ and $\boldsymbol{y}$. For observed time series $x(t)$ and $y(t)$ with significant period T, the response time delay of variable x to variable y can be estimated by the following formula:

$$\bar{\tau}_{xy} = \arg\max_{\tau \in B} Corr(\bar{y}(t \mid \tau), y(t)), \tag{3}$$

where $\bar{y}(t \mid \tau)$ are the estimated values of time series $y(t)$. Similarly, we can also obtain the estimated response time delay of variable y to variable x using the formula

$$\bar{\tau}_{yx} = \arg\max_{\tau \in B} Corr(\bar{x}(t \mid \tau), x(t)). \tag{4}$$

We consider the sign of $\bar{\tau}_{xy}$ and $\bar{\tau}_{yx}$ comprehensively to infer the causality between the variables $\boldsymbol{x}$ and $\boldsymbol{y}$. If $\bar{\tau}_{xy} \geq 0$ and $\bar{\tau}_{yx} < 0$, then variable $\boldsymbol{x}$ affects future values of $\boldsymbol{y}$ unidirectionally with time delay $-\bar{\tau}_{yx}$. If $\bar{\tau}_{xy} < 0$ and $\bar{\tau}_{yx} \geq 0$, then variable $\boldsymbol{y}$ affects future values of $\boldsymbol{x}$ unidirectionally with time delay $-\bar{\tau}_{xy}$. If $\bar{\tau}_{xy} < 0$ and $\bar{\tau}_{yx} < 0$, then $\boldsymbol{x}$ and $\boldsymbol{y}$ have two-way cause and effect, and the action time delay is $-\bar{\tau}_{yx}$ and $-\bar{\tau}_{xy}$, respectively. If $\bar{\tau}_{xy} \geq 0$ and $\bar{\tau}_{yx} \geq 0$, then we conclude that there is no causal evidence between variables $\boldsymbol{x}$ and $\boldsymbol{y}$. We choose the negative optimal cross-lag as the estimated time delay because CCM is a historical information-dominated method [28], which is also consistent with previous extension [35].

Collectively, we have made an adjustment on the basis of CCM, and this update makes up for the limitation of the extended CCM in inferring causality between periodic time series.

3. Results

3.1. Testing on an Infectious Disease Model

As the first step, we test the causal inference methods on an air quality index (AQI)-embedded susceptible–infectious–susceptible (SIS) epidemic model (Figure 2a). In this model, the total population (N) consists of classes of individuals that are susceptible (S) and infectious (I), yielding

$$\begin{aligned} S(t+1) &= f(N(t)) + \sigma\phi(\tfrac{I(t)}{N(t)}, \alpha F(t))S(t) + \gamma\sigma I(t), \\ I(t+1) &= \sigma(1 - \phi(\tfrac{I(t)}{N(t)}, \alpha F(t)))S(t) + (1-\gamma)\sigma I(t). \end{aligned} \tag{5}$$

where t is time, $f(N(t))$ is the density-dependent birth rate or recruitment according to the formula $f(N(t)) = N(t)exp(r - N(t))$, σ is the probability of survival, α is a modified parameter for the effect of air pollution on incidence, and γ is the recovery rate. We assume that the proportion of susceptible individuals that do not become infected at time t is $\phi(z(t), w(t)) = e^{-\beta z(t)}e^{-\beta w(t)}$ given the disease prevalence $z(t) = I(t)/N(t)$ and air pollution effect $w(t) = \alpha F(t)$, that is, encounters leading to infection are modeled via a Poisson process with the transmission constant β. The environmental driver $F(t)$ (i.e., air quality index) varies according to the following formula, which is a discrete time form of a continuous time system [49].

$$F(t+1) = \lambda(t)F(t) + C \tag{6}$$

where $\lambda(t) = a - b * sin(t/\omega)$ is the remaining proportion of mixed pollutants in the air from time step t to $t+1$; C is the constant rate of inflow of pollutants into the air, mainly depending on the persistent release of various air pollutants. We simulated the system with parameters setting in (Appendix A.1) and generated time series of the environmental factor and infectious individuals.

We first test CCM [28] using these simulated data, and we find that the CCM skill in both direction becomes better as the length of time series increases (Figure 2b), which implies a bidirectional causality between environmental factor and disease incidence [28] instead of the true unidirectional causality in our simulated system (Figure 2a). Thus, CCM is not suitable for inferring causality in the strongly coupled systems, because the strong coupling strength leads to a synchrony between response variable and driving variable, resulting in the dynamics of a response variable becoming dominated by those of the driving variable [35]. We next apply extended CCM [35] to identify the optimal cross-map lags between environmental factor and disease. In our numerical simulations, $\lambda(t)$ is a 4π-period function (Appendix A.1), so the period of time series $F(t)$ and $I(t)$ are approximately 12. The results of extended CCM show that the optimal time lag is not unique (Figure 2c), and the difference between two adjacent local optimal delays is around 6, which is consistent with Proposition 3 and the period of time series $F(t)$ and $I(t)$.

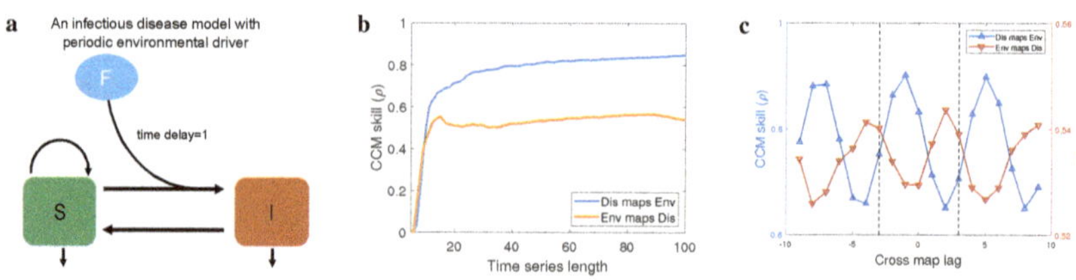

Figure 2. Numerical validation of theoretical results. (**a**) An environmental factor (F)−embedded susceptible−infectious−susceptible (SIS) epidemic model, in which the dynamics of environmental factor is periodic. The effect of environmental factor on disease incidence has a time delay 1. (**b**) The performance of CCM and the CCM skill as a function of the length of time series used to reconstruct the high−dimensional manifold. (**c**) The performance of extended CCM and the CCM skill as a function of the tested time delay. Here, the length of time series used to reconstruct the high−dimensional manifold is fixed.

In addition, by setting $B = (-3, 3)$ as shown by the vertical dashed lines in Figure 2c, we estimated that $\bar{\tau}_{Dis,Env} = -1$ and $\bar{\tau}_{Env,Dis} = 2$ using the Formulas (3) and (4). Therefore, our inference is that the environmental factor affects disease incidence with a time delay 1, which is consistent with the modeling (Figure 2a). Collectively, we showed the limitations of CCM and extended CCM in inferring the causality between periodic time series (Figure 2b,c), which are overcome by adding an estimation interval for the extended CCM (Formulas (3) and (4)).

3.2. Correlation Analysis and Wavelet Analysis of Real Data

As a comparison, before inferring the causality among respiratory infection, air pollution, temperature, and humidity using the real data in Xi'an (Figure 1), we analyzed the correlation between these data and provided statistic significance of the correlation (Figure 3a). Based on the result, we constructed a correlation network which is undirected

(Figure 3b). Edges in this network simply indicate that the variations in two connected variables are positively or negatively correlated, but do not distinguish between a driving variable and a response variable. In addition, we found that there is no significant correlation between air quality index (AQI) and relative humidity (Rhu) in Xi'an. According to the theoretical analysis (Proposition 3) and numerical analysis (Figure 2), the periodicity of observed time series affects the performance of extended CCM. Moreover, the minimum positive period of the time series also determines the setting of the estimation interval for the optimal time delay between two variables. Here, we investigated the periodicity of influenza-like illness (ILI) cases, air quality index (AQI), daily temperature, and relative humidity in Xi'an using the wavelet analysis ([48]; Figure 3c). The results of wavelet analysis [48] show that all time series have only a significant annual cycle (see Figure 3c), so we can detect the optimal time lag in a narrow window B with the width of no more than 180 days using extended CCM (Formulas (3) and (4)). In the following analysis, we detect the optimal lag in the estimation interval $(-50, 50)$.

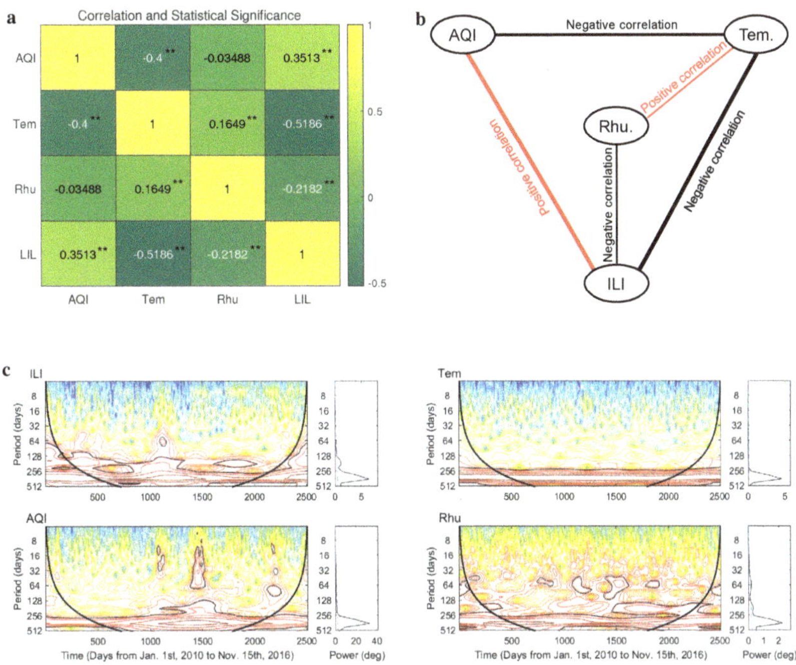

Figure 3. Correlation analysis and wavelet analysis of real data in Xi'an. (**a**) The correlation and statistical significance among the observed time series of influenza−like illness (ILI) cases, air quality index (AQI), lowest daily temperature, and relative humidity in Xi'an. p−values are < 0.01 (**). (**b**) The correlation network among the four variables we studied. (**c**) Wavelet analysis for time series of influenza−like illness (ILI) cases, air quality index (AQI), lowest daily temperature, and relative humidity. Wavelet power spectra are depicted on the left, and the right−hand panels show the mean spectra (vertical solid black line) with their significant threshold value of 0.05 (blue dashed line).

3.3. Causality Analysis of Real Data

In Figures 4a–c and 5a–c, we present the CCM skills using extended CCM in a narrow testing window. The cross-mapping skills between influenza-like illness and AQI time series indicate that there is a driving force from air pollution to respiratory infections with time delay of 11 days ($\bar{\tau}_{ILI,AQI} = -11$ and $\bar{\tau}_{AQI,ILI} = 9$; Figure 4a). The cross-mapping skills between influenza-like illness and temperature time series indicate that there is a driving force from temperature to respiratory infections with a delay of 14 days

($\bar{\tau}_{ILI,Tem} = -14$ and $\bar{\tau}_{Tem,ILI} = 11$; Figure 4b). Figure 4c shows the cross-mapping skills between influenza-like illness and relative humidity time series, which indicate that there is a driving force from relative humidity to respiratory infections with time delay of 4 days ($\bar{\tau}_{ILI,Rhu} = -4$ and $\bar{\tau}_{Rhu,ILI} = 7$). We further analyzed the causality between environmental factors (see Figure 5a–c) and obtained a causal network among the four variables studied (see Figure 4d). The sign on each side comes from the correlation analysis (Figure 3a). In contrast to the correlation network (Figure 3b), the causality network is a directed network where the edge distinguishes the driving variable and response variable (Figure 4d). From this directed network, we predict that increasing temperature increases relative humidity and decreases the air pollution degree as well as respiratory infections risk. More serious air pollution decreases relative humidity and increases respiratory infections risk, but higher relative humidity decreases respiratory infections risk. This indicates that in order to reduce the risk of respiratory infections, the indoor temperature and humidity can be improved by using air conditioners and air humidifiers.

Collectively, we inferred the causality between respiratory infections and environmental factors in Xi'an using the extended CCM by limiting the width of testing window for searching for the optimal time delay. The results enrich the studies on health effects of environmental factors.

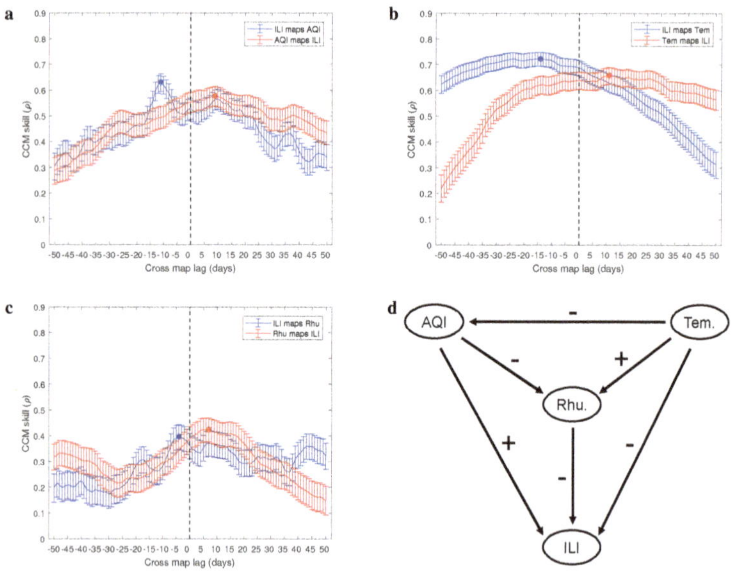

Figure 4. Causal evidence among four variables (ILI—influenza like illness, AQI—air quality index, Tem.—temperature and Rhu.—relative humidity). (**a–c**) The CCM skills between involved variables as a function of tested cross-map lag. The negative optimal cross-map lag is the estimated interaction delay between them, e.g., the estimated delay for air pollution to drive influenza—like illness cases is 11 days. (**d**) Estimated causal network. The signs associated with arrows represent positive or negative correlation between two nodes. A negative sign means that increasing the drive variable would inhibit the response variable, and a positive sign means that higher drive variable would promote the response variable.

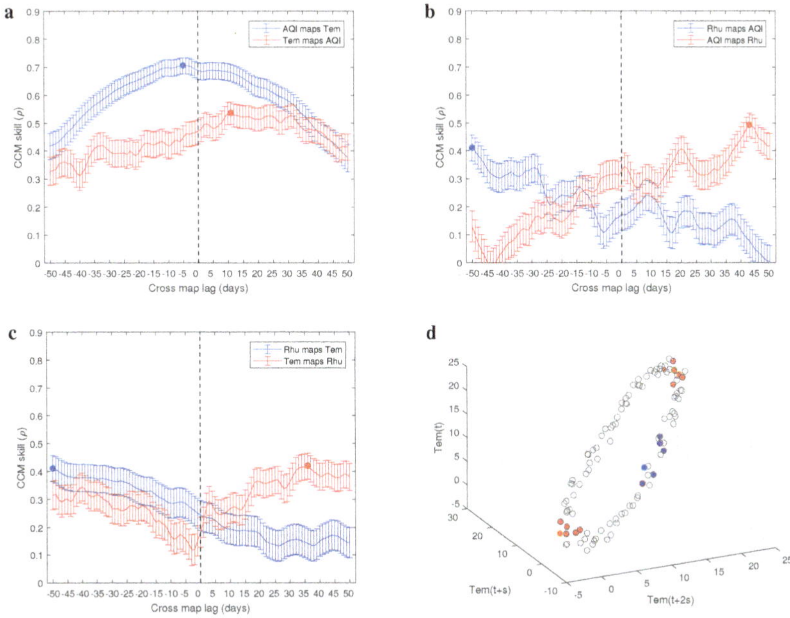

Figure 5. (**a–c**) Causal evidence between environmental factors. (**d**) Reconstructed manifold using the time series of temperature. Consistent with the theoretical analysis, the variations of points density in the reconstructed manifold is periodic (the blue points and red points are the 6 nearest neighbors of some points).

4. Discussion

In this study, we presented evidence (Figures 4 and 5) for a causal relationship between respiratory infection and several environmental factors such as air quality, temperature, and humidity by adopting and refining a published method, CCM (convergent cross-mapping [28]). Related to this, we first performed theoretical analysis, centered chiefly on the extended CCM [35], which supports the result that the estimated optimal time delay between driving variable and response variable is not unique as long as these variables show synchrony and periodicity [37]. In addition, our theoretical result also suggests an idea to overcome the limitation of the extended CCM in inferring causality between synchronized periodic variables, which is estimating the optimal time delay in a bounded testing window (Formulas (3) and (4)). Consistently, we illustrated the limitations of the CCM as well as the extended CCM in inferring a causal relationship, and visualized the theoretical results (Proposition 3) using the data generated from an epidemic model (Figure 2) and the real data (Figure 5d). To illustrate that the characteristics of the real data (Figure 1) are consistent with the assumptions in our theoretical result and fall within the scope of our refined approach, we evaluated the periodicity of the data using wavelet analysis (Figure 3c). The minimal period of real data determines the width of testing window for estimating the time delay between the driving variable and response variable (Formulas (3) and (4)). By performing causal analysis for the real data, we suggested that all of air quality, temperature, and humidity have an effect on the incidence of respiratory infections. In particular, taking the reporting delay into account, air pollution promotes the respiratory infections risk with a time delay of 11 days.

In China, air pollution has been a public issue for a long time [50]. In recent years, the number of respiratory infections has highly synchronized with the variations of air quality index in China [19]. Through analyzing the time series of influenza-like illness and some environmental factors in Xi'an from 1 January 2010 to 15 November 2016, one important result of our research is that air pollution fuels the risk of respiratory infections. Different from the significant correlation confirmed in previous studies [19], our study gives the causality between air pollution and respiratory infection, and identifies the detailed time delay. In addition, we found that lower temperature and humidity also fuel the respiratory infections risk. According to our estimated causal network (Figure 4d), temperature is located at the most upstream of the entire causal network and affects respiratory infections, air quality, and relative humidity. Because the temperature in the Northern Hemisphere is mainly affected by the relative position of the Earth and the sun, the variables we studied may come from a larger and more complex system.

In addition to respiratory diseases [51], air pollution also leads to 3.3 million premature deaths per year worldwide [52] and has a substantial role in many noncommunicable diseases [53] such as cancer [54], stroke [55], cardiovascular disease [56,57], and Alzheimer's disease [58,59]. Furthermore, available evidence suggests that air pollution can prevent the beneficial cardiopulmonary effects of walking in people with heart or chronic lung disease [60,61] and results in poor lung function in children [62,63]. Therefore, our results complement previous research on the health effects of air pollution, which strengthens the importance of improving air quality.

It is well known that the variables being correlated does not imply that they are causal. Comparing the causal analysis with correlation analysis (see Figures 3b and 4d), we find that the causality does not imply significant correlation either. The possible reason is that standard correlation analysis mainly captures the linear relationships between variables, while real data may arise from complex nonlinear systems in which ephemeral correlations are common [64,65]. By broadening the scope of application and improving the accuracy as we did in this study, CCM can help us understand the relationship between variables in complex systems such as molecular systems [66] and public health systems [49], in which the causality is useful for designing novel experiments and interventions, respectively.

It is worth noting that in order to ensure that the optimal cross-map lag of extended CCM is unique, we define a bounded testing window which depends on the period of time series (Formulas (3) and (4)). This means that the real time delay between driving variable and response variable should be in the testing window. Otherwise, we would give a wrong causality and a wrong time delay between two variables. Nonetheless, we are still confident that our work has a broad applicability in time series analysis. For seasonal diseases such as respiratory infections, the period of the time series is usually very long and the unit is years. Therefore, the testing window is wide enough to cover the real time delay between driving variable and response variable. In addition, due to the temporal decay of information in transfer process, when the extended CCM is used to infer causality, only a rough approximation of the action time delay can be estimated. In some cases, the estimates of action time delay may not be reliable (Figure 5b,c). Related to this, we inferred causality by following the rule that the values of the driving variable are better to estimate the future value of the response variable, whereas the values of the response variable are better to estimate the past value of the driving variable [35].

In summary, we refined a published method (CCM) for causal inference through theoretical analysis. Using this refined method to analyze the time series of influenza-like illness, air quality, temperature, and humidity in Xi'an, we established a causal network where the nodes are these variables. In this network, air pollution promotes respiratory infections risk while higher temperature and humidity limit the risk (Figure 4d). It will be of interest to test the robustness of this causal network using different datasets, and to determine how these results will impact the design of novel interventions against respiratory infections in populations.

Author Contributions: Conceptualization, D.C., X.S. and R.A.C.; methodology, D.C., X.S. and R.A.C.; software, D.C.; validation, D.C., X.S. and R.A.C.; formal analysis, D.C. and X.S.; investigation, D.C.; resources, X.S.; data curation, X.S.; writing—original draft preparation, D.C.; writing—review and editing, D.C., X.S. and R.A.C.; visualization, D.C.; supervision, X.S.; project administration, X.S.; funding acquisition, X.S. All authors have read and agreed to the published version of the manuscript.

Funding: This research was funded by the National Key R&D Program of China (2022YFA1003704), by the National Natural Science Foundation of China (12071366) and by the China Scholarship Council.

Institutional Review Board Statement: Not applicable.

Informed Consent Statement: Not applicable.

Data Availability Statement: Data sources are already included in the main text.

Acknowledgments: We would like to thank Yanni Xiao and Luonan Chen for discussions and advice.

Conflicts of Interest: The authors declare no conflict of interest.

Abbreviations

The following abbreviations are used in this manuscript:

Tem	Tempreture
AQI	Air quality index
Rhu	Relative humidity
ILI	Influenza–like illness

Appendix A

Appendix A.1. The Generation and Analysis of Simulated Data

The system (5) is initialized as $S(1) = 5$, $I(1) = 4$, and $F(1) = 5$, and run for 3500 time steps with the parameters $\lambda(t) = 0.6 - 0.3sin(t/2), r = 6, \sigma = 0.5, \alpha = 8, \beta = 0.01$, and $\gamma = 0.01$ to generate the time series of $I(t)$ and $F(t)$. These time series are analyzed using $s = 1$ and $\Pi = 3$ which ensure the requirements of Takens' embedding theorem [30,31]. We first test CCM [28] using these simulated data, selecting 100 pairs of 100 vectors of random libraries over time points 101–1000, computing the cross-map skill for each pair of libraries using time series length 7–100, and averaging out the cross-map skill of 100 random libraries, respectively. We then apply extended CCM [35] to identify the optimal cross-map lags, selecting 100 pairs of random libraries of 2000 vectors over time points 101–3000, computing cross-map skill for each pair of libraries with maximum length using different cross-map lag and averaging out the cross-map skill of these random libraries, respectively.

Appendix A.2. Kalman Filtering

Kalman filtering was achieved by using the function kalman in MATLAB (available from: https://www.mathworks.com/help/control/ref/ss.kalman.html accessed on 19 January 2021). The low–frequency component was derived first (Figure A1a) and this was subtracted from the original series (high-frequency component) to provide the residual. After standardization, we found that the residuals were fitted with a standard normal distribution (Figure A1b).

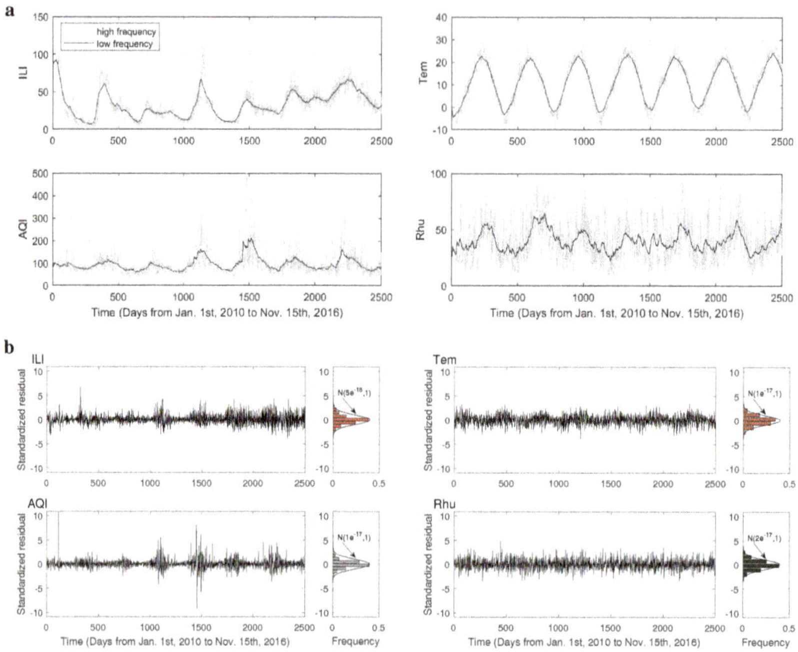

Figure A1. Results of Kalman filtering. (**a**) Data of the influenza−like illness (ILI) cases, air quality index (AQI), lowest daily temperature and relative humidity, low−frequency component, and original date (high−frequency component). (**b**) The time series and distribution of standardized residuals. The residuals were calculated by subtracting low−frequency component from the original series.

References

1. Jones, K.E.; Patel, N.G.; Levy, M.A.; Storeygard, A.; Balk, D.; Gittleman, J.L.; Daszak, P. Global trends in emerging infectious diseases. *Nature* **2008**, *451*, 990–993. [CrossRef] [PubMed]
2. Weiss, R.A.; McMichael, A.J. Social and environmental risk factors in the emergence of infectious diseases. *Nat. Med.* **2004**, *10*, S70–S76. [CrossRef] [PubMed]
3. McMichael, A.J. Environmental and social influences on emerging infectious diseases: Past, present and future. *Philos. Trans. R. Soc. London. Ser. B Biol. Sci.* **2004**, *359*, 1049–1058. [CrossRef] [PubMed]
4. Hay, S.; Tatem, A.; Graham, A.; Goetz, S.; Rogers, D. Global environmental data for mapping infectious disease distribution. *Adv. Parasitol.* **2006**, *62*, 37–77. [PubMed]
5. Eisenberg, J.N.; Desai, M.A.; Levy, K.; Bates, S.J.; Liang, S.; Naumoff, K.; Scott, J.C. Environmental determinants of infectious disease: A framework for tracking causal links and guiding public health research. *Environ. Health Perspect.* **2007**, *115*, 1216–1223. [CrossRef]
6. Koelle, K.; Rodó, X.; Pascual, M.; Yunus, M.; Mostafa, G. Refractory periods and climate forcing in cholera dynamics. *Nature* **2005**, *436*, 696–700. [CrossRef]
7. Mordecai, E.A.; Caldwell, J.M.; Grossman, M.K.; Lippi, C.A.; Johnson, L.R.; Neira, M.; Rohr, J.R.; Ryan, S.J.; Savage, V.; Shocket, M.S.; et al. Thermal biology of mosquito-borne disease. *Ecol. Lett.* **2019**, *22*, 1690–1708. [CrossRef]
8. Johansson, M.A.; Apfeldorf, K.M.; Dobson, S.; Devita, J.; Buczak, A.L.; Baugher, B.; Moniz, L.J.; Bagley, T.; Babin, S.M.; Guven, E.; et al. An open challenge to advance probabilistic forecasting for dengue epidemics. *Proc. Natl. Acad. Sci. USA* **2019**, *116*, 24268–24274. [CrossRef]
9. Shocket, M.S.; Ryan, S.J.; Mordecai, E.A. Temperature explains broad patterns of Ross River virus transmission. *eLife* **2018**, *7*, e37762. [CrossRef]
10. Deyle, E.R.; Maher, M.C.; Hernandez, R.D.; Basu, S.; Sugihara, G. Global environmental drivers of influenza. *Proc. Natl. Acad. Sci. USA* **2016**, *113*, 13081–13086. [CrossRef]
11. Ali, S.T.; Cowling, B.J.; Wong, J.Y.; Chen, D.; Shan, S.; Lau, E.H.; He, D.; Tian, L.; Li, Z.; Wu, P. Influenza seasonality and its environmental driving factors in mainland China and Hong Kong. *Sci. Total Environ.* **2022**, *818*, 151724. [CrossRef]
12. Sly, P.D.; Trottier, B.; Ikeda-Araki, A.; Vilcins, D. Environmental impacts on infectious disease: A literature view of epidemiological evidence. *Ann. Glob. Health* **2022**, *88*, 91. [CrossRef]

13. Lin, H.H.; Ezzati, M.; Murray, M. Tobacco smoke, indoor air pollution and tuberculosis: A systematic review and meta-analysis. *PLoS Med.* **2007**, *4*, e20. [CrossRef]
14. Xiang, K.; Xu, Z.; Hu, Y.Q.; He, Y.S.; Dan, Y.L.; Wu, Q.; Fang, X.H.; Pan, H.F. Association between ambient air pollution and tuberculosis risk: A systematic review and meta-analysis. *Chemosphere* **2021**, *277*, 130342. [CrossRef]
15. Wong, C.M.; Yang, L.; Thach, T.Q.; Chau, P.Y.K.; Chan, K.P.; Thomas, G.N.; Lam, T.H.; Wong, T.W.; Hedley, A.J.; Peiris, J.M. Modification by Influenza on Health Effects of Air Pollution in Hong Kong. *Environ. Health Perspect.* **2009**, *117*, 248–253. [CrossRef]
16. Liang, Y.; Fang, L.; Pan, H.; Zhang, K.; Kan, H.; Brook, J.R.; Sun, Q. PM 2.5 in Beijing–temporal pattern and its association with influenza. *Environ. Health* **2014**, *13*, 102. [CrossRef] [PubMed]
17. Chen, G.; Zhang, W.; Li, S.; Zhang, Y.; Williams, G.; Huxley, R.; Ren, H.; Cao, W.; Guo, Y. The impact of ambient fine particles on influenza transmission and the modification effects of temperature in China: A multi-city study. *Environ. Int.* **2017**, *98*, 82–88. [CrossRef]
18. Feng, C.; Li, J.; Sun, W.; Zhang, Y.; Wang, Q. Impact of ambient fine particulate matter (PM2.5) exposure on the risk of influenza-like-illness: A time-series analysis in Beijing, China. *Environ. Health* **2016**, *15*, 17. [CrossRef]
19. Tang, S.; Yan, Q.; Shi, W.; Wang, X.; Sun, X.; Yu, P.; Wu, J.; Xiao, Y. Measuring the impact of air pollution on respiratory infection risk in China. *Environ. Pollut.* **2018**, *232*, 477–486. [CrossRef]
20. Fattorini, D.; Regoli, F. Role of the chronic air pollution levels in the Covid-19 outbreak risk in Italy. *Environ. Pollut.* **2020**, *264*, 114732. [CrossRef] [PubMed]
21. Travaglio, M.; Yu, Y.; Popovic, R.; Selley, L.; Leal, N.S.; Martins, L.M. Links between air pollution and COVID-19 in England. *Environ. Pollut.* **2021**, *268*, 115859. [CrossRef]
22. Berkeley, G. *A Treatise Concerning the Principles of Human Knowledge*; JB Lippincott and Company: Philadelphia, NY, USA, 1881.
23. Mirsaeidi, M.; Motahari, H.; Taghizadeh Khamesi, M.; Sharifi, A.; Campos, M.; Schraufnagel, D.E. Climate change and respiratory infections. *Ann. Am. Thorac. Soc.* **2016**, *13*, 1223–1230. [CrossRef] [PubMed]
24. Eichler, M., Causal Inference in Time Series Analysis. In *Causality*; John Wiley and Sons, Ltd.: Hoboken, NJ, USA, 2012; Chapter 22, pp. 327–354.
25. Sugihara, G.; May, R.M. Nonlinear forecasting as a way of distinguishing chaos from measurement error in time series. *Nature* **1990**, *344*, 734–741. [CrossRef]
26. Sugihara, G. Nonlinear forecasting for the classification of natural time series. *Philos. Trans. R. Soc. London. Ser. A Phys. Eng. Sci.* **1994**, *348*, 477–495.
27. Dixon, P.A.; Milicich, M.J.; Sugihara, G. Episodic fluctuations in larval supply. *Science* **1999**, *283*, 1528–1530. [CrossRef]
28. Sugihara, G.; May, R.; Ye, H.; Hsieh, C.H.; Deyle, E.; Fogarty, M.; Munch, S. Detecting Causality in Complex Ecosystems. *Science* **2012**, *338*, 496–500. [CrossRef]
29. Ye, H.; Sugihara, G. Information leverage in interconnected ecosystems: Overcoming the curse of dimensionality. *Science* **2016**, *353*, 922–925. [CrossRef]
30. Takens, F. Detecting strange attractors in turbulence. In *Dynamical Systems and Turbulence*; Springer: Berlin/Heidelberg, Germany, 1981; pp. 366–381.
31. Stark, J. Delay Embeddings for Forced Systems. I. Deterministic Forcing. *J. Nonlinear Sci.* **1999**, *9*, 255–332. [CrossRef]
32. Runge, J.; Bathiany, S.; Bollt, E.; Camps-Valls, G.; Coumou, D.; Deyle, E.; Glymour, C.; Kretschmer, M.; Mahecha, M.D.; Muñoz-Marí, J.; et al. Inferring causation from time series in Earth system sciences. *Nat. Commun.* **2019**, *10*, 1–13. [CrossRef]
33. Cheke, R.A.; Young, S.; Wang, X.; Tratalos, J.A.; Tang, S.; Cressman, K. Evidence for a causal relationship between the solar cycle and locust abundance. *Agronomy* **2020**, *11*, 69. [CrossRef]
34. Doi, H.; Yasuhara, M.; Ushio, M. Causal analysis of the temperature impact on deep-sea biodiversity. *Biol. Lett.* **2021**, *17*, 20200666. [CrossRef] [PubMed]
35. Ye, H.; Deyle, E.R.; Gilarranz, L.J.; Sugihara, G. Distinguishing time-delayed causal interactions using convergent cross mapping. *Sci. Rep.* **2015**, *5*, 14750. [CrossRef]
36. Rulkov, N.F.; Sushchik, M.M.; Tsimring, L.S.; Abarbanel, H.D. Generalized synchronization of chaos in directionally coupled chaotic systems. *Phys. Rev. E* **1995**, *51*, 980. [CrossRef]
37. Sugihara, G.; Deyle, E.R.; Ye, H. Reply to Baskerville and Cobey: Misconceptions about causation with synchrony and seasonal drivers. *Proc. Natl. Acad. Sci. USA* **2017**, *114*, E2272–E2274. [CrossRef]
38. Bjørnstad, O.N.; Viboud, C. Timing and periodicity of influenza epidemics. *Proc. Natl. Acad. Sci. USA* **2016**, *113*, 12899–12901. [CrossRef]
39. wikipedia. Air Quality Index. 2022. Available online: https://en.wikipedia.org/wiki/Air_quality_index (accessed on 18 February 2020).
40. tianqihoubao. Air Quality Index. 2022. Available online: http://www.tianqihoubao.com/aqi/xian.html (accessed on 18 February 2020).
41. Administration, C.M. Meteorological Data. 2022. Available online: http://data.cma.cn (accessed on 18 February 2020).
42. Granger, C.W. Investigating causal relations by econometric models and cross-spectral methods. *Econom. J. Econom. Soc.* **1969**, *37*, 424–438. [CrossRef]

43. Tsonis, A.A.; Deyle, E.R.; May, R.M.; Sugihara, G.; Swanson, K.; Verbeten, J.D.; Wang, G. Dynamical evidence for causality between galactic cosmic rays and interannual variation in global temperature. *Proc. Natl. Acad. Sci. USA* **2015**, *112*, 3253–3256. [CrossRef]
44. Cobey, S.; Baskerville, E.B. Limits to causal inference with state-space reconstruction for infectious disease. *PLoS ONE* **2016**, *11*, e0169050. [CrossRef]
45. Southallzy, B.; Buxtony, B.; Marchant, J. Controllability and observability: Tools for Kalman filter design. In Proceedings of the British Machine Vision Conference, Southampton, UK, 14–17 September 1998; Volume 98, pp. 164–173.
46. Whitney, H. Differentiable manifolds. *Ann. Math.* **1936**, *37*, 645–680. [CrossRef]
47. Xia, F.; Deng, F.; Tian, H.; He, W.; Xiao, Y.; Sun, X. Estimation of the reproduction number and identification of periodicity for HFMD infections in northwest China. *J. Theor. Biol.* **2020**, *484*, 110027. [CrossRef]
48. Torrence, C.; Compo, G.P. A practical guide to wavelet analysis. *Bull. Am. Meteorol. Soc.* **1998**, *79*, 61–78. [CrossRef]
49. Chen, D.; Xiao, Y.; Tang, S. Air quality index induced nonsmooth system for respiratory infection. *J. Theor. Biol.* **2019**, *460*, 160–169. [CrossRef]
50. Li, M.; Zhang, L. Haze in China: Current and future challenges. *Environ. Pollut.* **2014**, *189*, 85–86. [CrossRef] [PubMed]
51. Guarnieri, M.; Balmes, J.R. Outdoor air pollution and asthma. *Lancet* **2014**, *383*, 1581–1592. [CrossRef] [PubMed]
52. Lelieveld, J.; Evans, J.S.; Fnais, M.; Giannadaki, D.; Pozzer, A. The contribution of outdoor air pollution sources to premature mortality on a global scale. *Nature* **2015**, *525*, 367–373. [CrossRef]
53. Maria Neira, A.P.U.; Mudu, P. Reduce air pollution to beat NCDs: From recognition to action. *Lancet* **2018**, *392*, 1178–1179. [CrossRef]
54. Loomis, D.; Grosse, Y.; Lauby-Secretan, B.; El Ghissassi, F.; Bouvard, V.; Benbrahim-Tallaa, L.; Guha, N.; Baan, R.; Mattock, H.; Straif, K. The carcinogenicity of outdoor air pollution. *Lancet Oncol.* **2013**, *14*, 1262–1263. [CrossRef]
55. Pandian, J.D.; Gall, S.L.; Kate, M.P.; Silva, G.S.; Akinyemi, R.O.; Ovbiagele, B.I.; Lavados, P.M.; Gandhi, D.B.C.; Thrift, A.G. Prevention of stroke: A global perspective. *Lancet* **2018**, *392*, 1269–1278. [CrossRef]
56. Xie, W.; Li, G.; Zhao, D.; Xie, X.; Wei, Z.; Wang, W.; Wang, M.; Li, G.; Liu, W.; Sun, J.; et al. Relationship between fine particulate air pollution and ischaemic heart disease morbidity and mortality. *Heart* **2015**, *101*, 257–263. [CrossRef] [PubMed]
57. Franklin, B.A.; Brook, R.; Arden Pope, C. Air Pollution and Cardiovascular Disease. *Curr. Probl. Cardiol.* **2015**, *40*, 207–238. [CrossRef]
58. Hautot, D.; Pankhurst, Q.A.; Khan, N.; Dobson, J. Preliminary evaluation of nanoscale biogenic magnetite in Alzheimer's disease brain tissue. *Proc. R. Soc. London. Ser. B Biol. Sci.* **2003**, *270*, S62–S64. [CrossRef] [PubMed]
59. Maher, B.A.; Ahmed, I.A.M.; Karloukovski, V.; MacLaren, D.A.; Foulds, P.G.; Allsop, D.; Mann, D.M.A.; Torres-Jardón, R.; Calderon-Garciduenas, L. Magnetite pollution nanoparticles in the human brain. *Proc. Natl. Acad. Sci. USA* **2016**, *113*, 10797–10801. [CrossRef]
60. Pope III, C.A.; Dockery, D.W. Health effects of fine particulate air pollution: Lines that connect. *J. Air Waste Manag. Assoc.* **2006**, *56*, 709–742. [CrossRef] [PubMed]
61. Sinharay, R.; Gong, J.; Barratt, B.; Ohman-Strickland, P.; Ernst, S.; Kelly, F.J.; Zhang, J.J.; Collins, P.; Cullinan, P.; Chung, K.F. Respiratory and cardiovascular responses to walking down a traffic-polluted road compared with walking in a traffic-free area in participants aged 60 years and older with chronic lung or heart disease and age-matched healthy controls: A randomised, crossover study. *Lancet* **2018**, *391*, 339–349.
62. Gauderman, W.J.; Urman, R.; Avol, E.; Berhane, K.; McConnell, R.; Rappaport, E.; Chang, R.; Lurmann, F.; Gilliland, F. Association of Improved Air Quality with Lung Development in Children. *N. Engl. J. Med.* **2015**, *372*, 905–913. [CrossRef] [PubMed]
63. Dockery, D.W.; Ware, J.H. Cleaner Air, Bigger Lungs. *N. Engl. J. Med.* **2015**, *372*, 970–972. [CrossRef]
64. Mysterud, A.; Stenseth, N.C.; Yoccoz, N.G.; Langvatn, R.; Steinheim, G. Nonlinear effects of large-scale climatic variability on wild and domestic herbivores. *Nature* **2001**, *410*, 1096–1099. [CrossRef]
65. Wagner, B.K.; Kitami, T.; Gilbert, T.J.; Peck, D.; Ramanathan, A.; Schreiber, S.L.; Golub, T.R.; Mootha, V.K. Large-scale chemical dissection of mitochondrial function. *Nat. Biotechnol.* **2008**, *26*, 343–351. [CrossRef]
66. Chen, D.; Forghany, Z.; Liu, X.; Wang, H.; Merks, R.M.; Baker, D.A. A new model of Notch signalling: Control of Notch receptor cis-inhibition via Notch ligand dimers. *PLoS Comput. Biol.* **2023**, *19*, e1010169. [CrossRef]

entropy

Article

Schizophrenia MEG Network Analysis Based on Kernel Granger Causality

Qiong Wang [1,2], Wenpo Yao [3,*], Dengxuan Bai [1], Wanyi Yi [1], Wei Yan [4] and Jun Wang [3,*]

1 School of Telecommunications and Information Engineering, Nanjing University of Posts and Telecommunications, Nanjing 210003, China
2 School of Physics and Information Engineering, Jiangsu Second Normal University, Nanjing 210013, China
3 Smart Health Big Data Analysis and Location Services Engineering Research Center of Jiangsu Province, School of Geographic and Biologic Information, Nanjing University of Posts and Telecommunications, Nanjing 210023, China
4 Department of Psychiatry, Affiliated Nanjing Brain Hospital, Nanjing Medical University, Nanjing 210029, China
* Correspondence: yaowp@njupt.edu.cn (W.Y.); wangj@njupt.edu.cn (J.W.)

Abstract: Network analysis is an important approach to explore complex brain structures under different pathological and physiological conditions. In this paper, we employ the multivariate inhomogeneous polynomial kernel Granger causality (MKGC) to construct directed weighted networks to characterize schizophrenia magnetoencephalography (MEG). We first generate data based on coupled autoregressive processes to test the effectiveness of MKGC in comparison with the bivariate linear Granger causality and bivariate inhomogeneous polynomial kernel Granger causality. The test results suggest that MKGC outperforms the other two methods. Based on these results, we apply MKGC to construct effective connectivity networks of MEG for patients with schizophrenia (SCZs). We measure three network features, i.e., strength, nonequilibrium, and complexity, to characterize schizophrenia MEG. Our results suggest that MEG of the healthy controls (HCs) has a denser effective connectivity network than that of SCZs. The most significant difference in the in-connectivity strength is observed in the right frontal network ($p = 0.001$). The strongest out-connectivity strength for all subjects occurs in the temporal area, with the most significant between-group difference in the left occipital area ($p = 0.0018$). The total connectivity strength of the frontal, temporal, and occipital areas of HCs exhibits higher values compared with SCZs. The nonequilibrium feature over the whole brain of SCZs is significantly higher than that of the HCs ($p = 0.012$); however, the results of Shannon entropy suggest that healthy MEG networks have higher complexity than schizophrenia networks. Overall, MKGC provides a reliable approach to construct MEG brain networks and characterize the network characteristics.

Keywords: kernel Granger causality; effective network; schizophrenia MEG; nonequilibrium; complexity

1. Introduction

Schizophrenia (SCZ) is a psychiatric disease characterized by significant impairments in the way reality is perceived, with delusions, hallucinations, and disorganized thinking and behavior [1]. In recent years, experts and scholars have held the view that SCZ may be related to aberrant brain network connections [2–5]. The human brain is a dynamic complex system, and each functional area does not work independently but achieves the purpose of completing a certain task through mutual coordination. The brain network can effectively quantify such coordinated interactions among various functional areas of the brain, making it particularly popular in elucidating complex brain dynamical structures. Complex network analysis [6–9], which could describe the brain as a network of nodes and edges, is a powerful tool to explore the characteristics of cerebral activity, especially in the brains of patients with psychiatric disorders [3,10,11]. With the development of neuroimaging, a thriving body of advanced techniques for understanding pathophysiological mechanisms has emerged, among which magnetoencephalography (MEG) stands out for its high temporal resolution and noninvasiveness [12,13]. A number of studies exploit MEG signals and brain network analysis to explore the dynamic features and underlying mechanisms of the SCZ brain. Houck et al. [14] utilized spatial independent component analysis and pairwise correlations between independent component timecourses to estimate the MEG network connectivity, and found that the patients with schizophrenia (SCZs) had abnormal connectivity within the frontal and temporal networks. Through assessing the characteristics of resting-state MEG networks using graph-theoretic analysis, Tagawa et al. [15] verified that the local networks of SCZs may disintegrate at both the microscale and macroscale levels, mainly in the beta band. Bai et al. [16] constructed the multiscale multidimensional recurrence plot for MEG signals of SCZs, and proved that the nonlinear dynamics of MEG signals in SCZs had lower predictability and laminarity. Lottman et al. [17] evaluated functional connectivity between resting-state MEG networks, and found that the delta band of SCZs revealed hypoconnectivity between sensorimotor and task-active networks.

Effective connectivity [18] is one of the approaches to construct physiological networks and represents the influence that one series exerts over another. It can provide directional and weighted information, which is helpful for tapping into the underlying structure of networks. Granger causality is a widely used measure of effective connectivity proposed by Granger [19] and has been used in economics [20], neuroscience [21], biology [22] and so on. When Granger causality was initially proposed, it was based on a linear model involving two variables. Considering the influence of other variables, conditional Granger causality [23] and partial Granger causality [24] have successively emerged. With the unremitting efforts of researchers, Granger causality has been generalized to the nonlinear analysis, namely kernel Granger causality [25–27], which is based on the theory of reproducing kernel Hilbert spaces, and performs linear relations in the feature space of suitable kernel functions by assuming an arbitrary degree of nonlinearity.

Network measures play an important role in exploring the characteristics and underlying structures of networks [6,7]. Weight [7,28] is an indispensable measure of an effective connectivity network, and the importance of a node can be measured by the in- , out- and total weight of a node. Moreover, for a complex and changeable physiological system, its structure is complex and constantly evolving, and the equilibrium and complexity measures of the network have the potential to better reveal the information interaction of the system. Equilibrium [29–31] refers to the constant performance of the statistical properties of a sequence over time or amplitude reversal. Entropy measures [32–35] are widely used to quantify the complexity of dynamical systems and can characterize the complexity of network information exchanges from an information-theoretic perspective.

In this paper, the MEG effective connectivity networks are constructed by multivariate inhomogeneous polynomial kernel Granger causality for SCZs and healthy controls (HCs). We adopt three measures (strength, nonequilibrium, and complexity) to explore the features of SCZ networks. The content is organized as follows: We describe the MEG data collection, Granger causality, and brain network measures in Section 2. A comparative test of multivariate inhomogeneous polynomial kernel Granger causality, bivariate linear Granger causality, and bivariate inhomogeneous polynomial kernel Granger causality is conducted in Section 3. Network analysis results are described in Section 4. The paper ends with a discussion in Section 5 and a brief conclusion in Section 6.

2. Materials and Methods

2.1. MEG Data

2.1.1. Subjects

This experiment included 31 right-handed (self-reported) subjects, including 17 SCZs (4 women, age 25 ± 8.32) and 14 HCs (3 women, age 25.79 ± 5.29). Before the experiments, all subjects were fully informed and signed written informed consent. The Ethics Committee of Nanjing Brain Hospital approved this study. Subjects with a history of head trauma or drug abuse were excluded from the study. There were no significant between-group differences in age or sex.

2.1.2. MEG Recording and Preprocessing

MEG recordings were obtained with a whole-head CTF MEG system with 275 channels (VSM Medical Technology Company, Coquitlam, BC, Canada), located in a magnetically shielded room at the Nanjing Brain Hospital. Prior to data acquisition, participants were instructed to remove all metallic wearables, lie in a supine position, remain awake but resting, and avoid blinking and making any eye or muscle movement. For each subject, MEG signals were recorded at a sampling frequency of 1200 Hz with a duration of 2 min. During the recording, if the participant was found to have made any movement that may have affected the accuracy of the result, the recorded signal was discarded and a new record made. All of the MEG datasets were preprocessed offline using the Fieldtrip toolbox [36] on MATLAB (version 2020b). The recordings containing artifacts were removed after manual checking and screening by experienced senior engineers. A bandpass filter of 0.1–200 Hz [37,38] was used to filter MEG data, and then direct current offset removal was achieved using a powerline filter (50 Hz and higher harmonics).

In our case, to avoid the multiple-comparison problems and computational limitations posed by this number of data, the 275 channels were grouped into five areas, namely the frontal (F), central (C), temporal (T), parietal (P), and occipital (O) areas. The temporal (T) area was divided into left and right regions, and the other four areas were divided into left, middle, and right regions. Consequently, the whole brain was divided into 14 regions, as illustrated in Figure 1.

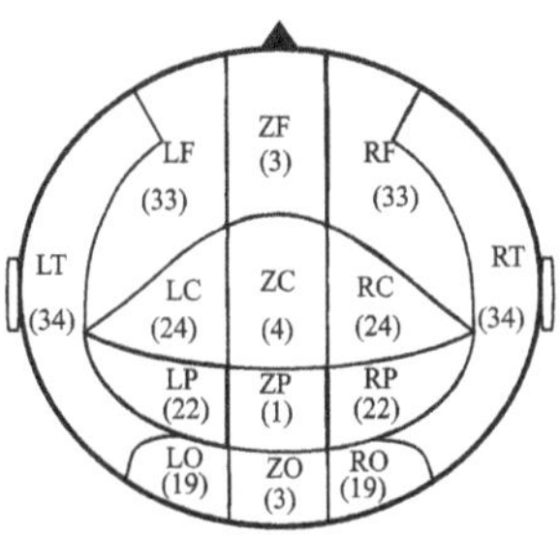

Figure 1. Layout of brain division of MEG recordings. Left frontal (LF), middle frontal (ZF), right frontal (RF), left central (LC), middle central (ZC), right central (RC), left temporal (LT), right temporal (RT), left parietal (LP), middle parietal (ZP), right parietal (RP), left occipital (LO), middle occipital (ZO), and right occipital (RO). The numbers represent the number of channels in each brain region.

2.2. *Granger Causality*

In this section, bivariate linear Granger causality (BLGC), bivariate inhomogeneous polynomial (IP) kernel Granger causality, and its multivariate pattern [25,26] are introduced.

2.2.1. Bivariate Linear Granger Causality

Suppose that $X_i = (\xi_i, \ldots, \xi_{i+m-1})^{\mathrm{T}}$, $Y_i = (\eta_i, \ldots, \eta_{i+m-1})^{\mathrm{T}}$, and $x_i = \xi_{i+m}$ (for $i = 1, \ldots, N$) are treated as N realizations of the stochastic variables $\mathbf{X}$, $\mathbf{Y}$ and $\mathbf{x}$, respectively. $\mathbf{X}$ is an $m \times N$ matrix, where X_i denotes the column, $\mathbf{Z}$ is a $2m \times N$ matrix with vectors $Z_i = \left(X_i^{\mathrm{T}}, Y_i^{\mathrm{T}}\right)^{\mathrm{T}}$, and $\mathbf{x}$ is a vector with elements x_i, i.e., $\mathbf{x} = (x_1, \ldots, x_N)^{\mathrm{T}}$. For each component of $\mathbf{X}$ and $\mathbf{Y}$, all values of the vector $\mathbf{x}$ have zero mean, and $\mathbf{x}$ is normalized, i.e., $\mathbf{x}^{\mathrm{T}}\mathbf{x} = 1$.

The vectors $\tilde{\mathbf{x}} = (\tilde{x}_1, \ldots, \tilde{x}_N)^{\mathrm{T}}$ and $\tilde{\mathbf{x}}' = \left(\tilde{x}'_1, \ldots, \tilde{x}'_N\right)^{\mathrm{T}}$ are estimated by the linear regressions $\tilde{x}_i = \sum_{j=1}^{m} A_j \xi_{i+m-j}$ and $\tilde{x}'_i = \sum_{j=1}^{m} A'_j \xi_{i+m-j} + \sum_{j=1}^{m} B_j \eta_{i+m-j}$, respectively.

$H \subseteq \Re^N$ is the range of the matrix $\mathbf{K} = \mathbf{X}^T\mathbf{X}$; then, $\tilde{\mathbf{x}}$ is the projection of $\mathbf{x}$ on H. That is, if $\boldsymbol{P}$ is the projector on the space H, then $\tilde{\mathbf{x}} = \boldsymbol{P}\mathbf{x}$. Analogously, $\boldsymbol{P}'$ is the projector on the $2m$-dimensional space $H' \subseteq \Re^N$ with the range of the matrix $\mathbf{K}' = \mathbf{Z}^T\mathbf{Z}$; then, $\tilde{\mathbf{x}}' = \mathbf{P}'\mathbf{x}$. H' can be decomposed as $H' = H \oplus H^{\perp}$, where $H^{\perp}$ is the space of all vectors of H' orthogonal to all vectors of H. $\mathbf{P}^{\perp}$ is the projector on $H^{\perp}$. Suppose that $\mathbf{y} = \mathbf{x} - \boldsymbol{P}\mathbf{x}$; then, the linear Granger causality index can be denoted as [25]

$$\delta = \frac{\left\|\mathbf{P}^{\perp}\mathbf{y}\right\|^2}{1 - \tilde{\mathbf{x}}^T\tilde{\mathbf{x}}} \tag{1}$$

where $H^{\perp}$, which corresponds to the additional features due to the inclusion of $\{\eta\}$ variables, is the range of the matrix $\tilde{\mathbf{K}} = \mathbf{K}' - \mathbf{PK}' - \mathbf{K}'\mathbf{P} + \mathbf{PK}'\mathbf{P}$. Suppose that $H^{\perp}$ is spanned by the set of eigenvectors $\{t_i\}$, which are the eigenvectors with nonvanishing eigenvalues of $\tilde{\mathbf{K}}$. Consequently, Equation (1) can be written as $\delta = \sum_{i=1}^{m} r_i^2$, where r_i is the Pearson's correlation coefficient of $\mathbf{y}$ and $\mathbf{t}_i$. To avoid overfitting, Fisher's r-to-z transformation and FDR correction are adopted to select the eigenvector $\mathbf{t}_i$. Then, a filtered linear Granger causality index δ_F is obtained by summing only the values of $\{r_i\}$ that pass the FDR test:

$$\delta_F = \sum_i r_{i'}^2 \tag{2}$$

where δ_F measures the causality $\eta \to \xi$. By exchanging the roles of the two time series, the causal interaction $\delta_F(\xi \to \eta)$ can be evaluated.

2.2.2. Bivariate IP Kernel Granger Causality

The IP kernel of integer order p is $K_p(X, X') = \left(1 + X^T X'\right)^p$. The bivariate IP Kernel Granger Causality (BKGC) is based on the theory of reproducing kernel Hilbert spaces [25,27]. In this case, $H \subseteq \Re^N$ is the range of the Gram matrix $\mathbf{K}$ with elements $K_{ij} = K_p(X_i, X_j)$ rather than the matrix $\mathbf{K} = \mathbf{X}^T\mathbf{X}$ in the linear case. Analogously, the Gram matrix $\mathbf{K}'$ is organized with elements $K'_{ij} = K(Z_i, Z_j)$ instead of $\mathbf{K}' = \mathbf{Z}^T\mathbf{Z}$. Note that when $p = 1$, it corresponds to the linear regression. Along the same line as described for the linear case, the BKGC only takes the eigenvectors of $\tilde{\mathbf{K}}$ that pass the FDR test into account:

$$\delta_F^K = \sum_{i'} r_{i'}^2 \tag{3}$$

2.2.3. Multivariate IP Kernel Granger Causality

On the basis of BKGC, to assess the causality $\{x(a)\} \to \{x(b)\}$, the Gram matrix $\mathbf{K}$ is evaluated as $K_{ij} = k(X_i, X_j)$ with elements $X_i = \left(x(1)_i^T, \ldots, x(M)_i^T\right)^T$ that contain all the input variables but those related to $\{x(a)\}$. The Gram matrix $\mathbf{K}'$ is then evaluated as $K'_{ij} = k(Z_i, Z_j)$ with elements $Z_i = \left(x(1)_i^T, \ldots, x(a)_i^T, \ldots, x(M)_i^T\right)^T$ that contain all the input variables [25]. The target vector is then $\mathbf{x} = \left(x(b)_{1+m}, \ldots, x(b)_{N+m}\right)^T$. Consequently, in this case, the causality index of Multivariate IP Kernel Granger Causality (MKGC) is then calculated, as in Equation (3).

2.3. *Brain Network Analysis*

Complex network analysis is widely used for physiological and pathological data analysis [8,9]. Several complex network measures can be used to characterize directed weighted brain networks. A brief description of the complex network measures used in this study is presented in the following subsection.

2.3.1. Weight

Given that N is the set of all nodes in the network, W is the weighted matrix of the network, and w_{ij} is the weight of the link from node i to j [7], the in-connectivity strength of node i is the sum of all input weights of that node and is computed as $w_i^{in} = \sum_{j\in N} w_{ji}$. The out-connectivity strength is the sum of all output weights of the node and is computed as $w_i^{out} = \sum_{j\in N} w_{ij}$. The total connectivity strength of node i, referred to as the node strength w_i, consists of in-connectivity strength w_i^{in} and out-connectivity strength w_i^{out} and can be written as $w_i = w_i^{in} + w_i^{out}$. The information exchange of the whole network $w_{sum} = \sum_{i\in N} w_i^{in} = \sum_{i\in N} w_i^{out}$ provides information on the total level of weighted connectivity over the whole network.

2.3.2. Network Nonequilibrium

The probability distributions of w_i^{in} and w_i^{out} of a node i are calculated as $p_i^{in} = w_i^{in}/w_{sum}$ and $p_i^{out} = w_i^{out}/w_{sum}$, respectively. The subtraction-based probabilistic difference parameter of in- and out-connectivity strength for a node i is formulated as [30,31]

$$Y_S =< p_i^{in}, p_i^{out} >= p_i^{in} \frac{p_i^{in} - p_i^{out}}{p_i^{in} + p_i^{out}} \tag{4}$$

where p_i^{in} should not be smaller than p_i^{out}. If $p_i^{in} < p_i^{out}$, the roles of p_i^{in} and p_i^{out} should be exchanged, that is, $\langle p_i^{out}, p_i^{in} \rangle$. If the in- or out-connectivity strength of a node does not exist, its corresponding probability distribution (p_i^{in} or p_i^{out}) is 0. Cases such as this would lead to unreliable results for the division-based parameters, i.e., the relative entropy. However, we employ the subtraction-based parameters Y_S in Equation (4) to avoid this situation.

The probability difference of in- and out-connectivity strength for a single node, called $Y_{S\_}L$, reflects the local nonequilibrium of the network, and we can assess the nonequilibrium of the whole network, called $Y_{S\_}W$, by summing the probability differences of each node.

2.3.3. Complexity Measure

Shannon entropy [32] is usually considered fundamental and most natural when dealing with information content, and is typically used to evaluate the information content of a system by means of a probability distribution function. Given any arbitrary discrete probability distribution $P = (p_i : i = 1 \ldots, M)$, Shannon's logarithmic information measure [32–34,39] is $En = -\sum_{i=1}^{M} p_i \log p_i$. Shannon entropy measures the uncertainty and randomness in a given quantity of information and, as a measure of complexity, has gained popularity in nonlinear analysis [34,35]. In our work, p_i^{in} and p_i^{out} are the probability distributions of the in- and out-connectivity strength of a node i, respectively. Consequently, the Shannon entropy measures of in- and out-connectivity strength for networks are given as follows:

$$\begin{aligned} En\_in &= -\sum_i p_i^{in} \log p_i^{in} \\ En\_out &= -\sum_i p_i^{out} \log p_i^{out} \end{aligned} \tag{5}$$

3. Model Data Tests

In this section, we construct models of five nonlinear time series using the coupled first-order autoregressive processes to verify the effectiveness of MKGC in comparison to BLGC and BKGC, as displayed in Equation (6):

$$
\begin{aligned}
x_1(t) &= (1-e)\left(1-ax_1^2(t-1)\right)+e\left(1-ax_2^2(t-1)\right)+s\tau_1(t)\\
x_2(t) &= 1-ax_2^2(t-1)+s\tau_2(t)\\
x_3(t) &= (1-e)\left(1-ax_3^2(t-1)\right)+e\left(1-ax_1^2(t-1)\right)+s\tau_3(t)\\
x_4(t) &= (1-e)\left(1-ax_4^2(t-1)\right)+e\left(1-ax_1^2(t-1)\right)+s\tau_4(t)\\
x_5(t) &= (1-e)\left(1-ax_5^2(t-1)\right)+e\left(1-ax_4^2(t-1)\right)+s\tau_5(t)
\end{aligned}
\tag{6}
$$

where $e = 0.2$, $a = 1.8$, $s = 0.02$, and $\tau's$ are unit variance Gaussian noise terms. The causal relationships implemented in these equations are 1→3, 1→4, 2→1, and 4→5, and are illustrated in Figure 2a. Analyzing segments of length $N = 1000$, we evaluate causality for all pairs of maps within the 200 simulation runs.

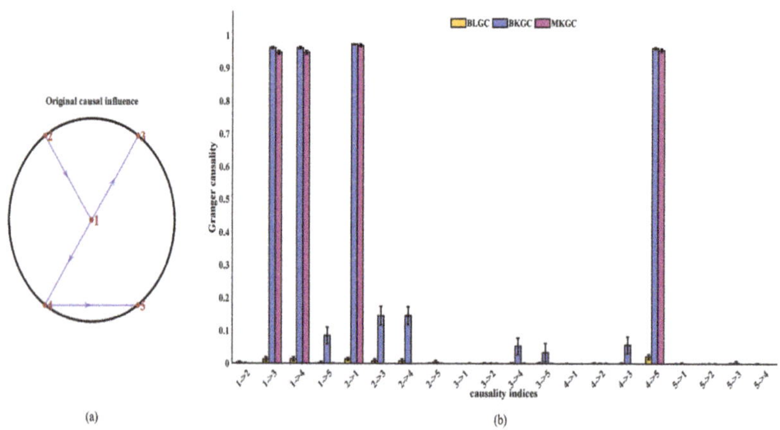

Figure 2. (**a**) Original causal influence of 1→3, 1→4, 2→1 and 4→5 between the five coupled autoregressive processes. (**b**) BLGC, BKGC and MKGC of the five coupled autoregressive processes. The order of autoregression is $m = 1$ chosen by the Bayesian information criterion; MKGC and BKGC analyses are performed with the IP kernel ($p = 2$); and vertical bars indicate estimated standard errors.

The model results for the three methods are shown in Figure 2b. The results of BLGC analysis show that the causality index of 1→3, 1→4, 2→1 and 4→5 is extremely low, with false causal influences for 2→3 and 2→4, which indicates that BLGC is not suitable for detecting the causal interaction of nonlinear time series. Both BKGC and MKGC analysis reveal the influences 1→3, 1→4, 2→1, and 4→5 with fairly large values. The slight causal interactions of 1→5, 2→3, 2→4, 3→4, 3→5 and 4→3, which are mediated by the other interactions, are only revealed by BKGC, while the MKGC indicates that they are nonsignificant (the causality index was equal to zero). The results suggest that bivariate evaluation has a limitation in that it cannot be used to discern whether the influence between two time series is direct or mediated by another one. MKGC not only has the ability to identify causal relationships between nonlinear time series but also distinguishes direct influences from indirect influences between time series.

To further analyze the validity of BLGC, BKGC and MKGC, the sensitivity, specificity, and Matthews correlation coefficient (*Mcc*) of the three methods are calculated. By comparing the rows of the target matrix with those of the actual matrix, we can obtain four parameters: true negative (*TN*), true positive (*TP*), false negative (*FN*), and false positive (*FP*). The sensitivity, specificity, and *Mcc* are evaluated as follows:

$$\begin{aligned} &Sensitivity(\%) = 100 \times TP/(TP + FN) \\ &Specificity(\%) = 100 \times TN/(TN + FP) \\ &Mcc(\%) = 100 \times \frac{TP \times TN - FP \times FN}{\sqrt{(TP + FP)(TP + FN)(TN + FP)(TN + FN)}} \end{aligned} \tag{7}$$

Table 1 quantitatively displays the performances of the average results from 200 runs with the parameters of sensitivity, specificity and *Mcc* with the three methods on the five time series above. Out of the three approaches, MKGC outperforms BLGC and BKGC.

Table 1. *Sensitivity*, *specificity*, and *Mcc* analysis of BLGC, BKGC, and MKGC.

Method	*Sensitivity*	*Specificity*	*Mcc*
MKGC	1 ± 0	0.9979 ± 0.0097	0.9945 ± 0.0260
BKGC	1 ± 0	0.5879 ± 0.0537	0.4329 ± 0.0402
BLGC	0.9653 ± 0.0866	0.8672 ± 0.0667	0.6890 ± 0.1369

In summary, compared with the other two methods, MKGC can more accurately identify pathways of causal interaction between nonlinear time series, thus providing a powerful tool for determining the effective connectivity between brain regions and for brain network construction.

4. Network Analysis on Schizophrenia MEG Data

For each individual brain dataset, the brain regions are defined as the nodes of the network, and the representative time series of each brain region is obtained by averaging the MEG time series across all channels within that brain region. We exploit MKGC to calculate the causal interactions at the regional level in MATLAB (version 2020b) , then construct directed weighted networks for MEG activities and characterize the effects of SCZ on network interactions. The order m of MKGC for the MEG data is set to 1 using Bayesian information criterion (BIC) [40]. According to Marinazzo et al. [25], Liao et al. [26], and the result of the model data test above, we choose $p = 2$ for the order of IP kernel. The Mann–Whitney U test is performed to find significant differences in the network parameters.

We adopt surrogate theory [41,42] to assess the statistical significance of effective connectivity constructed by MKGC. A total of 200 sets of surrogate data for each real dataset are generated using the improved amplitude-adjusted Fourier transform [43]. To detect whether the original MKGC connection is significantly different from the surrogate values, we calculate the statistic φ between the original and the mean surrogate value as $\varphi \equiv \frac{|Q_D - \mu_H|}{\sigma_H}$ according to J. Theiler [41]. The value $p = 0.05$ is employed as the significance level, and the non-significant effective connectivity level is removed [42,44].

4.1. MEG Effective Connectivity Network

The group average effective connectivity networks of HCs and SCZs are presented in Figure 3a,b. It is obvious that HCs have more and denser interregional connections than SCZs. The average value of effective connectivity over the whole brain of SCZs (0.008 ± 0.002) is lower than that over the whole brain of HCs (0.009 ± 0.002). Moreover, the Mann–Whitney U test is performed to investigate the between-group differences in each effective connection, and the connections with significant differences ($p < 0.05$) between HCs and SCZs are formed into the directed differential connectivity graph, as shown in Figure 3c. In total, 24 of all the effective connectivity values show significant differences, which mainly exist in the frontal temporal (FT) and occipital parietal (OP) subnetworks, among which ZC$\rightarrow$ZP ($p = 0.001$), ZP$\rightarrow$LO ($p = 0.004$), and ZF$\rightarrow$LF ($p = 0.006$) have more acceptable differences.

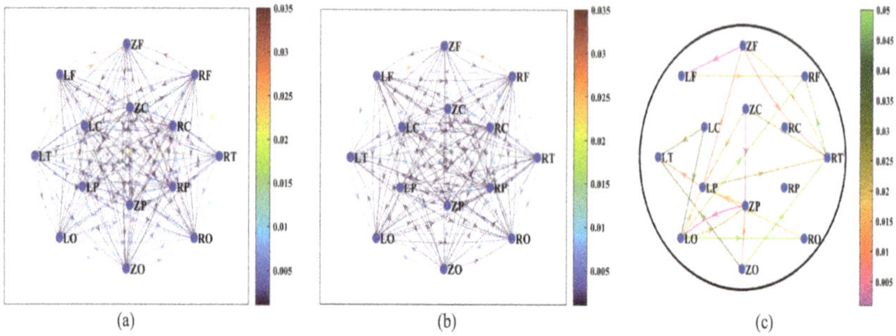

Figure 3. Effective connectivity network at group level for HCs (**a**) and SCZs (**b**). The nodes are the 14 brain regions. The colors of the links between nodes represent the interregional causal interactions, and the arrows indicate the directions of connections. (**c**) The directed differential connectivity graph between HCs and SCZs ($p < 0.05$). The colors of the links represent the p values obtained by the Mann–Whitney U test.

4.2. Network Connectivity Strength

The weights of the effective connectivity networks represent the strength of the causal interactions. Exploring the strength and their relationships is beneficial for comprehensively understanding the natural properties and underlying structures of the networks. To this end, we investigate the in-, out-, and total-connectivity strength of brain regions successively.

The maximum values of the in-connectivity strength are observed in ZF for both HCs (0.099) and SCZs (0.077). The in-connectivity strength of each brain region, excluding ZC and RC, of the HCs is greater than that of SCZs. Significantly reduced levels occur in the LF, ZF, RF, LT, RT, and LP regions of SCZs, among which RF exhibits the most significant difference ($p = 0.001$). In addition, significant differences are most widely distributed in the frontal (LF, ZF, and RF) and temporal (LT and RT) regions. However, there are no significant differences in the central and occipital regions (Figure 4).

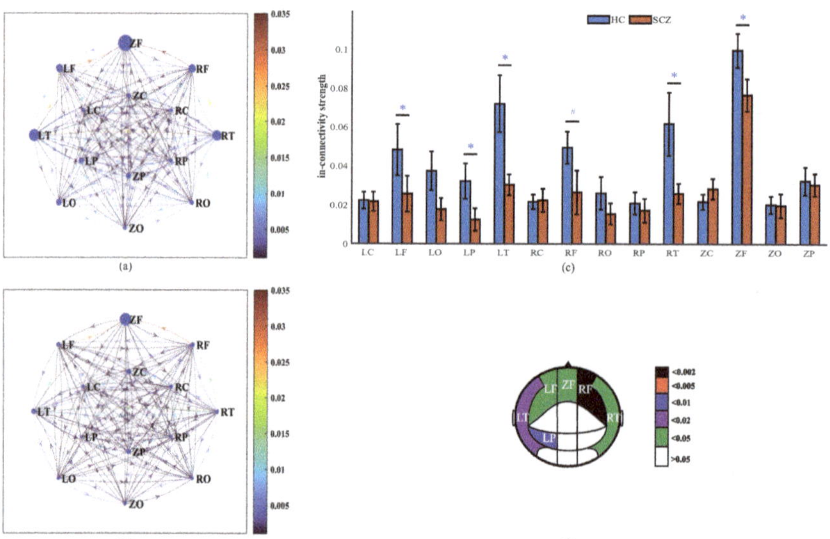

Figure 4. In-connectivity strength of brain regions. In-connectivity networks of HCs (**a**) and SCZs (**b**); the diameters of the nodes are positively related to the in-connectivity strength of the brain regions,

and the colors of the links between nodes represent the causal interactions between the brain regions. (**c**) In-connectivity strength of brain regions (mean ± standard error); # and ∗ indicate the statistical significance of $p < 0.002$ and $p < 0.05$ using the Mann–Whitney U test, respectively. (**d**) Brain regions with significant differences in in-connectivity strength. The fill color represents the p value obtained by the Mann–Whitney U test.

The strongest out-connectivity strength for all subjects occurs in the temporal area (including LT and RT), with out-connectivity strengths of RT for HCs and SCZs of 0.087 and 0.059, respectively, and out-connectivity strengths of LT for HCs and SCZs of 0.071 and 0.055. The out-connectivity strength of all regions of HCs is greater than that of SCZs, excluding RC and RP; the between-group differences are significant in the LF, ZF, ZP, LO, and ZO regions, among which LO exhibits the most significant difference ($p = 0.0018$). Furthermore, significant differences are most widely distributed in the frontal (LF and ZF) and occipital (LO and ZO) regions, while no significant differences are observed in the temporal and central regions (Figure 5).

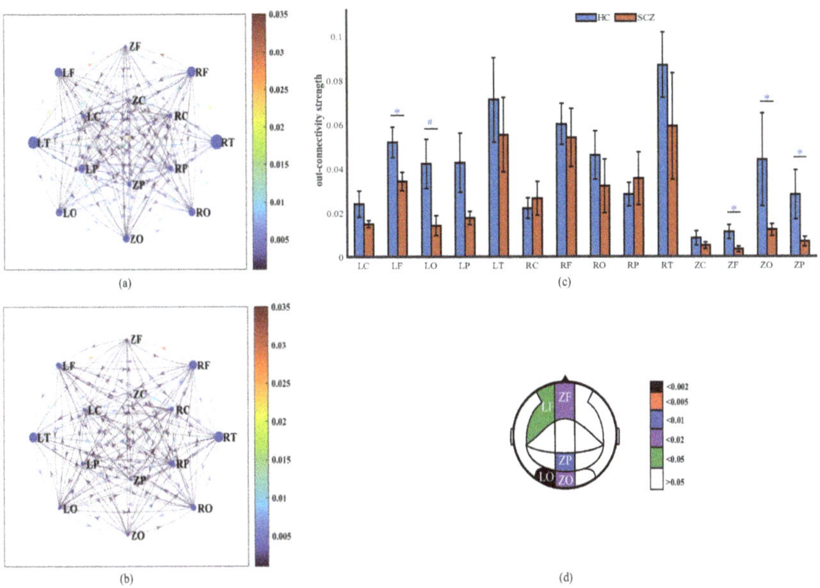

Figure 5. Out-connectivity strength of brain regions. Out-connectivity networks of HCs (**a**) and SCZs (**b**). The diameters of the nodes are positively related to the out-connectivity strengths of the brain regions and the colors of the links between nodes represent the interregional causal interactions. (**c**) The out-connectivity strength of brain regions (mean ± standard error); # and ∗ indicate the statistical significance of $p < 0.002$ and $p < 0.05$ using the Mann–Whitney U test, respectively. (**d**) Brain regions with significant differences in out-connectivity strengths. The fill color represents the p value obtained by the Mann–Whitney U test.

In another strength analysis, we focus on the total connectivity strength of brain regions. It is obvious that the total connectivity strength of brain regions is nonhomogeneous. Specifically, the total connectivity strength of the peripheral brain regions (LF, ZF, RF, LT, and RT) of the subjects is higher than that of the middle brain regions (LC, ZC, RC, LP, ZP, and RP). The total connectivity strength of the frontal (LF, ZF, and RF) and temporal (LT and RT) regions of all subjects exhibits higher values compared with other brain regions. Moreover, relative to that of the SCZs, the total connectivity strength is generally greater over the vast majority of the brain regions of HCs, and, in particular, significant differences in LO ($p = 0.004$), LF ($p = 0.009$), and RT ($p = 0.009$) exist, as displayed in Figure 6.

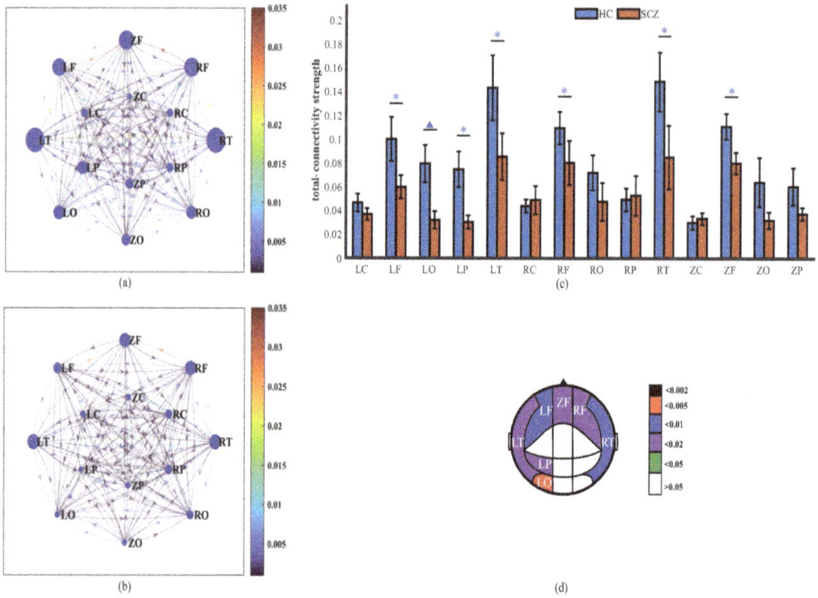

Figure 6. Total connectivity strength of brain regions. Total connectivity networks of HCs (**a**) and SCZs (**b**). The diameters of the nodes are positively related to the total connectivity strength of the brain regions, and the colors of the links between nodes represent the causal interactions between the brain regions. (**c**) Total connectivity strength of brain regions (mean ± standard error). △ and ∗ indicate the statistical significance of $p < 0.005$ and $p < 0.05$ using the Mann–Whitney U test, respectively. (**d**) Brain regions with significant differences in total connectivity strength. The fill color represents the p value obtained by the Mann–Whitney U test.

4.3. Network Nonequilibrium

The difference between the in-connectivity and out-connectivity strengths in a brain region reflects the increase or decrease in the amount of information in the brain region. Measuring the parameter $Y_{S\_}L$ [30,31] for each brain region, we can explore the local nonequilibrium of the network. The maximum value of $Y_{S\_}L$ is observed in ZF for both HCs and SCZs, and is 0.167 for the HCs and 0.232 for the SCZs, but there is no significant difference. The value of $Y_{S\_}L$ in the frontal (ZF, RF, and LF) region of SCZs is higher than that in the other four brain regions. However, LF, RF, ZC, and ZP all have acceptable discriminations between the two groups, and ZC ($p = 0.005$) has a better discrimination, as illustrated in Figure 7.

In addition, the parameter $Y_{S\_}W$ is employed to assess nonequilibrium features over the whole brain. The $Y_{S\_}W$ value of the MEG network constructed by the MKGC for the HCs is 0.741, and that of the SCZs is 0.937, which is significantly larger than that of the HCs ($p = 0.012$), as displayed in Figure 8.

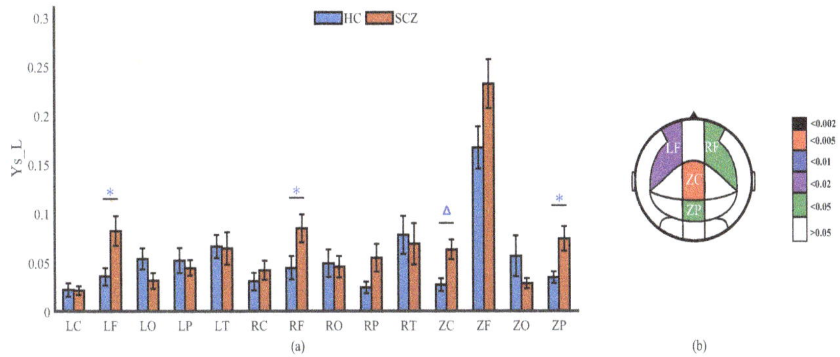

Figure 7. (**a**) Brain regional probabilistic difference $Y_{S\_}L$ of causal interactions (mean ± standard error). △ and ∗ indicate the levels of significance ($p < 0.005$ and $p < 0.05$) of the probabilistic difference across groups using the Mann–Whitney U test. (**b**) Brain regions with significant differences in $Y_{S\_}L$. The fill color represents the p value obtained by the Mann–Whitney U test.

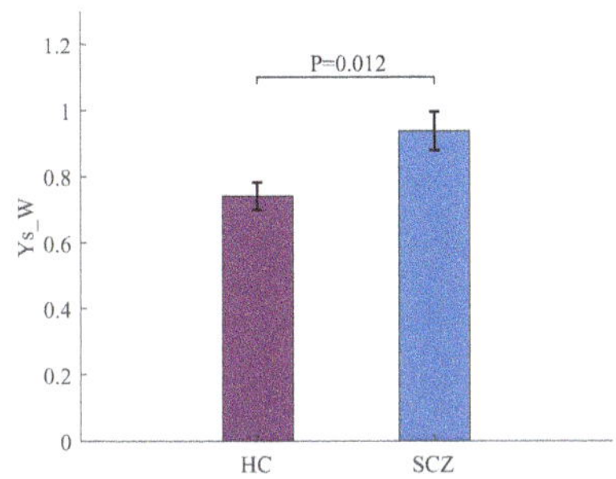

Figure 8. Nonequilibrium (mean ± standard error) of the MEG network constructed by MKGC over the whole brain for HCs and SCZs. The p value ($p = 0.012$) is obtained by the Mann–Whitney U test.

4.4. Network Complexity

Shannon entropy, one of the measures that characterize static complexity [34], can be exploited to express the amount of information in a network. We quantify the Shannon entropy of in-connectivity and out-connectivity strength for all brain regions. The Shannon entropy of the in-connectivity strength for HCs is 2.311 and that for SCZs is 2.227. No statistically significant difference ($p = 0.225$) is found between SCZs and HCs (Figure 9a). In addition, the Shannon entropy of the out-connectivity strength for HCs is 2.257, and that for SCZs is 2.224. The two groups do not have acceptable discrimination ($p = 0.593$) (Figure 9b).

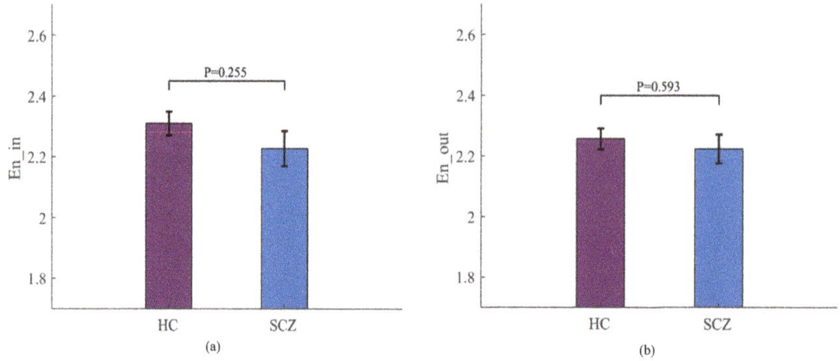

Figure 9. Shannon entropy of HCs' and SCZs' networks. (**a**) Shannon entropy of in-connectivity strength (mean ± standard error). (**b**) Shannon entropy of out-connectivity strength (mean ± standard error). p values are obtained by the Mann–Whitney U test.

From the above analysis, it can be seen that MKGC can effectively characterize the causal interactions between nonlinear time series. MKGC is a reliable tool to construct MEG networks for characterizing the physiological and pathological features of SCZs.

5. Discussion

The directed weighted networks based on MEG signals are constructed by exploiting MKGC to explore the dynamic structure and characteristics of schizophrenic brain networks. However, during the analysis, we found that there are some related issues that need further discussion.

From the above network strength analysis, it can be seen that the SCZ networks have lower values of in-, out- and total-connectivity strength in the frontal, temporal, occipital, and parietal regions, especially in the frontal regions. A wealth of SCZ studies on structural, functional and effective connectivity [4,45–47] hold similar opinions and have reported that a decreased level of connectivity was observed in SCZ networks. In addition, the frontal lobe is closely related to cognitive functions, and the abnormal performance of the frontal lobe indicates cognitive dysfunction in SCZs. Numerous neuroimaging studies have revealed that the frontal lobe exhibits abnormal performance in SCZs, for instance, an increased count of pathological myelinated fibers [48], reduced centrality [49], altered clustering [50], and longer path lengths [51]. In our findings, the network connectivity strength and local nonequilibrium of the frontal regions in SCZ networks are significantly different to those in healthy networks, which is consistent with the previous statements.

We then discuss the contradictory findings about the Shannon entropy and nonequilibrium measures. The nonequilibrium in the SCZs' network is significantly larger than that in the HCs' network, while the Shannon entropy of in-connectivity and out-connectivity in the SCZs' networks is smaller than that in the HCs' networks. The mathematical reason for this contradiction lies in the fact that nonequilibrium and Shannon entropy measure probabilistic distributions from different perspectives. The smaller the probabilistic differences, the smaller the nonequilibrium but the larger the entropy. Moreover, these contradictory results suggest that the nonequilibrium and entropy approaches, as information-theoretic approaches, target different aspects of complex systems. Shannon entropy characterizes complexity [34,35], whereas nonequilibrium [30,31] describes the features of the in–out fluctuations in network interactions. This comparative study at different levels for the characteristics of complex systems encourages us to better grasp features of the system from a broader perspective and have a deeper understanding of the specific properties of systems.

Another issue concerns the quantitative nonequilibrium for network interactions. Previous studies [52,53] have described network time irreversibility. It is important to note the differences between the concepts of network nonequilibrium and time irreversibility. Time reversibility describes the property whereby a process is invariant under the reverse time scale, which is an important approach to measure the characteristics of nonequilibrium. Statistically, time irreversibility can be measured by the probabilistic differences between forward and backward series or those between symmetric vectors. However, once a network is constructed, it is impossible to use the forward and reverse processes of time irreversibility to detect probability differences. Consequently, the research on the time irreversibility of a network essentially aims to measure a kind of nonequilibrium from a different perspective. Moreover, relative to time irreversibility, visibility graphs [52], fluctuations in the vector distance [54], etc., can detect nonequilibrium from different points of view.

Last but not least, as fundamental issues in cognitive neuroscience and neural information processing science, neural code [55,56] and neural communication [57] play an invaluable role in understanding the internal mechanisms of the brain and exploring certain medical conditions. In the complex nervous system, information is conveyed by spike trains, which are considered as elements of neural code. The exploration and detection of spike trains is a hot research field in neural code. For example, Mainen et al. [58] exploited recordings from neurons to detect the reliability of spike generation. Knoblauch et al. [59] examined the relationship between noise and inter-spike-interval statistics in real neurons in working brains. Pregowska [60] explored how spike fluctuations affect the information transmission rates. Moreover, how neurons communicate is also an important aspect of studying brain function. The frequencies and temporal dynamics of neural communication are associated with distinct behavioral states, and have an important impact on the flow of information in the brain [57]. Schizophrenia causes the abnormal function of neurons in the brain, which could exert an effect on neural code and communication [61,62]. The formation of brain networks based on MEG and the extraction of the network characteristics depend on the neural code and the communication between neurons. Consequently, the analysis of the brain MEG network for SCZs can provide powerful support for the exploration of the pathophysiological mechanisms of schizophrenia.

6. Conclusions

We examine the performance of three methods of Granger causality by model data test, and the results show that MKGC has a more satisfactory performance in characterizing nonlinear features. Then, MKGC is employed to construct the brain network of SCZs and HCs to explore the strength, nonequilibrium, and complexity of the SCZ MEG network. Compared with HCs, SCZs have decreased network strength, significantly increased nonequilibrium, and decreased complexity, suggesting that SCZ negatively affects brain network interactions. The network analysis based on MKGC could provide a reliable approach to identify the dynamic structure of the SCZ brain network and investigate the pathological and physiological mechanisms of SCZ.

Finally, we would like to emphasize that our findings have to be validated with a larger and more representative number of subjects, especially to check the performance of MKGC in the characterization of MEG-directed interaction networks.

Author Contributions: Methodology, writing—original draft preparation, software, formal analysis, Q.W.; conceptualization, writing—review and editing, W.Y. (Wenpo Yao); investigation, D.B. and W.Y. (Wanyi Yi); resources, W.Y. (Wei Yan); supervision, J.W. All authors have read and agreed to the published version of the manuscript.

Funding: This project is supported by the Postgraduate Research & Practice Innovation Program of Jiangsu Province (Project Number KYCX19_0902, KYCX21_0743, KYCX22_0952) and funding from Shandong Key Laboratory of Biophysics (TK221003).

Institutional Review Board Statement: The study was conducted in accordance with the Declaration of Helsinki, and the protocol was approved by the Ethics Committee of the Affiliated Brain Hospital of Nanjing Medical University (protocol code 2017-KY015 and 28 February 2017 approval).

Informed Consent Statement: Informed consent was obtained from all subjects involved in the study.

Data Availability Statement: Restrictions apply to the availability of these data. Data was obtained from the Affiliated Brain Hospital of Nanjing Medical University and are available from Wei Yan and Jun Wang with the permission of the Affiliated Brain Hospital of Nanjing Medical University.

Acknowledgments: We would like to thank everyone who participated in this investigation, and give thanks to the staff of the MEG Room in the Affiliated Brain Hospital of Nanjing Medical University for their assistance in this investigation.

Conflicts of Interest: The authors declare no competing interest.

Abbreviations

The following abbreviations are used in this manuscript:

MEG	Magnetoencephalogram
SCZs	Patients with schizophrenia
HC	Healthy controls
MKGC	Multivariate inhomogeneous polynomial kernel Granger causality
BLGC	Bivariate linear Granger causality
BKGC	Bivariate inhomogeneous polynomial kernel Granger causality
IP	Inhomogeneous polynomial
FDR	False discovery rate
Mcc	Matthews correlation coefficient
BIC	Bayesian information criterion

References

1. Schizophrenia. Available online: https://www.who.int/news-room/fact-sheets/detail/schizophrenia (accessed on 1 June 2023).
2. Friston, K.J. The disconnection hypothesis. *Schizophr. Res.* **1998**, *30*, 115–125. [CrossRef]
3. Lynall, M.E.; Bassett, D.S.; Kerwin, R.; McKenna, P.J.; Kitzbichler, M.; Muller, U.; Bullmore, E. Functional connectivity and brain networks in schizophrenia. *J. Neurosci.* **2010**, *30*, 9477–9487. [CrossRef] [PubMed]
4. Fornito, A.; Zalesky, A.; Pantelis, C.; Bullmore, E.T. Schizophrenia, neuroimaging and connectomics. *Neuroimage* **2012**, *62*, 2296–2314. [CrossRef] [PubMed]
5. van den Heuvel, M.P.; Fornito, A. Brain networks in schizophrenia. *Neuropsychol. Rev.* **2014**, *24*, 32–48. [CrossRef] [PubMed]
6. Bullmore, E.; Sporns, O. Complex brain networks: Graph theoretical analysis of structural and functional systems. *Nat. Rev. Neurosci.* **2009**, *10*, 186–198. [CrossRef]
7. Rubinov, M.; Sporns, O. Complex network measures of brain connectivity: Uses and interpretations. *Neuroimage* **2010**, *52*, 1059–1069. [CrossRef]
8. Bassett, D.S.; Sporns, O. Network neuroscience. *Nat. Neurosci.* **2017**, *20*, 353–364. [CrossRef]
9. Liao, W.; Ding, J.; Marinazzo, D.; Xu, Q.; Wang, Z.; Yuan, C.; Zhang, Z.; Lu, G.; Chen, H. Small-world directed networks in the human brain: Multivariate Granger causality analysis of resting-state fMRI. *Neuroimage* **2011**, *54*, 2683–2694. [CrossRef]
10. Dai, Z.; Yan, C.; Li, K.; Wang, Z.; Wang, J.; Cao, M.; Lin, Q.; Shu, N.; Xia, M.; Bi, Y.; et al. Identifying and mapping connectivity patterns of brain network hubs in Alzheimer's disease. *Cereb. Cortex* **2015**, *25*, 3723–3742. [CrossRef]
11. Wadhera, T. Brain network topology unraveling epilepsy and ASD Association: Automated EEG-based diagnostic model. *Expert Syst. Appl.* **2021**, *186*, 115762. [CrossRef]
12. Vrba, J.; Robinson, S.E. Signal processing in magnetoencephalography. *Methods* **2001**, *25*, 249–271. [CrossRef]
13. Gross, J.; Baillet, S.; Barnes, G.R.; Henson, R.N.; Hillebrand, A.; Jensen, O.; Jerbi, K.; Litvak, V.; Maess, B.; Oostenveld, R.; et al. Good practice for conducting and reporting MEG research. *Neuroimage* **2013**, *65*, 349–363. [CrossRef]
14. Houck, J.M.; Çetin, M.S.; Mayer, A.R.; Bustillo, J.R.; Stephen, J.; Aine, C.; Cañive, J.; Perrone-Bizzozero, N.; Thoma, R.J.; Brookes, M.J.; et al. Magnetoencephalographic and functional MRI connectomics in schizophrenia via intra-and inter-network connectivity. *Neuroimage* **2017**, *145*, 96–106. [CrossRef] [PubMed]
15. Tagawa, M.; Takei, Y.; Kato, Y.; Suto, T.; Hironaga, N.; Ohki, T.; Takahashi, Y.; Fujihara, K.; Sakurai, N.; Ujita, K.; et al. Disrupted local beta band networks in schizophrenia revealed through graph analysis: A magnetoencephalography study. *Psychiatry Clin. Neurosci.* **2022**, *76*, 309–320. [CrossRef] [PubMed]
16. Bai, D.; Yao, W.; Lv, Z.; Yan, W.; Wang, J. Multiscale multidimensional recurrence quantitative analysis for analysing MEG signals in patients with schizophrenia. *Biomed. Signal Process. Control* **2021**, *68*, 102586. [CrossRef]
17. Lottman, K.K.; Gawne, T.J.; Kraguljac, N.V.; Killen, J.F.; Lahti, A.C. Examining resting-state functional connectivity in first-episode schizophrenia with 7T fMRI and MEG. *NeuroImage Clin.* **2019**, *24*, 101959. [CrossRef]
18. Friston, K.J. Functional and effective connectivity in neuroimaging: A synthesis. *Hum. Brain Mapp.* **1994**, *2*, 56–78. [CrossRef]

19. Granger, C.W. Investigating causal relations by econometric models and cross-spectral methods. *Econom. J. Econom. Soc.* **1969**, *37*, 424–438. [CrossRef]
20. Troster, V.; Shahbaz, M.; Uddin, G.S. Renewable energy, oil prices, and economic activity: A Granger-causality in quantiles analysis. *Energy Econ.* **2018**, *70*, 440–452. [CrossRef]
21. Seth, A.K.; Barrett, A.B.; Barnett, L. Granger causality analysis in neuroscience and neuroimaging. *J. Neurosci.* **2015**, *35*, 3293–3297. [CrossRef]
22. Deshpande, A.; Chu, L.F.; Stewart, R.; Gitter, A. Network inference with granger causality ensembles on single-cell transcriptomics. *Cell Rep.* **2022**, *38*, 110–333. [CrossRef] [PubMed]
23. Ding, M.; Chen, Y.; Bressler, S.L. Granger causality: Basic theory and application to neuroscience. In *Handbook of Time Series Analysis: Recent Theoretical Developments and Applications*; Wiley: New York, NY, USA, 2006; pp. 437–460.
24. Guo, S.; Seth, A.K.; Kendrick, K.M.; Zhou, C.; Feng, J. Partial Granger causality-eliminating exogenous inputs and latent variables. *J. Neurosci. Methods* **2008**, *172*, 79–93. [CrossRef] [PubMed]
25. Marinazzo, D.; Pellicoro, M.; Stramaglia, S. Kernel-Granger causality and the analysis of dynamical networks. *Phys. Rev. E* **2008**, *77*, 056215. [CrossRef] [PubMed]
26. Liao, W.; Marinazzo, D.; Pan, Z.; Gong, Q.; Chen, H. Kernel Granger causality mapping effective connectivity on fMRI data. *IEEE Trans. Med. Imaging* **2009**, *28*, 1825–1835. [CrossRef] [PubMed]
27. Marinazzo, D.; Liao, W.; Chen, H.; Stramaglia, S. Nonlinear connectivity by Granger causality. *Neuroimage* **2011**, *58*, 330–338. [CrossRef]
28. Barrat, A.; Barthelemy, M.; Pastor-Satorras, R.; Vespignani, A. The architecture of complex weighted networks. *Proc. Natl. Acad. Sci. USA* **2004**, *101*, 3747–3752. [CrossRef]
29. Fang, X.; Kruse, K.; Lu, T.; Wang, J. Nonequilibrium physics in biology. *Rev. Mod. Phys.* **2019**, *91*, 045004. [CrossRef]
30. Yao, W.; Yao, W.; Wang, J.; Dai, J. Quantifying time irreversibility using probabilistic differences between symmetric permutations. *Phys. Lett. A* **2019**, *383*, 738–743. [CrossRef]
31. Yao, W.; Yao, W.; Wang, J. Equal heartbeat intervals and their effects on the nonlinearity of permutation-based time irreversibility in heart rate. *Phys. Lett. A* **2019**, *383*, 1764–1771. [CrossRef]
32. Shannon, C.E. A mathematical theory of communication. *Bell Syst. Tech. J.* **1948**, *27*, 379–423. [CrossRef]
33. Cover, T.M. *Elements of Information Theory*; John Wiley & Sons: New York, NY, USA, 1999.
34. Xiong, W.; Faes, L.; Ivanov, P.C. Entropy measures, entropy estimators, and their performance in quantifying complex dynamics: Effects of artifacts, nonstationarity, and long-range correlations. *Phys. Rev. E* **2017**, *95*, 062114. [CrossRef] [PubMed]
35. Yao, W.; Yao, W.; Yao, D.; Guo, D.; Wang, J. Shannon entropy and quantitative time irreversibility for different and even contradictory aspects of complex systems. *Appl. Phys. Lett.* **2020**, *116*, 014101. [CrossRef]
36. Fieldtrip. Available online: https://www.fieldtriptoolbox.org/ (accessed on 1 June 2023).
37. Sharon, D.; Hämäläinen, M.S.; Tootell, R.B.; Halgren, E.; Belliveau, J.W. The advantage of combining MEG and EEG: Comparison to fMRI in focally stimulated visual cortex. *Neuroimage* **2007**, *36*, 1225–1235. [CrossRef]
38. Taulu, S.; Hari, R. Removal of magnetoencephalographic artifacts with temporal signal-space separation: Demonstration with single-trial auditory-evoked responses. *Hum. Brain Mapp.* **2009**, *30*, 1524–1534. [CrossRef] [PubMed]
39. Brissaud, J.B. The meanings of entropy. *Entropy* **2005**, *7*, 68–96. [CrossRef]
40. Vrieze, S.I. Model selection and psychological theory: A discussion of the differences between the Akaike information criterion (AIC) and the Bayesian information criterion (BIC). *Psychol. Methods* **2012**, *17*, 228. [CrossRef]
41. Theiler, J.; Eubank, S.; Longtin, A.; Galdrikian, B.; Farmer, J.D. Testing for nonlinearity in time series: The method of surrogate data. *Phys. D Nonlinear Phenom.* **1992**, *58*, 77–94. [CrossRef]
42. Deshpande, G.; Hu, X.; Stilla, R.; Sathian, K. Effective connectivity during haptic perception: A study using Granger causality analysis of functional magnetic resonance imaging data. *Neuroimage* **2008**, *40*, 1807–1814. [CrossRef]
43. Schreiber, T.; Schmitz, A. Improved Surrogate Data for Nonlinearity Tests. *Phys. Rev. Lett.* **1996**, *77*, 635–638. [CrossRef]
44. Tana, M.G.; Sclocco, R.; Bianchi, A.M. GMAC: A Matlab toolbox for spectral Granger causality analysis of fMRI data. *Comput. Biol. Med.* **2012**, *42*, 943–956. [CrossRef]
45. Skudlarski, P.; Jagannathan, K.; Anderson, K.; Stevens, M.C.; Calhoun, V.D.; Skudlarska, B.A.; Pearlson, G. Brain connectivity is not only lower but different in schizophrenia: a combined anatomical and functional approach. *Biol. Psychiatry* **2010**, *68*, 61–69. [CrossRef]
46. van den Heuvel, M.P.; Kahn, R.S. Abnormal brain wiring as a pathogenetic mechanism in schizophrenia. *Biol. Psychiatry* **2011**, *70*, 1107–1108. [CrossRef]
47. Harmah, D.J.; Li, C.; Li, F.; Liao, Y.; Xu, P. Measuring the Non-linear Directed Information Flow in Schizophrenia by Multivariate Transfer Entropy. *Front. Comput. Neurosci.* **2020**, *13*, 1–15. [CrossRef]
48. Uranova, N.A.; Vikhreva, O.V.; Rachmanova, V.I.; Orlovskaya, D.D. Ultrastructural alterations of myelinated fibers and oligodendrocytes in the prefrontal cortex in schizophrenia: A postmortem morphometric study. *Schizophr. Res. Treat.* **2011**, *2011*, 325789. [CrossRef] [PubMed]
49. Zhang, Y.; Lin, L.; Lin, C.P.; Zhou, Y.; Chou, K.H.; Lo, C.Y.; Su, T.P.; Jiang, T. Abnormal topological organization of structural brain networks in schizophrenia. *Schizophr. Res.* **2012**, *141*, 109–118. [CrossRef] [PubMed]

50. Bassett, D.S.; Bullmore, E.; Verchinski, B.A.; Mattay, V.S.; Weinberger, D.R.; Meyer-Lindenberg, A. Hierarchical organization of human cortical networks in health and schizophrenia. *J. Neurosci.* **2008**, *28*, 9239–9248. [CrossRef]
51. van den Heuvel, M.P.; Mandl, R.C.; Stam, C.J.; Kahn, R.S.; Hulshoff Pol, H.E. Aberrant frontal and temporal complex network structure in schizophrenia: A graph theoretical analysis. *J. Neurosci.* **2010**, *30*, 15915–15926. [CrossRef] [PubMed]
52. Lacasa, L.; Flanagan, R. Time reversibility from visibility graphs of nonstationary processes. *Phys. Rev. E* **2015**, *92*, 022817. [CrossRef] [PubMed]
53. Flanagan, R.; Lacasa, L. Irreversibility of financial time series: A graph-theoretical approach. *Phys. Lett. A* **2016**, *380*, 1689–1697. [CrossRef]
54. Yao, W.; Yao, W.; Wang, J. A novel parameter for nonequilibrium analysis in reconstructed state spaces. *Chaos Solitons Fractals* **2021**, *153*, 111568. [CrossRef]
55. Van Hemmen, J.L.; Sejnowski, T.J. *23 Problems in Systems Neuroscience*; Oxford University Press: Oxford, UK, 2005.
56. Rieke, F.; Warland, D.; Van Steveninck, R.d.R.; Bialek, W. *Spikes: Exploring the Neural Code*; MIT Press: Cambridge, MA, USA, 1999.
57. Salinas, E.; Sejnowski, T.J. Correlated neuronal activity and the flow of neural information. *Nat. Rev. Neurosci.* **2001**, *2*, 539–550. [CrossRef] [PubMed]
58. Mainen, Z.F.; Sejnowski, T.J. Reliability of spike timing in neocortical neurons. *Science* **1995**, *268*, 1503–1506. [CrossRef] [PubMed]
59. Knoblauch, A.; Palm, G. What is signal and what is noise in the brain? *Biosystems* **2005**, *79*, 83–90. [CrossRef] [PubMed]
60. Pregowska, A. Signal fluctuations and the Information Transmission Rates in binary communication channels. *Entropy* **2021**, *23*, 92. [CrossRef]
61. Krystal, J.H.; Anticevic, A.; Yang, G.J.; Dragoi, G.; Driesen, N.R.; Wang, X.J.; Murray, J.D. Impaired tuning of neural ensembles and the pathophysiology of schizophrenia: A translational and computational neuroscience perspective. *Biol. Psychiatry* **2017**, *81*, 874–885. [CrossRef]
62. Krajcovic, B.; Fajnerova, I.; Horacek, J.; Kelemen, E.; Kubik, S.; Svoboda, J.; Stuchlik, A. Neural and neuronal discoordination in schizophrenia: From ensembles through networks to symptoms. *Acta Physiol.* **2019**, *226*, e13282. [CrossRef]

entropy

MDPI

Article

Detection of Anticipatory Dynamics between a Pair of Zebrafish

Wei-Jie Chen, I-Shih Ko, Chi-An Lin, Chun-Jen Chen †, Jiun-Shian Wu ‡ and C. K. Chan *

Institute of Physics, Academia Sinica, Taipei 115, Taiwan
* Correspondence: ckchan@gate.sinica.edu.tw
† Current address: Fachbereich Physik, Universität Konstanz, 78464 Konstanz, Germany.
‡ Current address: Department of Life Science, National Tsing Hua University, Hsinchu 300, Taiwan.

Abstract: Anticipatory dynamics (AD) is unusual in that responses from an information receiver can appear ahead of triggers from the source, and direction of information flow (DIF) is needed to establish causality. Although it is believed that anticipatory dynamics is important for animals' survival, natural examples are rare. Time series (trajectories) from a pair of interacting zebrafish are used to look for the existence of AD in natural systems. In order to obtain the DIF between the two trajectories, we have made use of a special experimental design to designate information source. However, we have also used common statistical tools such as Granger causality and transfer entropy to detect DIF. In our experiments, we found that a majority of the fish pairs do not show any anticipatory behaviors and only a few pairs displayed possible AD. Interestingly, for fish in this latter group, they do not display AD all the time. Our findings suggest that the formation of schooling of fish might not need the help of AD, and new tools are needed in the detection of causality in AD system.

Keywords: causality; direction of information flow; transfer entropy; anticipatory dynamics; zebrafish

1. Introduction

Active matters [1] can exhibit different collective phenomena because of their motions and induced interactions with their surroundings. Animals, as a form of active matter, are different from the usual physical active matters in that they can process information to avoid predators and join their mates. One counter-intuitive phenomenon arises from systems capable of information processing is anticipatory dynamics (AD), Ref. [2] in which an information receiving system can produce responses ahead of the information source. It is known that both physical and biological systems are capable of anticipating incoming events. For example, in the phenomenon of anticipating synchronization (AS) proposed by Voss [3], a slave system driven by a master can produce responses ahead of its master in time. Also, our retina [4] can produce responses ahead of predictable stimulation [5]. It is natural to ask if such AD are involved during flocking [6] in birds or schooling [7] in fish, phenomena that are still poorly understood. Presumably, during flocking or schooling, animals do not normally run into each other because they can anticipate the future positions of their group members. Therefore, it is natural to ask if AD can be detected during interactions between moving animals in nature.

If the trajectories of two interacting animals are given as $U(t)$ and $V(t)$, one would need to know how does one detect the existence of anticipatory dynamics between them. Because anticipatory dynamics is unusual in that causal events between the two time series is not ordered by time, if the events in times series $U(t)$ is found to be ahead of the time series $V(t)$, there are two possible scenarios: either "$V(t)$ follows $U(t)$" or "$U(t)$ anticipates $V(t)$". The correct scenario can only be resolved by knowing the direction of information flow (DIF) between them. In this example, if DIF is from $U(t)$ to $V(t)$, it is the case of anticipation; otherwise, it is just simply the case that later events in $V(t)$ follow earlier events in $U(t)$. However, the detection of information flow is non-trivial, and tools such as Granger causality, transfer entropy, etc., Ref. [8] have been developed for such purpose.

In this article, we report results of our experiments designed to test for the existence of anticipatory interaction between a pair of interacting zebrafish through their motion trajectories. The method of time lag mutual information (TLMI) [9] is used to first establish the temporal relation between $U(t)$ and $V(t)$. Then, usual methods of causality are applied to determined the DIF. We found that these methods just confirm the idea that information flows from leading events to following events and therefore do not indicate any AD in experiments. However, by allowing the fish to have a choice between two channels, we were able to determine which fish is in control of the interaction and therefore use it as a indicator of DIF. With this experimental method, we found that a majority of the fish pairs do not show any anticipatory behaviors, and only a few pairs displayed possible AD. Interestingly, for the latter group, the interaction between the fish pair is not always anticipatory. Our result suggests that (a) new tools are needed to detect AD between two time series, and (b) AD might not be needed for the formation of schooling.

2. Materials and Methods

In this section, we describe the experimental method and the information theoretic tools to determine the temporal order of the time series and the direction of information flow between them. These methods will help to distinguish between the cases of "anticipate" or "follow" when the two time series are correlated with some time lag. However, this method of anticipatory dynamic detection will fail when there is no significant time lag between the two time series. We will address this problem in Section 4 below.

2.1. Experiments of Fish Pairs

In the experiments, a pair of zebrafish is placed in a two-channel rectangular glass tank with the two channels separated by a wall with doors on it. The inner surface of the channels (in contact with water), including the wall, are all opaque and non-reflective, so the fish are not seeing their reflections from these surfaces. The doors allow the fish to choose in which channel to stay and therefore provide a means to detect the DIF between the two fish. The source must be the leading fish who is making the choice, whereas the follower should be on the information receiving end. The rectangular channels are of size 21.6 cm × 14 cm. The fish are 1∼1.5 years old and of length 3.5∼4 cm. The water levels in the two channels are kept around 2 cm deep. This depth was determined empirically to be deep enough to avoid the jumping of fish out of the water and shallow enough to allow the treatment of the channels as one-dimensional.

The tank is placed on top of a LCD monitor (40 cm × 70 cm), which is controlled by a computer to provide different spatially uniform illuminations for the two channels. A CCD camera (Basler, Ahrensburg, Germany acA4096-40um) placed 90 cm above the tank is used to capture images of the fish. An infra-red LED (940 nm) linear array is also used to provide illumination that is visible only to the CCD but not to the fish so that captured image quality can still be maintained even when visible illumination levels in the channels are low. The whole setup is kept inside a box with black walls, preventing the fish from detecting visual cues from the environment.

A total of more than 20 fish were kept in a large tank, and selected fish pairs were then placed into the tank for experiments. We found that a settlement time of 0, 2.5, 5, and 10 min before the start of an experiment recording did not affect the results of our experiments. Trajectories of the two fish during experiments were obtained from video images recorded at 30 or 60 frames per second (fps) with a spatial resolution of 1340 × 560 square pixels covering an area of 21.6 cm × 9 cm. The recording duration is always set to 500 s. For the health of the fish, the total experiment period per day is limited to 60 min. Trajectories of the fish are extracted from recorded images by the python package: idTracker [10].

All experiments were performed at 25 °C. Data reported below were obtained from experiments recorded at 30 fps; data from 60 fps recording gave similar results. Figure 1 shows typical images captured in our experiments. The x-component of the trajectories of one fish will be denoted by $U = \{u_0, u_1, u_2...u_n\} \equiv \{u_i\}$ with u_i being the position of the fish at the ith step. The time step size is determined by the frame rate. All the experiments reported below are of step size of 1/30 s. Similarly, $V = \{v_i\}$ is defined for the other fish. For the computation of time lag mutual information and transfer entropy described below, u_i and v_i are discretized to n bit resolution so that the horizontal span (x-component) of the tank is divided into 2^n states. Similarly, the y-component of the trajectories are discretized into two states (1 bit) to indicate in which channel (upper or lower) the fish is located.

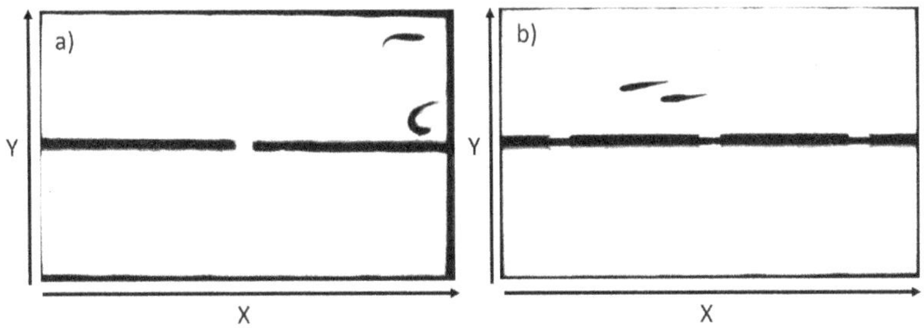

Figure 1. The tank used in the experiment with (**a**) one single door and (**b**) three doors. Directions along the length and the width of the channels are referred to as the X-direction and Y-direction, respectively, as shown in the figure. Note that the walls of the tanks are black.

2.2. Time Lag Mutual Information (TLMI)

As mentioned above, to establish anticipatory dynamics between two time series, we need: (a) the temporal order of events between them and (b) the direction of information flow. Usually, temporal order is the same as as DIF for normal behavior. However, for AD, they should be reversed. To investigate the temporal order between two time series U and V, we make use of the TLMI, which is defined as:

$$\mathcal{I}(U,V,\delta t) = \sum_{u_{t+\delta t},v_t} P(u_{t+\delta t},v_t)log[\frac{P(u_{t+\delta t},v_t)}{P(u_{t+\delta t})P(v_t)}] \quad (1)$$

where $P(\ldots)$ is the probability distribution or joint distribution of the variables in $(\ldots)$. It measures how much information is being shared between $\{u_i\}$ and $\{v_i\}$ when U is shifted j step ($\delta t = j\Delta t$) ahead of V. Maximum information is being shared between the two time series at the peak of $\mathcal{I}(U,V,\delta t)$.

The position of the peak in $\mathcal{I}(U,V,\delta t)$ as a function of δt will indicate the relation between similar events between the two time series. If the peak is at positive lag (δ_p), it indicates that the time series V is leading U by an amount of δt_p. We will label the TLMI between two different time series as the cross-TLMI and that between the same time series as auto-TLMI. Obviously, the peak of the auto-TLMI will always be at zero lag. By comparing the peak heights of auto-TLMI and and cross-TLMI, we will be able to quantify the strength of interaction between the two fish. If there is no sharing of information between the two fish, there will be no peak, and, therefore, peak height equals zero.

2.3. Detection of Direction of Information Flow (DIF)

Although the method of time lag mutual information described above can provide the temporal orders of events in the two time series U and V, it cannot distinguish between "anticipatory" and "following" dynamics. Both the cases of U anticipates V and V follows U give the same characteristic peak position in the cross-TLMI between U and V because in both cases U will be leading V. The two cases can be separated only when the direction of information flow (DIF) is known. For example, for the case of either U anticipates V or V follows U, it is the anticipatory case when information flow from V to U. Here, we employ three different methods for the detection of information flow. They are described briefly below.

2.3.1. Granger Causality (GC)

Intuitively, if a signal is predictable, one can make guesses about the future of the signal based on its past history. In 1948, Wiener [11] used this idea to predict u_i (auto-regression) with constant coefficients $\{a_i\}$ based on $\{u_{i-1}, u_{i-2}, \ldots\}$ as

$$u_i = \sum_{j=1}^{p} a_j u_{i-j} + \epsilon_i \tag{2}$$

where p is the history length or order of the auto-regression with $\{\epsilon_i\}$ being the error (residuals) of the linear regression model. If V is correlated with U, one can also use the past of V to help for the prediction of the future of U with constant coefficients $\{b_i\}$ based on $\{v_{i-1}, v_{i-2}, \ldots\}$ as:

$$u_i = \sum_{j=1}^{p} a_j u_{i-j} + \sum_{j=1}^{p} b_j v_{i-j} + \eta_i \tag{3}$$

where η_i are the residuals. The idea of GC is that if the inclusion of V can help to improve the prediction of the future of U, U is said to be GC-caused by V. One can then make use of the F-test to establish if $\sum \epsilon_i^2$ is significantly larger than $\sum \eta_i^2$. The F-test will return a p-value of the likelihood that the observed difference is caused by chance. Usually, a critical p-value of 0.05 is used, and we will use the same value here. Symmetrically, one can also interchange the roles of U and V to see if V is GC-caused by U. Here, we used the matlab package MVGC (Multi-Variate Granger Causality) [12] to detect the GC causal relation between U and V. Note that a quantity related to the F-test is used in MVGC to establish causality; namely $\mathcal{F}_{U \to V}$, which is defined as:

$$\mathcal{F}_{V \to U} = log_e \frac{|\Sigma'_{XX}|}{|\Sigma_{XX}|} \tag{4}$$

where $\Sigma'_{XX} = cov(\epsilon_i)$ and $\Sigma_{XX} = cov(\eta_i)$ are the residuals covariance matrices of models (2) and (3), respectively. With this method, GC is established as "U causes V" or DIF from U to V when $\mathcal{F}_{U \to V} > \mathcal{F}_{V \to U}$, and the likelihood is characterized by the corresponding p-value.

2.3.2. Liang's T Method

By considering the rate of information flow between U and V, Liang [13] derived a tight formula to describe the information flow between U and V using only the covariance between the four time series U, $\dot{U}$, V, and $\dot{V}$ as

$$T_{V \to U} = \frac{C_{UU} C_{UV} C_{V,\dot{U}} - C_{UV}^2 C_{U,\dot{U}}}{C_{UU}^2 C_{VV} - C_{UU} C_{UV}^2} \tag{5}$$

where $C_{ij} (i, j = U, V, \dot{U}, \dot{V})$ is the covariance between two time series, with $\dot{U}$ and $\dot{V}$ being the derivatives of U and V, respectively. Note that $\dot{U} = \{\dot{u}_i\}$, with $\dot{u}_i = \frac{u_{i+1} - u_i}{\Delta t}$, and similarly for $\dot{V}$. With this formulation, Liang was able to show that $T_{V \to U}$ is the maximum likelihood estimator for a linear system. For such a system, if $|T_{V \to U}|$ is non-zero, V is causal to U; otherwise, it is non-causal.

2.3.3. Transfer Entropy (TE)

We follow the definition of TE of Schreiber [14] and calculate the TE from time series U to V as

$$\mathcal{T}_{U\to V}(k,l,u) = H(V(t)|V_{t_{-1}}^{(k)};U_{t_{-1}}^{(k)}) - H(V(t)|V_{t_{-1}}^{(k)}) \tag{6}$$

where $H(|)$ denotes the conditional entropy. The notation $V_{t_{-1}}^{(k)} = \{v_{t-k}, v_{t-k+1}, ..., v_{t-1}\}$ represents the history of V with a length of k time step before the time bin t and similarly for U. This TE measures the reduction of entropy of the $V(t)$ by using both V's own history and that of U with history length k and l time step, respectively. If $\mathcal{T}_{U\to V}$ is positive, we will have information transfer from U to V. Since there might be information flow in both directions, the net information flow between U and V is the difference as $\Delta\mathcal{T}_{U\to V} \equiv \mathcal{T}_{U\to V} - \mathcal{T}_{V\to U}$. If $\Delta\mathcal{T}_{U\to V}$ is positive, there will be a net flow of information from U to V, and vice versa. To simplify analysis, we have set the history lengths in both U and V to be the same and labeled it as h. In the results reported below, we are using the python package PyInform [15].

2.4. Simulation of Anticipatory Data

It is known that one can generate anticipatory responses ($Z(t)$) from a predictable signal ($S(t)$) by using a negative group delay (NGD) filter [2]. This NGD model was later improved to understand the response from anticipatory dynamics of a retina [5], and the original model has the following form:

$$\dot{Z}(t) = -\alpha Z(t) + k(S(t) - Z(t - t_d)) \tag{7}$$

where α is a damping constant, with k being the gain of the system. One can think of $Z(t)$ is the response to drive $S(t)$ with a negative feedback ($Z(t - t_d)$) of delay t_d. We will use this model to generate anticipatory responses to verify validity of the causality tests mentioned above. The time series $S(t)$ is sometimes labeled as the master or "driver" signal and as slave or "target" signal for $Z(t)$.

3. Results

3.1. Trajectories in One- and Three-Door Tanks

Figure 2a,b show typical trajectories of the two fish in the tank with one and three doors, respectively and Table 1 is the measured probabilities of the choice of doors by the fish. It can be seen that, although there are two channels in the tank, the fish prefer to stay together. That is, when one of the fish choose to move to the other channel, the other fish will follow, indicating that there is some kind of attractive interaction between them. From the figure, it is clear that the main difference between the one-door and three-door tank is that the fish prefer not to use the doors located at the middle of the channel. This last observation can be understood by the observation that the fish spend most of their time at the ends of the channel, as the ends are bounded by three walls. If the probability of going through a door is a random process, the probability of choosing which door to use is then just proportional to the probability of the fish located in the vicinity of the door. Below, we will focus only on the results from the tank with a single door.

Since the channels are shaped as a quasi-1D system, we would assume that the dynamics in the X-direction and Y-direction are different. In the X-direction, the fish are interacting naturally. In the Y-direction, it is meaningful in the sense that the fish choose in which channel to stay. Therefore, we decompose the trajectories into their Y-direction time course and X-direction time course as shown in Figure 3 and Figure 4, respectively.

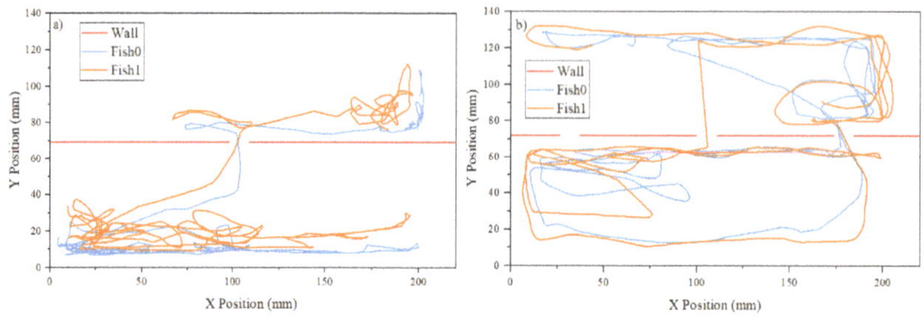

Figure 2. Trajectories of the two fish in (**a**) the tank with one door and (**b**) the tank with three doors. Note that the separation between the two channels is opaque so that the two fish can see each other only through the doors when they are located in different channels. The red horizontal line with openings in the figures indicates the separation between the two channels and the opening of the doors located at $y = 70$ mm. The fish can freely move between the two channels through the doors.

Table 1. Probability of the choice of doors by the fish measured in four experiments.

Experiment Number		Number of Passages	
	Left	Middle	Right
1	28	19	33
2	28	20	20
3	51	16	31
4	20	6	18
Probability	43.8%	21.0%	35.2%

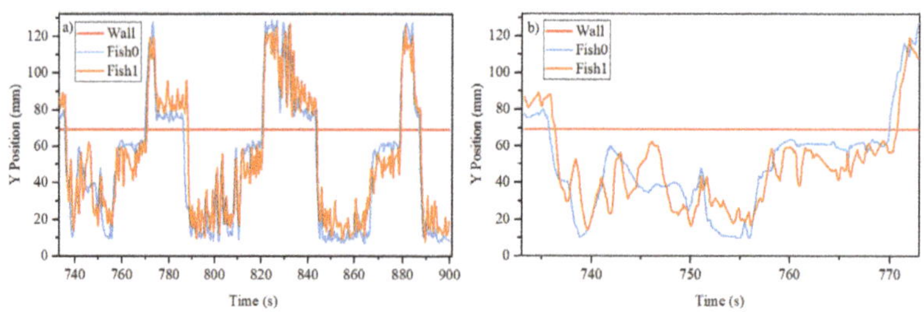

Figure 3. Typical time course of the y-component of the trajectories of the two fish in (**a**) long time scale and (**b**) in short time scale. It can be seen that Fish 1 has faster dynamics, swimming around Fish 0. It also follows Fish 0 from the lower channel to the upper channel. The red horizontal line in the figures indicates the opaque separation between the two channels located at $y = 70$ mm.

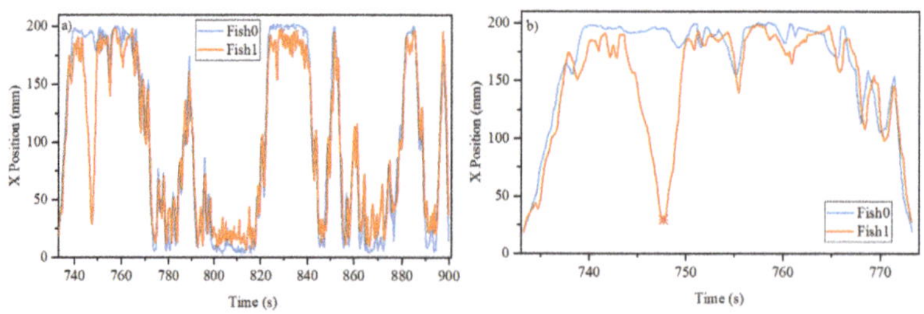

Figure 4. Time course of the x-component of the trajectories shown in Figure 3 of the two fish in (**a**) long time scale and (**b**) short time scale. The "*" marks the time point at which the two fish can be quite far apart.

It can be seen from Figure 3 that the two fish are in the same channel most of the time. They are in different channels only briefly, because once one fish starts to move into another channel, the other fish will invariably follow after some short period of time. This phenomenon can be seen as two closely spaced vertical lines in the figure when the fish change their channel. That is, the two fish always stay close together. Sometimes, the two fish can be quite far apart, as shown with the point * in Figure 4b. But very quickly, one of the fish will go the location of the other fish.

3.2. Time Lag Mutual Information from the X Component (xTLMI)

Figure 5a shows a typical result of the measured xTLMI between the two fish for trajectories similar those shown in Figure 4 when the two fish can swim freely in the tank with the door open. Note that the auto-TLMI always has a peak at zero time lag, and its decay time indicates how fast memory is fading in time. In Figure 5a, the measured auto-TLMI for both fish are similar, indicating that they have similar dynamics. A decay time of the order of second for the auto-TLMI suggests that the trajectories of the fish within a second is strongly correlated. It can also be seen from the figure that the two fish are interacting quite well because the cross-TLMI has a peak height close to 50% of that of the auto-TLMI. The observation that one fish is leading the other fish in the experiments can also be seen from the location of the peak at non-zero time lag.

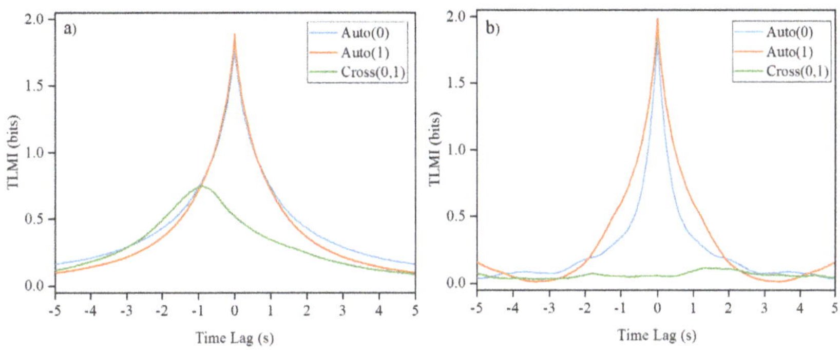

Figure 5. A typical TLMI based on the time course of x-component of the trajectories of the two fish when (**a**) the door in the tank is open and they are almost always in the same channel and (**b**) when the door is blocked and they are in different channels. It can be seen that there is little mutual information when the two fish are in separate channels with a blocked door because they cannot see each other. Auto(0): auto-TLMI of fish 0 and Cross(0,1): cross-TLMI between fish 0 and fish 1. The labels 0 and 1 are arbitrarily assigned to the two fish here.

In order calibrate the effect of interaction strength between the two fish, we have also performed experiments with the door blocked when the two fish were kept in different channels. Figure 5b shows the result of such an experiment. There are two two remarkable differences shown in Figure 5a,b. First, the auto-TLMI for two fish are quite different when they cannot see each other. This observation shows that the interaction between the two fish enable them to have similar dynamics. Second, the cross-TLMI has a prominent peak for the interacting case, whereas it is almost flat and close to zero when there is no interaction. The height of the peak indicates how strongly the two fish interact. Furthermore, we can use Figure 5b as the baseline of mutual interaction between the two fish.

Note that a 2-bit resolution for the computation of TLMI was used in Figure 5 and the theoretical value of the peak height is 2 bit. We have also checked that similar results can be obtained when a 4-bit resolution was used. However, for a 4-bit resolution, the measured results were more noisy because of the increased number of states in the trajectories. Results of xTLMI reported below are all based on 2-bit resolution.

3.3. yTLMI and DIF Detection

The results from xTLMI tell us about which fish is leading during their interaction. However, it does not tell us the direction of information flow. Here, we will use properties of the y-component of their trajectories to infer the DIF when they are interacting when the door is open. Since there are two channels in the system and the fish are free to move between them, we will treat the fish as being in two different states ("0" or "1") when they are in the upper or lower channel, respectively. With this description, the fish changes its state when they go from one channel to the other channel through the door. Our rationale is that the information emitting fish will decide which channel it will take, whereas the information receiving fish will just follow.

Figure 6a shows the time course of the y-component of the trajectories of the two fish in term of the states of the fish during the experiment. It can be seen that once a fish changed its state, the other fish follows suit. In other words, one of the fish will first decide to which channel it will go and then the other fish will follow. That means the leading fish is the information source and the following fish is the information receiver. If we assume that the role of the fish is constant in time (during experimental recording time), we can then use the yTLMI to determine the direction of information flow with the leader in the yTLMI as the information source. Figure 6b shows a typical result of the computed yTLMI from the time course of the state of the two fish.

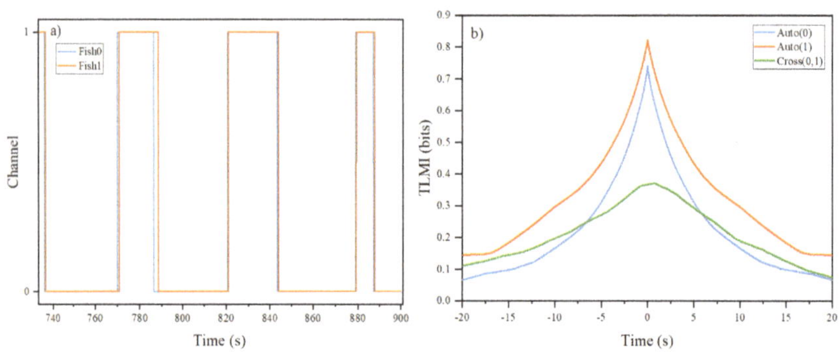

Figure 6. (**a**) A typical time course of the state of the two fish and (**b**) the computed yTLMI based on the time course of the states. The peak position of the yTLMI based on states confirms our observation in (**a**) that Fish 0 changes its state first.

One of the main differences between properties of xTLMI and yTLMI is that the decay time scales of their auto-TLMI are very different, as demonstrated by Figures 5 and 6. For xTLMI, the dynamics is dominated by the quasi-1d interaction between the two fish in a single channel. For the yTLMI, the dynamics is dominated by the decision of which channels to take by the leader fish. Intuitively, these two dynamics should be very different. For the xTLMI, the dynamics is determined by how fish interact in short term time scales when they want to be close to each other. As shown in Figure 5, it is on the order of 500 ms. For the yTLMI, the leading fish can choose which channel to take only when it is next to the door. Therefore, the time scale is much longer, on the order of a few seconds, in Figure 6. However, these differences in time scales of auto-TLMI does not impose any limitation to the peak positions of their corresponding cross-TLMI because the peak position of cross-TLMI is determined only by how fast one fish is responding to the other fish.

3.4. Summary of Experimental Results

Table 2 is a summary of the important properties of xTLMI and yTLMI obtained from experiments similar to those shown in Figures 5 and 6 above. Here, the peak values of xTLMI (yTLMI) are normalized by the peak height of the corresponding auto-TLMI. With this method, the peak value will be independent of the number of states used in the discretization of the trajectories. As mentioned above, the peak height indicates the strength of interaction between the two fish; we have only included data that have a x-TLMI peak value at least 10% of the peak of the auto-TLMI in the x-component.

Table 2. Summary of cross-TLMI of experimental data. There are a total of 16 experiments (Expt) reported, but there are only 12 pairs of fish. The peak height is reported as the ratio between peak heights from the cross and auto-TLMI. The decay time is taken as the half decay time of the auto-TLMI.

Expt Number	Fish Pair	Properties of Cross xTLMI			Properties of Cross yTLMI		
		Peak Position(s)	Peak Height	Decay Time(s)	Peak Position(s)	Peak Height	Decay Time(s)
1	A	−0.83	0.22	0.57	−1.10	0.41	6.13
2	B	0.63	0.09	0.53	−3.87	0.35	7.90
3	B	−0.23	0.31	0.53	−0.53	0.48	6.03
4	C	−0.60	0.12	0.87	−0.73	0.19	3.97
5	D	0.50	0.09	0.47	−3.30	0.28	9.30
6	D	−0.63	0.12	0.60	−11.17	0.20	19.97
7	E	−0.77	0.20	0.40	−1.43	0.36	19.97
8	F	0.47	0.13	0.50	−0.53	0.26	2.53
9	F	−0.27	0.16	0.53	−1.13	0.19	2.47
10	G	−0.63	0.22	0.63	−1.73	0.39	13.47
11	H	−0.60	0.26	0.63	−1.37	0.26	4.67
12	I	−0.30	0.17	1.23	−0.67	0.22	7.40
13	J	−0.43	0.25	0.47	−0.53	0.34	4.93
14	L	0.57	0.23	0.83	−0.33	0.30	17.53
15	L	−0.67	0.27	1.03	−1.33	0.31	9.47
16	M	−0.40	0.21	0.87	−1.43	0.23	3.73

When peak position takes a value other than zero, it indicates that one fish is leading the other. Since the labels of the fish are arbitrary, we have chosen the convention that the peak position of the cross y-TLMI is always negative. Therefore, when one also detects a negative peak position in the cross xTLMI, we have the same leading fish in both the x and y components of the trajectories. That means one fish just follows another fish (the case of "following" dynamics). However, when one detects a positive peak position in the cross xTLMI, one would have the situation that the follower in the y-component becomes the leader in the x-component. This is the situation of anticipatory dynamics (AD), because the leading fish in xTLMI is the information receiver while the other fish is the information source. Therefore, with this convention, any fish pair with a positive cross xTLMI peak position is an indication of anticipatory dynamics. For example, in experiment number 5, fish pair D produced a cross yTLMI with peak position at −3.3 s whereas the peak position of cross xTLMI is located at +0.5 s.

However, it can be also seen from the table that the same fish pair D in experiment 4 does not produce peak positions in xTLMI and yTLMI with different signs. This latter observation indicates that the leading fish in xTLMI is the same leading fish in yTLMI. Our finding suggests that the role of information receiver/source for a fish pair is not necessarily constant in time. Similar observations of changes in roles can also be seen for fish pairs B, F, and L. From our experimental observations, fish pairs that exhibit anticipatory dynamics also display follow behaviors. However, the reverse is not true. One interesting observation from Table 2 is that interaction strength is smaller for anticipatory pairs.

3.5. DIF Detection by Statistical Methods

As mentioned above, three statistical methods are used to determine DIF by the time series obtained in the experiments. The results of GC test and Liang's T test are summarized in Table 3. For the GC computation to obtain $\mathcal{F}$, one needs to determine the order (lag) used in the computation of GC in the models of Equations (2) and (3). Figure 7 shows the order (time lag) dependence of the Akaike information criterion (AIC) and Bayesian information criterion (BIC) using the code of MVGC. Ideally, the order of the model is determined by the location of the minimum of the AIC/BIC curve. As can be seen from the figure, there seems to be no minimum, only saturation. The order shown in the table is determined automatically by MVGC. We have checked that if we fixed the order to be 10, some numerical values of the table will be changed, but the conclusion from Table 3 discussed below will not be changed.

Table 3. Summary of GC test and Liang's T using data from experiments listed in Table 2.

Expt Number	Fish Pair	Order (BIC)	$\mathcal{F}$ (MVGC) $\mathcal{F}_{0\to1}$	$\mathcal{F}_{1\to0}$	p-Value (MVGC) $p_{0\to1}$	$p_{1\to0}$	Liang's T $T_{0\to1}$	$T_{1\to0}$
1	A	20	1.37×10^{-2}	1.90×10^{-4}	0.00×10^{0}	1.00×10^{0}	1.15×10^{-2}	1.04×10^{-2}
2	B	20	1.17×10^{-3}	6.13×10^{-3}	7.90×10^{-3}	4.61×10^{-7}	1.29×10^{-3}	1.49×10^{-3}
3	B	20	6.20×10^{-2}	3.78×10^{-3}	0.00×10^{0}	1.25×10^{-2}	4.20×10^{-2}	3.75×10^{-2}
4	C	15	6.48×10^{-3}	2.64×10^{-4}	1.43×10^{-7}	1.00×10^{0}	3.20×10^{-3}	2.97×10^{-3}
5	D	11	7.89×10^{-4}	1.02×10^{-2}	8.10×10^{-1}	2.22×10^{-16}	2.56×10^{-3}	2.73×10^{-3}
6	D	18	6.55×10^{-3}	3.15×10^{-4}	2.14×10^{-8}	1.00×10^{0}	1.55×10^{-3}	1.41×10^{-3}
7	E	20	19.91×10^{-2}	4.01×10^{-4}	0.00×10^{0}	1.00×10^{0}	1.20×10^{-2}	1.12×10^{-2}
8	F	14	1.26×10^{-3}	5.66×10^{-3}	5.35×10^{-1}	2.03×10^{-7}	2.92×10^{-3}	3.27×10^{-3}
9	F	20	6.45×10^{-3}	2.03×10^{-3}	6.01×10^{-6}	5.32×10^{-1}	2.50×10^{-3}	1.53×10^{-3}
10	G	20	1.72×10^{-2}	1.39×10^{-3}	0.00×10^{0}	6.03×10^{-1}	1.08×10^{-2}	1.01×10^{-2}
11	H	20	2.14×10^{-2}	1.77×10^{-4}	0.00×10^{0}	1.00×10^{0}	1.37×10^{-2}	1.22×10^{-2}
12	I	10	1.33×10^{-2}	1.07×10^{-3}	0.00×10^{0}	5.05×10^{-1}	4.48×10^{-3}	3.65×10^{-3}
13	J	20	2.39×10^{-2}	3.27×10^{-2}	0.00×10^{0}	4.35×10^{-2}	2.03×10^{-2}	1.82×10^{-2}
14	L	10	5.07×10^{-4}	6.16×10^{-3}	9.96×10^{-1}	3.30×10^{-8}	4.95×10^{-3}	5.89×10^{-3}
15	L	10	1.35×10^{-2}	2.22×10^{-4}	0.00×10^{0}	1.00×10^{0}	1.09×10^{-2}	9.95×10^{-3}
16	M	20	1.27×10^{-2}	1.97×10^{-4}	1.11×10^{-16}	1.00×10^{0}	8.84×10^{-3}	7.32×10^{-3}

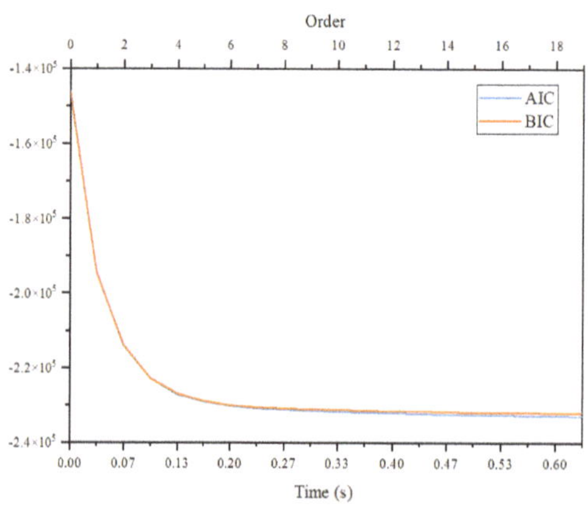

Figure 7. A typical estimation of order of auto-regressive model base on Bayesian information criterion (BIC) and Akaike information criterion (AIC) obtained from programs provided by the MVGC tool box. The order shown in the figure is related to the time step of our data of 1/30 s.

Figure 8a,b are the GC test results and the corresponding p-values from Table 3. A remarkable feature of Figure 8a is that all the $\mathcal{F}_{0\to1} > \mathcal{F}_{1\to0}$ for all the experiments except for experiment numbers 2, 5, 8, and 14. That means that the computed $\mathcal{F}$ values correctly predict that Fish 1 (follower) is receiving information from Fish 0 (leader) except for these four experiments. This difference is significant, as can also be seen from the p-value shown in Figure 8b.

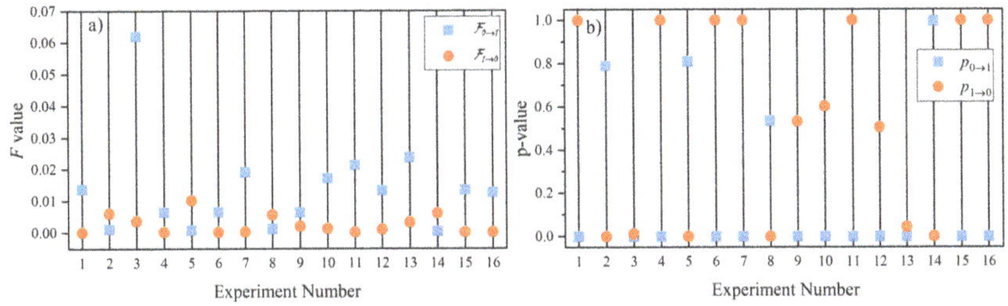

Figure 8. Results of $\mathcal{F}$ values from Granger causality based on the programs provided by MVGC. (**a**) $\mathcal{F}$ values for different experiments shown in Table 2 and (**b**) their responding p-value.

The implication of the results of the GC test for experiments 2, 5, 8, and 14 is interesting because they are the cases for anticipatory dynamics. That means if we merely look at the x-component for their trajectories, one could have concluded that Fish 1 is the leader. It is only through the y-component of their trajectories that we conclude that these are cases for anticipatory dynamics; namely, information flow from Fish 0 to Fish 1, but Fish 1 is leading in action. Therefore, the use of the GC test to detect direction of information flow fails for anticipatory dynamics.

Following Liang [13], we have also computed $|T_{0\to1}|$ and $|T_{1\to0}|$ for our experimental dataset, and they are also shown in Table 2 and Figure 9. It is clear that all T are non-zero and all $|T_{0\to1}|$ are close to $|T_{1\to0}|$. Therefore, there is no clear indication of causality. However, upon close examination, similar to the GC test, all the $|T_{0\to1}|$ are larger than $|T_{1\to0}|$ except for experiments 2, 5, 8, and 14. Although there is no clear indication of direction of information flow from using Liang's analysis, our results show that Liang's T method, similar to the GC test, fails to detect DIF in the cases of anticipatory dynamics.

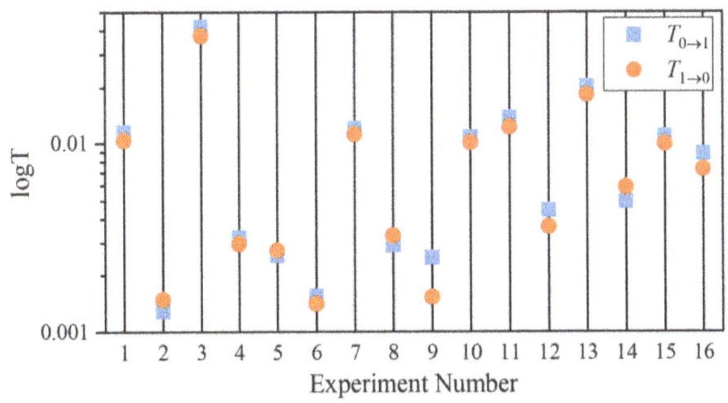

Figure 9. Results of Liang's T-value computation from experiments shown in Table 2. It can be seen that $T_{0\to1}$ are all larger than $T_{1\to0}$ except for experiments 2, 5, 8, and 14, similar to the finding of using GC.

We have also computed the TE between the two time series from the experiments. For the computation of TE from our experimental data, we need to first specify a history length that is similar to the order of the model in the method of GC. In the package of MVGC, the order is determined automatically by the package. However, for TE, we need to specify it manually when we use the python package PyInform to compute the TE. Since the number of permissible states in the system increases exponentially with history length, there will be a strong bias [16] because the data length is short or history length is long. For example, in our case of the trajectories in the X-direction divided into fiur states, the number of permissible states of the system will increase as 4^{h+1}, where h is the history length. For $h = 1, 2, 4$, and 8, the corresponding number of permissible states are $16, 64, 1024$, and 262,144, respectively. Since our data length is only 18,000, the results of TE computation will be unreliable when h is larger than 4. But in view of Figure 7, our history length should be chosen to be at least 5, which corresponds to a lag of about 165 ms.

Figure 10 shows the results of TE computation of data from Table 3 for different history lengths from 2 to 5. It can be seen from the figure that, in general, $\mathcal{T}_{0\to 1}$ is greater than $\mathcal{T}_{1\to 0}$, although their differences are small. This last finding shows that the DIF for most of the cases in the experiment are from 0 to 1. However, if we look closely at experiments 2, 5, 8, and 14, we find that $\mathcal{T}_{0\to 1}$ is either very close to or smaller than $\mathcal{T}_{1\to 0}$. The last finding shows that the DIF for these cases are from 1 to 0. Therefore, the DIF obtained from the method of TE are the same as those determined by the GC test and Liang's T. All these methods failed to detect the correct DIF for anticipatory dynamics.

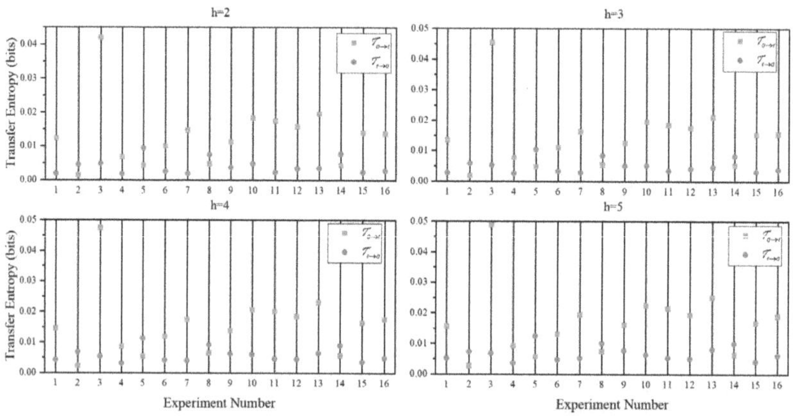

Figure 10. Computation of transfer entropy of experiments listed in Table 2 using the package PyInform. Here, h is the history length, and the two directions of transfer entropy are shown as blue and red. It can be seen that for most of the cases, TE is higher from 0 to 1, but the difference between the two directions are small. Similar to the computation of TLMI, the discretization here is also 2 bit, but a 4 bit discretization will give similar results but with different numerical values for the computed TE.

3.6. Testing of DIF Detection with Simulated Anticipatory Data

The results from the three methods (GC, Liang's T, and TE) are similar in that they all determine that the leading time series is detected as the information source and therefore fail to detect the possible anticipatory dynamics in experiments 2, 5, 8, and 14. To further demonstrate this property of these tools, we have also used simulated anticipatory dynamics for these tests. Our source signal, $S(t)$, is a lowpass Ornstein–Uhlenbeck time series that has been demonstrated to be able to produce anticipatory response from a negative group delay model [5]. The model of Equation (7) is then used to create the anticipatory responses $Z(t)$.

The simulation of Equation (7) and the corresponding TLMIs between $S(t)$ and $Z(t)$ are shown in Figure 11. From the peak position of the cross-TLMI, it is clear that $Z(t)$ is leading $S(t)$. This is exactly the situation for anticipatory dynamics: information flow from $S(t)$ to $Z(t)$ while $Z(t)$ is leading $S(t)$. When we perform the GC and the Liang's T analysis with these two signals, we find that $\mathcal{F}_{z\to s} > \mathcal{F}_{s\to z}$ and $|T_{z\to s}| > |T_{s\to z}|$. In other words, both GC and Liang's method fail to detect the correct direction of information flow. Therefore, the failure of the detection of AD in experiments 2, 5, 8, and 14 does not mean that there is absence of AD in these experiments. We have also computed the corresponding TE of this NGD model for various history lengths, and the result is shown in Figure 12. It can be seen clearly from the figure that the direction of information flow is wrong because TE from S to Z is always larger than those from Z to S. Note that the discretization of the trajectories used in Figures 11b and 12 are both 4 bit. Similar results can also be obtained when the discretization is changed to 2 bit.

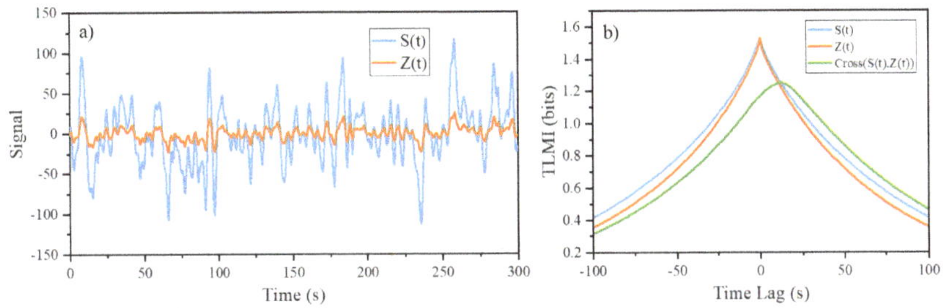

Figure 11. Simulation of anticipatory dynamics from Equation (7) with the following parameters: $\alpha = 20\text{s}^{-1}, k = 5\text{s}^{-1}$, and $t_d = 1\text{s}$. (**a**) The time course of lowpass OU signal, $S(t)$, and the output $Z(t)$. (**b**) The corresponding TLMI between $S(t)$ and $Z(t)$. Here, $S(t)$ is the lowpass (0.3 Hz) of $W(t)$ with $\dot{W}(t) = -W(t)/\tau + \sigma\zeta(t)$, where $\sigma = 63.2\text{s}^{-1}$, $\tau = 1$, and $\zeta(t)$ is a dimensionless Gaussian white noise with zero mean and unit variance. Note that $S(t)$, $Z(t)$, and $W(t)$ are all dimensionless, and both Equation (7) and $W(t)$ are obtained by using simple Euler's method with a time step size of 0.01 s. Similar results can also be obtained when a time step of 0.001 s is used. These results are obtained with a duration of 300 s of simulated time.

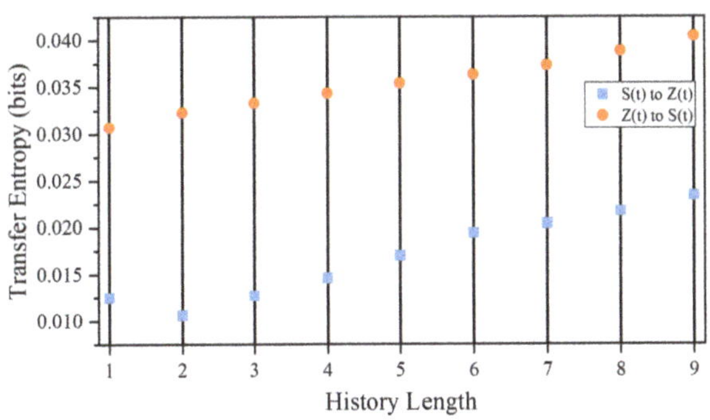

Figure 12. Measured TE between S and Z of the NGD model for various history length. It can be seen that TE from Z to S is always larger than that from the reverse direction. A history length is measured in a simulation step to be 0.01 s.

4. Limitations

4.1. Predictive and True Causality

The argument we used above to obtain the direction of information flow (causality) between two time series is based on the improvement of prediction of future values of one time series by the inclusion of values of the other time series. The causality established in this manner is also known, more precisely, as predictive causality [17]. It is natural that we choose this methodology here because AD is predictive. In fact, all three methods used here to detect direction of information flow are predictive in nature. However, we would like to stress that predictive causality can be different from true causality [17], which requires a direct cause-and-effect mechanism [18] between two agents. Therefore, our results of detection of AD between a pair of fish should be taken with caution. We did not present any experimental evidence of a direct cause-and-effect mechanism between the two fish. Data needed to establish true causality will require adequately designed intervention experiments [19]. The readers should keep in mind that anticipatory dynamics is predictive in nature and its detection does not imply that a biological cause-and-effect mechanism between the two fish has been inferred.

4.2. Detection of Anticipatory Dynamics

In this work, we are using the usual definition of AD in which information flows from the source to the receiver while the temporal order of the receiver is ahead of the source. In the case of a retina [4,5], it is clear that information flows from the visual stimulation to the retina. AD is said to be observed when the output the of the retina (receiver) is ahead of the stimulation (source). With this definition of AD, our claim of detection of AD is based on our observation that the motions of receiver fish is ahead of the source fish in some fish pairs. In our experiment, the source and receiver fish assignment is based on the passing order of the fish through the door and the assumption that the roles of the fish do not change during the experiment. However, the readers are reminded that these assumptions of the passing order and the constancy of the roles of the fish need to be further tested.

4.3. Issues of Entropy Based Causality

It is well known that one must be cautious when dealing with entropy, especially when it is used to deal with causality [20]. The counter-intuitive anticipatory dynamics under consideration here might even make matters worse. For example, in a simulation study of using TE to determine the direction of causality in coupled logistic maps with anticipatory properties, Hahs et al. [21] found that the direction of causality in this relatively simple case is dependent on the data resolution being used. Correct direction of causality can be found only when high enough data resolution is used to compute the transfer entropy. In fact, we have also checked that, for our simulation model above, the results could be quite different from that shown in Figure 12 if a higher data resolution is used in the computation of TE.

The two lines in Figure 12 will cross over at a certain history length when the data resolution is 6 bit or higher, suggesting that the direction of information flow is reversed. However, we find that this crossover can be removed by using longer simulated time (larger sample size). It is not clear if this phenomenon originates from the bias of sample size mentioned above or is related to the effect mentioned in Ref. [21]. Nevertheless, these results from the NGD model simulation clearly demonstrated that TE based causality must be taken with care. Unlike numerical simulations in which data resolution can be increased relatively easily, our experimental data resolution is fixed by the setup. The use of computed TE based causality in our experiments might not be conclusive. Of course, our assumption that the "driver" fish will go through the door first in the experiment also needs to be further tested.

4.4. Correlation and Causation

One common mistake in the study of causality between two time series is the confusion between correlation and causality. In Ref. [3], where anticipatory synchronization is considered, there is a master and a slave with identical intrinsic dynamics (before coupling). These two systems will synchronize with the slave system ahead of the master system. It would be easy to conclude that the slave system is the cause of the master system because its time course is ahead of that from the master. However, in such a case, there is no causal relation between them because, when the two systems are synchronized, there is no information flow between them. In fact, the coupling term vanishes when the two systems are synchronized. In such a case, these two systems are perfectly correlated, but there is no casual relation between them.

However, in the case of Ref. [2], the NGD model (Equation (7)) in our manuscript, $S(t)$ and $Z(t)$ are not only correlated but there is also a causal relation between them. Note that the intrinsic dynamics of $Z(t)$ is purely relaxation without the coupling term. It is the coupling delayed feedback, $k(S(t) - Z(t - t_d))$, which uses $S(t)$ as the drive for the system $Z(t)$. The system $Z(t)$ can produce anticipatory output of $S(t)$ because of the negative group delay properties of system $Z(t)$ as well as the predictability of signal $S(t)$ by using a lowpass filter on a random signal. Had $S(t)$ been totally random, there will be no anticipatory output from $Z(t)$. For this NGD model, the causal direction is clearly from $S(t)$ to $Z(t)$. This simple NGD model cannot be used to understand the interaction between the fish pair. It is used here simply to demonstrate that the common tools for causality used here fail to detect the correct DIF when anticipatory data of known DIF are fed into these tools. In our experiments, there is no common external stimulation to the fish pair. Presumably, their correlated but not synchronized motions are the results of information exchanges between them.

4.5. Problem of Bi-Directional Coupling

It should be stated again that our definition of anticipatory dynamics is quite narrow. For example, if there are bi-directional anticipatory interactions between the two fish with almost equal strength, the resultant cross-TLMI will peak very close to zero time lag. In such a case, there will be no obvious leader in the two resultant time series and our method will reach the wrong conclusion that there is no AD. Therefore, our method of detecting AD probably cannot be used to detect causality in a closed-loop control system, such as the coupling between heart rate and respiration rate [22] or auto-regulation of blood pressure [23]. In a closed-loop control system, different variables of the system are coupled directly or indirectly in such a way to maintain the system in some desirable state. Therefore, the causal effects of different variables in such a system are investigated because these causal relations might reveal the underlying control mechanism. Methods such as Granger indices [24] have been used to infer the types of interaction between different variables in the controlled system. However, such an approach is probably not suitable for our investigation of the interaction between two fish. It is not clear if their trajectories can be regarded as the result of some kind of control. We could have also extended our NGD simulation model to have a bi-directional coupling. But as mentioned above, our detection method would probably fail.

5. Discussion

Traditionally, causality refers to the relationship between cause and effect, where a cause precedes an effect in time. It implies that the cause happens first, leading to the subsequent occurrence of the effect. However, as shown above in our simple numerical simulation, in the context of anticipatory dynamics, causality is not ordered by time. This happens because the responding system can incorporate future information of the source into its present behavior. Here, the future information of the source can be learned/anticipated by the responding system as in the case of NDG model, or it may use internal models or predictions to guide its behavior based on expected future conditions as in the case of anticipatory synchronization [3].

Our challenge is: how do we determine the causality between two given correlated time series as in our experiments in the context of anticipatory dynamics? From the discussion above, it is clear that the method of TLMI can be used to detect the temporal order of events between the two time series. Ideally, if DIF can also be computed from the two time series, one will be able to distinguish between the cases of "anticipatory" or "following". However, it is non-trivial to determine DIF simply based on the data from the two times series as demonstrated by our experiment and simple simulation. In our experiments, we are able to tell the DIF because of the special design of using a door to determine which fish is the information source. Unfortunately, the methods of the GC test, Liang's T analysis, and TE all failed to detect DIF for both experiments and our NGD generated data. These tools seem to detect DIF based on temporal order of events in the two time series. It is not clear if the existence of AD can be detected based only on the data from two time series. If yes, new tools need to be developed to detect it.

One interesting aspect of anticipatory dynamics is that the leading in time course does not necessary means the "leader" [25] is in control. In the phenomenon of anticipating synchronization demonstrated in Ref [3], it can be clearly seen that the "leader" (time course) can be the slave because the slave is actively anticipating the future movements of the master. It is known that when birds flock, the birds from low pecking order can lead (in the sense of time course) for some time. Perhaps, these low pecking order birds are just anticipating the future position/movement of their masters (birds of high pecking order). We are still in the early stages of understanding these emerging behaviors from these active entities in the sense they are not only self-propelling but at the same time making active decisions. Our experimental finding that most of the fish pairs are interacting by "following" dynamics suggests that during the schooling of fish, perhaps, most of the fish are just following the trajectories of their neighbors. It would then be interesting to investigate if the direction of movement of a school of fish is determined by some leaders or it is just spontaneously reacting to the environment such as the currents in the sea or the location of prey and/or predators.

Finally, we would like to note that the method of analysis presented here can be further tested by using zebrafish with known altered behavior; for example, fish with neuro-degenerative disease [26]. Presumably, the dynamics of interaction between these fish might be quite different because of their impaired information processing capability.

Author Contributions: W.-J.C.: conduction of experiments and data analysis; I.-S.K.: coding and checking of computation of TE; C.-A.L.: editing, checking, and validation of data; C.-J.C. and J.-S.W.: early design concepts of experimental methodology; C.K.C.: supervision, writing, review, and editing. All authors have read and agreed to the published version of the manuscript.

Funding: This work has been supported by the MOST of ROC under the grant number 111-2112-M-001-032.

Institutional Review Board Statement: All the experiments with animals in this work were performed according to guidelines approved by Academia Sinica IACUC (Protocol:12-12-475).

Data Availability Statement: The datasets used or analyzed during the current study are available from the corresponding author on reasonable request.

Acknowledgments: One of the authors (CKC) would like to thank Vicsek for inspiring discussions.

Conflicts of Interest: The authors declare no conflict of interest.

Abbreviations and Symbols

AD	Anticipatory dynamics
DIF	Direction of information flow
Expt	Experiment
GC	Granger causality
NGD	Negative group delay
OU	Ornstein–Uhlenbeck
TE	Transfer Entropy
xTLMI	Time lag mutual information from the x component
U, V	Time series from the trajectories
S, Z	Source and target time series in the NGD model
W	Ornstein–Uhlenbeck noise
P	Probability distribution
η, ϵ	Error (residuals)
$\mathcal{F}$	F-test
p	p-value
T	Value of Liang's T mnethod
C	Covariance
$\mathcal{T}$	Value of transfer entropy
H	Entropy

References

1. Fodor, É.; Marchetti, M.C. The statistical physics of active matter: From self-catalytic colloids to living cells. *Phys. A Stat. Mech. Its Appl.* **2018**, *504*, 106–120. [CrossRef]
2. Voss, H.U. Signal prediction by anticipatory relaxation dynamics. *Phys. Rev. E* **2016**, *93*, 030201. [CrossRef] [PubMed]
3. Voss, H.U. Anticipating chaotic synchronization. *Phys. Rev. E* **2000**, *61*, 5115. [CrossRef] [PubMed]

Berry, M.J., II; Brivanlou, I.H.; Jordan, T.A.; Meister, M. Anticipation of moving stimuli by the retina. *Nature* **1999**, *398*, 334. [CrossRef] [PubMed]

Chou, P.Y.; Chien, J.F.; Chen, K.S.; Huang, Y.T.; Chen, C.C.; Chan, C. Anticipation and negative group delay in a retina. *Phys. Rev. E* **2021**, *103*, L020401. [CrossRef] [PubMed]

Vicsek, T.; Czirók, A.; Ben-Jacob, E.; Cohen, I.; Shochet, O. Novel type of phase transition in a system of self-driven particles. *Phys. Rev. Lett.* **1995**, *75*, 1226. [CrossRef] [PubMed]

Katz, Y.; Tunstrøm, K.; Ioannou, C.C.; Huepe, C.; Couzin, I.D. Inferring the structure and dynamics of interactions in schooling fish. *Proc. Natl. Acad. Sci. USA* **2011**, *108*, 18720–18725. [CrossRef]

Hlaváčková-Schindler, K.; Paluš, M.; Vejmelka, M.; Bhattacharya, J. Causality detection based on information—Theoretic approaches in time series analysis. *Phys. Rep.* **2007**, *441*, 1–46. [CrossRef]

Vastano, J.A.; Swinney, H.L. Information transport in spatiotemporal systems. *Phys. Rev. Lett.* **1988**, *60*, 1773. [CrossRef]

). Van der Walt, S.; Schönberger, J.L.; Nunez-Iglesias, J.; Boulogne, F.; Warner, J.D.; Yager, N.; Gouillart, E.; Yu, T. scikit-image: Image processing in Python. *PeerJ* **2014**, *2*, e453. [CrossRef]

1. Wiener, N. *Cybernetics or Control and Communication in the Animal and the Machine*; MIT Press: Cambridge, MA, USA , 2019.

2. Barnett, L.; Seth, A.K. The MVGC multivariate Granger causality toolbox: A new approach to Granger-causal inference. *J. Neurosci. Methods* **2014**, *223*, 50–68. [CrossRef] [PubMed]

3. San Liang, X. Unraveling the cause-effect relation between time series. *Phys. Rev. E* **2014**, *90*, 052150. [CrossRef] [PubMed]

4. Schreiber, T. Measuring information transfer. *Phys. Rev. Lett.* **2000**, *85*, 461. [CrossRef] [PubMed]

5. Moore, D.G.; Valentini, G.; Walker, S.I.; Levin, M. Inform: Efficient information-theoretic analysis of collective behaviors. *Front. Robot. AI* **2018**, *5*, 60. [CrossRef] [PubMed]

6. Wibral, M.; Vicente, R.; Lindner, M. Transfer entropy in neuroscience. In *Directed Information Measures in Neuroscience*; Springer: Berlin/Heidelberg, Germany, 2014; pp. 3–36.

7. Li, J.; Convertino, M. Inferring ecosystem networks as information flows. *Sci. Rep.* **2021**, *11*, 7094. [CrossRef] [PubMed]

8. Pearl, J. *Models, Reasoning and Inference*; Cambridge University Press: Cambridge, UK, 2000; Volume 19, p. 3.

9. Hyttinen, A.; Eberhardt, F.; Hoyer, P.O. Experiment selection for causal discovery. *J. Mach. Learn. Res.* **2013**, *14*, 3041–3071.

0. Zenil, H.; Kiani, N.A.; Tegnér, J. Low-algorithmic-complexity entropy-deceiving graphs. *Phys. Rev. E* **2017**, *96*, 012308. [CrossRef]

1. Hahs, D.W.; Pethel, S.D. Distinguishing anticipation from causality: Anticipatory bias in the estimation of information flow. *Phys. Rev. Lett.* **2011**, *107*, 128701. [CrossRef]

2. Porta, A.; Castiglioni, P.; Di Rienzo, M.; Bassani, T.; Bari, V.; Faes, L.; Nollo, G.; Cividjan, A.; Quintin, L. Cardiovascular control and time domain Granger causality: Insights from selective autonomic blockade. *Philos. Trans. R. Soc. A Math. Phys. Eng. Sci.* **2013**, *371*, 20120161. [CrossRef]

3. Gelpi, F.; Bari, V.; Cairo, B.; De Maria, B.; Tonon, D.; Rossato, G.; Faes, L.; Porta, A. Dynamic cerebrovascular autoregulation in patients prone to postural syncope: Comparison of techniques assessing the autoregulation index from spontaneous variability series. *Auton. Neurosci.* **2022**, *237*, 102920. [CrossRef]

4. Porta, A.; Catai, A.M.; Takahashi, A.C.; Magagnin, V.; Bassani, T.; Tobaldini, E.; Van De Borne, P.; Montano, N. Causal relationships between heart period and systolic arterial pressure during graded head-up tilt. *Am. J. Physiol.-Regul. Integr. Comp. Physiol.* **2011**, *300*, R378–R386. [CrossRef] [PubMed]

5. Nagy, M.; Akos, Z.; Biro, D.; Vicsek, T. Hierarchical group dynamics in pigeon flocks. *Nature* **2010**, *464*, 890. [CrossRef] [PubMed]

6. Bashirzade, A.A.; Zabegalov, K.N.; Volgin, A.D.; Belova, A.S.; Demin, K.A.; de Abreu, M.S.; Babchenko, V.Y.; Bashirzade, K.A.; Yenkoyan, K.B.; Tikhonova, M.A.; et al. Modeling neurodegenerative disorders in zebrafish. *Neurosci. Biobehav. Rev.* **2022**, *138*, 104679. [CrossRef] [PubMed]

entropy

MDPI

Article

Robust Model-Free Identification of the Causal Networks Underlying Complex Nonlinear Systems

Guanxue Yang [1,*], Shimin Lei [1] and Guanxiao Yang [2]

1 School of Electrical and Information Engineering, Jiangsu University, Zhenjiang 212013, China; 2222207067@stmail.ujs.edu.cn
2 College of Automation, Jiangsu University of Science and Technology, Zhenjiang 212100, China; dxxy@just.edu.cn
* Correspondence: gxyang@ujs.edu.cn

Abstract: Inferring causal networks from noisy observations is of vital importance in various fields. Due to the complexity of system modeling, the way in which universal and feasible inference algorithms are studied is a key challenge for network reconstruction. In this study, without any assumptions, we develop a novel model-free framework to uncover only the direct relationships in networked systems from observations of their nonlinear dynamics. Our proposed methods are termed multiple-order Polynomial Conditional Granger Causality (PCGC) and sparse PCGC (SPCGC). PCGC mainly adopts polynomial functions to approximate the whole system model, which can be used to judge the interactions among nodes through subsequent nonlinear Granger causality analysis. For SPCGC, Lasso optimization is first used for dimension reduction, and then PCGC is executed to obtain the final network. Specifically, the conditional variables are fused in this general, model-free framework regardless of their formulations in the system model, which could effectively reconcile the inference of direct interactions with an indirect influence. Based on many classical dynamical systems, the performances of PCGC and SPCGC are analyzed and verified. Generally, the proposed framework could be quite promising for the provision of certain guidance for data-driven modeling with an unknown model.

Keywords: model-free; data-driven; causal inference; Granger causality; nonlinear dynamics

1. Introduction

Grasping the structure and dynamics of a networked system is crucial for understanding the functionality and influence mechanisms of these systems, which could lay the foundation for better controlling complex networked systems. To date, advances in data science and machine learning have promoted the prosperity and development of network science. As is well known, networks are represented not only by their structures, but also by the dynamical information taking place on the structures. Network reconstruction, as an important aspect of research on complex networks, has attracted the attention of many researchers from various fields, including biological, electrical, physical, financial, and ecological sciences, the study of social networks, and so on [1–5]. Multidisciplinary studies have led to the emergence of technological means based on the understanding and analysis of big data. However, the transient evolution of real complex systems is often accompanied by high complexity and nonlinearity. There is, in actuality, a lack of unified physical models for dynamical processes from complex data, where the dynamical laws underlying the real systems are usually elusive. Hence, in view of the large amount of data and complex laws, data-driven modeling and causal discoveries from system dynamics are expected to play an important part in the era of big data.

Over the last decade, a great deal of methods have been developed to infer networks from observational datasets, such as ordinary differential equations, nonlinear dynamic modeling methods, similarity-based methods, Granger causality, and so on. Many of these methods suppose that a model of the system dynamics is known in advance. Based on predefined or known mathematical models, the identification of undetermined parameters or the inference of network topology is relatively easy [5–8]. The methods based on these models sometimes do not work well, as most related modeling assumptions and conditions may not be satisfied and may be unavailable in real experimental studies. In linear dynamic modeling, many methods for network reconstruction only adopt a linear model to fit the data. These methods only consider the dynamical evolution of complex systems under a linear ordinary differential equation [9,10]. If the dynamic trajectories of a system vary from transients toward steady states, some of the related methods could also involve a linear regression method based on the datasets of steady states [11]. In actuality, these linear modeling methods cannot satisfy the demands and characteristics of complex nonlinear networked systems. As such, an adaptive differentiation scheme and pre-filtration step were introduced to linear ordinary differential equations, in order to tackle the challenge of inferring large-scale complex nonlinear networks, and this method was able to outperform some current state-of-the-art methods [12]. However, there is still a great deal of work to be carried out on network inference for complex nonlinear systems.

For unknown complex dynamical systems, many nonlinear dynamic modeling methods have been presented, and the nonlinear forms are different for different applications. Specifically, some works—which intend to build spaces of all possible basis functions for the subsequent model selection with sparse-promoting methods, if such nonlinear system dynamics can be sparsely represented by the proposed basis functions—have developed a novel framework to identify a dynamical system governed by nonlinear equations [13–15]. Although these methods could resort to using some basic knowledge and information about the physical laws of specific systems, it is worth mentioning that the reasonable choice of the function basis is not always explicit. Another approach determines the topology of networks based on the assumption that the network dynamics are a combination of self-dynamics and coupling dynamics, the crucial idea of which is to approximate a node's self-dynamics and coupling dynamics with complete orthogonal bases (e.g., the Legendre or Chebyshev polynomials or the Fourier basis) [16]. Furthermore, a novel model-free inference method was posed as a multivariate regression problem by systematically decomposing each unit's dynamics into pairwise, three-point, and higher-order interactions with other units in the network, as well as by introducing an explicit dependency matrix in combination with a block-orthogonal regression algorithm [17]. However, it is inevitable that this method would also require the network dynamics to be additive among multiple-order interactions and, sometimes, the system's dynamical model will not be able to decompose combinations of multiple-order interacting items. Therefore, these types of assumptions are restricted to some real fields of science and engineering.

In addition, similarity-based indicators are the basis of some popular methods in statistical science, the basic theories and technologies of which are correlation coefficients, mutual information, transfer entropy, and so on. They are usually used to extrapolate the causality and correlation among datasets. For pairwise relationships, there exist correlation coefficients and mutual information for linear and nonlinear cases, respectively. However, these methods result in indirect links when the number of nodes increases. As such, partial mutual information and partial correlation coefficients, which are designed to silence indirect relationships through the influence of common external inputs induced by other nodes in the whole network, have been proposed for this purpose [18–20]. In addition, these correlation coefficient and mutual information methods are only designed based on the consideration of the correlation, which cannot be used for causal inference. Hence, transfer entropy based on information theory was developed to uncover causality using time series data. Transfer entropy was first proposed to find the nonlinear causal interactions between bivariate time series [21]. Then, conditional transfer entropy [22,23] was put forward to eliminate the indirect influence of other variables in the multivariate case. For information theory methods, when the dimension of the variable increases, the calculation of the probability density function becomes difficult and complicated. Moreover, when used for the general judgment of statistical dependencies, the ability of these similarity-based methods should be further improved for specialized fields.

As an equivalent companion of transfer entropy for Gaussian variables [24], Granger causality is another popular and powerful causality detection method that is usually designed to find the temporal interactions among time–course variables in complex multivariate systems [25–28]. As a heuristic statistical prediction concept based on the vector autoregressive (VAR) model, Granger causality was originally presented in econometrics with the aim of determining whether or not the past observations of a process help to predict the future values of another process [29]. Accordingly, conditional Granger causality was introduced to distinguish direct interactions from indirect ones [30]. Then, formulations of Granger causality in the frequency domain were proposed, such as directed transfer functions, partially directed coherence, and so on [31–33]. In order to deal with nonlinear relationships, some nonlinear Granger causality methods have also been proposed based on some kernel functions and copula theory, such as kernel Granger causality [34–36] and copula Granger causality [37].

In order to make up for the deficiency of current Granger causality methods, recent works on Granger causality are still at the forefront of scientific research on network inference [38–40]. Additionally, in order to deal with the problem of small sample sizes for large-scale networks, many sparse-promoting methods can be applied to traditional Granger causality methods, such as truncated Lasso Granger causality [41], grouped Lasso graphical Granger [42], and an improved backward conditional Granger causality (mBTSCGC) [43]. Direct comparisons of many penalized regression approaches have been extensively conducted to provide guidelines for further applications [44]. However, these sparse Granger causality methods are mainly proposed based on linear VAR models. For the consideration of nonlinear modeling, group Lasso nonlinear conditional Granger causality (GLasso-NCGC) was proposed for nonlinear causal inference [45], the nonlinear formulation of which is only for certain types of systems. As the nonlinear variant of mBTSCGC, rpCGCI was further proposed, where the mBTS scheme was applied to the polynomial VAR model for Granger causality inference [46]. However, rpCGCI only focuses on model formulation up to second-order polynomial products, and the second-order polynomial approximation is not sufficient for highly complex nonlinear systems. Furthermore, LASSO regression was used in a VAR framework and state-space model to compute the information dynamics [47]. Then, artificial neural networks (ANNs) were combined with state-space models for Granger causality analysis [48].

In this study, we put forward a new and unified framework for identifying causal networks and predicting nonlinear dynamics from noisy observational datasets in complex nonlinear systems. Rather than identifying parameters of complex systems governed by predefined and known models or taking some polynomial, rational, or other basis functions as prior information for the subsequent model selection, we first propose Granger causality based on the general nonlinear dynamical framework, which is termed Polynomial Conditonal Granger Causality (PCGC) and Sparse Polynomial Conditional Granger Causality (SPCGC); these not only consider the nonlinearity and causality of mutual interactions, but also reconcile the inference of direct interactions with the influence of indirect links. In particular, in our PCGC model, the polynomial approximation can be extended to multiple-order products for the demands of highly complex nonlinear systems, which are not limited to the second order. The network dynamics in our nonlinear framework are not simply additive between the self-dynamics and the coupling dynamics (pairwise, three-point, and other higher-order interactions among nodes in the network). We investigate our approach in many different types of complex nonlinear systems and verify the performance of several standard classical dynamical models, the system trajectories of which contain dynamical behaviors from transients towards steady states and from transients to periodic dynamics, in addition to non-periodic dynamical trajectories and chaotic dynamical trajectories. All of the simulation results demonstrate the effectiveness and robustness of the proposed method when there is a specific polynomial order and a proper size of observations.

2. Materials and Methods

2.1. Polynomial Conditional Granger Causality Model

The dynamical behavior of complex networked systems is governed by the interactions among a population of units (nodes). For each state variable in a complex system, the dynamical response or evolution is determined by the driving variables on the right side of the equation.

In general, nonlinear dynamical systems can be described using the following general differential equations:

$$\begin{cases} \dot{x}_1 = f_1(x_1, x_2, \ldots, x_n) \\ \dot{x}_2 = f_2(x_1, x_2, \ldots, x_n) \\ \quad\vdots \\ \dot{x}_n = f_n(x_1, x_2, \ldots, x_n) \end{cases}, \tag{1}$$

where x_i is the state variable and $i = 1, 2, \ldots, n$; n is the dimension of the system; $\dot{x}_i$ describes the time derivative of x_i; and the nonlinear function $f_i(\bullet)$ represents the dynamical law of the system.

In detail, for each target variable x_i, Equation (2) can be obtained as follows:

$$\dot{x}_i = f_i(x_1, x_2, \ldots, x_n). \tag{2}$$

Obviously, this is a unified manner of establishing a nonlinear framework for all complex networked systems. In order to investigate the causal relationship between the set of driving variables $\{x_1, x_2, \ldots, x_n\}$ and the target variable x_i, the exact identification of the nonlinear function $f_i(\bullet)$ is of crucial importance. Here, we use the r-th-order polynomial function to fit the nonlinear function $f_i(\bullet)$. Generally, the nonlinear function $f_i(x_1, x_2, \ldots, x_n)$ can consist of polynomials from the driving variable set $\{x_1, x_2, \ldots, x_n\}$. Then, $f_i(x_1, x_2, \ldots, x_n)$ can be denoted as shown in Equation (3).

$$\begin{aligned} f_i(x_1, x_2, \ldots, x_n) &= \mathbf{\Phi}\mathbf{a}_i \\ &= \sum_{k_1, k_2, \ldots, k_n} a_{k_1, k_2, \ldots, k_n} x_1^{k_1} x_2^{k_2} \cdots x_n^{k_n}, \end{aligned} \tag{3}$$

where $\mathbf{\Phi}$ is a vector of polynomial basis; $\mathbf{a}_i$ is an unknown parameter; $\{k_1, k_2, \ldots, k_n\} \subset \mathbb{N}$; and $k_1 + k_2 + \cdots + k_n \leq r$. r is the order of the polynomial. In detail, the candidate function library $\mathbf{\Phi}$ can be expressed as follows:

$$\mathbf{\Phi} = \begin{bmatrix} 1 & \mathbf{x}^{p_1} & \mathbf{x}^{p_2} & \mathbf{x}^{p_3} & \cdots & \mathbf{x}^{p_r} \end{bmatrix}, \tag{4}$$

where $\mathbf{x}^{p_r}$ can be taken to obtain the r-th-order polynomial, which includes the set of r-th-order monomials relating to $\{x_1, x_2, \ldots, x_n\}$. Here, $\mathbf{x}^{p_r}$ is defined as the r-th-order polynomial vector. For example, the first-order vector and the second-order vector can be described as follows:

$$\begin{aligned} \mathbf{x}^{p_1} &= \begin{bmatrix} x_1 & x_2 & \cdots & x_n \end{bmatrix}, \\ \mathbf{x}^{p_2} &= \begin{bmatrix} x_1^2 & x_1x_2 & \cdots & x_1x_n & x_2^2 & x_2x_3 & \cdots & x_n^2 \end{bmatrix}. \end{aligned}$$

Other higher-order polynomial vectors (e.g., $\mathbf{x}^{p_3}$, $\mathbf{x}^{p_4}$, etc.) can be expressed similarly. As shown in Equation (4), when the polynomial order r is given, $\mathbf{\Phi}$ includes all related polynomial items whose order is less than or equal to r.

Next, based on the theory of Granger causality, our nonlinear causal index is proposed for a nonlinear dynamical system as follows. For Equation (2), the complete set of all variables in the system is denoted as $\Gamma = \{x_1, x_2, \ldots, x_n\}$. For each target variable x_i, the unrestricted model can be described as shown in Equation (5).

$$\dot{x}_i = f_i(\Gamma) + \xi_i. \tag{5}$$

In order to judge which driving variable x_j in Γ causally influences the target variable x_i, the restricted model can be written as shown in Equation (6).

$$\dot{x}_i = f_i(\Gamma \backslash x_j) + \xi_j, \tag{6}$$

where $\Gamma \backslash x_j$ means removing the variable x_j in Γ, i.e., $\Gamma \backslash x_j = \{x_1, x_2, \ldots, x_{j-1}, x_{j+1}, \ldots, x_n\}$. Accordingly, for the nonlinear function $f_i(\Gamma \backslash x_j)$, all relevant items of x_j in $f_i(\Gamma)$ are removed. Then, the residual ξ_i of the unrestricted model and the residual ξ_j of the restricted model are calculated. In this case, it is worth noting that the inference of the causal relationship between x_j and x_i is conditioned on the set of other nodes in the network $\Gamma \backslash x_j$, which is designed to silence the indirect relationships through the influence of common external inputs induced by other nodes in the entire network. The conditional variables are not just explicitly added to the driving variable, but they are latently integrated into the nonlinear function, which has already involved the driving variable.

Finally, the nonlinear causal index (PCGC) is calculated as follows:

$$\mathbf{PCGC}_{x_j \to x_i} = \ln \frac{\sigma_j^2}{\sigma_i^2}, \tag{7}$$

where σ_i^2 and σ_j^2 are the variances in error ξ_i and ξ_j, respectively. Generally, if PCGC is greater than the given threshold value δ, this confirms that x_j causes x_i, i.e., there exists a link $x_j \to x_i$.

In theory, an unrestricted model with more parameters will always be able to fit the data at least as well as a restricted model with fewer parameters. So, an unrestricted model with lower error will result in a better fit to the data than a restricted model. Meanwhile, in order to determine whether the unrestricted model gives a significantly better fit to the data, the F-statistic hypothesis is taken when obtaining the final network. The F-statistic value should be smaller than the given significance level P_{val}. The formulation of the F-statistic hypothesis is defined as

$$F = \frac{\left(||\xi_i||^2 - ||\xi_j||^2\right) / (n_i - n_j)}{||\xi_i||^2 / (n_i - M)}, \tag{8}$$

where $||\xi_i||^2$ and $||\xi_j||^2$ are the residual sums of squares in the unrestricted model and the restricted model, respectively. n_i and n_j are the total numbers of parameters in the unrestricted and restricted models, respectively. M is the number of observations.

In order to determine the interactions among variables in the system, all of the time histories of state variables x_i $(i = 1, 2, \ldots, n)$ are collected, and the derivatives $\dot{x}_i$ can be measured directly or approximated using several methods, such as the Euler and Runge–Kutta methods.

Furthermore, suppose that the data are sampled several times, and T time points are obtained at each measurement. The state matrix $\mathbf{X}$ and derivative matrix $\dot{\mathbf{X}}$ are collected as follows:

$$\dot{\mathbf{X}} = \begin{bmatrix} \dot{x}_{1,1} & \dot{x}_{2,1} & \cdots & \dot{x}_{n,1} \\ \dot{x}_{1,2} & \dot{x}_{2,2} & \cdots & \dot{x}_{n,2} \\ \vdots & \vdots & \ddots & \vdots \\ \dot{x}_{1,T} & \dot{x}_{2,T} & \cdots & \dot{x}_{n,T} \end{bmatrix} \quad and \quad \mathbf{X} = \begin{bmatrix} x_{1,1} & x_{2,1} & \cdots & x_{n,1} \\ x_{1,2} & x_{2,2} & \cdots & x_{n,2} \\ \vdots & \vdots & \ddots & \vdots \\ x_{1,T} & x_{2,T} & \cdots & x_{n,T} \end{bmatrix},$$

where $x_{i,t}$ denotes the data point of x_i that is sampled at moment t, and $\dot{x}_{i,t}$ denotes the value of the derivative $\dot{x}_i$ that is measured or estimated at moment t.

Sometimes, in order to ensure a variety of datasets, multiple measurements are carried out under different conditions (random initial values, adding perturbations, removing nodes, etc.). Here, the number of multiple measurements is set to m. Then, the total number of observations is set to $M = mT$. Then, data matrices ($\dot{\mathbf{X}}$ and $\mathbf{X}$) with $M \times n$ are collected, i.e.,

$$\dot{\mathbf{X}} = \begin{bmatrix} \dot{\mathbf{X}}^{[1]} \\ \dot{\mathbf{X}}^{[2]} \\ \vdots \\ \dot{\mathbf{X}}^{[m]} \end{bmatrix} \quad and \quad \mathbf{X} = \begin{bmatrix} \mathbf{X}^{[1]} \\ \mathbf{X}^{[2]} \\ \vdots \\ \mathbf{X}^{[m]} \end{bmatrix},$$

where, at the m-th measurement, $\dot{\mathbf{X}}^{[m]}$ and $\mathbf{X}^{[m]}$ are denoted as

$$\dot{\mathbf{X}}^{[m]} = \begin{bmatrix} \dot{x}_{1,1}^{[m]} & \dot{x}_{2,1}^{[m]} & \cdots & \dot{x}_{n,1}^{[m]} \\ \dot{x}_{1,2}^{[m]} & \dot{x}_{2,2}^{[m]} & \cdots & \dot{x}_{n,2}^{[m]} \\ \vdots & \vdots & \ddots & \vdots \\ \dot{x}_{1,T}^{[m]} & \dot{x}_{2,T}^{[m]} & \cdots & \dot{x}_{n,T}^{[m]} \end{bmatrix} \quad and \quad \mathbf{X}^{[m]} = \begin{bmatrix} x_{1,1}^{[m]} & x_{2,1}^{[m]} & \cdots & x_{n,1}^{[m]} \\ x_{1,2}^{[m]} & x_{2,2}^{[m]} & \cdots & x_{n,2}^{[m]} \\ \vdots & \vdots & \ddots & \vdots \\ x_{1,T}^{[m]} & x_{2,T}^{[m]} & \cdots & x_{n,T}^{[m]} \end{bmatrix}.$$

Next, for the target variable x_i, the matrix formulation of Equation (2) is shown in Equation (9).

$$\dot{\mathbf{X}}_i = f(\mathbf{X}) = \mathbf{\Theta}\mathbf{a}_i + \Xi_i, \tag{9}$$

where $\dot{\mathbf{X}}_i = \begin{bmatrix} \dot{x}_{i,1}^{[1]} & \cdots & \dot{x}_{i,T}^{[1]} & \cdots & \dot{x}_{i,1}^{[m]} & \cdots & \dot{x}_{i,T}^{[m]} \end{bmatrix}^{\mathrm{T}}$ is the i-th column of $\dot{\mathbf{X}}$, which corresponds to the derivative data of variable i. $\mathbf{\Theta}$ is a nonlinear data matrix under the polynomial basis $\mathbf{\Phi}$. $\mathbf{a}_i$ is the coefficient to be solved. Ξ_i is the vector of the model error.

Taking a Lorenz oscillator system as an example, a flowchart of Polynomial Conditional Granger Causality based on the results of a simulation of this classical chaotic system is illustrated in Figure 1. Firstly, a benchmark network is obtained from the equation of the Lorenz oscillator system for comparison. In order to obtain the inferred network, the identification of the whole network is decomposed into the selection of neighbors for each target node. For example, to investigate the relationship of x with all of the variables in the system (a self-loop is also considered), unrestricted and restricted regression models are jointly constructed. In detail, to explore the impact of the driving variable y on the target variable x, an unrestricted model of the complete space of polynomials in (x, y, z) and a restricted model of the subspace of polynomials in (x, z) are constructed. The corresponding dynamic trajectories of x predicted by the unrestricted model in (x, y, z) and the restricted model in (x, z) are illustrated. From the errors of regression (r_{xyz} and r_{xz}), we find that the accuracy of curve fitting decreases when the past information of y is excluded. Hence, the causal inference from y to x ($y \rightarrow x$) is found. Similarly, the corresponding dynamic trajectories of x predicted by the restricted model in (y, z) and (x, y) are also plotted. The accuracy sharply decreases when the past information of x is removed. In this case, the self-loop of x is inferred. However, high accuracy is also obtained without the past information of z, which means that z is not the cause of x. So, a subnetwork relating to target node x is formed. In the same way, the entire network is obtained, and the Granger causal strength is marked on each link by calculating the nonlinear causal index. Meanwhile, the P_{val} matrix is obtained based on the F-statistic test. The significance level P_{val} is found to be 10^{-10}. In Figure 1, we find that the inferred network perfectly matches the benchmark network, with high causal strength and high confidence.

2.2. Sparse Polynomial Conditional Granger Causality

In general, the classical least squares method can be used to deal with Equations (5) and (6). However, the solution procedure for these equations may be problematic and inexact when the number of nonlinear basis functions is larger than the number of available observations. In fact, typically, not all basis function terms can influence the target variable. Most equations of real systems are governed by only a few relevant terms (or variables) that define the dynamical behaviors of target variables, which makes the system equations sparse in a high-dimensional space of a nonlinear basis function, especially for large networked systems. Actually, the consideration of all of the basis functions (including other unrelated terms) may lead to the deterioration of prediction performance in the whole system. In this case, Sparse Polynomial Conditional Granger Causality (SPCGC) is proposed, a flowchart of which is shown in Figure 2 based on the results of the simulation of a Lorenz 96 system with $N = 10$ nodes. A benchmark network is obtained from the system model. Both the area under the receiver operating characteristic curve (AUROC) and the area under the precision–recall curve (AUPR) are utilized as standard metrics for evaluation.

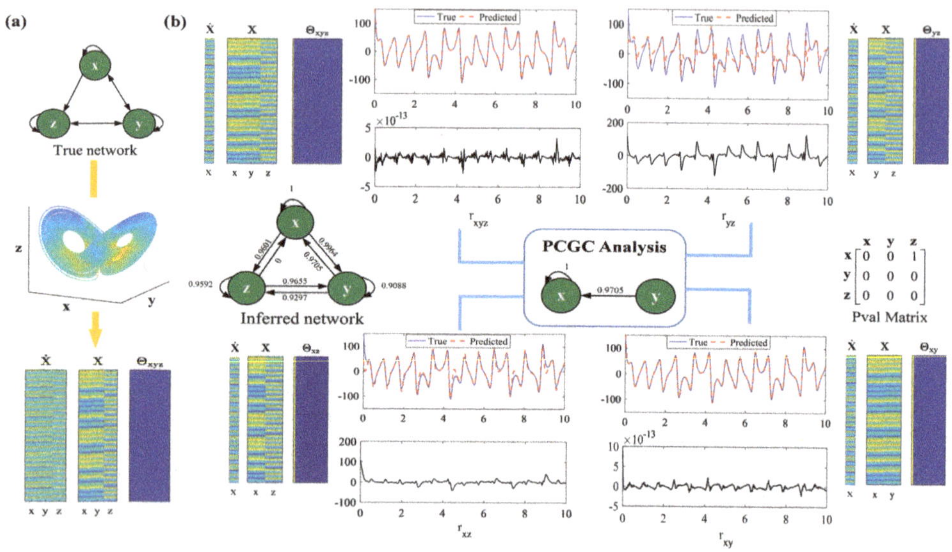

Figure 1. A flowchart of Polynomial Conditional Granger Causality based on the results of a simulation of a Lorenz oscillator system. (**a**) Datasets ($\mathbf{X}$ and $\dot{\mathbf{X}}$) are generated from the Lorenz system equations. The noise strength σ is set to zero. Here, $m = 1$ and $T = 2000$; that is, data are collected from the interval $t \in [0, 20]$ with the time step $\Delta t = 0.01$. $\mathbf{\Theta}$ is a nonlinear data matrix with the polynomial basis $\mathbf{\Phi}$. The unrestricted model of the Lorenz system is initially constructed in the complete space of polynomials in (x, y, z) up to the fifth order, and the corresponding nonlinear data matrix is $\mathbf{\Theta}_{xyz}$. (**b**) For the target variable x, the derivative vector $\dot{\mathbf{x}}$ is arranged to be the output variable of both the unrestricted model and the restricted model. Then, three restricted models are obtained to judge which driving variable causally influences the target variable. In detail, the restricted models of the system are constructed in the subspace of polynomials in (y, z), (x, z), and (x, y) up to the fifth order. The corresponding nonlinear data matrixes are $\mathbf{\Theta}_{yz}$, $\mathbf{\Theta}_{xz}$, and $\mathbf{\Theta}_{xy}$, respectively. The dynamic trajectories of x in different cases are plotted, and the respective errors of prediction are analyzed. The Lorenz oscillator system is shown in Equation (A1) in Appendix A.

The process of SPCGC can be divided into two steps. Datasets ($\dot{\mathbf{X}}$ and $\mathbf{X}$) are generated from the system model. Based on the datasets of $\mathbf{X}$ and the polynomial order r, a nonlinear data matrix $\mathbf{\Theta}$ is obtained with the candidate basis function library $\mathbf{\Phi}$. For each target variable i, the regression model underlying the derivative $\dot{\mathbf{X}}_i$ and nonlinear data matrix $\mathbf{\Theta}$ is first formulated, and the coefficient $\mathbf{a}_i$ of this can be solved using the sparse optimization shown in Equation (10).

$$\hat{\mathbf{a}}_i = \arg\min_{\mathbf{a}_i} \left(\|\dot{\mathbf{X}}_i - \mathbf{\Theta}\mathbf{a}_i\|_2^2 + \lambda \|\mathbf{a}_i\|_1 \right), \tag{10}$$

where λ is a sparse penalty parameter. Based on the results of Equation (10), the basis function terms corresponding to the nonzero elements in the vector of coefficient $\mathbf{a}_i$ are fetched to form a new set of basis functions. Then, we obtain the candidate variable sets for each $\dot{\mathbf{X}}_i$ according to the new set of basis functions. Next, we rearrange $\mathbf{\Theta}$ with the candidate variable sets, which are expressed as the new nonlinear data matrix Θ_i', and reform the regression model of the PCGC model. Finally, we execute Granger causality analysis with the F-test in terms of the given significance level and confirm the causal variables of the target variable i. Another subnetwork can be inferred in a similar way. As a result, the whole network can be identified. The detailed procedure of the SPCGC algorithm can be illustrated as follows.

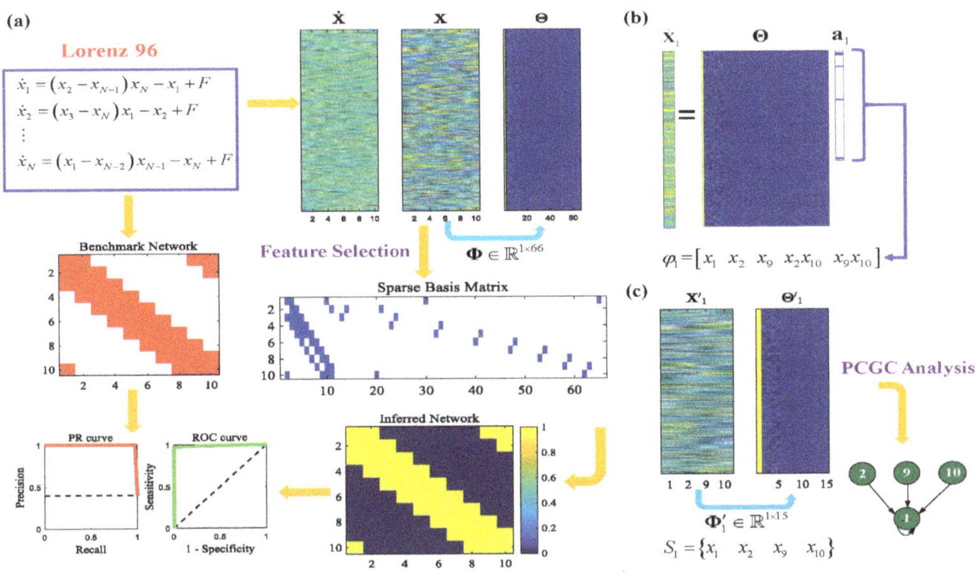

Figure 2. A flowchart of Sparse Polynomial Conditional Granger Causality based on the results of the simulation of a Lorenz 96 system with $N = 10$. Here, $m = 300$, $T = 3$, $r = 2$, $\lambda = 0.001$, and $P_{val} = 10^{-10}$. (**a**) Datasets ($\dot{\mathbf{X}}$ and $\mathbf{X}$) are generated from the Lorenz 96 system. Based on $\mathbf{X}$, Θ under $\Phi \in \mathbb{R}^{1\times 66}$ is obtained. Then, feature selection based on sparse optimization is executed to select the contributing items in Φ, and a sparse basis matrix is acquired. Next, with the analysis of PCGC, the inferred network is compared with the benchmark network in terms of the PR and ROC curves. (**b**) Taking node no. 1 as an example, the regression equation underlying $\dot{\mathbf{X}}_1$ and Θ is solved through sparse optimization. The nonzero elements in the vector of coefficient $\mathbf{a}_1$ are fetched to form φ_1. (**c**) Then, the corresponding set of nodes S_1 is refined. Based on S_1, a nonlinear data matrix Θ_1' is obtained from $\mathbf{X}_1'$ with the new basis function library $\Phi_1' \in \mathbb{R}^{1\times 15}$. The new regression equation underlying $\dot{\mathbf{X}}_1$ and Θ_1' is constructed. As a result, the final subnetwork of node no. 1 is judged using the PCGC analysis.

Step 1: Based on Equation (2), a feature selection method is first used to select the columns of Θ for dimensionality reduction. Actually, this is equivalent to selecting the candidate set of polynomial items from Φ. Here, the feature selection method is formulated based on the Lasso optimization in Equation (10). The candidate set of polynomial items C corresponds to the nonzero elements in the vector of coefficient $\mathbf{a}_i$.

Step 2: Based on the candidate set of polynomial items C, the corresponding driving variables are denoted as D_j, $j = 1, 2, \ldots, K$, where K is the number of driving variables fetched from C. The polynomial items related to D_j in C are denoted as C^{D_j}.

Step 3: Based on the set of driving variables $D = \{D_1, D_2, \ldots, D_K\}$, the corresponding unrestricted model can be reformulated. For each target variable x_i, let $\mathbf{y}_i = \dot{\mathbf{X}}_i$; the corresponding unrestricted model is shown in Equation (11).

$$\mathbf{y}_i = \Theta_D \mathbf{a}_i + \Xi_i, \tag{11}$$

where $\mathbf{\Theta}_D$ is the nonlinear data matrix with the polynomial basis of driving variables D. Then, the residual Ξ_i can be calculated as follows:

$$\Xi_i = \mathbf{y}_i - \mathbf{\Theta}_D \mathbf{\Theta}_D^{\dagger} \mathbf{y}_i, \tag{12}$$

where the pseudo-inverse $\mathbf{\Theta}_D^{\dagger} = \left(\mathbf{\Theta}_D^{\mathrm{T}} \mathbf{\Theta}_D\right)^{-1} \mathbf{\Theta}_D^{\mathrm{T}}$.

Step 4: Then, the restricted model should be formulated as shown in Equation (13).

$$\mathbf{y}_i = \mathbf{\Theta}_{D \backslash D_j} \mathbf{a}'_i + \Xi'_i, \tag{13}$$

where $D \backslash D_j = \{D_1, D_2, \ldots, D_{j-1}, D_{j+1}, \ldots, D_K\}$, and $D \backslash D_j$ means removing all of the related polynomial items C^{D_j} in the candidate set C. Then, $\mathbf{\Theta}_{D \backslash D_j}$ is constructed based on the basis $C^{D \backslash D_j}$. So, for each D_j, the residual Ξ'_i can be calculated as follows:

$$\Xi'_i = \mathbf{y}_i - \mathbf{\Theta}_{D \backslash D_j} \mathbf{\Theta}_{D \backslash D_j}^{\dagger} \mathbf{y}_i, \tag{14}$$

where the pseudo-inverse $\mathbf{\Theta}_{D \backslash D_j}^{\dagger} = \left(\mathbf{\Theta}_{D \backslash D_j}^{\mathrm{T}} \mathbf{\Theta}_{D \backslash D_j}\right)^{-1} \mathbf{\Theta}_{D \backslash D_j}^{\mathrm{T}}$.

Step 5: In order to judge the causal relationship between node D_j and node i, the PCGC index is calculated as follows:

$$PCGC_{D_j \to x_i} = \ln \frac{\sigma^2(\Xi'_i)}{\sigma^2(\Xi_i)}. \tag{15}$$

If $\sigma^2(\Xi'_i) > \sigma^2(\Xi_i)$, i.e., removing the effect of D_j will increase the error variance of the prediction of x_i, there exists a link $D_j \to x_i$. A positive threshold $0 < \delta < 1$ can be set for the extraction of causal links with larger Granger causal weights. In addition, F-statistic tests can be performed to confirm the significance level for each link.

2.3. Selection of the Polynomial Order r and Sparse Penalty Parameter λ

As is well known, for the determination of models that provide better predictions, overfitting and generalization are critical factors for judging which model performs better. Cross-validation and regularization are two classical ways of restraining the complexity of a model. In our work, the performance of our proposed methods (PCGC and SPCGC) is also based on the selection of the following parameters: the polynomial order r and the sparse penalty parameter λ, respectively. Although these parameters can be selected according to practical experience, an automatic selection scheme should be introduced and analyzed.

For PCGC, in order to ensure the fitting precision of nonlinear system equations and avoid overfitting, a proper polynomial order r is vital for dynamical prediction and Granger causality analysis. Here, K-fold cross-validation is adopted. Firstly, a cross-validation partition is created for data, and this can be used to define a specified size of training sets and test sets for validating the effectiveness of a statistical model based on cross-validation. In detail, all M observations are divided into K disjoint subsamples (folds) using a random partition with a roughly equal size. Then, through randomly repeated cross-validations, we minimize the cost function of the error to determine the best model.

In addition, for the simulation of SPCGC, the selection of the sparse penalty parameter λ in the regularization is important. Here, the Hannan–Quinn criterion (HQC) [49] can be used for the selection of the sparse penalty parameter. In detail, the HQC is adopted to balance the model complexity and model accuracy and to seek the best model's ability to describe datasets. For our case, based on the basic idea of the HQC, its detailed definition for the selection of λ is shown as follows:

$$HQC(\lambda) = \ln\left|\sigma_\lambda^2\right| + \frac{2n_\lambda \ln(\ln M)}{M}, \tag{16}$$

where M is the size of the data, n_λ is the number of variables, and σ_λ^2 is the variance in the error. n_λ and σ_λ^2 can be computed for each value of λ to search for the optimal solution.

3. Results

In order to verify the performance of our proposed methods, different nonlinear system models were collected and employed, including dynamical trajectories displaying transients towards steady states, dynamical trajectories exhibiting transients toward periodic dynamics, non-periodic dynamical trajectories, and chaotic dynamical trajectories [17].

These different nonlinear systems were categorized and verified according to their different types of dynamical trajectories. For dynamical trajectories from transients towards steady states, we employed a gene regulation network model with Michaelis Menten kinetics [50] and a metabolic network model (yeast glycolysis) [15]. For dynamical trajectories from transients to periodic dynamics, we simulated another two biological models: another metabolic network model (glycolytic oscillator) [13,17,51–53] and a biochemical reaction network model [14]. For non-periodic dynamical trajectories, we adopted two networked models: a Kuramoto oscillator and a phase-coupled oscillator [17]. For chaotic dynamical trajectories, we tested the Lorenz oscillator system and Rössler oscillator system. To verify the reconstruction performance of the larger networks, we also utilized the Lorenz 96 networked system. All of the system models are described in Appendix A.

3.1. Detailed Case Description of PCGC: Glycolytic Oscillator Network

In this section, we consider the inference of a metabolic network based on the glycolytic oscillator model. The complex formulations of the equations in this model are composed of constant, polynomial, and fractional terms. This is a classical benchmark problem for model prediction, automatic inference, and system identification. The glycolytic oscillator model is set to describe the dynamical behavior of metabolic networks. Accelerating the inference of metabolic networks would aid interventions in metabolic diseases.

First, to illustrate the effectiveness of our proposed PCGC method in the case of dynamical trajectories from transients to periodic dynamics, the following simulation is based on the nonlinear dynamical equations of a glycolytic oscillator with $n = 7$ nodes (variables). In Figure 3a, a benchmark adjacency matrix and a directed graph are drawn from the given equations of the system model. For the adjacency matrix, the red squares are existent links among nodes, and the white areas are nonexistent links.

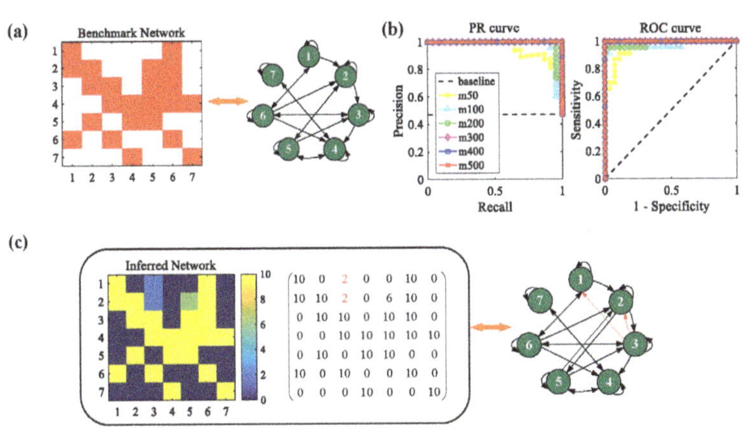

Figure 3. Simulation results for the glycolytic oscillator model. Here, $T = 2$, $r = 5$, $P_{val} = 10^{-10}$, and $\sigma = 0.01$. (**a**) Benchmark network together with the corresponding directed graph. (**b**) The curves of the ROC and PR with different numbers of samples. (**c**) Discovery rate matrix inferred from 10 realizations and the corresponding directed graph.

Then, synthetic datasets are derived, the related parameters of which in the simulation are shown in Figure 3. In Figure 3b, the curves of the ROC and PR are plotted with different numbers of observations. Here, the number of time points $T = 2$ is kept unchanged, and the number of measurements is taken from the set $m = \{50, 100, 200, 300, 400, 500\}$. We can see that the values of the AUROC and AUPR are relatively lower when $m = 50$. As m increases, the performance becomes better and better, and perfect reconstruction is realized when $m = \{300, 400, 500\}$. Next, the performance of robust estimation with noise is investigated. The Gaussian noise variance is set to $\sigma = 0.01$. In this case, multiple realizations are carried out, and the number of realizations is set to 10. Based on the PCGC analysis with $P_{val} = 10^{-10}$, the final network is inferred. In Figure 3c, the discovery rate matrix inferred from 10 realizations in the glycolytic oscillator model is demonstrated (the discovery rate means the total number of links that are rightly discovered over multiple realizations). It is obvious that the true positive links are always found, except for link $5 \to 2$, which has a 60% discovery rate. Meanwhile, there are two false positive links with a 20% discovery rate ($3 \to 1$ and $3 \to 2$). In Figure 3c the final directed graph is plotted from the discovery rate matrix, where the thickness of the line indicates the value of the discovery rate. In general, the results as a whole demonstrate the robust performance of the PCGC method.

3.2. Comparison of PCGC and SPCGC: Gene Regulatory Network

As mentioned above, PCGC is a method based on a nonlinear regression model. If the number of nonlinear basis functions is greater than the number of observations, the regression equation for Granger causality analysis is an underdetermined problem, and the exact solution will not be obtained. In order to verify the validity and necessity of SPCGC, a comparison between PCGC and SPCGC is made by executing a simulation of a gene regulatory dynamical system with Michaelis Menten kinetics. We first apply our proposed methods to reconstruct a gene regulatory network with $N = 10$ nodes. The generation of a benchmark network follows the mechanism using an approximate power-law output degree distribution with an average degree of $\langle k \rangle = 3$. Then, synthetic datasets with $M = mT$ observations are obtained. Here, the time points are kept unchanged at each measurement ($T = 2$). In order to investigate how the number of observations influences the performance of our method, the number of multiple measurements m is set to 400 and 700. Other related parameters are given as follows: Gaussian noise strength $\sigma = 0.01$, the polynomial order $r = 5$, and the sparse penalty parameter $\lambda = 0.001$.

In Figure 4a, the Granger causality matrixes of PCGC and SPCGC are demonstrated in the cases of $M = 1400$ and $M = 800$ observations, respectively. With adequate observations ($M = 1400$), the two methods could find all existent links, especially the existent links in the Granger causality matrix of SPCGC with a higher causal strength. For PCGC, compared with SPCGC, the causal strength of many existent links is relatively smaller. Meanwhile, all of the nonexistent links have a small causal strength, which can be eliminated by setting a specific threshold. In this case, both PCGC and SPCGC can achieve a perfect reconstruction. With insufficient observations ($M = 800$), PCGC obviously loses its function in reconstructing the network, as all of the links in the Granger causality matrix of PCGC have a high causal strength. However, although there are a few nonexistent links with slight causal intensity, SPCGC still maintains a good performance. In the following section, the performance of robust estimation with different numbers of samples is explored. Robust estimation is verified by running over 10 realizations. In particular, the elements in the Granger causality matrixes reconstructed using PCGC and SPCGC methods over 10 realizations are exhibited in Figure 4b. As shown in Figure 4b, both PCGC and SPCGC achieve perfect reconstruction when $M = 1400$. The existent links and nonexistent links can be divided using a given threshold. When $M = 800$, we find that PCGC largely mixes existent links with nonexistent links. This is short of a certain threshold for distinguishing existent links from nonexistent links. However, in this case, an almost perfect separation by SPCGC can also be seen when the number of samples is smaller than the number of nonlinear basis functions. The average values (standard deviations) of the AUROC and

AUPR over 10 realizations are computed and shown in Figure 4c. Overall, it is worth emphasizing that SPCGC demonstrates perfect performance with different numbers of observations, even when the number of samples is smaller than the number of nonlinear basis functions, i.e., the regression equation is underdetermined.

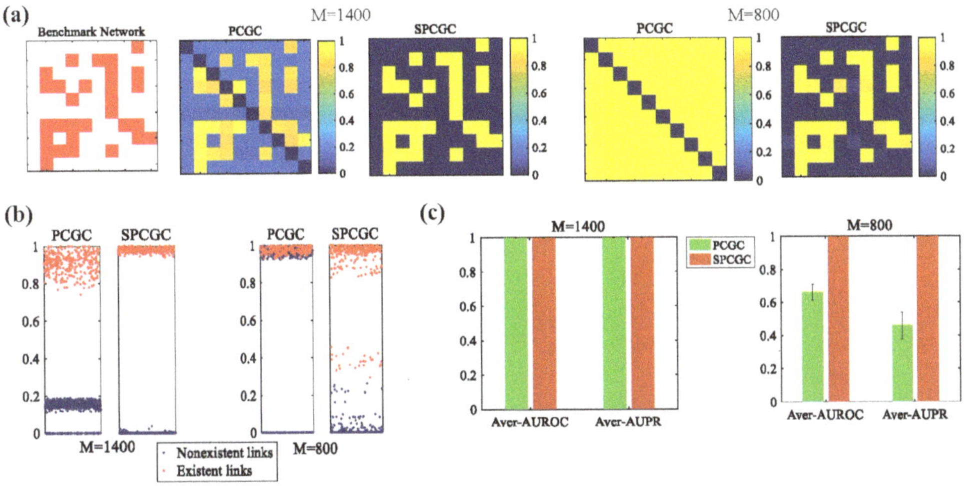

Figure 4. Simulation results for the comparison of PCGC and SPCGC in different cases by using $M = 1400$ and $M = 800$ observations. (**a**) The benchmark network of a gene regulation network with $N = 10$ nodes and the Granger causality index matrixes obtained by using $M = 1400$ and $M = 800$ observations. (**b**) Granger causality indexes of reconstructed elements in the matrixes recovered using PCGC and SPCGC over 10 realizations. (**c**) The average values with standard deviations of the AUROC and AUPR over 10 realizations.

3.3. Robust Results of Classical Models in Different Cases

To further assess the performance of our proposed method, both the AUROC and the AUPR were utilized to evaluate our proposed method in different classical models. These models include a biochemical reaction network, glycolytic oscillator network, yeast glycolysis network, gene regulatory network, Kuramoto oscillator network, and phase-coupled oscillator network, as well as the Lorenz 96, Lorenz, and Rössler networks.

Firstly, the simulation of different models with different numbers of observations was carried out. The detailed parameter settings of the simulations of these different models for different numbers of observations are shown in Table 1, and they include m, T, σ, and r. The values of the average AUROC and average AUPR were computed by averaging over 10 independent realizations. In detail, the inference results of different models under different conditions were explored. The different conditions involve only one parameter being changed while the others are kept the same. In Table 1, the "-" sign means that these parameters vary in the simulations. Here, a different number of observations (m or T) is used for detailed comparisons, and the specific ranges of values are shown in Figure 5. As is known, most of the benchmark network topologies can be derived from system models, except for the gene regulatory network, Kuramoto oscillator network, and phase-coupled oscillator network. The network topologies of these three models should be given in advance as the benchmark networks. Here, the preset topology follows the scale-free generative mechanism, in which the output degree of the network approximates a popular power-law degree distribution with $N = 10$ and $\langle k \rangle = 3$. For the PCGC method, the simulation results of different models with different numbers of observations are shown in Figure 5. As shown in Figure 5, the performance trend rises overall with the increase in the number of samples. As we have seen, with a certain number of samples, nearly perfect reconstruction is realized.

Table 1. Parametric settings of simulations of different models with different numbers of observations. Among these parameters, m is the number of measurements, T is the number of time points at each measurement, σ is the strength of Gaussian noise, and r is the polynomial order. Based on m and T, the total number of observations M is collected ($M = mT$). The "-" sign means that parameters vary in the simulations.

Model	m	T	σ	r
Lorenz oscillator	1	-	0.01	5
Rössler oscillator	1	-	0.01	5
Lorenz 96	-	2	0.01	4
Biochemical reaction network	-	2	0.01	4
Glycolytic oscillator	-	2	0.01	5
Yeast glycolysis	-	2	0.01	5
Gene regulatory network	-	2	0.01	4
Kuramoto oscillator	-	2	0.01	4
Phase-coupled oscillator	-	2	0.01	4

Next, in order to further address the robustness to uncertainties in data, a simulation with different noise intensities σ should be considered for the further verification of PCGC. The simulation results of different models at different noise intensities σ are shown in Figure 6. All of the values of the AUROC and AUPR are averaged over 10 realizations. The related parametric settings of the simulations in Figure 6 are listed in Table 2. The values of m, T, and r are fixed, while σ is taken from the set $\{0.01; 0.05; 0.1; 0.5; 1\}$. With the increase in σ, the performance of PCGC on these classical system models is generally stable, except for the gene regulation network and Rössler oscillator system. In the simulation of the gene regulation network and Rössler oscillator, the performance of PCGC goes down quite sharply with the increase in σ, especially for the gene regulation network. For the Kuramoto oscillator, phase-coupled oscillator, Lorenz oscillator, and Lorenz 96 model, both the average AUROC and average AUPR of PCGC over 10 realizations basically stay at the maximum value, which indicates that PCGC has strong robustness in the case of different values of σ. For the biochemical reaction network, glycolytic oscillator network, and yeast glycolysis network, the performance of PCGC slightly decreases when σ is high. In general, the robustness of PCGC is demonstrated in the case of different values of σ.

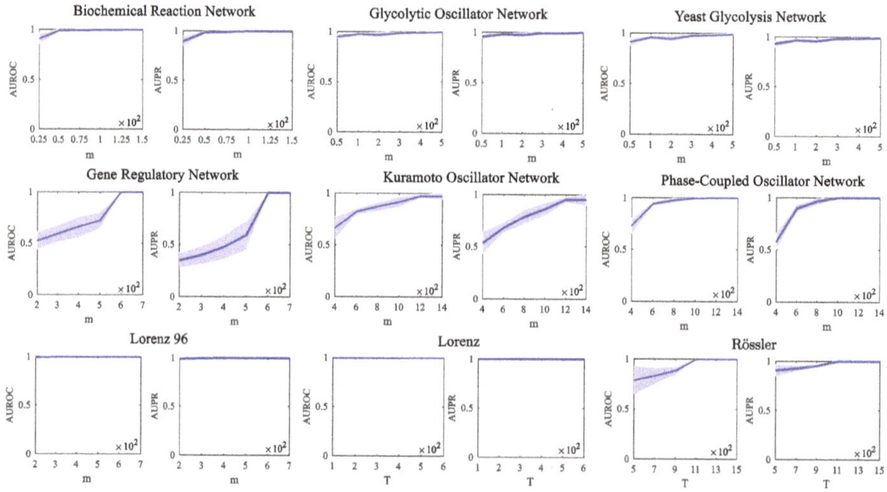

Figure 5. Simulation results of different models with different numbers of observations (m or T). All of the values of the AUROC and AUPR are averaged over 10 realizations. The blue-shaded area is the error bound of the AUROC or AUPR over 10 realizations.

Table 2. Parametric settings of simulations of different models with different noise intensities σ.

Model	m	T	σ	r
Lorenz oscillator	1	600	$\{0.01; 0.05; 0.1; 0.5; 1\}$	5
Rössler oscillator	1	1500	$\{0.01; 0.05; 0.1; 0.5; 1\}$	5
Lorenz 96	700	2	$\{0.01; 0.05; 0.1; 0.5; 1\}$	4
Biochemical reaction network	150	2	$\{0.01; 0.05; 0.1; 0.5; 1\}$	4
Glycolytic oscillator	500	2	$\{0.01; 0.05; 0.1; 0.5; 1\}$	5
Yeast glycolysis	500	2	$\{0.01; 0.05; 0.1; 0.5; 1\}$	5
Gene regulatory network	700	2	$\{0.01; 0.05; 0.1; 0.5; 1\}$	4
Kuramoto oscillator	1400	2	$\{0.01; 0.05; 0.1; 0.5; 1\}$	4
Phase-coupled oscillator	1400	2	$\{0.01; 0.05; 0.1; 0.5; 1\}$	4

Finally, in the case of a higher polynomial order with relatively insufficient samples, the nonlinear regression equation for PCGC will be underdetermined. Then, high performance will be not guaranteed. To some extent, it will even become very poor. Meanwhile, even if the number of variables (nodes) is small, the polynomial space might also be very large with a higher polynomial order. In this way, it is necessary to propose SPCGC for dimension reduction to improve the reconstruction performance. Simulations comparing the PCGC and SPCGC methods are demonstrated in Figure 7. Here, Lorenz 96, the gene regulatory network, the Kuramoto oscillator network, and the phase-coupled oscillator network are taken for further investigation; the network generation mechanism and network parameter settings are the same as those in the simulation in Figure 5. The other parameters for the simulations in Figure 7 are listed in Table 3. As shown in Figure 7, based on the average AUROC and average AUPR over multiple realizations, the performance of SPCGC is higher than that of PCGC as a whole. In particular, for the Lorenz 96 network, unlike PCGC, SPCGC has almost the same values for the AUROC and AUPR. However, the final reconstructed network of SPCGC has more exact and reliable causal weights with higher confidence levels. In this case, a similar comparison between SPCGC and PCGC can be performed by referring to the analysis in Figure 4.

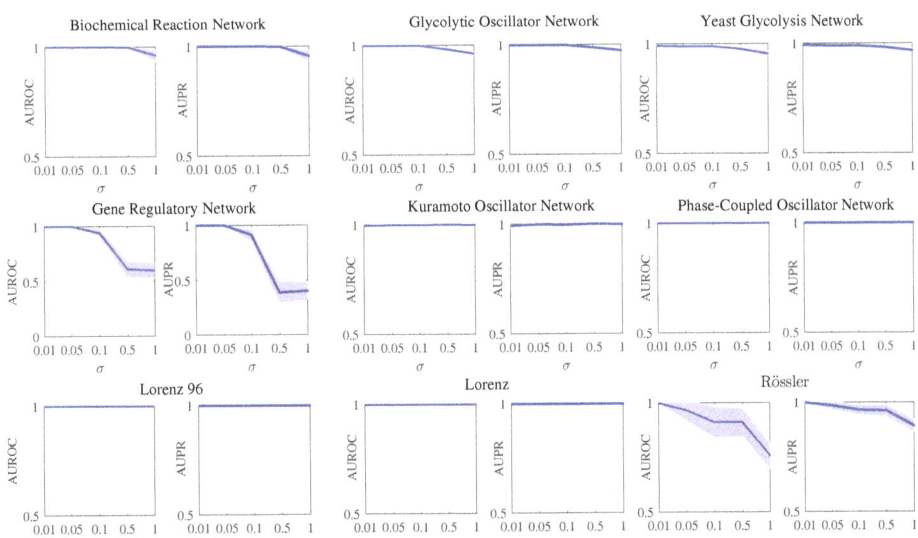

Figure 6. Simulation results of different models at different noise intensities σ. All of the values of the AUROC and AUPR are averaged over 10 realizations. The blue-shaded area is the error bound of the AUROC or AUPR over 10 realizations.

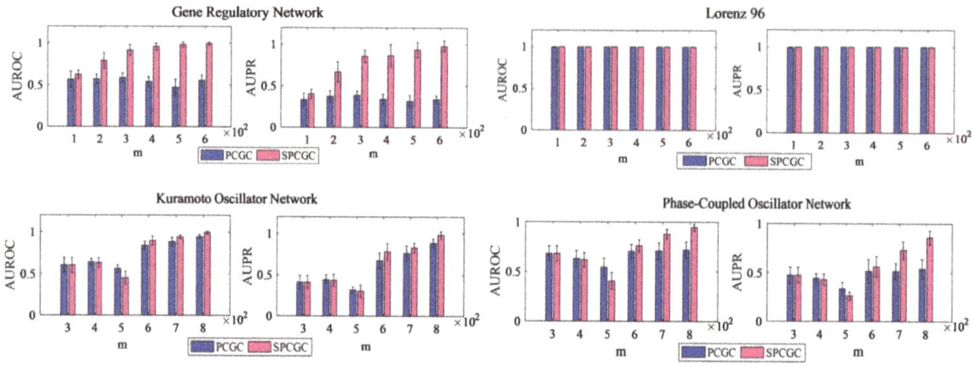

Figure 7. Simulation results of different models for the comparison of PCGC and SPCGC. All of the values of the AUROC and AUPR are averaged over 10 realizations.

Table 3. Parametric settings of simulations of different models for the comparison of PCGC and SPCGC. Here, m is the number of measurements, T is the number of time points at each measurement, σ is the strength of noise, r is the polynomial order, and λ is the sparse penalty parameter.

Model	m	T	σ	r	λ
Gene regulatory network	{100; 200; 300; 400; 500; 600}	2	0.01	5	0.002
Lorenz 96	{100; 200; 300; 400; 500; 600}	2	0.01	5	0.001
Kuramoto oscillator	{300; 400; 500; 600; 700; 800}	2	0.01	5	0.003
Phase-coupled oscillator	{300; 400; 500; 600; 700; 800}	2	0.01	5	0.003

4. Discussion

The traditional Granger causality method was proposed based on a linear VAR model, which often cannot achieve good results under the condition of an insufficient sample size. Based on the consideration of nonlinearity, sparsity, and causality, the model-free PCGC and SPCGC methods are presented in this study and, based on the simulation of different complex nonlinear networked systems, the robustness and effectiveness of our proposed method are verified. However, the following questions still need to be addressed and discussed.

(1) The heterogeneity and diversity of data can guarantee the performance and quality of causal inference methods. Therefore, different initial values under different conditions are used to collect data using a scheme with multiple measurements. In this case, our proposed methods are generally proven to be effective and robust in simulations of many system models. However, some issues should be addressed. In Figure 5, for the gene regulatory network and Kuramoto oscillator network, when the sample size is relatively small, the heterogeneity of the data is not adequate. This is also the reason why our proposed method PCGC obtains lower AUROC and AUPR values in the simulations of the gene regulatory network and Kuramoto oscillator network. However, as the sample size increases, the performance of PCGC is greatly improved. On the other hand, the Lorenz 96 and the Lorenz systems have chaotic dynamic trajectories. The data generated from them are heterogeneous enough. So, PCGC still achieves good performance even with a relatively smaller sample size in the simulation of Lorenz 96 and the Lorenz systems. The AUROC and AUPR of PCGC reach stable values as the sample size increases. In particular, we conducted a detailed comparison between PCGC and SPCGC in a gene regulatory network, as shown in Figure 4. The performance of methods varies greatly as the sample size increases. We attempted to analyze the reasons in detail to make this study more representative. Of course, other models can be used for the same analysis and comparison.

(2) The focus of our theoretical research is not to specifically study the impact of the presence of measurement noise on Granger causality inference, but to consider the

robustness of our method in the presence of certain measurement noise. For this reason, we also performed some simulation studies in the case of different noise intensities. The robustness to uncertainties in the data was addressed; see Figure 6. Figure 6 provides the simulation results of different models at different noise intensities. We discuss this problem of measurement noise on Granger causality analysis [54,55] and refer to some works that have already attempted to explore this aspect [56,57]. Based on the consideration of noise, we believe that a combination of state-space modeling and some filtering methods for our PCGC framework would work well.

(3) To improve the performance of our proposed method, the choice of method parameters is also a crucial issue. In general, for a complex system, the same polynomial order r can be set for all system equations. In particular, for most networked systems, due to the difference in the complexity of the system equation for each node, it is necessary to give a specific polynomial order to different system equations. In this way, the respective complexity of the system equations can be roughly estimated by determining different polynomial orders of the system equations. Similarly, for a complex system, the same penalty parameter λ can be set for all system equations. For different equations of a system with heterogeneous complexity, it is more reasonable to choose different values of λ for different target nodes (with the respective equations of the system model) rather than using the same value of λ.

(4) In our study, we specifically focus on the proposed methods to verify their performance from different perspectives in detail, such as different types of models, different types of data, different sample sizes, and different noise intensities. In the future, the proposed methods will be compared and analyzed with existing advanced causal network inference methods. For further perspectives, the Lasso selection in SPCGC can be replaced with other compressed sensing algorithms for the investigation of better performance. We can make a similar comparison of penalized regression methods, as shown in [44]. On the other hand, based on a summary of some existing Granger causality methods [38–40], including an analysis of causal methods based on information theory [58,59], we should obtain an idea of solving causal network inference. In particular, a similar method should be pointed out, as it was proposed based on software space intervention analysis, and it is named algorithmic information dynamics. It might be considered as an alternative to our causal approach, but it uses computer programs rather than polynomial differential equations [59], and this needs to be studied in our future work.

5. Conclusions

In brief, the exact identification and dynamic prediction of causal networks from data were demonstrated by our proposed methods, one of which is termed Polynomial Conditional Granger Causality (PCGC), while the other is its expanded sparse-promoting version (SPCGC). These methods do not require assumptions on the specific form of the nonlinear system equations. In particular, a general polynomial approximation is adopted to fit the relationships among nodes, which has the superiority of turning the nonlinearity of complex systems into some additive terms. Then, SPCGC combines nonlinear regression based on Granger causality with sparse optimization, which is fit for larger high-dimensional systems with a relatively smaller number of samples.

From the point of view of network science, all real systems can be represented by networks. Due to the complexity of real systems, the mathematical model of a real system is often indistinct or unavailable. Therefore, for networked systems, it is necessary to develop a data-driven causal inference method that can provide a foundation for subsequent network analysis. In general, as a simple and effective method, this model-free framework can, to some extent, provide new prospects, and represents an attempt to develop a basis for network reconstruction methods in the future.

Author Contributions: Conceptualization, G.Y. (Guanxue Yang), S.L. and G.Y. (Guanxiao Yang); investigation, G.Y. (Guanxue Yang) and S.L.; writing—original draft preparation, G.Y. (Guanxue Yang) and S.L.; writing—review and editing, G.Y. (Guanxue Yang), S.L. and G.Y. (Guanxiao Yang); funding acquisition, G.Y. (Guanxue Yang). All authors have read and agreed to the published version of the manuscript.

Funding: This research was funded by the National Natural Science Foundation of China under grant number 61903161.

Data Availability Statement: The original contributions presented in the study are included in this article, further information can be available on request from the corresponding author.

Conflicts of Interest: The authors declare no conflicts of interest.

Appendix A. Nonlinear System Models for Simulation

Appendix A.1. Lorenz Oscillator

The system model of the Lorenz oscillator is formulated as shown in Equation (A1).

$$\begin{aligned} \dot{x} &= \sigma(y - x) + \xi_x \\ \dot{y} &= x(\rho - z) - y + \xi_y \\ \dot{z} &= xy - \beta z + \xi_z \end{aligned} \tag{A1}$$

where the standard parameters are $\sigma = 10$, $\rho = 28$, and $\beta = 8/3$. ξ_x, ξ_y, and ξ_z are zero-mean uncorrelated Gaussian noise terms with identical unit variance ($\xi \sim \mathcal{N}(0, \sigma^2)$).

Appendix A.2. Rössler Oscillator

The system model of the Rössler oscillator is formulated as shown in Equation (A2).

$$\begin{aligned} \dot{x} &= -y - z + \xi_x \\ \dot{y} &= x + ay + \xi_y \\ \dot{z} &= b + z(x - c) + \xi_z \end{aligned} \tag{A2}$$

where $a = 0.1$, $b = 0.1$, and $c = 14$. ξ_x, ξ_y, and ξ_z are zero-mean uncorrelated Gaussian noise terms with identical unit variance ($\xi \sim \mathcal{N}(0, \sigma^2)$).

Appendix A.3. Lorenz 96

The Lorenz 96 model is a dynamical system formulated by Edward Lorenz in 1996, and it is defined as shown in Equation (A3).

$$\dot{x}_i = (x_{i+1} - x_{i-2})x_{i-1} - x_i + F + \xi_i, \tag{A3}$$

where $i = 1, 2, ..., N$; $x_{-1} = x_{N-1}$, $x_0 = x_N$, and $x_1 = x_{N+1}$. x_i is the state of the system, and F is a forcing constant. $F = 8$ is a common value known to cause chaotic behavior. ξ_i is a zero-mean uncorrelated Gaussian noise term with identical unit variance ($\xi_i \sim \mathcal{N}(0, \sigma^2)$).

Appendix A.4. Biochemical Reaction Network

The system model of the biochemical reaction network is formulated as shown in Equation (A4).

$$
\begin{aligned}
\dot{x}_1 &= -\gamma_1 x_1 + \frac{\alpha_1}{1 + x_6^{n_1}} + \xi_1 \\
\dot{x}_2 &= -\gamma_2 x_2 + \frac{\alpha_2}{1 + x_4^{n_2}} + \xi_2 \\
\dot{x}_3 &= -\gamma_3 x_3 + \frac{\alpha_3}{1 + x_5^{n_3}} + \xi_3 \\
\dot{x}_4 &= -\gamma_4 x_4 + \beta_1 x_1 + \xi_4 \\
\dot{x}_5 &= -\gamma_5 x_5 + \beta_2 x_2 + \xi_5 \\
\dot{x}_6 &= -\gamma_6 x_6 + \beta_3 x_3 + \xi_6
\end{aligned} \tag{A4}
$$

where x_1, x_2, and x_3 are concentrations of the mRNA transcripts of genes 1, 2, and 3, respectively; x_4, x_5, and x_6 are concentrations of the proteins of genes 1, 2, and 3, respectively; α_1, α_2, and α_3 are the maximum promoter strengths for the corresponding genes; γ_1, γ_2, and γ_3 are mRNA decay rates; γ_4, γ_5, and γ_6 are protein decay rates; β_1, β_2, and β_3 are protein production rates; and n_1, n_2, and n_3 are hill coefficients. ξ_i is a zero-mean uncorrelated Gaussian noise term with identical unit variance ($\xi_i \sim \mathcal{N}(0, \sigma^2)$). The parameters of Equation (A4) are given in Table A1.

Table A1. Parameter settings in the biochemical reaction network.

$\alpha_1 = 4$	$\alpha_2 = 3$	$\alpha_3 = 5$			
$\gamma_1 = 0.3$	$\gamma_2 = 0.4$	$\gamma_3 = 0.5$	$\gamma_4 = 0.2$	$\gamma_5 = 0.4$	$\gamma_6 = 0.6$
$\beta_1 = 1.4$	$\beta_2 = 1.5$	$\beta_3 = 1.6$			
$n_1 = 4$	$n_2 = 4$	$n_3 = 4$			

Appendix A.5. Metabolic Network 1: Glycolytic Oscillator

The system model of the glycolytic oscillator is formulated as shown in Equation (A5).

$$
\begin{aligned}
\dot{x}_1 &= J_0 - \frac{k_1 x_1 x_6}{1 + (x_6/K_1)^4} + \xi_1 \\
\dot{x}_2 &= \frac{2k_1 x_1 x_6}{1 + (x_6/K_1)^4} - k_2 x_2 (N - x_5) - k_6 x_2 x_5 + \xi_2 \\
\dot{x}_3 &= k_2 x_2 (N - x_5) - k_3 x_3 (A - x_6) + \xi_3 \\
\dot{x}_4 &= k_3 x_3 (A - x_6) - k_4 x_4 x_5 - \kappa (x_4 - x_7) + \xi_4 \\
\dot{x}_5 &= k_2 x_2 (N - x_5) - k_4 x_4 x_5 - k_6 x_2 x_5 + \xi_5 \\
\dot{x}_6 &= \frac{-2k_1 x_1 x_6}{1 + (x_6/K_1)^4} + 2k_3 x_3 (A - x_6) - k_5 x_6 + \xi_6 \\
\dot{x}_7 &= \psi \kappa (x_4 - x_7) - k x_7 + \xi_7
\end{aligned} \tag{A5}
$$

where x_1 is the concentration of glucose; x_2 is a pool compounded of triose phosphates, glyceraldehyde 3-phosphate, and dihydroxyacetone phosphate; x_3 is the concentration of 1,3-bisphosphoglycerate; x_4 is a pooled compound of pyruvate and acetaldehyde; x_5 is the concentration of NADH; x_6 is the concentration of ATP; and x_7 is the concentration of extracellular coupling substances [51,52]. ξ_i is a zero-mean uncorrelated Gaussian noise term with identical unit variance ($\xi_i \sim \mathcal{N}(0, \sigma^2)$). The parameters of Equation (A5) are given in Table A2.

Table A2. Parameter settings in the glycolytic oscillator model.

$J_0 = 2.5$;	$k = 1.8$;	$\psi = 0.1$;	$\kappa = 13$	
$K_1 = 0.52$;	$N = 1$;	$A = 4$;	$k_1 = 100$	
$k_2 = 6$;	$k_3 = 16$;	$k_4 = 100$;	$k_5 = 1.28$;	$k_6 = 12$

Appendix A.6. Metabolic Network 2: Yeast Glycolysis

The system model of yeast glycolysis is formulated as shown in Equation (A6).

$$\begin{aligned}
\dot{x}_1 &= a_1 + \frac{a_2 x_1 x_6}{1 + a_3 x_6^4} + \xi_1 \\
\dot{x}_2 &= \frac{b_1 x_1 x_6}{1 + b_2 x_6^4} + b_3 x_2 - b_4 x_2 x_7 + \xi_2 \\
\dot{x}_3 &= c_1 x_2 + c_2 x_3 + c_3 x_2 x_7 + c_4 x_3 x_6 + \xi_3 \\
\dot{x}_4 &= d_1 x_3 + d_2 x_4 + d_3 x_5 + d_4 x_3 x_6 + d_5 x_4 x_7 + \xi_4 \\
\dot{x}_5 &= e_1 x_4 + e_2 x_5 + \xi_5 \\
\dot{x}_6 &= \frac{f_1 x_1 x_6}{1 + f_2 x_6^4} + f_3 x_3 + f_4 x_3 x_7 + f_5 x_6 + \xi_6 \\
\dot{x}_7 &= g_1 x_2 + g_2 x_2 x_7 + g_3 x_4 x_7 + \xi_7
\end{aligned} \tag{A6}$$

where the description of x_i $(i = 1, 2, ..., 7)$ is the same as above. ξ_i is a zero-mean uncorrelated Gaussian noise term with identical unit variance ($\xi_i \sim \mathcal{N}(0, \sigma^2)$). The parameters of Equation (A6) are given in Table A3.

Table A3. Parameter settings in the yeast glycolysis model.

$a_1 = 2.5$;	$a_2 = -100$;	$a_3 = 13.6769$		
$b_1 = 200$;	$b_2 = 13.6769$;	$b_3 = -6$;	$b_4 = -6$	
$c_1 = 6$;	$c_2 = -64$;	$c_3 = 6$;	$c_4 = 16$	
$d_1 = 64$;	$d_2 = -13$;	$d_3 = 13$;	$d_4 = -16$;	$d_5 = -100$
$e_1 = 1.3$;	$e_2 = -3.1$			
$f_1 = -200$;	$f_2 = 13.6769$;	$f_3 = 128$;	$f_4 = -1.28$;	$f_5 = -32$
$g_1 = 6$;	$g_2 = -18$;	$g_3 = -100$		

Appendix A.7. Gene Regulatory Network

Suppose that gene interactions are modeled by the Michaelis–Menten equation, as shown in Equation (A7). This is a popular system of equations for gene networks.

$$\dot{x}_i = -x_i^f + \sum_{j=1}^{N} b_{ij} \frac{x_j^h}{x_j^h + 1} + \xi_i, \tag{A7}$$

where $f = 1$ and $h = 2$. Let $\mathbf{B} = [b_{ij}]_{N \times N}$ be the adjacency matrix, which characterizes the interactions among nodes. $b_{ij} \neq 0$ if the j-th variable connects to the i-th one; otherwise, $b_{ij} = 0$. ξ_i is a zero-mean uncorrelated Gaussian noise term with identical unit variance ($\xi_i \sim \mathcal{N}(0, \sigma^2)$).

Appendix A.8. Kuramoto Oscillator

The system model of the Kuramoto oscillator is formulated as shown in Equation (A8).

$$\dot{x}_i = \omega_i + \sum_{j=1}^{N} b_{ij} \sin(x_j - x_i) + \xi_i, \tag{A8}$$

where ω_i is a constant natural frequency. The second term describes the interactions between variable i and its interacting partners j. The nonlinear functions $sin(\bullet)$ represent the dynamical laws that govern the variables of the system. $\mathbf{B} = [b_{ij}]_{N\times N}$ is an adjacency matrix that describes the interactions among variables. $b_{ij} \neq 0$ if the j-th variable connects to the i-th one; otherwise, $b_{ij} = 0$. ξ_i is a zero-mean uncorrelated Gaussian noise term with identical unit variance ($\xi_i \sim \mathcal{N}(0, \sigma^2)$).

Appendix A.9. Phase-Coupled Oscillator

The model of a phase-coupled oscillator is given with coupling functions that have two Fourier items in Equation (A9).

$$\dot{x}_i = \omega_i + \sum_{j=1}^{N} b_{ij}\left[\sin\left(x_j - x_i - 1.05\right) + 0.33\sin\left(2\left(x_j - x_i\right)\right)\right] + \xi_i, \tag{A9}$$

where ω_i is a constant natural frequency. The two Fourier modes describe the interactions between variable i and its interacting partners j. The nonlinear functions $sin(\bullet)$ represent the dynamical laws that govern the variables of the system. $\mathbf{B} = [b_{ij}]_{N\times N}$ is an adjacency matrix that describes the interactions among variables. $b_{ij} \neq 0$ if the j-th variable connects to the i-th one; otherwise, $b_{ij} = 0$. ξ_i is a zero-mean uncorrelated Gaussian noise term with identical unit variance ($\xi_i \sim \mathcal{N}(0, \sigma^2)$).

eferences

1. Marbach, D.; Costello, J.C.; Küffner, R.; Vega, N.M.; Prill, R.J.; Camacho, D.M.; Allison, K.R.; Kellis, M.; Collins, J.J.; Stolovitzky, G. Wisdom of crowds for robust gene network inference. *Nat. Methods* **2012**, *9*, 796–804. [CrossRef] [PubMed]
2. Ahmed, A.; Xing, E.P. Recovering time-varying networks of dependencies in social and biological studies. *Proc. Natl. Acad. Sci. USA* **2009**, *106*, 11878–11883. [CrossRef] [PubMed]
3. Pratapa, A.; Jalihal, A.P.; Law, J.N.; Bharadwaj, A.; Murali, T. Benchmarking algorithms for gene regulatory network inference from single-cell transcriptomic data. *Nat. Methods* **2020**, *17*, 147–154. [CrossRef]
4. Runge, J.; Petoukhov, V.; Donges, J.F.; Hlinka, J.; Jajcay, N.; Vejmelka, M.; Hartman, D.; Marwan, N.; Paluš, M.; Kurths, J. Identifying causal gateways and mediators in complex spatio-temporal systems. *Nat. Commun.* **2015**, *6*, 8502. [CrossRef]
5. Wang, W.X.; Lai, Y.C.; Grebogi, C. Data based identification and prediction of nonlinear and complex dynamical systems. *Phys. Rep.* **2016**, *644*, 1–76. [CrossRef]
6. Chang, Y.H.; Gray, J.W.; Tomlin, C.J. Exact reconstruction of gene regulatory networks using compressive sensing. *BMC Bioinform.* **2014**, *15*, 400. [CrossRef]
7. Shen, Z.; Wang, W.X.; Fan, Y.; Di, Z.; Lai, Y.C. Reconstructing propagation networks with natural diversity and identifying hidden sources. *Nat. Commun.* **2014**, *5*, 4323. [CrossRef]
8. Mei, G.; Wu, X.; Wang, Y.; Mi, H.; Lu, J.A.; Chen, G. Compressive-sensing-based structure identification for multilayer networks. *IEEE Trans. Cybern.* **2017**, *48*, 754–764. [CrossRef]
9. Yeung, M.S.; Tegnér, J.; Collins, J.J. Reverse engineering gene networks using singular value decomposition and robust regression. *Proc. Natl. Acad. Sci. USA* **2002**, *99*, 6163–6168. [CrossRef]
10. Alter, O.; Brown, P.O.; Botstein, D. Singular value decomposition for genome-wide expression data processing and modeling. *Proc. Natl. Acad. Sci. USA* **2000**, *97*, 10101–10106. [CrossRef]
11. Rogers, S.; Girolami, M. A Bayesian regression approach to the inference of regulatory networks from gene expression data. *Bioinformatics* **2005**, *21*, 3131–3137. [CrossRef] [PubMed]
12. Deng, Y.; Zenil, H.; Tegnér, J.; Kiani, N.A. HiDi: An efficient reverse engineering schema for large-scale dynamic regulatory network reconstruction using adaptive differentiation. *Bioinformatics* **2017**, *33*, 3964–3972. [CrossRef] [PubMed]
13. Brunton, S.L.; Proctor, J.L.; Kutz, J.N. Discovering governing equations from data by sparse identification of nonlinear dynamical systems. *Proc. Natl. Acad. Sci. USA* **2016**, *113*, 3932–3937. [CrossRef] [PubMed]
14. Pan, W.; Yuan, Y.; Gonçalves, J.; Stan, G.B. A sparse Bayesian approach to the identification of nonlinear state-space systems. *IEEE Trans. Autom. Control* **2015**, *61*, 182–187. [CrossRef]
15. Mangan, N.M.; Brunton, S.L.; Proctor, J.L.; Kutz, J.N. Inferring biological networks by sparse identification of nonlinear dynamics. *IEEE Trans. Mol. Biol. Multi-Scale Commun.* **2016**, *2*, 52–63. [CrossRef]
16. Wang, S.; Herzog, E.D.; Kiss, I.Z.; Schwartz, W.J.; Bloch, G.; Sebek, M.; Granados-Fuentes, D.; Wang, L.; Li, J.S. Inferring dynamic topology for decoding spatiotemporal structures in complex heterogeneous networks. *Proc. Natl. Acad. Sci. USA* **2018**, *115*, 9300–9305. [CrossRef]
17. Casadiego, J.; Nitzan, M.; Hallerberg, S.; Timme, M. Model-free inference of direct network interactions from nonlinear collective dynamics. *Nat. Commun.* **2017**, *8*, 2192. [CrossRef]

18. Rice, J.J.; Tu, Y.; Stolovitzky, G. Reconstructing biological networks using conditional correlation analysis. *Bioinformatics* **200** *21*, 765–773. [CrossRef]
19. De La Fuente, A.; Bing, N.; Hoeschele, I.; Mendes, P. Discovery of meaningful associations in genomic data using parti correlation coefficients. *Bioinformatics* **2004**, *20*, 3565–3574. [CrossRef]
20. Frenzel, S.; Pompe, B. Partial mutual information for coupling analysis of multivariate time series. *Phys. Rev. Lett.* **200** *99*, 204101. [CrossRef]
21. Schreiber, T. Measuring information transfer. *Phys. Rev. Lett.* **2000**, *85*, 461. [CrossRef] [PubMed]
22. Faes, L.; Nollo, G.; Porta, A. Information-based detection of nonlinear Granger causality in multivariate processes via nonuniform embedding technique. *Phys. Rev. E* **2011**, *83*, 051112. [CrossRef]
23. Kugiumtzis, D. Partial transfer entropy on rank vectors. *Eur. Phys. J. Spec. Top.* **2013**, *222*, 401–420. [CrossRef]
24. Barnett, L.; Barrett, A.B.; Seth, A.K. Granger causality and transfer entropy are equivalent for Gaussian variables. *Phys. Rev. Let* **2009**, *103*, 238701. [CrossRef] [PubMed]
25. Youssofzadeh, V.; Prasad, G.; Naeem, M.; Wong-Lin, K. Temporal information of directed causal connectivity in multi-trial ER data using partial Granger causality. *Neuroinformatics* **2016**, *14*, 99–120. [CrossRef]
26. Zhou, D.; Xiao, Y.; Zhang, Y.; Xu, Z.; Cai, D. Causal and structural connectivity of pulse-coupled nonlinear networks. *Phys. Re Lett.* **2013**, *111*, 054102. [CrossRef]
27. Lusch, B.; Maia, P.D.; Kutz, J.N. Inferring connectivity in networked dynamical systems: Challenges using Granger causalit *Phys. Rev. E* **2016**, *94*, 032220. [CrossRef]
28. Wu, X.; Wang, W.; Zheng, W.X. Inferring topologies of complex networks with hidden variables. *Phys. Rev. E* **2012**, *86*, 04610 [CrossRef]
29. Granger, C.W. Investigating causal relations by econometric models and cross-spectral methods. *Econom. J. Econom. Soc.* **196** *37*, 424–438. [CrossRef]
30. Geweke, J.F. Measures of conditional linear dependence and feedback between time series. *J. Am. Stat. Assoc.* **1984**, *79*, 907–91 [CrossRef]
31. Dhamala, M.; Rangarajan, G.; Ding, M. Estimating Granger causality from fourier and wavelet transforms of time series dat *Phys. Rev. Lett.* **2008**, *100*, 018701. [CrossRef] [PubMed]
32. Baccala, L.A.; Takahashi, D.Y.; Sameshima, K. Directed Transfer Function: Unified Asymptotic Theory and Some of its Implication *IEEE Trans. Biomed. Eng.* **2016**, *63*, 2450–2460. [CrossRef] [PubMed]
33. Omidvarnia, A.; Azemi, G.; Boashash, B.; Colditz, P.B.; Vanhatalo, S. Orthogonalized Partial Directed Coherence: Measurin time-varying interactions within EEG channels. *IEEE Trans. Bio-Med Eng.* **2014**, *61*, 680–693. [CrossRef]
34. Tao, C.; Feng, J. Nonlinear association criterion, nonlinear Granger causality and related issues with applications to neuroimag studies. *J. Neurosci. Methods* **2016**, *262*, 110–132. [CrossRef]
35. Marinazzo, D.; Pellicoro, M.; Stramaglia, S. Kernel method for nonlinear Granger causality. *Phys. Rev. Lett.* **2008**, *100*, 14410 [CrossRef]
36. Ancona, N.; Marinazzo, D.; Stramaglia, S. Radial basis function approach to nonlinear Granger causality of time serie *Phys. Rev. E* **2004**, *70*, 056221. [CrossRef]
37. Hu, M.; Liang, H. A copula approach to assessing Granger causality. *Neuroimage* **2014**, *100*, 125–134. [CrossRef]
38. Finkle, J.D.; Wu, J.J.; Bagheri, N. Windowed granger causal inference strategy improves discovery of gene regulatory networks *Proc. Natl. Acad. Sci. USA* **2018**, *115*, 2252–2257. [CrossRef]
39. Stokes, P.A.; Purdon, P.L. A study of problems encountered in Granger causality analysis from a neuroscience perspective *Proc. Natl. Acad. Sci. USA* **2017**, *114*, E7063–E7072. [CrossRef]
40. Sheikhattar, A.; Miran, S.; Liu, J.; Fritz, J.B.; Shamma, S.A.; Kanold, P.O.; Babadi, B. Extracting neuronal functional networ dynamics via adaptive Granger causality analysis. *Proc. Natl. Acad. Sci. USA* **2018**, *115*, E3869–E3878. [CrossRef]
41. Shojaie, A.; Michailidis, G. Discovering graphical Granger causality using the truncating lasso penalty. *Bioinformatics* **2010** *26*, i517–i523. [CrossRef] [PubMed]
42. Lozano, A.C.; Abe, N.; Liu, Y.; Rosset, S. Grouped graphical Granger modeling for gene expression regulatory networks discovery *Bioinformatics* **2009**, *25*, i110–i118. [CrossRef] [PubMed]
43. Siggiridou, E.; Kugiumtzis, D. Granger causality in multivariate time series using a time-ordered restricted vector autoregressive model. *IEEE Trans. Signal Process.* **2015**, *64*, 1759–1773. [CrossRef]
44. Antonacci, Y.; Toppi, J.; Pietrabissa, A.; Anzolin, A.; Astolfi, L. Measuring connectivity in linear multivariate processes with penalized regression techniques. *IEEE Access* **2024**, *12*, 30638–30652. [CrossRef]
45. Yang, G.; Wang, L.; Wang, X. Reconstruction of complex directional networks with group lasso nonlinear conditional granger causality. *Sci. Rep.* **2017**, *7*, 2991. [CrossRef]
46. Siggiridou, E.; Kugiumtzis, D. Dimension reduction of polynomial regression models for the estimation of Granger causality in high-dimensional time series. *IEEE Trans. Signal Process.* **2021**, *69*, 5638–5650. [CrossRef]
47. Antonacci, Y.; Astolfi, L.; Nollo, G.; Faes, L. Information transfer in linear multivariate processes assessed through penalized regression techniques: Validation and application to physiological networks. *Entropy* **2020**, *22*, 732. [CrossRef]

48. Antonacci, Y.; Minati, L.; Faes, L.; Pernice, R.; Nollo, G.; Toppi, J.; Pietrabissa, A.; Astolfi, L. Estimation of Granger causality through Artificial Neural Networks: applications to physiological systems and chaotic electronic oscillators. *PeerJ Comput. Sci.* **2021**, *7*, e429. [CrossRef]
49. Dong, C.Y.; Shin, D.; Joo, S.; Nam, Y.; Cho, K.H. Identification of feedback loops in neural networks based on multi-step Granger causality. *Bioinformatics* **2012**, *28*, 2146–2153. [CrossRef]
50. Gao, J.; Barzel, B.; Barabási, A.L. Universal resilience patterns in complex networks. *Nature* **2016**, *530*, 307–312. [CrossRef]
51. Wolf, J.; Heinrich, R. Effect of cellular interaction on glycolytic oscillations in yeast: A theoretical investigation. *Biochem. J.* **2000**, *345*, 321–334. [CrossRef] [PubMed]
52. Ruoff, P.; Christensen, M.K.; Wolf, J.; Heinrich, R. Temperature dependency and temperature compensation in a model of yeast glycolytic oscillations. *Biophys. Chem.* **2003**, *106*, 179–192. [CrossRef] [PubMed]
53. Daniels, B.C.; Nemenman, I. Efficient inference of parsimonious phenomenological models of cellular dynamics using S-systems and alternating regression. *PLoS ONE* **2015**, *10*, e0119821. [CrossRef] [PubMed]
54. Nalatore, H.; N, S.; Rangarajan, G. Effect of measurement noise on Granger causality. *Phys. Rev. E* **2014**, *90*, 062127. [CrossRef]
55. Vinck, M.; Huurdeman, L.; Bosman, C.A.; Fries, P.; Battaglia, F.P.; Pennartz, C.M.; Tiesinga, P.H. How to detect the Granger-causal flow direction in the presence of additive noise? *Neuroimage* **2015**, *108*, 301–318. [CrossRef]
56. Sommerlade, L.; Thiel, M.; Platt, B.; Plano, A.; Riedel, G.; Grebogi, C.; Timmer, J.; Schelter, B. Inference of Granger causal time-dependent influences in noisy multivariate time series. *J. Neurosci. Methods* **2012**, *203*, 173–185. [CrossRef]
57. Ahmadi, S.; Nair, G.N.; Weyer, E. Granger causality of Gaussian signals from noisy or filtered measurements. *IFAC-PapersOnLine* **2020**, *53*, 506–511. [CrossRef]
58. Zenil, H.; Kiani, N.A.; Tegnér, J. Low-algorithmic-complexity entropy-deceiving graphs. *Phys. Rev. E* **2017**, *96*, 012308. [CrossRef]
59. Zenil, H.; Kiani, N.A.; Marabita, F.; Deng, Y.; Elias, S.; Schmidt, A.; Ball, G.; Tegner, J. An algorithmic information calculus for causal discovery and reprogramming systems. *Iscience* **2019**, *19*, 1160–1172. [CrossRef]

entropy MDPI

Article

Causal Factor Disentanglement for Few-Shot Domain Adaptation in Video Prediction

Nathan Cornille *, Katrien Laenen, Jingyuan Sun and Marie-Francine Moens

Language Intelligence and Information Retrieval (LIIR) Lab, Department of Computer Science KU Leuven, 3001 Leuven, Belgium; katrien.laenen@kuleuven.be (K.L.); jingyuan.sun@kuleuven.be (J.S.); sien.moens@kuleuven.be (M.-F.M.)

* Correspondence: nathan.cornille@kuleuven.be

Abstract: An important challenge in machine learning is performing with accuracy when few training samples are available from the target distribution. If a large number of training samples from a related distribution are available, transfer learning can be used to improve the performance. This paper investigates how to do transfer learning more effectively if the source and target distributions are related through a Sparse Mechanism Shift for the application of next-frame prediction. We create Sparse Mechanism Shift-TempoRal Intervened Sequences (SMS-TRIS), a benchmark to evaluate transfer learning for next-frame prediction derived from the TRIS datasets. We then propose to exploit the Sparse Mechanism Shift property of the distribution shift by disentangling the model parameters with regard to the true causal mechanisms underlying the data. We use the Causal Identifiability from TempoRal Intervened Sequences (CITRIS) model to achieve this disentanglement via causal representation learning. We show that encouraging disentanglement with the CITRIS extensions can improve performance, but their effectiveness varies depending on the dataset and backbone used. We find that it is effective only when encouraging disentanglement actually succeeds in increasing disentanglement. We also show that an alternative method designed for domain adaptation does not help, indicating the challenging nature of the SMS-TRIS benchmark.

Keywords: causal representation learning; video prediction; transfer learning; few-shot learning

1. Introduction

Applications such as self-driving cars [1], weather prediction [2], or camera-equipped household robots [3] all benefit from the accurate prediction of high-dimensional future timesteps such as video frames or satellite imagery. A particularly challenging task is to make such predictions accurate when there are few samples to learn from. While it is typically expensive to gather enough frames from a new environment, many frames of a different-but-related environment *are* often available (such as a different location or different sensory equipment). This motivates us to propose a method to better enable a learner to make use of the related 'old' (in-domain or ID) data to increase prediction accuracy on the target 'new' (out-of-domain or OOD) dataset.

A naïve approach is simply training a model to be as accurate as possible on the ID data and subsequently fine-tuning it on the OOD data. Researchers have tried to improve on this approach by making certain assumptions about *how* the ID and OOD data are related. If y is the prediction target and x the input, typical assumptions are that only $P(x)$ changes but $P(y|x)$ stays the same ('covariate shift'), or that $P(y|x)$ changes but we can split x into $x_{variant}, x_{invariant}$ such that $P(y|x_{invariant})$ stays the same [4–7]. One type of relatedness between the ID and OOD data is still underexplored, however, except in the case where there is a Sparse Mechanism Shift [8]. In this setting, the high-dimensional observables (like video frames) are views of lower-dimensional factors (such as the position of a pedestrian) evolving over time according to causal mechanisms that are fixed within one distribution (e.g., whenever the traffic light turns green, the pedestrians in front of it move forward in subsequent timesteps). The ID and OOD distributions, then, are different in only a small subset of these mechanisms. It is a technique that is able to improve the speed of the adaptation under the Sparse Mechanism Assumption, which can have significant implications for real-world applications. For example, when a robot undergoes a change in a sensor or actuator [9], such a technique would improve how quickly it can accurately predict future observations again. It can also help in a biological context by improving the predictability of gene expressions in new pathways, where the Sparse Mechanism Shift assumption has shown to be useful for disentangling biological processes [10]. The reasonableness of the Sparse Mechanism Shift hypothesis is motivated in [8]. In this work, we will take this hypothesis as true and explore how to improve few-shot prediction accuracy in a scenario that is true.

We develop a novel benchmark to test few-shot domain adaptation when the Sparse Mechanism Shift is true, called "SMS-TRIS". It is derived from the TRIS datasets [11], which are synthetic datasets of video frames rendered from latent causal factors that evolve over time via stationary causal mechanisms, along with occasional interventions on the factors. SMS-TRIS consists of variants of the TRIS datasets in which one stationary mechanism is different per variant. We exploit the fact that the ID and OOD data are related through a Sparse Mechanism Shift by disentangling certain model parameters with regard to the true causal mechanisms. Specifically, we use CITRIS [11] to achieve this disentanglement, a method that leverages access to intervention information to guarantee disentanglement. If this succeeds, then a model of the ID data only needs to update the parameters that correspond to the subset of mechanisms that shifted. Based on the results from [12], this is hypothesized to increase speed-of-adaption, as a smaller number of parameters need to be updated, reducing the effective dimensionality of the hypothesis search space.

Experimental results indicate that the CITRIS extensions can improve performance, but that this improvement is brittle: it is dependent on the particular dataset, as well on the particular backbone (i.e., the basic model architecture to which the CITRIS extensions are added) that is used. Specifically, we find that the CITRIS extensions only improve the prediction performance when they succeed in significantly improving disentanglement.

A comparison with an alternative Domain Adaptation method (Deep CORAL [13]) indicates that it is not consistently effective either, indicating that SMS-TRIS is a challenging benchmark.

In summary, our contributions are as follows:

- We generate and make available SMS-TRIS, a new benchmark for evaluating few-shot domain adaptation for next-frame prediction under the Sparse Mechanism Shift assumption (The code to generate the datasets and reproduce our experiments as well as links to the dataset artifacts can be found at https://github.com/Natithan/SMS-TRIS (accessed on 21 August 2023.)
- We show that encouraging disentanglement during pretraining for few-shot domain adaptation can benefit prediction accuracy, but only if the disentanglement encouragement succeeds in leading to strong disentanglement.
- We show that an external baseline (Deep CORAL) does not improve over a naïve baseline, underlining the need for customized algorithms to exploit the Sparse Mechanism Shift assumption.

The remainder of the article is structured as follows: We position our work in the context of related work in Section 2. We detail our problem setup and explain our method in Section 3. We then describe the datasets and models we use in our experimental setup in Section 4. Finally, we discuss our experimental findings in Section 5 and conclude in Section 6.

2. Related Work

2.1. Causal/Disentangled Representation Learning

While the focus of our study is on leveraging disentanglement to improve few-shot performance, disentangling latent variables has often been of interest as a goal in itself.

CITRIS is proposed by [11], with the goal of creating latent representations that are disentangled with regard to true causal factors. We build on this by evaluating the usefulness of such disentanglement for domain adaptation. Another work that disentangles latent representations using extra information is iVAE [14], which we include as a baseline under the name "Standard VAE". Work such as [15] aims to improve disentanglement, stating that this can be useful for transfer learning or zero-shot learning. However, they assume independent factors of variation, which is not realistic when factors of interest can have common causes, as in our data. In [12], causal representation learning and domain adaptation are linked, but with reversed goals: they make use of speed-of-domain adaptation to achieve disentanglement with regard to the underlying causal structure; we achieve this disentanglement through other means (i.e., making use of intervention vectors as CITRIS does) and subsequently evaluate whether such disentanglement improves speed-of-domain adaptation.

2.2. *Causality for Distribution Shifts*

Researchers have investigated whether ideas from causality can benefit performance after a distribution shift. In [8], the authors motivate how causal representation learning could be relevant for machine learning purposes, such as domain adaptation, if the Sparse Parameter Shift assumption holds. However, they do not perform empirical experiments. There are a number of works [5,16–18] that make use of causal representation learning for distribution shifts, but they focus on domain *generalization* rather than domain adaptation. They typically have one mechanism of interest (that is, the target variable) and assume that this mechanism is invariant in distribution shifts, while the mechanisms of covariates are allowed to change. In contrast, this paper is interested in modeling mechanisms of multiple causal factors, assumes that a small number of them can change, and aims to improve the adaptation of the model to that change, rather than hoping to remain unaffected by it. Few-shot domain adaptation is performed in [4], but they assume known factors. They also do not assume a Sparse Mechanism Shift, but rather that no causal mechanisms shifted, and the distribution shift is due to a shift in the noise variable distributions. They then intend to learn a model that fits *both* the source-domain and target-domain data (a 'conservative' setting), while we intend to *adapt* the model (a 'non-conservative' setting). Moreover, they require access to multiple source domains.

2.3. *Domain Adaptation*

A substantial body of work shares the goal of performing domain adaptation, without using causality as a tool.

Many works focus on the classification setting, such as for images ([4,13,19,20] or for labeling activities in videos [21,22]). In Deep CORAL [13], the authors aim to improve the model performance on the OOD data based on access to the ID data and some OOD data. They align the covariance of latent features of the ID and OOD data, whereas we align the mechanisms and parameters for the ID data and investigate whether that improves the fine-tuning on the OOD data. It is complementary to encouraging disentanglement. We compared the effect of Deep CORAL to the effect of encouraging disentanglement in our experiments. A similar idea of aligning certain views of the samples from the source and target domain, but for videos, is used in [22]. Other works try to address domain adaptation for classification in a way that relies on having access to categorical labels [19–21]. Those techniques are not applicable for next-frame prediction, however.

Other settings in which domain adaptation has been tackled include semantic segmentation, language modeling, or keypoint detection [23]. In semantic segmentation, the meta-learning framework is common [24,25], in which training happens on a series of few-shot domain adaptation episodes, rather than the transfer learning setting in this work, in which we train on one big source domain and adapt to one target domain. In language modeling, parameter-efficient fine-tuning has been shown to be an effective approach for few-shot domain adaptation [26].

3. Methodology

We first detail the problem setup by formalizing the kind of data, the type of distribution shift, and the kind of models we consider. We then explain and motivate our method.

3.1. Problem Setup

The task under consideration is next-frame prediction, and for our purposes, we assume the frames come out of a Mechanisms-Induced Distribution:

Definition 1 (Mechanisms-Induced Distribution). *A Mechanisms-Induced Distribution D is characterized by the following:*

- $P_{c_0} : \mathbb{R}^{\sum_{k=1}^{K} \zeta_k} \to \mathbb{R}^+$*: A distribution from which the set of true, unobserved causal factors* $\mathbf{c}^t = (c_k^t \in \mathbb{R}^{\zeta_k})_{k=1}^K$ *at the first time* $t = 0$ *are sampled, where* ζ_k *is the dimension of factor* $\mathbf{c}_k^t$;
- $P_{u_X} : \mathbb{R}^{\zeta_{u_X}} \to \mathbb{R}^+$*: A distribution from which the rendering noise* u_X^t *is sampled at each timestep, where* ζ_{u_X} *is the dimension of* u_X^t;
- $P_u : \mathbb{R}^{\sum_{k=1}^{K} v_k} \to \mathbb{R}^+$*: A distribution from which the set of factor noises* $\mathbf{u}^{t+1} = (u_k^{t+1} \in \mathbb{R}^{v_k})_{k=1}^K$ *is sampled at each timestep, where* v_k *is the dimension of* u_k^{t+1}*. The* u_k^{t+1} *are assumed to be independent of each other:* $P_u(u_1^{t+1}, \ldots, u_K^{t+1}) = \prod_{k=1}^K P_{u_k}(u_k^{t+1})$;
- $f_k, k \in \{1 \ldots K\}$*: The true causal mechanisms that determine how factors evolve:* $\mathbf{c}_k^{t+1} = f_k(\mathbf{c}^t, u_k^{t+1})$*. They are stationary;*
- $\mathbf{X}^t$*: The observed video frame at time t, deterministically 'rendered' from a combination of* $\mathbf{c}^t$ *and* u_X^t *by some observation function h:* $\mathbf{X}^t = h(\mathbf{c}^t, u_X^t)$.

It is possible that a factor $\mathbf{c}_k^{t+1} = f_k(\mathbf{c}^t, u_k^{t+1})$ depends only on a subset of factors $Pa(\mathbf{c}_k^{t+1})$:

$$Pa(\mathbf{c}_k^{t+1}) = \{\mathbf{c}_l^t | 1 \le l \le K, \exists \mathbf{c}^t, u_k^{t+1} : \frac{\partial f_k(\mathbf{c}^t, u_k^{t+1})}{\partial \mathbf{c}_l^t} \neq 0\} \tag{1}$$

We call this subset the parents of $\mathbf{c}_k^{t+1}$.

We assume the two distributions are related by a Sparse Mechanism Shift:

Definition 2 (Sparse Mechanism Shift (SMS)). *We define a Sparse Mechanism Shift as a Boolean property of two Mechanisms-Induced Distributions,* D_1 *and* D_2*, and an integer s that is true if and only if* D_1 *and* D_2 *are equal in all characteristics except in the subset S of all K true causal mechanisms,* $S = \{f_i | 1 \le i \le K, |S| = s\}$.

In the rest of the paper, we will be informal and leave out the s argument when we just mean that s is a small fraction of all K mechanisms. We will model the data with Encoder-Transition models:

Definition 3 (Encoder-Transition Model). *An Encoder-Transition Model M is characterized by:*

- *An invertible encoder* e_θ*, with inverse function* e_θ^{-1}*, that maps between* $\mathbf{X}^t$ *and a latent representation* $z^t = e_\theta(\mathbf{X}^t)$, $\hat{\mathbf{X}}^{t+1} = e_\theta^{-1}(\hat{z}^{t+1})$.
- *A transition prior* p_ϕ *that predicts the next timestep in the latent space:* $\hat{z}^{t+1} = p_\phi(z^t)$.

Such a two-component model is a natural fit when the true Mechanisms-Induced Distribution can also be partitioned along the observation function h and the mechanisms f_k.

3.2. Our Method: Causal Mechanism Disentanglement for Few-Shot Domain Adaptation

Our approach to improve few-shot next-frame prediction after a Sparse Mechanism Shift in order to encourage the parameters of the transition prior p_ϕ to being disentangled with regard to the true mechanisms f_k. We refer to such disentanglement as Causal Mechanism Disentanglement.

We will first detail Causal Mechanism Disentanglement and then discuss why it is expected to improve few-shot next-frame prediction after a Sparse Mechanism Shift.

3.2.1. Causal Mechanism Disentanglement

Figure 1a illustrates Causal Mechanism Disentanglement with regard to a Mechanism-Induced Distribution in an Encoder-Transition Model.

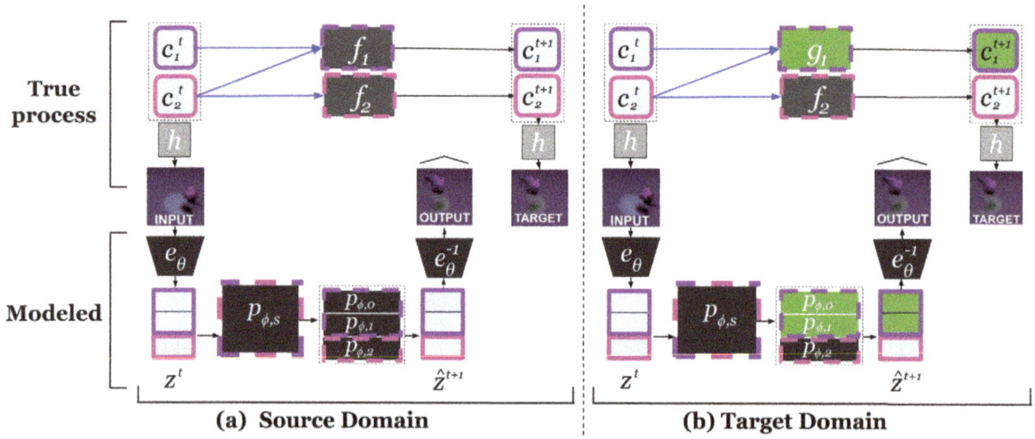

Figure 1. (**a**) Causal mechanism disentanglement for three latent dimensions of $\boldsymbol{z}^t$ and two true causal factors c_k^t, with sample frames from the Shapes dataset. The top part shows the true factors and mechanisms along with the observation function h that produces the observed frames. The bottom part shows the modeled latents and parameters. The alignment between true factors $\boldsymbol{c}_k^t$ and disentangled dimensions of the model activations $\boldsymbol{z}_i^t$ is indicated with full bold-colored outlines (purple for factor 1 and $\boldsymbol{z}^t$ dimensions 0 and 1; pink for factor 2 and $\boldsymbol{z}^t$ dimension 2). (**b**) In the target domain, the shifted mechanism g_1, with a green background, leads to a shift in $P(\boldsymbol{c}_1^{t+1} \mid Pa(\boldsymbol{c}_1^{t+1}))$. If the encoder e_θ disentangles different causal factors into different subsets of the latent $\boldsymbol{z}^t$, this leads to a shift only in $P(\boldsymbol{z}_{\psi_1}^{t+1} \mid Pa(\boldsymbol{z}_{\psi_1}^{t+1}))$. It is then possible to adapt to this change during transfer learning by updating only p_{ϕ,ψ_1}. This work evaluates whether this isolation of the parameters that need to update can be exploited to improve few-shot domain adaptation.

To define Causal Mechanism Disentanglement, consider the following variables:

- An Encoder-Transition Model M with encoder e_θ and transition prior p_ϕ;
- A Mechanisms-Induced Distribution D;
- An assignment function $\psi : J \to K, J \geq K$ that assigns dimensions of $\boldsymbol{z}^t$ to an index k in $\{1, \ldots, K\}$. In other words, ψ partitions the dimensions of $\boldsymbol{z}^t$ into K subsets, where each subset is assigned to one of the K true factors.
  For a certain ψ, we can consider p_ϕ as the composition of two parts:
  - $p_{\phi,shared}$: A shared part whose parameters affect all dimensions of $\hat{\boldsymbol{z}}^{t+1}$;
  - $p_{\phi,\psi_k}, k \in 1 \ldots K$: A set of K parts, where the parameters of the part with index k affect only the dimensions of $\hat{\boldsymbol{z}}^{t+1}$ that are assigned to factor k.

We then say a model M has achieved Causal Mechanism Disentanglement with regard to distribution D if there exists an assignment function ψ such that two requirements hold: First, there exists a set of deterministic functions $\{\eta_k : \mathbb{R}^{\#\psi_k} \to \mathbb{R}^{\zeta_k}\}_{k=1}^K$ such that $\eta_k(\boldsymbol{z}_{\psi_k}^t) = \boldsymbol{c}_k^t$ for all $k \in \{1, \ldots, K\}$, where $\psi_k = \{j \mid j \in \{1 \ldots J\}, \psi(j) = k\}$ corresponds to the dimensions of $\boldsymbol{z}^t$ that are assigned to causal factor k, and $\#\psi_k$ is the number of elements in ψ_k. Second, the model's transition prior p_ϕ accurately predicts the next-step latents:

$$\forall \boldsymbol{c}^t : e_\theta \circ h(\boldsymbol{c}_1^{t+1}, \ldots, \boldsymbol{c}_k^{t+1}) = p_\phi \circ e_\theta \circ h(\boldsymbol{c}_1^t, \ldots, \boldsymbol{c}_k^t) \tag{2}$$

Here, $\circ$ indicates the function composition: $f \circ g(x) = f(g(x))$.

The first requirement corresponds to causal representation learning as defined in [11]. We use Causal *Factor* Disentanglement as a synonym for causal representation learning, as it concerns disentangling latent activations $\mathbf{z}^t$ with regard to the true causal factors $\mathbf{c}^t$. Furthermore, if $\mathbf{c}_j^t \in Pa(\mathbf{c}_i^{t+1})$, $k \in \psi_j$ and $l \in \psi_i$, we simply write $z_k^t \in Pa(z_l^{t+1})$.

In order to fulfill the first requirement (i.e., achieve Causal Factor Disentanglement), we use the CITRIS model [11]. To achieve Causal Mechanism Disentanglement with regard to the ID mechanisms, we fulfill the second requirement by training the model to accurately predict the next frame in the ID data.

3.2.2. Relevance to Few-Shot Next-Frame Prediction

Informally, Causal Mechanism Disentanglement is about making distinct subsets of the parameters of p_ϕ responsible for modeling distinct true causal mechanisms f_t. If the Sparse Mechanism Shift assumption holds, successful Causal Mechanism Disentanglement entails that only the subset of parameters that modeled the shifted mechanisms needs to change in response. The parameters that model mechanisms that did not shift can remain the same. Causal Mechanism Disentanglement thus reduces the expected number of parameters that need to update.

Figure 1a illustrates this. It shows a target distribution that is shifted with regard to the one shown in Figure 1b that was caused by a single causal mechanism change, indicated in green. Gradient descent in a smaller parameter search space is then expected to adapt the model to a good solution more quickly, a property that has been empirically observed in [12].

3.2.3. Shared Parameters

A restriction of our setup concerns shared parameters. Consider model parameters that are shared across all latent predictions (i.e., the shared parameters in the transition parameter p_ϕ, as well as all parameters of the encoder e_θ). If these shared parameters already 'specialize' to particular source-domain causal mechanisms, it restricts the extent to which the model can 'get away' with only updating the nonshared parameters. Addressing this specialization is an interesting avenue for future work.

4. Experimental Setup

In this section, we detail our benchmark datasets, the models we compare, and our evaluation metrics.

4.1. Datasets

4.1.1. TRIS Datasets

Our benchmark is derived from the Temporal Intervened Sequences (TRIS) datasets [11]. We select these datasets for two reasons. First, they satisfy the property of being Mechanisms-Induced. They are generated as one long sequence of observable video frames, where the mechanisms dictate how the latent causal factors evolve from those at the previous timestep, and the rendering function determines how that translates into observed frames. Note that this entails that the underlying causal factors are typically not mutually independent.

The second reason for starting from the TRIS datasets is that they include extra information that allows a model to disentangle the underlying causal factors. This disentanglement is key to the way in which we exploit the Sparse Mechanism Shift assumption. Specifically, they include the presence of a binary soft-intervention value $\iota_k^{t+1} \in \{0,1\}$ for each factor k at each timestep $t+1$ that changes the natural mechanism f_k into an intervened mechanism $f_k^\iota : Pa(\mathbf{c}_k^{t+1}) \times u_k \to \mathbf{c}_k^{t+1}$ if equal to 1. This kind of extra information can be realistic for learning agents, where the interventions might correspond to the actions of the agent (For example, the natural mechanism of a pie in a hot oven might be to transform a pie at one timestep into a slightly expanded pie at the next timestep, but if the agent intervenes by turning off the oven, the mechanism will take the same input pie but produce a smaller one over time).

In this work, we assume that for a given time t, the ι_k^t for different factors c_k^t are sampled independently.

This extra information is also necessary to achieve Causal Factor Disentanglement.

The task for this dataset is then to predict the next-timestep frame X^{t+1}, based on the current-timestep frame X^t and the intervention vector ι^{t+1}.

Figure 2 shows an example for $K = 2$, $Pa(c_1^{t+1}) = \{c_1^t, c_2^t\}$ and $Pa(c_2^{t+1}) = \{c_2^t\}$.

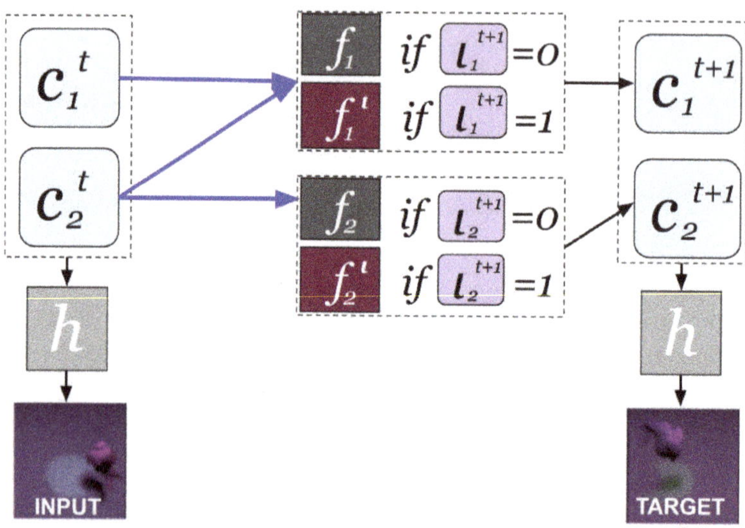

Figure 2. Temporal Intervened Sequence (TRIS) data setup for $K = 2$ causal factors, for which $Pa(c_1^{t+1}) = \{c_1^t, c_2^t\}$ and $Pa(c_2^{t+1}) = c_2^t$. The mechanism governing the evolution of the causal factors is the natural mechanism f_k if $\iota_k^{t+1} = 1$, and the intervened mechanism f_k^t is otherwise.

We use the two TRIS datasets reported in [11]: Temporal Causal3DIdent (Shapes) (For Shapes, we use the same object shapes as [11]: Cow [27], Head [28], Dragon [29], Hare [30], Armadillo [31], Horse [32], and Teapot [33]. We do not use the Teapot-only variant, but the variant with all seven shapes) and Pong. Both are synthetic datasets, where the true causal factors and mechanisms are known. Shapes consists of 250,000 frames at a resolution of 64 × 64. It displays a three-dimensional object varying in position/orientation/color, which makes it representative for real-life applications involving three-dimensional objects such as a robot manipulating certain household objects. Pong consists of 100,000 frames at a resolution of 32 × 32. It shows frames of an adaptation of the Atari game of Pong [34], making it relevant for applications that involve game-playing. We show examples of the Shapes and Pong datasets in Figures A1 and A2 in Appendix A.

4.1.2. SMS-TRIS Benchmark

We create out-of-distribution versions of these datasets by changing the causal mechanisms of one factor at a time. The ID mechanisms correspond to those in the original TRIS datasets. We generate nine OOD variants of the Shapes dataset and eight OOD variants of the Pong dataset, each of which differ from the original dataset in one mechanism. Following the original TRIS dataset, we generate each variant as one long sequence. For both Shapes and Pong, we generate 10,000 frames for each OOD variant.

For the Shapes dataset, the original causal mechanisms and the OOD-shifted mechanisms are shown in Table 1 for the position, rotation, and hue values.

Table 1. OOD mechanisms for position, rotation, and hue values. They cover different kinds of distribution shifts: ones that keep the same input, ones that depend on different inputs, and one in which a relation is changed from linear to non-linear. Red text highlights the difference between ID mechanism and OOD mechanism. The function $f(a,b,c) = \frac{a-b}{2} + c$ and u-variables are independently sampled from a Gaussian distribution as described in [11]. For HUE_O_ID_GOAL and HUE_O_OOD_GOAL, see ID object hue goal and OOD object hue goal, respectively, in Table 2.

Factor	ID Mechanism	OOD Mechanism
pos_x^{t+1}	$f(1.5 \cdot sin(rot\_\beta^t), pos\_x^t, u_X^t)$	$f(1.5 \cdot cos(rot\_\beta^t), pos\_x^t, u_X^t)$
pos_y^{t+1}	$f(1.5 \cdot sin(rot\_\alpha^t), pos\_y^t, u_y^t)$	$f(-1.5 \cdot cos(rot\_\alpha^t), pos\_y^t, u_y^t)$
pos_z^{t+1}	$f(1.5 \cdot cos(rot\_\alpha^t), pos\_z^t, u_z^t)$	$f(1.5 \cdot sin(rot\_\beta^t), pos\_z^t, u_z^t)$
rot_α^{t+1}	$f(hue\_b, rot\_\alpha^t, u_\alpha^t)$	$f(hue\_o, rot\_\alpha^t, u_\alpha^t)$
rot_β^{t+1}	$f(hue\_o, rot\_\beta^t, u_\beta^t)$	$f(hue\_b, rot\_\beta^t, u_\beta^t)$
rot_s^{t+1}	$f(atan2(pos\_x^{t+1}, pos\_y^{t+1}), rot\_s^t, u_{rs}^t)$	$f(atan2(pos\_y^{t+1}, pos\_z^{t+1}), rot\_s^t, u_{rs}^t)$
hue_s^{t+1}	$f(2\pi - hue\_b^t, hue\_s^t, u_{hs}^t)$	$f(2\pi - hue\_b^t \cdot hue\_s^t, hue\_s^t, u_{hs}^t)$
hue_b^{t+1}	$hue\_b^t + u_{hb}^t$	$hue\_b^t + u_{hb}^t + hue\_o^t$
hue_o^{t+1}	$f(\text{HUE}_\text{O}\text{\_ID\_GOAL}, hue\_o^t, u_{ho}^t)$	$f(\text{HUE}_\text{O}\text{\_OOD\_GOAL}, hue\_o^t, u_{ho}^t)$

For object hue, the mechanism can be described as trying to achieve a particular hue value depending on the object shape. The OOD-shifted-mechanism changes this target hue value, as shown in Table 2.

Table 2. OOD mechanisms for object hue. We choose the changes so that the inherent difficulty is not changed.

Object Shape	ID Object Hue Goal	OOD Object Hue Goal
Teapot	0	π
Armadillo	$\frac{1}{5} \cdot 2\pi$	0
Hare	avg(hue spot, hue back)	avg(hue spot, hue back) + π
Cow	$\frac{2}{5} \cdot 2\pi$	$\frac{3}{5} \cdot 2\pi$
Dragon	avg(hue spot, hue back) + π	avg(hue spot, hue back)
Head	$\frac{3}{5} \cdot 2\pi$	$\frac{2}{5} \cdot 2\pi$
Horse	$\frac{4}{5} \cdot 2\pi$	$\frac{4.5}{5} \cdot 2\pi$

Table 3 shows the changes in the causal mechanisms of the factors in Pong.

In the SMS-TRIS benchmark, the latent causal factors correspond to human-interpretable factors such as color, position, etc. For disentanglement to benefit domain adaptation, human-interpretability is in itself not a required property of the factors that the model disentangles. Their only required property is that the distribution shift of interest is sparse in the space of mechanisms that generate them. An avenue for future work is to evaluate the effectiveness of disentanglement when latent factors are not human-interpretable.

Table 3. Changes in the causal mechanisms of the factors in Pong. Since a Pong timestep plays out in multiple stages, we need to ensure that a mechanism change always only affects only one variable given its causal parents.

Factor	OOD Mechanism Change
Ball x-position	The ball now teleports horizontally over a middle section whose width is half the inter-paddle horizontal distance.
Ball y-position	The ball now teleports vertically over a middle section whose width is one-fifth of the inter-wall vertical distance.
Ball velocity direction	When a ball collides with a paddle, instead of only having the x-component of its velocity direction flipped, now the y-component also flips, flipping the velocity direction by 180 degrees.
Ball velocity magnitude	Ball velocity is doubled when in the lower half of the playing field.
Paddle left y-position	After a paddle–ball collision, the paddle now teleports a distance equal to half the inter-wall vertical distance up, if the collision was in the lower half, and down, if the collision was in the upper half.
Paddle right y-position	Same as for paddle left y-position.
Score left	When a score of 5 is reached, the score now resets to 1 instead of 0.
Score right	Same as for score left.

4.2. Models

Our hypothesis is that we can improve the few-shot OOD prediction accuracy of a model by not only training it to predict accurately on the source-domain data, but also encouraging it to be disentangled. To achieve this disentanglement, we use the Causal-Factor-Disentanglement-encouraging extensions proposed in [11], which we refer to as 'CITRIS CFD extensions'. We compare models with CITRIS CFD extensions ('CITRIS') to baseline models ('Standard') with the same backbone, but none of the extensions. As in [11], we do this for two backbone variations: an Auto-Encoder + Normalizing Flow (NF) and a Varatiational Auto-Encoder (VAE). This results in four models: CITRIS-NF, CITRIS-VAE, Standard-NF, and Standard-VAE.

Additionally, we compare the effect that disentanglement encouragement has with the effect of Deep Correlation Alignment (Deep CORAL [13]), an alternative method designed to improve the domain adaptation performance that is not designed to exploit the Sparse Mechanism Shift assumption.

We now detail the backbones, summarize the CITRIS CFD extensions, and explain the DeepCORAL baseline.

4.2.1. Backbones

The Variational Auto-Encoder backbone consists of an encoder e_θ, a decoder d_ι, and a transition prior p_ϕ. Following [11], the decoder d_ι is an approximation of the inverse encoder e_θ^{-1}. Each of these components predict a probability distribution by predicting the mean and standard deviation of a normal distribution. We indicate the predicted probability distributions of these components as P_θ, P_ι, and P_ϕ, respectively. The VAE objective then consists of a reconstruction term and a Kullback–Leibler (KL) divergence term:

$$
\begin{aligned}
L_{VAE} = & -\mathbb{E}_{\boldsymbol{z}^{t+1}\sim P_\theta(\boldsymbol{z}^{t+1}|\boldsymbol{X}^{t+1})}\left(\log P_\iota(\boldsymbol{X}^{t+1}|\boldsymbol{z}^{t+1})\right)+ \\
& \mathbb{E}_{\boldsymbol{z}^{t}\sim P_\theta(\boldsymbol{z}^{t}|\boldsymbol{X}^{t}),\boldsymbol{z}^{t+1}\sim P_\theta(\boldsymbol{z}^{t+1}|\boldsymbol{X}^{t+1})}\left(D_{KL}(P_\theta(\boldsymbol{z}^{t+1}|\boldsymbol{X}^{t+1})||P_\phi(\boldsymbol{z}^{t+1}|\boldsymbol{z}^{t},\iota^{t+1})\right)
\end{aligned} \quad (3)
$$

The Normalizing Flow backbone does not operate on $\boldsymbol{X}^t$ directly. Rather, an autoencoder $\{e_{AE}, d_{AE}\}$ is first trained with a reconstruction objective (where d_{AE} again approximates e_{AE}^{-1}), and the model then operates on the encoded images $\boldsymbol{y}^t = e_{AE}(\boldsymbol{X}^t)$. Another encoder e_θ is then trained to map $\boldsymbol{y}^t$ to a $\boldsymbol{z}^t$ that is intended to be disentangled with regard to the causal factors $\boldsymbol{c}^t$. This latter encoder e_θ is implemented via an invertible multilayer normalizing flow (NF) network. The encoder e_θ is responsible for ensuring Causal Factor Disentanglement, i.e., the information about different true factors c_k^t is stored in separate dimensions of z^t.

The transition prior part of the model (p_ϕ) then predicts a mean and log standard deviation for the next timestep in the z^t-space and uses this to optimize for the Negative Log Likelihood (NLL) of y^{t+1} after rescaling with the help of the Jacobian of the flow network e_θ.

For both backbones, we follow [11] in using an autoregressive transition prior.

4.2.2. CITRIS CFD Extensions

To achieve Causal Factor Disentanglement, CITRIS consists of a number of extensions to the basic KL-Divergence/NLL objective. We summarize the extensions here and refer to [11] for an in-depth explanation.

Three extensions are about restricting information about the input based on the learned assignment function ψ when predicting the NLL (for a Normalizing Flow) or KL-Divergence (for a VAE).

First, CITRIS restricts access to the information in the intervention vector ι^{t+1} during the prediction of a particular z_i^{t+1}. Specifically, it only allows access to the element in ι^{t+1} to which that particular z_i^{t+1} is assigned by ψ. The motivation is that whatever properties of the observed data that the *encoder* stores in a particular z_i^{t+1}, the *transition prior* will need to be able to predict that property as accurately as possible using z^t and *only one part of* ι^{t+1}. Each part of ι^{t+1} contains information relevant for the prediction of properties corresponding to one true causal factor. Hence, the encoder allows the transition prior to make the best possible prediction of a dimension z_i^{t+1} by letting that dimension contain only properties corresponding to the causal factor it is assigned to. This encourages the encoder to disentangle the information in its output z^{t+1} with regard to the causal factors by making use of the information ι^{t+1} has on the causal factors.

Second, CITRIS restricts access to the information in the previous timestep z^t during the prediction of a particular z_i^{t+1}. Consider the case where z_i^{t+1} is assigned by ψ to the first element of ι^{t+1} and that first element in ι^{t+1} indicates whether the 'object-color' was intervened on. If that first element of ι^{t+1} equals 1, the 'object-color' was indeed intervened on, meaning that its value is no longer correlated with the previous frame. In that case, it is not useful for the model to let its predictions of the z^{t+1}-dimensions that are mapped by ψ to the 'object-color' depend on the previous frame. Accordingly, CITRIS erases the information about the previous timestep for the prediction of a z_i^{t+1} that is mapped by ψ to a causal factor for which ι^{t+1} equals 1.

Third, the transition prior is autoregressive *per group of z^t-dimensions assigned to the same factor*. Empirically, restricting the autoregression in this way is important for improving disentanglement.

Two further extensions add additional terms to the loss besides the KL-Divergence/NLL objective.

First is a target classifier: an added MLP trained to predict each element in the intervention vector ι^{t+1} from z^t and different subsets of z^{t+1}. The encoder e_θ is then encouraged to allow the target classifier to be maximally accurate when predicting an element of ι^{t+1} from the subset of z^{t+1} that matches it according to ψ, but less accurate (only up to predicting the average value) when predicting it from a nonmatching subset. Since this loss term is quite involved, we refer to appendix C.3.3 in [11] for its detailed description.

Second is a term that is intended for the situation when not all the information in the video frames is predicted by the causal factors that the model can disentangle with the help of the intervention vector. The term biases ψ to reserving some dimensions of z^{t+1} for this 'extra information':

$$L_{bias} = \lambda_{bias}\frac{1}{L}\sum_{l=1}^{L}\left(1 - \frac{e^{\Psi_{0,l}}}{\sum_{j=0}^{K} e^{\Psi_{j,l}}}\right) \tag{4}$$

Here, λ_{bias} is a hyperparameter (set to 0.01 in [11] and in this work), L is the number of dimensions of z^{t+1}, K is the number of causal factors, and Ψ is a $K+1$ by the L parameter matrix containing logits that are used to assign each of the L dimension of z^{t+1} to a causal factor (rows 1 to K) or to reserve it for this 'extra information' (row 0).

The Standard models leave out all of the CITRIS CFD extensions. This means this model is no longer biased to be more disentangled than what is useful for the ID prediction objective.

The Standard model with the VAE backbone is equivalent to Identifiable VAE (iVAE [14]), in which the conditioning information consists of the previous timestep along with the intervention information.

4.2.3. Deep CORAL

To place the impact of the CITRIS CFD extensions on few-shot domain adaptation into context, we compare its impact to that of an existing method designed for domain adaptation. For our problem setup, the method needs to be applicable to non-categorical prediction targets and needs to be able to work with access to only one source distribution. We select Deep CORAL [13] as an external baseline that is compatible with our problem setup.

Deep CORAL works by accessing the OOD data *during* ID training and encouraging the covariance matrices of latent activations of the ID and OOD batches to be close to each other. Since this is orthogonal to the CITRIS extensions, we report CITRISNF, Standard, CITRISNF + Deep CORAL, and Standard + Deep CORAL.

The variants using Deep CORAL cannot reuse the same ID-pretrained model for different OOD shifts. That is because they need access to the ID and OOD data *at the same time* during pretraining, so each pretrained model is specific to one OOD shift. Since we evaluate many OOD shifts, this significantly increases the computational requirements. Hence, we pretrain for a maximum of 50 epochs in the experiments that compare the effect of CFD encouragement to the effect of Deep CORAL, whereas we pretrain for 500 epochs in the other experiments. We select the pretrained checkpoint based on the best ID prediction performance.

4.3. *Evaluation*

To investigate the relation between Causal Factor Disentanglement (CFD), Causal Mechanism Disentanglement (CMD), and the OOD next-timestep-prediction performance, we report a number of metrics.

4.3.1. Causal Factor Disentanglement (CFD)

To quantify the level of disentanglement of the latents (z^t) with regard to the true causal factors (c^t) for different models after ID training, we use the correlation metrics and triplet evaluation used in [11].

For the correlation metrics, a mapping $m_{k,j}$ is learned to predict each $\hat{c}^t_k = m_{k,j}(z^t_{\psi_j})$ from each group of latents $z^t_{\psi_j}, 1 \le j \le K$ (so not only from the 'matching' group of latents $z^t_{\psi_k}$). Note that this mapping $m_{k,j}$ is not part of the model, but is learned purely for evaluation purposes. The correlation between the prediction $m_{k,j}(z^t_{\psi_j})$ and the true factor c^t_k is then reported. A well-disentangled model should have high correlation values for $k = j$, and low values otherwise. The R^2 coefficient of determination [35] and the Spearman's rank correlation coefficient [36] are reported. Since the TRIS and SMS-TRIS datasets are generated sequentially, factors in each frame can be correlated, which can skew the interpretation of these correlation metrics. Hence, the correlation metrics are evaluated on independently sampled video frames. For the 'Standard' models, ψ is not learned. Hence, each latent dimension is assigned to the causal factor that it has the highest correlation with.

We also report the triplet distance, calculated as follows. A separate evaluation dataset is rendered consisting of triplets of frames: two randomly sampled images and a third image rendered using a mix of causal factors of the other two images. The model then computes the latents for the two original images, and a third latent is made by using the same mix of groups of latent dimensions assigned to a particular causal factor. The model is then tasked to decode this third latent to an image, which is compared to the rendered third image. The comparison is not reported in the pixel space but in the causal-factor space. To do so, a mapping from images $\boldsymbol{X}^t$ to causal factors $\boldsymbol{c}^t$ is learned in a supervised fashion. For categorical causal factors (such as shape), accuracy is used, while absolute difference is used for continuous variables. Each distance is normalized to fall between 0 and 1.

Note that both the independently sampled frames used for the correlation metrics and the triplets of frames used for the triplet distance do not consist of frames related over time through causal mechanisms. Hence, the same CFD score applies to both the in-domain and out-of-domain datasets.

Measuring Causal Factor Disentanglement is possible only because the true causal factors are known in the TRIS datasets. For real applications, we might not have access to the true causal factors. We are, however, still interested in measuring CFD to evaluate the effectiveness of encouraging CFD as a tool to reduce few-shot prediction error. Such a tool is useful for real applications, even if we cannot verify the level of disentanglement in real applications.

4.3.2. Prediction Error

We report the OOD prediction error for different models after transfer learning. After pretraining the models on the ID data, we fine-tune them on the OOD data with a varying number of available OOD samples. We report the results for differing choices of the ID-training checkpoint to start fine-tuning from. We freeze e_θ during this fine-tuning and only train the transition prior: in line with the argument for Causal Mechanism Disentanglement made in Section 3, the model should be able to learn to predict the OOD data by adapting only (a subset of) the parameters of the transition prior. While the number of available samples varies, we fine-tune for a fixed number of epochs (50).

We evaluate the models on a held-out test set of the OOD data. We measure errors in the causal factor space, in the same way as for the triplet evaluation.

5. Results and Discussion

5.1. Causal Factor Disentanglement (CFD)

Table 4 shows the disentanglement metrics for both models for the Shapes and Pong datasets.

Table 4. Disentanglement metrics for the Shapes and Pong data. R^2 is the R^2 coefficient of determination and Sp is Spearman's rank correlation coefficient. *diag* corresponds to the average correlation score of the predicted causal factor $m_{k,k}(z^t_{\psi_k})$ and its matching true factor c^t_k (best value is 1); *offdiag* corresponds to the average of the maximum correlation score of a predicted causal factor $m_{i,k}(z^t_{\psi_k})$ and a non-matching true factor c^t_i, $i \neq k$ (best value is 0). For triplet distances, the mean over all causal factors is reported (Triplet mean). CFD score is the average of all other metrics (using 1 minus [metric] for the metrics for which lower is better).

	Model	R^2 Diag ↑	R^2 Sep ↓	Sp Diag ↑	Sp Sep ↓	Triplet Mean ↓	CFD Score ↑
Shapes	CITRIS-NF	0.95 ± 0.011	0.08 ± 0.020	0.95 ± 0.017	0.10 ± 0.016	0.05 ± 0.008	0.93 ± 0.014
	Standard-NF	0.26 ± 0.001	0.62 ± 0.003	0.29 ± 0.001	0.61 ± 0.004	0.21 ± 0.000	0.42 ± 0.001
	CITRIS-VAE	0.63 ± 0.022	0.25 ± 0.062	0.63 ± 0.028	0.28 ± 0.050	0.34 ± 0.010	0.68 ± 0.031
	Standard-VAE	0.60 ± 0.016	0.46 ± 0.015	0.61 ± 0.014	0.47 ± 0.004	0.23 ± 0.001	0.61 ± 0.005
Pong	CITRIS-NF	0.64 ± 0.064	0.39 ± 0.046	0.62 ± 0.068	0.41 ± 0.045	0.31 ± 0.168	0.63 ± 0.070
	Standard-NF	0.13 ± 0.004	0.85 ± 0.006	0.13 ± 0.003	0.85 ± 0.002	0.25 ± 0.001	0.26 ± 0.001
	CITRIS-VAE	0.77 ± 0.085	0.25 ± 0.118	0.77 ± 0.086	0.31 ± 0.136	0.26 ± 0.030	0.75 ± 0.081
	Standard-VAE	0.83 ± 0.124	0.37 ± 0.081	0.83 ± 0.115	0.39 ± 0.054	0.25 ± 0.001	0.73 ± 0.060

We are only able to reproduce the strong improvement in the level of disentanglement reported in [11] for the Shapes dataset and the NF backbone. Hence, we expect the CITRIS CFD extensions to improve few-shot accuracy only in that setting. For Shapes, the most challenging factors to disentangle were usually those concerning the rotation of the object. For Pong, the most challenging was to disentangle both paddle positions into separate dimensions, as their movements are very correlated.

5.2. Prediction Error

We show three perspectives on the prediction error. In the first perspective, we vary the pretraining epoch (between 1 and 500) used as a starting point for the few-shot domain adaptation and show the prediction error for one number of available shots (i.e., 200 shots). In the second perspective, we select one pretraining epoch (i.e., epoch 500) and show the prediction error for various numbers of available shots (i.e., 20, 100, 1000, and 10,000 shots). Finally, we also show a scatterplot comparing the CFD score to the prediction error at one number of shots (i.e., 100) and one pretraining epoch (i.e., 500).

5.2.1. Varying Pretraining Epoch

Figure 3 shows the evolution of the target-domain error with source-domain epochs for both SMS-TRIS datasets.

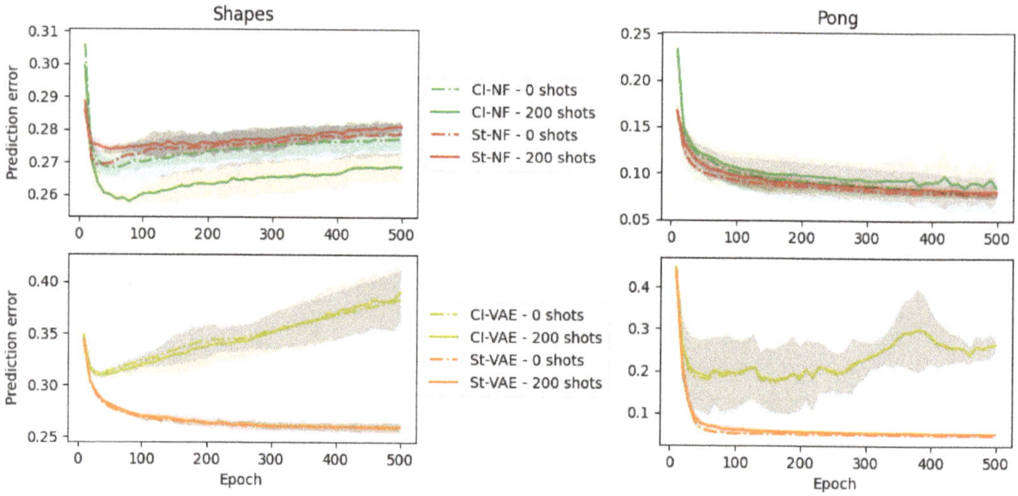

Figure 3. The 0-shot OOD error and 200-shot OOD error (lower is better) that a model achieves if the source-domain pretraining checkpoint at the epoch indicated on the x-axis is taken. The Standard models (St-VAE and St-NF) are shown in orange/red and the CITRIS models (CI-VAE and CI-NF) in green/olive. The left figures show results for the Shapes dataset and the right for the Pong dataset. The top figures show the Normalizing flow backbone and the bottom figures the VAE backbone. The line indicates the average of five runs, with the shaded areas indicating the standard deviation.

For Shapes and the NF backbone, we see that CITRIS-NF obtains the best performance. We also see that CITRIS-NF is the only variant for which the 200-shot performance (full lines) is significantly better than the 0-shot (dotted lines) performance. This is in line with our hypothesis that successful disentanglement improves few-shot domain adaptation.

For the VAE-models, the CITRIS-CFD extensions are not beneficial and Standard-VAE (which is equivalent to iVAE) is significantly better. This can be explained by the limited success of CITRIS-VAE in improving Causal Factor Disentanglement over Standard-VAE, as observed in Table 4.

For Pong, we also do not see that the CITRIS-CFD extensions are beneficial. This is again in line with the observation in Table 4 that the CITRIS-CFD extensions fail to improve Causal Factor Disentanglement. This indicates that finding more robust disentanglement encouragement is an avenue to more robustly improving few-shot domain adaptation prediction accuracy.

5.2.2. Varying Number of Shots

Figure 4 also shows the error, but displays the number of shots on the x-axis, rather than the pretraining epoch as in Figure 3. The pretraining epoch is fixed to 500.

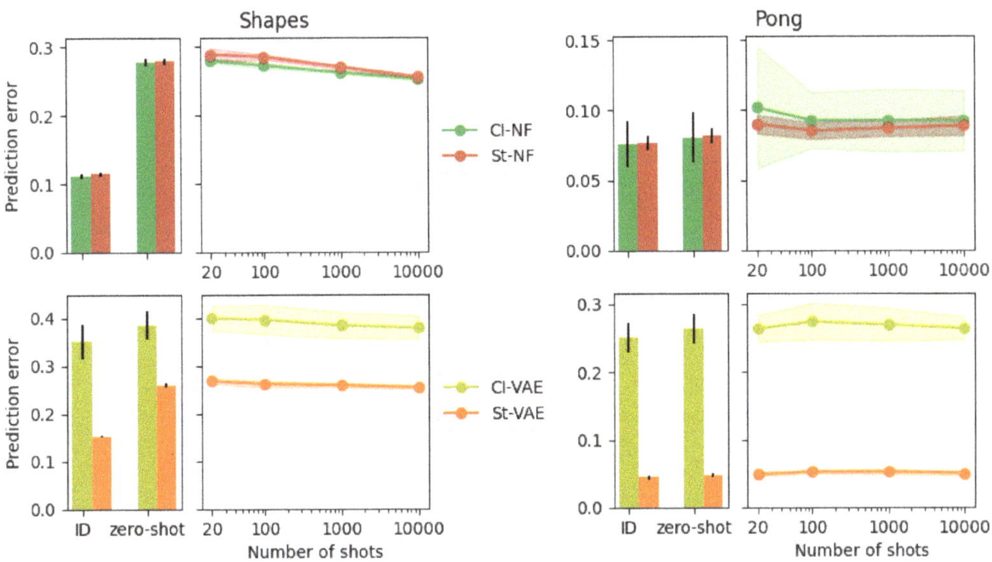

Figure 4. In-domain error, 0-shot error, and few-shot error of models after pretraining for 500 epochs. The Standard models are shown in red/orange and the CITRIS models in green/olive. The left figures show results for the Shapes dataset and the right for the Pong dataset. The top figures show the NF backbone and the bottom figures the VAE backbone. The average of five runs is shown, with the error bars/shaded areas indicating the standard deviation. The x-axis indicates in-domain or zero-shot out-of-domain for the bar charts and the number of shots used for the line plots.

For Shapes, it confirms the observation from Figure 3 that CITRIS-NF sees the biggest improvement compared to its zero-shot performance. For Pong, we see that none of the models are able to improve over their zero-shot performance, indicating that adaptation in SMS-Pong is more challenging than in SMS-Shapes.

5.3. *Causal Factor Disentanglement versus Prediction Error*

Figure 5 shows the correlation between few-shot prediction performance and Causal Factor Disentanglement.

It shows that while adding CITRIS does not consistently improve the CFD score, a higher CFD score is positively correlated with a lower prediction error, regardless of how it was achieved. This again indicates that finding more robust disentanglement encouragement is a promising avenue.

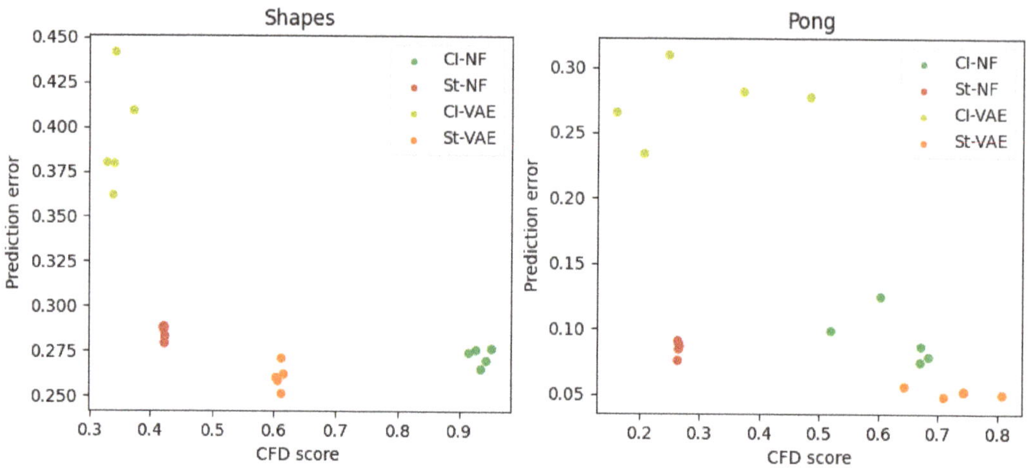

Figure 5. Correlation between few-shot prediction performance and Causal Factor Disentanglement. The y-axis shows 100-shot prediction error after pretraining for 500 epochs. The x-axis shows the CFD Score. Results for the Shapes dataset are on the left, and for Pong, on the right.

5.4. Comparison to Deep CORAL

Figure 6 evaluates the effect of including the Deep CORAL objective. We only consider the Normalizing Flow backbone, as it showed the most consistent few-shot learning. Since using Deep CORAL is complementary to the use of CITRIS CFD encouragement, we show four variations: CITRIS-NF, CITRIS-NF + Deep CORAL, Standard-NF, and Standard-NF + Deep CORAL. The results show that the Deep CORAL objective is *not* helpful for the SMS-TRIS benchmark, highlighting the need for alternative methods to exploit the SMS assumption.

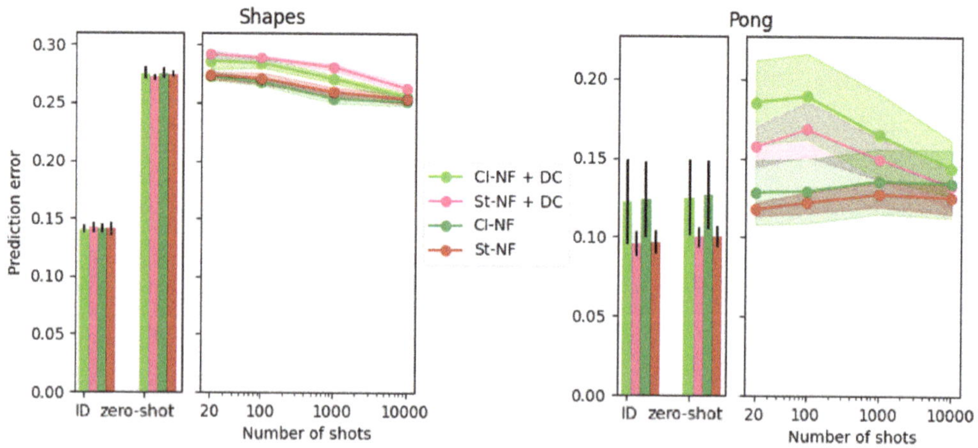

Figure 6. The effect of Deep CORAL on in-domain error, 0-shot error, and few-shot error of models after pretraining for 50 epochs. The Standard models are shown in shades of red and the CITRIS models in shades of green. The left figure shows results for the Shapes dataset and the right for the Pong dataset. The average of five runs is shown, with the error bars/shaded areas indicating the standard deviation. The x-axis indicates in-domain or zero-shot out-of-domain for the bar charts and the number of shots used for the line plots.

5.5. Discussion

We observe that CFD encouragement, using the CITRIS CFD extensions, does not improve the CFD score consistently across different backbones and datasets. This indicates that a more robust way of improving the CFD score is important when leveraging disentanglement for few-shot domain adaptation.

Our results indicate that CFD encouragement can help specifically in improving the relative improvement of *few-shot* performance over *zero-shot* performance, which is in line with the observations made in [12]. However, adding the CFD encouragement sometimes damages the zero-shot performance.

One factor that might be limiting the benefits of disentanglement is that shared parameters in the encoder and transition prior specialize to source-domain mechanisms. If that happens, the model cannot "get away" with only updating the nonshared parameters that are disentangled with regard to the shifted mechanism. Hence, it can be valuable to achieve disentanglement without being influenced by specific ID mechanisms.

6. Conclusions

This paper proposed a method to improve accuracy in the challenging problem of transfer learning for few-shot video prediction. Specifically, we aim to exploit the situation where the source and target domains are related through a Sparse Mechanism Shift. In this situation, we study the idea of encouraging the model to be disentangled with regard to causal mechanisms, allowing it to improve their few-shot prediction performance. We argue that successful Causal Representation Learning can enable such disentanglement. To experimentally investigate this connection, we created a novel benchmark called SMS-TRIS that consists of datasets with source-domain and target-domain variants that vary by a single distribution shift. Using this benchmark, we compare the effect of Causal Representation Learning using the CITRIS extensions proposed in [11] on a number of baselines.

Our results suggest that including CITRIS extensions benefits few-shot target-domain accuracy *if* those extensions allow the model to reach a sufficient level of Causal Factor Disentanglement on the source-domain data. Our experiments also indicate that few-shot learning in general is a hard problem and that it is often hard to beat the simple baseline of not using the few available target-domain samples at all.

We hope this work can spark research that further looks into the best ways to leverage the Sparse Mechanism Shift assumption for few-shot domain adaptation.

Author Contributions: Conceptualization: N.C.; methodology: N.C.; software: N.C.; validation: N.C.; formal analysis: N.C.; investigation: N.C.; resources: N.C.; data curation: N.C.; writing—original draft preparation: N.C., M.-F.M., K.L. and J.S.; writing—review and editing: N.C., M.-F.M., K.L. and J.S.; visualization: N.C.; supervision: M.-F.M., K.L. and J.S.; project administration: M.-F.M.; funding acquisition: M.-F.M. All authors have read and agreed to the published version of the manuscript.

Funding: This research is financed by the CALCULUS project—Commonsense and Anticipation enriched Learning of Continuous representations—of the European Research Council Advanced Grant H2020-ERC-2017-ADG 788506, https://calculus-project.eu/ (accessed on 21 August 2023). K.L. was supported by a Research Foundation—Flanders (FWO) junior postdoctoral fellowship no. 12B0623N during their work on this paper.

Institutional Review Board Statement: Not applicable.

Data Availability Statement: Data are contained within the article.

Conflicts of Interest: The authors declare no conflict of interest.

Appendix A. Example Subsequence of Shapes and Pong Datasets

Figures A1 and A2 show example subsequences of the Shapes and Pong datasets, respectively.

Figure A1. Example subsequence of the Shapes dataset.

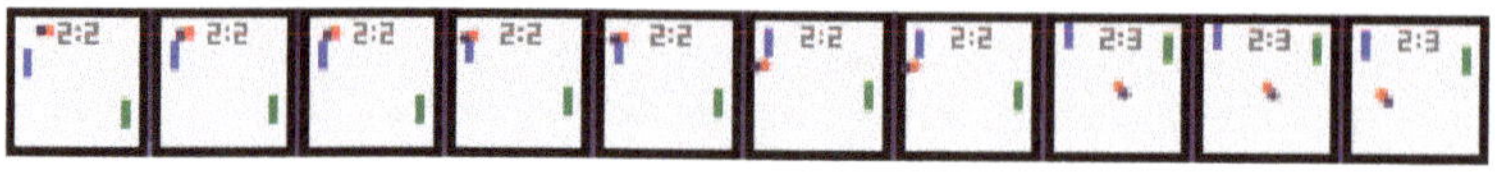

Figure A2. Example subsequence of the Pong dataset.

References

1. Filos, A.; Tigkas, P.; McAllister, R.; Rhinehart, N.; Levine, S.; Gal, Y. Can autonomous vehicles identify, recover from, and adapt to distribution shifts? In Proceedings of the International Conference on Machine Learning, PMLR, Virtual, 13–18 July 2020; pp. 3145–3153.
2. Guariso, G.; Nunnari, G.; Sangiorgio, M. Multi-step solar irradiance forecasting and domain adaptation of deep neural networks. *Energies* **2020**, *13*, 3987. [CrossRef]
3. Rothfuss, J.; Ferreira, F.; Aksoy, E.E.; Zhou, Y.; Asfour, T. Deep Episodic Memory: Encoding, Recalling, and Predicting Episodic Experiences for Robot Action Execution. *IEEE Robot. Autom. Lett.* **2018**, *3*, 4007–4014. [CrossRef]
4. Teshima, T.; Sato, I.; Sugiyama, M. Few-shot Domain Adaptation by Causal Mechanism Transfer. In Proceedings of the 37th International Conference on Machine Learning, PMLR, Virtual, 13–18 July 2020; pp. 9458–9469. ISSN 2640-3498.
5. Arjovsky, M.; Bottou, L.; Gulrajani, I.; Lopez-Paz, D. Invariant Risk Minimization. *arXiv* **2019**, arXiv:1907.02893.
6. Liu, C.; Sun, X.; Wang, J.; Tang, H.; Li, T.; Qin, T.; Chen, W.; Liu, T.Y. Learning causal semantic representation for out-of-distribution prediction. *Adv. Neural Inf. Process. Syst.* **2021**, *34*, 6155–6170.
7. Wang, R.; Yi, M.; Chen, Z.; Zhu, S. Out-of-distribution Generalization with Causal Invariant Transformations. In Proceedings of the IEEE/CVF Conference on Computer Vision and Pattern Recognition, CVPR 2022, New Orleans, LA, USA, 18–24 June 2022; pp. 375–385. [CrossRef]
8. Schölkopf, B.; Locatello, F.; Bauer, S.; Ke, N.R.; Kalchbrenner, N.; Goyal, A.; Bengio, Y. Toward causal representation learning. *Proc. IEEE* **2021**, *109*, 612–634. [CrossRef]
9. Kozhubaev, Y.; Ovchinnikova, E.; Viacheslav, I.; Krotova, S. Incremental Machine Learning for Soft Pneumatic Actuators with Symmetrical Chambers. *Symmetry* **2023**, *15*, 1206. [CrossRef]
10. Lopez, R.; Tagasovska, N.; Ra, S.; Cho, K.; Pritchard, J.; Regev, A. Learning Causal Representations of Single Cells via Sparse Mechanism Shift Modeling. In Proceedings of the Second Conference on Causal Learning and Reasoning, PMLR, Tübingen, Germany, 11–14 April 2023; pp. 662–691. ISSN 2640-3498.
11. Lippe, P.; Magliacane, S.; Löwe, S.; Asano, Y.M.; Cohen, T.; Gavves, S. Citris: Causal identifiability from temporal intervened sequences. In Proceedings of the International Conference on Machine Learning, PMLR, Baltimore, MD, USA, 17–23 July 2022; pp. 13557–13603.
12. Bengio, Y.; Deleu, T.; Rahaman, N.; Ke, N.R.; Lachapelle, S.; Bilaniuk, O.; Goyal, A.; Pal, C.J. A Meta-Transfer Objective for Learning to Disentangle Causal Mechanisms. In Proceedings of the 8th International Conference on Learning Representations, ICLR 2020, Addis Ababa, Ethiopia, 26–30 April 2020.
13. Sun, B.; Saenko, K. Deep CORAL: Correlation Alignment for Deep Domain Adaptation. In Proceedings of the Computer Vision—ECCV 2016 Workshops, Amsterdam, The Netherlands, 8–10, 15–16 October 2016.
14. Khemakhem, I.; Kingma, D.P.; Monti, R.P.; Hyvärinen, A. Variational Autoencoders and Nonlinear ICA: A Unifying Framework. In Proceedings of the 23rd International Conference on Artificial Intelligence and Statistics, Online, 26–28 August 2020; Chiappa, S., Calandra, R., Eds.; Volume 108, pp. 2207–2217.
15. Kim, H.; Mnih, A. Disentangling by Factorising. In Proceedings of the 35th International Conference on Machine Learning, ICML 2018, Stockholm, Sweden, 10–15 July 2018; Dy, J.G., Krause, A., Eds.; Volume 80, pp. 2654–2663.
16. Lu, C.; Wu, Y.; Hernández-Lobato, J.M.; Schölkopf, B. Nonlinear Invariant Risk Minimization: A Causal Approach. *arXiv* **2021**, arXiv:2102.12353.
17. Krueger, D.; Caballero, E.; Jacobsen, J.H.; Zhang, A.; Binas, J.; Zhang, D.; Priol, R.L.; Courville, A. Out-of-Distribution Generalization via Risk Extrapolation (REx). In Proceedings of the 38th International Conference on Machine Learning. PMLR, Virtual, 18–24 July 2021; pp. 5815–5826. ISSN 2640-3498.
18. Rojas-Carulla, M.; Scholkopf, B.; Turner, R.; Peters, J. Invariant Models for Causal Transfer Learning. *J. Mach. Learn. Res.* **2018**, *19*, 1–34.
19. Shu, R.; Bui, H.H.; Narui, H.; Ermon, S. A DIRT-T Approach to Unsupervised Domain Adaptation. In Proceedings of the 6th International Conference on Learning Representations, ICLR 2018, Vancouver, BC, Canada, 30 April–3 May 2018.
20. Yoon, J.; Kang, D.; Cho, M. Semi-supervised domain adaptation via sample-to-sample self-distillation. In Proceedings of the IEEE/CVF Winter Conference on Applications of Computer Vision, Waikoloa, HI, USA, 3–8 January 2022; pp. 1978–1987.
21. Peng, K.; Wen, D.; Schneider, D.; Zhang, J.; Yang, K.; Sarfraz, M.S.; Stiefelhagen, R.; Roitberg, A. FeatFSDA: Towards Few-shot Domain Adaptation for Video-based Activity Recognition. *arXiv* **2023**, arXiv:2305.08420.

2. Xu, Y.; Yang, J.; Zhou, Y.; Chen, Z.; Wu, M.; Li, X. Augmenting and Aligning Snippets for Few-Shot Video Domain Adaptation. *arXiv* **2023**, arXiv:2303.10451.
3. Jiang, J.; Ji, Y.; Wang, X.; Liu, Y.; Wang, J.; Long, M. Regressive domain adaptation for unsupervised keypoint detection. In Proceedings of the IEEE/CVF Conference on Computer Vision and Pattern Recognition, Nashville, TN, USA, 20–25 June 2021; pp. 6780–6789.
4. Lang, C.; Cheng, G.; Tu, B.; Li, C.; Han, J. Base and meta: A new perspective on few-shot segmentation. *IEEE Trans. Pattern Anal. Mach. Intell.* **2023**, *45*, 10669–10686. [CrossRef] [PubMed]
5. Tian, Z.; Zhao, H.; Shu, M.; Yang, Z.; Li, R.; Jia, J. Prior guided feature enrichment network for few-shot segmentation. *IEEE Trans. Pattern Anal. Mach. Intell.* **2020**, *44*, 1050–1065. [CrossRef] [PubMed]
6. Liu, H.; Tam, D.; Muqeeth, M.; Mohta, J.; Huang, T.; Bansal, M.; Raffel, C. Few-Shot Parameter-Efficient Fine-Tuning is Better and Cheaper than In-Context Learning. In Proceedings of the NeurIPS, New Orleans, LA, USA, 28 November–9 December 2022.
7. Crane, K. Keenan's 3D Model Repository. Available online: https://www.cs.cmu.edu/~kmcrane/Projects/ModelRepository/ (accessed on 1 January 2021).
8. Rusinkiewicz, S.; DeCarlo, D.; Finkelstein, A.; Santella, A. Suggestive Contour Gallery. Available online: https://gfx.cs.princeton.edu/proj/sugcon/models/ (accessed on 1 January 2021).
9. Curless, B.; Levoy, M. A volumetric method for building complex models from range images. In Proceedings of the 23rd Annual Conference on Computer Graphics and Interactive Techniques, New Orleans, LA, USA, 4–9 August 1996; pp. 303–312.
0. Turk, G.; Levoy, M. Zippered polygon meshes from range images. In Proceedings of the 21st Annual Conference on Computer Graphics and Interactive Techniques, Orlando, FL, USA, 24–29 July 1994; pp. 311–318.
1. Krishnamurthy, V.; Levoy, M. Fitting smooth surfaces to dense polygon meshes. In Proceedings of the 23rd Annual Conference on Computer Graphics and Interactive Techniques, New Orleans, LA, USA, 4–9 August 1996; pp. 313–324.
2. Praun, E.; Finkelstein, A.; Hoppe, H. Lapped textures. In Proceedings of the 27th Annual Conference on Computer Graphics and Interactive Techniques, New Orleans, LA, USA, 23–28 July 2000; pp. 465–470.
3. Newell, M.E. The Utilization of Procedure Models in Digital Image Synthesis. Ph.D. Thesis, The University of Utah, Salt Lake City, UT, USA, 1975.
4. Bellemare, M.G.; Naddaf, Y.; Veness, J.; Bowling, M. The arcade learning environment: An evaluation platform for general agents. *J. Artif. Intell. Res.* **2013**, *47*, 253–279. [CrossRef]
5. Wright, S. Correlation and causation. *J. Agric. Res.* **1921**, *20*, 557–585.
6. Spearman, C. The proof and measurement of association between two things. *Am. J. Psychol.* **1987**, *100*, 441–471. [CrossRef] [PubMed]

entropy

MDPI

Article

Information-Theoretical Analysis of Team Dynamics in Footbal Matches

Yi-Shan Cheng [1,*], Acer Yu-Chan Chang [2] and Kenji Doya [1]

1 Okinawa Institute of Science and Technology, Okinawa 9040412, Japan; doya@oist.jp
2 Department of Psychology, College of Contemporary Psychology, Rikkyo University, Tokyo 1718501, Japan; acercyc@rikkyo.ac.jp
* Correspondence: yi-shan.cheng2@oist.jp

Abstract: Team dynamics significantly influence the outcomes of modern football matches. This study employs an information-theoretical approach, specifically causal emergence, combined with graph theory to explore how team-level dynamics arise from complex interactions among players, utilizing tracking data from 34 J-League matches. We focused on how collective behaviors arise from the interdependence of individual actions, examining team coordination and dynamics through player positions and movements to identify emergent properties. Specifically, we selected relative distance to the field's center, center of mass (CoM) and clustering coefficients based on velocity similarity and inverse distance as macroscopic features to capture the key aspects of team structure, coordination, and spatial relationships. Relative distance and CoM represent the collective positioning of the team, while clustering coefficients provide insights into localized cooperation and movement similarity among the players. The results indicate that average causal emergence with relative distance and CoM as a macroscopic feature across entire games shows a strong correlation with differences in ball possession rate between home and away teams. In contrast, clustering coefficients based on inverse distance and velocity similarity showed moderate to weak correlations with ball possession rate, indicating that these metrics may capture localized interactions that are less directly tied to team-level emergent behavior compared to CoM. Additionally, relative distance and CoM as macroscopic features yield higher causal emergence in attacking phases than in defending phases before shooting, suggesting that the collective positioning of players may play a more significant role in facilitating successful attacks than in defensive stability. This study offers a novel perspective on team coordination in football, suggesting that effective team coordination may be characterized by emergent patterns arising from collective positioning. These findings have practical implications for understanding coordinated team behaviors and inform coaching and performance analysis focused on enhancing team dynamics.

Keywords: team dynamics; causal emergence; information theory; graph theory; football analytics; collective behavior

1. Introduction

In modern football, team dynamics play a crucial role in determining the outcome of matches [1,2]. Understanding how players interact on the field, cooperate, and execute tactical plans is key to optimizing team performance. Recent advances in data analytics and tracking technologies have enabled detailed analysis of player movements and interactions [3], yet quantifying teamwork remains a complex challenge.

Despite the availability of substantial amounts of player tracking data, current methods often fall short in capturing the complexity of team cooperation. Traditional metrics focused on individual players' physical ability [4], performance [5], and the training [6] or coaching [7], which may overlook the emergent properties that arise from the complex interactions within a team. These methods fail to adequately reflect the dynamic, collective behaviors that contribute to team success, which are often greater than the sum of the individual players' actions. Therefore, there is a need for new approaches that can accurately represent the collective coordination and emergent dynamics that underpin successful teamwork.

Emergence, a key concept in complex systems, describes how macroscopic behaviors or properties arise from the interactions of individual components, often resulting in patterns that cannot be fully understood by analyzing each component in isolation. For example, Seth demonstrated that migratory bird flocks do not act as mere aggregates of individual birds but form cohesive, coordinated groups where shared directionality and collective decision making emerge from interactions between individuals [8]. Collective behaviors are observed in the swarming of soldier crabs [9], fish schools [10] and other natural group phenomena. These examples illustrate emergence as a property of systems in which behaviors at the macroscopic level arise from the interactions of individual microscopic elements, resulting in patterns that cannot be fully understood by examining each component in isolation [11,12].

Causal emergence builds upon traditional emergence, which describes how macroscopic properties arise from the interactions of individual components in a system. Emergence, while providing descriptive insights, lacks a quantitative framework to evaluate how macroscopic properties influence system behavior. Causal emergence addresses this limitation by providing a method to compare macro-level and micro-level models in terms of their ability to explain or predict system dynamics. Hoel et al. [13] introduced causal emergence as a framework for analyzing when macro-level models capture causal patterns that are not evident at the micro-level. Their work has been applied in various domains to identify conditions under which macro-level properties provide additional explanatory value. Yuan et al. [14] reviewed recent advancements in causal emergence theory, summarizing its theoretical and applied developments in analyzing complex systems. In football, macro-level properties such as formations, passing networks, and coordinated movements are critical to understanding match outcomes. These properties are difficult to fully capture through micro-level analysis of individual players' actions. This study applies causal emergence theory to investigate how macro-level structures contribute to team coordination and performance, offering insights that cannot be obtained from micro-level data alone.

To analyze causal emergence within team dynamics, we adopt the framework developed by Rosas et al. [15], which uses information-theoretic methods to quantify emergent behaviors. This framework applies Partial Information Decomposition (PID) to decompose shared information between variables into unique, redundant, and synergistic components [16]. Synergy represents information that arises from the joint state of multiple variables and cannot be assigned to any single variable, while redundancy reflects information that is shared across variables and can be attributed to multiple sources. By examining both synergy and redundancy, this framework provides a detailed view of how team-level coordination emerges from micro-level interactions among football players.

In this study, we also consider network interaction generated from graph theory to analyze team dynamics. These metrics emphasize relational dynamics and quantify structural and functional properties within the team's network, providing insights into coordination patterns. Network science has been applied in various studies to analyze the structure and performance of football teams. For example, graph theory has been used to evaluate the passing networks of teams during the FIFA World Cup [17], demonstrating that high clustering coefficients were associated with successful teams, particularly in possession-dominant styles. Similarly, Buldú et al. applied network metrics to analyze team coordination, showing how the clustering coefficient can highlight the ability of players to maintain ball circulation and control [18]. These studies underscore the importance of network-based metrics in capturing the collective properties of teams.

By incorporating weighted clustering coefficients into football analysis [19], this study aims to highlight these network metrics not merely as descriptive indicators of team performance but as potential emergent properties arising from the interactions of individual players. Specifically, clustering coefficients, derived from micro-level features of velocity similarity and physical distance between players, are treated as collective features that reflect the coordinated behaviors of the team as a whole. This approach shifts the focus from evaluating how these metrics correlate with team success to investigating whether they capture emergent dynamics that cannot be fully explained by individual-level attributes alone. By doing so, we aim to explore the extent to which these metrics represent higher-order properties of team coordination and their role in the causal emergence of team performance.

The primary objective of this study is to investigate how causal emergence reveals macro-level team coordination arising from micro-level player interactions in football. Specifically, we explore how variations in causal emergence may be influenced by both synergy and redundancy, acknowledging their potential combined contributions to emergent team behaviors. This approach provides a framework for analyzing how team dynamics emerge, offering a deeper understanding of the mechanisms driving effective coordination.

This research merges causal emergence theory with network-based metrics, aiming to identify the role of emergent properties in team performance. By integrating information-theoretic tools with clustering coefficients, we analyze the interplay between micro-level interactions and macro-level patterns, contributing to both sports analytics and the broader field of complex systems research.

This study addresses the following key research questions:

1. How does causal emergence reflect emergent team coordination in football?
2. Can weighted clustering coefficients, derived from velocity similarity and physical distance, be interpreted as emergent properties of collective team behavior?
3. What role do emergent properties play in shaping successful team performance in terms of coordinated movements and match outcomes?

The structure of this paper is organized as follows: Section 2 introduces the theoretical framework and methodology. Section 3 presents the results, focusing on the relationship between causal emergence and possession rate, including different choices of macro-level features Section 4 discusses the implications of these findings for understanding team dynamics and their broader applications. Finally, Section 5 concludes with a summary with key insights and suggestions for future research directions.

2. Materials and Methods

2.1. Data Preparation

The dataset used in this study was provided by DataStadium Inc., Tokyo, Japan, under an agreement with the J-League. These proprietary tracking data include 34 J-League matches from the 2022 season, with usage approved by DataStadium Inc. and in compliance with all legal and ethical standards.

Preprocessing

The original player tracking data include positional information recorded at 25 Hz. The data were first down-sampled to 1 Hz. Since velocity information was not provided directly, the x and y velocity components for each player were calculated as the difference in position coordinates between consecutive seconds.

To determine the start and end frames of each half, event data were utilized. Event data included timestamps for match-specific actions such as passes, shots, fouls, and substitutions, providing a temporal reference to segment the tracking data. This ensured that only the frames corresponding to each half were extracted, allowing for precise alignment of positional data with gameplay phases.

During player substitutions, event data were also used to ensure that positional data for ten outfield players from each team remained available, excluding goalkeepers due to their unique role and restricted movement range. Furthermore, data from match periods involving red card incidents were excluded to maintain consistency with ten players per team for subsequent analyses.

2.2. Causal Emergence

To measure causal emergence in this study, we adopted the framework introduced by Rosas et al. [15]. This framework considers causal emergence as grounded in the unique causal power exhibited by macroscopic features V_t at time t in predicting the system's future state $X_{t'}$ at time $t\prime$. To capture the concept of unique causal power, this framework utilizes Partial Information Decomposition (PID). PID, introduced by Williams and Beer, decomposes the total information that a set of source variables provides about a target variable into the following distinct components: unique, redundant, and synergistic information [16]. For example, consider two variables X_1 and X_2 as sources of information about a target variable Y. PID decomposes the total mutual information between (X_1, X_2) and Y into the following: unique information, which is the part of Y that is predicted only by X_1 or only by X_2; redundant information, which represents the information about Y that is shared by both X_1 and X_2; and synergistic information, which captures the information about Y that is not present in either X_1 or X_2 individually but emerges from their combined state.

In the context of causal emergence, unique information captures the part of the macroscopic feature V_t that provides predictive power beyond what is available at the next future microscopic state $X_{t'}$. Therefore, the formal definition of causal emergence, as proposed by Rosas et al. [15], is as follows: In a system described by X_t, a supervenient feature V_t exhibits causal emergence of order l if:

$$\mathrm{Un}^{(l)}(V_t; X_{t'}|X_t) > 0 \tag{1}$$

where $\mathrm{Un}^{(l)}(V_t; X_{t'}|X_t)$ represents the unique information of V_t about $X_{t'}$ given X_t. at order l. Order l specifies the level of decomposition used in the analysis and determines the maximum subset size of microscopic variables considered when evaluating causal emergence. This definition captures the idea that a macroscopic feature V_t exhibits causal emergence if it contains predictive information about the system's future that is not available in any subset of its microscopic components X_t.

In practical application, to address computational limitations, a practical criterion of causal emergence was used, comparing the mutual information $I(V_t; V_{t'})$ at the macroscopic level with the aggregate $\Sigma_{i \in s} I(X_t^i; V_{t'})$ across microscopic features.

Therefore, the practical criteria used to measure causal emergence Ψ as proposed by Rosas et al. [15], is defined as follows:

$$\Psi^{l}_{t,t'}(V) := I(V_t; V_{t'}) - \Sigma_{i \in s} I\big(X^{i}_{t}; V_{t'}\big), \tag{2}$$

where $I(V_t; V_{t'})$ represents the mutual information between the macroscopic feature V at two time steps, t and a step after t', but not all of the time steps before t'. The second term, $\Sigma_{i \in s} I(X^{i}_{t}; V_{t'})$, is the sum of the mutual information between each microscopic feature X^{i} at time t and the macroscopic feature V at the subsequent time $t\prime$. Here, i indexes each microscopic feature within the set s of all microscopic feature s, allowing us to assess the combined contribution of all microscopic components relative to the macroscopic state. The practical criterion is particularly useful for empirical studies because it provides a computable metric that preserves the core concept of causal emergence. To estimate the mutual information terms here, we used the Gaussian mutual information estimator implemented in the publicly available toolbox provided by Rosas et al. [15]. This estimator assumes that variables are jointly Gaussian-distributed and provides an efficient closed-form computation of mutual information [20].

Note that we restricted our analysis to order $l = 1$, meaning we only considered the contributions of individual microscopic features in explaining the predictive power of the macroscopic feature. Higher orders of l (e.g., $l = 2$ or greater) that consider combinations of two or more microscopic features were not included in this study.

In the original proposal by Rosas et al. [15], causal emergence is identified when Ψ is positive, indicating that the macroscopic level provides sufficiently greater predictive power regarding the future state than the sum of the contributions from the microscopic components. Positive values of Ψ suggest that the macroscopic state captures emergent patterns and interactions that cannot be fully explained by the collective contributions of individual microscopic features. However, in our study, we also considered cases where Ψ is negative, focusing on the dynamics of causal emergence rather than only its positive manifestations.

Real-world systems, including team dynamics, often exhibit substantial redundancy, where overlapping information between system components contributes to the robustness and coordination of the system. Redundancy can lead to negative values of Ψ, reflecting scenarios where the macroscopic state retains less predictive power to the future macro-state than the total contributions of the predictive power of individual components to the future macro-state. Importantly, in the context of the current study, redundancy does not imply a lack of collective behavior but instead highlights the shared information among players that supports the overall system's functionality. This shared information can enhance team coordination and resilience, even when the predictive power of individual components to the future macro-state exceeds that of the macroscopic feature.

Understanding redundancy is critical for interpreting collective behaviors in team sports. It provides insight into how shared information among players contributes to robust coordination and adaptability under various game conditions. By examining both positive and negative values of Ψ, this study aims to capture the full spectrum of causal emergence dynamics, providing a more comprehensive understanding of how team-level behaviors arise from the interplay of individual interactions.

Microscopic and Macroscopic Feature Selection

Microscopic Feature Selection

In the context of our causal emergence analysis, the selection of appropriate microscopic variables is essential as they form the foundation for deriving macroscopic features and identifying emergent team behaviors. For this study, we chose player positions, velocities, and distance to the field center as our primary microscopic features (illustrated in Figure 1). Player positions, represented by their x and y coordinates on the field, capture the spatial configuration of the team and are used to derive the macroscopic feature center of mass and the clustering coefficient of inverse distance from network analysis (see below). Player velocities, derived from the change in position over time, reflect the dynamic aspects of individual player movements and are used to compute the macro feature, the clustering coefficient of velocity similarity. Additionally, we included each player's distance to the field's center to account for their spatial relationship to a key reference point on the field; this is aggregated to form the macroscopic feature, relative distance. These microscopic variables were chosen because they directly represent the actions and spatial context of individual players. They provide a detailed, granular perspective on individual contributions before we aggregate them into team-level macroscopic features to explore emergent properties.

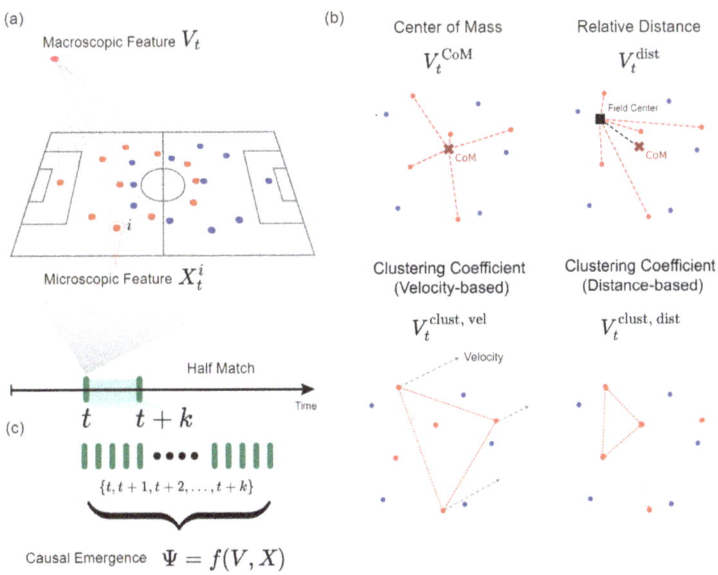

Figure 1. Framework for macroscopic feature selection and causal emergence analysis in football team dynamics. (**a**) Generation macroscopic feature V_t from microscopic features X_t^i. (**b**) Schematic of macroscopic features based on CoM (V_t^{CoM}), which was generated from players' positions as microscopic features; distance from CoM to the field's center (V_t^{dist}), which was generated from players' distances to the field's center as microscopic features; clustering coefficient of velocity similarity ($V^{\text{clust, vel}}$), which was generated from players' velocities as microscopic features; and inverse distance ($V^{\text{clust, dist}}$), which was generated from players' positions as microscopic features. The red and blue dots presented the players' positions in different teams and the lines are the distances between two objects. (**c**) Causal emergence Ψ analysis with interval $\{t, t+k\}$.

Macroscopic Feature Selection

In this study, the selection of macroscopic features and their corresponding microscopic variables, as presented in Figure 1, is pivotal for capturing the emergent team behaviors that arise from the complex interactions between individual players. These features serve as aggregated representations of team-level dynamics, providing insights that are not evident from analyzing individual components alone. We focus on two main categories of macroscopic features: aggregate positioning metrics and network interaction metrics.

Aggregate Positioning Metrics

Aggregate positioning metrics emphasize the collective positioning and spatial organization of the team. These features are derived from geometric configurations of player positions and capture the overall team structure. The selected metrics in this category include the following:

Center of Mass (V^{CoM}):

The microscopic features used to compute the center of mass are the x and y coordinates of all players on the field. The macroscopic feature is obtained by averaging these individual player positions, resulting in a two-dimensional representation of the team's spatial structure. This approach captures overall team positioning, offering a direct measure of collective spatial dynamics.

Relative Distance (V^{dist}):

For each player, the distance to the field's center was used as a microscopic feature, while the distance from the CoM to the field center served as a one-dimensional macroscopic feature. This representation highlights the team's spatial orientation relative to a fixed reference point.

Network Interaction Metrics

Network interaction metrics are derived from graph theory and emphasize the relational dynamics and interactions among players. Specifically, we focus on the clustering coefficient, a metric that measures the degree of local clustering or interconnectedness within a network [21]. To construct graphs, we consider each player as a node and take two approaches to defining the edges of the graph: velocity-based similarity and distance-based proximity.

Velocity-Based Edge Construction:

To capture the degree of local coordination based on the players' velocity, we calculated the clustering coefficient for each second from player's velocity components in the x and y directions as the microscopic features. Each player's velocity and movement direction were derived by calculating the distance and angle between consecutive positions. For each second, a weighted, undirected graph was constructed with nodes representing individual players and edges representing the relationships between the players. These relationships were weighted based on relative velocity and angular differences between the players, allowing us to reflect synchronization in player movements.

The weight of an edge between two players u and v was calculated as follows:

$$Weight(u,v) = S_u \times S_v \times (cos(\Delta\theta) + 1), \tag{3}$$

where S_u and S_v represent the players' velocity, and $\Delta\theta$ is the difference in their movement angles. This approach ensures that two players with higher movement velocities and similar moving directions are assigned higher weights to their edges, indicating greater synchronization.

Distance-Based Edge Construction:

To capture spatial cooperation among players, we used each player's Euclidean coordinates as the microscopic features and computed the clustering coefficient based on inverse distance metrics as the macroscopic feature. This approach assigns stronger edges to players who are physically closer, reflecting a higher likelihood of interaction. Here, edges were weighted by the inverse Euclidean distance between players u and v as follows:

$$Weight(u,v) = \frac{1}{Distance(u,v)}, \tag{4}$$

where u and v represent two players, and $Distance(u,v)$ is the Euclidean distance between their respective positions at a given second.

Compute clustering coefficients from a graph

The clustering coefficient $V_i^{\text{clust,}}$ for a node (player) i in a weighted graph is defined as follows:

$$V_i^{\text{clust}} = \frac{1}{k_i(k_i-1)} \sum_{j,k} \frac{w_{ij}+w_{ik}}{2} a_{jk}, \tag{5}$$

where k_i is the degree of node i, which represents the number of neighbors connected to node i, and w_{ij} and w_{ik} are the weights of the edges connecting node i to nodes j and k, respectively. The last term a_{jk} is an indicator function, which is 1 if there is an edge between nodes j and k, and 0 otherwise.

The global clustering coefficient is then calculated by taking the average of individual clustering coefficients across all players within a team, as floolows:

$$V^{\text{clust}} = \frac{1}{N}\sum_{i=1}^{N} V_i^{\text{clust}} \tag{6}$$

where N is the total number of players in the team.

Using the velocity- and distance-based edge calculations described above, we can derive two macroscopic features, as follows: $V^{clust,vel}$, clustering coefficient based on velocity similarity, and $V^{clust,dist}$ clustering coefficient based on inverse distance. These metrics capture different aspects of team coordination and spatial organization. NetworkX library in Python [21] was used in the implementation of the analysis.

2.3. Causal Emergence and Possession Rates

To investigate how team-level emergent dynamics relates to team performance, we examined the relationship between causal emergence and possession rates. The possession rate, defined as the percentage of time a team maintains control of the ball, is a pivotal metric often considered a decisive factor in determining match outcomes. By focusing on the differences between home and away teams, this analysis aimed to uncover the extent to which emergent team dynamics contribute to maintaining control of the ball, a key aspect of successful gameplay.

Causal emergence values were derived using macroscopic features based on player tracking data, including relative distance (V_t^{dist}), CoM (V_t^{CoM}), the clustering coefficient of inverse distance ($V_t^{\text{clust, dist}}$), and velocity similarity ($V_t^{\text{clust, vel}}$). For each match, the difference in average causal emergence values between the home and away teams was computed separately for the first and second halves. Similarly, the differences in possession rates between home and away teams were obtained for the same periods.

We correlated these paired differences (home vs. away) to assess the relationship between causal emergence and possession rates. Pearson's correlation coefficient (R) and the corresponding p-values were used to quantify the strength and statistical significance of these relationships, providing insights into how emergent team dynamics is related to ball control.

2.4. Causal Emergence Before Shooting

To analyze causal emergence before shooting events, a sliding window approach was employed to segment and compare the emergence values over time. This method aimed to capture the dynamic coordination patterns leading up to shooting events.

For each shooting event, a 60-s interval of emergence data preceding the event was extracted. The window size of calculating each causal emergence was set to 60 s to ensure sufficient temporal resolution for identifying emergent patterns, while the step size was defined as 1 s to provide granular temporal alignment. The shooting event served as the temporal anchor (time-lock), allowing consistent alignment of emergence values across all analyzed segments. Specifically, the 60-s interval began exactly 60 s before the recorded frame of the shooting event and ended at the frame immediately preceding the shot.

To establish a baseline for comparison, random 60-s intervals were selected from the same half of the game where the shooting event occurred. These segments were chosen randomly within the start and end frames of each half. The baseline segments were generated using the same sliding window parameters (60-s window size and 1-s step size) to maintain consistency in data structure and temporal granularity.

Although the defending teams occasionally regained possession during the analyzed windows, the labels of the shooting teams were maintained for clarity and consistency. This approach allowed this study to focus on the emergent behaviors of the attacking team, regardless of temporary disruptions in ball possession rate.

For each match, emergence values were extracted from preprocessed positional data and aligned with shooting events. The shooting frames were identified using event data, which recorded match-specific actions, including passes, fouls, and shots. Frames corresponding to the start of the first half, the start of the second half, and their respective end frames were used to segment the emergence data. For each shooting event, the corresponding team and half were identified to ensure correct alignment between emergence values and event data.

The emergence values from shooting intervals and their respective baseline segments were aggregated for subsequent statistical analysis. This comparison provided insights into whether patterns of causal emergence differed significantly between shooting scenarios and randomly selected segments, revealing critical features of team coordination and dynamics leading to shots.

3. Results

3.1. Match-Level Analysis: Degree of Causal Emergence Correlates with Possession Rate

To investigate how the degree of causal emergence relates to team performance, we conducted a match-level analysis examining the relationship between causal emergence and possession rates. Possession rate, defined as the percentage of time a team controls the ball, is a pivotal metric often regarded as a decisive factor in determining match outcomes [22]. This analysis aimed to uncover the extent to which emergent team dynamics, as quantified by causal emergence, contribute to a team's ability to maintain ball possession, a critical component of effective gameplay and overall success.

In this analysis, our objective was to understand how collective behaviors emerge in football teams by examining causal emergence in relation to the players' positions and velocities. To represent team coherence at a higher level, we first used relative distance and CoM as macroscopic features, capturing the collective movement of players on the field. Previous studies have shown that CoM is an effective indicator of team coordination and collective behavior, especially in scoring zones where spatial organization and coordinated actions are crucial for success [23].

We examined the relationship between causal emergence and ball possession rate across the first and second halves of multiple matches. Specifically, causal emergence was calculated using the following macroscopic features: relative distance (V_t^{dist}), CoM (V_t^{CoM}), inverse distance ($V_t^{\text{clust, dist}}$), and velocity ($V_t^{\text{clust, vel}}$).

To account for the variability between the two halves of each match, we computed the differences in average causal emergence values and possession rates between the home and away teams for each half. This approach ensures a standardized comparison by mitigating the effects of game-specific conditions and strategic variations across halves.

In Figure 2, the results demonstrate a strong relationship between ball possession rate and causal emergence metrics derived from aggregate positioning metrics. Teams with higher causal emergence values indicative of greater synergistic team dynamics tend to achieve higher ball possession rates. This finding highlights that spatial structure, as captured by macroscopic features, plays a crucial role in facilitating ball retention. The high correlation ($R = 0.79$) observed with relative distance (V_t^{dist}) as macroscopic features suggest that emergent team-level dynamics, as captured by relative positioning, play a critical role in maintaining possession. Teams in possession of the ball likely exhibit higher synergy, as their spatial arrangements reflect coordinated offensive structures that promote ball retention and passing options.

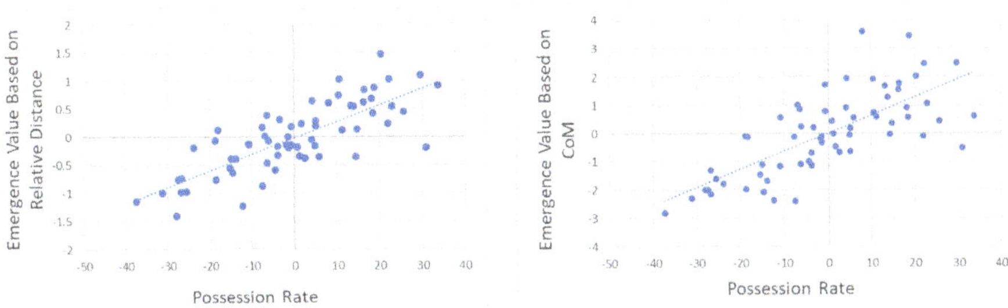

(a) (b)

Figure 2. Correlation of differences in causal emergence based on aggregate positioning metrics and ball possession rates. (**a**) Causal emergence based on relative distance exhibits a high correlation with ball possession rate, with $R = 0.79$ ($p < 0.001$). (**b**) Causal emergence based on CoM shows a similar strong correlation with possession rate at $R = 0.74$ ($p < 0.001$).

Causal emergence based on CoM (V_t^{CoM}) also exhibits a strong correlation with the ball possession rate ($R = 0.74$), indicating that when a team possesses the ball, their macroscopic configuration reflects a higher level of coordinated interaction, or synergy, compared to the opposing team. This emergent synergy likely arises as the possessing team dynamically adjusts its structure to create passing lanes, maintain spacing, and responds to the opposing team's defensive movements.

In Figure 3, causal emergence derived from the clustering coefficient of inverse distance ($V_t^{\text{clust, dist}}$) demonstrated a moderate positive correlation with possession rate differences ($R = 0.58$). This result shows that higher $V_t^{\text{clust, dist}}$, which reflects stronger local spatial interconnectedness within the team's positional network, is associated with higher possession rates. This finding suggests that spatial arrangement plays a critical role in sustaining ball control.

In contrast, causal emergence derived from the clustering coefficient of velocity similarity ($V_t^{\text{clust, vel}}$) showed no meaningful correlation with the ball possession rate ($R = 0.06$, $p = 0.71$). This lack of significant correlation suggests that player velocity alignment alone is not strongly associated with the ball possession rate. While velocity synchronization might reflect localized tactical coordination, it does not appear to directly contribute to the team-level emergent dynamics required for sustained possession.

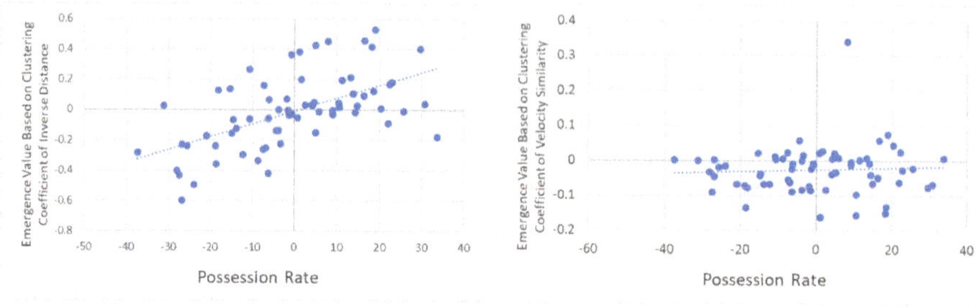

(**a**) (**b**)

Figure 3. Correlation of differences in causal emergence based on network interaction metrics with ball possession rates. (**a**) The correlation between causal emergence based on the clustering coefficient of inverse distance and possession rate yielded a moderate correlation of $R = 0.58$ ($p < 0.01$). (**b**) The correlation between causal emergence based on clustering coefficient of velocity similarity and possession rate showed a near-zero correlation, with $R = 0.06$ ($p = 0.71$).

The analysis reveals that causal emergence, as quantified through various macroscopic features, especially from spatial organization, correlates strongly with possession rate, underscoring the critical role of emergent team dynamics in effective ball control. However, it also suggests that velocity alignment alone is insufficient to capture the emergent team dynamics necessary for maintaining ball control.

In the next section, we will focus on the critical event of shooting, examining the detailed changes in causal emergence leading up to pivotal moments.

3.2. Causal Emergence over Players' Positions

In this analysis, we compared two macroscopic features based on player tracking data, including relative distance (V_t^{dist}), and CoM (V_t^{CoM}). For the relative distance calculation, we defined each player's distance from the center of the field as the microscopic feature. The macroscopic feature was represented by the average distance of all players' positions to the center of the field. This approach captures the spatial coherence of players relative to a fixed reference point (i.e., the center of the field), simplifying the representation of team dynamics.

Our analysis focused on evaluating causal emergence values before shooting, using relative distance and CoM as the macroscopic features. As shown in Figure 4, for both (a) relative distance and (b) CoM analyses, the attacking team exhibits an increasing trend in causal emergence values as the shot approaches, while the defending team shows a decreasing trend.

To quantitatively assess trends in causal emergence, we conducted linear regression analyses for each condition across both relative distance and CoM representations. For the relative distance analysis, for the attacking team, the regression analysis yielded a significant positive slope, $\beta = 0.0035$, $R^2 = 0.822$, $p < 0.001$, indicating a strong increase in causal emergence values over time. In contrast, the defending team exhibited a significant negative slope, $\beta = -0.0080$, $R^2 = 0.967$, $p < 0.001$, indicating a significant decrease in causal emergence values. Random intervals serve as a baseline, showing flatter trends with smaller slope values than attacking and defending. For the random attacking intervals, the slope was $\beta = 0.0004$, $R^2 = 0.037$, $p = 0.139$, which does not display strong directional trends. This baseline comparison underscores that the increasing and decreasing trends in causal emergence are specific to shooting phases rather than non-shooting phases.

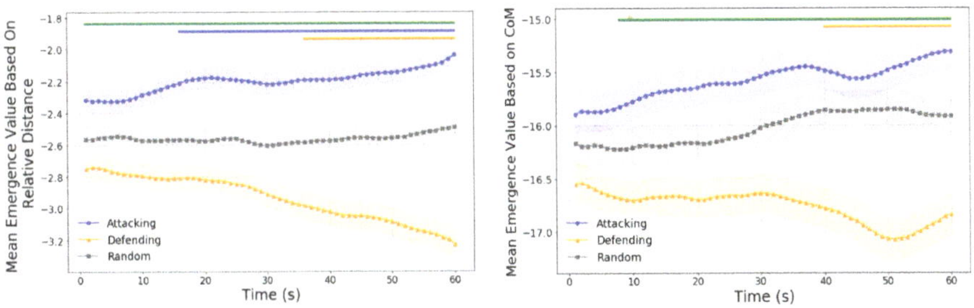

(a) (b)

Figure 4. Causal emergence with (**a**) relative distance and (**b**) CoM as macro features within the 60 s leading up to a shot. Each data point represents the causal emergence calculated using a 60-s time interval ending at the point of measurement. Shaded regions indicate the standard error of the mean (SEM) for each data point across all events. The blue lines represent values for the team that took the shot (attacking team), while the orange lines represent values for the opposing team (defending team). The gray lines depict the average causal emergence values during randomly selected 60-s intervals, matched in number to the actual shooting events. This provides a baseline comparison between dynamics before shooting events and neutral or random phases of play. Colored ribbons on top of the graph indicate statistically significant differences between groups, with Bonferroni correction for multiple comparisons. The green ribbon denotes significant differences between the attacking team (blue line) and defending team (orange line). The blue ribbon indicates significant differences between the attacking team (blue line) and random intervals (gray line). The orange ribbon marks significant differences between the defending team (orange line) and random intervals (gray line).

The increasing causal emergence in the attacking team suggests coordinated and synergistic movement patterns likely driven by structured offensive strategies as they progress toward a shot. Conversely, the defending team appears to react to the attackers, resulting in an increase in redundancy in the seconds leading up to the shot. This difference in causal emergence trends illustrates how team coordination evolves distinctly in offensive versus defensive contexts.

Similarly, for the CoM analysis (Figure 4b), the attacking team exhibited a significant positive slope, $\beta = 0.0084$, $R^2 = 0.883$, $p < 0.001$, indicating a strong upward trend in causal emergence values. The defending team showed a significant negative slope, $\beta = -0.0071$, $R^2 = 0.707$, $p < 0.001$, reflecting a downward trend. However, unlike the relative distance, the random intervals in the CoM analysis also displayed slope values. For the random attacking intervals, the slope was $\beta = 0.0076$, $R^2 = 0.848$, $p < 0.001$. Although these intervals showed significant trends, they were not as pronounced as those observed during shooting phases.

These findings suggest that, while baseline spatial coordination is present in both teams, the emergence dynamics during shooting intervals are distinct, with the attacking team demonstrating the strongest positive trend in causal emergence and the defending team showing a clear negative trend.

Both the relative distance and CoM analyses reveal consistent trends, with increasing causal emergence in the attacking team and decreasing values in the defending team. This consistency across CoM representations confirms that CoM is an effective macroscopic feature for analyzing emergent behavior in team dynamics. The observed trends likely reflect coordinated offensive movements that rely on coherence actions to create scoring opportunities, while the defending team's responses may result in a breakdown of coherence.

3.3. *Clustering Coefficients as an Emergent Feature*

3.3.1. Causal Emergence of Clustering Coefficients Based on Velocity Similarity

We used clustering coefficients based on velocity similarity to analyze local coordination among players, focusing on the similarity in their movement velocities and directions. By examining velocity similarity, we aimed to understand how closely players align their movement patterns, which is essential for maintaining coordinated formations and responding to tactical demands. Connections between players were weighted based on velocity and directional similarity, providing a measure of how synchronized the players are in their movement as they approach key moments like a shot.

In Figure 5, the clustering coefficients based on velocity similarity provide insights into the local coherence of player movements. Higher values indicate closer alignment in velocity and direction among neighboring players, often associated with a cohesive structure.

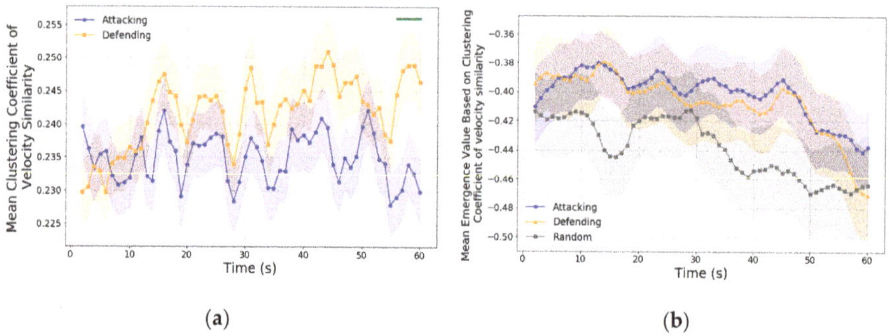

Figure 5. (**a**) Clustering coefficient of velocity similarity for the attacking team (blue) and defending team (orange) over the 60 s leading up to a shot. Shaded regions represent the standard error of the mean (SEM). While the defending team generally exhibits higher clustering coefficients, statistically significant differences were only observed in the final seconds before the shot, indicated by the green ribbon on top ($\alpha = 0.05$). (**b**) Causal emergence values based on clustering coefficients of velocity similarity over the same interval, capturing the emergent properties of velocity coherence.

In terms of causal emergence, this analysis focuses on whether the dynamics of the clustering coefficient itself can be explained by microscopic features of velocity and direction, or if the clustering coefficient exhibits emergent properties that provide additional predictive power beyond the microscale. Both the attacking and defending teams exhibited a downward trend in causal emergence values over time. Specifically, the attacking team (blue) exhibited a mild downward trend with a slope of $\beta = -0.0024$ $(R^2 = 0.091,\ p = 0.019)$, and the defending team (orange) showed a similar downward trend with a slope of $\beta = -0.0028$ $(R^2 = 0.109,\ p = 0.010)$. Random intervals also displayed a downward trend, with slope of $\beta = -0.0010$ $(R^2 = 0.742,\ p < 0.001)$.

This decline in causal emergence values suggests that, as the shot approaches, the dynamics of the clustering coefficient based on velocity similarity become increasingly predictable by the microscopic features (velocity and direction). In other words, local coherence in velocity aligns more closely with individual-level movement patterns, indicating a shift from synergistic, emergent contributions toward more constrained and predictable movement patterns. This trend likely reflects the tactical adjustments made by both teams, as follows: the attacking team seeks to maximize forward momentum, while the defending team adopts structured formations to counteract offensive advances. As a result, the clustering coefficient's predictive power becomes more tied to individual movement, limiting its emergent properties.

Interestingly, this trend in causal emergence based on velocity similarity contrasts with findings from the analysis of positional coherence, where causal emergence values for the attacking team increased as they approached the shot. This difference suggests that positional adjustments, compared to velocity alignment, may offer greater potential for emergent team-wide dynamics.

Unlike velocity similarity, which primarily supports immediate and localized coordination, positional coherence facilitates long-term strategies and anticipates complex interactions across the team. Thus, positional coherence can be considered better in terms of its ability to capture emergent behaviors that are not directly reducible to microscopic features. These emergent patterns likely play a critical role in creating scoring opportunities by leveraging the collective spatial dynamics of the team, a feature that is less pronounced in velocity-based analyses.

3.3.2. Causal Emergence of Clustering Coefficients Based on Inverse Distance

To understand how spatial coordination contributes to team behavior during critical moments, we used player positions as the microscopic features and calculated clustering coefficients based on the inverse of the distances between players. This approach highlights how close positioning among players contributes to collective team dynamics. Previous studies have shown that, in team sports, spatial arrangement and compactness play a crucial role in enabling cohesive defensive or offensive structures, which directly impact emergent collective behaviors during crucial phases of play. By using the inverse distances among players, we can assess how tightly aligned or dispersed each team is, providing insights into the coordination level within the team.

As shown in Figure 6, the causal emergence values for both teams exhibit discernible patterns over the 60 s before a shot. In the first 30 s, neither team's causal emergence deviates significantly from the values observed in randomly selected intervals, suggesting that their positioning dynamics do not substantially enhance overall emergent behavior during this initial period.

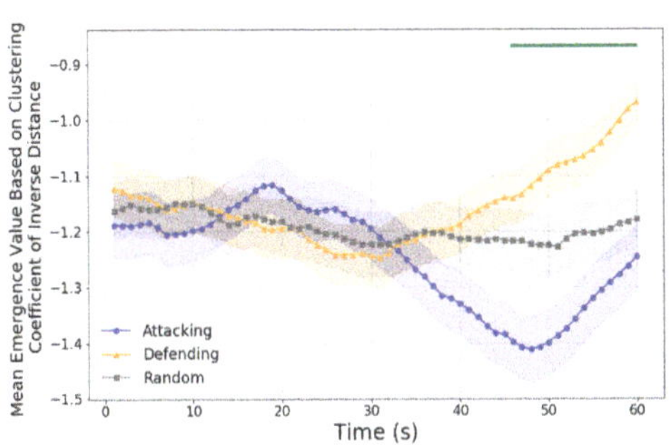

Figure 6. Causal emergence values with clustering coefficients based on inverse distances within the 60 s leading up to a shot. Shaded regions represent the standard error of the mean (SEM). Statistical significance is indicated by the green ribbon on top, which marks significant differences between the attacking team (blue line) and defending team (orange line) from the 45-s mark onward (Bonferroni corrected). Linear regression analysis for the last 30 s of the defending team suggests a consistent upward trend in causal emergence. For the attacking team, analysis over the last 10 s shows a steep increase in causal emergence just before the shot.

After the 30-s mark, the defending team begins to show a marked increase in causal emergence, statistically exceeding that of the attacking team from approximately the 40-s mark onward (indicated by the green ribbon on top). The upward trend in the defending team's causal emergence, as confirmed by the linear regression results with slope $\beta = 0.0089$, $(R^2 = 0.976,\ p < 0.001)$, indicates that their positioning dynamics become increasingly predictive of team-level coherence. This increase likely reflects their effort to maintain a compact defensive structure as they adapt their positioning to counteract the attacking team's movements. The higher causal emergence values suggest that the collective positioning of defending players becomes more tightly aligned, creating an emergent pattern that enhances their ability to block potential shooting opportunities and maintain spatial control.

For the attacking team, a noticeable increase in causal emergence only appears within the last 10 s before the shot, as indicated by the steep slope from the linear regression where slope $\beta = 0.0158$, $(R^2 = 0.998,\ p < 0.001)$. This dynamic follows a U-shaped trend, where causal emergence values initially decrease during the earlier phase of the 60-s window before rising sharply in the final moments. This U-shaped pattern reflects a shift in the attacking team's spatial dynamics, as follows: the initial dip may indicate a period of spatial adjustment as players transition from broader formations into more focused attacking configurations. The late surge in causal emergence suggests that players achieve a level of spatial coherence characterized by strategic positioning that maximizes scoring opportunities.

In summary, the causal emergence values based on inverse distances reveal that the defending team enhances their spatial coherence earlier, responding proactively to the attacking threat, while the attacking team's emergent behavior becomes more pronounced only in the critical seconds before a shot. This pattern underscores the tactical adjustments made by each team, with the defending team maintaining compact formations to limit scoring opportunities and the attacking team intensifying their positional coherence to maximize goal-scoring potential in the final moments.

4. Discussion

4.1. Discussion About the Current Result

This study applies the concept of causal emergence to the analysis of football match dynamics, providing a novel framework to understand how team-level behaviors emerge from individual player interactions. To examine different aspects of team collective behavior, we derive causal emergence using the following four different macroscopic features: relative distance, CoM, clustering coefficient of inverse distance, and velocity similarity.

When relative distance (V_t^{dist}) and center of mass (V_t^{CoM}) were used as macroscopic features, both showed strong positive correlations between casual emergence and ball possession rate. The findings imply that teams with higher causal emergence, which manifested through well-structured relative positions and collective movements, are better equipped to sustain possession. This observation could result from higher player cohesion than opposite team, or adaptive in-game decision making. In the context of shooting dynamics, causal emergence derived from V_t^{dist} and V_t^{CoM} exhibited similar trends, as follows: for attacking teams, causal emergence increased significantly as they approached a shot, reflecting improved coordination and spatial organization during offensive phases. Conversely, for defending teams, a decline in causal emergence was observed for both features, indicating an increase in redundancy at the micro level. This suggests that defending teams rely more on synchronized and predictable actions among players to maintain stability in defensive formations. These results highlight the distinct dynamics between offensive and defensive phases, demonstrating how macro-level spatial coherence relates to team strategies and possession outcomes.

When clustering coefficients derived from inverse distance ($V^{clust,dist}$) were used as the macroscopic feature, a moderate positive correlation between casual emergence and ball possession rate was observed. This suggests that localized spatial formations contribute to higher-level emergent dynamics that are critical for sustaining possession than that of the opposite team. This reflects the ability of teams to integrate local proximities into cohesive, system-wide behaviors that enhance ball control and adaptability during gameplay. In the context of shooting dynamics, causal emergence for the defending team showed a steady increase after the 30-s mark. For the attacking team, a sharp rise in causal emergence occurred in the final 10 s before the shot, contrasting with the relatively stable values observed earlier.

For clustering coefficients derived from velocity similarity ($V^{clust,vel}$), no significant correlation with ball possession rate was found. Additionally, before shooting events, velocity-based clustering coefficients showed minimal variation. These findings suggest that player velocity alignment, while reflecting localized synchronization during specific tactical moments (e.g., attacking from own half or counterattacks), does not strongly contribute to emergent, system-level dynamics critical for sustained possession or defensive coordination in pivotal moments. This lack of correlation implies that velocity similarity alone may capture short-term, transient tactical behaviors rather than long-term or stable emergent patterns integral to overall team strategy. In the context of possession, spatial organization (as reflected in relative distances, CoM, or clustering based on inverse distance) may play a greater role in team coherence and emergent dynamics than simple velocity alignment.

Taken together, these findings reveal distinct patterns of causal emergence across different macroscopic features, highlighting spatial coherence as a key driver of emergent team dynamics during possession and shooting phases, while underscoring the limitations of velocity-based metrics in capturing the complexity of team strategies. More broadly, it demonstrates the value of causal emergence as a framework for analyzing complex, real-world systems where interdependent components interact to produce collective behaviors. This research thus establishes a foundation for using causal emergence as a new metric in sports analytics, offering coaches and analysts an innovative perspective on team coordination and game strategies.

4.2. Link to Other Literature

From the perspective of theoretical frameworks of emergence, this study highlights the dynamic interplay between synergy and redundancy in shaping team-level behaviors. Previous works from Hoel et al. [13] and Rosas et al. [15] have formally shown that macro-level properties often provide additional predictive power that cannot be fully explained by micro-level components alone. However, these studies primarily emphasized synergistic phenomena, focusing on how macro-level coordination emerges from micro-level interactions. Our analysis considers the dynamics between redundancy and synergy, a factor critical in real-world environments like football games. In the context of football, redundancy is inherently present, as players must maintain a degree of synchronization to form cohesive attacking or defensive structures. Synergy could emerge when individual player contributions combine in non-linear ways to enhance overall team effectiveness. Our findings suggest that the interplay between these two forces dynamically shifts, with attacking teams demonstrating higher causal emergence metrics before shooting events, reflecting a transition from redundancy-dominated formations to synergy-driven coordination.

By integrating these theoretical principles into the analysis of team sports, our study provides a practical application of causal emergence. It demonstrates how macro-level coordination, quantified through causal emergence metrics, contributes to an understanding of coordinated human behaviors in high-pressure, competitive environments.

Our findings offer a perspective that complements previous research emphasizing the role of team dynamics in sports science. Duarte et al. highlighted that irregularities in individual player synchronization can contribute to stabilizing team-level coordination by allowing localized variability to support collective behavior [1]. This concept aligns with our observation of increasing causal emergence derived from relative distance and the center of mass (CoM) for attacking teams before shooting. Our results suggest that these emergent properties may reflect how localized spatial adjustments among players enhance macro-level coordination, thereby facilitating effective offensive actions.

Another possible interpretation of the observed differences in causal emergence based on aggregate positioning metrics between attacking and defending teams is the distinction of exploratory and exploitation [24]. We could consider attacking as a process of exploration, where players adjust their positioning and passing to identify potential weaknesses of the opponents to attack. On the other hand, defensive strategies, in contrast, often exhibit a more exploitative structure, as teams rely on pre-established defensive formations and strategies.

For the low correlation of possession rate and causal emergence based on clustering coefficients, one possible way of considering it is the constraints of human coordination capacity. Studies suggest that human groups typically coordinate most effectively within subgroups of approximately five to six individuals, beyond which coordination becomes increasingly difficult without a hierarchical structure or simplified decision-making processes [25–27]. In the context of football, this limitation may explain why localized coordination measured by clustering coefficients at the whole team level does not strongly correspond to possession rate. To better capture the role of hierarchical and subgroup-based coordination, future studies could consider partitioning players into functional subgroups based on their roles (i.e., defenders, midfielders, and forwards) and then calculating causal emergence within these units.

One behavioral interpretation of why the field center plays a crucial role in the causal emergence of team coordination in our analysis is that it acts as a naturally emergent spatial structure that shapes collective movement. This concept aligns with stigmergy, where individuals coordinate indirectly by interacting with modifications in their environment rather than through direct communication [28]. In football, the field center provides a shared spatial reference that influences team formations and movement patterns. Players dynamically adjust their positioning in response to their teammates, opponents, and their relation to the field center, creating coordinated movement patterns. This self-organized process enables teams to maintain coherence without constant direct communication, emphasizing the significance of macro-level spatial features in team dynamics.

From a team behavior perspective, negative values of causal emergence ($\Psi < 0$) may offer additional insights into the learning and adaptation processes underlying team coordination. Specifically, negative Ψ values indicate that individual-level information redundancy outweighs macro-level predictive power. The behavioral interpretation of this phenomenon remains open. One possible explanation for this is that these negative values reflect the players' learning and adaptation, leading to localized synchronization rather than emergent team-wide coordination. This aligns with research on team learning and coordination, which suggests that high-performing teams develop shared cognitive models through repeated interaction rather than relying solely on individual skill diversity [29,30].

Future research could further investigate the relationship between information redundancy, synchronization, and adaptive team behavior.

Recent studies have further explored the application of collective behavior metrics in team sports. For example, a collective movement analysis demonstrated how coordination tactics among football players emerge through spatiotemporal dynamics during gameplay [31]. Our findings align with this perspective by showing how spatial metrics like relative distance and CoM reveal emergent team behaviors that are critical for sustaining possession and enhancing offensive coordination. Additionally, a systematic review of collective tactical behaviors in football using positional data highlighted the importance of spatial metrics, such as player distance and movement patterns in understanding team performance [32]. Our work builds on this foundation by explicitly linking these spatial metrics to emergent team dynamics, demonstrating their relevance not only for performance evaluation, but also for understanding distinct offensive and defensive strategies.

Research in network science applied to football and water polo has demonstrated that passing interactions among players play a crucial role in performance outcomes [33,34]. While these studies focus on static passing-based edges, our approach utilizes a moving window of seconds to calculate clustering coefficients, forming dynamic graphs that evolve continuously throughout gameplay. This method captures continuous spatiotemporal interactions among players, providing a more detailed view of how emergent team dynamics change during match events. Additionally, multilevel hypernetworks have been employed to analyze team synergies, offering a comprehensive framework to quantify interactions across different levels of complexity. This approach highlights how tactical configurations, local interactions (e.g., two vs. one scenarios), and key player contributions collectively shape team dynamics, providing valuable insights into the emergent properties of competitive team performance [35]. Studies in rugby have also investigated the emergence of collective states, demonstrating how defensive formations exhibit higher order and compactness compared to the more dispersed and dynamic structures during attacks, thereby highlighting the universality of collective behavior metrics across different team-based activities [36]. Our result aligns with this perspective, as we also observed that clustering coefficients derived from velocity similarity were higher during defensive phases than offensive phases. This suggests that defensive strategies may prioritize synchronized and compact formations, while offensive behaviors rely more on dynamic spatial organization. These parallels highlight the relevance of collective behavior metrics across sports, offering a shared framework to explore emergent team dynamics.

Our findings also align with the broader perspectives on team synergies and collective behavior in sports science. Araújo and Davids emphasized the theoretical framework of team synergies, describing them as emergent properties arising from interactions within the team [37]. Similarly, the concept of sports teams as superorganisms emphasizes how individual contributions and interactions within a team operate similarly to biological systems, such as ant colonies or bee hives, where collective behaviors arise from local interactions [38].

By integrating these perspectives, our study builds on existing frameworks while providing a novel approach to analyzing macro-level team strategies through causal emergence metrics. This research underscores the potential of these metrics to provide deeper insights into team coordination, possession strategies, and broader collective dynamics in football.

4.3. Limitations

This study primarily focused on intra-team interactions, examining how individual players' behaviors contribute to macro-level team dynamics. However, in competitive environments, emergent behaviors within one team are heavily influenced by inter-team interactions. The opposing teams' strategies and spatial arrangements can significantly shape the dynamics of play, particularly during critical phases such as transitions or set plays. Future research should integrate inter-team dynamics to better capture the mutual influences and adaptive strategies between competing teams.

Our analysis considers individual players as the first-order micro-level components and examines how their interactions contribute to macro-level team behaviors. However, we do not explicitly account for higher-order dynamics like the combined influence of multiple players or interactions within subgroups. Rosas et al.'s framework for causal emergence includes higher-order interactions, such as pairwise or subgroup-level combinations, as micro-level contributors [15]. By focusing solely on individual players versus the whole team, our approach may overlook the interdependencies that arise from these higher-order structures, potentially underestimating the complexity of team coordination. Extending causal emergence metrics to include these higher-order interactions would provide a more comprehensive understanding of team dynamics.

Another limitation is that the causal emergence metrics employed in this study provide relative comparisons between synergy and redundancy, but they do not yield absolute measures of these quantities. This limitation restricts the application of such metrics for cross-contextual comparisons, such as benchmarking team performance across different contexts, matches, or sports. Developing absolute measures of synergy and redundancy is an active area of research, particularly within the framework of Partial Information Decomposition (PID) [16]. By adopting or extending PID methodologies, future research could establish absolute metrics for causal emergence, enabling robust cross-contextual analyses and advancing the generalizability of causal emergence as an analytical framework for team dynamics.

4.4. Future Directions

The study of causal emergent team dynamics in sports presents several directions for future research. One important direction involves the integration of machine learning techniques to model and predict emergent behaviors based on spatiotemporal player data. Advanced algorithms, such as neural networks and graph-based models, could uncover hidden patterns in player interactions, providing deeper insights into how micro-level behaviors scale into team-level dynamics. These methods would enable the development of predictive models that enhance the understanding of emergent behaviors under various tactical and environmental conditions.

Another critical area for exploration is the application of causal emergence metrics across different sports contexts. Sports such as rugby, basketball, and water polo exhibit distinct spatiotemporal and interaction dynamics compared to football. Comparative analyses could validate and refine causal emergence methodologies, identifying universal principles of collective coordination and adaptation. These studies would also highlight context-specific variations, offering a broader perspective on the role of emergent dynamics in diverse team-based activities.

Temporal analysis of emergent dynamics is another valuable direction. Understanding how causal emergence evolves throughout matches, particularly during critical phases such as transitions between offense and defense, high-pressure situations, or set plays could provide a richer understanding of team adaptability. Longitudinal studies that track these dynamics over entire games or seasons would elucidate how emergent properties evolve and stabilize under changing contexts, contributing to the development of time-sensitive models of team performance.

5. Conclusions

This study employs causal emergence to investigate collective team dynamics in football, analyzing macroscopic features derived from player tracking data to quantify how collective behaviors emerge from individual interactions. The findings demonstrate that causal emergence successfully captures team coordination, exhibiting a strong correlation with ball possession rates and increased emergence during attacking phases. These results suggest that collective spatial organization and coherence are required for successful offensive actions.

The results identify key distinctions in the mechanisms driving offensive and defensive team behaviors. Offensive strategies leverage synergy to achieve coordinated movements and exploit spatial opportunities, while defensive strategies rely more on redundancy to maintain structural stability. The use of causal emergence as a quantitative framework provides a detailed method for linking micro-level interactions with macro-level team dynamics

These findings advance our understanding of the role of emergent dynamics in shaping team performance and strategies.

Author Contributions: Conceptualization, Y.-S.C. and A.Y.-C.C.; methodology, Y.-S.C., A.Y.-C.C. and K.D.; software, Y.-S.C.; formal analysis, Y.-S.C.; resources, K.D.; writing—original draft preparation, Y.-S.C. and A.Y.-C.C.; writing—review and editing, Y.-S.C., A.Y.-C.C. and K.D; visualization, Y.-S.C. and A.C; supervision, A.Y.-C.C. and K.D.; funding acquisition, K.D and A.Y.-C.C. All authors have read and agreed to the published version of the manuscript.

Funding: This work was funded by JST (Japan Science and Technology Agency) COI-NEXT, Grant Number JPMJPF2205 and JSPS KAKENHI, Grant Number 24H00707.

Data Availability Statement: The dataset analyzed in this study was provided by DataStadium Inc. under a licensing agreement and is not publicly accessible. Any requests for data access are subject to the terms and conditions set by DataStadium Inc.

Acknowledgments: We gratefully acknowledge Katja Sangati and Sébastien Lerique for their invaluable support with data visualization and insightful discussion. We would also like to extend our gratitude to Tom Froese for his initial involvement in this work.

Conflicts of Interest: The authors declare no conflicts of interest.

References

1. Duarte, R.; Araújo, D.; Correia, V.; Davids, K.; Marques, P.; Richardson, M.J. Competing Together: Assessing the Dynamics of Team–Team and Player–Team Synchrony in Professional Association Football. *Hum. Mov. Sci.* **2013**, *32*, 555–566. [CrossRef] [PubMed]
2. McEwan, D.; Beauchamp, M.R. Teamwork in Sport: A Theoretical and Integrative Review. *Int. Rev. Sport Exerc. Psychol.* **2014**, *7*, 229–250. [CrossRef]
3. Ferraz, A.; Duarte-Mendes, P.; Sarmento, H.; Valente-Dos-Santos, J.; Travassos, B. Tracking Devices and Physical Performance Analysis in Team Sports: A Comprehensive Framework for Research—Trends and Future Directions. *Front. Sports Act. Living* **2023**, *5*, 1284086. [CrossRef] [PubMed]
4. Benítez Sillero, J.D.; Da Silva-Grigoletto, M.E.; Muñoz Herrera, E.; Morente Montero, A.; Guillén Del Castillo, M. Capacidades Físicas En Jugadores de Fútbol Formativo de Un Club Profesional/Physical Capacity in Youth Football Players of a Profesional Club. *Rev. Int. Med. Cienc. Act. Fis. Deporte* **2015**, *58*, 289–307. [CrossRef]
5. Tiedemann, T.; Francksen, T.; Latacz-Lohmann, U. Assessing the Performance of German Bundesliga Football Players: A Non-Parametric Metafrontier Approach. *Cent. Eur. J. Oper. Res.* **2011**, *19*, 571–587. [CrossRef]
6. Sawyer, D.T.; Ostarello, J.Z.; Suess, E.A.; Dempsey, M. Relationship Between Football Playing Ability and Selected Performance Measures. *J. Strength Cond. Res.* **2002**, *16*, 611. [CrossRef] [PubMed]
7. Sarmento, H.; Anguera, M.T.; Pereira, A.; Araújo, D. Talent Identification and Development in Male Football: A Systematic Review. *Sports Med.* **2018**, *48*, 907–931. [CrossRef]
8. Seth, A.K. Measuring Autonomy and Emergence via Granger Causality. *Artif. Life* **2010**, *16*, 179–196. [CrossRef]

9. Murakami, H.; Tomaru, T.; Nishiyama, Y.; Moriyama, T.; Niizato, T.; Gunji, Y.-P. Emergent Runaway into an Avoidance Area in Swarm of Soldier Crabs. *PLoS ONE* **2014**, *9*, e97870. [CrossRef]
10. Niizato, T.; Sakamoto, K.; Mototake, Y.; Murakami, H.; Tomaru, T.; Hoshika, T.; Fukushima, T. Finding Continuity ar Discontinuity in Fish Schools via Integrated Information Theory. *PLoS ONE* **2020**, *15*, e0229573. [CrossRef]
11. Jaffe, K. Quantifying Social Synergy in Insect and Human Societies. *Behav. Ecol. Sociobiol.* **2010**, *64*, 1721–1724. [CrossRef]
12. Zhang, J.; Tao, R.; Leong, K.H.; Yang, M.; Yuan, B. Dynamical Reversibility and A New Theory of Causal Emergence. *npj Comple* **2024**, *2*, 3. [CrossRef]
13. Hoel, E.P.; Albantakis, L.; Tononi, G. Quantifying Causal Emergence Shows That Macro Can Beat Micro. *Proc. Natl. Acad. Sc USA* **2013**, *110*, 19790–19795. [CrossRef]
14. Yuan, B.; Zhang, J.; Lyu, A.; Wu, J.; Wang, Z.; Yang, M.; Liu, K.; Mou, M.; Cui, P. Emergence and Causality in Complex Systems: Survey of Causal Emergence and Related Quantitative Studies. *Entropy* **2024**, *26*, 108. [CrossRef]
15. Rosas, F.E.; Mediano, P.A.M.; Jensen, H.J.; Seth, A.K.; Barrett, A.B.; Carhart-Harris, R.L.; Bor, D. Reconciling Emergences: A Information-Theoretic Approach to Identify Causal Emergence in Multivariate Data. *PLoS Comput. Biol.* **2020**, *16*, e100828 [CrossRef]
16. Williams, P.L.; Beer, R.D. Nonnegative Decomposition of Multivariate Information. *arXiv* **2010**, arXiv:1004.2515.
17. Cotta, C.; Mora, A.M.; Merelo, J.J.; Merelo-Molina, C. A Network Analysis of the 2010 FIFA World Cup Champion Team Play. *Syst. Sci. Complex.* **2013**, *26*, 21–42. [CrossRef]
18. Buldú, J.M.; Busquets, J.; Martínez, J.H.; Herrera-Diestra, J.L.; Echegoyen, I.; Galeano, J.; Luque, J. Using Network Science t Analyse Football Passing Networks: Dynamics, Space, Time, and the Multilayer Nature of the Game. *Front. Psychol.* **2018**, *9*, 190 [CrossRef]
19. Saramäki, J.; Kivelä, M.; Onnela, J.-P.; Kaski, K.; Kertész, J. Generalizations of the Clustering Coefficient to Weighted Comple Networks. *Phys. Rev. E* **2007**, *75*, 027105. [CrossRef]
20. Barrett, A.B.; Seth, A.K. Practical Measures of Integrated Information for Time-Series Data. *PLoS Comput. Biol.* **2011**, *7*, e100105 [CrossRef]
21. Bothorel, C.; Cruz, J.D.; Magnani, M.; Micenková, B. Clustering Attributed Graphs: Models, Measures and Methods. *Netw. Sc* **2015**, *3*, 408–444. [CrossRef]
22. Sarkar, S.; Chakrabarti, A.; Mukherjee, D.P. Generation of Ball Possession Statistics in Soccer Using Minimum-Cost Flow Network In Proceedings of the 2019 IEEE/CVF Conference on Computer Vision and Pattern Recognition Workshops (CVPRW), Lon Beach, CA, USA, 16–17 June 2019; pp. 2515–2523.
23. Duarte, R.; Araújo, D.; Freire, L.; Folgado, H.; Fernandes, O.; Davids, K. Intra- and Inter-Group Coordination Patterns Revea Collective Behaviors of Football Players near the Scoring Zone. *Hum. Mov. Sci.* **2012**, *31*, 1639–1651. [CrossRef]
24. March, J.G. Exploration and Exploitation in Organizational Learning. *Organ. Sci.* **1991**, *2*, 71–87. [CrossRef]
25. Dunbar, R.I.M.; Duncan, N.D.C.; Nettle, D. Size and Structure of Freely Forming Conversational Groups. *Hum. Nat.* **1995**, *6* 67–78. [CrossRef]
26. James, J. A Preliminary Study of the Size Determinant in Small Group Interaction. *Am. Sociol. Rev.* **1951**, *16*, 474. [CrossRef]
27. Bakeman, R.; Beck, S. The Size of Informal Groups in Public. *Environ. Behav.* **1974**, *6*, 378–390. [CrossRef]
28. Garnier, S.; Gautrais, J.; Theraulaz, G. The Biological Principles of Swarm Intelligence. *Swarm Intell.* **2007**, *1*, 3–31. [CrossRef]
29. Klein, G.A. *Sources of Power: How People Make Decisions*, 20th Anniversary ed.; MIT Press: Cambridge, MA, 2017; ISBN 978-0-262-53429-1.
30. Heath, C.; Staudenmayer, N. Coordination Neglect: How Lay Theories of Organizing Complicate Coordination in Organizations *Res. Organ. Behav.* **2000**, *22*, 153–191. [CrossRef]
31. Marcelino, R.; Sampaio, J.; Amichay, G.; Gonçalves, B.; Couzin, I.D.; Nagy, M. Collective Movement Analysis Reveals Coordination Tactics of Team Players in Football Matches. *Chaos Solitons Fractals* **2020**, *138*, 109831. [CrossRef]
32. Low, B.; Coutinho, D.; Gonçalves, B.; Rein, R.; Memmert, D.; Sampaio, J. A Systematic Review of Collective Tactical Behaviours in Football Using Positional Data. *Sports Med.* **2020**, *50*, 343–385. [CrossRef]
33. Passos, P.; Davids, K.; Araújo, D.; Paz, N.; Minguéns, J.; Mendes, J. Networks as a Novel Tool for Studying Team Ball Sports as Complex Social Systems. *J. Sci. Med. Sport* **2011**, *14*, 170–176. [CrossRef] [PubMed]
34. Grund, T.U. Network Structure and Team Performance: The Case of English Premier League Soccer Teams. *Soc. Netw.* **2012**, *34*, 682–690. [CrossRef]
35. Ribeiro, J.; Silva, P.; Davids, K.; Araújo, D.; Ramos, J.; Lopes, R.J.; Garganta, J. A Multilevel Hypernetworks Approach to Capture Properties of Team Synergies at Higher Complexity Levels. *Eur. J. Sport Sci.* **2020**, *20*, 1318–1328. [CrossRef] [PubMed]
36. Koudela, H.; Schaerf, T.M.; Lathlean, T.; Murphy, A.; Welch, M. Investigating the Emergence of Collective States Within Rugby Sevens Gameplay. *J. Sports Sci.* **2024**, 1–12. [CrossRef]

7. Araújo, D.; Davids, K. Team Synergies in Sport: Theory and Measures. *Front. Psychol.* **2016**, *7*, 1449. [CrossRef]
8. Duarte, R.; Araújo, D.; Correia, V.; Davids, K. Sports Teams as Superorganisms: Implications of Sociobiological Models of Behaviour for Research and Practice in Team Sports Performance Analysis. *Sports Med.* **2012**, *42*, 633–642. [CrossRef]

MDPI AG
Grosspeteranlage 5
4052 Basel
Switzerland
Tel.: +41 61 683 77 34

Entropy Editorial Office
E-mail: entropy@mdpi.com
www.mdpi.com/journal/entropy

www.ingramcontent.com/pod-product-compliance
Lightning Source LLC
Chambersburg PA
CBHW041938260926
51850CB00018B/264
* 9 7 8 3 7 2 5 8 6 7 9 0 5 *